The Law of
International Cartels

The Law of
International Cartels

HEINRICH KRONSTEIN

Cornell University Press

ITHACA AND LONDON

74-8675

International Standard Book Number 0-8014-0627-7
Library of Congress Catalog Card Number 73-164642

Printed in the United States of America by Vail-Ballou Press, Inc.

Librarians: Library of Congress cataloging information appears on the last page of the book.

Publisher's Note

Heinrich Kronstein died at Bern, Switzerland, on September 27, 1972. That he had the pleasure, before his death, of seeing the galley proofs of his book is especially gratifying to us, his publisher.

Professor Kronstein through the years was tireless in his search for the facts of his discipline, and he was dedicated to making known, to those who might alter the conduct of men and nations, the world-wide consequences of present practices. This book has become a final judgment and plea at the end of a long and fruitful life.

CORNELL UNIVERSITY PRESS

Acknowledgments

The basic concepts in this book were first elaborated in *Das Recht der Internationalen Kartelle*, published in Germany by J. Schweitzer Verlag (1967). The present book is not, however, merely a translation of the German edition. It is a revision of that work and includes developments which have occurred since the first publication.

I would like to express again my gratitude to those people who helped in the preparation of the German edition, mentioned in the Preface thereto. In addition, many people helped in editing this text for publication in English. I am most grateful to Jochen Volhard and to the following students at Georgetown University Law Center who were active in this work, Wardlaw Hamilton, Thomas Grooms, Jochen Jahn, and John Wintrol, as well as to E. Bruce Butler, under whose direction the editing was accomplished. I would also extend my warmest thanks to Mrs. Erika Schoenhoefer, whose tireless efforts were invaluable in the completion of this edition.

H. K.

Frankfurt am Main

Contents

Abbreviations

A.	Atlantic Reporter
A.B.A.J.	*American Bar Association Journal*
A.C.	Appeals Case
AEG	Allgemeine Elektrizitaets-Gesellschaft
Alcoa	Aluminum Corporation of America
All E.R.	All England Reports
AM. J. Comp. L.	*American Journal of Comparative Law*
Am. Jur.	*American Jurisprudence*
A.M.R.	American Market Reporter
Am. R.	American Reports
AWD	Aussenwirtschaftsdienst des Betriebs-Beraters
BAG	Bundesarbeitsgericht
BG	Schweizerisches Bundesgericht
BGB	Bürgerliches Gesetzbuch
BGBl.	Bundesgesetzblatt
BGE	Entscheidungen des Schweizerischen Bundesgerichts
BGH	Bundesgerichtshof
BGHZ	Entscheidungen des Bundesgerichtshofs in Zivilsachen
Biss.	Bissel's U.S. Circuit Court Reports
B.I.S.D.	Basic Instruments and Selected Documents
BKartA	Bundeskartellamt
BKartA/E	Entscheidungen des Bundeskartellamtes
BP	British Petroleum Company
B.T.	Bundestag
B.Y.I.L.	*British Yearbook of International Law*
C.A.	Court of Appeals
Camp. Rep.	Campbell's Reports
Can. Bar. Rev.	*Canadian Bar Review*
Cass. civ.	Cour de cassation
C.C.	Code Civil
CCH	Commerce Clearing House

CCH Trade Cas.	Commerce Clearing House Trade Cases
CCH Trade Reg. Rep.	Commerce Clearing House Trade Regulation Reports
C.C.P.A.	Court of Customs and Patent Appeals Report
CEA	Compagnie Européenne d'Automatism
C.F.P.	Compagnie Française des Pétroles
C.F.R.	Court of Federal Regulations
CGE	Compagnie Générale d'Electricité
CGTSF	Compagnie Générale de Télégraphie sans Fils
Ch.	Chancery
Ch. D.	Chancery Division
Cir.	U.S. Circuit Court of Appeals
Cmnd.	Command
Colum. L. Rev.	*Columbia Law Review*
C.P.L.R.	Civil Practice Law and Rules (N.Y.)
CPO	Zivilprozessordnung (Code of Civil Procedure)
D.C.N.Y.	District Court New York
D.L.R.	Dominion Law Reports
D.N.J.	District Court New Jersey
Duke L. Rev.	*Duke University Law Review*
E.C.	European Commission; Economic Cooperation
E/Conf.	European Conference
ECOSOC	Economic and Social Council
E.D.	Eastern District
EEC	European Economic Community
F.	Federal Reporter
FAO	Food and Agriculture Organization of the United Nations
F.A.Z.	*Frankfurter Allgemeine Zeitung*
FDIR	Federal Direct Investment Regulation
Fed. Bar J.	*Federal Bar Journal*
F.R.	Federal Rules
F. Supp.	Federal Supplement
F.T.C.	Federal Trade Commission
G.A.	Geneva Agreement
GATT	General Agreement on Tariffs and Trade
GemK.	Gemeinschaftskommentar
Geo.	King George
Geo. L.J.	*Georgetown Law Journal*
Geo. Wash. L. Rev.	*George Washington Law Review*

Gov't Cont. Rep.	Government Continued Report
GSA	Government Services Administration
GWB	Gesetz gegen Wettbewerbsbeschränkungen
H and N	Hurlstone and Norman's Reports
Harv. L. Rev.	*Harvard Law Review*
H. Bl.	Handelsblatt: H. Blackstone's Reports of Common Pleas
ICC	International Chamber of Commerce
ICI	Imperial Chemical Industries, Ltd.
I.C.J. Rep.	International Court of Justice Reports
I.L.A.	International Law Association
I.M.C.O.	Intergovernmental Maritime Concertative Organization
IMF	International Monetary Fund
Int. and Comp. L.Q.	*International and Comparative Law Quarterly*
IPC	Iraq Petroleum Company, Ltd.
J. Pat. Off. Soc'y	*Journal of the Patent Office Society*
KartA	Kartellamt
KartRdsch.	Kartell-Rundschau
K.B.	King's Bench
L	Law
Law and Cont. Prob.	*Law and Contemporary Problems*
LL.R.	Lloyds Law Reports
L.N.T.S.	League of Nations Treaty Series
L.Q. Rev.	*Law Quarterly Review*
M.D.	Middle District
Moo. P.C.	Moore's Privy Council Cases
N.E.	North Eastern (Reporter)
N.Y.(S.)	New York (Supplement)
N.Y.U. L. Rev.	*New York University Law Review*
OECD	Organization for Economic Cooperation and Development
O.G.	Official Gazette
O.P.E.C.	Organization of the Petroleum Exporting Countries
P	Pacific
Pat. and T.M. Rev.	*Patent and Trademark Review*
P.C.	Privy Council
P.L.	Public Law
Q.B.	Queen's Bench
RAG	Reichsarbeitsgericht
RCA	Radio Corporation of America

Reg.	Regulation
Rep.	Report(s), Reporter
RG	Reichsgericht (German Supreme Court before World War II)
RST	Roan Selection Trust
S.Ct.	Supreme Court
S.D.	Southern District
S.E.	South Eastern (Reporter)
SEC	Securities and Exchange Commission
sec.	section
Sen.	Senate
Sess.	Session
Stat.	Statute
S.W.	South Western (Reporter)
T.C.	Tariff Commission
TD./Tin	UNCTAD Record on Tin
T.E.A.	(UN) Treaty on Economics and Agriculture
T.I.A.S.	Treaty and other International Agreement Series
T.L.R.	Times Law Report
T.S.	Treaty Series
U.C.C.	Uniform Commercial Code
U.N.	United Nations
UNCTAD	United Nations Conference on Trade and Development
U.N.G.A.O.R.	United Nations General Assembly Official Record
U.N.T.S.	United Nations Treaty Series
U.S.C.(A)	United States Code (Annotated)
U.S.C.S.	United States Code Supplement
U.S.L.W.	United States Law Weekly
U.S.T.	United States Treaties
Va. L. Rev.	Virginia Law Review
W.D.	Western District
Wis. L. Rev.	*Wisconsin Law Review*
W.L.R.	Weekly Law Reports
WuW	Wirtschaft und Wettbewerb
WZG	Warenzeichengesetz

The Law of
International Cartels

I ~~~~~~~~~

Introduction

The formal framework of United States international trade is presently undergoing another of the attacks to which it is periodically subject. In the field of public international trade law, proponents of freer trade and advocates of restrictive arrangements, such as quotas, have presented their briefs. A thoroughgoing revision of private market regulation has been called for, to be made by a new commission proposed in both Houses of Congress.[1] Sponsors of the bill apparently hope to limit the "extraterritorial effect" of American antitrust laws, which allegedly discriminate against American enterprises operating abroad, where foreign businesses seem so much more unrestricted. This activity and concern call for a basic reassessment of the present organization of international markets.

Following World War II, a privately organized balance of power outside the Communist world developed, by means of a new kind of international-market regulating organization, to reconcile the often contradictory forces operating in the present international market.

With the development of modern systems of communication, the world has become a single network with every point instantly accessible. Modern transportation allows any center of economic activity, wherever it may be, to send and receive goods from any other point. Modern distribution and merchandising systems, using international communication and transportation, trade symbols, and world advertising, establish larger and larger markets. An integrated world market has developed to some extent in almost every economic sector: raw materials, technology, and industrial products. In a parallel development, the business concerns carrying on the trade, some under public control, are becoming increasingly integrated industrially, both territorially and vertically or horizontally within their businesses. Among these integrated business organizations, cooperation most often takes the form of tacit understandings.

Yet there is no longer any doubt that the economic-technological

[1] *Congress. Rec.* HI556, S2606 ff. (daily ed. Mar. 11, 1969).

dynamism of modern economics has not been followed by a similar political-economic integration. While in the period immediately following World War II one was willing to accept the East-West disintegration and to wait for the economies of the so-called developing countries to reach a competitive level, today these problems seem chronic. "Markets" have become limited by the reach of one or another currency or tariff system; differing policies of social security, especially with regard to full employment, subject each industry or economy to special rules, so that the international market disintegrates into a relatively large number of units. In developed economies, unemployment, balance-of-payments deficits, dollar shortages, distribution of defense orders, and security demands are symptoms of this disintegration. Meanwhile, the problems of the developing continents seem to increase.

Usually when these problems are discussed, the elements of disintegration are treated as merely temporary phenomena. As a matter of fact, immediately after World War II, the draftsmen of the International Trade Organization (ITO), the predecessor of the General Agreement on Tariffs and Trade (GATT), of the International Monetary Fund (IMF), and of the Organization for Economic Cooperation and Development (OECD) intended to encourage the integration of markets and expected that political cooperation would inevitably result from technological and market integration. A coordinately monetary system appeared an absolute necessity; a coordinated monitoring of public and private trade restrictions and trade regulation should logically follow.

The establishment of a European Common Market (EEC) and the European Free Trade Association (EFTA) appeared a further step toward an integrated market, politically coordinated and closely connected with the concept of an Atlantic Community. Preparations made for a coordinated system of industrial property protection involved patents, trademarks, and copyrights. They certainly did not seem the tools for the disintegration of markets. But the results are evident.

A synthesis of the integrating and disintegrating forces of international market regulation has become a necessity. Organized balance-of-power systems have developed in each sector of international trade to affect this synthesis. An organized international economy now stands above the nation-states, guaranteeing that those engaged in international trade can take full advantage of the business opportunities the integrated aspects of modern markets offer them.

A careful analysis of this development is necessary to show American business how "free" it actually is and to indicate to American officials and legislators to what extent American law and policies can influence or modify this new international order. There is certainly a historic relation between today's development and the cartelizing trend observed between the two world wars, but this should not suggest that the present development is nothing but a resurrection of that international cartel system.

The dynamism resulting from the second industrial revolution of the post–World War II period brings out the contrast to the purpose of the pre–World War II market regulation: the primary task of economic policy then was viewed as one of stabilization. This was attempted by parallel action in establishing multilateral private business organizations whose main objective was a market division along geographic and product lines, and by governmental bilateral barter agreements. This policy necessarily achieved stabilization at the expense of outsiders.

The foundations of the new order are maintained by individual nations and by international organizations. Indeed, despite certain liberalizing tendencies, the influence of the state on economic matters is generally increasing rather than decreasing, not only in developing nations and countries with a socialist-planned economy, but also in many Western industrial states. Standing beside the state or the international organization in the creation of this order, however, is the private business economic organization. An attentive observer of the international economy is bound to notice the particular effect that the enterprises formally or informally under a unifying control have on the development and functioning of the international economy.

Occasionally the activities of a single business enterprise exert influence, but more often several independent enterprises, working together under a formal agreement, or perhaps with only an informal understanding, shape the economic order. These private alliances of enterprises, which we shall call cartels (with the proviso that a more detailed definition will be given later) operate behind the windbreak of state power. They may decide to remove a market from the ordinary economic order and subject it to one of their own making; they may use their own private market power to force those within and without the group to respect their order; and they may establish a judicial and administrative regulation clearly separate and increasingly independent from that of the state. All aspects of business and economic organization may be subjected to this quasi-governmental order.

Organizers of modern international market regulations utilize various national legal institutions, legal rules, and court decisions to create and to secure their system of regulation. This is accomplished primarily through the use of the international and national law of contracts, the choice of forum and of arbitration courts, and the use of international corporation law and of the national and international law of industrial property. An analysis of these various institutions will explain the development of extensive international private economic orders whose different facets regulate relations between the enterprises themselves and the relations with third parties. These orders have established independent systems of legal protection, undisturbed by state authority. To be sure, a token grounding in some national law is still considered necessary, but this connection is largely perfunctory. National law is merely a peg upon which the organizers of a given order hang their justification for complete autonomy. This is not to question the validity of national laws in these matters, but to acknowledge the problem which has developed in practice and which must be dealt with.

As the most international of arrangements, one would expect these private orders to organize according to international law. But international law would only interest them if it allowed more freedom than municipal law. If international law were more restrictive, it would be in the interest of the organizers to choose among many "sovereign" national legal orders, so as to use many independent legal institutions to establish and to secure their order.

In this study, the use of existing concepts and terms poses a problem. Legal concepts developed in national economic legislation are inappropriate for an analysis of a new private order in the international economy.

Concepts must be devised to fit the new circumstances. Economic studies might be examined for concepts to replace those of national legislation that are obsolete. Concepts must evolve with the facts, which is the problem with attempts to establish definitive formulations.

The economist's freedom and facility in adjusting his notions of the facts are very attractive to a lawyer, for even with all the freedom that interpretation grants, it is much more difficult to adjust legal than economic concepts to new facts. Law requires uniformity. Legal terms such as *cartel, restrictive agreement,* and *trust,* once written into law, can be redefined only with great difficulty. In analyzing both international enterprises and modern international market regulation, we will find economic concepts that have become legal terms even though their legal meaning differs from their meaning to the economist. To use these concepts without distinction would be to ignore realities. If we improve or modify them, we could be accused of abusing them. We can only use these concepts as we find them and adjust them for our purpose.

In the United States during World War II, congressional committees, such as the Temporary National Economic Committee (TNEC), the group preparing the International Trade Organization (ITO), and the Governmental Cartel Committee under Edward Mason of Harvard, demonstrated a pronounced understanding of the mutual effects of governmental and private regulation of trade.[2]

Legal analysis at the time was heavily influenced by the "functionalists," jurists who analyzed the function of legal institutions, such as contracts, industrial property, or corporation, within the context of society.

It is surprising that the new post–World War II role of legal institutions in international market regulation has not been followed with more attention, and even more surprising that the disputes on conflict of law or on questionable arrangements in industrial property and arbitration have not analyzed the function of these legal institutions in "cartels." A number of factors contributed to this change in analytic emphasis.

First, the postwar generation was convinced that the prewar world

[2] G. Stocking and M. W. Watkins, *Cartels in Action* (New York, 1946) and *Cartels or Competition?* (New York, 1948); E. S. Mason, *Controlling World Trade: Cartels and Commodity Agreements* (New York, 1946); U.S. Cong., Temporary National Economic Committee (TNEC), *Concentration of Economic Power,* Monograph No. 16, 76th Cong., 3d Sess. (1940); J. W. F. Rowe, *Markets and Men: A Study of Artificial Control Schemes in some Primary Industries* (New York, 1936); W. Y. Elliott, *International Control in the Non-Ferrous Metals* (New York, 1937); U.S. Cong., Senate, *The International Petroleum Cartel,* Staff Report of the Federal Trade Commission, submitted to the Subcomm. on Small Business, 82d Cong., 2d Sess. (1952).

of separate, national, autarchic economies was over, that treaties had established a uniform monetary system, and that GATT and other ideas of ITO had established at least a road leading toward an open market, free from qualitative and quantitative restrictions and subject only to a controlled system of tariffs. The United States, the leading trader, seemed dedicated to opening world markets with free trade. The OECD treaty formally embodied all these principles, including control of cartels. The antitrust idea was included in the Treaty of Rome, establishing the European Economic Community as well as in German and other European national legislation. A free market operating with a liberal industrial policy seemed bound to perpetuate itself by the force of competition. In the light of these developments, it was tempting to treat disturbing factors that threatened the process of integration as merely temporary discrepancies.

Also, both the method and theory of American legal and economic scholarship delayed full recognition of the actual developments in the organization of international market regulation and their inevitable impact on legal institutions. The model method of economic analysis, which uses mathematics and games theory, whatever its value for economic theory, is not sufficiently supported by factual analysis and investigation of the mechanisms of trade to use as a basis for legal and political decisions.

The functional approach to the study of legal institutions and their utilization in society—a teleological investigation of rules of law—has been replaced by a pragmatic case-by-case determination of the course of action. Accompanying this has been a broad transfer of the power to determine the law of private organizations: in contract, arbitration, and the utilization of corporations.

A sound new U.S. policy in respect to public or private international market regulation requires a clarification of current facts. Many countries have prepared excellent factual material, notably the hearings held by the U.S. Congressional committees, Senate as well as House (e.g., the Senate Antitrust Subcommittee on Economic Concentration, 1968, or the House Antitrust Subcommittee on Conglomerates, 1969). The German cartel office, as a part of the Commerce Ministry of the Bundesrepublik, for instance, in an investigation of the organization and the oil and fuel trade in Germany, has raised the important question of the interrelation between the national market and international market regulation. The international agencies, such as

OECD and UNCTAD, have undertaken important inquiries, which should be helpful when published.

This book, based on material available to anyone, contains developments in international trade at the governmental and private levels. Most frequently, sources are the commodity papers, the annual reports of leading companies, and the publications of governmental agencies of the leading industrial countries, especially the United States, Canada, England, Australia, Japan, and France, which investigate and describe the international organization of the market.

This information is subjected to two sorts of analysis: a description of the existing international market regulatory order, which results from a combination of operations and activities by both governments and outside private organizations; and an analysis of the utilization of legal institutions in this international market order by its organizers.

An investigation of the private use of legal institutions would be incomplete if it were limited to the current situation: it is necessary to examine the historical background of these institutions to determine whether their present use is consonant with their original purpose. In the second part of the book, therefore, when we discuss the questions of choice of law, choice of forum, choice of an arbitration tribunal, or industrial property or corporation law in a given jurisdiction, we must also examine the historical origins of these institutions. The lawyer must know not only what is and can be done with the national legal system, but also how the structure of society limits that legal order.

This book undertakes a triple task: to present sufficient examples of modern market regulations to show the existence and operations of these organizations; to show the legal institutions used in this international market regulation; and to analyze, in the case of the most important legal institutions, how this development and utilization became possible. The important purposes of such an analysis are to clarify the limits existing even for a country as powerful as the United States to change the present market regulation by national legislation; to consider how a coordination between the powers of these international market regulations with public organizations is possible and necessary; and to clarify to what extent the legal institutions of the United States are being put to use for purposes entirely different from those they were created for, and to consider the consequences.

Above all, this is a book written by a lawyer for practitioners in, as well as theoretical observers of, the present system. I believe the best possible presentation of the facts is to use examples. Here we use the technological cartel as the basic type, since today more market regulations use technological or related devices than any other. However, we also present the raw-material, industrial-products, and the so-called defensive cartels.

My aim is to describe the different types of market regulations operating in the international market today, the legal organizations and mechanics through which they function, and their interrelationship with legal institutions in the United States and elsewhere. Not only the United States is planning a redrafting of regulatory laws (such as antitrust and patent laws); parallel plans exist in England and the Common Market, in Australia and the developing countries. A purely national solution of this problem is apt to be ineffective and rather dangerous, since, as this book will show, a very strong international market regulation exists. It is rather doubtful, in short, that national laws, present or future, can cope with the problem.

2

Governmental Regulation in
International Markets

The organizations controlling private market regulation are not only mutually interdependent; they also interact closely with government bodies. Many writers hold that, since World War II, the function of a free government has been to enforce free trade by enacting anticartel or similar legislation and to regulate its own economy. The extent to which the different measures of various governments, including antitrust laws, can be used by the organizers of private international market regulations for their own purpose has not been sufficiently recognized. Therefore, it seems advisable to open this inquiry with a discussion of some of the governmental measures available in different countries for use by private market organizers.

International cartels regulate international trade on the basis of mutual understandings and the common policy of enterprises operating in different states. Governmental measures regulating the same economy pose a problem to them: such regulations may themselves regulate the free flow of goods and thereby restrict the area of private market regulations. However, in many cases private regulators can use governmental measures to create and maintain the order serving their own purposes.

The complex interrelationship between governmental and private market regulation is strengthened by the constantly increasing interpenetration of state and private economy.[1] This is one of the most important differences between the present structure of world trade and that prior to World War II: there were then many instances of governmental interference, especially in foreign trade, but interpenetration was much less pronounced.

The interrelationship between governmental and private regulations may come into play on the basis of: (1) international treaties or agreements between governments, which directly or indirectly establish public regulation of a given market; (2) the coordinated effect of

[1] A. Schoenfield, *The Changing Balance of Public and Private Power* (1965), p. 439.

measures by several governments regarding their foreign trade, whether intentional or not; (3) the unilateral measures of a government, which affect its own foreign trade; and (4) general bi- and multi-lateral agreements regulating and affecting general principles of trade.

International Public Market-Regulating Agreements

Direct Market-Regulating Effects

International agreements exist which regulate one or more of the significant elements of the market (production, price, or consumption) or which attempt to regulate a particular market as a whole. Some of these agreements have been enacted within the framework of the United Nations or the General Agreement on Tariffs and Trade (GATT),[2] while others are simply multilateral agreements. Regulation of a market *as a whole* takes that market out of regular channels of trade and puts it under governmental control, presumably making private market regulation impossible. But if the governmental agreement regulates only particular aspects of the market, a private regulatory structure can be built around this agreement. In some instances, private regulation only becomes effective when supplemented by public regulation, especially if private regulation proves too weak to achieve the desired stabilization. Indeed, it is most helpful if public and private agreements, or both, are under permanent review by the participating parties and they must meet continually to check each other's policy. The negotiations in the preparation of commodity agreements in copper and zinc appear to have been utilized in this manner.

Five international commodity agreements exist today, four covering agricultural products and one an industrial raw material: the International Wheat Trade Convention of 1968;[3] the International Sugar Agreement of 1958;[4] the International Coffee Agreement of 1967, in

[2] GATT, concluded at Geneva, Oct. 30, 1947; entered into force for the United States Jan. 1, 1948, 61 Stat., A3, A51, T.I.A.S. 1700, 55-61 U.N.T.S.

[3] T.I.A.S., Series 5115, 5844, 6057, and 6537. See also F. H. Sanderson, "The International Grain Arrangement," 58 *Dept. of State Bull.* 590 (1968); *Congress. Rec.* S7106–22 (daily ed. June 27, 1968) and *Congress. Rec.* E7004 (daily ed. July 26, 1968). This convention followed the basic framework of prior conventions of 1949, 1953, 1956, 1959, and 1962.

[4] International Sugar Agreement, Dec. 1, 1958, 10 U.S.T. 2188, T.I.A.S. 4389.

effect since December 30, 1968; [5] the International Olive Oil Agreement of 1963; [6] and the International Tin Agreement of 1965.[7]

It is interesting to compare this list with pre–World War II commodity agreements: wheat, London, August 25, 1933, between importing and exporting countries; sugar, London, May 6, 1937; tea, London, February 9, 1936, replaced August 25, 1938; coffee—Interamerican Coffee Agreement—November 28, 1940; beef, 1937; timber, 1935; tin, 1931; and rubber, 1934.[8] Recent attempts to reach a world cotton and a cocoa commodity agreement have failed. The GATT Cotton Textile Agreement is dealt with later in this chapter.

In November 1967, a conference to deal with tariff preferences for developing nations, called by the Secretary General of the United Nations Conference on Trade and Development (UNCTAD) in Geneva, proved fruitless, and the negotiations were adjourned.[9] The same fate befell such discussions at UNCTAD's second conference at New Delhi in 1968.

In the industrial raw material sector experts periodically meet under the auspices of the United Nations to discuss the eventual establishment of public market regulation for zinc, lead, and copper. These meetings fulfill an important function from the point of view of private "mutual understanding on market policy."

The role of the United Nations in the preparation of new commodity agreements is based on a recommendation of the U.N. Social and Economic Committee that the ITO principles on commodity agreements be used as a general guide; [10] these have formed the basis

[5] International Coffee Agreement, T.I.A.S. 6584.

[6] International Olive Oil Agreement, Apr. 20, 1963, 495 U.N.T.S. 3.

[7] Third International Tin Agreement of 1965, United Nations Conference on Trade and Development (UNCTAD), TD/TIN 3/L.I. Apr. 20, 1965; TD/TIN 3/4 May 10, 1965. The United States is not a participant but does consult on an informal basis. In connection with commodity agreements, see Stabilization of International Commodity Markets, UNCTAD, E/Conf. 46/8 Mar. 19, 1964; J. W. F. Rowe, *Primary Commodities in International Trade* (Cambridge, 1965).

[8] International Labor Office, Intergovernmental Commodity Control Agreements I and II (Montreal 1943).

[9] Commission of the European Communities, *First General Report of the Activities of the European Commission of 1967* (Brussels 1968) p. 405.

[10] Economic and Social Council (ECOSOC) Res. 30 (iv) of Mar. 28, 1947. See Staff Papers, Presented to the Commission on Foreign Economic Policy, pp. 189–190 (1954); see also G.A. Res. 623, 7 U.N.G.A.O.R. Supp. 20, p. 15, U.N. Doc. A/2361 (1952), which endorsed the desirability of having stability agreements in the area of raw materials.

of all the commodity agreements concluded to date. The "findings" that have constituted the genesis for each of the agreements have been based on the "findings" required by Article 62 of the ITO charter.[11]

Articles 60 and 63 of the charter set out two basic procedural principles for the conclusion and operation of commodity agreements, and these principles have been uniformly adhered to in negotiating these agreements. First, participation is open to those countries "substantially interested," and second, those countries mainly interested in imports have voting power on substantive matters equal to those countries mainly interested in exports. This principle is considered to be a vast improvement over pre–World War II private cartels, where consumers did not take part in decisions that affected their interests.

The official objective of all five commodity agreements is twofold: to take the price of raw materials out of the market price resulting from offer and demand, and to give each of the producing countries a fixed quota of the international market in export and import.

These objectives may be accomplished by different devices depending on the nature of the commodity in question, and there are several types of international commodity agreements: [12] (1) The agreement can take the form of a buffer stock arrangement, such as the international tin agreements, which are designed to maintain prices within a given range through purchases by empowering the buffer when the market price drops to a certain level and sales when the market price moves too high.[13] (2) The agreement may establish export quotas for each producing country. Under the new cotton agreement excess exports lead to substantial penalties for the exporting countries. (3) The agreement may provide for maximum and minimum export prices. The new Wheat Convention provides for FOB U.S. Gulf "posted prices" (published from time to time in selected papers). (4) Combinations of buffer stock arrangements joined with

---

[11] The requisite "findings" under this article are either (a) a burdensome surplus of the primary commodity, undue hardship to small producers, and price inelasticity, or (b) widespread unemployment, undue hardship to workers, and price inelasticity.

[12] No. 7 above; see also R. F. Mikesell, "Commodity Agreements and Aid to Developing Countries," 28 *Law and Contemp. Prob.* 294 (1963); H. Brodie, "Commodity Agreements—A Partial Answer to the Trade Problems of Developing Countries," 53 *Dept. of State Bull.* 111 (1965).

[13] See also Chapter 4, for a discussion of the arrangements with respect to tin.

quotas regulating the quantities of the raw material to be purchased by the buffer stock management also exist. Another device is the combination of export quotas with development of minimum and maximum prices, as in wheat.

A critical new study of the effects of public commodity agreements on national or international trade, especially when operating in conjunction with private regulation, is imperative.

There is a strong tendency to extend this system of commodity agreements.[14] These agreements are being recommended again and again as novel legal-economic "procedures." Similar methods, as mentioned, have been used under the auspices of the League of Nations.

There is good reason to assume that present agreements will lead to some dangers already apparent in the commodity agreements of the late twenties and early thirties: (1) On renewal every three or five years, each agreement establishes progressively stricter regulation. For instance, in 1968 the coffee agreement enforced the maintenance of export quotas, which the 1965 agreement did not. The 1968 wheat agreement provided for maximum and minimum prices 12 per cent higher than the 1962 agreement and effectively imposed the prices of the convention on nonmembers, in contrast to earlier agreements. (2) The mere expectation of price increases in this kind of negotiation apparently influences the price development: while the 1968 International Sugar Convention was meeting, prices increased by 30 per cent. (3) Since price decreases under the agreement are subject to stringent procedures, all parties have to consider the very real danger of unilateral action by countries exporting cheaper than the fixed price or even than the production costs.[15] (4) In one important point, public raw-material regulation proves weaker than private regulation: private regulators have many devices to shut out newcomers. In public regulation, the experiences of the twenties and the thirties indicate that a higher price for sugar or wheat usually leads to an increase in sugar and wheat production, even in countries that have not previously produced, or at least not exported.[16]

[14] These programs are being undertaken by both the World Bank and UNCTAD.

[15] For example, see the adverse effects which have already been reported as a result of the International Grains Agreement, *Congress. Rec.* 8141 (daily ed. Sept. 20, 1968), and *Congress. Rec.* 7004 (daily ed. July 26, 1968).

[16] M. Palyi, "Fears of World Wheat Shortage Are Unfounded," *Commercial and Financial Chronicle*, Nov. 7, 1968, p. 3.

On the other hand, Pierre E. Trudeau, Prime Minister of Canada, presented the purpose of the Wheat Convention in full when it came under attack by United States farming interests:

Our Canadian answer to this is that the price was set after a great deal of discussion and debate. It is perhaps easy or tempting now to say the price was too high because of the current situation of the producing nations and the surpluses in grain. But this is the basis of all commodity agreements. If we did not have an agreement, we might be able to probably say the price is too high now; but in years of shortage, then the price would probably appear too low to us and we would be tempted, all of us exporters, to up the price considerably to the consuming nations. And that is why a balance must be established in all these international commodities, commodities which are internationally traded, and that is why we have this approach.[17]

In 1962 the leading import and export nations executed an International Cotton Textile Agreement within the framework of GATT.[18] This agreement, designed to meet the special problems of the cotton textile trade, was unique in its approach. Faced with a disruption or threat of disruption in its market, the importing country can request the exporting country to make arrangements to counter the disruptions. If such a bilateral agreement is not reached within sixty days, the importing country can unilaterally limit imports.[19] This GATT Cotton Textile Agreement is certainly much weaker than other commodity agreements (at present in force, it covers about 13 per cent of domestic consumption). A report approved by the International Cotton Advisory Committee pointed out:

The question of a study of an International Cotton Agreement was fully explored. Some producers considered that it would be useful and desirable to undertake a fresh and impartial study of a cotton agreement for the stabilization of the world cotton market and that such agreement might prevent the detrimental effects of unilateral action. The general impression

[17] Reprinted in *Congress. Rec.* S3203 (daily ed. Mar. 26, 1969).

[18] Long-Term Agreement Regarding International Trade in Cotton Textiles, 1962, entered into force for the United States Sept. 26, 1962, 13 U.S.T. 2673, T.I.A.S. 5240, 471 U.N.T.S. 296; protocol for extension until Sept. 30, 1970, T.I.A.S. 6289.

[19] Understandably the developing countries are critical of this agreement. "Exports [of the United Arabian Republic] to the countries which had signed the GATT Long-Term International Agreement for the Organization of World Trade in Cotton Textiles dropped again in 1966" (*Industrial Egypt*, 43, No. 3, p. 29 [1967]).

of many delegates was that in the initial stages at least, a cotton agreement would tend to be restrictive in nature and that limiting of production or exports would not be in the interests of developing nations nor in the best interests of cotton in its efforts to meet the competition from the man-made fibres. The consensus of the meeting was that a study should not be undertaken.[20]

The United States had repeatedly supported an international commodity agreement of cotton.[21]

The Organization of Petroleum Exporting Countries (OPEC) is an agreement among the major petroleum-producing countries to stabilize the world petroleum price.[22] Members include Abu Dhabi, Indonesia, Iran, Iraq, Kuwait, Libya, Quatar, Saudi Arabia, and Venezuela.[23] An economic commission was established in Vienna to aid the organization in promoting stability in international petroleum prices at equitable levels, in keeping with the spirit and principles set out in the Organization's Resolutions I. 1, IV. 32, and V. 42.[24]

Resolution IV. 32 of 1962 clarifies the OPEC's attitude toward the cartellike "posted prices" of the oil companies. According to this resolution, the membership countries shall enter into negotiations "with a view to ensuring that oil produced in Member Countries shall be paid for on the basis of posted prices not lower than those which applied prior to August 1960." Such agreements were partly implemented; because of the international decline of prices, however, some of the oil companies refused to recognize the high 1960 price. Therefore, in Resolution VII. 49 of 1964, OPEC again emphasized, "the Member Countries which accepted the royalty settlement hereby declare that they, with the other Member Countries, are prepared to continue the struggle for the realization of the stand taken concerning crude-oil prices as laid down in Resolution IV. 32 with all the conse-

[20] Annex to proceedings of the 25th Plenary Meeting of the International Cotton Advisory Committee, Pt. 3, pp. 18–28 (1966). GATT long-term cotton textile agreement in force; at present about 30 per cent of domestic consumption.

[21] Id., Pt. 2, pp. 10 ff.

[22] The aim of the organization is to curb competition which it feels is at the root of price weakness; see Statement of the Secretary General of the OPEC to the Second International Symposium on Energy, held at Rome, Mar. 11–13, 1968 (OPEC Bull., Apr. 1968).

[23] The OPEC was established by Iran, Iraq, Kuwait, Saudi Arabia, and Venezuela in Sept. 1960; see Resolutions Adopted at the Conference of the OPEC (1960).

[24] OPEC Res. VIII. 55 (1964).

quences, and are prepared to take action in the interest of it." The posted prices of the oil companies are used not only as a basis for computing license fees but also, according to Resolution X. 64 of 1965, for the purpose of taxing the oil companies in each country participating in the treaty. By 1968 the Organization had effectively stabilized posted crude-oil prices, supported mainly by the private cartel organization of the oil companies. Threats of a boycott or other action against the uncooperative oil companies appear to have been successful. The OPEC has also explored the possibility of imposing maximum quotas for production and exportation of crude-oil.

The Council of Copper Exporting Countries (CIPEC), (Chile, Congo, Peru, and Zambia) controlled about half of the world copper export outside the Communist Bloc in 1967.[25] The Council is at present engaged in establishing in Paris an organization similar to the OPEC with the approval of the governments involved. The interest of the private companies and the governments in securing the highest profits will presumably promote cooperation.

The governments of Ghana, Nigeria, Brazil, Ivory Coast, Cameroun Republic, and Togo, which produced 79 per cent of the world crop in 1960 and 1965, established the Cocoa Producers Alliance.[26] This organization tried to control prices and other market conditions but failed in 1966. It tried to withhold the 1964–1965 crop until prices rose to 26.6 cents per pound. Some of the producers did not withhold all their supply, and purchasers were sceptical about the eventual success of the agreement and had sufficient supplies to withstand the boycott.

Another form of international agreement with direct market-regulating effect is the North Atlantic Treaty Organization (NATO), which provides that regulation defense contracts for NATO requirements can be given only to contractors who reside in a member state and a majority of whose stockholders reside in member states.[27]

Trade with Communist Bloc countries is usually transacted according to the system that governed international trade between the world wars: modified barter agreements involving mutual concessions. The effect of these barter agreements even on competition within each state

[25] See "Copper Vacuum," *Mining J.*, May 10, 1968.

[26] J. R. Behrmann, "Monopolistic Cocoa Pricing," 50 *Am. J. of Agriculture and Economics* 702 (1968).

[27] U.S. Government Contracts Reports (1958–1965 ed., 7-25-61), p. 511.

is evident. First, as in the case of aluminum,[28] the quantity involved in these exchanges is controlled so as not to disturb the home market. Second, the negotiations and consultations of the domestic supplier with his government are an excellent starting point for working out their own common action or tacit agreements.

The American-Canadian Agreement on Continental American Oil Policy was described by Pierre E. Trudeau, Prime Minister of Canada, at the National Press Club in Washington, March 25, 1969, in reporting on his meeting with President Nixon:

> We have a continental oil policy of sorts. It was set up in the past and worked reasonably well. The technical details of it are perhaps a bit elaborate, but essentially it means that Canadian oil producers sell to Western Canada and sell to the United States an amount roughly equivalent to the amount of oil that Eastern Canada purchases overseas and notably from the Venezuelan producers. It is a deal between the American government and the Canadian government with its cost savings for both parties. . . . I think we have arguments for the United States in the sense that our oil is not only cheaper but it is more secure in terms of defense in any future conflict. It is continental oil, it is more easy of access.[29]

As a matter of fact, this "deal" between governments can only be understood in relation to the unilateral American oil regulation. From the point of view of U.S. constitutional law it would be quite interesting to examine what type of agreement or treaty this "deal" is.

Indirect Market-Regulating Effects

Other international agreements do not specifically regulate international trade between private enterprises but affect world trade indirectly when used as an element of private market regulation structure. These agreements include the following types: (1) agreements leading to a customs union or a free trade area, for example, the Treaty of Rome, establishing the European Economic Community or the European Free Trade Area Convention; (2) agreements on the gradual abolition of import restrictions, such as GATT, and agreements on double taxation; (3) ageements on the establishment and maintenance of monetary order, especially the Bretton Woods Agreement, the International Monetary Fund, and subsequent agreements in this field; (4) agree-

---

[28] The Benelux countries fix a quota for Russian aluminum imports; other states use import licensing. See press release of Mar. 1964, Metallgesellschaft AG, Z/1.

[29] Reprinted in *Congress. Rec.* S3199 (daily ed. Mar. 26, 1969).

ments on safety measures and standardization of products in international trade; (5) agreements on the protection of industrial property rights (patents and trade marks) in international trade.

The most far-reaching is the General Agreement on Tariffs and Trade (GATT). The 1967 Geneva Protocol concluding the so-called Kennedy Round continued arrangements to harmonize market conditions to avoid governmental interferences through quantitative and qualitative restrictions in reducing tariffs. Of special importance in the relationship between private and public regulation are the antidumping rules, especially the implementation of Article 6 of the GATT. This agreement came into force on July 1, 1968.[30]

Coordination among Governments and with International Agreements

International market regulation can be strengthened by coordination of the individual measures of a government with international agreements or with the individual measures of other governments. While such coordination may narrow the scope of private systems of regulation, it may also give enterprises an opportunity to develop their own private market-regulating activity under the protection of the public market regulations.

Petroleum

The power of the Organization of Petroleum Exporting Countries by itself to influence international petroleum trade of the independent oil companies is very limited. However, countries that import and produce petroleum have established their own regulations to protect their domestic reserves and market, and in effect these regulations have strengthened the OPEC. Great influence has also been exerted by the export restrictions of the individual oil-producing countries.

Domestically, even though the production of crude oil in the United States is within the jurisdiction of each producing state, the Texas Railroad Commission (that state's oil regulatory agency) has exercised a dominant influence beyond the boundaries of Texas.[31] The Commis-

[30] GATT, Legal Instruments Embodying the Results of the 1964–67 Trade Conference, H.R. Doc. No. 184, 90th Cong., 1st Sess. (1967).

[31] See in this connection A. Schoenfield, n. 1 above, p. 439; statement of the Chairman of the Texas Petroleum Research Comm., U.S. Cong. House Select Comm. on Small Business, *Hearings on Small Business Problems Created by Petroleum Imports*, 87th Cong., 1st Sess., p. 105, (1961); see also U.S. Cong.,

sion establishes monthly production quotas for all producers in Texas; it sets the number of working days during which the producers are permitted to pump their wells to full capacity.[32] The other oil-producing states adapt themselves to these quotas (with the exception of California, which does not use any rationing system) because all the states know that if these guidelines should be significantly breached, Texas could flood the market with its tremendous capacity.[33]

In establishing the quotas, the Railroad Commission requests an estimate of demand from the oil companies. This system of balance between supply and demand, called "market demand proration," is justified as being in the security interests of the United States. However, the fact that the production quota is based on the estimated demand of the largest oil companies and that other producers are bound by it, invites doubt whether security and protection against waste of United States products actually prevail. Nobody fixes the price, yet it is obvious that what exists here is a completely regulated market. The prices are artificially kept high and the strongest enterprises with the help of government become the "policemen."

To understand the full effect of "oil conservation" on prices, it is necessary to take into account U.S. petroleum import restrictions.[34] Section 8 of the Trade Agreements Extension Act of 1958 [35] and Section 232 of the Trade Expansion Act of 1962 [36] have given the President authority to establish quotas for petroleum imports. The

House Comm. on Small Business, Subcomm. No. 4, *Hearings on FTC Industry Conference on Marketing of Automotive Gasoline* (statement of W. E. Turner), 89th Cong., 1st Sess., Pt. 1, App. 1, p. 50 (1965).

[32] In effect it sets a certain percentage of permitted capacity allowed; for example, in Apr. 1968, the output from regulated wells was set at 46.7 per cent of permitted capacity (*Wall Street J.*, Apr. 18, 1968).

[33] Texas is a member of the Interstate Oil Compact whose Commission acts as an agency for the exchange of information on oil conservation (77 Stat. 145) (1963). The Commission itself has not undertaken to direct the activities of any of the state members and the regulatory system accomplishes only an indirect and partial balancing of overall crude oil supply, which permits higher prices to be established than would normally prevail if no controls existed; see *Report of the Attorney General, Pursuant to Sec. 2 of the Joint Res. of Sept. 6, 1963, Consenting to an Interstate Compact to Conserve Oil and Gas*, Report 16-8 (1967).

[34] U.S. Dept. of Interior, Oil Import Administration, *Brief History and Description of Oil Import Program* (Aug. 3, 1964).

[35] 19 U.S.C. §1351 (1964).

[36] 19 U.S.C. §1801 (1964). See also Proclamation of U.S. Dept. of Interior, Oil Import Administration, Oil Reg. 1, Rev. 4, Amends. 1-5.

quota is based on estimates by refineries of their requirements for the
cheaper foreign oil for the types of products into which the oil will be
converted.[37] In determining the quota, the decisive factor may very
well be the protection and preservation of an adequate price for the
domestic market.

It is clear that the import restrictions of the United States are not
welcomed as such by the members of the OPEC, but the resulting price
maintenance enables them to more easily stabilize their own export
prices. Therefore, the member countries in Resolution II. 14 of 1961
expressed their hope that agreements could be reached "in order to
arrive at satisfactory solutions and thus promote mutual understandings for the protection of the interests of both exporting and importing
countries." Furthermore, the public regulations of American oil production and imports are a decisive factor in the international private
market regulations of the oil companies. In *United States v. Standard
Oil of Indiana* the court noted that the federal government of the
United States, "together with the regulatory agencies in the principal
producing states, exercises considerable influence over crude oil prices.
By controlling the amount of domestic production and imports, State
and Federal authorities determine the total available crude oil supply
which, in turn, governs the level of crude oil prices." [38] The oil companies can therefore rely on the government's planned figures and can
build them into their own system. It will be shown later that such a
system exists and is not eliminated by governmental regulations.

The American-Canadian government oil deal referred to above is an
international arrangement for the purpose of maintaining the American
domestic governmental oil policy, namely the maintenance of strategic
reserves within the American continent, while Canada purchases in
Venezuela. At the same time, this deal is a protective device for the
American owners of the Venezuelan firms.[39]

On April 21, 1953, the United States government brought suit

[37] The oil import quota is established at the beginning of each year by the
U.S. Dept. of Interior, Oil Import Administration. The Department announces
the allocation of these quotas under the mandatory oil import program on a
six-month basis in order to assure a stable level of imports throughout the year.
See U.S. Dept. of Interior Press Release, Feb. 14, 1968.

[38] CCH Trade Cas. ¶71,215 at 79,841 (N.D. Cal. 1964).

[39] There are some cases which may be on the borderline between unilateral
action (discussed in the next section), and coordinated action of governments, as,
for example, with sugar.

against the Standard Oil Company of New Jersey, Socony Mobil Oil Company, Texaco, and Gulf Oil Corporation.[40] The government alleged that the defendants had tacitly continued the 1928 international cartel agreement (the Achnacarry Agreement) between themselves, British Petroleum Corporation, Royal Dutch Petroleum Company, Shell Transport and Trading Company, and others. The suit was terminated by consent judgments [41] prohibiting the American companies from observing the agreement. This judgment also applied to all corporations under the control of the defendants.

The permissive provisions of the consent judgment rendered on July 29, 1963, against Texaco [42] are representative of the general approach used to settle these cases. Neither Texaco nor the companies under its control were required to violate foreign law in satisfying the terms of the judgment. Texaco was allowed to participate in any agreement restricting competition when such an agreement is required either by law of the foreign nation, or by the decree of any supranational authority having jurisdiction over the agreement, or by the official pronouncement of the foreign government's policy where failure to comply with the policy would expose Texaco to the risk of present or future loss of business in the foreign nation.

These broad exceptions from the consent decree are practically a blank check for bypassing consent judgments.[43] Here it may be sufficient to refer to the clauses dealing with the OPEC. The firmly expressed "desire" of the petroleum producing countries, like that expressed in the resolution quoted above, is obviously covered by the "saving clause" of the consent judgment even though the acts are beyond the territorial reach of the OPEC. Practically all forms of market regulation used by the oil companies—which will be discussed later—are covered by this "saving clause." This is especially true of the posted prices system, which is of great importance to the price stabilization policy of OPEC's members.

---

[40] U.S. District Court for the District of Columbia, Civil Action No. 86-27. For a discussion of this procedure see H. Kronstein, "Staat und private Macht in der neueren amerikanischen Rechtsentwicklung," in *Festschrift zum 70. Geburtstag von Franz Böhm* (Karlsruhe, 1965).

[41] Kronstein, *id.*, p. 155, n. 80.

[42] United States v. Standard Oil Co. (New Jersey) (Texaco Inc.) 1963, Trade Cas. ¶70,819 at 78,309 (S.D.N.Y. 1963).

[43] Kronstein, n. 40 above, pp. 157 ff.

Cotton Textiles, Zinc, and Sugar

A certain coordination of the individual measures of government and international agreements is also apparent in the field of cotton textiles. Some countries, upon execution of the Cotton Textile Agreement, enacted domestic legislation for trade with countries not members of this agreement. These measures for nonmember states were practically the same as the bilateral import quotas established by treaty according to the textile agreement provisions.[44]

Zinc is an example of the coordinated effect of individual measures by different governments. From 1958 to 1965 U.S. law provided absolute import quotas for zinc apportioned among those countries exporting to the United States.[45] Sales of zinc from the strategic reserves in the United States were also severely restricted until July 1964.[46] Since USSR zinc production was subject to the Soviet plan, it also remained a predictable factor for years in the planning of the major zinc producers. These two governmental measures established reliable constants for the zinc market, enabling the private regulators to carry out regulation of the area. A much more modest program has also been undertaken by the United States to stabilize prices for small domestic producers of lead and zinc.[47] If a producer qualifies as a "small domestic producer," he is eligible for "stabilization payments." These subsidy payments have only limited effect on the market.[48]

Sugar is an especially interesting example of the coordinated effect of planning by individual governments (for their own country as well as their neighbors) and international commodity agreements.

World sugar trade can be classified in two categories: free market trade and trade outside the free market. If trade subject to regulation of quantity, direction, and price is included in the second category, then this category accounted for about 50 per cent of world sugar exports over the period 1954 to 1962. Such regulated trade includes

[44] N. 19 above.

[45] In this connection see Exec. Order No. 3257, 3 C.F.R., 1954–58 Cong., p. 165; U.S. Tariff Commission: *Lead and Zinc, Report to the President on Investigation No. TEA-1A-3.* ¶*351(d) (2) of Trade Expansion Act of 1962.* TC Publ. 157, Table 1 (June 1965).

[46] U.S. Tariff Commission, *id.*, p. 13.

[47] P.L. 87-345, 75 Stat. 766 (1961) as modified by P.L. 89-238, 79 Stat. 925 (1965).

[48] Report of the Secretary of the Interior on the Lead and Zinc Mining Stabilization Program, reprinted in *Congress. Rec.* S2532 (daily ed. Mar. 10, 1969).

transactions under the Commonwealth Sugar Agreement, the United States Sugar Act, the French Sugar Bloc Agreement, and the Portuguese Sugar Bloc Agreement.[49] The United States Sugar Act provides for the division of the U.S. market between domestic production and specific quotas allocated to other countries.[50]

The Common Market of Europe is bringing into force parallel sugar legislation, and the Commonwealth Sugar Agreement is already in existence. The commodity agreement on sugar has not been signed by the United States and the European Common Market. It is clear, however, that the study of the total regulation of the sugar market is understandable only if the national restrictions are considered in connection with the commodity agreements. The international organizers of the sugar market and the partners to the international sugar agreement can rely on the existence of the domestic organization of the United States and EEC markets.

Unilateral Measures of Governments

Unilateral governmental measures taken to regulate foreign trade or which affect the foreign trade of a particular state can also become a significant element for international market regulation. As was true with intergovernmental agreements and the coordination of individual measures, such unilateral measures can restrict the area in which private industry can establish its own regulation, but often they are used as a tool to create or maintain private market regulations. In discussing this aspect of the problem, it is necessary to distinguish between short- and long-range effects of such measures.[51]

Measures Intended to Affect Foreign Trade

Aid to developing countries

During and immediately after World War II, one of the main objectives of American trade policy was to break up the division of the markets of South America, Asia, and Africa which then existed. This policy had special consequences for aid to developing countries. However, under the pressures created by balance-of-payments problems and for other reasons as well, a revival and even a strengthening of the old

[49] 50 *Am. J. of Agriculture and Economics* 531 (1968).   [50] *Id.*, table p. 523.
[51] This discussion of unilateral measures which achieve a market regulation must rely on specific examples to a even greater extent than was true with international arrangements or coordinated actions of governments. Indeed, all measures in regard to taxes, financial matters, and labor may become pertinent.

market divisions of the developing countries has occurred. Market division as a result of aid to developing countries has, to a large extent, replaced the classical market divisions of cartel agreements, tariff policies, and quantitative restrictions.

One example of this new form of market division can be seen in foreign aid policy of the United States. Under the Foreign Assistance Act of 1961, the President is required to take into consideration the possible effects upon the United States of the loan or the grant.[52] This provision is implemented by Section 604, which provides that goods purchased under the American foreign aid program may be obtained outside of the United States only when the President determines that this purchase will not have damaging consequences for the economy of the United States and when the price of the goods purchased abroad (taking into account differences in transportation costs, quality, and conditions of payment) is lower than the prevailing market price in the United States.[53] The result of this proviso was that in 1965, 80 per cent of the available aid to developing countries was tied to American supplies.[54]

Further, an important tying clause with respect to ocean transportation exists within the framework of American aid to developing countries. The Agency for International Development (AID) and the Department of Agriculture (under their P.L. 480 sales) [55] are required to ship 50 per cent of the goods purchased under their programs on American vessels if such vessels are available at fair and reasonable rates. In practice, however, neither AID nor the Department of Agriculture examines whether American freight rates are reasonable. If the American freight rates rise above foreign rates, the Department covers this difference in 50 per cent of its shipments, leaving the foreign importer to pay only the foreign freight rate. As a result, 70 per cent of the U.S. government cargoes generated under these two programs are shipped on American vessels.[56]

The use of such tying clauses in the U.S. foreign-aid program not

[52] See Foreign Assistance Act of 1961, 22 U.S.C. §2161(b)(6).

[53] Id., §2354.

[54] U.S. Cong. House Comm. on Foreign Affairs, Hearings on Foreign Assistance Act of 1965, 89th Cong., 1st Sess., Pt. 2, p. 278 (1965).

[55] 7 U.S.C. §§1722, 1732 (1964). See also report on the extent to which these laws are complied with; Congress. Rec. S2195 (daily ed. Feb. 28, 1969).

[56] U.S. Cong. Joint Economic Comm., Subcomm. on Federal Procurement and Regulation Hearings on Discriminatory Ocean Freight Rates and the Balance of Payments, 89th Cong., 1st Sess., Pt. 1, pp. 1–19 (1965).

only protects American enterprises from foreign competition but also offers an excellent opportunity for American enterprises to limit competition among themselves within this protected market. For example, an agreement among American producers of concentrated phosphate fertilizer provided for artificially high prices and for the allocation of foreign aid shipments to South Korea among these producers.[57] These agreements were particularly advantageous to the few American enterprises involved because of the protection against foreign competition offered by the tying clauses. In the absence of such a clause, the price of American goods would not have been competitive with the price offered by foreign suppliers, who would have had shorter shipping distances.

Further evidence of similar agreements is provided in the hearings of the Federal Maritime Commission in 1964.[58] American exporters testified that they generally delivered goods only to countries that maintained relations with AID. The exporters stated that they did not have to fear foreign competition and that competition among domestic enterprises was dealt with "properly."

Other countries show parallel developments. The Federal Republic of Germany officially ties only 20 per cent of its foreign aid by specifically restricting bids to its own country; however, the approximate percentage of foreign aid actually spent in Germany is about 80.[59] This high percentage is based, in part, on the fact that under German practice foreign aid is generally tied to a particular project. Also, the developing countries—probably correctly—assume that the involvement of German enterprises in a prospective project substantially increases their chance of receiving foreign aid.[60] In addition, an important factor in larger shipments and installations is that replacement parts can usually be obtained more easily from the original supplier. Another reason is that German industry exerts pressure to obtain the greatest benefits possible for itself from German foreign

[57] United States v. Concentrated Phosphate Export Ass'n, 273 F. Supp. 263 (S.D.N.Y. 1967).

[58] Docket No. 1114, Federal Maritime Commission, V and VI, pp. 534 ff. (1964).

[59] Statement by Federal Minister for Foreign Aid of the Federal Republic of Germany, BT-Drucksache IV/3772, p. 1; Walter Trautmann, "Entwicklungshilfe-Deutsche Weltbankmilliarden," Der Volkswirt, Mar. 26, 1965; F. K. Vialon, Entwicklungshilfe in der Diskussion, Sonderdruck im Auftrag des Bundesministeriums für wirtschaftliche Zusammenarbeit (Bonn, 1964), p. 29.

[60] Statement by Federal Minister for Foreign Aid, n. 59 above.

aid. Similarly, in other European countries, such as Great Britain and France, the share of tied foreign aid also appears to be very great.

In addition to the wide prevalence of tying clauses within the foreign aid framework, it should also be noted that a reluctance to use multilateral aid exists in all states.[61] One obvious reason for this is that each country fears that its control over the use of the aid funds will be impaired.

From the above analysis, it is reasonable to conclude that the similar aid practices of the granting states close whole markets and remove them from the international marketplace. Even the multinational development programs, especially those connected with the International Development Association and the World Bank, where competitive bids are invited, do not affect this situation significantly. First, the amount of foreign aid from these programs is relatively small. Second, many projects are only partially financed multilaterally with the balance financed nationally. Because of the economic-technical considerations in a particular project, companies of the countries that jointly finance the project on the national level have a competitive advantage in the award of contracts on the whole project. And finally, agreements among producers of like commodities to submit their bid jointly rather than individually can restrict competition.[62]

Of course, there are instances of competition among enterprises of different industrial countries involving foreign aid to the developing countries. India is an example. But this is more a desire to share the uncertainties of trade with a partner. In short, the removal of entire markets from the normal international market by means of foreign aid and the subsequent diversion of trade flow must be considered in all discussions of the cartel issue.

Monetary control

In 1969, just as between the first and second world wars, political and governmental control over monetary policy, whether to maintain domestic purchasing power or to regulate relationships with other currencies, led to a practical division of markets or at least established sufficient elements for use in public and private agreements. The Bretton Woods Agreement indicates an optimism on the part of its signers in regard to the establishment of a stable monetary relationship between nations. In spite of the requirement to consult the International Mone-

[61] *Id.*, pp. 3–4; F. K. Vialon, n. 59 above, p. 31.   [62] N. 57 above.

tary Fund before interference in the stability of currency, the agreement does permit unilateral action if absolutely necessary and obliges other members to recognize such action, even if such a step will seriously interfere with the free flow of trade. After the war, the difference in buying power and exchange rates of the Deutsche Mark (DM) and the dollar decisively influenced the great expansion of American industry in Germany.[63] The increase in valuation of the DM by 5 per cent in 1961 adversely affected the competitive ability of German industry in export markets for a period of time,[64] whereas one of the avowed purposes of the devaluation of the pound sterling was to increase exports from Great Britain.[65]

Another opportunity that exists for countries to use their currency sovereignty to influence international competition and which provides a starting point for private regulation of international trade is through foreign exchange control. While the Bretton Woods Agreement of 1945 [66] restricts the use of this device by individual countries, it does permit national regulations to exist in certain areas, and all member states of the International Monetary Fund are bound to recognize within their own territory the use of these restrictions by other countries.[67] The IMF Agreement specifically permits national regulation of capital transactions.[68]

Tariff authority

International market divisions are greatly controlled by tariff walls.[69] This is especially true in a country like the United States that maintains

[63] With respect to American investment abroad see E. Benoit, "Interdependence on a Small Planet," 6 *Atlantic Community Q.* 80 (1968).

[64] With respect to problems in revaluation of currency, see J. Robinson, *Readings in the Theory of International Trade* (Philadelphia, 1949), p. 393.

[65] Speech of Prime Minister Wilson announcing the devaluation of the pound, reprinted in *New York Times,* Nov. 20, 1967.

[66] Articles of agreement of the International Monetary Fund, Dec. 27, 1945, 60 Stat. 1401, T.I.A.S. 1501; 2 U.N.T.S. 39.

[67] *Id.,* Art. 8(2)(b). See J. Gold, "The Fund Agreement in the Courts," VII, 9 *IMF Staff Papers* No. 2, p. 264 (1962), and VIII, 11 *IMF Staff Papers* No. 3, p. 465 (1964), and J. Gold, *The International Monetary Fund and Private Business Transactions: Some Legal Effects of the Articles of Agreement* (Washington, 1965); also Banco do Brasil, S.A. v. A.C. Israel Commodity Co., Inc., 12 N.Y. 2d 371, 190 N.E. 2d 235 (1963).

[68] IMF Agreement, Art. 6(3).

[69] For a general discussion of this problem, see E. Hexner, *International Cartels* (Chapel Hill, 1945), p. 127.

relatively high protective tariffs. Consequently, any changes in tariff rates can lead to changes in the market division. Such changes occur when a concession granted by one country is withdrawn in accordance with the GATT rules because it considers that reciprocal concessions granted to it have been impaired or when a country reduces its tariff rates unilaterally.[70] For example, Section 252 of the Foreign Assistance Act of 1962 [71] gives the President of the United States authority to increase tariffs on exports from other countries in retaliation for the imposition of tariffs or nontariff barriers by that country.

A second method of erecting tariff barriers is through an artificial increase in the basis upon which a tariff rate is determined. This is aptly illustrated by the "American Selling Price" (ASP) system utilized to protect certain domestic products in the chemical field. In dealing with a limited number of products, the ASP system uses the wholesale price of the American product as the basis upon which the computation of a customs duty is made rather than using the wholesale value of the goods in the country of origin. The ASP is almost always higher than the invoice price of the item in question [72] and for that reason became a major issue from the onset of the Kennedy Round of trade negotiations. Finally, on June 30, 1967, the American negotiators agreed to seek Congressional approval of the elimination of the ASP on benzenoid chemicals [73] (the most significant item to which ASP was applied) in return for a substantial tariff reduction for exports of U.S. chemicals [74] and for the removal of a number of nontariff trade barriers that adversely affect the exports of other U.S. products, such as tobacco [75] and automobiles.[76]

The regulating effect of tariff quotas is also very apparent. A tariff quota generally imposes a favorable duty rate on the import of a specified amount of goods from one or more countries. Imports in excess of this quota are subject to a prohibitively higher customs rate. The German quota for coal is a good example.[77] The tariff quota

---

[70] GATT, Jan. 1, 1948, Art. 23, 61 Stat. Pts. (5–6), T.I.A.S. 1700 (1947), as amended 62 Stat. (Pt. 3) 3680, T.I.A.S. 1890 (1948), 55–61 U.N.T.S.

[71] 19 U.S.C. §1351 (1964).

[72] W. Roth, "What Comes Next in the U.S.," 5 *Atlantic Community Q.* 358, 360–365 (1967).

[73] Agreement Relating Principally to Chemicals, Supplementary to the Geneva (1967) Protocol to the GATT, Pt. II, Subpt. A, Art. 2.

[74] *Id.*, Pt. III, Subpt. A, Art. 6.   [75] *Id.*, Pt. IV, Subpt. B, Art. 9.

[76] *Id.*, Pt. III, Subpt. B, Art. 7.   [77] Cf. AWD 1959, p. 42; 1963, p. 20.

guarantees an outlet for a specific quantity of cheaper American coal but, by setting a prohibitively high tariff for American coal above the quota, assures that the remainder of German needs will be provided by domestic producers of other member states of the European Coal and Steel Community (ECSC) cartel organizations.

Cartels granted legislative and administrative sanction

Many countries actually permit export cartels or grant exemptions in specific cases. Except for the United States, where the so-called Webb-Pomerene export cartels are not allowed to participate in international arrangements,[78] the members of export cartels are permitted to arrange any kind of restraint with each other, with other enterprises, or with other export cartels. Such governmental sanction opens the door for far-reaching international market regulation.[79] This is especially true when the enterprises of the country permitting the cartel have a strong position in the exportation of a particular product. And this sanction becomes even more significant if a number of the most important exporting countries permit export cartels for a specific product, for there is a strong tendency to coordinate the policies of the different cartels into an oligopolistic structure. By permitting and even encouraging export cartels in the interest of expanded foreign trade, without sufficient consideration to the structure of a particular export market, a country often creates the basis for a powerful private market regulation which may have harmful effects on its own economy in the long run.[80]

An unusual aspect in private market regulation by cartel arrangements is the Japanese export cartels for textiles, steel, aluminum, and photographic supplies. Because low-priced Japanese goods were disrupting the Western markets, especially the American market, the United States recommended that the Japanese enterprises enter into export cartels to insure that minimum prices and maximum quantities would be established in their exports to the United States in order to

---

[78] See United States v. United States Alkali Export Ass'n, 86 F. Supp. 59 (S.D.N.Y. 1949).

[79] In this connection, see especially H. Kronstein, "Conflicts Resulting from the Extraterritorial Effects of the Antitrust Legislation of Different Countries," in *Legal Essays in Honor of Hessel E. Yntema* (Leyden, 1961), pp. 432 ff.; K. Brewster, Jr., "Complementary Remarks to Problems Posed by Import and Export Associations," 2 *Cartel and Monopoly in Modern Law* 743 ff. (1961).

[80] See Kronstein, *id.*

forestall the imposition of antidumping duties. This was a special type of export cartel created to insure the ability to export, rather than an arrangement for the purpose of regulating an export market, as is the case under normal German and American practice.

A Swiss statute regulating the export of watches and the subsequent private agreements among the largest exporters of wrist watches have many of the characteristics of a cartel.[81] Until recently, the government not only controlled investment, but also established the quantities for export and set other export regulations. Within the framework of the Swiss statutes a cartellike organization was established which regulated exports, particularly to the United States, the largest importer of Swiss watches. This system not only restricted exports from Switzerland but also stimulated German and Austrian competitors to coordinate their actions with the Swiss producers.

Another example of governmental sanctions of restrictive practices involved the approval of shipping conferences by the various nations. For example, in the United States, the Shipping Act of 1916 provides for an exemption from the antitrust laws for all shipping conference agreements regulated under that act.[82] These conferences are subject to regulation, however. The United States Federal Maritime Commission exercises jurisdiction over shipping conferences affecting trade with the United States. If these conferences discriminate against shipping lines which are not members of the conference, or establish higher freight rates for shipments from the United States to Europe than for trade in the opposite direction,[83] the Commission can disapprove the agreement and subject the parties to the American antitrust statutes. The Federal Maritime Commission thus exercises a genuine market-regulating function, but even so it was done as a defense against private market-restraining agreements.

[81] In this connection see United States v. Watchmakers of Switzerland Information Center, Inc., 1962 CCH Trade Cas. (S.D.N.Y. 1962), ¶69,988.

[82] At present there are 90 to 100 carrier shipping conferences and an additional 30 rate agreements which are similar to conferences. Information given by the Federal Maritime Board, April 1971. Shipping Act of 1916 still in force.

[83] In connection with the Shipping Act as amended in 1961, which laid down the regulation of shipping conferences, and with respect to investigations led by the Federal Maritime Commission according to the Shipping Act, see T. J. May, "The Status of Federal Maritime Commission Shipping Regulations Under Principles of International Law," 54 Geo. L.J. 794–856 (1966); see also Hearings on Discriminatory Ocean Freight Rates, n. 56 above, p. 3; S. Rep. No. 1, 89th Cong., 1st Sess. (1963).

Secondary Measures Which Affect Foreign Trade

Of particular interest in this study are a number of heterogeneous measures designed primarily to regulate internal trade but which affect foreign trade, or measures which are designed to regulate one particular aspect of foreign trade but which have side effects on other aspects of foreign trade.

Governmental procurement policies

After World War II, governments became increasingly involved in contracting with private industry for services and supplies. This led to significant changes in the demand structure of some markets.[84] For example, the United States spent 70 billion dollars for procurements for military purposes in 1967.[85] An additional $5.4 billion was spent for research and development in that year.[86] These two sums in themselves were almost 50 per cent of the total public expenditures.

While the effects of governmental procurement policies upon internal markets is not of concern at this point, it is of importance to note that these policies have a significant effect upon foreign trade. It is only natural that governments and government-controlled enterprises whose procurement policies follow those of the government will favor domestic enterprises in placing orders. Political considerations, such as those which exist in the Federal Republic of Germany, may suggest a more flexible policy, but this is an exceptional circumstance.

In addition, many governments are legally bound to make, or have established the practice of making, their purchases from domestic enterprises. One clear example is the Buy American Act, which provides that materials to be used in the United States must, as a rule, come from American enterprises. The "Buy National" policy of the majority of other industrial countries is not defined as openly as that of the United States, but the history of administrative practice shows favoritism toward domestic firms. Foreign firms are discouraged by the numerous

---

[84] Compare U.S. Cong., Joint Economic Comm., *Economic Impact of Federal Procurement, Report of the Subcomm. on Federal Procurement and Reg.*, 89th Cong., 1st Sess. (Joint Comm. on Printing, 1965), and J. Whelan, "Public Contracts of the United Kingdom Government: A Comparative Survey and Introduction," 32 *Geo. Wash. L. Rev.* 82 (1963).

[85] U.S. Bureau of the Budget, *The Budget in Brief*, for Fiscal Year 1969, p. 17.

[86] *Id.* These figures should be compared with earlier figures. For example, in 1964, $26 billion was spent for military procurements and $14.5 billion for research and development.

technical regulations and by the lack of public notice in placing government orders. As a result, foreign firms are used only in very minor ways or are excluded entirely from certain orders.[87]

While the purchasing power of the government is a potential counterweight to the power of private industrial organizations, such power has not really deterred the power of the private sector, but rather has been utilized by it. One example of this is the procurement policies of the European governmental postal administrations. In theory these administrations should have been able to rely upon competition among the various bidders in order to elicit the best offer. It has been more practical, however, for the postal administrations to place orders exclusively with the powerful group of enterprises that control the national and international field through exchanges of patents and know-how.[88]

The same is true with government orders for military equipment. In the United States, the procurement agencies often consider it more reasonable to buy from the larger enterprises with considerable production and development capacities.[89] Thus, the smaller enterprises are brought into procurement arrangements only as subcontractors, with the large enterprises doing the main work.

Investment control

Governmental control over investments occurs not only in the less developed countries but also in England, the United States, and France,[90] with significant effects on the economy. This investment

[87] All the regulations are compiled in *Congress. Rec.* 20279–20346 (daily ed. Aug. 19, 1964). For a discussion of the "Buy American" policies, see Michael Baram, "Buy American," 8 *Boston College Ind. and Com. L. Rev.* 269 (1966).

[88] In connection with the procurement policy of the German Bundespost (which deals in postal affairs, telephone, and telegraph), see Rudolf Meierrose and Gerd Wiegand, *Jahrbuch des elektrischen Fernmeldewesens* (Bonn, 1965), pp. 9, 20, 25, 28, 38, 51.

[89] Almost half of the prime contracts awarded by the Department of Defense go to 25 companies (*Business Week*, June 22, 1968, p. 48).

[90] In regard to the situation in France, see J. Fourastié and J. P. Courthéoux, *La Planification économique en France* (Paris, 1963). The situation in England is characterized by the establishment of the National Economic Development Council, which regularly publishes economic analysis and programs based thereon; compare *Growth of the United Kingdom Economy to 1966* (London, 1963), *Conditions Favourable to Faster Growth* (London, 1963), and *The Growth of the Economy* (London, 1964).

control must be considered in the private as well as the public regulation of international trade.

Nearly all countries exercise control over investments in their own territory.[91] This is particularly true of industries extracting raw materials such as coal, crude oil, and natural gas. Usually a regulatory statute will provide for the establishment of an institution to which planned investments must be submitted.[92] This institution is then authorized to examine the planned investments to insure their compatibility with governmental aims.[93] Another governmental method often utilized is registration of all foreign investments made in the country. Before the registration is allowed, the planned investment is subject to an examination of its legality and desirability.[94]

An even more important factor to be considered in international regulation is the investment control that countries exercise over foreign investments of their own residents. Immediately after World War II, the tendency was to give all possible freedom to private investment. Today, with a few exceptions such as Germany, the situation is nearly reversed. For example, in the United States, under the Interest Equalization Tax, the purchase of foreign securities by private investors or banks is subject to a graduated excise tax of 15 per cent, and loans to foreign enterprises are subject to a tax ranging from 2¾ to 15 per cent.[95] In addition, on January 1, 1968, under 5(b) of the Trading-With-the-Enemy Act, mandatory controls over foreign investments were promulgated by the President of the United States. These mandatory controls are basically twofold: they limit the transfer of capital abroad unless authorized under the regulations or licensed by the

[91] In this connection, see H. Aufricht, "A Study of Foreign Investment Law: A Cross-Section View of the Foreign Investment Laws in Force in 1957," in J. Starkes, *Protection and Encouragement in Private Foreign Investment* (Washington, D.C., 1966), p. 23.

[92] For instance, in Afghanistan (Rules and Regulations Governing the Investment of Foreign Capital, Art. 12, 1954); Chile (Act No. 437, Arts. 8, 9, 11, Feb. 2, 1954); China (Stat. for Investment by Foreign Nationals, Art. 6, July 14, 1954); Greece (Act No. 2687, Art. 3, published in *Official Gazette*, Nov. 10, 1953); Israel (Law for the Encouragement of Capital Investment in Israel, Art. 8, 1955).

[93] Compare Afghanistan, Art. 13, with Chile, Art. 11, with China, Art. 6, of the regulations cited in n. 92 above.

[94] For example, in Colombia (Act No. 8, Art. 2, July 18, 1952). Sometimes the granting of certain advantages depends on the registration; for example, in Argentina (Act No. 14, Art. 5, Aug. 26, 1953).

[95] Interest Equalization Tax, 26 U.S.C. §4911 (1964).

Secretary of Commerce;[96] and they require the repatriation of a substantial portion of earnings from abroad and the reduction of bank deposits and other short-term financial assets abroad.[97]

Stockpiles

The United States, in particular, has maintained an immense supply of strategically important raw materials and ready-made articles, so-called stockpiles,[98] for a long time. Originally, only those products that were scarce in the United States and had to be imported were stocked, such as tin and copper. Later, however, the stockpile was significantly expanded and today it contains goods having a value of 6.6 billion dollars.[99]

After the Korean War, when large quantities of goods were stock-piled, the market-regulating capabilities of stockpiling were observable for the first time. On the one hand, the problem of reducing stockpiles without affecting stability of foreign markets arose. On the other hand, pressure groups interested in preventing a market surplus of iron, copper, and oil were urging that the United States increase it stock-piles. As a result of this pressure, Congress initiated legislation requiring that the stockpiles be reduced only with the approval of Congress, only after a period of six months from the date of such approval, and only in such amounts and in such a manner that normal market move-ments would not be disturbed. Later, the stockpile legislation was amended to give the President the exclusive power to dissolve stock-piles, and the time period was shortened to two months, but all the other requirements for disposal of the stockpile remained the same.[100]

Under these provisions, the stockpiles, which developed on a national basis, established "buffer-stocks," which became very important in balancing the supply and demand on the international commodity markets. Whenever the quantity of stockpiled material is large, the General Services Administration, which is in charge of the stockpiles,

[96] Exec. Order No. 11387, 33 Fed. Reg. 47 Subpt. B, §1000.201 (1968).

[97] Id., §§1000.202, 100.203. See C. J. Kingston, "Investment in Western Europe under the Foreign Direct Investment Regulations: Repatriation, Taxes and Bor-rowings," 69 Colum. L. Rev. 1 (1969).

[98] Report of Senator Mansfield, S. Rep. No. 56, 89th Cong., 1st Sess. (1965).

[99] Office of Emergency Planning, Stockpile Report, July–Dec. 1967, p. 1.

[100] 50 U.S.C. §98d (1964). See Senator Mansfield, n. 98 above, p. 4. Compare debates and hearings on the new bill, Hearings on S. 2272 before a Subcomm. of the Senate Armed Services Comm., 88th Cong., 2d Sess., Pt. 1, pp. 2–12, and Pt. 2, p. 84 (1966).

is able to significantly influence the domestic American market and, in some cases, the world market also.[101] In addition, numerous possibilities for coordinating governmental actions with private international market regulations are created. The organizers of these regulations, using their knowledge of sales rates and their knowledge that the General Services Administration will use stockpiles for the purpose of stabilization, acquire a tremendous advantage in market planning and distribution.

This important factor of modern market regulations will be dealt with more extensively in the chapter dealing with raw-material cartels. For present purposes, it need only be noted that in a few cases the General Services Administration directly cooperated with cartel organizations.[102]

In 1965, the United States Secretary of Defense threatened to release quantities of aluminum from the U.S. stockpile to counteract a price increase planned by the industry. An agreement was subsequently reached between the stockpile administrator and the major American and Canadian firms under which these producers agreed to take specific quantities of the stockpile releases, based upon production capacity for American firms and imports into the United States for Canadian firms. These agreements not only informed each of the producers of their competitors' relative capacities but, in effect, recognized and sanctioned the existence of a clearly organized and carefully regulated market.[103]

Tax law

It is now well established that tax laws influence the competitive conditions of domestic markets.[104] In addition, they have considerable consequences on the flow of international trade. This can be shown by

[101] In this connection, see Congressman Whitten's criticisms concerning the sales policy of the administration with respect to cotton stockpiles; the administration did not sell the cotton surplus on the world market for world market prices (*Congress. Rec.* H8927) (daily ed. Apr. 26, 1966).

[102] For example, in the case of quinine; the General Services Administration sold the surpluses to the Dutch-Indonesia cartel and not to American companies, allegedly in order not to disturb the political relation of the countries concerned (*Hearings on S. 191 before the Subcomm. on Antitrust and Monopoly of the Senate Comm. on the Judiciary,* 89th Cong., 2nd Sess., pp. 3-35) (1966).

[103] Testimony of H. Kronstein, U.S. Cong., Senate Comm. on the Judiciary, Subcomm. on Antitrust and Monopoly, *Hearings on Economic Concentration outside the United States,* 90th Cong., 2d Sess., pp. 3657-3658 (1968).

[104] M. Moore, *Taxes and Exports* (Toronto, 1963).

the following examples, although they do not indicate the complete picture.

Under an earlier version of the German-American double taxation treaty, German enterprises were subject to the normal corporation tax at the rate of 51 per cent for all profits retained for financing purposes or distributed to the parent firm but which were reinvested. However, for American concerns in Germany, a corporate tax of 15 per cent in Germany and 15 per cent in the United States was imposed on re-invested profits. This gave an American enterprise the opportunity to reinvest profits of its German subsidiary for the purpose of expansion without the additional tax burden, which was applicable to a German concern reinvesting a similar profit. The revised protocol to the double-tax treaty that came into force at the end of 1965 eliminated the favor-able treatment previously granted to the American enterprises for reinvested profits and applied the normal rate of 25 per cent for earned income.[105]

A second example of the effect of taxation on the flow of interna-tional trade and on the competitive position of a firm is the taxation of the internal movement of goods of an international company. This problem is difficult to solve, especially for the less developed countries, because subsidiaries domiciled in these countries export raw materials to the foreign parent at very low prices. This enables the parent to realize a substantially higher profit upon further manufacturing of the product or through the sale abroad of ready-made articles of other subsidiaries of the same concern. Therefore, the less developed coun-tries tend to base their rate of taxation on a reference price that is higher than the actual parent-subsidiary price. One example is the effort of the OPEC members to base their rate of taxation on the posted prices of the oil companies to secure a more adequate tax return within the country, because such prices are higher than the effective market prices.[106]

Also of special importance are the turnover tax systems, which exist in numerous countries and which result in a higher tax burden for imported goods than for goods produced domestically. This is espe-cially true of the French value-added tax. The United States has taken the position that the new German value-added tax has a similar effect.

[105] Convention for the avoidance of double taxation with the Federal Republic of Germany, July 22, 1954, 5 U.S.T. 2768, T.I.A.S. 3133, 239 U.N.T.S. 3; protocol modifying the convention, Sept. 17, 1965, 16 U.S.T. 1875, T.I.A.S. 5920 (effective Dec. 27, 1965).
[106] OPEC Res. X, Apr. 1965.

Safety, quality, and standardization regulations

Even before World War I, a number of countries had enacted laws providing that certain goods had to meet specific safety requirements. Although a requirement that foreign suppliers adhere to certain safety standards is not in itself a restraint of trade, it may operate as a significant restraint on international trade if the quality or safety-mark for an imported product must be acquired from a private association before it can be traded. The American legislation dealing with safety requirements for automobiles is an example of this problem.[107]

Similarly, in the field of pharmaceuticals, complications can arise because of the rigid saftey inspection requirements to which foreign drugs are subjected even though the drugs have been tested abroad for a long period of time. The resulting delays imposed upon imported drugs have caused foreign companies to license domestic firms or to establish their own domestic subsidiaries to produce these drugs in order to expedite the administrative procedures.

Regulations also exist in all countries establishing standards and packaging requirements for consumer products. All of these regulations have market-restraining effects if foreign suppliers are unable to meet the requirements.[108] The similar effects of trademarks and country-of-origin markings will be discussed in other connections.

Admission of foreign corporations to do business and of foreign control of domestic corporations

It is possible for a government to restrict the legal protection granted to foreign enterprises as compared with the protection offered to domestic competitors. This type of discrimination is often eliminated by the inclusion of a provision calling for national treatment of foreign enterprises in friendship, commerce, and navigation treaties. Where no such treaty exists, the domestic enterprise has a considerable advantage over the foreign enterprise in competing for the domestic markets.[109]

National laws often prohibit a foreigner from having a majority interest in a domestic corporation, or at least prohibit his control of the

---

[107] National Traffic and Motor Vehicle Safety Act of 1966, 15 U.S.C. §§1301 n., 1381 ff., 1403 n.; 23 U.S.C. §313 n. (Supp. II, 1965–1966).

[108] Press release of the Commission of the Common Market, IP (66) 50, May 17, 1960.

[109] For instance, Treaty of Friendship, Commerce, and Navigation with the Federal Republic of Germany, Art. VII, Oct. 29, 1954, 7 U.S.T. 1839, T.I.A.S. 3593, 273 U.N.T.S. 3.

management of the corporation. Such legislation is often enacted by countries sensitive to foreign participation in their economies, particularly the less developed countries of Africa and Asia, and some South American countries. Isolated cases of similar regulations exist in industrial countries such as Switzerland.[110] In addition, the American Communication Satellite Act of 1962, COMSAT, limits foreign participation to 20 per cent of the project.[111]

The preceding review indicates that governmental trade regulation is generally only undertaken by individual governments. International regulations exist in only a relatively few areas, and even these seldom include the entire world market. Generally, an enterprise whose parts are spread over the whole world in the legal form of a corporation is confronted by individual governments separately. While the management of the enterprise can steer its worldwide operations toward a specific goal, each government must necessarily be restricted to protecting its own particular interests and each is limited by the legal and factual setting of the problem. Thus, it is not surprising that while various efforts of individual nations directed against the existence and policies of private market regulation can be found, in reality very little is accomplished. As the measures of individual states cannot regulate all aspects of the international market, the organizers of private market regulations can anticipate them. While it is certainly true that the individual governmental regulations restrict the areas available for private market regulation, it is often the case that the organizers of private market regulation cleverly use the governmental measures for their own purposes. In some instances, private market regulation is possible only because one or more governments took special measures in the field of international trade.

Modern Cartels

The phenomenon of modern international cartels cannot be successfully analyzed in terms of traditional antitrust and cartel legislation

---

[110] Schweizer Obligationenrecht (Swiss Law of Contracts), Art. 711.

[111] 47 U.S.C. §734(a) (1964). In 1964, a worldwide international convention, the Agreement Establishing a Global Commercial Communications Satellite System, was concluded. On the basis of this agreement, plus a Special Agreement, the participation of the nations concerned or the private or public telecommunications designated by the respective government is permitted (Agreement Establishing a Global Commercial Communications Satellite System, Aug. 20, 1964, Art. IIa, 15 U.S.T. 1705, T.I.A.S. 5646, 514 U.N.T.S. 26).

and literature. Even setting aside considerations of the significant differences between these concepts, the fact remains that they deal with
conditions that developed before World War II. National regulatory
legislation and cartel literature envisage an arrangement founded on the
classical cartel contract—a detailed agreement between several enterprises that provides for sanctions, arbitration agreements, and other
precautions to enforce it. As far as these contracts are concerned, the
definitions in the cartel laws and literature are meaningful when they
define a cartel as a contractual agreement for the purpose of influencing
or regulating the market by enterprises maintaining their autonomy.[112]

Of course, cartel contracts formulated in detail can still be found
today, but they have become relatively rare at the international level.
Steadily growing vertical and horizontal concentration in international
trade and industry and stricter regulatory legislation have caused
formal cartel agreements to fall into disuse. But the old contract remains the basis for continuous private market regulation, although the
formal relation no longer exists. Parties so inclined may use agreements
not directly concerned with competitive behavior; or covert, non-
compulsory agreements may be based on entanglements or friendly relationships between firms. In any case, the effect may be to establish a
parallelism fully as regulatory as the old formal cartel.

It would not be realistic to use the concept of oligopolistic market
behavior to cover all these forms of cooperation.[113] The coordination
of oligopolistic enterprises depends upon independent decisions by each
enterprise, based on the economic laws of oligopolistic competition,
which are reviewed at every change of market conditions. Each enterprise assumes that its behavior will influence its competitors, but this
is an external influence. The different forms of enterprise cooperation
mentioned above, however, exercise an internal influence on the

---

[112] See, for example, G. Stocking and M. Watkins, *Cartels or Competition?*
(New York, 1948); E. Hexner, *International Cartels* (Chapel Hill, 1946), pp. 19
ff.; and Organization for Economic Cooperation and Development (OECD),
Glossary of Terms Relating to Restrictive Business Practices (Paris, 1965), p. 29.

[113] See especially F. Machlup, *The Economics of Seller's Competition* (Baltimore, 1952), pp. 414 ff.; with respect to the term "oligopoly" see E. H. Chamber-
lin, *The Theory of Monopolistic Competition* (8th ed.; Cambridge, 1956), pp.
30 ff.; G. W. Stocking, *Workable Competition and Antitrust Policy* (Nashville,
1961), pp. 27 ff.; see also United States v. U.S. Steel Corp., 251 U.S. 417 (1920);
United States v. Int'l Harvester Co., 274 U.S. 693 (1927) with respect to the
American law; and L. Wilberforce, A. Campbell, and N. Elles, *The Law of Restrictive Trade Practices and Monopolies* (2d ed.; London, 1966), p. 238, with
respect to British law.

decision-making of competitors by force of custom, entanglements, or contracts. In view of the situation today, it does not seem reasonable to exclude agreements of this sort from the concept of a cartel merely because there is no cartel agreement in standard form. If the coordination of the market behavior of several enterprises results in market regulation due not to the free decision of the enterprises, but to outside influences from other enterprises (that is, if it is based upon any form of consent to outside influence), this coordination should be called a cartel even if prevailing terminology does not agree.

Therefore, the first characteristic of the modern cartel is the consent of the parties to isolate a special market from normal market discipline and to submit it to an artificial order. Secondly, this consent of the parties must induce parallel or complementary economic behavior that influences or regulates the market. All other matters can be coordinated between those poles but may also be subject to formal agreements.

To include only coordination directly concerning market behavior, as cartel literature often requires,[114] would be too limited an approach. It is enough if there are indirect effects upon the market behavior of the parties concerned, as for example agreements concerning pricing information or joint development work. In examining the different types of cartels, further analysis will be based upon these considerations.

Coordination must lead to a market regulation. To define this it is necessary to first tackle the familiar concept of the relevant market.[115] This concept in modern economic conditions needs fundamental amplification. Preparatory work has already been done in the American antitrust law, where Walton Hamilton [116] early recognized that even the behavior of a firm that is concentrated in one market can have effects in any other independent field in which the firm may be engaged. The American discussion concerning conglomerate mergers [117] has sup-

---

[114] Especially in the German literature, see H. Müller-Henneberg and G. Schwartz, *Gesetz gegen Wettbewerbsbeschränkungen und Europäisches Kartellrecht (Gemeinschaftskommentar)* (2d ed.; Cologne, 1963), §1GWB, 20 ff. with citations.

[115] See United States v. Brown Shoe Co., 370 U.S. 294, 325–326, 336 (1962); I. K. Barnes, "Legal Issues and Economic Evidence in Cartel Law," 2 *Cartel and Monopoly in Modern Law*, 822 ff. (1961).

[116] W. H. Hamilton and Associates, *Price and Price Policies* (New York, (1938), pp. 2 ff.

[117] U.S. Cong. Senate Comm. on the Judiciary, Subcomm. on Antitrust and Monopoly, *Hearings on Economic Concentration*, Pt. 1 (Overall and Conglom-

ported Hamilton's thesis. Agreements that seem to be restricted to one particular product, and therefore to the limited market for this product, can also have effects upon other markets in which the parties to the agreement are engaged. Therefore these markets too must be comprehended within the concept of the "relevant market."

Using this approach, we can speak of a market regulation if the cartel partners subject other competitors (of the regulated or adjoining markets) or members of the industry at different vertical levels to their will. This is clearly the case where the market regulation directly affects dealings with third persons. In addition, the members of modern international cartels increasingly draw up rules which govern their own economic behavior, but as part of their purpose they induce reflex action by nonparty third persons. The technological cartel and the restriction of paid-in capital or capital surplus indirectly affect business dealings with third persons. These internal regulations affect the course of business to the same extent as external regulations, if they are backed up by the kind of power at the disposal of an international cartel. Therefore, here again it is possible to speak of a market regulation.

The modern cartel, then, may be defined as a coordination of the economic behavior of independent partners, based upon their consent, which results in regulation of one or more markets. This working definition will be the point of departure for an analysis of the individual types of cartels, a discussion of the cartel agreements and the types of agreements found in international cartels, and a consideration of the parties and of those affected by the cartel.

We are concerned here only with international cartels. These, according to traditional interpretation, are cartels with partners in different nations. The concept, therefore, does not cover national cartels with extranational effects, such as export cartels, which are included in traditional cartel concepts. This investigation focuses on the phenomenon of international cartels with their own independent existence and their own laws. Only when enterprises of several nations are involved in the agreement are the parties able to take advantage of variations in the rules of international private law, choice of forum, arbitration, establishment of corporations, and the use of industrial property rights. For this reason national cartel agreements with extraterritorial

erate Aspects), 88th. Cong., 2d Sess. (1963); Procter and Gamble Co. v. FTC, 386 U.S. 361 (1967), and Reynolds Metals v. FTC, 309 F. 2d 223 (D.C. Cir. 1962).

effects are not regarded in this book as international cartels. This limitation will be generally observed in setting forth the concepts of the practice of cartels. In connection with the defensive cartel, however, questions of national cartels with extraterritorial effects will arise.

3 ~~~~~~~~~~

The Technological Cartel

In the international field, as in the national sphere, an increasing number of enterprises form joint ventures for pure or applied research and development. Pure or basic research seeks to understand the laws of nature without consideration of practical utility. Applied research is much more utilitarian and tries to discover some economic application, even if very general, for the knowledge acquired.[1] Development is the systematic use of research knowledge to produce useful prototypes, materials, tools, systems, methods, or procedures.[2] Unlike research, development generally focuses on the end product to be obtained. It is not static but depends upon the relative stage of technological and economic knowledge of a particular enterprise or enterprises and of the particular country involved. For example, the point of departure in the development of the radio industry in an underdeveloped country is quite different from that for the same industry in a modern country. While the former concentrates on the initial development of transmitters and receivers, the latter is concerned more with improving its defensive position against intrusion by competitors from industries where substitution is possible.[3]

Cooperation in technological development may be very beneficial to the general economy[4] by preventing the inefficient duplication of expertise and capital in the same development project. The technologi-

---

[1] Of course, this distinction is not exact. Pure or basic research is often carried out with the belief that the knowledge obtained will be of practical use and applied research can produce basic knowledge.

[2] For definitions, see National Science Foundation, *Federal Funds for Research, Development and Other Scientific Activities,* fiscal years 1963, 1964, and 1965, Vol. XIII (Survey of Science Resources), *Surveys of Science Series Research and Development Programs* 129 (1965) (hereafter cited as Study No. 6).

[3] Hazeltine Co. v. Zenith Corp., 1965 CCH Trade Cas. ¶71,335 (N.D. Ill. 1965), reversed on other grounds.

[4] "Technology" covers production and use of goods and energies of all kinds—for example, apparatus, methods, and procedures for production and use—and should be distinguished from the development of "economic" methods which would concern, for example, the economic structure of the less developed countries or the trade between states or between different economic systems.

cal data of several enterprises can be correlated, and the cooperating firms best able to incorporate the new data into their production plans and corporate facilities can develop new processes and products. Especially today, in the second industrial revolution, characterized by automation, discovery of new energy sources, rapid means of communication, and space technology, cooperation among enterprises in the task of research and development is often the only economically feasible method of technological and economic progress.

Through cooperation, the regulation of technological research and development becomes possible, and this regulation provides the participating enterprises with direct means of controlling certain aspects of the economy. It is only natural that agreements concerning technical research and development, the so-called immaterial commodities of industry, have come to replace the classical cartel agreement in those sectors of the international economy where regulation formerly concerned only special products. Indeed, combined results of research and technology become an "asset" usable for market regulation. Parallel to this development is the influence on the entire modern social process of the participating personnel changes. Businesses previously run by only "businessmen," even branches of business which have not kept pace with the second industrial revolution, are today characterized by a technological and economic dynamism that has greatly affected their structure. The technician or the scientist is now on an equal, if not more favorable, footing with the businessman on the boards of large enterprises. The emphasis of the enterprise toward production and sales is now complemented by emphasis on technical research and development. This importance is indicated by expenditures.

In 1969, the total sum spent in the United States for technical research and development was about 15.9 billion dollars, of which private industry contributed 8.0 billion.[5] The share of government-sponsored total research has declined since 1968.[6] It remains to be seen whether this trend is going to be continued.

It is of considerable importance, within the scope of this investigation, to inquire whether the restrictions resulting from common development projects can be utilized to control a market. The question of

[5] U.S. Census Bureau: *Statistical Abstract for the United States* (1967), p. 537.
[6] G. Bylinsky, "U.S. Science Enters a Not-So-Golden Era," *Fortune*, Nov. 1968, pp. 144, 147. See also analysis of the research budget for the fiscal year 1969/70 in *Congress. Rec.* H2767 (daily ed. Apr. 17, 1969).

whether these agreements are prohibited under various antitrust laws, such as Article 1 of the Sherman Act, Article 85 of the EEC Treaty, or Section 1 GWB in the German law, is not at issue here. Analysis of the factual international market regulation, as undertaken here, is especially necessary because the problem of consistency or inconsistency with national provisions on antitrust or similar laws became practically the exclusive problem in the discussion during the last twenty years.

Exactly when are agreements concerning technological cooperation covered by the concept of an international cartel? Three requirements are necessary: the parties concerned must impose parallel self-restrictions on their economic behavior; the agreements must be in a relatively new field or branch of an industry; and these restrictions must have the effect of market regulation.

The restrictions that members of the cartel impose upon themselves can cover every phase of research work as well as development of the results. Since any restriction results in some market regulation, it must be a restriction on research and development work that may have direct effects upon the market. Consequently, contracts concerning pure research must be excluded. In this area, enterprises may participate jointly in financing and control of pure research because of the possibility that they may be able to utilize some of the findings of this research to develop their own procedures or in the production of special goods.[7] For example, the United States Navy is interested in pure research in the field of underwater acoustics, whereas enterprises in the electrical industry may be interested in pure research with respect to acoustics in general, without reaping any direct economic benefits or achieving any market regulation by use of the knowledge acquired in this research.

The concept of direct effects on the market should not, however, be restricted solely to the effects upon the final product that enters the market as the result of certain development work. One characteristic of much of the newest economic developmental research is that it is not related directly to the marketing of specific goods, services, or, in special cases, of narrowly defined procedures, but rather is a special

---

[7] "Study No. 6," n. 2 above, p. 129, which emphasizes the importance of basic research. See also the report on the capital market No. 9 (1965) of Bayerische Hypotheken- und Wechselbank, Munich, which states: "The lack of basic theories within a certain area of problem leads to vague and expensive experiments and in addition, to the retardation of development."

technological know-how acquired by a limited number of enterprises, which is of value in itself, apart from specific products, services, or narrowly defined procedures.

Prior to the second industrial revolution, which arose out of World War II, the role of technology was different. At that time, the technological agreements covered only one or more final products. The lightbulb cartel agreement, for instance, provided merely that all production methods and discoveries relating to product improvement be covered by the cartel. Apart from the concrete purposes of the agreement relating to the particular product, the cartel partners were under no restrictions.[8] But today, research and development embraces more than the specific final product. Specific research covering an entire field of technology has taken its place. Since this type of research requires an existing high level of technological proficiency, the prior accumulation of considerable technological know-how as well as the most advanced machinery and qualified experts is necessary before cooperation is possible. Only a relatively few enterprises can fulfill these requirements in their respective fields. These enterprises thus have a competitive advantage over other firms and may affect the market of an entire economic sector rather than just the market for one specific product.

As was already mentioned, not all agreements on common developmental research with resulting market regulation are technical cartels. The final requirement is that the agreement concern a young industry, or a young branch of an industry, where innovation is paramount and the pattern of growth is decided by developmental research. Such agreements should be distinguished from those in which the common development is within the older, more established industries and serves only to strengthen existing situations and to improve the existing superiority of products against the competition of substitutive products. The latter is the normal industrial product cartel and will be discussed in Chapter 5.[9] Note, however, that one industry may contain

[8] W. Meinhardt, *Kartellfragen* (Berlin, 1929), p. 100; G. Stocking and M. Watkins, *Cartels in Action* (New York, 1946), pp. 6–7.

[9] One distinction between the technical cartel and the industrial product cartel is that among the latter the public and private development expenses, as well as the number of employed scientists, are considerably lower. According to *Christ und Welt*, May 21, 1965, the Federal Republic of Germany in 1963 spent the following amounts of money for research and development: DM 859,471,633 (approximately $215 million) by the industrial research group of the electrical,

both elements. For example, in electronics, radio and black-and-white television represent an old industry, but the transistor and computer industry represent a new field of development. Further illustrations can be discerned in the chemical industry.

Since development is independent of the final product, the technological expertise and potential of an enterprise may itself become a product.[10] Anyone following the rapid increase of technological agreements in the postwar period can hardly reach any other conclusion. Know-how and development potential is being acquired regularly in exchanges between enterprises, sometimes with a cash payment added to the exchange. Only in rare situations is it possible for an enterprise with a strong capital basis to buy development potential. The uniqueness of this market lies in the fact that it is open only to the few enterprises that can be considered exchange partners. This market, therefore, is not an open market.

Where enterprises exchange or merge their total know-how and development potential in a specific technological field, market regulation is inherent, because these agreements lead to the exclusion of third parties. But if the agreement only concerns common development in a very limited field, then the resulting market regulation will, in all probability, affect only the final product. For example, the utility of a certain synthetic material for a specific class of electrical machines might be examined. If this research yields satisfactory results, the material will be analyzed further in the hope that it may prove adaptable for numerous purposes in these machines. There are a number of intermediate positions between development that directly serves the process of production and the totally free research of fundamental principles. Thus, each case must be examined individually to determine whether or not the agreement fulfills our definition of a cartel.

The potential for market regulation in control of the results of developmental research must be studied in relation to the aims of the

---

mechanical, and opitical industries, and DM 167,015,758 (approximately $42 million) by the metal industry; in the U.S., $2.98 billion was spent by the electrical, mechanical, and optical industries (of which government participation amounted to $1.794 billion), and $253 million was spent by the metal industry (of which the government contributed $41 million) ("Study No. 6," n. 2 above, pp. 56–57).

[10] The agreements between Siemens and the Radio Corporation of America in the field of computers form an impressive example of the situation today ("Siemens will stärker in die Datenverarbeitung gehen"), *F.A.Z.*, Jan. 27, 1965).

enterprises participating in such regulations and the effects on the national as well as the international economy.

Participating Enterprises

The market-regulating effects of agreements on technological research and development are controlled by two factors: first, the economic or market power of the participating enterprises individually and, second, the combined power and control due to joint research and monopolization of its results.

Economic Power of Enterprises Participating in Development Agreements

Common research work—even when not tied in with restrictions regarding products developed from the work—has the immediate market-regulating effect of concentrating research in a few enterprises and forcing other enterprises into a subordinate role. In fields such as the chemical, pharmaceutical, or electrical industries, for example, one or two firms in the United States, England, France, and the Federal Republic of Germany have a strong enough position to make them desirable partners in joint research and development. To determine the extent to which these agreements can lead to a regulation of the market, the market or technological position of each of the participating enterprises, as well as the position of the group as a whole, must first be determined.

The ability of an enterprise to undertake, on its own, large-scale and technically sophisticated research is a decisive factor in assessing its position. This, together with other individual elements, such as production and processing know-how, and the experience of personnel, make up the "research position" of an enterprise; this research position is somewhat like the concept of good will. Just as it is possible to separate a firm's good will from its assets, it is also possible to transfer a firm's research position without transferring those individual factors that create it, such as special processes and the knowledge of experts.

There is considerable variation among the research positions of enterprises. While in some industries, such as electronics and aircraft, almost every enterprise in the industry is in a position to collaborate in advanced research, in other industries only a few such strong enterprises have the capability.

Enterprises strong enough to take part in national patent and know-how exchange agreements or in international technological cartels during the time between the wars had an unusually strong technological position at the onset of World War II, even in some areas far outside their own particular field.[11] When other firms came to them seeking this specialized information, the established enterprises were able to demand in return access to all subsequent research and development made by the newer firms. The established firms could then pass this new information on through the national exchange agreements or international cartels to which they belonged.

Later, when preparations began for war, new research and development had to be undertaken to prepare for military and civil contingencies. For example, the United States government and the chemical and oil industries entered into an agreement to accelerate all research in the production of synthetic rubber. All such research was to be financed by the government.[12] Another illustration was the arrangement of the American military authorities with several pharmaceutical companies to secure a medicine for malaria.[13] Naturally, the U.S. government turned to the most experienced firms, which could be expected to make the most rapid progress. It is important to note that these firms were primarily those that even prior to World War I had taken part in exchange agreements or corporate relationships with German, English, and French pharmaceutical companies.

Since the war, these positions of dominance have also been strengthened in many countries by the expenditure of state funds for research and development. In the United States, payments were at first only made from the Department of Defense, NASA, and the Atomic Energy Commission budgets. Now lesser funds come from other budgets. It is estimated that in 1968 research and development by private industry cost some 17.3 billion dollars. Of this, the federal government paid about 9.1 billion dollars, or roughly 53 per cent. To this must be added the government's own research and develop-

---

[11] A comparison of Hazeltine Co. v. Zenith Corp., n. 3 above, with the old cases in the field of electric bulbs, for example, United States v. General Electric Co., 82 F. Supp. 753 (D.N.J. 1949), shows that the cartel parties in the electrical industry are always the same enterprises.

[12] Ch. F. Phillips, Jr., *Competition in the Synthetic Rubber Industry* (Chapel Hill, 1961), pp. 39 ff.

[13] Cf. R. Coatney, "Pitfalls in a Discovery: The Chronicle of Chloroquine," 12 *Am. J. of Tropical Medicine and Hygiene*, pp. 121 ff. (1963).

ment expenditures and its contributions to universities and similar organizations in the amount of some 4.2 billion dollars. Private industry contributed only 33 per cent of the total national research and development cost of 25 billion dollars. The research and development work done by industrial organizations in cooperation with the federal government, especially the Department of Defense, NASA, and the Atomic Energy Commission, strengthens the technological position of the enterprises involved and allows them to force other newcomers into a position as subcontractor or other subordinated roles. During World War II and the Cold War standard contracts developed where the federal government reimbursed the industrial enterprises for their costs.[14]

In several western European states, especially Great Britain and France, which encourage research for defense purposes, the expenses of industry are relatively low in relation to the total research and development expense of the nation. In 1962 this fraction in Great Britain was 36 per cent, and in France, 30 per cent. On the other hand, in the Federal Republic of Germany industry participation amounted in the same year to 60 per cent. The aircraft and electronics industries are in the foreground in Great Britain and France, while developments in chemistry hold first position in the Federal Republic of Germany.[15] With all these figures, one must keep in mind that development expenses in the industrial sector of all the states mentioned were more than 10 per cent below the development expenses in the United States.

In the Federal Republic of Germany, another method of cooperation between government and industry has been developed over the last fifteen or twenty years. The German method does not include the cost-plus-fee method. However, industry calculates in each field that a certain percentage of the total turnover should be expressly spent for research and that in the relationship to the government, industry should

14 C. H. Danhof, *Government Contracting and Technological Change* (Washington, 1968), pp. 162 ff. See also statement of General A. D. Starbird before the U.S. Cong. House Subcomm. of the Comm. on Appropriations, *Hearings on Appropriations for 1969*, 90th Cong., 2d Sess., p. 1 (1969).

15 C. Freeman and A. Young, *The Research and Development Effort in Western Europe, North America and the Soviet Union* (Paris, 1965), pp. 472–473. According to a report of the Federal Republic of Germany on research, the West German public administration's share in research programs is over 50 per cent; Bundesregierung, *Bericht über Stand und Zusammenhang aller Massnahmen des Bundes zur Förderung der wissenschaftlichen Forschung* I, 142.

obtain a price for the completed good or technique that is considered equitable to all parties.

These differences between the German and American method occurred because the United States has maintained the war-financing method, while in Germany the growth of research and development happened after the mid-fifties. In Germany, leading participants of the industrial organizations have rejected the cost-plus-fee system after careful consideration. A comparative study of these methods would be quite interesting. There is a certain tendency in the United States to overlook the catastrophe of 1945 in the long run and to recognize that one can learn today from other countries, even in the relationship between government and industry in research and development.

Putting aside the question of who obtains the rights to inventions and patents developed with these funds, participation alone in these projects greatly strengthens the research position of the participating enterprises. It is of special value for the industrial research position of the cartel that the initiative and presentation of problems is apparently worked out by industry and presented to the government rather than the reverse situation being true and, since large enterprises are favored in this participation, their positions are strengthened. In 1964, only 300 companies out of the 13,400 firms doing research and development accounted for 97 per cent of the federally financed research and development in the United States.[16]

Positions of power in research are also strengthened by industrial concentration. Each acquisition of control over a production plant engaged in research and development means control and use of researchers and current processes of the acquired firm. The know-how of the acquired firm has often been obtained through technological

[16] C. H. Danhof, n. 14 above, p. 226. For example, in the field of atomic research and development in the U.S., where all the patents are granted by the government, the important inventions were made by only 14 companies. The largest shares were contributed by General Electric, Western Electric, Westinghouse, Monsanto, and North American Aircraft. See U.S. Cong. Joint Comm. on Atomic Research. Subcomm. on Legislation Hearings on Atomic Energy, *86th Cong., 1st Sess.*, p. 76 (1959); see in addition "Study No. 6," n. 2 above, pp. 63 ff., for a list of the government grants to corporations that participate in governmental programs. A further example is mentioned by Senator Long, *Congress. Rec.* S9343 (daily ed. May 4, 1965). RCA was in control of a patent for color television. Hence, only RCA participated in the development of color television which was subsidized by the government; its competitor, CBS, which had developed a system as well, but whose patent position was not as powerful, did not participate.

collaboration with its national competitors or other firms. Thus, the acquiring firm obtains not only the benefits which the acquired firm received from agreements with its competitors or others but also the future benefits which these agreements bring.

When these international research and development associations were slowly forming after World War II, only enterprises with a relatively strong independent research and development position of their own could gain entry. They alone could offer real challenges to the relatively small number of important research and development experts. There are fewer really important development experts than one might think. Around 1933, approximately three hundred chemists in the German pharmaceutical industry were working exclusively in research. The wide dispersal of this group cost the German pharmaceutical industry its world leadership in this field for a long time. In the United States, now certainly the largest development center, 303,800 research and development scientists and engineers are available in private industry. Of this group, however, only 11,800 are listed as physical scientists; 220,900 are engineers.[17] In Great Britain, France, and Germany combined, there were about 127,000 scientists working in the field of research and development in 1962. Only an estimated 60 to 70 per cent, however, were employed in private industry.[18]

In short, while capital was previously considered the decisive factor for market power, today the research position of an enterprise is vital for market control. Capital has become a much more fungible ingredient, since capital can flow from various directions, including government subsidization.[19] But in research, only those enterprises that have acquired adequately trained personnel during the last decade are able to join the exclusive coterie formed by agreements on joint research and development work. Each partner is admitted only if he will bring new advantages to all. This concentration of specialists, technology, and know-how benefits only these partners. While the members of the development association make use of research and development results they would not have obtained alone (or at least not so inexpensively),

17 U.S. Cong., Select House Comm. on Government Research, *Study No. 2, Manpower for Research and Development*, Under H. Res. Report Study No. 2, 504 by Select House Comm. on Government Research, 88th Cong., 2d Sess., p. 23 (1964).

18 Freeman and Young, n. 15 above, p. 72.

19 A company's technical equipment and know-how are also important, however.

enterprises excluded from the association remain in subordinate positions.

Research and Development Programs

Joint research and development [20] strengthens market power not only in a particular product area but also in other markets often seemingly distant, because of the interrelationship of research and development programs in general. This fosters industrial concentration, and the economic power of the participating enterprise is greatly broadened and strengthened. For example, the relationship between aspirin and dyestuffs extends the pharmaceutical industry into other fields of the chemical industry.

Generally, enterprises with prior experience in research and development in any field have a great advantage, even an exclusive power and position, when research and development in other fields is undertaken.

The interrelationship between different research and development programs proves most effective in the development of research procedures and methods of analysis, which may be used in developing many different lines of products.

Correct elaboration of the results of research and development projects is a prime element in this interrelationship of programs. For example, participation in governmental research and development, particularly in the military field, can benefit the enterprise, even though the end result of that research, such as patents, will belong to the government. An often-cited case is where research on the usefulness of new synthetic materials for military purposes produces valuable information on nonmilitary uses as a byproduct.[21] More important, however, is the fact that enterprises working for the Department of Defense obtain valuable technological know-how and a basis for inquiry into other fields in the process.[22]

Another important example of interrelationship of research and development is the concentration of such work in the field of natural raw materials and synthetic substitutes for them and of products using these materials. To maintain his dominance in the substitutable product,

[20] Concerning the interrelationship of different research programs see "Study No. 6," n. 2 above, p. 127; Stocking and Watkins, n. 8 above, pp. 426–427.

[21] Freeman and Young, n. 15 above, p. 11.

[22] See "Der Höhenflug der amerikanischen Raumfahrtindustrie," *F.A.Z.*, "Blick durch die Wirtschaft," June 14, 1965; "Der Griff nach den Sternen," *F.A.Z.*, June 4, 1966; "Study No. 6," n. 2 above, p. 132.

a producer must control its synthetic replacements, which he does by controlling the new research. The field of natural and synthetic rubber is one example, cotton and synthetic fibers another.[23]

From these examples it can be seen that while their goals and purposes differ widely, all research and development projects have an interrelationship, for the knowledge of procedures and methods of analysis gained in one carry over into another. Further, this relationship has a cumulative effect resulting in an ever increasing market advantage to the participants in a research and development association over those outside of the association. This is a very important aspect of the present movement toward conglomerate mergers.

Potential Uses of Research Results

While joint research and development causes market concentration by reinforcing existing market power and by extending that power into other markets, there is a correspondingly important relationship in the opportunities for exploitation of the various research results by the enterprises. This effect may be shown by the following examples:

1. Suppose a research program results in a new process for transforming bauxite into the primary product alumina, which is necessary for producing aluminum. This information could best be utilized only by one who could relate it with research in the transformation of alumina into aluminum.

2. Research and development on production processes, in automation for example, can be transplanted easily from one production line into another. Therefore, an enterprise with a wide field of activity stands to benefit manyfold from the experience gained from any one process.

3. Research results in the area of production can also lead to important results for further research methods generally. The larger the enterprise's sphere of activity, the greater is its potential utilization of such results and the more valuable is its participation in joint research projects. Conversely, the enterprise with the potential to make use of research results is an attractive partner for the other members of a technological agreement.

Market-Regulating Agreements

Let us examine both the nature of agreements on joint research and development operations, and their market-regulating effects. The high

[23] London *Times*, Mar. 19, 1969 (special issue on rubber).

level of development costs, the scarcity of specialists and of applicable know-how, and the risk that a development program or specific project will not prove productive are extremely burdensome. Therefore, it is not surprising that firms concerned with research and development have a strong tendency to coordinate their efforts and, above all, the application of the results.

General Agreements Concerning Joint Research and Development

In general, research and development agreements include the following specific clauses of understandings: [24]

(1) Clauses defining and limiting contents and objectives of research and development and investigation connected with it. These are clauses confining the development of the project to particular agreed limits, either because of already existing parallel research projects or of eventual adverse competitive effects. In this connection, agreements concerning the scheduling of projects can be utilized to delay developments where such restrictions are in the interest of the participating enterprises.

(2) Clauses concerning the carrying out of research and development. The most important clause is an express statement that allocates the costs, methods, machines, apparatus, materials, and experts to be utilized for the purpose of the research. Some participants may be admitted to contribute money or other consideration instead of research or know-how.[25]

(3) Clauses providing the place of research and development. The express statement concerning where research and development may or may not take place may be necessary to assure concerns that their know-how does not come into countries from which they wish it either completely or partially excluded. The determination of the location is often of importance in research and development undertaken in underdeveloped countries for the specific purposes of these countries, for example, prevention of newly developed competitive enterprises.

The three types of clauses mentioned above are closely related. By

[24] Unfortunately the agreements described below cannot always be proven with published material, but are often based upon knowledge gathered by the author in confidential talks. Therefore, a more abstract and general way of description has been chosen.

[25] Such a "service" in the cooperation between Siemens and RCA is, for example, to put Siemens' system of distribution at the disposal of RCA.

regulating the use by participating enterprises of specific procedures and development results of prior research, the areas of research and its application are automatically limited. By agreeing that developmental research will be undertaken in a country where certain technical prerequisites do not yet exist, a factual limitation is placed upon research and development and indirectly upon the procedures and means that should be available.

When the coordination or contractual regulation of research and development undertaken is in a newly defined field, the area of new research programs is at first relatively limited. These systems of contracts, however, offer many possibilities for expansion of research and development. This can result simply from the close relationship of the management of the enterprises or from the relationship of the directors of the different research departments in decisions concerning the various factors of input and, perhaps, the location to be chosen.

In general, enterprises that cooperate with each other over a long period can rely on less restrictive agreements with respect to cooperation on new development programs.[26] They know the extent of the other parties' general research and development and are assured that any decision made will take into account the interests of everyone concerned. In situations in which firms outside the inner group participate it is important to define the extent of the project.[27] This is another reason why it is rather difficult for an enterprise not already engaged in general research and development, or at least in a particular field, to become an equal partner in technological cooperation. In some cases, monetary payments have been accepted by enterprises in consideration of admitting a newcomer.

In addition to the main obligations set forth above, under certain conditions these agreements occasionally include a series of collateral obligations. The partners may agree not to start individual research and development programs or to participate in projects with other firms if the programs or their results would conflict with those covered

[26] This is especially true of the cooperation between Siemens and RCA; see n. 10 above.

[27] For example, it has been stated in the agreement between the Compagnie Européenne d'Automatisme (CEA) to which belong the French CGE and CGTSF as well as British producers, the British General Electric, and the Scientific Data Systems of America, that the cooperation in the field of computers should cover development, production, and distribution.

by the agreement. This obligation can extend to highly skilled employees or to third parties contracting with one of the participating enterprises. These special agreements on individual development projects are of great importance in determining the extent to which individual enterprises are excluded from participating in competing projects.[28]

Another collateral obligation may prohibit participating enterprises from giving any information to third parties concerning the initiation, progress, or results of a research project. The extent to which subsidiaries, other controlled companies, or even licensees are to be regarded as third parties can be of considerable importance in this context.

Types of coordination

Coordination of research and development can assume different economic and juridical forms which can be summarized in the following categories: [29]

Centralization: The research and development in a specific field is centrally directed and performed. For this purpose, the participating enterprises can either constitute a managing committee, or may place central management in a corporation specially created for that purpose.[30] A joint venture often offers the most effective vehicle for management to distribute the work and supervise its execution. Since the management in this type of coordination is hierarchical in form, the various projects and research groups learn of each other only at the discretion of the management.

Decentralization: Under this type of cooperation the specific devel-

[28] An example is the cooperation between Siemens and RCA; see note 10 above. Apparently here Siemens is not limited to carrying out its own competitive research programs, which specifically have to do with the fact that the firm has contracts with International Computers and Tabulators.

[29] Such agreements, of course, are not always available from published material and therefore a more abstract and general way of description has been chosen.

[30] This seems to be the case for the planned cooperation of Schneider-LeCreusot and Westinghouse; see "Eine gemeinsame Gründung Westinghouse-Schneider," *Neue Zürcher Zeitung*, May 16, 1964. This is similar to the cooperation of the British General Electric and CITEC, a joint enterprise of the French CGE and the CGTSF which established the Compagnies Européennes d'Automatisme; see "French Aiming at Independent Computer Industry," London *Times*, June 18, 1965. For a discussion of the cooperation of German and Dutch electronic enterprises in the field of electronics for shipping, see "Gemeinsame Elektronik-Forschung," *F.A.Z.*, May 20, 1966.

opment project is initially outlined by the management of the enterprise, but research on the various aspects of the problem is divided
among the various laboratories and other departments of the participating enterprises. Naturally, some consideration has to be given to the
nature of each enterprise's previous work in order to utilize each
department in the most appropriate and effective way. To assure that
the project develops uniformly, the concerned departments or enterprises keep each other closely informed on their progress. The managing technicians make periodic visits to the various research and development centers, and other devices for exchange of information are
used, but only to such a degree that the advantages of decentralization
are not lost.

Specialization: The participating enterprises agree that one or more
individual enterprises will undertake the research and development of
a project on behalf of all the enterprises participating in the agreement.[31] Supplementary agreements provide that in consideration for
the research work done, this member-firm is beneficiary of the work
done in other projects by other member-firms on behalf of the group.
All members have access to the development results. Very often the
recipient of such information has to guarantee to utilize the findings
of the research only for a particular product or field.

Coordination of the Use of Research Results. The enterprises may
simply come to an agreement on the exchange of results of research in
one of the patterns described above.[32] This type of coordination is
used, however, only if coordination of research and development is
already a fact or if an oligopolistic structure exists. The agreement
itself is an important element in channeling the research operation of
the participating enterprises in a specific direction.

Agreements Concerning Use of Research Results

The method of carrying out research is closely related to the manner
in which the results obtained are to be used by the participating enter-

[31] This was the case in the cooperation of Bell Telephone Laboratories, American Telephone and Telegraph Co., and Western Electric Co. from 1948 in the
field of transistors. See In re Western Electronic Corp., Letters Patent No.
694,021, High Court of Justice, Chancery Division, reprinted in *T.L.R.*, Jan. 12,
1965.

[32] Such a case may well exist for the agreements between Siemens and RCA
in the field of computers; see n. 10 above. A similar situation seems to exist in
the case of the agreement concerning the exchange of experience and licenses
between AEG and General Electric; see "Gemeinsame Tochter AEG-General
Electric," *F.A.Z.*, June 3, 1965.

prises. While enterprises sometimes only agree to use their research results in a specific manner,[33] most often the parties are very much concerned that no other enterprise obtain an advantage in the field of development. For this reason, an understanding among the parties on the distribution of results of a project becomes important.

Definition of results of research

When negotiating an agreement, the enterprises face the difficult question of how the word *result* is to be defined. The wider the scope of the research, the more difficult it is to define the results. Enterprises entering very broad fields of research and development expect that all technical data and know-how acquired by the participating technicians will be made available to each of the participating parties. As long as large enterprises have these advantages with respect to research and development, there are not likely to be differences of opinion on the definition of the research results. However, the interpretation of the meaning of the "research results" becomes very important if one of the parties believes that it can derive very few additional benefits from research in a particular field or if it believes that it can obtain better results through cooperation with third parties.

Specific types of agreements

The participating enterprises can agree to leave it to each individual enterprise to use any aspect of the research results, regardless of whether technical expertise or the production of a new product is concerned.[34]

The participating enterprises can agree, in connection with the basic agreement undertaking research, to use certain results only after the expiration of a certain period of time or only with the consent of the other parties concerned.

The participating enterprises can agree to use the results of their research and development, especially technical procedures, only in designated market sectors—and in other market sectors only with the special license of other members.

The participating enterprises can agree, especially in the case of new products, not to compete with other members either in particular countries or markets allocated to other members.

The participating enterprises can agree to distribute the new products developed by common research and development through common

---

[33] *Id.*   [34] This is obvious in the agreement between Siemens and RCA.

sales agencies or even to establish common manufacturing plants in different parts of the world.[35]

The participating enterprises can agree to establish the prices and the conditions of sale for the new products developed by this research.

Agreements Dealing with Relationships to Third Parties

Agreements coordinating research and development and the application of the results also prescribe, partly explicitly and partly by implication, how the participants are to act in their relationships with third parties regarding the immediate and subsequent research programs and their results. The more permanent the relationship between the participating enterprises, the less specific these obligations have to be. But isolated agreements, for instance where special research programs are undertaken by one large and one medium-sized enterprise, more often contain detailed clauses of this kind.

Agreements concerning current or future research and development

The enterprises are under an obligation not to give any information to others on the goal and progress of the research and development and to guarantee that none of the employees or other experts working on the research project will disclose this information. As was noted previously, the extent to which subsidiaries, other controlled companies, or licensees are to be regarded as third parties is of special importance.

The enterprises are under an obligation not to undertake any joint research and development with third parties in areas where the program or its results would conflict with those covered by the agreement. Or they may agree to undertake further research and development in one sector of the economy only with firms that participate in the contractually regulated research, provided certain preconditions are fulfilled.

Agreements concerning the research results (procedures and products)

The enterprises agree to transfer to third parties the methods and products developed or the know-how acquired during the course of

---

[35] The latter is the case in the cooperation between AEG and General Electric in the field of the construction of atomic reactors; see "Gemeinsame Tochter AEG-General Electric," n. 32 above; the French-British-American agreement on computers provides joint manufacture and joint distribution; see n. 27 above.

the research only with the consent of the other participating enterprises or under established conditions applicable to all customers.

Numerous conditions are often placed upon the transfer of methods or know-how: the third party must agree to apply these methods only for very specific purposes in a specific manner, or to use machinery or raw materials to be delivered by the participating enterprises. In certain cases, the third party will have to accept limitations upon the geographic area in which the method may be utilized.

The third party must inform the enterprises that participate in the development agreement of any improvements it makes in the methods made available to it. In certain cases, it even has to agree to inform the enterprises of any inventions that it develops in the entire economic sector to which the disclosed research results belong. Thus, the obligations of a third party are very similar to those of a member of the agreement.

These parties must also assume the same obligations for products and services offered or produced in accordance with the methods disclosed by the participating partners as those set forth below for products developed by this research and later transferred to third parties.

With respect to products or services that either result from the research program or from methods based upon the research program, the participating enterprises agree to impose upon third parties certain obligations if the products or services are made available in such a way that they can be produced or carried on by these parties. The customers must observe agreed-upon conditions regarding all elements of delivery of the products or furnishing of services, such as means, prices, quantity, quality, and time and place of delivery.

The enterprises can solicit from the third parties obtaining information from them, as well as third parties supplied by them, an agreement to impose similar obligations on their customers, if possible.

Role of Patents in the Research Position of the Cartel

In other parts of the book, the use of patents together with other industrial property rights to protect a cartel will be discussed.[36] A patent entitles its owner to prevent anyone from producing, selling, or using the protected object. It follows that a patent owner can forbid a research project if it requires the use, no matter how minor, of a patented object or process.

[36] Chapter 12.

A single patent is rarely strong enough to prevent research in important development areas. Nevertheless, there are cases in which individual patents have permitted control over research and development in vast areas. For instance, for a long time the patent protecting the use of a special wire in the construction of radios blocked development of all radio research projects.[37] But generally, the degree of protection which a patent affords depends upon the market power of its owner and the interrelationship of research projects. It should be noted that certain enterprises, by cooperation in the international cartels of the prewar years, by working with the defense authorities before and especially after World War II, and, finally, by cooperation with other enterprises of the most important industrial nations, have obtained experience in research and development and have an exceptionally strong patent position, maintained by a great number of individual patents. At the beginning of World War II, the Radio Corporation of America, for instance, disposed of more than three thousand patents in the field of radio production. This included self-developed patents and the American patents of European competitors, which were surrendered to RCA on the basis of agreements. To this was added the power of RCA to use the radio patents of General Electric, Westinghouse Corporation, and the American Telephone and Telegraph Company, on the basis of various agreements. Conversely, the other enterprises were allowed to use RCA's patents for their own work.[38] The patent power resulting from these contracts is enormous.

The feasibility of an outside research and development program depends to a considerable extent on whether the research might conflict with these patents, especially those concerning processes. Furthermore, the outsider must consider how far research results could be applied without collision with product patents. The negotiating position of those participating in the patent group, therefore, is extremely strong.

Especially in the postwar years, the practice developed in the United States and abroad of granting enterprises doing government research foreign and sometimes local patent protection or granting exclusive

[37] The importance of patent protection as a safeguard against new developments in the electrical industry becomes obvious in the case Hazeltine Co. v. Zenith Corp., n. 3 above; and In re Western Electronic Co., n. 31 above.

[38] United States v. General Electric Co., note 11 above; Hazeltine Co. v. Zenith Corp., n. 3 above.

licenses from the government.[39] One exception is the Atomic Energy Program in the United States.[40] Since participation in government research is predominantly carried out by powerful enterprises, this additionally strengthens the patent positions of these firms.[41]

When deciding whether an enterprise is to be admitted into a group doing research, the patent position of the applicant is of great importance, for it can serve to protect the research of the others against dangers from outside. As mentioned above, the protection against the influence of third parties on research and development is seldom based on one single patent but usually on a large number of patents concentrated in one hand or in the hands of a group by ownership or licensing. In the interrelationship between the enterprises of the research group, however, negotiating positions are based on extent of know-how and development potential.

Apart from the position of power resulting from a complete patent protection in the execution of the research project is the power obtained by an integration of all patents relative to the utilization of research results. It cannot be assumed that an enterprise will decide to participate in a common research project if it is clear from the beginning that the patent situation does not permit the group of enterprises as a whole, on the basis of all its patents, to utilize the expected results. Thus, when a group of enterprises starts in a new area of development or engages in the improvement of existing development projects, it is

[39] The important provisions and forms of agreement of the U.S. are printed in Patent Advisory Panel, *Progress Report to the Federal Council for Science and Technology*, June 1964, App. A, pp. 11 ff. Which party gets the patent is decided by whether the firm already had other patents and technical knowledge in the field (if this is the case the enterprise gets the patents) or whether it is an entirely new development (in this case the government gets the patents in order to prevent monopolization). See Patent Advisory Panel, *Statement of Government Patent Policy*, issued Oct. 10, 1963, App. B, pp. 32 ff.

[40] Atomic Energy Act of 1954 §151(a) and 152, 42 U.S.C. §§2182–2201 (1964); see also *Hearings on Atomic Energy Patents*, n. 16 above, pp. 14 ff., 23 ff. In former times the situation in space research was similar; however, nowadays the contract firms get the patents. See "Der Höhenflug der amerikanischen Raumfahrtindustrie," n. 22 above.

[41] The considerable head start of American enterprises compared to their European competitors is to a large extent based hereupon. According to Freeman and Young, n. 15 above, pp. 11, 31, the expenses for military purposes and space research of the U.S. and the Western European countries (Great Britain, the Federal Republic of Germany, France, Belgium, and the Netherlands) is at a ratio of 4:1 (research cost rate) [7:1 official exchange rate] but only in the ratio 1½:1 [2½:1] in the case of military research and development; see also *id.*, p. 51.

unimportant whether it concerns process or product patents. What must be clear is whether the development results can be used effectively and whether or not utilization can be prevented by a concentration of patents in a third party. For example, the producers of color film own sufficient patents in that field to prevent other self-developing methods for the production of color films from entering the market. It is very difficult to develop a procedure that does not in one way or another enter into conflict with already existing patents. Furthermore, the importance of existing patents for the protection of possible research results depends also on how the research group proceeds later on with the results and the patents procured thereby. This factor will be discussed in the succeeding section.

It is obvious that protection against infringement of patent rights, especially by third parties, is an important element in securing market control. The participating enterprises provide in the contracts among themselves to seek the widest possible protection of patents against infringement. The acquired patents are used not only to proceed against troublemakers through infringement suits, but also to protect the agreements with third parties.

Since the patents derived from the work of the development group can be used only under license, it is relatively simple to make the distribution of licenses dependent upon acceptance of the obligations described above. Some of these obligations involve also a determination of the area where the licensed methods or products are needed or can be introduced into the market.[42] In addition to protection afforded to patent rights, trademarks also play an important part in the protection of development results from unauthorized use by third parties.

Market Regulation by Common Research and Development and Distribution of Research Results

Not every agreement relating to joint development is a technological cartel, but as was already explained, only those agreements in which the contracting parties use the totality of development and the control of research results as a base for market regulation. The discussion in the section dealing with the market power of the participating enterprises and the effect upon economic concentration of common development work by interrelated research programs and results should prove to be helpful in working out usable tests.

[42] The proceedings of the cartel partners in the case Hazeltine Co. v. Zenith Corp., n. 3 above, are instructive.

The Relevant Market

In determining the relevant market, an important consideration is that today, in many instances, the field of technology represents a market that is separable from the products and services resulting from this research. He who controls the developmental research that influences large industrial areas can impose his will upon third parties, not only in research and development, but also in the area of production and services depending upon this research. For example, control of research and development in the field of electronics gives the power to exclude others not only from this area of development, but also from the next step, as for instance with respect to telephones, cable, or other production. Control of research and development in any large market, in practical terms, guarantees access to investigations conducted in a given field of production because, in the long run, it is almost impossible to develop specific areas successfully without access to the technology of the total field.

It might be useful to point out once more the extent of the field of "technology." The United States annually spends many billions of dollars for industrial research and development. Very real market power is derived from the power to exclude other parties from this activity and to dictate to other participants in this research the conditions and methods under which they must work.[43] The markets (fields and territories) affected by such powers may of course change from time to time in individual cases.

With respect to the application of national antitrust laws by governmental authorities, it is necessary to examine the actual setting in which market regulation takes place. The power to determine the market regulated or influenced by the cartel—the so-called "relevant market" within the United States domestic or foreign market—has proved difficult for the national antitrust agencies to establish. In the analysis of the social phenomenon of the international cartel and the relationships of the cartel parties, however, an exact description of the relevant market is not as necessary as it is for the national regulatory laws. It is sufficient if the agreement, or, more precisely, the economic power

[43] "CGTSF—Compagnie Générale de Télégraphie Sans Fils," London *Times*, July 7, 1965. In this article on CGTSF it is stated that the American enterprises, due to the large number of government orders, is in a position "to create, and often to impose, markets over a wide field"; see also Freeman and Young, n. 15 above, pp. 51 ff.

obtained through the cooperation in research and the exploration of research results, can be used for the regulation of one or several specific markets. The exact market limits, especially when considering the question of the success of the market regulation, are of practical importance only where "weak" cartels are concerned.

Firms may exercise "oligopolistic" control beyond the existing agreements. However, a multitude of technological agreements may have some effect on the market. In this type of structure a minimum number of agreements are necessary since the enterprises compete among themselves in only subordinate areas, and competition with third parties is negligible.

Types of Market Regulation

In the simplest instance, research and development cooperation leads to the regulation of a specific market for a developed product, such as a new pharmaceutical product for a specific disease. Apart from patent or trademark protection, the enterprises participating in the research program have a considerable advantage in the development and in adaptation of the product to the market, for they have observed all phases of the research. This position will often be strong enough to permit the enterprises to fix the quantity or price of the product or to apportion sales distribution in individual countries among themselves. At least for a certain period of time, this dominance of the market often makes it imprudent for competitors to undertake research and development and thus leads to even greater market regulation by the cartel group.

The interrelationship between the product that is developed and other products, not only of the same type but often of very different types, as well as the range of business interests of the participating enterprises, often extending over several economic sectors, can also make the regulation of other markets possible. The market-regulating effects of the developed product can encompass those product groups with common methods of procedure or potential common use. Since he who controls the research and development now will in all likelihood control it in the future, he can keep the research results (procedures and products of the same group) continuously under market control. This is also true of a product belonging to another market that depends on the production methods of the research group. Finally, there are also ways of effective market control of third party products even if the products of the associated group are only partly identical with those of the third party.

In this situation, the possibilities for regulation increase. Under certain circumstances, the regulation of research and development in a special technological field can ultimately lead to control of the economy in large fields.[44] The interrelationship of different fields of industry, for example the common interests of chemical, pharmaceutical, petrochemical, and synthetic product industries, as well as the relationship between these and the steel industry, gives some indication of the extent of market control that can be exercised on the basis of the joint research and development enterprises.

Relationship between Regulation of Research and Development and Market Control

In areas subject to a rapid technical development, such as electronics and the pharmaceutical industry, each enterprise that is excluded from research and development is, for all practical purposes, excluded from production or access to the new achievements in its representative field. If not completely eliminated, the enterprise is at least subject to an unbearable competitive disadvantage. This is true regardless of whether the technological cooperation is in the form of joint research and development or by exchange of research results. Further, it is not necessary that the primary inventions in the respective fields be held by the research group for this disadvantage to affect the third party. It is sufficient that the research group own certain production methods and systems to which an outsider has no access. And even if an outsider should assemble a staff of outstanding experts, such a staff would be opposed by the experts of all of the enterprises in the cartel, who in addition to their own know-how also have access to the latest technology of other participating enterprises, which would not be available to the outsider's experts.

The widespread interests of the enterprises in the cartel grant them a superior range of uses for research results. On the one hand, they can bring together all the experience they have gained in various fields and apply it in the production of a specific product. On the other hand, they can utilize the knowledge gained in the development and production of a specific product in other fields in which the group is engaged. This advantage alone, coupled with the role of patents, makes

[44] "CGTSF," n. 43 above.

it difficult for newcomers to succeed. If they do succeed, it is only in a limited field.

Exclusive cooperation in research and development gives to the participating enterprises the power to decide when, where, how, and even whether to employ the collected data or the newly developed product. Thus, a newcomer seeking to intrude into their market can release the totally new, low-priced product, or they can subject the intruder to sharp competition in other fields in which he is sensitive.

Significance of corporate devices for the market control

Any subjection of any outsider, or any influence on the market by corporate devices, increases the scope of technological control over particular markets whenever the enterprises brought under control have been engaged in research and development. The general impact of corporate devices on cartels are dealt with in a special chapter of this book, since this impact can be felt in all types of cartels.[45] Thus, the acquiring firm either increases its control in particular fields or permits it to enter the field.

Relationship between Market Control by Control of Research and Development and the Course of Research and Development

Market control secured through cooperative research and development not only includes control over production and sales but also includes control over the present and future course of research and development. In order to evaluate the economic advantages and disadvantages of technological cartels, the actual control exercised over the course of research and development must be considered. Such a consideration is best approached from the point of view of the interests involved.

---

[45] U.S. Cong., Senate Committee on the Judiciary, Subcomm. on Antitrust and Monopoly, *Hearings on Economic Concentration*, 89th Cong., 2d Sess. Pt. 3 (Concentration, Invention, and Innovation) (1965). If, indeed, the development of modern technology takes place in the manner suggested by Dr. Blair and others in this report (p. 1118) in the small plants owned or controlled by independent inventors, nothing can be more harmful to the public interest with respect to rapid access to technological development than the agreements described here. See also *Hearings on Economic Concentration*, 91st Cong., 1st Sess. Pt. 6 (Technologies and Concentration) (1967).

Interests of the joint participants in the research
and development association

In deciding how to use research results ιto change products and methods, enterprises controlling a market on the basis of research and development seek to secure a reasonable return on their previous investments and also to increase their competitive position in the marketplace. Thus, by regulating the time and sequence of research and development, the enterprises can avoid a market crisis that would result from too rapid research and development growth and can, as a result, assure themselves a stable but increasing growth rate.

These enterprises may instead restrict ιthe quantity of the products under their control in such a way that they make a high profit which will fully or partially finance their current research projects. For example, the profit the German nitrogen producers gained from the international nitrogen cartel between the two world wars was sufficient to cover the expensive research projects in the field of synthetic petroleum and synthetic rubber.

Especially important in a time of industrial revolution, the participating enterprises can also protect secondary manufacturers, wholesalers, and retailers against rapid technological change, yet assure them access to new products. Also, the attainment of market control gives each enterprise a time of relative peace from competition, enabling it not only to concentrate on further joint research and development but also to continue individual projects undisturbed. Thus, a greater stability is achieved for the research and development programs of the respective enterprises.

The market control of the enterprises participating in the technological cartel also enables them to regulate the flow of information to underdeveloped countries. The participating enterprises can make the results of the research available under conditions that permit industrial development while restricting the local enterprises so created or aided in order to prevent disruption of the world market because of uncontrolled competition. This is accomplished through the imposition of restrictions on their technical information, which results in control of the speed of local development in the recipient country and makes impossible the establishment of these enterprises as competitors in other countries. In this area, patents become important, not only as a means of protection against outsiders, but also as a means to limit the agree-

ment with the partners of the cartel enterprises in the developing
countries to the strict purpose for which those arrangements were
conceived. Each violation of the individual contracts concerning the
transfer of research and development data has, at the same time, to be
a violation of the patents that belong to the cartel enterprises in the
developing countries. The quarrel between the Indian government and
certain American industries with respect to how far the Indian government is entitled, within the framework of the existing international
agreements, to abolish the patent protection for certain sectors [46] aptly
illustrates the danger the enterprises of the industrial countries fear
most—loss of market control through loss of patent protection.

> The interests of the industrial countries where the enterprises
>   participating in the research and development group
>   have their seat

It is extremely important to every state that at least one of its
enterprises have access to research projects and results in as wide an
economic sector as possible. This is true for all industrial fields, especially in defense and space research, where governmental interests are
predominant. Furthermore, it is important for the economy of the
individual states that the market not be disrupted by unregulated
development, but that a stability be maintained in the domestic economy while at the same time allowing as full a profit return from the
introduction of new research and development as possible.

Each state gains from the strong position of its enterprises in technological exchange and in technological cartels because the state is then
in a better position in negotiating trade agreements and tariff reductions either within the framework of GATT or outside this organization.

At the same time, market control through regulated research can
affect a national economy most unfavorably. If the cartel is very

[46] A limitation of the patent protection is planned initially for pharmaceutical
and food patents. The original plan to completely eliminate patent protection has
been abandoned under pressure from the Western industrial complexes. See the
opinion of the Indian government where it is explained that the patent system
brings about disadvantages to the underdeveloped countries because the Indian
patents granted to foreign enterprises are generally used to protect exports to
India but do not serve to start production in India. United Nations, Economic
and Social Council, Comm. for Industrial Development, *The Role of Patents in
the Transfer of Technology to Developing Countries*, U.N. Doc. ECOSOC, Report of Secretary General E/13861/Rev. 1 [1964], p. 19).

restrictive in its exploitation of research and development, the economic advancement of a country is stifled, particularly when potential entrants with sufficient know-how are excluded from the market by the barriers imposed by the cartel members. This regulation of newcomers affects not only the narrow area under market control, but also other areas. The power of the cartel group hampers research or attempted development by a competing enterprise or enterprises. The government itself has considerable difficulties in its own research projects if it does not come to an agreement with the cartel. This is true in spite of the power of governmental intervention, such as the grant of compulsory licenses or the power of governments to use patents for public purposes.

Research and development by cartels established in older industries indirectly affects the new developments because new research depends on whether the enterprises are established in the regulated economic sector, as is the case in the postwar development of the steel industry in the United States. Certainly, it is within the interest of every country that new developments which are technically feasible are carried through and that the market division controlling the market of the old product does not prevent new research projects for the development of new products within the country for years.

The interests of the developing countries

The developing countries often support special research programs of industries in other developing countries because their stages of development are comparable. In these cases they rely in part on the knowledge acquired by the research groups of the industrialized countries.

Individual enterprises participating in the technological cartel are able to give information and technological assistance to industries in the developing country and may collaborate in the establishment of local shareholding companies or government enterprises without having to fear that the cartel enterprises will disregard their interests in other sectors. This situation often has unfavorable effects on the developing countries. As noted, a usual prerequisite for the utilization of the research results and for the pursuit of research in the developing countries is that the enterprises receiving access to this know-how will not compete with the other cartel members in other geographic areas or expand into other economic fields.

The close cooperation of the enterprises is especially unfavorable for the developing countries as any possibility of playing off one enterprise against the other is eliminated.

Even the conflict between the East and the West presents little opportunity for the enterprises or governments of developing countries to play off the two Blocs against each other.

Another unfavorable effect of the technological cartel on the developing countries is that the members of the cartel can, owing to their market control, sell their products, such as specialized machinery, or can license their technical resources, at high prices. These prices do not always correspond to the price changes of raw materials that the developing countries can supply and upon which they depend to raise the capital to finance industrial development. This discrepancy between costs for technological products and receipts for raw materials is one of the reasons for the economic difficulties existing in numerous developing countries.

Role of the governments in the development of international technological cartels

Governments have a special interest in promoting research and development related to defense, space research, medicine, pharmacology, and automation, because of the direct relationship of those fields to the public interest. Thus, the United States government gives direct financial support of developmental research.[47] As the government is interested in concrete results, it is most often prudent to give preference to the enterprises participating in the technological cartel as their participation in the cartel has given them access to research projects and research results that other enterprises do not have. In awarding contracts for research and development to members of the technological cartels, each government must be aware that the cartel members may gain knowledge which can easily be utilized by other economic sectors. Owing to the interrelationship between research and development projects in general, the enterprise that does research in a special field on a government order obtains considerable advantages even though the research results belong to the contracting government. In addition, enterprises that did research for the United States government were allowed, under the prevailing cost-plus system, to construct all the buildings, plans, machinery, and so forth, and maintain them

[47] "Study No. 6," n. 2 above, p. 53; Freeman and Young, n. 15 above, pp. 31 ff.

for future use, if in their opinions they were useful for the realization of the research and development project undertaken for the government. This system also provided practically free training of experts, since the government reimbursed the salaries of those employees who had to obtain extensive background knowledge in order to work on the government projects. The enterprises could, however, later utilize the experts in any suitable position.[48] Thus, the enterprises with research and development contracts from the government receive numerous advantages they can pass on to the technological cartel.[49]

In short, while the various governments are, on the one hand, beneficiaries of the technological cartel, on the other hand, they are promoters and perpetuators of it. This is reflected in the statistics on government participation in research and development. In 1962, the amount of governmentally financed research and development in the industrial sector was a little less than 50 per cent in the United States, about 40 per cent in Great Britain, about 33 per cent in France, and about 15 per cent in the Federal Republic of Germany.[50] These differences are not only based on the differences in the size of defense expenditures of these states, but above all, on differences in supply and demand in the different states. Until recently, the Federal Republic of Germany and Switzerland felt that expenses for research and development, even of interest to the government, should be paid for by industry. The government then paid the industry for the research results or for the developed product.[51] Today, in general, an additional charge of 15 per cent above the invoice price is paid by the government for research and development undertaken. The expenses for the research and development may then be deducted for tax purposes.

[48] However, recently the system of cost-plus (refunding of the cost plus a certain percentage of the cost) has been modified with respect to salaries for these experts, where specific time limits within which these wages may be paid have been included in government contracts.

[49] Therefore it must also be taken into consideration that the European subsidiaries of the enterprises which are particularly favored sometimes obtain the knowledge of the procedures and the products that have been developed by the producing company. However, this process must not be imagined to be too fast because the international holdings have a retarding effect; see Freeman and Young, n. 15 above, p. 52.

[50] *Id.*, pp. 55, 72. The estimated share of government-sponsored research and development in the United States in 1968 was almost 53 per cent. National Science Foundation, *National Patterns of Research and Development Resources* (Washington, 1967), pp. 22-23.

[51] National Science Foundation, *id.*, p. 45.

The governments or banks controlled by the governments in the industrialized countries also make available large amounts of capital on especially favorable terms to enterprises in all fields of development. This is of importance to the participants in the technological cartels. In addition, the capital given by the Western governments to the underdeveloped countries helps the cartels increase their influence. This capital may be given directly or through the International Development Corporation or the World Bank. It may be utilized in an underdeveloped country to acquire technology from an industrialized country, or for new research development by the country itself;[52] in either case, the enterprises participating in the technological cartel are the indirect beneficiaries of this grant of funds because of their advantageous position in the research and development work in the area in question.

The various governments of the industrialized countries also have important technological information of their own to sell or exchange. This includes not only research done by the governmental authorities themselves, but also research and development undertaken by industrial enterprises on behalf of the government, which includes a stipulation that the information uncovered not be exchanged with other enterprises.[53] The governments are, therefore, potential suppliers of technological information. This gives them the opportunity to participate in the technological cartels while at the same time giving them partial control of these monopolistic enterprises. It is thus possible for governments, through capital grants and government-owned technological information, to either actively aid in the development of technological cartels or to actively protect itself by giving such grants or information to enterprises in a position to resist this special cartel or which have formed a defensive technological cartel. For example, a defensive cartel of large French, German, and American firms was established to combat the monopoly position of IBM.[54] The

---

[52] Concerning the transfer of technology in industrialized countries, see *The Role of Patents in the Transfer of Technology to Developing Countries*, n. 46 above.

[53] "Der Höhenflug der amerikanischen Raumfahrtindustrie," n. 22 above.

[54] This cartel consists of a large number of individual agreements. Partners on the German side are mainly AEG and Siemens, on the French side, Compagnie Générale d'Electricité (CGE) and Compagnie Générale de Télégraphie Sans Fils (CGTSF), partly by their common subsidiary CITEC; on the British side, General Electric Company and ICT (cooperation exists between the French and

French government apparently has not only made funds available but also supplied technological know-how.[55]

Governments in a number of cases have united their technological knowledge in a manner similar to that of a technological cartel. For example, the NATO governments exchange technological know-how and research results in special fields and also undertake common research projects in certain cases. The agreements usually provide for the exclusion of all those enterprises which do not belong to a member state of NATO or which are controlled by citizens of nonmember states of NATO.[56] In these cases a certain competition between government cartels and private technological cartels exists. At the same time, the government cartels are in some measure dependent on the know-how power of the technological cartel. Conversely, the technological cartels want to acquire the research and development background that cooperation of the government affords.

Agreements concerning common research and development between governments of the developing countries or between countries technologically deficient in a certain field are analogous to defensive cartels. An interesting example of this is the cooperation of the Western European countries in the field of space research in order to reduce the enormous lead of the United States and the Soviet Union in this field. The manner of cooperation is in the concentration on one project and the specialization of participating enterprises on some of the complementary research projects.[57] Another example is the coopera-

---

the British companies via Compagnie Européenne d'Automatisme, CEA); and on the American side, RCA, Scientific Data Systems, Westinghouse, Honeywell, and Univac. See "Questions on Computers," London *Times*, Mar. 3, 1965; "French Aiming at Independent Computer Industry," London *Times*, June 18, 1965; CGTSF—Compagnie Générale de Télégraphie Sans Fils, London *Times*, July 7, 1965.

[55] "French Avionics Industry Expands in Size and Diversity," and "French Nationalism vs. U.S. Technology," *Aviation Week and Space Technology*, June 14, 1965, pp. 118, 120.

[56] U.S. Government Cont. Rep. §§4045, 4048. Bilateral cooperation between the United States and the Federal Republic of Germany seems to be prepared in the field of space research; see address of Ambassador McGhee before the University of Bonn, *Die Welt*, Jan. 28, 1968.

[57] In the European Launcher Development Organization (ELDO), the participants are the Federal Republic of Germany, France, Great Britain, Italy, Belgium, the Netherlands, and Australia. See Wilhelm Seuss, "Der Schuss ins All—oder ins Nichts," *F.A.Z.*, Jan. 11, 1966; Bundesregierung: Forschung, Bd. I, pp. 60–61, cf. n. 15 above.

tion, particularly between France and Great Britain, in the field of airplane production. Such cooperation is directed against the present United States superiority in this area.[58] And finally, agreements of the governments of underdeveloped countries (especially in South America) pledging to exchange technological know-how in certain fields in order to restrict the dominance of the great powers can be found. Moreover, these agreements provide that public laws will be promulgated to assure the utilization of the successful results of the cooperative research and development even if such results have not reached the point where they are economically competitive with products or methods already developed and in use by the industrialized countries.[59]

The governments of the industrialized and the underdeveloped countries have the power to promote or to delay the technical development in their state territory by legislation or administrative action. They can grant patents, but they can also force an enterprise to grant licenses to other enterprises. They can promote, delay, or prevent the establishment of enterprises for research and development or of manufacturing plants. As suppliers of raw material, they can influence decisively the quantity of raw material disposal or the conditions on which they are brought into the market. Especially for medium-sized industrial countries or underdeveloped countries, these authorizations can represent important means for the promotion of technological and other cartels. The price an underdeveloped country pays, for example, to have an aluminum plant established generally includes the promise of the concerned government to act in accordance within the total structure of the aluminum industry.

[58] Report of the Committee of Inquiry into the Aircraft Industry, Appointed by the Minister of Aviation under the Chairmanship of Lord Plowden (the "Plowden Report"), 1964–65 Cmnd. 2853; see further "France to Join in Research on Proton," London *Times*, Feb. 16, 1965; "Le Bourget 1965," *F.A.Z.*, June 10, 1965; "Englisch-französische Luftfahrtehe," *id.*, Mar. 15, 1965; "Parliament Tuesday, April 13," London *Times*, Apr. 14, 1965.

[59] U.N. Conference on Trade and Development, Report by the Secretariat of the U.N. Economic Commission for Latin America, U.N. Doc. UNCTAD E/Conf. 46/60 (1964), pp. 24–25.

4 ﹏﹏﹏﹏

The Raw Material Cartel

Since the end of World War I, international raw material cartels have played an important part in international trade owing to the greatly increased demand for raw materials in the modern industrial countries. The colonies, which formerly provided the industrial countries with the raw materials, have gained their independence and become necessary copartners in any system of regulation. By an international raw material cartel, enterprises of different nationalities seek to regulate the market for a specific raw material. The definition does not include the frequent governmental agreements in this area.[1] The limits between private and public market regulation are, however, fluid and vague, and international cartels often supplement or form the basis for governmental agreements.[2] Once judicial or executive pressure in one country on parties to an agreement regulating a particular field is being felt, governments often adopt their own regulation to maintain the existing conditions. Governments further influence raw material markets by concluding supply contracts and by granting exclusive rights to members of raw material cartels. Therefore, an analysis of these cartels must also focus on the importance of governmental intervention.

[1] Chapter 2 above.

[2] The tin agreements concluded before World War II are an example. In 1931, the most important producing countries (90 per cent of the world production) concluded the First International Tin Agreement. This agreement provided for a restriction of the tin production. Nevertheless, the tin deposits kept increasing. In addition, private enterprises founded an international tin pool to buy tin surpluses on the market and to resell in time. This pool was dissolved in 1933–1934, bringing considerable profits to its members; K. O. Titze, *Internationale Planungen auf den Weltrohstoffmärkten* (Darmstadt, 1958), pp. 127–128. In 1934, the Second International Tin Agreement came into force, which was supplemented by the International Bufferstock Agreement concluded by the producing countries on July 10, 1934. The situation was a similar one in the thirties in the sugar market. In 1931, the producer associations of nine sugar-exporting countries joined into a private cartel, which was called the Chadbourne Plan. As the cartel members failed to stabilize prices by reducing the production, the producer countries endeavored to conclude a governmental sugar agreement following the monetary and economic world conference in 1933. In 1937, they concluded the First International Sugar Agreement.

For purposes of this discussion raw material is defined as "a product exploited from nature," for example, iron ore, crude oil, or gas. In addition, this definition includes pure raw material extracted or refined from the natural raw material by simple chemical-technical processes prior to any significant addition of other materials. By strict definition, agreements with respect to processed raw materials are not raw material cartels. There is no reason, however, to distinguish between natural raw materials and processed raw materials, since the production of both is generally concentrated in the same enterprise and conditions of production and distribution are similar. Regulation of raw material markets often requires the inclusion in the cartel agreement of additional products that fall outside the definition of a raw material. This is the case with modern synthetic products that replace the raw material product, for instance man-made fibers or synthetic rubber. Regulation of these synthetics is part of the raw material cartel because its purpose is to regulate the raw material market.

The principal aim of international raw material cartels has been the stabilization of the market in order to control price fluctuations caused by economic cycles, and in particular to obviate the risks of price declines. In many cases this aim of stabilization has not been achieved, particularly in today's extremely dynamic economy.

Participating Enterprises

The power of enterprises to regulate raw material markets may be based on property title, on contracts, on associate relationships with the legal owner, manufacturers, or distributors, or upon exclusive rights granted by a government.

The influence of these enterprises may be exerted on the raw material itself; on the transformation of the natural raw material into a processed raw material; on the transportation of the pure or processed raw material to the market areas; on the manufacture of the pure or processed raw material into semifinished products; on the distribution of these products; or on the production or distribution of synthetic products substituted for these raw materials.

The level of market power or the degree of vertical concentration an enterprise has to attain in order to become an attractive partner for a raw material cartel will vary. Occasionally, market power at only one of the stages mentioned above will suffice; sometimes it will require market power at each of these stages, thus requiring a fully integrated operation.

Conditions vary from industry to industry. For instance, in the field of diamonds, the South African De Beers Consolidated Mines, Ltd., is a cartel partner primarily because of its strong position as a diamond producer and because of its extensive research in the exploitation of diamonds from the sea as well as their synthetic production.[3] On the other hand, the Aluminum Company of America (ALCOA),[4] Standard Oil of New Jersey,[5] and American copper producers [6] are especially desirable cartel partners because of their far-reaching vertical integration. Because market power and economic concentration are subject to temporal modifications, the potential cartel partners may change. For example, initially, the coal and petroleum producers had a very strong market position. They entered into cartel agreements, fixing prices and establishing quotas, which were adhered to no matter how significant their customers were. These customers included the chemical, steel, and oil-refining industries.[7] In subsequent years the producers lost their controlling position. Many coal mines were acquired by the steel and chemical industries.[8] In Germany, however, some owners of coal mines invaded the steel industry instead,[9] and thus avoided the loss of power by vertical integration. In the United States, Standard Oil of Ohio was strengthened through the expansion of its interests beyond the petroleum industry.[10] The company grew from solely an oil-refining enterprise, gradually contracting with the

---

[3] The Annual Report of De Beers Consolidated Mines, Ltd., for 1962 states an annual production of 5.05 million carats (inclusive of subsidiaries) (pp. 15, 33, 35). The world production was estimated at 32 million carats for 1962 ("A Brighter Sparkle in Diamond Sales," *Financial Times*, Sept. 7, 1964). Furthermore, a subsidiary of the De Beers group, named Diamond Corporation, Ltd., concluded sale contracts with most of the other diamond producers in the world ("The Diamond Industry," an address by H. F. Oppenheimer to the 7th Commonwealth Mining and Metallurgical Congress, Apr. 12, 1961, p. 21).

[4] United States v. Aluminum Co. of America, 148 F. 2d 416, 422 (2d Cir. 1945).

[5] The Esso Standard Oil Co. refines the crude oil which it produces, in approximately 60 refineries. In 1962, it sold 14.5 per cent of the world consumption of oil products through its own distributing organizations. At the same time, it controlled 10 per cent of the world tanker tonnage and participated in 45 pipeline systems all over the world.

[6] United States v. Kennecott Copper Corp., 231 F. Supp. 95 (D.C.N.Y. 1964).

[7] Compare I. Tarbell, *The History of the Standard Oil Company*, I (New York, 1925), pp. 70 ff.; H. Kronstein, "Die Politik des Wettbewerbs in den Vereinigten Staaten von Amerika," 3 *ORDO* 75 ff. (1950).

[8] O. Lenel, *Ursachen der Konzentration unter besonderer Beruecksichtigung der deutschen Verhältnisse* (Tübingen, 1962), p. 100.

[9] The Thyssen and Haniel groups are examples. See also *id.*

[10] Standard Oil Co. v. United States, 221 U.S. 1, 31 ff. (1910).

railroad companies for preferential tariffs and discounts, and ultimately brought the pipelines under its control. With these competitive advantages, the company was in a position either to purchase most of the crude-oil-producing enterprises or at least to force them into mergers during the period from 1872 to 1888. By about 1890, Standard Oil of Ohio controlled more than 90 per cent of the production, refining, sale, and distribution of crude oil in the United States.

Trade is no longer divided into autonomous functions, such as producing or retailing. Many producers or manufacturers distribute their products through their own, or dependent wholesale and retail systems. For example, the petroleum and motor oil producers sell their products through gasoline stations, which are either owned by these producers or under long-term contractual obligations to them.[11] The present wave of conglomerate mergers in the United States could expand this process.

This same blurring of function has occurred between the producer or manufacturer and the wholesaler. The difficulties of the large London copper-trading firms, which endure, at least until today, are an example of this.[12] London is the headquarters of the copper trade influenced by copper producers such as Anaconda Company. It may be sufficient to refer to the heading of the last annual report of Anaconda, "From Mining to Consumer." In addition, producers of raw materials, especially in petroleum and bauxite, have gained influence in the transportation industry. Hence, shipping or pipeline enterprises have failed to establish systems of market regulation of their own.[13]

In spite of extensive vertical concentration in the raw material markets, the economic position of the producers may be threatened by competition from synthetic products. The chemical industry has be-

[11] Oil Co. of California v. United States, 337 U.S. 293, 295 (1945); or the British case, Petrofina 2 W.L.R. 1299 (1965).

[12] "What Now for Copper," *Mining J.*, Apr. 12, 1966.

[13] With respect to Esso Standard Oil Co. see n. 5 above. The Socony Vacuum Oil Co. controlled 4 per cent of the world tanker tonnage in 1962. The Royal Dutch/Shell group holds 14 per cent of the world tanker tonnage (see H. Nolte, "Geschichte der Riesen," *F.A.Z.*, June 15, 1963). With respect to the Aluminum Co. of America, see the Annual Report of Alcoa, 1964, p. 4. According to this report the Alcoa Steamship Co., which is a 100 per cent subsidiary of Alcoa, undertakes all bauxite transports of the company from Central and South America to the refineries in the United States. The steamship company also undertakes transports for third enterprises. With respect to Aluminum, Ltd., compare 1962 Annual Report, according to which its subsidiary, Saguenay Shipping, Ltd., has 40 ships.

come a significant competitor of raw material cartels in many areas. The raw material producers have taken some countermeasures, however. Because of their strong economic power they are in a position either to suppress the development of synthetic products or to secure a well-balanced market development of the raw material and the competitive synthetic product by participating in a cartel that includes producers of the synthetic material. For example, the leading producers of diamonds and the most important copper producers are themselves engaged in developing synthetic substitutes.[14]

The position of the producers and enterprises or groups of enterprises with exclusive access to the raw material would appear to be paramount. It is interesting that even after nationalization of copper by expropriation in certain countries the same firms remain in an unfavorable supply position: the nationalizing governments in Congo and Zambia gave the former owners a preference in the distribution and acquisition of their copper (see Chapter 14).

Market-Regulating Agreements

The market regulation of the international raw material cartels may result by influencing any step from production through distribution. As was true of the technological cartels, close correlation exists between different economic levels in the raw material sector. The market-regulating effects of these agreements differ in intensity but not in their nature. This correlation should be kept in mind in the following discussion of market-regulating agreements.

Agreements on Joint Production of Raw Materials

No regulation of production is more pervasive than joint administration or even joint ownership of certain sources of raw materials, since all conditions of sale may be set effectively by a control agency.[15] Nevertheless, this type of market regulation is not found as frequently as in the field of technological cartels. Because of the unstable nature of this type of cartel, producers try to avoid too close connections with each other. The power of this cartel depends on the continuously strong position of the same raw material producers. Joint production occurs in such fields as crude oil, however, where joint enterprises

---

[14] See "Search for New Uses," London *Times*, Jan. 22, 1964.

[15] The market regulation is still more effective when producers exert joint control of manufacturing plants and distribution systems as well.

have existed for a long time, especially in the developing countries.[16] A similar development can also be found in the field of bauxite production, where it is an especially important aspect of market regulation.[17]

Agreements on Quantity of Production

Before World War II, international raw material cartels often utilized long-term agreements on the distribution of production quotas.[18] This type of agreement is rare today, although some commodity agreements are returning to a quota system.[19] A stable market and sufficient market controls are necessary for a system of production quotas to work. Long-term production quotas are especially difficult in today's dynamic market, where constant fluctuations in demand require a system that can adapt quickly to changes in market conditions. Thus, quota agreements are practical in most cases, if the products are sold through a joint marketing agency. However, producers are generally unable or unwilling to enter into such an arrangement.

Recently, producers have apparently limited production by ad hoc agreements or decisions that reflect the market conditions evaluated by interested parties at that time, whatever the actual conditions have been. Thus, for example, in the fall of 1960 the leading copper producers limited production by as much as 10 or 15 per cent with the result that the copper offered on the world market dropped by 30,000 tons per year.[20] The increased organization power of copper-export-

---

[16] Iraq Petroleum Company, Ltd. (IPC), and her two subsidiaries, Mosul Petroleum Co. and Basrah Petroleum Co., Ltd., hold 75-year concessions for all oil fields in Iraq. Shareholders of the IPC are: Royal Dutch/Shell, BP, the Compagnie Française des Pétroles S.A. (CFP), the Near East Development Co. (a joint enterprise of Esso and Mobil Oil) and the Gulbenkian Erben; see U.S. Cong., Senate, *The International Petroleum Cartel, Staff Report to the Federal Trade Commission,* submitted to the Subcomm. on Small Business, 82d Cong. 2d Sess. (1952), p. 46; Ch. W. Hamilton, *Americans and Oil in the Middle East* (Houston, 1962), pp. 93 ff.

[17] "Latin America's First Large Aluminum Plant," London *Times,* July 15, 1963; "The Battle of Gove," *Mining J.,* Mar. 26, 1965. According to these articles, the large producers have established joint ventures in cooperation with domestic enterprises to exploit the new bauxite fields in Africa, Australia, and South America. See also testimony of H. Kronstein, U.S. Cong. Senate Comm. on the Judiciary, Subcomm. on Antitrust and Monopoly, *Hearings on Economic Concentration Outside the United States,* 90th Cong., 2d Sess., p. 3656 (1968).

[18] See generally E. Hexner, *International Cartels* (Chapel Hill, 1945).

[19] Chapter 2.   [20] See *Neue Zürcher Zeitung,* May 22, 1964.

ing countries opens a new method for restricting production.[21] A comparison between the commodity agreements on sugar, tin, and coffee and their relationship to domestic laws in different countries indicates an interesting trend. An agreement of this type may aim at excluding cheaper, lower-quality goods, even if a number of customers are interested in just this supply. Similar agreements can be found among the producers of zinc and lead.[22]

Agreements on Quality of Raw Materials

International agreements also exist with respect to the quality of raw materials. These agreements generally are designed to meet the competition from synthetic products and other raw materials. The agreement with respect to natural rubber is an example of this type of market regulation.[23]

Agreements on Joint Sale of Raw Materials

Joint sales agencies, generally called syndicates, can often be found in national cartel systems, as in the German coal, fertilizer, or cement industries. However, this type of arrangement is rare in international raw material cartels. Producers are generally unwilling to renounce such an important part of their business activity. National political considerations also play a part in this reluctance.

The only significant exception is in the diamond industry. Under the leadership of De Beers' Consolidated Mines, Ltd., a central sales agency, the Central Selling Organization, sells at least 80 per cent of the world production of raw diamonds.[24] Because of its controlling market position, the diamond syndicate is able to stabilize prices by restricting the supply of industrial diamonds as well as the supply of diamonds to the diamond grinders, operating primarily in the Nether-

[21] See discussion in Chapter 2.
[22] Statement made by M. F. R. Potter at the meeting of the British Non-Ferrous Metals Federation, printed in the daily bulletin of Metallgesellschaft AG, Dec. 16, 1963.
[23] See the statement of I. V. Burgess, Chairman of the Rubber Trade Association of London, London Times, Mar. 1, 1965.
[24] "A Brighter Sparkle in Diamond Sales," n. 3 above. The quotas are fixed by the Diamond Producers Association, in which three representatives of De Beers and of the Diamond Corporation, Ltd. (the most important subsidiary of De Beers), and two representatives of South Africa participate. J. Balfour, The Evolution of the Central Selling Organization for Diamonds (London, 1962), p. 5, and H. F. Oppenheimer, "The Diamond Industry," n. 3 above.

lands and Israel.[25] The syndicate was able to reach an agreement with the only other important producer of raw diamonds, the Soviet Union, whose production was marketed by the syndicate for a period of time.[26] Even after the Soviet Union withdrew from this arrangement there were no disturbances of the market.

Other Agreements on Sale of Raw Materials

Elimination of the distribution level

One current type of market-regulating agreement that did not exist in prewar cartels is the obligation of producers to supply their main clients, including manufacturers, directly. The product exchanges and middlemen are thus eliminated as a regulatory element, and the direct relationship created between the producer and its primary clients is not exposed to fluctuations in market conditions. In recent years the important producers of copper, lead, and zinc have agreed not to sell to their primary clients through the normal channels of trade, especially the London Metal Exchange and its merchants, but have agreed to undertake their sales directly.[27] Only small quantities of these raw materials, coming partly from main producers participating in this agreement and partly from other sources, are sold via the London Metal Exchange to the regular big customers. Thus, the system of "double prices," recently adopted in the gold market, became more and more effective.

Agreements on supplies to certain countries

Prewar cartels occasionally contained agreements on the allotment of national markets.[28] This type of agreement is rare in the field of raw materials today. However, the very far-reaching extension of the system of vertical integration and concentration of producers of raw material, such as copper, and the manufacturers of certain finished products, such as cable, amounts to a practical allotment of countries to the owner of the integrated enterprises.[29] There are, however, agreements granting preferential treatment to certain enterprises in supplying specific countries. On the other hand, enterprises in some states that purchase raw materials are prejudiced because they are not able to secure favorable long-term contracts with these producers.

[25] *Deutsche Zeitung,* July 20–21, 1963.   [26] *Die Zeit,* July 19, 1963.
[27] *Neue Zürcher Zeitung,* Aug. 11, 1964.
[28] See Hexner, n. 18 above, pp. 372 ff.
[29] See testimony of H. Kronstein, n. 17 above, p. 3654.

It would appear that at least some of the principal producers of iron ore have agreed that customers from those states having the greatest financial interest in the producers will be preferred in times of limited supply. This preferential treatment benefits the British economy especially.[30] Another example of this appeared in the copper market. Until April 1966, the most important producers excluded several small states from obtaining copper at the favorable producer prices through similar contractual definitions of the concept of a "main customer." [31]

To a limited extent, producers may agree to sales quotas with respect to individual countries if this is required by market conditions or political circumstances. Thus, the agreements repeatedly made by the oil industry with the Federal Republic of Germany guaranteeing the importation of a certain maximum amount of fuel oil or other oil into the Federal Republic [32] presuppose an agreement among the participating firms allocating, among the individual producers, the quota of oil to be imported. The German government apparently tolerates this agreement since an arrangement with the oil industry would otherwise not be possible.

Agreements Regarding Transformation of Natural Raw Materials into Processed Raw Materials

Joint manufacturing plants

As in production, joint operations in the transformation of natural raw materials into processed raw materials are very rare, apparently because the participating enterprises generally consider this form of cooperation undesirable because participation at this level implies abandonment of important elements of control. Nevertheless, there are some examples of these arrangements. Producers of crude oil operate refineries jointly in many countries.[33] Joint enterprises of this type also exist in the petrochemical industry,[34] the steel industry,[35] and the aluminum industry.[36]

[30] Statement by Sir Douglas Waring, C.B.E., at the 19th Annual General Meeting of British Overseas Mining Association, London *Times*, Dec. 31, 1964.

[31] 1965 *Metall* 49 ff.; 1964 *Metall* 108.   [32] *F.A.Z.*, Dec. 7, 1964.

[33] These are mainly in the new African countries (*F.A.Z.*, "Blick durch die Wirtschaft," Dec. 16, 1964).

[34] The Bayer-Werke and the British Petroleum Co. have a joint petrochemical enterprise in Dormagen (*F.A.Z.*, June 3, 1966).

[35] Leading German enterprises have entered into a joint venture with a Dutch company for the production of steel in the Netherlands (*id.*, May 27-28, 1965).

[36] Cf. n. 17 above.

Agreements on supply of raw materials for manufacturing plants

It was noted earlier that potential partners in a market regulation system often show a high degree of vertical integration. Consequently enterprises that transform natural raw materials into processed raw materials are not only customers but also are potential competitors of the producers. Thus, for many producers of raw materials it is appropriate to regulate the relationship with these firms in such a way that competition with outsiders can be controlled. In this area the producers may utilize quantitative restrictions together with the allocation of customers among the producers. Agreements exist in the field of crude oil allocating the supply of independent refineries in certain countries to a single production group.[37] To a certain extent this group thus holds an exclusive position.

Agreements on Price of Raw or Processed Raw Materials

Direct price agreements

Direct price agreements explicitly fixing prices or price ranges for certain periods are one of the classic means of market regulation. The first agreements of this kind after World War II occurred in the copper and zinc industries. The price agreement among copper producers, which was in existence until April 1966,[38] has two interesting aspects. Preferential prices were fixed under this agreement only with respect to deliveries to preferred customers such as the electrical industry, re-

[37] See provisions contained in the London Draft Memorandum of Principles, Jan. 1, 1934 (reprinted in *The International Petroleum Cartel*, n. 16 above, p. 263).

[38] The system of fixed copper prices, established by the producers in addition to the London Exchange prices, was overturned by Chile, which increased the price of Chilean copper by approximately £160 per long ton on Apr. 14, 1966 ("Chile sprengt das System der Kupferfestpreise," *F.A.Z.,* Apr. 16). Furthermore, Chile passed a bill in which minimum prices were fixed for exports of copper at 70 per cent of the average London Exchange prices; this bill came into force on Apr. 29, 1966 ("Chilean Copper Law in Force," London *Times,* May 2). Nearly all big copper producers followed the Chilean example in a short time. The Zambian producers, Roan Selection Trust, and the Anglo-American Corp. adapted their prices to the London Metal Exchange price on Apr. 25, 1966 (*Tagesnachrichten,* Apr. 25); the Union Minière du Haut Katanga, Republic of Congo, on Apr. 26, 1966 (*id.,* Apr. 27; the Noranda Sales Corp., Canada, increased its fixed prices in a similar way as the Chilean producers on Apr. 28, 1966 (*id.,* Apr. 28); and the International Nickel Co. of Canada on May 10, 1966 (*id.,* May 10). Only the American and Australian copper prices did not change.

portedly under two-year supply contracts.[39] The prices for deliveries to other customers were not fixed. Their regulation was left to the London Metal Exchange.[40] The contracts with the preferred customers contained specific provisions that any resale by the preferred customers would be made at the exchange prices.[41] In addition, these principal customers guaranteed that they would supply copper only to integrally related subsidiaries domiciled in the same country as the purchaser. This price structure can be shown by developments in the copper industry in 1964. On January 16, 1964, the producer price was fixed at £236 per long ton.[42] On March 13, 1964, the price was raised to £244, and on August 13, 1964, to £260.[43] A further price rise occurred in October 1964 with respect to copper produced in Chile.[44] Copper not produced for the principal customers was sold on the London Metal Exchange on November 6, 1964, for instance, at a maximum price of £531 per long ton.[45]

The situation in the international zinc market is similar. Here also the price quoted on the London Exchange governs prices in most sales outside of the United States.[46] When the London Exchange price increased in July 1964, the most important producers retreated from the zinc exchange. While the London Exchange price went up to approximately £140 per long ton, the Imperial Smelting Corporation, a subsidiary of the Rio-Tinto Zinc Corporation, announced that it intended to supply its regular customers at a fixed price of £125.[47] Canadian and Australian producers immediately followed a similar course of action, and French and Belgian refiners followed very shortly thereafter. The most important American producers, American Metal Climax and American Smelting and Refining Company, did not directly participate in this action as their sales on the European market are very limited.[48]

[39] See *Neue Zürcher Zeitung*, Feb. 2, 1964.　　[40] *Id.*
[41] *Id.;* see also 51 *Metallstatistik* 1 ff. (1964), published by the Metallgesellschaft AG, Frankfurt.
[42] Cf. *Metallstatistik, id.*　　[43] *Neue Zürcher Zeitung*, Sept. 23, 1964.
[44] "Copper Price Protest," London *Times*, Oct. 6, 1964, and "American Copper Prices Rise," *id.*, Oct. 8.
[45] *F.A.Z.*, "Blick durch die Wirtschaft," Nov. 11, 1964. The regulation of the copper mining prices remained about the same in 1969, permitting different prices for principal customers. This is only possible if an effective market regulation exists (*Mining J.*, Apr. 12, Dec. 6, 1968).
[46] U.S. Tariff Commission, *Lead and Zinc: Report to the President on Investigation No. TEA-IA-3 ¶351(d)(2) of Trade Expansion Act of 1962;* TC Publ. 157, p. 26 (June 1965).
[47] "Zinc after the Change," *Metal Bull.*, July 27, 1964.　　[48] *Id.*

The exchange price immediately increased to £155, but then dropped below the producer price. The producer price was then reduced to £110 per long ton under the leadership of the Imperial Smelting Company.[49] For a long time thereafter the exchange price was higher than the fixed producer price.[50] The fact that the two prices do not differ greatly can be attributed to the release of zinc from the strategic stockpile reserves of the United States and to the expected growth of production capacity in the United States, Australia, Japan, and Ireland.[51]

Price agreements utilizing product exchanges

In principle, no institution permits freer competition than the product exchanges, where the interplay of offer and demand establishes market prices. The international product exchanges, and particularly the London Metal Exchange, generally served this function of market regulation in the period prior to World War II.[52] After the war, however, members of international raw material cartels appear to have utilized these product exchanges for their own system of private market regulation. This development was possible primarily because the number of suppliers had greatly decreased. The important producers of copper, lead, zinc, and tin managed to keep the exchange price at a certain level through market agreements. The situation in the copper and zinc markets during the period from 1961 to 1963 illustrates this. In 1961, the exchange price for copper was stabilized at £234 per long ton.[53] This action was apparently initiated by two Rhodesian producers, Anglo-American Corporation and the Roan Selection Trust. During 1962 and 1963, approximately 160,000 long tons of copper were purchased by cartel members on the copper exchange in order to stabilize the exchange price.[54] It is interesting to note that when a copper shortage developed in 1964 these 160,000 long tons were not available for sale, apparently because they had been disposed of outside the normal market channels, particularly to the Soviet Union and Japan.[55] The purchase of copper on the exchange market in order to stabilize prices over a long period of time is possible only if the purchaser is relatively certain that the supply will continue to be limited.

49 *Neue Zürcher Zeitung*, Sept. 5, 1964.
50 *F.A.Z.*, "Blick durch die Wirtschaft," July 19, 1965.
51 See *id.* of Jan. 1, 1965; and *Handelsblatt*, Dec. 31, 1968.
52 *Neue Zürcher Zeitung*, Aug. 17, 1963.   53 *Id.*
54 *Id.*, Aug. 23, 1964.   55 *F.A.Z.*, "Blick durch die Wirtschaft," Feb. 9, 1965.

Zinc producers have also supported exchange prices. Even after the introduction of fixed producer prices they continued this policy.[56] They did so primarily to avert a decline in the exchange price as the result of a large supply of Russian zinc offered on the London market, which threatened the fixed price of £110.[57] It was easier to accomplish this policy in the zinc market than in the copper market because zinc scrap is much less important on the London Exchange than copper scrap.[58] And yet, the few powerful firms in control of copper and copper scrap manage to establish a most effective control. With respect to zinc it was necessary to establish a more widely branched and more formal organization because of the large number of producers.[59] The zinc producers initially attempted to support sales prices by establishing a formal cartel under Swiss law.[60] When this plan failed, the producers created a fund and appointed a common agent to purchase Russian zinc on behalf of the cartel members. These purchases of zinc occasionally amounted to 10,000 long tons and were resold, primarily to Communist China, because the high costs connected with the support purchases made them noncompetitive in Western markets.[61] As in the case of copper, the quantities purchased and resold were unavailable for stabilization of the market when demand increased.

At the same time, the producers agreed to restrict their production and fixed production quotas because of their fear of a crisis in the zinc market.

Agreements utilizing "administered prices"

In American economic literature, the concept of administered prices has come to mean the parallel price policy of enterprises in oligopolistic markets. These prices are not sensitive to changes in the market. Changes in demand are reflected by changes in sales and production rather than by changes in price. One can assume here that new price agreements still exist but that prices are maintained and, if necessary, changed in a uniform way by the autonomous parallel price policies of individual oligopolistic enterprises.[62]

[56] Id., July 1, 1963.   [57] Id., Nov. 1, 1965.
[58] "Zinc Producers' Collective Front," New York Times, July 21, 1964.
[59] "Mr. R. L. Stubbs Continues His World Zinc Review," Metal Bull., Apr. 28, 1959.
[60] Handelsblatt, July 28, 1965.   [61] F.A.Z., n. 55 above.
[62] See generally, H. Kronstein, J. T. Miller, Jr., and P. Dommer, Major American Antitrust Laws (New York, 1965), pp. 91–98; U.S. Cong., Senate Comm. on the Judiciary, Subcomm. on Antitrust and Monopoly, Hearings on Administered

Administered prices in national markets may play a part in the market policies of an international raw material market cartel. When this happens, the cartel partners agree to respect the administered prices in a specific national market, whereas the national producers adapt to the conditions imposed by the cartel in their dealings in foreign markets.

The situation in the copper market can again serve as an example. The domestic price for copper in the United States from May 1962 until March 1964 was maintained at 31 cents per pound.[63] On March 13, 1964, the same day on which the two large Rhodesian producers increased their selling prices on the London Exchange, American Smelting and Refining Company (ASARCO) raised its price to 34 cents.[64] Anaconda, Kennecott, and Phelps Dodge followed with price rises within a short period of time. At the same time, the American firms, particularly Anaconda, adhered to the producer prices of the international cartel in their export trade, which, because of the stabilization measures, was considerably lower than the domestic United States price.[65] On the other hand, very little copper was delivered to the United States from Africa, despite the fact that imports in greater amounts would have been profitable in spite of American import duties.[66] The same has been true in recent years, especially in the first months of 1969.[67]

The American market for zinc is isolated in a similar manner. In addition to the New York market price, which is dependent on the London price, American zinc producers have fixed a special producer price that does not depend upon the London quotations.[68] This price is usually published in the *Engineering and Mining Journal* and was generally higher than the London Exchange price until the middle of 1964. After this time it was generally lower than the London price. Nevertheless, American zinc exports in 1964 were 10 per cent smaller than in 1963, and 34 per cent smaller than the average exports during the years 1959 to 1963.[69]

Prices: A Compendium on Public Policy, 88th Cong., 1st Sess. (Comm. Print 1963).

[63] *Der Metallmarkt*, Jan. 18, 1964.

[64] U.S. Dept. of Interior, Bureau of Mines, "Copper in 1964," 1964 *Mineral Industry Surveys* 2.

[65] "Copper Price Protest," London *Times*, June 10, 1964.   [66] *Id.*, Sept. 6.

[67] N. 45 above.

[68] Report of the U.S. Tariff Commission, n. 46 above, pp. 24 ff.

[69] See text at nn. 52–56 above.

The Canadian zinc price can be characterized as an administered price as well. This price is set by the leading Canadian producer, the Consolidated Mining and Smelting Company of Canada (COMINCO), in the journal *The Northern Miner* and closely follows the intra-American zinc price.[70]

The observer of the international trade structure often may find indications of international administered prices and may conclude that the market is regulated by a purely oligopolistic harmonization of enterprises. This conclusion may be erroneous, since enterprises actually participating in a cartel agreement may merely create the illusion of an administered price structure. Each individual case must be scrutinized closely in order to ascertain whether the "concerted action" of enterprises in a market is based on a cartel agreement or is truly parallel behavior not covered under existing cartel laws.[71]

The situation in the oil industry can serve as an example. For many years, the United States Gulf Coast price was the prevailing price and "customary in industry." [72] After 1960, this special type of freight base price system was replaced by the so-called posted price system. Under this system, the major oil companies—Esso, Shell, Standard Oil of California, Gulf, Texaco, Socony, and British Petroleum—announced their prices for different grades of petroleum and different geographical markets, for instance in London in the *Petroleum Press Service*. Prices for all these companies were the same. Originally they were applied to sales to all independent refineries or other customers; later, however, competition from crude oil produced by those outside this arrangement became so intense that the parties were forced to make their posted prices applicable only to sales within the concerns.[73]

The importance of these posted prices is greater today, especially since they are utilized in long-term, exclusive contracts that the large oil companies have with a great many other customers, particularly gas stations. Even if the oil companies did not bind the resale price of their products, the posted prices would influence these resale prices

[70] Canada, Dep't of Justice, *Report of the Canadian Restrictive Trade Practices Commission Concerning the Production, Distribution and Sale of Zinc Oxide* (Ottawa, 1958). See also "Mr. R. L. Stubbs Continues His World Zinc Review," n. 59 above.

[71] Concerted action is not even prohibited by all nations under their restrictive practices legislation.

[72] *The International Petroleum Cartel*, n. 16 above, pp. 349 ff.

[73] "The Boiling World of Oil," *Fortune*, Feb. 1965, pp. 126, 129 ff., 218 ff.

because they must be used as a basis for calculations of these prices. The close relationship between the large oil companies and their principal customers prevents effective competition by outsiders.[74]

It is true that the joint use of a base point system—an agreed calculation of transport costs on the basis of an assumed, not necessarily real, place of departure—for participation in an organization collecting price information does not necessarily justify the conclusion that an agreement exists to hide contractual price-fixing by giving the appearance of mere oligopolistic behavior. On the other hand, the antitrust division of the United States Department of Justice did bring suit shortly after World War II against the seven leading producers of petroleum on the grounds that the producers had agreed, in the so-called Achnacarry Agreement of 1928, to maintain the then existing market divisions and to respect the existing price structure through the use of the United States Gulf Coast prices.[75] Although the producers subsequently ceased to rely on the Gulf Coast prices, they have apparently maintained their system of posted prices through prices established in the *Petroleum Press Service* in London.[76] The Justice Department referred to this as an illustration of the fact that the leading crude oil producers and refinery operators worked together and controlled the systems of distribution to the ultimate consumer.[77] Because of this pervasive control of production, manufacturing, transportation, and distribution of oil, the enterprises have many opportunities to engage in price-fixing agreements. Even if the external price policy of the large oil companies appears to be purely oligopolistic, this should not prevent further investigation as to whether informal price agreements arranged in business meetings or through joint subsidiaries do exist.

The nebulous line between price agreements and administered prices can also be seen in the aluminum market, which at first glance appears to be a situation in which genuine oligopolistic price leadership exists.[78]

[74] For example, with respect to Great Britain see *Monopolies and Restrictive Business Commission: Petrol. A Report on the Supply of Petrol to Retailers in the United Kingdom* (July 22, 1965), *passim*, esp. pp. 29 ff.

[75] U.S. District Court, District of Columbia, Civ. Action 86-27.

[76] *The International Petroleum Cartel*, n. 16 above, p. 266.

[77] Nn. 5, 13, and 16 above.

[78] At the meeting of the British Non-Ferrous Metals Federation, the purchasing manager of M. F. R. Potter, a subsidiary of Pirelli, explicitly termed the aluminum price an "administered price" (*Tagesnachrichten*, Dec. 16, 1963; *Neue Zürcher Zeitung*, Feb. 21, 1963; "French Aluminum Up," *Mining J.*, Apr. 15, 1965).

On the one hand, prices in the national aluminum markets differ, partly because of divergent costs for electricity and raw materials, and partly because of protectionist measures of individual governments. On the other hand, prices in international trade are unusually stable. The world price is basically influenced by the export price of Aluminum, Ltd., a Canadian firm, which is by far the largest exporter of raw aluminum in the Western hemisphere.[79]

It should be remembered that a worldwide cartel existed for aluminum prior to World War II.[80] This cartel agreement was facilitated by far-reaching horizontal and vertical concentration in the aluminum industry, and this concentration still exists. More than 85 per cent of Western aluminum capacity is controlled by the six largest Western aluminum enterprises.[81] Cooperation among these large enterprises continued to exist after World War II, as can be shown by several examples.

The tendency toward cooperation is very strong in the production of bauxite, alumina, and aluminum. Often several large producers cooperate in the same venture; for example, Kaiser (52 per cent), Aluminum, Ltd. (20 per cent), Pechiney (20 per cent), and Conzine Riotinto of Australia (8 per cent) all participate in the Queensland Alumina Company, Ltd., venture in Australia.[82]

Further evidence of cooperation among the large Western enterprises is their joint policy toward the Soviet Union and Japan. Because Soviet aluminum sales in Western markets had exerted a downward pressure on prices since 1958, the major Western producers concluded an agreement with the Soviet government in 1963 under which they agreed to purchase specific quantities of Russian aluminum and to use it in their own fabricating plants and to sell it to nonintegrated producers under their normal terms of sale.[83] This agreement was re-

[79] H. Bachmann, *Aluminum as an Export Industry*, UNCTAD (United Nations Conference on Trade and Development) E/Conf. 46 (1964), p. 69; the export prices of Aluminum, Ltd., between 1958 and 1964 were as follows: Apr. 1958 to Dec. 1959, 22.5 cents per pound; to Feb. 1962, 23.25 cents per pound; to Oct. 1963, 22.5 cents per pound; to Mar. 1964, 23 cents per pound; to Nov. 1964, 24.5 cents per pound.

[80] In connection with prewar aluminum cartels, see "International Aluminum Cartel," *Metal Bull.*, Feb. 28 and Mar. 7, 1961. In addition, see United States v. Aluminum Co. of America, 44 F. Supp. 97, 279 ff. (S.D.N.Y. 1940); 148 F. 2d 416, 440 ff. (2d Cir. 1945).

[81] Bachmann, n. 79 above, p. 65.   [82] "The Battle of Gove," n. 17 above.

[83] "What's Russia Up To?" *Metal Bull.*, Oct. 18, 1963; "Gentlemen's Agreement in Aluminum," *Financial Times*, Nov. 7.

negotiated in the spring of 1966 and extended through 1967.[84] Another interference with the free market appears to have occurred with
respect to Japanese raw aluminum. Aluminum exports from Japan to
Europe produced strong reaction in the European aluminum industry
and eventually led to the establishment of an export cartel for raw
aluminum in Japan. After the establishment of this cartel, Japanese
exports to Europe stopped completely in 1963 and 1964. These facts
would appear to indicate that through the use of this cartel a regional
market division with respect to Europe was accomplished, especially if
the trade between Japan on the one hand and the United States and
South America on the other is observed.[85]

In addition, it is doubtful whether the cooperation between Aluminum, Ltd., and Alcoa, which was attacked by the Department of
Justice in *United States v. Aluminum Corp. of America*,[86] has ceased
to exist. Since the divestiture ordered by the court in 1951 has been
completed there is indeed no common ownership between the two
companies.[87] The divestiture, however, does not seem to have changed
the cooperation between the two corporations at all; they still utilize
the same bank, the First Boston Corporation, and in 1955 they applied
jointly, together with other aluminum enterprises, for a license to
construct a large aluminum plant in Surinam.[88]

The market policy of both enterprises provides further indications
of their close cooperation, since Aluminum, Ltd., sells in the American
domestic market only at the price used there. In 1955 the agents of
Aluminum, Ltd., declared their intention not to decrease their prices
in the event that import duties were suspended and apparently were
not even willing to make sales on the American market at the lower
Canadian prices.[89] Only once, in 1961, did Aluminum, Ltd., change
its policy and induce price decreases on the American market by
offering cheap Canadian aluminum.[90]

[84] See *Metal Bull.*, Jan. 4, Feb. 4, Mar. 18, May 5, 1966; Mar. 3, Mar. 17, 1967.

[85] "Japanese Export Cartels Approved," *id.*, May 3, 1963; "Japan Plans Aluminum Cartel," *Financial Times*, Mar. 8.

[86] 44 F. Supp. 97 (S.D.N.Y. 1941); 148 F. 2d 416 (2d Cir. 1945); 91 F. Supp. 333
(S.D.N.Y. 1950).

[87] Aluminum, Ltd., Annual Report for 1960, p. 15.

[88] Daily bulletin of Metallgesellschaft AG, July 21, 1965; the application was
rejected.

[89] U.S. Cong., House. Select Comm. on Small Business, *Hearings on the Aluminum Industry*, H. Res. 114, 84th Cong., 1st Sess., Pt. 1, pp. 157 ff. (1956).

[90] Aluminum, Ltd., Annual Report for 1961, p. 15; Alcoa, Annual Report for
1961, p. 9.

One final striking parallelism in the policy of the two enterprises is that since December 1962 the export price of Aluminum, Ltd., the American domestic price (which is decisively influenced by Alcoa), and the American export price have been essentially at the same level.[91]

Certain remarks by American aluminum producers when discussing the acquisition of aluminum stockpiles from the American government corroborate this statement. They assured the government officials that they would prevent a flow-back of the aluminum sold abroad at low prices. Prohibitions against resale seem to be common in international aluminum trade and are generally included in contracts concluded by Aluminum, Ltd.[92]

These few examples show clearly that the concept of the "oligopolistic" aluminum market cannot be accepted unequivocably, for it is not comprehensive enough to describe the various agreements and understandings that are also possible in this type of market.

Agreements on the application of uniform sales conditions

To protect price regulations, the partners of international raw material cartels often impose uniform business conditions to prevent their customers from disturbing the price policy through resale of non-manufactured and manufactured goods. Sometimes the producers also attempt to subject substitutional products, especially scrap, to this regulation.

To use the copper market as an example again, the producers have obligated their wholesalers to insert the following conditions into their retail contracts: [93]

(1) Buyers who are also manufacturers are not allowed to resell the copper as such (this provision does not apply when resales are made to completely controlled domestic subsidiaries).

(2) The buyers are obligated not to charge fixed prices for products which they sell and which contain copper. Rather, their prices are to be based on the producer price on the day of delivery.

(3) The producers are entitled to revoke the supply contract at any time within the first year of its existence, while the buyers are not given a similar option.

(4) Buyers who are distributors are obligated to resell at the prices

[91] Aluminum, Ltd., Annual Reports, 1961–1964.

[92] Statement of M. Hickman, U.S. Cong., Senate Select Comm. on Small Business, *The Aluminum Industry*, 88th Cong., 2d Sess., S. 2272, pp. 123, 125, 128 ff. (1964).

[93] *Neue Zürcher Zeitung*, Feb. 2, 1964.

established on the London Metal Exchange rather than at the producer prices.

In addition, producers have also tried to force primary clients who are distributors to offer the producer price for scrap copper in sales to those enterprises that obtain producer prices in raw copper sales. This attempt to regulate the scrap market price has failed, however, because the enterprises concerned generally sell scrap through third persons.

Agreements also exist without any connection to specific sales contracts, but they generally are not very effective. The agreement among four hundred enterprises of the World Cotton Trade [94] with respect to the establishment of uniform sales conditions is worthy of mention.

Market Regulation by Agreements on Raw Material

Market control by raw material cartels is easier to define than that by technological cartels. Raw material cartels cover a limited number of products in specific markets while the technological cartel may cover a great variety of items each sold in a different market.

Two kinds of market regulation should be distinguished: that aimed only at the raw material itself; and that affecting not only the raw material but also processed raw materials and finished products or even competitive synthetic products. The second type may even include other products that do not contain this raw material but that are dependent upon methods which cannot be developed or applied except in connection with raw material or processed raw material.

In both cases, three types of markets are distinguished:

(1) Markets in which all producers are primarily concerned with the production and distribution of the specific raw material and do not exert any influence on its use. This is the case with diamonds, platinum, and nickel.[95]

(2) Markets in which the raw material producers control operations using the raw material and thereby control the processed raw materials or finished products. Only the excess material is sold on the open market. This is the case with the American copper producers Anaconda, Kennecott, and Phelps Dodge, which control production in

---

[94] C. Edwards, *Cartelization in Western Europe* (Washington, 1964), p. 30.

[95] In connection with diamonds see "A Brighter Sparkle in Diamond Sales," n. 3 above; with respect to nickel, see "International's Dominant Position in the World Nickel Picture," *Magazine of Wall Street*, July 2, 1961.

the United States and in Chile, but which require most of the copper they produce for their own manufacturing operations.[96] On the other hand, African copper producers have no interest in manufacturing plants except for a few refineries. There appears to be a new cooperation between governments that have nationalized the raw material mines and the former owners, whose vertical integration assures the maintenance of the present situation.

The petroleum industry provides another example. Here the refineries belong to the raw material enterprises that in many cases not only control the refining of crude oil into fuel oil and gasoline, but also produce a large number of important by-products for the petro-chemical industry.[97] Here one finds cases of the joint interests of raw material producers in manufacturing plants or in the distribution of goods to the ultimate customer.

(3) Markets in which some types of raw materials are exploited in countries where the export trade is restricted by tariffs, import quotas, or other governmental regulations. These measures have the effect of dissolving the international market into seemingly closed national markets. The regulations concerning oil conservation in the different states in the United States, the corresponding regulations of other oil-producing countries, and the U.S. import quotas for oil are measures of this type.[98]

Market Regulation of Raw Materials

International raw material cartels are one of the oldest systems of international private market regulation. Prior to World War II, nearly all raw materials were controlled by international cartels. The prewar cartels, although no longer existing formally, did exercise an influence as soon as the economic and political preconditions were sufficiently reestablished. During World War II and the early postwar years, raw materials were extremely scarce and were subject to government regulation. Because of this scarcity and because of the political climate, international cartels were to a large extent eliminated. Only in the mid-fifties were governmental regulations abandoned and a free world market reestablished. At the same time, however, the trend toward private market regulation revived in some sectors formerly governed

[96] For example, United States v. Kennecott Copper Corp., 231 F. Supp. 95 (S.D.N.Y. 1964).

[97] *Industriekurier*, Aug. 27, 1963.   [98] Chapter 2, above.

by cartels. An historical investigation of the copper, zinc, and oil world markets shows that postwar cartels are not genuinely new organizations. They represent a natural structural organism founded upon basic decisions made a long time ago. Raw material traffic moves according to the rules of this organism, which are individually adapted to prevalent economic situations.

The factual limits of market control within the raw material cartel

The international raw material cartels of the prewar years generally cover the entire market. Because of the relationship between prewar and postwar cartels, the modern raw material cartels obviously would like to reestablish total market regulation. This pervasive control, however, does not seem possible today for a number of reasons: the availability of scrap metals; the existence of substitute products that can fill some of the demand for the raw material; the existence or threatened development of synthetic products that can be substituted entirely or partially for the raw material; and the potentially large reservoir of untapped resources, especially through further exploitation of the sea, as for example in the fields of diamonds or petroleum.[99] These factors have created specific limits to the market control of international raw material cartels.

In the fields of copper, lead, and iron ore, and, to a limited extent in tin and zinc also, the market regulation is complete only if it includes the scrap metal that serves as the respective substitute. Thus, for example, copper producers attempted to bind customers buying the primary products to sell scrap only to other favorite primary customers and only at the producer prices. The producers attempted to prevent sales of copper scrap at prices lying between the producer and the exchange prices. This attempt failed, however, because the enterprises involved disposed of their scrap through third persons.

Even if there is no agreement on scrap, regulation of the raw material itself may affect the whole market if the market share of scrap is very small or if its utility as a substitute is limited. If, on the other hand, scrap has a considerable market share or is useful as an alternate product, the raw material cartel agreement may be ineffective. The situation in most raw material markets generally lies somewhere between these two. The copper market between 1963 and April 1966 can be used as an example. Although cartel members were unable to

[99] *Deutsche Zeitung*, Feb. 26, 1964.

gain control over the distribution of scrap copper and controlled only 70 per cent of the new raw material offered on the world market, they exerted a decisive influence on world market prices.[100] By entering into long-term contracts with their primary customers, giving them a priority on potential supplies, and by granting preferential prices that were not subject to the price fluctuations of the London Metal Exchange, the producers were able to restrict the amount of copper available on the free market. Thus, copper purchasers who were not members of the cartel agreement were severely discriminated against. For example, West German consumers had to buy 50 to 60 per cent of their requirements at the high exchange prices, and consumers from other countries outside of the United States had to make 30 per cent of their purchases on the exchange.[101] This discrimination was the consequence of an effective regulation of the whole copper market.

The regulators of the raw material markets are, in some instances, restricted by the threat from substitutive raw materials, depending upon price and cost considerations. This threat is alleviated to some extent by the considerable investment costs, such as retooling, arising out of the changeover to a new material. Such a changeover also raises a number of technical problems. For example, an aluminum cable must be much heavier than a copper cable if it is to transmit the same capacity of electricity.

Thus, price is not the only consideration involved in turning to a substitute product. Nevertheless, alternate products present a danger for the raw material cartel members. These market regulators may protect themselves against such a changeover by stabilizing prices for the raw material at a competitive level or by applying new methods that make their product more profitable. For example, the copper and zinc producers temporarily grant price reductions to those primary clients capable of converting to the substitute product and thus make such substitution unprofitable. Customers unable to bear change-over costs for financial or technical reasons must pay higher prices.

A raw material cartel does not necessarily lose its market-regulating effects merely because a substitute product is successfully introduced upon the market, since the cartel members still have the opportunity to extend their market regulation to the alternate raw material. In other cases, the substitute itself is subject to special market regulation. Market regulation of substitutive raw materials thus takes form,

---

[100] 1964 *Metall* 1006, 1008.   [101] *Id.*

with free competition between the two materials only one of many possibilities.

Enterprises participating in international raw material cartels must also consider possible competition from synthetic substitutes. The 1964 United Nations Conference on Trade and Development in Geneva showed that the producer countries were aware of this danger.[102] The synthetic product plays a decisive role as a competitive substitute only if it is sold at lower or more stable prices than the natural product, and if sold in considerable quantities. In this case, the participating enterprises may attempt to establish market regulations covering both the raw material and its synthetic substitute. If they do not succeed, significant competition between the raw material and its synthetic substitute may result. It is also possible that the competitive position of either the synthetic or natural product may become strong enough to indirectly subject the other to regulation.

Generally, some accommodation between the interests of raw material producers and those of the synthetic product is reached. The raw material producers may participate from the beginning in research programs and in the development of the synthetic product. They thus often have the opportunity to adapt their production and distribution of the synthetic substitutes to market-regulating agreements governing the respective raw materials. A number of interesting combinations between technological and raw material cartels can result in this area. For example, in three different fields, the diamond enterprise of De Beers, a large copper firm, and the steel industry, companies are working to develop different synthetic substitutes.[103]

An especially interesting official recognition of this relationship between natural product and synthetic product exists in the case of man-made fiber and cotton. The possibility of "some form of modus vivendi between man-made fibers" and cotton "was proposed to the GATT Committee on Trade and Development last November by the member countries of the Association of African and Malgache States (AAMS). Such an agreement, if successful, would open new perspectives of incalculable importance for the developing countries." [104]

[102] UNCTAD E/Conf. 46/28, June 16, 1964, pp. 9, 53.

[103] With respect to the manufacturing of synthetic diamonds see "A Brighter Sparkle in Diamond Sales," n. 3 above; "Search for New Uses," London Times, Jan. 22, 1964.

[104] Statement of the Brazilian delegate to the International Cotton Advisory Committee Twenty-Fifth Plenary Meeting, Annex to Proceedings (1966), pp. 56, 60.

Another aspect is that the sudden introduction of new synthetic products is very unlikely. For example, General Electric worked for at least ten years until it was possible, in 1955, to produce synthetic diamonds in sufficient quantities and at low enough costs to compete with natural diamonds.[105] Of the five producers of artificial diamonds, General Electric, De Beers, and Swedish, Soviet Russian, and Japanese enterprises, only De Beers utilizes the Central Selling Organization to sell their artificial diamonds; the other producers offer their products on the free market.[106] The share of synthetic diamonds in total production is very small, however, and does not significantly affect the diamond market as a whole, because the only synthetic diamonds that can be economically produced are very small and have a relatively restricted applicability, for instance in record players.

Even if the synthetic product can be applied with the same utility as the raw material, the production of synthetic products generally passes through a phase in which its production is more expensive than that of the natural product. In the field of nitrogen, for example, the synthetic product was at first considerably more expensive than the natural product. When nitrogen was in short supply during World War I, producers of synthetic nitrogen expanded their share of the market rapidly and hence amortized their development costs very quickly. The synthetic producers were even in a position to undercut the prices of natural nitrogen. Nevertheless, they eventually established price regulations which enabled the Chilean producers of natural niter, whose market share had gradually dwindled, to maintain a position in the market.[107] The prewar agreement on nitrogen among the synthetic producers also included natural nitrogen, and this caused a higher price for the synthetic product.

In the field of petroleum, Standard Oil agreed with IG-Farbenindustrie in 1934 to raise the price of its natural products in Europe so that the European firm could produce synthetic petroleum.[108] In return, Standard Oil obtained access to the methods for production of synthetic petroleum which later proved significant, particularly for the production of airplane fuel. This is an unusual case in which the price of the natural product was raised to give the synthetic product a chance to enter the market.

[105] "A Brighter Sparkle in Diamond Sales," n. 3 above.   [106] *Id.*
[107] See 1934 *Kartell-Rundschau*, 558 ff.
[108] United States v. Standard Oil, et al., U.S. District Court, District of New Jersey, Criminal Action No. 682; United States v. Standard Oil Co. (N.J.), 1941–1943 CCH Trade Reg. Rep. §52, 768 (D.N.J. 1942).

Synthetic India rubber was developed in Russia in the beginning of the 1920's, and also in Germany by IG-Farbenindustrie (Buna) in 1929–1930. This development was stimulated by the artificial restriction of the production of natural rubber. The American firms such as DuPont (Neoprem) and Standard Oil of New Jersey (Butyl) developed their own synthetic rubber about 1940. At this time, Germany and the Soviet Union were the significant producers of synthetic rubber.[109] The development of synthetic products in the United States had been restricted by cartel agreements among IG-Farbenindustrie, Standard Oil, and DuPont.[110] In 1942, the United States government succeeded, through criminal and civil suits brought against Standard Oil and DuPont, in securing a consent decree placing the patents on Buna and Butyl at the disposal of Standard Oil subsidiaries.[111] Despite this order and the resulting permission to utilize these patents, the primary responsibility for the development of synthetic rubber in the United States during the war years and until 1955 lay with the United States government.[112] In 1955 the United States government decided to turn its synthetic rubber plants over to the public. The tire producers and chemical concerns were able to secure control over production of synthetic rubber. These industries had always shown a trend toward cartelization [113] since ten concerns supply 80 per cent of the world market for rubber.[114]

Following the return of synthetic rubber production to private industry, output increased considerably. In 1969 the ratio between consumption of natural and synthetic rubber was already 1:3.1 in the United States, while in other countries, except Canada and the USSR, natural rubber was predominant.[115] In 1971 the world consumption amounted to 2.99 million long tons of natural rubber and to nearly 5

[109] C. F. Phillips, Jr., *Competition in the Synthetic Rubber Industry* (Chapel Hill, 1961), pp. 17 ff.

[110] *Id.*, pp. 30 ff.; G. Stocking and M. Watkins, *Cartels in Action* (New York, 1946), pp. 114 ff.

[111] Cases cited in n. 108 above; Phillips, n. 109 above, p. 37.

[112] Phillips, *id.*, pp. 55 ff.

[113] Disapproval of Proposed Sale of Government-Owned Rubber Producing Facilities, S. Rep. No. 117, 84th Cong., 1st Sess., pp. 19, 21 (1957).

[114] According to a speech made by Mr. Friedrich, general director of the Phönixgummiwerke AG at the shareholders' meeting of the corporation on June 11, 1964.

[115] F.A.O., *Commodity Review and Outlook 1969–70* (Rome, 1970) pp. 116, 118.

million long tons of synthetic rubber; the world ratio between natural and synthetic rubber was 1:1.67.[116] Although natural rubber has continuously been losing its market position, rubber producers have not, as yet, experienced difficulty in selling their product.[117] On the contrary, absolute production has increased in recent years. This development is based on several factors. First, the producers have endeavored to improve the quality of natural rubber. Second, natural rubber has certain technical advantages synthetic rubber does not have. And third, the demand for natural and synthetic rubber still exceeds production.[118]

It is difficult to determine the extent to which an international cartel influences the rubber market today. It is clear that private market regulation of natural rubber extends only to its quality.[119] On the other hand, since the production of natural rubber is very inelastic, synthetic rubber producers are in a position to achieve a partial regulation of the market.[120]

To summarize, in certain cases the synthetic product has provided significant competition to the raw material, for example, in rubber and a number of metals. The threat of synthetic products, however, is a greater danger to the market share of a single enterprise than it is to the system of market regulation itself. In most instances, the prevailing market regulation system has shifted to the stronger substitutive product, or, if it was not clearly superior, to the whole market.

The exploitation of new deposits by independent enterprises constitutes an additional factor threatening the private market regulation system, if the newcomers are sufficiently strong to undertake the necessary investments. In 1964, the extraction of diamonds from the bottom of the sea amounted to approximately 850 carats per day.[121]

[116] Daily bulletin of Metallgesellschaft, May 2, 1972.

[117] Statement of George R. Vila, reprinted in *Rubber Age*, Dec. 1959, p. 475.

[118] Production increased from 2,050,000 long tons (1961) to 2,635,000 long tons (1968); see n. 116 above; and B. Anossow, "Der internationale Kautschukmarkt," in *Aussenhandel* 4/1972.

[119] I. V. Burgess, n. 23 above.

[120] According to Friedrich's report, n. 114 above, a "realistic" conception prevailed at the last meeting of the International Rubber Study Group. The participants adopted the view that it is not possible to restrict the production of synthetic rubber; the only way to meet its competition is to increase the productivity of the plantations, to adapt the products to the technological needs of the manufacturers, and to eliminate gradually the existing trade barriers.

[121] "De Beers and Marine Diamonds," *Mining J.*, Feb. 5, 1965.

These diamonds have generally been taken from the sea near South Africa and South-West Africa by the Marine Diamond Corporation and by the South African firm General Mining and Financing Corporation, Ltd.[122] De Beers, however, has been able to take over the distribution of these diamonds.

The primary natural resource extracted from the sea in recent years has been petroleum.[123] The impact of these new resources on the existing market regulation for crude oil is not yet clear.

Geographic limits of market regulation

The preceding discussion has clearly shown that it is impossible to discuss regulation of a particular raw material without considering scrap metal, substitute products, and synthetic products. How far can an agreement concluded to control one part of the world market affect geographical markets not directly subject to this agreement? An international raw material cartel may exclude certain geographical markets from the agreement because of national antitrust laws or because of specific economic barriers. In general, a market policy referring to one country applies to the areas excluded from the cartel agreement. This does not mean, however, that these areas are not affected by the cartel in some manner. The situation in the crude oil, zinc, and copper markets shows the existence of such effects.

American legislation authorizes the President to establish import quotas for petroleum.[124] In addition, American laws and governmental regulations establish quotas for the production of crude oil from American resources.[125] These regulations are significant of the organizers of an international petroleum cartel. Because there is no American oil available for exports to other countries, no disturbances of the international market can originate from the United States. Furthermore, the cartel members, knowing the volume to be offered on the American market and the resulting prices, can take American prices into consideration when they fix posted prices for petroleum sold on the world market. The American market thus represents a known

---

[122] Statement of Mr. H. F. Oppenheimer, Chairman of De Beers Consolidated Mines, Ltd., printed in London *Times,* May 21, 1965.

[123] "Boiling World of Oil," n. 73 above, p. 130.

[124] U.S. Tariff Commission. Trade Agreement Extension Act 1958, §8; Trade Expansion Act 1962, §232. See also the Report of the President's Special Representative for Trade Negotiations, Future U.S. Trade Policy (1969), p. 2.

[125] Chapter 2 above; see also Oil Import Regulation 32A C.F.R., Ch. X (1968).

quantity that can be taken into consideration in the same way as if the United States and its enterprises had been actually participating in the cartel agreement.

In 1958, the U.S. government fixed quarterly quotas for zinc imports in order to counteract market disturbances caused by overproduction in the United States.[126] These quotas remained practically unchanged until they were lifted in 1965.[127] The regulations did not include U.S. government imports and imports of duty-free zinc articles. The amount of zinc offered on the American market was thus restricted and was increased only when the sale of zinc from the U.S. strategic stockpiles was undertaken in July 1964.[128]

The situation in the U.S. copper market is somewhat different. The United States government does not fix quotas for domestic copper sales. Nevertheless, the price of copper has remained extremely stable since the end of the war, especially after the wartime controls were removed. The total production of Phelps Dodge and 90 per cent of the production of the two international copper enterprises, Anaconda and Kennecott, is sold to their subsidiaries. In the United States, 80 to 90 per cent of the copper produced was sold at producer prices, compared with only 40 per cent in the Federal Republic of Germany. Furthermore, the principal exporters of copper to the United States, the Chilean producers, are under the control of American firms who thus can regulate this production as well as the total amount of imports to the United States.[129] Because of the structure of the American copper industry, American copper exports do not exert a significant influence on the world market or upon the regulation of world market prices. This is left to the members of the copper cartel. There are indications of occasional agreements between the cartel members and the American firms to prevent price disturbances and to establish certain principles of cooperation. From the middle of May 1962, until March 15, 1964, the American price was stabilized at 31 cents per pound.[130]

[126] Presidential Proclamation 3257, 1958, 48 C.F.R., Pt. 15 (1968).
[127] Report of the U.S. Tariff Commission, n. 46 above, Table 1.
[128] *Id.*, p. 13.
[129] F. L. Wideman, "Copper," a reprint from U.S. Dept. of the Interior, Bureau of Mines, 1963 *Minerals Yearbook* 443; "The Chileanization of Copper," *Engineering and Mining J.*, Dec. 28, 1964; the subsidiaries are Chile Exploration Co., Andes Copper Mining Co., Santiago Mining Co. (Anaconda), Braden Copper Co. (Kennecott). It is not clear what effects the participation of the Chilean government in these corporations will have.
[130] N. 63 above.

This price was held even when the European price was lower and when the European price would have been even much lower if it had not been for the price support program of the African firms on the London Metal Exchange. Nevertheless, only small amounts of copper were exported from Africa and Europe to the United States.[131] These low prices and the low tariff barriers for copper indicate that exports to the United States would have been profitable, especially since Rhodesian producers had taken 160,000 tons off the market in order to stabilize prices. Instead of selling in the United States, however, these copper supplies were sold to the Soviet Union and Japan at prices below the American market price.[132]

On the other hand, the increase of the world market price does affect copper prices in the United States. On March 16, 1964, the American price was 34 cents per pound, which corresponded exactly to the European producer price of £244 per long ton.[133] The small amount of American copper not sold at producer prices is not normally subject to the price fluctuations of the London Metal Exchange. The price difference between the American free price and the producer price, however, reached similar levels. At the end of 1964 it amounted to roughly 25 cents per pound and thus meant extremely strong pressures upon independent manufacturers.[134] So, even if the United States government and the American producers maintain high prices in the United States, notwithstanding price declines on the world market, the United States domestic trade is nevertheless affected by the market regulation of private cartels. While wild price races occurred on the London Metal Exchange, the American domestic prices as well as the European producer prices remain relatively low. As already pointed out, this suggests that there is an actual division of markets between the United States and Europe and other markets.

[131] N. 66 above. From 1960 to 1963, 5 to 12 per cent of the annual North and South American copper imports came from Africa (Wideman, n. 129 above, pp. 463 ff.). The stability of the United States market was not disturbed by imports from other North or South American countries because the Chilean and Canadian copper is controlled by United States corporations.
[132] See Wideman, n. 129 above.   [133] N. 64 above.
[134] Remarks of Senators Mansfield and Symington, *Congress. Rec.* S280–82 (daily ed. Feb. 19, 1966). According to Sir Ronald L. Prain, chief manager of the Rhodesian Selection Trust, this twofold system of prices has existed in the U.S.A. and Canada for a long time (speech of Oct. 24, 1964, annex to 1964 Annual Report of the Rhodesian Selection Trust).

The effects of vertical integration on raw material markets

International raw material cartels are even more detrimental to free trade if the members of the cartel show an interest in manufacturing through vertical integration. In this case a cartel not only leads to a price increase but also provides the integrated raw material cartel with a considerable competitive advantage at the manufacturing level. Thus, the nonintegrated manufacturers feel the brunt of the anticompetitive practices of the cartel. If the cartel members charge a split price for delivery to third parties, as the partners in the international copper cartel did temporarily, the cartel primarily affects those enterprises not supplied at the lower producer price. But the producer price for the primary clients was also a high cartel price. In addition, these primary clients were obligated to establish the price for the copper parts of their finished products on the basis of the producer price at the time of delivery. Thus, the integrated enterprises maintained a competitive advantage even with respect to these large firms. These larger enterprises, however, had an advantage over other less-favored producers.

Market Regulation of Processed Raw Materials or Semifinished Products through Agreements on Raw Materials

The market regulation of a raw material often extends to treated raw materials. This is especially true when the difference between the pure raw material and the processed raw material is so slight that it is not possible to speak of separate markets, as for instance with copper. Here a regulation of only the pure raw material would be ineffective.

The situation is different where the pure raw material and processed raw materials are sold on different markets, especially where there are many processed raw materials, as for example in the field of crude oil, which is processed into gasoline and numerous petrochemical materials. Here the enterprises at the processing level must base their calculations upon the oil prices fixed by the international cartel. Market regulation at the manufacturing level, however, is an entirely different matter. Because of their strong position as suppliers, the producers of pure raw materials clearly have the power to regulate the subsequent market for processed raw materials. In general, they will use this power only if they have an interest in the market through vertical integration, as for example in the fields of crude oil and copper.[135] The greater the vertical integration of the cartel partners, the more important it is to include processed raw materials in the system of market regulation. If the situation that exists today in the American copper market, where a considerable part of imports and production is sold directly to subsidiaries, existed also in other parts of the world, a pure raw material regulation would no longer be necessary. In this case, the cartel members naturally try to regulate the market for the processed goods through different methods. At first they may merely discriminate against the nonintegrated clients with respect to sales price or conditions, thus giving their own manufacturing firms considerable competitive advantages. Then, they may restrict the quantities or types of finished products produced by their own manufacturing plants or those of third enterprises supplied at preference prices. Finally, the parties may influence the price of the finished product. Since the enterprises supplied at the free market price are generally not competitive, the cartel members are in a position to combine preference prices and market restrictions on finished products to assure sufficient sales of their raw materials and also to guarantee that their primary clients do not compete with their own manufacturing plants. This often requires national rather than international market regulation because of the need for vertical concentration of producers in every country. The national cartels in the manufacturing sector thus must be examined together with raw material cartels.

Role of Governments in Developing
International Raw Material Cartels

Public international agreements also play a part in the regulation of raw material markets. Countries participating in production and consumption of raw materials have concluded a number of commodity agreements.[136] It is generally argued that the regulation of pure raw materials and processed raw materials by governmental agreements can serve as a substitute for private raw material cartels because these agreements have been concluded under the auspices of the United Nations treaty provisions, that guarantee equal representation to the consumer and producer interests and thus theoretically protect the public interest as well as the interests of the economically weaker

[135] *Neue Zürcher Zeitung*, Dec. 4, 1964.   [136] See Chapter 2, n. 3–8.

party.[137] It is thus argued that these governmental agreements should be used to replace the private systems of market regulation. Analysis of the system of market regulation for raw materials shows that this assumption is doubtful. As a matter of fact, commodity agreements are generally based on prior private international market regulations, and these private regulations generally reappear once the governmental regulation has ceased.[138] Often private market regulation remains within the framework of the governmental agreements, which are used only to establish a barrier against price decreases. In addition, a formal equality of votes between producer and consumer countries does not take into consideration those instances where the interests of some consumer countries are similar to those of the producing nations. Because of these factors, commodity agreements do not appear to be appropriate instruments to protect the consumer interests.

The Tin Market

The interrelationship between governmental agreements and private market regulation can be shown with respect to the tin market. After numerous attempts to regulate the international tin market through private agreements in the 1930's, the First International Tin Agreement was concluded in New York in 1953 within the framework of the United Nations treaty. The Second Tin Agreement followed in 1960 at the expiration of the first. The Third Tin Agreement, in which the United States government did not participate, was concluded on April 20, 1965, and remained in force until June 30, 1971. The Fourth International Tin Agreement was adopted by the United Nations Tin Conference in Geneva on April 13, 1970, and came into force on July 1, 1971.[139] New members of the Fourth Agreement are the USSR and Western Germany, while the United States again did not join the agreement.

The producing and consuming countries in the Fourth Agreement are as follows:

[137] UNCTAD, International Commodity Problems, E/Conf. 46/8 (Mar. 19, 1964), p. 4.
[138] Note 2 above.
[139] U.N. Doc. TD/TIN. 4/7 Rev. 1. The international tin agreements are used here for two reasons. The United States is not a member and therefore the relationship of regulation of the domestic American market as far as it can be shown is not necessarily a result of the commodity agreement. Furthermore, the facts around this case show very clearly the actual interrelation between the administration of the commodity agreement and the operation of private cartels.

PRODUCERS		CONSUMERS			
Country	*Votes*	*Country*	*Votes*	*Country*	*Votes*
Australia	33	Austria	10	India	42
Bolivia	182	Belg./Luxem.	29	Italy	58
Congo	43	Bulgaria	10	Japan	204
Indonesia	117	Canada	40	Netherlands	45
Malaysia	440	Taiwan [140]	8	Poland	34
Nigeria	52	Czechoslovakia	34	Korea	7
Thailand	133	Denmark	11	Spain	24
		W. Germany	111	UK	147
		France	90	USSR	65
		Hungary	15	Yugoslavia	16

These agreements contain two important points. First, if there is a tin surplus, the International Tin Council is authorized to establish export quotas and thus to regulate the amount of tin sold on the international markets.[141] Although this method permits regulation of the supply of tin, this metal is more difficult to regulate by private agreement than copper and zinc because of the many states that participate in its production and influence any regulation of the market. It is much easier in some geographic areas to open new tin mines and to increase tin production than it is to increase copper production. While in each producing country the tin producer has an oligopolistic structure, the world situation is much less concentrated than in the copper case.

On the other hand, export control is facilitated by the fact that primary tin producers—Bolivia, Congo, Indonesia, Malaysia (which controls 40 per cent of the entire free world tin production), Nigeria and Thailand—have to ship their products by ocean transportation to the primary consumer countries, such as Great Britain, the Federal Republic of Germany, France, Japan, and the United States. For a long time Britain and the Netherlands used their control over corporations in certain colonies or foreign countries to subject any shipment consigned to foreign refineries, especially United States installations, to extra taxes. Between the two world wars, this assured the control and

[140] In the meantime Taiwan withdrew from the agreement, so that the association of the votes of the consuming countries slightly changed.

[141] Art. 33-35, Fourth Tin Agreement.

strong position of the tin smelter in Britain and his comparatively weaker position in the United States.[142]

Under the second important provision of these agreements, the participating countries obligated themselves to establish both a monetary reserve and a supply of tin. The manager of the tin pool is obligated to use this monetary reserve to buy tin if the established floor price is reached and to sell from the supply of tin if the fixed maximum price is exceeded.[143]

The officers of the International Tin Council must observe the objectives laid down in Article I of the Fourth International Tin Agreement:

(a) To provide for adjustment between world production and consumption of tin and to alleviate serious difficulties arising from surplus or shortage of tin;

(b) To prevent excessive fluctuations in the price of tin and in export earnings from tin;

(c) To make arrangements which will help to increase the export earnings from tin, especially those of the developing producing countries, thereby helping to provide such countries with resources for accelerated economic growth and social development, while at the

[142] "Oligopoly in Tin," 26 *Am. J. of Economics and Sociology* 13, 17 (1967).
[143] Art. 250 of the Fourth Tin Agreement provides:
"(c) If the market price of tin:
"(i) Is equal to or greater than the ceiling price the Manager shall, unless otherwise instructed by the Council, if he has tin at his disposal and subject to articles 26 and 27, offer tin for sale on the London Metal Exchange at the market price, until the market price of tin falls below the ceiling price or the tin at his disposal is exhausted;
"(ii) Is in the upper sector of the range between the floor and ceiling prices, the Manager may operate on the London Metal Exchange at the market price if he considers it necessary to prevent the market price from rising too steeply, provided he is a net seller of tin;
"(iii) Is in the middle sector of the range between the floor and ceiling prices, the Manager may buy and/or sell tin only on special authorisation by the Council;
"(iv) Is in the lower sector of the range between the floor and ceiling prices, the Manager may operate on the London Metal Exchange at the market price if he considers it necessary to prevent the market price from falling too steeply, provided he is a net buyer of tin;
"(v) Is equal to or less than the floor price, the Manager shall, unless otherwise instructed by the Council, if he has funds at his disposal and subject to articles 26 and 27, offer to buy tin on the London Metal Exchange at the floor price until the market price of tin is above the floor price or the funds at his disposal are exhausted."

same time taking into account the interests of consumers in importing countries;

(d) To ensure conditions which will help to achieve a dynamic and rising rate of production of tin on the basis of a remunerative return to producers, which will help to secure an adequate supply at prices fair to consumers and to provide a long-term equilibrium between production and consumption;

(e) To prevent widespread unemployment or under-employment and other serious difficulties which may result from maladjustments between the supply of and the demand for tin;

(f) In the event of a shortage of supplies of tin occurring or being expected to occur, to take steps to secure an increase in the production of tin and a fair distribution of tin metal in order to mitigate serious difficulties which consuming countries might encounter;

(g) In the event of a surplus of supplies of tin occurring or being expected to occur, to take steps to mitigate serious difficulties which producing countries might encounter;

(h) To review disposals of noncommercial stocks of tin by Governments and to take steps which would avoid any uncertainties and difficulties which might arise;

(i) To keep under review the need for the development and exploitation of new deposits of tin and for the promotion, through, inter alia, the technical and financial assistance resources of the United States and other organisations within the United Nations system, of the most efficient methods of mining, concentration and smelting of tin ores; and

(j) To continue the work of the International Tin Council under the First, Second and Third International Tin Agreements.

Market effects

Even though the tin agreement has as one of its objectives the stabilization of tin prices on the world market, the participating parties were unable to accomplish this. When the world tin price exceeded the fixed limits of the agreement, the pool manager did not have sufficient supplies of tin at his disposal to sell on the market in order to lower prices.[144] This situation occurred in 1964, although the floor price had been fixed at £850 per long ton on December 5, 1963, and the

---

[144] The Fourth Agreement fixed the limits as ceiling £1650, floor £1350. At the end of 1971 there were 6,637 tons of tin remaining in the bufferstock (daily bulletin of Metallgesellschaft, March 24, 1972).

ceiling price set at £1,000 per long ton on November 12, 1964.[145] Despite these limits, the price on the London Metal Exchange in the middle of November mounted to £1,420 [146] and later even exceeded this amount after occasional price declines.[147] During this period the pool did not have any tin reserves because the pool manager had previously sold all the supplies allocated to him to meet earlier price increases. In any event, the intervention of the pool would have been meaningless because of the impossibility of forcing a price decrease to the maximum limit established in the agreement.[148]

Another development that may frustrate the objectives of the tin agreement is the increased use of long-term contracts granting preferential conditions to primary customers,[149] despite the multitude of new tin producers.[150] On the basis of a mutual understanding, tin producers purchased tin on the world market when prices were low and prevented the pool manager from obtaining a sufficient supply of tin, since under the provisions of the tin agreement he was permitted to purchase tin only when the world market price reached a fixed minimum level. Because the tin producers purchased tin at prices in excess of this fixed minimum, the pool manager, when market conditions unexpected by the agreement required him to do so, did not have a sufficient supply of tin to prevent the price from later rising above the fixed maximum. Under these circumstances the tin producers made a significant profit on the tin they had previously purchased.[151]

The partners in such a cartel must take into consideration the situation in the United States as well as the influence of China and Russia on the fixed amount of tin to be sold on the world market. After World War II, the United States began stockpiling large quantities of tin to establish a strategic reserve. In March 1962, the United States government disclosed that its stockpile had a surplus of 164,000 long tons.[152] If the U.S. government had disposed of this surplus rapidly, it probably would have reduced the world market price below the floor price of the pool.[153]

[145] Neue Zürcher Zeitung, Sept. 6, 1964.   [146] Id., Dec. 8.
[147] In January the price went down to £1187 per long ton; in May it increased to £1607.50; then it fell again to £1441.25 on June 22, 1965; see id., May 23, 1965.
[148] Id.   [149] Daily bulletin of Metallgesellschaft, Dec. 12, 1964.
[150] N. 146 above.   [151] F.A.Z., Dec. 23, 1963.
[152] The International Tin Council, Statistical Yearbook, 1962, p. 14.
[153] Id. Until recently, the United States government could only release materials from the stockpiles upon the authorization of Congress.

Following negotiations with the producer countries and representatives of the Tin Council, the United States agreed in 1962 to sell its tin surplus gradually in accordance with market conditions and in moderate quantities. Under United States law, merchandise could only be released from the stockpile under Congressional authorization. Congress at first authorized the release of only 50,000 tons.[154] The United States Department of State gave further assurances in 1963 that its sales from the stockpiles would not unnecessarily disturb the raw material market but would attempt to maintain existing price levels.[155] The situation changed somewhat in 1964 because of the scarcity of tin. Considerable pressure was exerted on the United States to release larger quantities from its stockpiles, but the government preferred to proceed slowly.[156] In the spring of 1971 the government announced that the United States would stop sales from the stockpile for an indefinite time.[157] This situation suggests that the private regulation of the tin market above the ceiling prices of the tin pool cannot be disturbed by the United States, at least not at the present time.

The Eastern Bloc countries are also in a position to disturb the tin market. The threat to the market posed by their exports was resolved by an agreement between those countries and the International Tin Council. These export restrictions have had favorable effects in critical periods.[158]

On balance, the international tin agreements have turned out to be more favorable for producers than for consumers [159] and, because of restrictive export policies of the participating countries, have created a scarcity of tin supplies.[160] This is due primarily to the fact that the international tin agreements could not eliminate the private market regulation structure, but rather helped create an atmosphere of freedom

154 Id.   155 "GSA Steps Up Sales," 1963 Metal Bull.

156 Discussion before the Senate of the United States on the Stockpile Act of 1965, Congress. Rec. S2311, S2314, S2316, S2319 (daily ed. July 2, 1966). To meet the scarcity of copper, a bill was introduced providing for the sale of 100,000 short tons of copper from the stockpile to American copper producers upon the condition that the amount of copper received be replaced in the stockpile within 60 days, Congress. Rec. S280 (daily ed. Feb. 14, 1966).

157 Daily bulletin of Metallgesellschaft, April 13, 1971.

158 R. Broh, "Zinnrat—Zinnmarkt," 1963 Metall 843.

159 F.A.Z., Dec. 23, 1963.

160 Neue Zürcher Zeitung, Mar. 21, 1965. For the first six months of 1972 the International Tin Council estimated a deficit of 3,500 tons (daily bulletin of Metallgesellschaft, Mar. 23, 1972).

in which the private system of market regulation can impose artificially high prices.

On the other hand, the tin agreements have proven especially effective in preventing price declines. Since the floor price for tin has not been tested for many years, the evidence is not conclusive, but from October 1957 until September 1958 the manager of the tin pool was to maintain the tin price above the fixed floor price.[161] On the other hand, the manager of the tin pool is powerless against efforts by the tin producers to maintain high prices. Since the costs of tin production are relatively low, tin producers can adapt to a decreasing demand much faster than the producers of other raw materials, merely by restricting their production. They are thus in a strong position, knowing that there is little danger of price declines and that efforts to regulate high prices will generally be fruitless. Further evidence is the fact that, because the tin market has been regulated by governmental and private measures since the thirties, tin production has not increased to any considerable extent despite the availability of sufficient tin deposits,[162] nor has the efficiency in exploiting existing deposits been satisfactory. Protection against real economic loss has led to very uneconomical results. This policy of protection of the producer's market was strengthened by the decision of the International Tin Council at its ninth meeting under the Third International Tin Agreement (September 1968) to introduce quotas to restrict export and production of tin. The quotas had been introduced for a 104-day period, from September 19 through December 31, 1968, and were set at a level equivalent to an annual export of 152,000 tons. This figure equalled the production of the six producer members of the agreement during 1967.[163]

In 1967, under entirely different conditions, quotas were established under Article VII, 6a, of the Third Tin Agreement. It was expected that under the new quota figures the production and export in 1969 would be reduced by about two thousand tons. This restriction of export limited the quantity of offers to the buffer stock manager and was another general device to prevent tin prices from dropping below a certain minimum level.

[161] During the period from October 1957 until September 1958, the manager of the tin pool was able to keep the price of tin above the fixed floor prices. On Sept. 18, 1958, a small price occurred which severely threatened the financial resources of the pool.

[162] *Neue Zürcher Zeitung*, Dec. 8, 1964.

[163] *Mining J.*, Sept. 7 and 20, 1968.

It is alleged that a price increase might induce the United States to release some of its stockpile; however, the United States government is very reluctant to make releases from its stockpile for the purpose of keeping the price at a certain level.

It is very interesting to observe that from time to time the markets in many raw materials, for instance copper and tin, come under pressure because of rumors that at a certain date a depression of prices is to be expected. That was the case in 1956 and is now again the case, especially with respect to an eventual end of the hostilities in Vietnam.

One other factor in connection with the tin market should not be overlooked; that is, the significant competition offered to tin by substitute products. At the present time, 40 per cent of the total tin supply is utilized in the packaging industry.[164] In recent years, however, aluminum has made significant inroads in this industry. It will become very important to observe what would occur should any significant breakthrough for these new products take place and should the old, strictly regulated product begin to lose its place in the market.

The influence of the producer group under the tin agreement can be further explained by the specific situation. This favoritism exists despite the provisions of the United Nations treaty with respect to commodity agreements that consumer and producer countries are to be equally represented in the International Tin Council; the producing group as well as the consuming group have at least one thousand votes.[165] Although these votes have been allocated between producer and consumer countries, nevertheless Great Britain, a consumer country, and probably also the Netherlands, which control 147 and 45 votes respectively, have considerable interests in the tin-producing countries, especially in Indonesia and Malaysia.[166] Therefore, the voting of these two consumer countries is influenced not only by their interest as consumers but also by considerations reflecting the producer's interests. Thus the interest of the producers generally prevails even within the auspices of the commodity agreement.[167]

[164] *Neue Zürcher Zeitung*, Dec. 3, 1964.

[165] Second and Third International Tin Agreements, Art. IV c.

[166] According to Annex B of the Third Tin Agreement, the votes of the main consuming countries are allocated as follows: Australia, 33; Belgium, 25; Canada, 34; Federal Republic of Germany, 76; India, 33; Italy, 40; Japan, 100; the Netherlands, 27; the United Kingdom, 129; the United States, 344.

[167] Daily bulletin of Metallgesellschaft, Jan. 7, 1965, reporting on a meeting of raw material experts from the Common Market states.

Today it would appear that the difference between the effects of a mere private regulation and those of a government agreement are not decisive. This is especially true in view of the fact that some of the politically weaker countries such as Bolivia, Indonesia, and Malaysia generally agree with the outlook of the producing enterprises, either because the government has nationalized a specific industry or because it is in the national interest of that country to do so. It would appear that the producers have established a carefully coordinated entity in composing both the governmental agreement and their private arrangements. While the governmental agreement guarantees a floor price, they are in practice not bound by a ceiling price, but are in a position to frustrate the objectives of the tin pool in cases where these objectives would be disadvantageous to them. In addition, they have been in a position to establish monopoly prices by concluding long-term contracts.

The Zinc Market

Another example of the relationship between commodity agreements and private market regulation can be found in the zinc market. Since November 1958, the International Lead and Zinc Research Group, an organization within the United Nations structure, has attempted to coordinate supply and demand in the zinc market. The most important producer and consumer countries belong to this research group. In meetings of the research group in March and May of 1962, a number of countries indicated their willingness to limit production.[168] The Soviet Union announced that its exports to Western countries in 1962 would not exceed exports for 1961.[169] At a meeting of a special working group of fourteen countries in March 1963, an agreement on export controls was considered.[170] The representatives of the most important producing enterprises were invited to participate in the meetings of the research group as governmental experts.[171]

[168] Press Release No. EC/Zinc/12, Mar. 21, 1962, of Information Service, European Office, United Nations; and Press Release No. EC/2122, May 31, 1962, Office of Public Information, United Nations.

[169] Tariff Commission, *Lead and Zinc: Report to the President on Investigation No. TEA-IA-3*, ¶351 (d)(2) of the Trade Expansion Act of 1962; TC Publ. 71, p. 12 (Oct. 1962).

[170] U.S. Tariff Commission, *Lead and Zinc: Report to the President on Investigation No. TEA-IR-8-63*, ¶351 (d)(1) of the Trade Expansion Act of 1962; TC Publ. 111, pp. 21–22 (Oct. 1963).

[171] Edwards, n. 94 above, p. 28.

When these efforts proved unsuccessful, however, the producers
then tried to stabilize prices themselves by withdrawing from the
commodity exchange [172] and by introducing a fixed price system.
Since this private action led to relative stability in the zinc market,[173]
the research group began to show readiness to conclude a governmental agreement.[174] A draft agreement was submitted by the special
committee; it called for the establishment of a pool for sales and
purchases within the framework of ceiling and floor prices supported
by governmental control of production and exports. Nevertheless,
the ninth meeting of the Research Group in Tokyo from October 25
to November 5, 1965, produced no agreement. As a result, the leading
lead and zinc producers in the Western hemisphere founded the
International Lead/Zinc Research Organization (ILZRO) in Tokyo
on November 6, 1965. The purpose of this group is to promote economic stability in the lead and zinc industries through research and
development.[175]

[172] See text at nn. 52–61 above.   [173] *Id.*   [174] 1965 *Metall* 1020.
[175] Daily bulletin of Metallgesellschaft, Dec. 1, 1964.

5 ~~~~~~~~~~

The Industrial Products Cartel

The dominant type of cartel during the period between the two world wars was that formed for the regulation of industrial products markets. This form of cartel includes the regulation of semifinished and finished products as well as the industrial processed raw materials, also discussed in connection with raw material cartels.[1] The primary purpose of this regulation was to prevent decline in price, production, or sales. The dynamics of economic development after World War II, however, have changed the aims of these cartels. Today they often serve either as a bridge during a transition period of technological or economic development or as a means to protect large investments against the flow of further dynamic development. Though of less importance economically than before the war, they are still very common. Indeed, every further disintegration of world markets, as the result of the balance-of-payments problems or similar political-economic reasons, encourages new steps toward industrial products cartels.

In an economy noted for dynamic technological development, the technological agreement must be of primary importance.[2] In a rapidly changing area of the economy, market regulation that relates directly to the products can rarely be found for purely economic reasons. The industrial products industry, however, has become relatively static and the cartels reflect this to the extent that political-economic factors permit. Characteristically, their main goal has been the conservation of what has already been achieved.

There are two differences between the industrial products cartel and the raw material cartel. First, the potential market effects of raw material cartels are far-reaching, since they affect the production process at the outset. They thus can often exert great influence and

[1] Processed raw materials include refined oil, copper, and aluminum; for a detailed description of the differences between pure raw materials and processed raw materials, see Chapter 4.

[2] See Chapter 3 for a discussion of the technological cartel.

control on all levels of production and distribution. Second, despite their potential, the aim of raw material cartels—stabilization of the market—has not often been achieved for long periods of time, while stabilization of the industrial products market has usually been successful.

Steel is one of the traditional products subjected to national and international market regulating agreements. In March 1969, after long negotiations between the United States government and European and Japanese steel producers, an agreement was concluded for a voluntary export quota of fourteen million tons for 1969 and a 5 per cent annual increase in this quota.[3] The agreement was negotiated under the threat of mandatory import quota legislation in the United States should the voluntary agreement not be concluded. This voluntary agreement is only the latest in a long series of agreements, particularly among Japanese steel producers, allocating markets or limiting exports.

Participating Enterprises

The industries best suited to participate in a technological cartel are those dynamic enterprises that have grasped the fundamental principles in developing fields or that have a legally superior position technologically, owing to their control over patents. On the other hand, the industrial products cartel attracts those enterprises whose sole aim is to retain their present position in the production and distribution of their products in the different markets. Such enterprises are noted by their organization, their relation to third parties, their utilization of patents, and their reliance on normal technological development. While it is not as important for the industrial products cartel to control technological development, their control over the distribution of raw materials can be decisive.

The following types of enterprises can form industrial products cartels:

(1) Enterprises with a controlling position in certain geographical or product areas, or with certain groups of buyers based on market division agreements made prior to World War II. Owing to their dominant position, they can contribute to international regulation of industrial products by advertising, by control of trademarks and other property rights, and by regulating their wholesale and retail outlets.

[3] *The Economist*, Jan. 18, 1969, pp. 68–69.

(2) Enterprises that are influential in several markets, either because of their structure, their trademarks control, or their sales methods. These can contribute to a regulation of certain industrial products in the international field.

(3) Enterprises with an important influence on the supply of raw and processed raw materials, on patent procedures, or on the means of transportation which can regulate different levels of production and distribution.

(4) Enterprises that have a protected or preferred position in specific markets because of governmental protection, often undertaken for balance-of-payments reasons or in order to guarantee a market for particular enterprises.

(5) Enterprises that have already agreed with other enterprises on the market regulation of a certain product or a certain trade area. These agreements facilitate collaboration in further regulation.

(6) Enterprises that have common manufacturing plants with other enterprises in certain countries and thereby influence local distribution in those countries.

(7) Enterprises associated with other enterprises in unions and federations that fix common business conditions or control courts of arbitration and thereby influence market regulation of industrial products.

Marketing-Regulating Agreements

The industrial products cartels involve the classical forms of agreements and are used in both national and international market regulation. These agreements include the apportionment of certain markets, goods, or groups of buyers to one or several enterprises; the establishment of quantities for production and distribution; the establishment of quality standards for certain groups of buyers; the establishment of prices and distribution conditions and channels; and restrictions on the utilization of the merchandise, for instance, requirements that the products be used only with certain other products or with specific machinery.

Division of Markets and Groups of Buyers

Before World War II, markets or groups of buyers in the pharmaceutical and electrical industries had long been allocated in such a way that certain enterprises controlled a given group of regional markets or a group of buyers, but were excluded from other markets or other groups of buyers. After the war, a market division in the international area granted an exclusive or at least a favorable position to those enterprises that before the war had been dominant. The scarcity of merchandise immediately after the war limited the area of possible activity. This allocation of markets reflected availability of supply more than grants of preferential position. As soon as this was eliminated, market divisions again went into effect but to a lesser extent. The following examples, while typical, are by no means exhaustive.[4] The market division as such will be examined here but not the use of the means for the division (such as the distribution of patents and trademarks), which will be detailed in a subsequent chapter.[5]

An effective international market division can be found in the television industry, especially in the color television market. This market division developed organically from the original division of the radio market that had been effective until the 1950's.[6] The market division in this field was based on the classical methods in use since the beginning of this century: contracts between national patent pools on one hand and coordination of patents or of important individual producers on the other hand. National patent pools in Great Britain, Canada, and Australia (in which subsidiaries of American producers participate) owe their controlling position to the collection of all important patents for radio and television production in the specific national market. These national pools granted global licenses—from the licenses collected within the pool—on the condition that the licensee neither import radio or television sets into the specific national market nor export them from that market. The important producers in the United States, Hazeltine and Radio Corporation of America, cooperate

[4] For further examples see C. Edwards, *Cartelization in Western Europe*, (Washington, 1964), p. 30.

[5] Chapter 12.

[6] The agreement on the division of the radio market is not in force today because of the antitrust actions taken by the U.S. government and because of the expiration of the important patents. In connection with these agreements see [British] Monopolies and Restrictive Practices Commission, *Report on the Supply of Electric Lamps* (Oct. 4, 1951). Also see the important case Hazeltine Research, Inc. v. Zenith Radio Corp. 239 F. Supp. 51 (D.C.Ill. 1965); 388 F. 2d 25 (7th C.A. 1967). The Appellate Court overturned the District Court decision and ruled that Zenith had not proven it was actually damaged by the activities of the foreign patent pool in which Hazeltine, a domestic competitor, participated. Reversed and affirmed in part, 37 U.S.L.W. 4424 (May 20, 1969).

THE INDUSTRIAL PRODUCTS CARTEL

with the pools by making their own property rights, and the property rights licensed to them by the pools, available to other American enterprises only if they agree to abide by the strict restrictions on importing to and exporting from the American market. Enterprises of other countries (for example, Germany) indirectly participate in the market division under contracts between these firms and other members of the cartel that call for the exchange of information and patents. Because of import-export restrictions, the market-controlling position of the pool, and the monopoly of the most important patents, this agreement leads to a complete division of the individual national markets.

In the field of medicine, there is a worldwide market division involving the important American producers and the important European producers, especially those from Germany, France, Switzerland, and Great Britain. This particular market regulation is unique. For newly discovered medicines a relatively restricted group of producers grants licenses for their home markets or their shares of interest in other markets to certain competitors. These are purely license contracts for certain products which, according to national cartel laws, are protected by their respective patents. Taken together, all these contracts form numerous intertwining restrictions of competition in which the same enterprises almost always participate, one time as licensee and another time as licensor. They cover the whole world, involve all the important newly developed medicines, and accomplish a perfect territorial division of markets. This territorial protection specifically covers the domestic markets of the larger producers. The discoverer of a new medicine generally avoids competing with the big competitors in these markets even though he would be in a good position to do so because of his patent rights. The contractual, almost institutionalized, exchange of new patents seems to show a typically oligopolistic state of mind among the large firms. In a real oligopolistic situation, however, no contractual agreement is necessary.[7] An example of this type of agreement is the market division between the Farbwerken Hoechst AG and the Upjohn Company with respect to a new oral medicine for diabetes, Tolbutamid, discovered by Hoechst.[8]

[7] F. Machlup, *The Economics of Seller's Competition* (Baltimore, 1952), pp. 414, 441, 475.

[8] U.S. Cong., Senate Comm. on the Judiciary, Subcomm. on Antitrust and Monopoly, *Hearings on Administered Prices*, 86th Cong., 2d Sess., Pt. 20, pp. 11065, 11257 (1960).

Under a 1958 agreement, the market for this medicine was so divided that in the United States it was distributed exclusively by Upjohn, in Europe by Hoechst (though in some countries it was distributed by Boehringer under a sublicense and with a different trademark but at the same price), and in Canada by a jointly owned subsidiary, the Hoechst Pharmaceutical Company of Canada. The method of this market division is twofold: first, the control of the different national patents for Tolbutamid by Upjohn and Hoechst, and second, the division of the trademarks, so that Upjohn sells in the United States under the trademark "Orinase" and Hoechst in Germany under the trademark "Rastinon." Owing to this control of patents and trademarks, a disturbance of the agreed-upon market division is impossible either by the parties themselves or from the outside. The market division is effective since the prices in the individual national markets are completely different.[9] The product is retailed in the United States for $4.17, in Canada for $3.75 and in Germany for $1.85. Such a market division, however, does not protect the company against competition from other newly discovered medicines. In the United States, Tolbutamid is in growing competition with Chlorpropamid, distributed by Charles Pfizer and Company under the trade name "Diabinese." But in Europe, Chlorpropamid, which apparently depends on a patent held by Hoechst, has not yet been introduced.

Antibiotics are another example of a market division in the field of medicine. In the case of Tetracyclin, the American firm Bristol, as licensee of American Cyanamid and Pfizer, granted sublicenses under a plan similar to the one described above, to Bayer, Société Industrielle pour la Fabrication des Antibiotiqua, Squibb (Italy), and Bayer Pharmaceutical Company. Hoechst received the exclusive right to produce and distribute Tetracyclin in Germany and Austria. In addition, the company was granted the right to manufacture and distribute these pills in some overseas countries. Hoechst had to market the drug under its own trade name, "Hortacyclin," and the agreement is protected by export prohibitions.[10] It is interesting that, in the United

[9] *Id.*, p. 11061. These price differences do not result from higher development costs. In the British Geigy-Biorex Case (which concerned "Emypramin") the development costs were estimated at only 8 per cent. Actually it is the sales promotion costs, spent to induce physicians to prescribe certain trademark medicines, which increase the prices of these medicines.

[10] *Id.*, Pt. 26, pp. 15356, 15458 (1961).

States, Upjohn did not receive an exclusive license for Tetracyclin.[11] There are many other examples of market division agreements in the field of antibiotics.[12]

In the field of textiles, market divisions exist, especially in the field of synthetic fibers. Strict market allocations were established, aided in part by control of certain patents, and continued for a time even after the patents expired. These producers were naturally exposed to competition in their allocated market from other artificial fibers. To prevent or moderate such competition, special agreements between patent owners were necessary. Such agreements were difficult to achieve, and the strongest agreement that could be accomplished restricted overcapacity.

New forms of market division have been established by producing enterprises for less developed countries. Four foreign producers contracted to establish joint subsidiaries for the production of electric lamps in India.[13] Each agreement fixed the prices the subsidiary would charge, restricted the subsidiary to its national territory, gave it access to all technological developments, and included exclusive supply agreements for necessary processed raw materials.[14] A similar agreement exists between an Indian producer of electric lamps for radios and one Dutch and five British producers (including the subsidiary of an American producer), which restricts the territorial market of the Indian lamp producer.[15]

Market divisions between parent and subsidiaries exist in the markets of highly industrialized countries. For example, in the automobile market, the Adam Opel AG is a 100 per cent subsidiary of General Motors. It does not face real competition from the American parent or from other European subsidiaries even though it withholds from the German market important new inventions that have been included in cars of similar price range in the United States for a long time.

A similar form of market division is seen in the production of

[11] *Id.*, p. 15331.

[12] A great amount of material can be found in *id.*, Pts. 25 and 26. In the German market, the licensing of the synthetic chloramphenicals produced by Parke, Davis & Co. is an interesting example. It is distributed in Germany by Bayer ("Leukonycin"), Boehringer ("Paraxin"), and Iptor ("Cobedor"), and their market share of antibiotics totals approximately 50 per cent.

[13] The producers also agreed on similar contracts for developed countries such as Australia, New Zealand, and South Africa.

[14] Edwards, n. 4 above, p. 28.   [15] *Id.*

urethane (plastic) foam, an important processed raw material used in the manufacturing of synthetic products.[16] From 1954 until challenged by the Department of Justice, the Monsanto Chemical Company of St. Louis and Farbenfabriken Bayer divided the market for this product. The United States was supplied exclusively by a common subsidiary, the Mobay Chemical Company in Pittsburgh, and the other countries were supplied by Bayer. Bayer granted to Mobay coownership of its American patents, and Monsanto gave its trademark "Merlon" to Mobay, both of which were to be used in producing this specific product.[17]

In order to protect a market division when patent protection is not possible, agreements restricting indirect sale in a specific foreign market or prohibiting resale arrangements that could affect the market division are often concluded. Whenever enterprises have an agreement on the division of markets in some parts of the world, there is an implied agreement protecting the home market of each of the enterprises against import from abroad, or against imports exceeding minimum figures, or providing for importation only with the permission and consent of enterprises operating in the market involved. An example of such an agreement, which provided extensive protection for individual home markets, is the cartel among a number of Dutch and Belgian producers of cleaning products.[18]

Agreements on Quantitative Restrictions and Joint Sales

Production and sales quotas

Between the two world wars, market divisions based on quotas were frequently used with syndicates and other similar means of distribution. Today, sale of industrial products by a syndicate or by

[16] Flexible urethane foam is widely used as cushioning and padding in automobiles and furniture, and as a lightweight lining for clothing. Rigid urethane foam is used as insulating and structural material in the construction industry. Production of urethane foam increased from about 1,000,000 pounds in 1955 to 300,000,000 pounds in 1965.

[17] United States v. Monsanto Co., Farbenfabriken Bayer AG, and Mobay Chemical Co., Trade Cas. ¶72,001, p. 83,553 (W.D.Pa. 1967). The court entered a consent judgment requiring Monsanto to sell its interests in Mobay to Bayer and prohibiting Monsanto from having any common officers or directors with Mobay, from competing with Mobay, or from restricting Bayer's operation of Mobay. Monsanto was also prohibited from acquiring for 10 years any facility being used to produce plastic foam.

[18] European Economic Community, press release (65) 148, July 26, 1965.

an open market division based on quotas has become relatively rare.[19] An important reason for this development is that if American export trade is directly involved, American enterprises cannot participate in international agreements that contain a market division based on quotas.[20] The American Export Associations, permitted under the Webb-Pomerene Act,[21] may not participate in these international agreements, even though they can work out a quota distribution for their own exports among themselves.[22]

An example of an open system of production quotas is the attempt to regulate the Western European cement market. The agreement was extremely successful after 1957. This effort started with the Paris Agreement of 1950 and continued in the 1953 and 1957 agreements (Noordwijks Cement Accord), which regulated the market in the Benelux countries. The cartel pattern used here—the syndicate form —involves joint sales agencies, price fixing, quota restrictions, and division of production.[23] Apparently the Benelux agreements were only one branch of a larger entwining cartel system reaching as far as Great Britain.

Producers of nitrogen-based fertilizer have agreed on production quotas for the world fertilizer market. In 1962, Nitrex, a European export association dealing with nitrogen, was established. The official purpose of this cartel was to cope with American and Japanese competition in third markets.[24] Nitrex originally included firms in Germany, Belgium, France, Italy, the Netherlands, Norway, and Switzerland. It is possible that British producers subsequently joined. The association agreement allocates export profits among the syndicate members on sales in third countries. The syndicate sells directly in countries with a centralized, state-controlled commerce; in other countries the profits are merely concentrated in a pool. The great price differences and the

[19] Contrast this with the case of diamonds in the raw material field, Chapter 4 above.

[20] H. Kronstein, J. T. Miller, Jr., and P. Dommer, *Major American Antitrust Laws* (New York, 1965), pp. 373–375.

[21] 15 U.S.C. §§61–65 (1964). Also see in this connection K. Brewster, Jr., *Antitrust and American Business Abroad* (New York, 1958), p. 454, which recommends repeal of the Act, arguing that only export cooperation which has neither the purpose nor effect of curtailing exports or restraining domestic competition should be lawful.

[22] United States v. United States Alkali Export Association, 86 F. Supp. 59 (S.D.N.Y. 1949); also see Kronstein *et al.*, n. 20 above.

[23] Edwards, n. 4 above.　　　　　[24] *Id.*

lack of competition in the individual home markets suggest that there is some kind of market division within Europe itself.[25] The syndicate's share of the overseas market is 60 per cent.[26] Normally a uniform price is quoted, subject to a uniform 12½ per cent discount. However, at times the market situation has forced the discount up to 20 per cent of the sales price.[27] Therefore, it would appear that the cartel has not yet actually succeeded in price stabilization.

On the other hand, there do not appear to be any European agreements on sales and quotas for phosphate, one of the most important types of fertilizer. However, there do seem to be cartel agreements of a different kind that are related to American cartel organizations. The European producers appear to fix individual prices at the annual meeting of their organization. They also apparently divide the markets and prevent competition from cheap phosphate sources. (The cheapest superphosphate comes from a Belgian plant and a Tunesian plant, but they are owned by members of the phosphate cartel and are prevented from becoming a real competitive threat.) [28]

In the potash field,[29] a common international sales organization and a quota division of the market appears to exist among the European producers.[30] Members of this organization include the French state-owned potash industry, the German and British potash syndicates, and producers from Israel as well as private and state-owned producers in Spain. The cartel has been able to influence most of the new producers to join one of its sales organizations, especially the producers from Spain and Israel. It was also able to use two of its subsidiaries to bring newly discovered Canadian potash deposits under the cartel's influence.

A further example of a distribution of sales quotas is the agreement between two producers of matches, the Swedish Zündholz monopolgesellschaft and the British Match Corporation, in which the overseas markets were divided according to continents.[31] This agreement

[25] W. Albers, *Marktlage, Preise, und Preispolitik für Düngemittel in den EFG-Ländern und ihre Bedeutung für Produktionskosten der Landwirtschaft* (Bonn, 1963), pp. 5, 32.
[26] Edwards, n. 4 above.   [27] *Id.*   [28] *Id.*, p. 28.
[29] Potash is a processed raw material; it is included in this chapter only because of its connection with chemical fertilizers.
[30] Edwards, *id.*, p. 29.
[31] *Id.*, p. 30; Monopolies and Restrictive Practices Commission, *Report on the Supply and Export of Matches and the Supply of Match-Making Machinery* (May 17, 1953), p. 100.

is important, for it seems to have survived every market fluctuation.

In the United States a Webb-Pomerene Export Association for potash [32] existed until June 30, 1966, and there are still export organizations for the different phosphate fertilizers. They are constructed similarly to the European export organizations. The phosphate exporters have chosen a common agent who distributes the quantities for export according to quotas.[33] An exception is made in this arrangement for superphosphate, since the contracts in this field are related in part to American foreign aid. Governments of less developed countries are supplied within the foreign aid framework through a joint sales organization that fixes prices and divides sales according to quotas.[34] There have also been price agreements for sales to Western Europe and Japan.[35]

There is no proof that European and American producers openly work together on the world markets. Nevertheless, the coordination of both the European and American enterprises each into a cartel creates two economic units related in an oligopolistic structure that can easily produce an understanding. In the nitrogen field, however, Japanese producers appear to be competitive on the export markets and thus upset this oligopolistic structure somewhat.[36]

These examples show that the parallelism of national export cartels must be taken into account when considering the problems of international cartels. One conclusion that can be drawn from this discussion is that between the two world wars the international agreements were open, whereas today there are hidden international market divisions based primarily on quota allocations. Parallel national agreements fall

[32] Edwards, *id.*, p. 30; also see n. 21 above.
[33] United States v. International Ore & Fertilizer Corp. (M.D.Fla.), Civil No. 64-34, Feb. 11, 1964, CCH Trade Reg. Rep. ¶45,064, p. 52,547 (1965).
[34] United States v. The Concentrated Phosphate Export Association, Inc. (S.D.N.Y.), Civil No. 64-3914, Sept. 21, 1964, CCH Trade Reg. Rep. ¶45,064; and United States v. International Ore & Fertilizer Corp. (S.D.N.Y.), 63 C.R. 927, Nov. 7, 1963, CCH Trade Reg. Rep. ¶45063, p. 52,538 (1965).
[35] C. Edwards, n. 4 above, p. 30. The Canadian enterprise, International Minerals & Chemical Corporation, is the greatest exporter of potash in the world. This corporation is under U.S. control; see "Expanding Markets for Fertilizer Minerals," *Mining J.*, Apr. 30, 1965.
[36] United States v. International Minerals & Chemical Corp., et al. (S.D.N.Y.), 63 C.R. 927, Nov. 7, 1963, CCH *Trade Reg. Rep.* ¶45064, p. 52,538 (1965). The producers pleaded *nolo contendere* to the charge of entering into a price-fixing agreement to establish artificially high prices for phosphate exported to Western Europe and Japan.

within the definition of an international cartel established in this book
when this parallel behavior arises not merely from a purely oligopolistic
market structure but rather is based upon agreements among the
parties, even if the outward appearance of an oligopoly is maintained.

Parallel national agreements are not necessary in every case. It is also
possible to establish a private international market division based upon
governmental measures in the industrial products field without ever
having a formal comprehensive agreement involving the governmental
regulations. Thus, for example, a system of private market regulation
can be built upon the import quotas for goods from low-priced countries found in the long Term Arrangement Regarding International
Trade in Cotton Textiles.[37] This approach is similar to the one discussed in connection with raw material cartels, where it was noted that
the American import quotas for petroleum were a fixed element that
could be used by a cartel in establishing its system of market regulation.[38]

Other forms of quantitative restrictions

In addition to production and sales quotas, other forms of quantitative restrictions are frequently applied when the competition to be
regulated is in regional markets: (1) The enterprises involved agree to
supply only specifically defined quantities for certain regional markets
or for certain sales agencies in the import states. (2) The enterprises
agree to sell only enough raw material or semifinished products, or to
grant licenses for patents and procedures, so that only a certain amount
of the finished products will be available in a particular market. (3) The
enterprises agree to limit sales of facilities for transportation of certain
products (including pipelines), to specific quantities, or to require an
increased fee if the quantity is exceeded. These quantitative restrictions
thus not only affect the product directly regulated, but they also
indirectly cover other products.

Agreements on specialization of production

Actual agreements for specialization in the production of industrial
products are usually found not at the international but on the national
level. An example of this is the agreement between the Farbenfabriken

[37] Compare "Japan's Textile Industry," 12 *Fuji Bank Bull.* No. 8, pp. 166, 171
(1964).
[38] Chapter 4, at n. 126.

Bayer AG and the Schering AG intended to restrict the growing American competition in Europe.[39] But the very nature of these national agreements causes them to be of some international significance.

Agreements on restricting the supply of certain products

The regulation of quantity of production is not the only form of restriction that can be placed upon the cartel members. Often it is agreed that in certain markets and with certain groups of buyers only specified types of products meeting set standards of quality and packaging can be sold. There is usually a supplementary agreement that the same product will not appear on the market under any other condition. The Hoechst-Upjohn restrictive agreement is an example of this.[40] It was specified that Hoechst could sell the oral diabetic medicine, Tolbutamid, in the United States only in its manufactured capsules under its own trade name.[41] The purpose of this restriction was to prevent competition in the reserved American market by smaller companies with their own pill production trademarks and distribution system through bulk purchases of the medicine from Hoechst and later resale. Retail stores and pharmacies are supplied with the manufactured pills, which can only be sold by prescription. The prescriptions are usually written out under the trade name for a product, rather than under its generic name. Thus, the Hoechst product, sold only under its trade name, has been automatically excluded from the market since prescriptions are filled out regularly under the trade name "Upjohn." The exclusion of delivery to the American market of the same product in any other form than the agreed-upon pill form means an effective restriction of the market and a strong fortification of the market division explained above.

A similar form of regulation can be shown in the agreements of companies to supply certain articles (such as electric cables and apparatus) for specific markets only under certain standards. An example of this is the very strict agreement of the copper cable producers to supply Canada only with cables that meet a specific standard.[42] Experi-

---

[39] Speech given by M. Hansen, General Director of Bayer, at the Hanover Fair, "German Firms Link to Beat U.S. Competition," London Times, May 4, 1965. Professor Hansen said that his corporation "had nothing to do with the cartel question, but that it was rather a matter of common sense."

[40] See text at n. 8 above.   [41] Hearings on Administered Prices, n. 8 above.

[42] Canadian Dept. of Justice, Report on Electrical Wire and Cable Products, pp. 237–239 (1953).

ence has shown that the public utility companies, on their own, demand the observance of these standards as a condition for supplying electricity. An effective regulation of the electrical products market is thus produced.

Agreements on quality standards for products in the textile industry are less stringent and restrictive. They often result from manufacturing or distributional considerations.[43] One example of this type of agreement involves enterprises primarily drawn from Great Britain and the Commonwealth countries; however, it also contains an agreement on the exchange of know-how and certain restrictions upon competition among the parties to the agreement.[44]

A special type of agreement in this general category relates to the point of time at which products of a certain quality will appear on certain markets. Considering the varying rates of technical development of individual countries, it is of considerable economic importance that the business partners agree on the date at which technical developments (such as new machines or machine parts) are put at the disposal of the different markets. The leading firms sell the newest products to the developing countries only when the machinery has been depreciated or when there is a competitive pressure from another side. The automobile and electrical industries are examples of this.[45] In highly concentrated industries these practices are often based on tacit understandings of the parties.

In practice, there are agreements to sell certain products on certain markets or to certain groups of buyers only when these products have special equipment or are sold under special trademarks.[46] Such agreements are especially effective for mass-produced and trademarked articles and can actually replace a formal division of the market.

[43] Edwards, n. 4 above. For example, there is an agreement among 76 producers on the quality of certain synthetic fiber products.

[44] Id.

[45] The German producers of washing machines did not introduce the higher American standards despite agreements for the exchange of information. They passed through a slower development phase which is comparable to development in the United States 10 to 15 years earlier. There was a similar situation in the field of automatic transmissions.

[46] Agreement between Upjohn and Hoechst whereby Tolbutamid is distributed in the United States under the trademark "Orinase" and in Germany under the trademark "Rastinon" (*Hearings on Administered Prices*, n. 8 above).

Agreements to supply products only for specific purposes and to distribute them only according to certain methods

In connection with the restrictive agreements relating to quality standards, discussed above, a requirement is often included restricting the use of the products sold for clearly defined purposes. This type of clause can be found in the fields of manufacturing, fabricating, or resale. The supply of semimanufactured goods is often dependent on such conditions. Thus, the restriction on the use of products is an important means of market stabilization.

In many cases, the restriction on utilization is joined with a restriction on the number of companies to be supplied. Thus, the Gulf Oil Corporation has established common sales agencies in the petrochemical industry with other large oil companies as well as joint plants for the refining of petroleum and the production of petrochemical products.[47] These plants are supplied exclusively by the participating oil companies and are only to be used for specific manufacturing schemes. It is not necessary that these companies be dependent on the producers of the crude oil. There are enough cases in which entirely independent enterprise are supplied in international trade only for certain purposes.

There are also agreements in which certain items are supplied on the condition that the manufactured product is to be sold on the domestic markets in a certain way and under special circumstances. These circumstances include the methods of distribution by wholesalers and retailers.

Agreements on prices

All of the agreements discussed so far have an indirect effect on prices of the regulated products. However, there are also agreements directly affecting prices in the international sphere.

Such agreements are found wherever enterprises have agreed on a joint sales agency. Cement, nitrogen, and potash are the most immediate examples of this type of arrangement.[48] Direct price agreements can often be found in connection with pure market division agreements. Phosphates and electric light bulbs are examples of this.[49]

The best example of a price agreement in the postwar period is the

[47] United States v. Standard Oil Co. (New Jersey), CCH Trade Cas. ¶69,849, p. 77,335 (1960).
[48] Nn. 24–28 above.   [49] Nn. 14 and 28 above.

minimum or suggested price agreement for third-country markets of the European steel industry.[50] On March 29, 1953, a few months after the European Coal and Steel Community Treaty went into force, the French, Belgian, and Luxembourgian producers of iron and steel founded the Brussels Export Convention. Dutch, German, and later Italian producers joined. The Convention established an executive commission of participating organizations (the so-called Marketing Commission) to examine the export conditions in the steel business and to fix obligations, minimum prices, surcharges, and conditions of payment. The decision-making power on the basic questions facing the Community rested in the President's Committee.[51]

The trade policy of the Export Convention has varied over the years. The Commission has adopted various measures, from the fixing of obligatory minimum prices, to agreement on recommended prices, to the simple exchange of sales price information. At first the Convention only fixed minimum prices. Until the end of 1955, various minimum prices had been agreed upon for the United States, Canada, Switzerland, and other third countries. In the case of several steel products, the prices for exports to the United States and Canada were considerably below the minimum prices set for the other sales areas.

From 1956 to April 1958, there were uniform minimum prices for all sales areas. As a result of the price deterioration on several export markets, which set in at the beginning of 1958, the Marketing Commission lowered the minimum prices several times. In spite of this, there was repeated price-cutting by individual exporters in the member countries. During the August 1958 meeting, the Commission agreed to shelve both the plans for further fixing of minimum prices and the plans for the establishment of a quota system. It was agreed only to request the members to give information on sales prices.

The German producers favored a system of more effective coopera-

[50] The question of the extent of the cartel's effect on the european coal and steel community, especially the question of whether there are production programs and market divisions, will not be discussed. Compare, however, the investigations into this question by the High Authority in *Official Report of the European Coal and Steel Community*, p. 202 (1953).

[51] The Convention covered the following products: semifinished products, steel rods, profiles (I and U), wide flank carrier, rolling steel, cube stripes, rolled wire, fine and crude sheet metal, universal steel, hot and cold rolled (under 3 mm.). Carbon fine steels and refined steels were excluded. For a survey of the Export Convention see M. J. Rosen, "The Brussels Entente: Export Combination in the World Steel Market," 106 *U. Pa. L. Rev.* 1079 (1958).

tion, and in February 1959 a suggested price system was introduced. Contrary to the price structure in the former minimum price system, here the prices of individual steel products exported to the United States were above the suggested retail prices for the other sales areas. However, the suggested price system was dropped in September of 1959 because the majority of the members of the Convention felt that the existing boom in the steel market should not be fortified by a suggested price system.

Furthermore, the global suggested price system had proven to be inflexible in the face of the varying offer-demand structures in individual countries. The system was also considered too vulnerable to American competition in view of the expected termination of the steel strike in the United States. Therefore, the Commission again limited itself only to the simple exchange of information on market prices.

There was an attempt in April 1960 to return to the suggested price system. One month later, in the face of continued underselling, members of the Commission restricted their cooperation to the exchange of price information. In September 1961, as a result of the continued price deterioration, the members agreed again to fix minimum prices. However, this minimum price system could not be sustained for any length of time due to the strong price pressure of foreign competition. As a result, the minimum prices began to function like the suggested price system. During the sixties and up to the present day, the steel exporters of the European Coal and Steel Community repeatedly tried to fix minimum prices for their exports. Though the success of these measures varied, one can say the Brussels Export Convention by and large continues to function.[52]

Since 1956 an agreement has existed between Coal and Steel Community exporters and Austrian exporters not to undersell each other in their respective domestic markets. This agreement resulted from the initiative of the Brussels Export Convention. It is possible that the Export Convention cooperated with British and Japanese exporters on the splitting of export markets.[53]

Apart from the creation of joint sales agencies to fix prices, price-fixing agreements can also be concluded to allocate markets. The processed raw material market for copper is an example. This market was the subject of the Lausanne Agreement of 1946 and included

[52] Compare Edwards, n. 4 above, p. 27.   [53] *Id.*

various European producers, both public and private.[54] For deliveries
to member countries, the partners agreed to abide by the price established in that country. The existing price in all cases was to be requested
from the producer organization there.[55] Owing to this procedure,
foreign participating producers cannot use price-cutting techniques to
break into other national markets. This price-setting agreement
achieved its desired market allocation. It was also agreed that list
prices (in effect minimum prices) would be used in supplying those
countries that were not members of the agreement but with whom the
members had come to terms. Deviations from the list prices were
allowed only in special cases (to combat competition from Japan or
Germany) or in specific markets (such as the United States or
Canada).[56] The provisions of the Lausanne Agreement dealing with the
established domestic prices of member countries was later limited because some of the governments involved doubted its legality.[57] However, the fixing of minimum prices for exports to nonmember countries remained in force.[58]

Another example of indirect market distribution through price-fixing
is the agreement between a Swedish producer and several German,
French, Swiss, and British producers of Polyvinyl Chloride, which
implies that the prices set by the Swedish company have to be maintained by the foreign producers in their exports to Sweden.[59]

The price agreement need not fix the market price at the beginning
of the contract. There can be a clause in the contract that calls for
adjustments in the market prices when there are cost increases in the
time between the signing of the contract and delivery of the product.

[54] This agreement replaced an international export cartel arrangement which
used a quota system.

[55] Compare Monopolies and Restrictive Practices Commission, *Report on the
Supply of Insulated Electric Wires and Cables* (June 6, 1952), p. 50, and *Report
on the Supply and Export of Certain Semi-Manufactures of Copper and Copper-
Based Alloys* (July 27, 1955), p. 59.

[56] *Id.*

[57] *Report on the Supply of Insulated Electric Wires and Cables*, n. 55 above,
p. 51.

[58] Further discussions concerning the price situation in member countries have
been held under the auspices of the International Wrought Nonferrous Metals
Council founded in 1953 by the national organizations. See *Report on the Supply
and Export of . . . Copper-Based Alloys*, n. 55 above, p. 64.

[59] Edwards, n. 4 above, p. 31.

The copper cartels use these adjustment clauses, as do the American phosphate cartels.[60]

It is customary in international business affairs to have explicit or silent agreements to inform business partners of price changes or not to introduce price changes until after the partners have been informed.[61] Article 60 of the European Coal and Steel Community Treaty requires that price change information be given beforehand. Experience has shown that an actual price agreement is involved. Only in very rare cases will one of the participating enterprises refuse to join the price change. It is not an oligopolistic measure. The previous price announcement shows the existence of an actual, even if indirect, price agreement.[62]

For products where the cost of materials is a very large percentage of total costs or for mass-produced products, agreements of suppliers on discounts or rebates are of such great importance that they have the same effect as vertical price agreements. Though the agreements do not fix the total price of the article, they are such an important element in price-fixing that they should be considered price agreements.

This group of price agreements also includes agreements on additional factors that affect prices, such as FOB and CIF clauses. This is especially true of those clauses establishing uniform freight rates.

Agreements on general business conditions

Even where several enterprises remain in competition in a particular market, it is not uncommon for them to agree to insert clauses in their contracts regarding the use of general business practices as the standard of conduct, or to be members of an association that requires the insertion of such clauses and regulates their application. These agreements are closely connected to price-fixing agreements. One example of agreement on common business conditions relates to the sale of bathtubs in the Danish market.[63] Other known contracts of this type deal with machinery for paper production and with acetate made by several

---

[60] United States v. International Ore & Fertilizer Corp., n. 33 above.

[61] United States v. Driver Harris Co., CCH Trade Cas. ¶71,169, p. 79,642 (D.N.J. 1964).

[62] This was the position taken by the Department of Justice in the Driver Harris case, *id.*, where the participating enterprises requested a consent judgment.

[63] This agreement is among German, French, Dutch, Swedish, Finnish, and Danish producers (Edwards, n. 4 above, p. 32).

producers and their joint subsidiaries, and in one case the agreement includes a provision not to purchase the base product from certain enterprises.[64]

The most important condition for which provision is often made in the contract concerns the use of arbitration courts. The interpretation, development, and often even the definition of general business conditions is left to the arbitrators. Their importance is due to the fact that the decisions of the arbitrators are widely reported and are adapted as fast as possible as general business practices by the individual enterprises. This important matter is discussed in greater detail in a subsequent chapter.[65]

Agreements on common research and development

Research and development in well-established industries is generally used to refine long-existing procedures or to reduce the production costs of products that have been on the market for some time. Research is actually directed more toward production and sale techniques than toward pure development. The industries do feel it is of great importance to protect products already on the market against competition from substitutes.

This type of research and development is done not only by individual enterprises but also by enterprises acting in concert with others in the international sphere. An example is the agreement for closer cooperation in research and development between the French Compagnie de Saint Gobain and the Belgian Glaceries de Saint Roch, both of which are involved in glass production. A jointly owned subsidiary in Germany apparently used to carry out the agreements. In addition to joint research and development, these agreements also give Saint Roch the right to use the distribution system of Saint Gobain, and make provisions for certain investments by the parties. In related developments arising out of this agreement, Saint Gobain has taken over subsidiaries of Saint Roch, while the latter firm has acquired an interest in subsidiaries of Saint Gobain.[66]

An example of complete autonomy in research and development— but with agreement for exchange of the development results—is the Lamp Agreement between leading British producers of electronic

---

[64] Id., p. 31.   [65] Chapter 13.
[66] Overberg, "Glasgesellschaften überwiegend in ausländischem Besitz," 1965 Das Wertpapier, pp. 812–814 (1965).

pipes and the Dutch Philips Company. The agreement was concluded in 1948 but is no longer in effect. This contract (which followed the old Phoebus Cartel) provided for a market division of specific overseas markets based on quotas. The cartel partners exchanged know-how and investments in the same fields that the previous cartel agreement had covered.[67]

Similar arrangements can be found in the cartel agreement between the British Metal Corporation and the Svendska Taendsticks Aktiebolaget. This quota cartel also provides for the exchange of know-how, procedures, and inventions in the production of mathces and match machinery.[68]

Market Regulation by Agreements on Industrial Products

Regulated Markets

Often the market-regulating effect of an industrial products cartel is restricted to the product that is the subject of the agreement. The congruity between the subject of the anticompetitive agreement and its market effect is greatly aided by product differentiation, especially in the consumer goods industry, and hence by the formation of numerous special markets.

On the other hand, the market effect can extend to related markets. The Canadian Cable Case is an example.[69] Here the restriction on types of cables influences the markets for specific electrical products and also influences the relationship between the supplying enterprises—the main buyers of these products—and their customers.

A similar extension to related markets is found when products needed for a particular service must meet certain requirements of type, quality, or price. It is necessary to determine whether these effects on related markets fall within the concept of a cartel agreement. Such a decision will depend on whether these market effects were intended or not. The parties must have at least considered such an indirect market effect beyond the directly regulated product. If this is the case, then not only the market explicitly covered by the agreement

---

[67] Art. 4 of the agreement reprinted in *Report on the Supply of Electric Lamps*, n. 6 above, p. 152.

[68] Art. 10 of the agreement reprinted in *Report on the Supply and Export of Matches . . .* , n. 31 above, p. 100.

[69] *Report on Electrical Wire and Cable Products*, n. 42 above.

but even the market indirectly affected is considered a regulated market.

There is also a mutual interdependence of market effects in a geographical sense. Industrial products cartels can regulate the markets of certain countries or regions and therefore appear isolated. However, there actually may be an interplay between these different cartels that leads to worldwide market regulation. For example, the prices of industrial products are regulated by national cartels in order to secure the prices fixed by the international cartel for the world market. Therefore, this national cartel is an element of the overall international market regulation.

Effectiveness of the Market Regulation

Not every international agreement in which the parties restrict their economic activity in regard to a specific industrial product achieves a real market regulation. In order to do so, all or at least the most important enterprises in a specific market must participate in the agreement. The ideal effect of a market division would be to have in one geographical market area only the enterprise assigned to that market. Usually this is not the case. A market division can still have a real market-regulating effect, however, if the preferred enterprises are strong enough in the area assigned to them to influence the decisive market elements such as price and quality of goods. There is a tendency today to call every market oligopolistic. This should not be done without first determining whether the oligopolistic firms owe their position in the individual national markets to international market-regulating agreements.

The same standard is valid for agreements other than market divisions if the enterprise in the position assigned to it by the agreement is strong enough to influence the decisive elements of the market. This has to be decided according to the circumstances of each case. Difficulties arise in determining how strong market effects must be in cases where only the competition for incidental services is regulated. In oligopolistic markets, competition is usually possible only with respect to incidental services. Its removal through agreements would mean the complete elimination of competition as such and, therefore, an absolute market regulation. In cases of different market structures, the restriction on competition of incidental services can lead to effective market regulation.[70] Certain types of products, such as electric typewriters or

[70] Id.

cash registers, may be subject to effective market regulation if the cartel enterprise controls the access to repair work or export materials and thereby exercises such a position of dominance that the other enterprises, unable to implement similar restrictions, are excluded from the market or from an important part of it. Because of the strong differentiation of products, the relevant market for a product is often identical to the regulated market for the product. If there is substitution competition, the cartel's share of the whole relevant market is important. If it seems necessary, the members of the cartel may try to influence the producers of the competitive substitute product to join their cartel. Or they could begin production of the substitute product itself. The steel industry is an example, producers having joined in the production and manufacturing of synthetic products.

General Economic Effects of Industrial Products Cartels

The general economic effects of industrial products cartels depend on the importance the regulated product or the market affected by the regulation has in the economy. General rules cannot be established.

Agreement on the specialization of production and agreements on joint research and development lead to simplification and can be very helpful, especially if the advantages of simplification are passed on to the buyers. However, in the long run all cartels for industrial products will hinder economic progress, especially when such cartels stifle technical development and thus prevent further dynamic development. This might be justified by the enterprise as amortization of its investments. From an economic standpoint, however, such artificial stagnation is dangerous since it can delay and hinder the national economy's development in competition with other economies.

The examination of the market effects of industrial products cartels shows how necessary for purposes of investigation is classification of cartels by types. At the same time, it is necessary to point out the interdependencies of the different types of cartels. In the examination of the raw material cartel, its interrelationship with the industrial products cartel was explained. In many cases technological cartels change into industrial products cartels when the participating enterprises reach a certain level of development. Once this point has been reached the parties want to retain the fruits of their research as long as possible.

6

The Defensive Cartel

An unusual form of cartel, the defensive cartel, calls for a special analysis.[1] By creating parallel market regulation structures in several countries, members exclude competitors from all countries outside the cartel structure and establish a more favorable bargaining position for their dealings with powerful customers and suppliers. The specific purpose of the parallel action is to discriminate against, or to exclude from the market, a specific enterprise, whereas in other types of cartels the discrimination or exclusion is only a device to accomplish a regulation of the market.

There are many reasons to establish defensive cartels. Very often political motives are involved; the cartel may be created to prevent foreign enterprises from using their economic power to obtain significant political power. On the other hand, the cartel partners may seek to increase the political power of their own states to protect their own strong economic position.

A defensive cartel may be established for technological reasons. Enterprises in a defensive cartel might not be able to compete at the same technological levels with competitors from a third country and therefore cannot permit the market to be regulated by normal conditions of supply and demand. Thus, an agreement is reached, perhaps even encompassing third parties such as power or transportation companies or banks, not to assist in the importation of certain goods or services or to limit imports to a fixed amount until the domestic enterprises have reached a competitive technological level. This type of cartel very often is created when enterprises situated in third countries

---

[1] In respect to the terminology, compare E. Hoppmann, "Der volkswirtschaftliche Inhalt der Ausnahmeregelung für Exportkartelle im Gesetz gegen Wettbewerbsbeschränkungen," 11 *Jahrbuch für Sozialwissenschaften* 298 ff. (1960); E. Hoppmann, "Die Anwendung des Territorialitätsprinzips auf reine Exportkartelle im GWB als volkswirtschaftliches Problem," in *Festschrift fur Herman Nottarp* (Karlsruhe, 1961), pp. 291 ff., and in H. Eichler, E. Hoppmann, and E. Schaefer, *Exportkartell und Wettbewerb* (Cologne and Opladen, 1964), pp. 75 ff.

are not willing to enter licensing agreements or other similar arrangements with the cartel partners.

A defensive cartel can also be established for commercial reasons. General economic considerations in a third country, such as balance-of-payments problems or a threat of cartelized or monopolistic suppliers, may influence enterprises in different nations to enter into a cartel agreement.[2] These cartels are similar to those established to deal with enterprises that have gained a powerful market position for certain products or services in a third country. Generally, these are export cartels formed to create a more favorable bargaining position in negotiations with monopolistic enterprises or state monopolies or in negotiations in domestic or export markets characterized by cartelized competition.

It is one of the peculiar characteristics of defensive cartels that governmental measures upon which these cartels are based, as well as the regulatory measures of the states concerned, play a considerable part in the establishment and continuation of cartel agreements. This type of cartel, by its very nature, is closely related to politics. Nevertheless, the use by defensive cartels of governmental measures must be distinguished from cases where the protective policy is accomplished exclusively by governmental actions, as, for example, in the case of high tariff barriers. The concept of a defensive cartel relates only to cooperation among enterprises, although the parties may make use of governmental measures in the creation of their regulatory structure. There are many economic and political reasons why the individual governments may not enact defensive measures themselves. For example, the General Agreement on Tariffs and Trade regulates, and in some cases prohibits, governmental interference with the principle of open markets by devices such as duties or quantitative restrictions, but it does not prohibit private agreements accomplishing the same purposes.[3]

[2] There are only a few international defensive import cartels. Examples of national import cartels are the German cartel for mine beams and braces (*Wirtschaft und Wettbewerb, Entscheidungssammlung zum Kartellrecht, Bundeskartellamt*, p. 447) and the British cartel for sulphuric acid (In re National Sulphuric Acid Association's Agreement, L.R. 4 R.P. 169 ff. [1963]).

[3] According to the decision of the GATT Group of Experts on Restrictive Business Practices of Nov. 18, 1960 (see Basic Instruments and Selected Documents [BISD], 9th Supp. 28 [1961]), the committee recognized that certain business practices which restricted competition could hamper world trade but that it was not practicable for the members of GATT at that time to undertake any form of control of these practices or to provide for investigations (E. Reh-

A government which looks benignly upon private market regulating systems thus can thwart the principles of the GATT treaty.

Participating Enterprises

The participating enterprises in a defensive cartel very often are not as powerful as the participants in other types of cartels. They can be relatively small enterprises. The following types of firms may participate in defensive cartels: (1) enterprises that have good relationships with the governments in the area controlled by the cartel and which are strong enough (either alone or in cooperation with other firms) to counter the infllence on these governments exerted by the foreign competitors because of their economic power; (2) enterprises threatened by technological developments abroad, yet which are strong enough not to be reliant upon this foreign technology; (3) enterprises whose domestic or export markets are threatened by competition from other cartels or enterprises with a strong economic position; (4) enterprises dealing with state trading agencies and their monopolistic buying practices.

In defensive cartels, the decentralization of a single enterprise into several independent juridical persons with different nationalities is important. This involves the question of how the subsidiaries of enterprises directly or indirectly opposed by the defensive cartel should react. In principle, this is not a legal question but rather one of enterprise policy. Between the two world wars, the central management of these enterprises was often divided. Some parts of the enterprise or some subsidiaries were helped by the defensive cartels, while others were adversely affected. This is one of the rare cases in which the management of the different units of the enterprise each uses the diffierence in juridical persons of the various subsidiaries for its own purposes and where these parts tend, temporarily, to go in different directions without disturbing the overall unity of purpose of the enterprise. This is true not only for subsidiaries of American corporations in Europe but also for subsidiaries of European firms in South America and Asia.

---

binder, *Extraterritoriale Wirkungen des deutschen Kartellrechts* [Baden-Baden, 1965], p. 163). See also H. Kronstein, "Conflicts Resulting from the Extraterritorial Effects of Antitrust Legislation of Different Countries," *Legal Essays in Honor of Hessel E. Yntema* (Leyden, 1961), pp. 447 ff.

Marketing-Regulating Agreements

Since defensive cartels have a very heterogeneous nature, the basic market-regulating agreements pertaining to these cartels differ widely. Certain common characteristics, however, distinguish them from the other types of cartels discussed previously. The purpose of the defensive cartel is not merely market regulation, but rather the limitation or exclusion of competitors from the market. These restrictions may affect the supply of goods and services, including technology and capital in home markets or in domestic markets. Defensive agreements can be concluded among suppliers or among purchasers. The defensive measures may be directed against other enterprises in the chain of production and distribution or against competitors.

Today defensive agreements occur most frequently in three main sectors of the world economy: in the supply of industrial products to the United States and Europe from minimum-price countries, such as Japan or Hong Kong; in the supply of industrial products, the capital markets, and the licensing of patents and technical know-how between the United States and Europe; and in the supply of goods and services from the Western industrialized nations to governmental buying agencies, such as those in the Eastern Bloc or underdeveloped countries. There are also defensive agreements in different fields which correspond to the local market structure. This group includes most of the export cartels.

Defensive Agreements against Competition from Minimum-Price Countries

Because of their low wage rates, the industrialized areas of Asia (Japan, Hong Kong, and, in recent years, Korea) enjoy a competitive advantage and are therefore in a position to disturb the domestic and export market structure of the industrialized nations of Europe and America. Shortly after World War II, the Western nations decided to oppose this threat jointly. Recently, however, this opposition has become less important, because the increase in Japanese wage rates and the rapid development of social welfare legislation have led to increased Japanese prices. In addition, a new market division has occurred as a result of Japanese penetration of "traditional" markets, particularly in Asia and Australia.

Exclusive licensing agreements

Exclusive licensing agreements, to be discussed in more detail later, are of considerable importance in protecting competitors in the industrialized nations of Europe and America from the intense competition offered by firms in low-price countries. The case of *United States v. Singer Manufacturing Co.* is an example of this approach.[4] In this case, American, Swiss, and Italian manufacturers of sewing machines entered into cross-licensing arrangements for the purpose of enabling the American firm to enforce patent rights of all of the parties against Japanese imports.

There are also more subtle methods of restricting competition from low-price countries. For example, the cartel members may grant key patent and know-how licenses to enterprises in low-price countries only if these firms agree to restrict their production to definite levels, or agree not to supply certain markets or to supply them only on specific conditions, such as at prices that will not disturb the market situation of the cartel members. In this way, the cartel members can protect both their domestic and export markets.

Interrelationship between suppliers and customers

In certain markets, especially with respect to capital goods and in some interrelationships with customers, the cartel partners can exclude firms of low-price countries by a different method. The members of the cartel often cooperate so closely with each other and with their principal customers on technical and commercial matters that it is almost impossible for third parties to gain a significant foothold in the market. This occurred especially in situations where market division existed in the prewar years. Today it is possible to restrict, but not necessarily to exclude, foreign firms by mere commercial cooperation. This occurs not only where a commercial or technical interrelationship exists between the customer and supplier but also where capital goods are involved, because these goods are regularly purchased by those wholesalers that can keep the market under permanent control through their local residency and ability to provide services.

[4] 205 F. Supp. 394 (S.D.N.Y. 1962); 374 U.S. 174 (1963).

Agreements concerning business quotas

There are also less restrictive agreements that lead to a partial exclusion of minimum-price competitors. The cartel partners may agree to secure a commitment from their purchasers or any sales organization with which they deal that the enterprises disturbing the market will be limited to a specific quota of the market, or they may agree to secure a commitment from their customers that they will give at least one of the cartel members the opportunity to make a new offer before an approach is made to an enterprise in the excluded group. The cartel partners may also demand that these customers accept an offer from a cartel member if it is within a certain percentage of an offer made by an enterprise in the excluded group. For obvious reasons, the excluded group is not mentioned specifically, but there are sufficient indications so that an "insider" has no doubt as to the identity of its members.

The use of governmental measures

A number of governmental measures are used by the participating enterprises to assist in carrying out the defensive agreement. For instance, the International Cotton and Textile Agreement, which permits the imposition of import quotas, provides an opportunity for the cartel partners to establish a regional defensive arrangement with the cooperation of their own governments.[5]

A second governmental measure that should be mentioned is the safety restrictions some governments place on certain technical material. For instance, in the period between the two world wars, guidelines were established providing that, for reasons of safety, certain goods could only be supplied if they had an approved trademark. A more recent example is the requirement in Germany that certain electrical appliances have specific safety features, which as a practical matter can only be supplied by firms from certain countries.[6]

[5] See Chapter 2.

[6] See, for example, the letter of the German Chancellor's office concerning "Doppelstecker" (multiple outlet cube tap) (*Wirtschaft und Wettbewerb Entscheidungssammlung Zum Kartellrecht*, Bundeskartellamt, pp. 145 ff.), which does not even mention the possible restrictive effects resulting from allegedly necessary safety provisions.

Defensive Agreements of European Enterprises against Competition from the United States

In the postwar years, American industry has gained a considerable competitive advantage in those industries where technological development is decisive for economic growth. The primary reason for this advantage is the significant participation by American industry in the military development and space research programs of the United States government, while the European governments either were not willing to refund the development costs of private industry or else did not undertake extensive research and development at all. Also, in static markets, where capital investment is decisive, the large American enterprises have a competitive advantage because of their capital strength in the domestic market. In these cases, European firms seek different ways of cooperating, often with smaller U.S. firms. Thus, the cooperating enterprises may agree not to buy certain products or services from large American firms, even if they are offered on considerably more favorable terms.[7]

Technological agreements

One example of cooperation in the technological field is the challenge by American and European firms of the dominant position of the International Business Machines Corporation (IBM) in the field of computers.[8] Another example is the attempt of the French and English airplane manufacturers, with the cooperation of German firms, to establish a stronger position in the air transport industry through joint development projects.[9] Although it would appear that the European national aeronautic industries cannot survive without this type of cooperation, fusion, or merger, they can achieve important advances in some specialized fields by developing their own working models of motors and parts rather than depending upon American know-how and deliveries. Some agreements for cooperation have been concluded, for example Britain and France on the Concorde, and France, Germany,

[7] Similar agreements seem to exist in the developing countries, in order to gain an independent technological position by excluding offers from the industrial states.

[8] See Chapter 3, n. 54 above.

[9] See the Report of the Committee of Inquiry into the Aircraft Industry, appointed by the Minister of Aviation under the Chairmanship of Lord Plowden (the "Plowden Report"), 1964–65 Cmnd. 2853.

and Spain on the Airbus. These agreements for cooperation, which appear so necessary, would be a form of defensive cartel, concerned more with establishing an independent production rather than purchasing from the cheapest and most technically advanced sources.

As these examples indicate, the main purpose of the defensive cartel is not to exclude the competitor from the market, but rather to strengthen the position and technological power of the cartel partners. The members of this type of cartel accomplish this purpose through the exchange of inventions and know-how and especially through the creation of a favorable credit system. The governments of the participating enterprises play a decisive role in these efforts. Without active support of the participating governments, defensive cartels of this type would have only a slight chance of success.

One example of a proposed defensive cartel with respect to industrial products is the attempt by Italian and French automobile manufacturers to cooperate in restricting the penetration of the European market by American firms and their European subsidiaries.[10] This attempt has been opposed because of the fear of the Volkswagen Company that such a plan would impair its position in the American market.

Agreements concerning access to capital markets

European firms have recently created defensive cartels against American enterprises in the European money markets because demand for capital has increased considerably on these markets. This increased demand is created largely by the measures the United States has been forced to take to protect its balance-of-payments position. One of these measures is the Interest Equalization Tax,[11] which is levied on the acquisition by American purchasers of foreign stocks and bonds. This tax increases the cost of raising money in the United States by foreign enterprises and thus has forced many firms to raise money in the European market instead. The second measure that has increased demand on the European market is the foreign direct investment restrictions imposed by President Johnson on January 1, 1968,[12] and implemented by the Foreign Direct Investment Regulations of the Department of Commerce.[13] These regulations restrict the transfer of

[10] See "Tour d'horizon der europäischen Automobilindustrie," *Neue Zürcher Zeitung*, Mar. 3, 1966.
[11] 26 U.S.C. 4911 ff. (1964).   [12] Exec. Order 11387, 33 Fed. Reg. 47 (1968).
[13] 33 Fed. Reg. No. 1, Pt. II, pp. 15, 41, 49, 79, 81, 84, 100 (1968).

capital from the United States and also require the repatriation of earnings to the United States by U.S. firms, thus forcing these firms to seek additional capital in the European money markets as well.

In Europe, this additional demand has increased the shortage in an already limited capital market. On the one hand, European banks and other financial institutions have recognized the advantages in opening the strongly isolated European capital market to deposits from foreign countries. On the other hand, they have tried to limit the demand on the capital market of any single European country. An understanding has been reached among the participating financial institutions that distribute the stocks and bonds of American corporations according to fixed quotas, regardless of which institutions have been the initial underwriters. The role of the central banks in this arrangement is not clear.

Agreements establishing the minimum conditions that American firms have to meet in order to obtain money from European capital markets are of similar importance.[14] It would appear that American firms are able to receive money only on a shorter term basis than is true for European firms. Europeans are thus able to restrict the expansion of American firms. The effect of this capital market situation on the technological balance is not clear.

Defensive Agreements against States with Central Purchasing Organizations

Agreements regarding trade with Eastern Bloc countries

Where a defenisve cartel is only increased in the opening of export markets, the private defensive agreements are directed not only against private agreements and private power, but also against governmental measures and the concentration of economic power by these governments. This is especially true with sales and the grant of lines of credit negotiated with countries having a planned economy and where control of all foreign trade is centralized. The methods utilized by Western enterprises in negotiations with the centralized purchasing agencies of the Eastern Bloc countries is a good example.[15] Especially in the case of the licensing of patents and company secrets, the West-

---

[14] According to personal information of the author.

[15] "Milliardenkredit an Moskau gefährdet die Berner Union," *F.A.Z.*, Aug. 22, 1966; and "Unveränderte Bonner Kreditpolitikgegenüber dem Osten," *id.*, Aug. 23, 1966.

ern enterprises are often restricted by agreements among themselves, which may on occasion be adapted to the laws and regulations of other Western countries. The experiences of the 1920's and the world economic crises that followed showed what would happen if suppliers attempted to deal with centralized purchasing organizations individually. At that time, suppliers were often forced to accept long-term contracts at little or no profit so they would be able to employ their workers. In addition, the credit terms offered to the Eastern Bloc countries, and to the developing countries as well, are agreed upon by the various suppliers often under strong political pressure from their governments.

Agreements on trade with developing countries

Cartel agreements made with respect to trade with developing countries,[16] referred to in the section on governmental measures, should also be discussed at this point. In these cases also, enterprises of the industrialized countries find themselves confronted with attempts of developing countries to place orders that cannot possibly be fulfilled in economic terms. It is not surprising that suppliers from industrialized countries try to prevent the playing off of one enterprise against another. Naturally, in some cases this argument is only a pretext to cover the real motive of the cartel agreement.

This shows that in transactions between enterprises belonging to different economic orders, the free movement of supply and demand does not take place. Alternative rules thus must be developed by the parties.

Other Forms of Defensive Cartels

Defensive cartels are frequently concluded by smaller enterprises to meet the competition of a large firm or a group of cartelized firms in an export market. Only in a few cases do genuine international agreements exist. The German-Dutch Lithophone cartel is such an international agreement. Most members of this cartel are, however, German enterprises.[17] Export cartels are generally made up of firms of the same nationality.

Similar agreements exist on the demand side. Here, also, international

[16] See United States v. The Concentrated Phosphate Export Association, Inc., et al., 393 U.S. 199 (1968). See consent decree 1969 CCH Trade Cas. ¶72,719 (D.C.N.Y. 1969).

[17] *Bundesanzeiger* No. 227, Nov. 24, 1960.

cartels are relatively rare. It should be pointed out that the members of export and import cartels very often only pretend to be in a defensive position to conceal their genuine objective, which is to conquer new markets. Therefore, export cartels are often of an agressive nature, although according to many national regulations, cartels are only permitted if there is an indication of a need for a defensive position in the market.[18]

Market Regulation by Defensive Cartels

The main purpose of defensive cartels is not to subject the functioning of the market to privately set rules. The real purpose of the parties to a defensive cartel is to reestablish the balance of power that has been disturbed by technological or economic power or by the use of the power of a particular state. As in the case of military conflicts, it is often very difficult to distinguish between defensive and aggressive measures. Certainly there are defensive cartels that give the participating enterprises a chance to maintain or increase their competitive influence despite distortions of competition. Often, however, the competitive advantage of outside enterprises is merely used as a pretext to justify the exclusion of a potential competitor. Certainly in the relationship to Japanese industry, some defensive cartels can be considered highly aggressive.

In evaluating the market-regulating effect of defensive cartels, it must also be noted that a defensive cartel can not really operate if its purpose is merely to exclude a third enterprise. Necessarily it is bound to lead to a market regulation among the participating firms. Even within the total cartel regulation, this limited market regulation can be observed. Furthermore, a natural result of an offensive market strategy of a defensive cartel, even if initiated for defensive purposes, leads to retaliation by the enterprises in the third countries or their governments. These countermeasures can involve the creation of a new cartel organization on the other side. In such a struggle, the defensive cartel will often lose its character; it changes into a new type of cartel, which includes enterprises from third countries originally attacked, as for example into a market division with respect to industrial products or into a technological cartel. What was originally an agreement for purposes of defense becomes, even if in a different form, an agreed regulation between the attacker and the attacked.

[18] See n. 2 above.

These tendencies can be noticed especially in cases where the enterprises in the states outside the defensive cartels have subsidiaries in the states that have merged into this cartel. Initially, the tendency of the domestic enterprises is to treat the subsidiary as a foreign company. Later, however, these parties often seek to include the subsidiary within the defensive group. Since this is not possible without the approval or silent consent of the parent company, the defensive cartel easily becomes an international cartel that can be compared with the other types of cartels. Of course, there are also instances in which the defensive measures did not create the foundations of a new cartel, but merely a temporary situation in the struggle of a group of enterprises of different nationalities within an older system of market regulation. This leads to a new balance of power and to a new equilibrium within the total system of regulation.

7 ~~~~~~~~

The Cartel Agreement

The preceding analysis of the different types of cartels regulating international trade provides sufficient illustrative material to permit an analysis of the contractual system that is the foundation of today's international cartel. Within the framework of these agreements, important markets have been subjected to regulation. In many cases, the organizers of these international cartels were able to develop a new system of regulation from an existing contractual order. They could change objectives of market regulation or establish new cartel institutions and devices or transform existing ones. The cartel organizers, by vertical agreements, were able to impose the will of the organizing group upon others in the chain of distribution and thereby effectuate the intended market regulation.

In some international cartels operating in certain geographical areas, especially in those in which borders had been altered by the outcome of World War II, the organizers found it necessary to establish an entirely new organization. They had to establish themselves as a cartel group on the international market and to decide on the aim of their market regulation and the methods to be used. They also had to establish institutions and devices to implement and enforce the planned market regulation. Vertical agreements were often used to enforce the market-regulating agreements. The increasing integration of the geographical markets and the fields of production and trade under the control of the cartel groups resulted in the continuous enlargement of the markets influenced by the agreement beyond those specifically described in the contract.

An actual hierarchy of groups and a contractual system for each exists on every level of production and trade. An international agreement on the market regulation of a certain raw material may lead to an international agreement on all semifinished or finished products made from this raw material. Agreements on one level have to be examined in light of the total hierarchy. They have an inseparable connection with each other even if the contracts did not anticipate such a hierarchy. Regional international agreements can only be fully understood as one element of more far-reaching global international agreements. Even many national agreements are often only one element in the implementation and enforcement of an international agreement.

A cartel agreement, consensus, or understanding was defined in an earlier chapter [1] as any type of joint decision by a few enterprises to establish, implement, or direct an international cartel.[2] No other definition adequately describes the joint decision of at least two partners to operate together to achieve the agreed market regulation. In analyzing the social phenomenon of the international cartel, it is only important whether the members of the international cartel consider the provisions of their cartel agreement binding. It is not as important whether the provisions are valid according to the laws of the various countries involved, since the international cartels establish their own legal order. Therefore, the so-called gentlemen's agreements, concerted action, or other forms of collusion dependent upon joint decisions are included within the concept of the contract.[3]

Phases of the Contractual System

The international cartel was initially defined for purposes of describing the different types of cartels as a contract among independent enterprises from different states leading to the coordinated behavior of each partner in the market. It is in fact more complex than that. There are three clearly distinguishable phases, especially in those international cartels that either regulate the entire world market or organize markets for products that had been subject to cartel regulation prior to World War II. The primary understanding obligates the cartel members to act together to regulate the intended market rather than permit its regulation by the general laws of the marketplace. This preliminary agreement, the basic requirement for each international cartel agreement, is termed the "basic regulatory agreement." Just as government agencies regulate business transactions through regulatory decisions, the basic regulatory agreement provides the necessary environment for

[1] Chapter 3.
[2] Chapters 9–14 examine the problem of whether the general concept of a contract adequately covers the character of a modern international cartel.
[3] A recent English decision, based on another type of market regulation, collective bargaining, comes to similar results (Ford Motor Company, Ltd. v. Amalgamated Union of Engineering and Foundry Workers, the Queen's Bench Division [Law Report III/6/1969], reprinted in London *Times*, March 7, 1969).

economic planning. Once this basic agreement has been reached, the cartel members must define, in view of existing economic conditions, which goals are to be pursued and which methods are to be used. This agreement as to plan and method is called a "planning agreement." Then the cartel members have to impose their plan agreement on firms operating on the different economic levels. A large number of vertical agreements, adapted to the condition of the cartel and called "cartel implementation agreements," will be necessary.[4]

Basic Regulatory Agreement

Basic points of agreement

A basic agreement, often concluded many years previously, is required for each market regulation. At least two enterprises agree to form a cartel group and to regulate a certain market by removing it from the competitive framework desired by the various governments concerned. The parties agree initially to control this market and regulate it according to their own rules. But such an agreement to set aside the general market forces is not sufficient by itself to establish a cartel group. A minimum of organization and institutionalization is unavoidable. This institutionalization may be nothng more than the creation of a council, composed of members of the cartel group, which is to meet and to settle all disputes on a case-by-case basis so as to accomplish regulation of the market. This understanding is an example of a basic regulatory agreement.

The analysis of private market regulation in the postwar period showed that effective market regulation was based on previously existing basic regulatory agreements. In some cases it is possible to fix almost exactly the date on which the group entered this agreement. For example, in the petroleum field the signing of the Achnacarry Agreement marked the beginning of the basic regulatory contract. Although the specific provisions of the agreement on the distribution of markets did not come into force as intended, the oil producers formed a definite group with fixed institutions able to establish new and necessary plans to replace the normal regulations and functions of the market.

Aluminum, developed during and immediately after World War I,

---

[4] F. Machlup, *The Economics of Seller's Competition* (Baltimore, 1952), pp. 414, 441, 475. This is a very controversial issue in connection with the national cartel laws.

was so controlled through the use of patents that the product was effectively removed from normal market regulation.[5] After World War II, the organizers based their further development on this previously existing arrangement and were easily able to adapt their plans to the economic changes that had occurred, in spite of the existence of new enterprises.

Even in a few of the very old industrial fields, such as copper, it can truly be said that the general market forces have never been effective. Here also, the participating enterprises after World War II were bound by a fundamental contractual system.

There has been a different development in the newly emerging technologies such as television and electronics. Here the cartel members sometimes used the basic regulatory agreement in contiguous fields to broaden the area of regulation. For example, television agreements were based on the old radio cartel arrangements, which had in turn evolved from the electric light bulb cartels. In other fields new basic regulatory agreements appeared to regulate the market, either when a new group appeared, when a former basic regulatory agreement broke down (necessitating an entirely new agreement), or when the old group was not sufficiently organized to achieve the desired regulation. The last situation is often the case in international cartels of regional or limited character, which are often temporary in nature.

These basic regulatory agreements, admittedly a new legal concept,[6] form the structure of the cartel. These contracts are often of long standing and allow the establishment of new market regulations and the adaptation of these regulations to changing economic and political situations. Without taking into consideration that cartel members often feel bound by the existing order, it might be concluded that the members are continuously making new agreements, entirely different from the former market regulations, or are even going through periods entirely free from agreements. Development of the present copper cartel in the postwar period can only be explained in terms of its earlier development. Without the knowledge of the existence of this basic regulation concerning the organization of the group, there is no way to

[5] See G. Stocking and M. Watkins, *Cartels in Action* (New York, 1946), pp. 227–273.

[6] As a lawyer who has always regarded with great skepticism the use of legal conceptualism, I find it ironic that it should become necessary to introduce a new concept—"the basic regulatory agreement." The justification for using this concept will be shown in the text.

understand the effects on the market after a long-term cartel regulation has ended. The market resulting from this cartel regulation might appear to the observer to be a competitive or at least an oligopolistic market. However, as a matter of fact, the market is still under the permanent supervision of the cartel group, united by the basic regulatory agreement, and still affected by the old planning agreements.[7]

The extent to which each point of the planning agreement is carried out is closely connected with the basic regulatory agreement. In the aluminum field, the Canadian export price determines the world market price, because the cartel group sufficiently controls market development and can intervene if necessary with a modified planning agreement. The purchase of cheaper Russian aluminum in Western Europe is an example of such intervention.

Originally, the basic group of the international cartel was often formed simultaneously with the establishment of the market regulation plan. These two phases of the cartel agreement are evident immediately. The regulatory agreement became the basic order of the group and was clearly separated from the planning agreement, which can be changed depending upon economic developments. However, even today for regionally restricted international cartels the basic regulatory agreement and the planning agreement can be identical. Here the parties will often make their agreement to form a group dependent on an agreement concerning the plan. But even with this dependence the two phases are completely different in character and in substance. It is important to note that the cartel group can remain in existence even if the planning agreement becomes unenforceable owing to changing economic or political conditions. This justifies the distinction made between the two phases.

Today at the international level in many important industries there are only a very few enterprises acting on the market either as single corporations or as international industrial combinations. In these situations with a limited number of enterprises, it is necessary only to explain how such a group was organized and how its planning agreements were fixed and implemented. Both the basic regulatory agreement and the planning agreement exist here. The only detailed agreements are found in the implementation agreements, however, and these are not easily understood or interpreted unless seen within the framework of the international cartel's basic structure.

[7] Machlup, n. 4 above.

The agreements leading to market regulation have been described from the view of those who have formed and worked with the regulations. For the members of this group the provisions of the basic regulatory agreement and the planning agreements are the result of their intentional, coordinated actions, and the parties abide by them. The outsider, such as the government authority or the scholar, is restricted in his observations to the well-known, publicized agreements (usually the implementation agreements), to knowledge of the existence of cartel institutions, and to signs of coordination between cartel partners.

Certain terms used here are similar to terminology used in the Soviet Union's centralized economic planning system. This is appropriate because the private international cartels remove one segment of the economy from the normal market situation and subject it to their planning contracts just as the government does in a planned economy. However, the concepts "basic regulatory agreement" and "planning agreement" do not mean here exactly what they would mean in Soviet terminology.[8] The reason for this distinction is that within the international cartel framework the planning and control is private, but in the Soviet centralized system the planning is governmental. Under the state-planning system, the agreement for implementing the plan is of minor importance. Private planning by several enterprises, however, can only follow such agreements. Thus, though there are certain differences in the meanings of these concepts, they are acceptable here because the similarities in the fact of planning as such are more important.

Organization

A degree of organization or institutionalization is necessary to keep the cartel group together. Sometimes the members simply come to an understanding that they will work together. But if they want a stronger organization, they usually form a permanent organ for coordination and decision-making. Often the creation of a cartel institution that is more than a coordinator is necessary. For example, a corporation may be established which functions as an agent, assuming

[8] In the Soviet-Socialist bloc countries, the basic regulatory agreement (i.e., the Economic Plan) determines the extent of the entire production and the amount of the entire costs; A. Weber, *Sowjetwirtschaft und Weltwirtschaft* (Berlin, 1959), p. 245. The Economic Plan is realized by a single planning contract.

a number of activities on behalf of the cartel within the framework of the basic regulatory agreement, the planning agreement, and the implementation agreement. The most far-reaching cartel institution, in the corporation form, is the syndicate, which may handle all sales and purchases for the cartel members according to the respective planning agreements. In this way the planning agreements are implemented without any difficulty. Today only in the field of diamonds is regulation by the syndicate complete.[9]

Patent-holding companies are another example of this corporation type of cartel institution. They "hold" patents and dispose of them to exert desired influence in accordance with the planning agreements.

As a result of postwar anticartel legislation, the extensive, powerful cartel administrations—which existed in the international sphere during the prewar years—did not openly reappear. Today the only cartel agencies are those absolutely necessary to enable the cartel members to interfere within the market effectively. These include price agencies, agencies for exchange of information, and agencies for scientific cooperation. The most important agency is the arbitration tribunal, which can be used by the group as a means of conciliation.[10]

The basic regulatory agreement, by removing specific markets from normal market regulation and subjecting them to certain planning agreements, has a similar function for cartels as the *contrat social* had for the doctrine of natural law in the understanding of the establishment of a permanent human society.[11] It is not possible nor necessary to set forth detailed provisions of this agreement. The crucial point is that by this agreement enterprises formally agree to cooperate in the future. They establish a basic constitution whose objective is to control the market by private regulation and to establish a certain basic organization for this market.

Planning Agreement

Basic points of agreement

The second phase in the development of international market regulation is the planning agreement. The parties decide, in light of the specific economic situation, what concrete aim their coordination should

9 For further discussion of the diamond cartel see Chapter 5.

10 A detailed examination of arbitration tribunals and their connection with international cartels can be found in Chapter 13.

11 In this connection see E. Wolf, *Das Problem der Naturrechtslehre* (Karlsruhe, 1964), p. 150.

serve and what methods should be employed. In effect they decide on a plan for market regulation. The planning agreement is the vehicle by which the participating enterprises directly determine, for a certain economic period, the behavior of the participating firms in the market and indirectly determine the behavior of third parties. The organizers of the international cartel (the partners in the basic regulatory agreement) use the planning agreement to decide which method of international market regulation to use. For example, they fix the quantity to be produced or sold, the distribution procedures, the price range, and other conditions in such a way that the goals of the plan can be realized. The planning agreement leads to a coordination or parallelism in the market behavior of the interested parties. This appears either in a general way, such as in a price-setting agreement, or in a supplementary way, such as in a distribution of markets. This plan can be established by a formal contract or by an informal agreement. It should be emphasized again, however, that the parallel but autonomous decisions of enterprises do not constitute such a contract.

In the copper cartel, the participating enterprises anticipated a market collapse and a product surplus in 1956, and planned accordingly. An agreement was concluded to restrict production or sale of copper products in certain markets and to fix prices. This agreement can be termed a planning contract and was fixed for the period in which the collapse of the market was expected. Each of the parties also had another purpose in the agreement: to avoid a price drop and the resulting depression. In 1963 a different situation occurred. Instead of an anticipated surplus and market collapse, there was a shortage of copper. Therefore, it was necessary to conclude a new planning contract, based on the "split price" practice, to achieve a new market regulation.[12]

It would be wrong to conclude from the cancelling of the copper cartel's 1956 planning agreement that an oligopolistic situation replaced the cartel regulation in the market. The whole system of market regulation must be examined. Just as the planning agreement is considered within the framework of the basic regulatory agreement, so each new planning agreement must be seen in connection with prior planning agreements. It is possible that no specific formal agreements were concluded concerning a set "producer's" price nor concerning the enforcement of this price on the various economic levels. Considering the small number of participating enterprises, it is possible that this is

[12] For a discussion of "split prices," see Chapter 4 on the raw material cartel.

merely coordinated action similar to oligopolistic practices. However, what happened in 1963 can not be separated from what happened in 1956. The planned success of the production restrictions had occurred. As a direct consequence of the old contract, individual enterprises were now able to allow both a policy of producer prices and a policy of free market prices. Even without further agreement, the parties could use the base established by the expired planning agreement. Within the framework of the basic regulatory agreement, the parties intervened as soon as the structure showed signs of deterioration.

Many methods of market regulation, such as market divisions, may be maintained in the same way by the participating parties without concluding a new planning agreement. For example, if a planning agreement divided the world market so that the American market was supplied only by American enterprises, this division could continue even if the contract were suspended. Or if, for example, patents are the basis of the planning agreement and are so distributed that they can only be applied in a specific way, then the organizers of the new planning agreement can base their decisions on these older contracts. Another example is the exclusive dealing contract in the petroleum industry, where an implementation agreement for a certain planning agreement is effective against third parties and remains as a useful instrument of the cartel organization even after cancellation of the planning agreement.

During the period between the two world wars, many international cartels included provisions with respect to individual countries that a variance in the economic situation would lead to a formal change in the agreement. Usually a special committee or arbitration tribunal was established to reach agreement on the changes necessary to accomplish the goal of the cartel. Today, as a result of strong horizontal and vertical integration of industry, detailed contracts are no longer necessary. The few members need only fix the direction and outline of the plan. This can be done by an informal agreement.

Hierarchy of planning agreements

Because of the close integration of the different economic levels (producers, manufacturers, distributors, and retailers), planning agreements are related to each other in a hierarchical structure. This hierarchy is based on the stages in the development of a product, from raw material to use by a consumer. Vertically integrated enterprises may coordinate the planning agreements on different economic levels. This coordination may take place where enterprises on one level actually depend on their distributional enterprises, such as retailers or wholesalers. For instance, raw material cartels may not only fix production quotas and prices, they may also prescribe that manufacturers using this raw material on a subsequent economic level shall be given the "producer price" advantage on the raw material. Thus, the planning agreement is in essence only an implementation agreement inseparable from the planning agreement on the raw material level.

A similar relationship is seen in international planning agreements that correspond to national planning agreements in the different industries. For example, raw material manufacturers can agree with their buyers on the basis of a cartel arrangement that the price of the finished product will depend on the price of the raw material on the day of delivery. In form these are national planning agreements. Actually, however, these are implementation agreements for the international planning agreement. It is of great legal and economic importance to examine how these national planning agreements are related to international planning agreements or to examine how a coordinated series of national planning agreements actually represents an international market regulation.

Types of planning agreements

By the use of planning agreements, the organizers of international cartels remove at least one of the elements of market development from the laws of the marketplace. The planning agreement attempts to resolve the following questions with respect to production, distribution, services, and technological development: whether the economic activity is to take place; where and when this activity is to occur; how it is to occur, including methods of production, distribution, transportation, and technological development; and how much economic activity should take place, including the quantities to be produced by that activity.

Owing to the close interrelationship of production, distribution, services, and technological development, an individual factor can exert influence not only in its own field but, under certain circumstances, in several fields of economic endeavor. By a planning agreement this one factor of production, distribution, services, or technological development is directly controlled, and thus, under certain circumstances, the whole economic field is regulated. For example, the quantity of articles to be disposed of can be regulated by the amount of packaging material available.[13] Another example is the agreement on the total amount of banking credits given for certain technological development. This agreement can be used to control and regulate this development.

The aim of the plan

The regulation of at least one factor in production, sales, services, or technological development is generally the objective of the particular plan. For a specific economic situation, the parties want a form of market regulation that will best suit their interests. The copper market is an example. If the producers face a dangerous flood of the market (as the copper producers did in 1956) the aim of their planning agreement will be to restrict the supply on the market and thereby retain certain minimum prices. Or if a scarcity of supply on the market is anticipated (as was the case in the copper market in 1963–1964), the aim of the producers' planning agreement will be either to equalize distribution of the product or to create and sustain a condition that would allow certain groups of buyers to acquire a preferred supply of the product at relatively favorable prices and force other buyers to use the "free" market.

Another example is the television market, where the important producers regulate the appearance of new types of products. The market can be saturated with the old product, such as black and white television, before the new product, such as color television, is introduced. The planning agreement determines the time at which the different types are to be sold in the various individual markets. The aim of the plan is maximum exploitation of the market for the old types before the new product is introduced.

Elements of organization

Within the framework of the basic regulatory agreement the parties at times create cartel instruments which serve the group's permanent organization but which can also be used for a specific planning agreement. The cartel partners also often establish within the planning agreement framework (by means of specific horizontal agreements of an associative nature) instruments not necessary for the basic organization of the cartel but which fulfill exclusive purposes of that

[13] H. Kronstein and J. T. Miller, Jr., *Regulation of Trade* (New York, 1953), p. 12.

planning agreement. The parties can also use institutions that have a completely different task, such as product exchanges, as an instrument of the planning agreement. The first two types of cartel instrument include: (1) syndicates that exist for the joint purchase or sale of specific products, such as diamonds; (2) patent-holding companies that control and grant exclusive licenses for a large number of the patents that form the basis for the regulation of specific markets; the Swiss patent-holding company that controls the patents for a special steel manufacturing procedure is an example; [14] (3) price-controlling and price-fixing agencies, especially market research agencies, which investigate and control the development of specific markets; also in this category are trust companies, which are used for special price fixing agreements, and clearing houses of all kinds; (4) technological advisory boards; (5) trade associations.

The syndicate, the coordination into one autonomous corporation of purchases and sales of the cartel members, has become rare in international trade. Today the only perfectly developed syndicate is found in the field of diamonds. Syndicates of a more regional character, such as Nitrex AG, the syndicate of European producers of nitrogen, and certain cement syndicates, do exist however.

Syndicates can also be instruments of the cartel group's inner organization, within the framework of the basic regulatory agreement. This enables one or more of the important members of the group to control the other members. More often, however, the syndicate has been chosen as the planning agreement's instrument for regulation of the cartel's outside relationships. This of course saves distribution costs. But more importantly, it produces a common front among the cartel members in dealing with important clients. This is clearly seen in the case of Nitrex AG, which appears as a syndicate in deals with state trading countries, but which in other cases merely supervises the pooling of the profits individual cartel members have made from their own sales.

In international trade, there can be numerous syndicate forms.[15] The modern cartels, however, have not developed new forms. This fact and the relatively rare use of the syndicate by cartels in international trade today obviates a description of the individual syndicate forms.

Patent-holding companies have today become an extremely im-

[14] See Chapter 12 at n. 64, for a further discussion of this device.

[15] J. Flechtheim, *Die rechtliche Organisation der Kartelle* (Mannheim, 1923), p. 13.

portant means of international cartelization. They are examined in the chapter concerning the application of patents for market regulation.[16]

Agencies for price control and price fixing stand in clear contrast to the syndicate. They do not attempt to concentrate purchases and sales, but rather they create certain uniform conditions under which the individual parties can make their own purchases and sales. The best-known form is the price registration agency that provides information on the prices charged by the individual enterprises or on the average prices.[17] In oligopolistic markets, the announcement of the prices of competitors or of an average price is already a restriction of competition. In these cases, the restriction of competition is not merely an unwanted side-effect resulting from the coincidence of price announcement and natural oligopolistic behavior. Often a group formed by the basic regulatory agreement is behind the price registration agency. And usually the participating enterprises are obligated not only to announce their prices but also to undertake a price change only after they have informed the price registration agency in advance.

The cartel members may also use instruments that are not a part of the cartel organization to fix prices indirectly. An example is the use of product exchanges, such as the London Metal Exchange, where the strong producers act as representatives for all the cartel members and regulate the exchange price by their purchases and sales. In this case, the exchange serves as a price agency for the members of the cartel.

In addition to these instruments affecting price fixing, there are also agencies for price control and market investigation that have important functions for the fulfillment of the planning agreement. This will be discussed when the implementation of cartel agreements is examined.

Various types of technological advisory boards to assist in market regulation also exist. Sometimes their aim is only to give information to the concerned parties so that they can make full use of the existing technological exchange agreements. These agencies can also restrict competition, however, by forcing producers to follow the agreements on restrictions of production or sale of newly developed products.

Trade associations serve a twofold purpose. They act to maintain friendly relations among the various enterprises of the industrial branch involved and to represent the interests of these enterprises in dealings with third parties. They can, however, be the base for actual restric-

16 Chapter 12.
17 F. Machlup, *The Political Economy of Monopoly* (Baltimore, 1952), p. 88.

tions of competition if all or some of the members are united in a group by a basic regulatory agreement. From merely informative talks about prospective plans to informal price or protection agreements, the associations have a wide field of possibilities, which are commonly used in the international arena.

Implementation Agreements

Essential implementation agreements which affect
relationships with third parties

The agreements among cartel members laid down in the basic regulatory agreement and the planning agreements in effect regulate the relationships between the cartel members and third parties. It is crucial in international market regulations that each cartel member abide by the horizontal cartel agreement when it concludes contracts with buyers or sellers. The content of each contract with third parties is, therefore, influenced by the horizontal market regulation. This is also true with planning agreements, which do not regulate contracts with third parties but merely provide for production restrictions or market divisions. These agreements may commit the cartel members not to conclude contracts with certain buyers in a given territory beyond a fixed amount. In these cases, the possibility of third parties concluding contracts is directly affected by the cartel agreement and, in addition, the contents of the contract may be indirectly influenced.[18]

These two types of contracts with third parties have several characteristics. First, they implement the market regulation and are directly or indirectly influenced by the planning agreements. Second, the regulation of the market only comes into effect after the conclusion of these contracts with the third parties. The planning agreement shows the interrelationship between the participating cartel members. It also affects third parties by restricting their chances of favorable business transactions and by exerting long-term influences on the economy.

All of these effects on third parties can be termed market regulation.[19] In this context the term market regulation presumes that the participating parties are strong enough to implement their agreements and substitute their order for the normal laws of the marketplace. If not, then the operation is merely a "paper" cartel. This does not mean that the cartel has to control a certain percentage of the market, as

[18] R. Lukes, *Der Kartellvertrag* (Munich, 1959), p. 135.   [19] *Id.*

for example 75 per cent, which some have contended is necessary.[20] Cartels controlling a considerably smaller share of the market can achieve an effective market regulation depending on the structure of that market.

Implementing contracts that have no direct restrictive effect on third parties enable one of the parties to perform its normal business activities within the market and still remain loyal to the cartel agreement. For example, these agreements can involve the establishment of new factories or laboratories for research and development within the terms and purpose of the cartel agreement. The availability of credit for the realization of the cartel aims is another example.

Autonomous implementation contracts

A large number of regular vertical contracts are necessary to implement the desired market regulation with respect to the parties participating in the basic regulatory contract and the planning contracts. There can be cases in which the necessary implementing contracts, such as sale contracts for regulated products, coincide with implementation agreements protecting international market regulation. For example, a buyer can be restricted in the distribution or use of the product in such a way that the market regulation can be enforced and eventually extended. Such contracts can be included in planning agreements as regulations and are necessary as implementation agreements. They can also be based on a general, implied authorization within the planning agreements, in which case they would have been agreed upon by the individual cartel members. Finally, they can be totally based on the individual economic decision of one or several members of the cartel; these are the real autonomous implementation agreements.

These agreements, implementing the market regulations, are concerned with the following questions of production, distribution, services, and technological development: whether this economic activity occurs at all; where and when it takes place; how it occurs, including the methods of production, distribution (especially sales conditions), and transportation, and the methods of technological research and development to be used; and how much of this economic activity takes place, including the quantities to be produced.

---

[20] W. Heuser, *Die Entwicklung und Bedeutung internationaler Kartelle* (Baden-Baden, 1929), pp. 7, 27.

The agreements through which market regulation is implemented, protected, and transferred to further economic levels can have different legal forms and can be part of various types of contracts. The chapters on the arbitration tribunal and the application of patents will discuss contract forms by which many of the above-mentioned points can be regulated.[21] Here it is sufficient merely to examine how some basic types of contracts, especially vertical contracts, can be used to implement and then protect the market regulation. For example, sales contracts can include: the obligation of the buyer to purchase only the seller's product; a restriction on the buyer on his use and resale of the purchased products; a restriction on the buyer concerning the application of specific technologically patented or unpatented procedures necessary for the manufacture of certain products; a price regulation or price-fixing agreement for the resale of the products; a regulation concerning the application of specific trademarks in case of manufacture or resale; the obligation of the buyer to secure similar obligations from buyers on the next level; and a restriction on the areas in which either finished or unfinished products can be sold.

Specific obligations can easily be passed on to customers in licensing contracts involving patents or trademarks. Similar obligations can be found in agreements concerning the appointment of sales agents.

Implementation and Enforcement of the Contractual Systems

In any contractual situation difficulties arise when the participating parties no longer observe the agreed-upon rules. Within the cartel's contractual system, such difficulties are especially dangerous, not because the cartel members' internal relationships are involved, but because the contracts establish regulations that affect third parties. Organizers of international cartels try to solve these problems either by legal or by factual means. Between the cartel members themselves, the market regulations are usually enforced by factual means. In their relationship with third parties, however, the cartel members apply the usual methods for legal enforcement of contractual claims.

Enforcement of the Contractual System among Cartel Members
Self-enforcement

Today international cartel contracts are not worked out in detail, and disagreements between the members rarely are the subject of

[21] Chapters 12 and 13.

court decisions. The partners to the basic regulatory agreement and the planning agreement are relatively few, but these are concluded by big and important enterprises that can use other methods to enforce the contracts. Thus, it might be assumed that the contracts or contract claims would not be enforced or settled through the use of the legal process. However, this is not the case.

The methods used for enforcement of the contractual system in the face of a violation of the basic regulatory agreement or of the planning agreement are very similar to the methods employed by governments in international controversies. The parties will negotiate a solution if persistent disregard of the agreement occurs or if circumstances change, requiring new planning agreements. In very important cases, a 'summit conference' of managers of the enterprises participating in the market regulation is called to discuss the situation. In other cases, there will only be meetings of the representatives of the cartel partners. These difficulties, which concern the basic questions of the cartel organization, are the result of private agreements and are thus of a highly political nature, and the methods used to solve these problems are similar to those used in politics.

This method of resolving disputes in most cases leads to an institutionalization of the conflict. The cartel members set up an agency to restore the undisturbed functioning of the market regulation. Thus, the cartel members are almost always able to reach an agreement on controversial questions. Although this might seem strange, it must be realized that the interested parties, especially the relatively small enterprises,—often have no choice but to act according to the agreement. They must agree to changes in the planning agreement since any attempt to withdraw from the cartel would be met by countermeasures. For example, in the technological cartel the large participating enterprises entering negotiations have bargaining power based on patents, technical expertise, and export controls. This power can be used not only at the beginning of the negotiations but at any time during the cartel's existence. A withdrawal from the cartel is really possible only if a new and unusual technological development has been accomplished by the particular enterprise wishing to withdraw.

The same is true for both the raw material cartel and the industrial product cartel. Each of the participating enterprises, even the large ones, must consider that, should it withdraw from the basic regulatory agreement or from the planning agreement, its competitors can flood its market with products at lower prices or can lower the prices on that part of the market where it is most vulnerable. In these cartels a withdrawal would be possible if an enterprise discovered or invented an important new procedure. For example, the aluminum cartel would break apart if one of its members invented a procedure to manufacture bauxite directly into aluminum, and a considerable time lag would be involved before its competitors could catch up.

Despite the possibility of withdrawals from the cartel, this has, in fact, rarely happened. When nonmember parties appear on the market, the question arises whether the existing planning agreement is effective enough to maintain the market regulation. The cartel can sometimes lose its position of power to regulate the market effectively without ceasing to be an important factor in the market. The posted price system in the petroleum industry is an example. Often these are only temporary developments that can later be changed into a definite market regulation.

Forms of implementation

To a large extent the implementation of these agreements is autonomous. However, the instruments of the basic regulatory agreement and of the planning agreements give the organizers of international cartels further possibilities of implementing these agreements. For example, the syndicate controlling the sale of diamonds has sufficient influence either to interfere in the market itself or to force the leading enterprise to interfere. Another example is a patent-holding company that not only achieves the desired regulation through the distribution of licenses for patents but which must also determine that the licensed patents were used in accordance with the agreement. If these cartel institutions intervene, real legal questions are being solved. The administrative conflicts found in the daily functioning of the cartel lie within the competence of these institutions. General political conflicts within the contractual system, however, are settled not according to law, but according to political considerations and the needs of the cartel.

The legalization of such conflicts means that arbitration tribunals often give the final decision. The arbitration tribunals can have jurisdiction to determine the rights and obligations between the cartel members on the one hand and cartel institutions on the other, and between either of these and third parties. Thus, a uniform interpretation of the whole contractual system is obtained. Arbitration tribunals can also function as "criminal courts" and can impose penalties on those parties that violate the agreements. More important today than this penal power is the presentation of legal, arbitral opinions, prepared either by the arbitration tribunals or by official or unofficial settlement agencies, concerning the relationships between the cartel members themselves, or between the members, the cartel institutions, and third parties. These arbitral opinions are used to prepare for meetings held by the cartel management when there has been a violation of the basic regulatory agreement or of the individual planning agreements, or when a change in the plan is required. The lawyer here acts as an arbitral expert. To be sure, the more important the problems in question, the less the parties consider themselves bound by this arbitral opinion. These basic conflicts have to be solved politically.

Termination of the cartel

There is a legal way to dissolve the cartel, just as it was possible legally to inaugurate the international market regulation. However, actual termination of a market regulation system as a whole is very rare. The planning agreement may be changed either because the aims of the cartel have been altered by changes in the economic situation, or because the cartel realizes that its temporary planning aims have been achieved. The latter situation occurred in 1963 in the copper cartel when, from the point of view of the cartel, the market was brought into a "temporary stabilized condition." Furthermore, the methods of implementing the cooperation, the least permanent aspect of the cartel agreements, are changed often without having any effect on the underlying agreements.

Because few enterprises are involved in international cartels today, the question of one enterprise giving notice of some action to the other enterprises—which in earlier times was so important that disputes were taken to arbitration tribunals—has become relatively meaningless. As in international politics, the large enterprises can conclude an international agreement for fifty years and obligate themselves for this period; however, one of the firms can at any time, in effect, end this contractual relationship merely by not applying the contract. A formal notice is not necessary. It is not possible to term this international market regulation an oligopoly just because the implementation of the agreement depends either on the willingness of the participants to fulfill their obligation or on the prerequisite that the economic situation does not change. These are positive contractual arrangements.

International market regulations display an extraordinary vitality. Actual dissolutions of the contract or actual refusals of a party to continue the agreement are relatively rare. The most important reason for such a refusal is a governmental antitrust prosecution. In the cartel members' internal relationships such interferences are factual elements that disturb the balance of power but do not force the cartel group to break apart. None of the participating enterprises is forced to violate its own national law. Each enterprise tries, however, to eliminate the disturbances within its own sphere of influence, sometimes by setting up new subsidiaries. A settlement among all the parties must be attempted when the disturbances cannot be worked out among the individual concerns. In this situation, the planning agreement is temporarily set aside. The cartel is said to have changed temporarily into an oligopoly. Actually, however, the cartel continues to function effectively; the basic regulatory agreement continues to operate to achieve a new regulation with new aims and methods of implementation. Characteristic of this attitude is the fact that during World War II the leading international cartels were considered "suspended" for the duration of the war. The international phosphate cartel is an example. As soon as the Allied Forces had recaptured North Africa, the parties to the cartel (especially American Cyanamid and the French firms) agreed that the suspended cartel had been reestablished. Later, however, it was realized that a complete reorganization of the cartel would be necessary, due to the divided condition of Europe.

In another more recent example, the parties agreed, after dissolution was enforced by cartel legislation, that an interim committee hold consultations as long as necessary until a new agreement was reached. The difference between mere consultations and the actual functioning of a system of market regulation is not very important. The parties keep a line of communication open even if they fail to achieve results. The structure of international market regulation today is so strong that one has to admit that organizations have begun to lead their own lives.

Enforcement of the Contractual System against Third Parties
Factual means

Boycotts and blacklisting have been used in the past to enforce a cartel's contractual system against third parties, and even today these devices still have some importance. More importantly, however, the changes of the cartel's contractual system into a mere understanding among the parties, without any specific form, parallel the changes in the methods of enforcement of the system against third parties. Today the parties use far more subtle methods to protect and enforce their contracts with third parties.

Where the buyers of cartel products or services are also strong enough to influence the structure of the market, a kind of autonomous self-enforcement of the cartel contracts by the large enterprises results; and this does not permit third parties to make successful offers. Examples are the technological contracts that have existed for a long time between an economically strong customer and one or more enterprises of the cartel. Thus, the outsider not only finds a closed circle he can never enter, but he must also recognize that the important customer will put his own technological know-how at the disposal only of the enterprises in the cartel. Therefore, the opportunity to do business with that enterprise does not in fact exist for the third party.

Furthermore, in spite of all technological changes, the leading enterprises in technological developments of the past are still the leaders today. This means that the outsider will find it quite difficult to compete except in very specialized fields.

It is also possible that the nature of the product or of the service forecloses the third party's entrance into the market. For example, the repair of machinery or similar products cannot be successfully undertaken if the repair material or spare parts are exclusively manufactured by cartel enterprises. Whoever purchases such a product is technically excluded from buying the repair material or spare parts from third parties. Thus a third party finds that the market is in fact closed despite the lack of formal agreements. And the exclusive position of the cartel enterprises can be substantially strengthened by regulations that restrict the outsider.

The vertical integration of large enterprises is one of the most effective devices for excluding third parties from the market. The vertically integrated cartel enterprise has so many variations in its policy compared to the outsider, who is merely active at one economic level, that competition is practically impossible. This is especially true if the outsider is supplied by the integrated enterprise. A contractual subjection of the outsider is not necessary to obtain the enforcement of the cartel order.[22]

[22] See testimony of H. Kronstein, U.S. Cong., Senate Comm. on the Judiciary, Subcomm. on Antitrust and Monopoly, *Hearings on Economic Concentration outside the United States*, 90th Cong., 2d Sess., p. 3651 (1968).

Similar effects result from the business policy of an enterprise that has extended its activity into a large number of different products (conglomerate enterprises). This enterprise can enforce that cartel contract which regulates one sphere of its activity by imposing more difficult business conditions on the outsiders in other fields of activity in case of violation of the cartel's contractual system.

The possibilities of enforcing the cartel's contractual system result not only from the business policy of each individual cartel member but also from the business policy of the cartel itself. This is seen when customers, because of their business dealings with the cartel, are placed in a more favorable position than could be obtained in dealings with third parties. An outsider's penetration of the market is impossible unless the cartel enterprises include the outsider in their contractual system. An example is the shipping conferences that grant their customers special premiums if they transport their goods exclusively in cartel ships. If only one nonconference shipper is used, the freight costs increase greatly. Thus, here also the outsider finds a closed market.

Use of exclusive property rights and governmental measures without contractual obligation

Another important method of cartel enforcement against third parties is the utilization of industrial property rights owned by a cartel member or by the cartel itself. As the details will be discussed in a later chapter,[23] it is sufficient here to note that by the use of patents and the threat of litigation the cartel contract can be enforced. It is often enough for the cartel to own one or two exclusive property rights without which the third party cannot be competitive. The patent today no longer has a great importance in the relationship between the parties. However, it is an excellent device to protect the cartel's contractual system against outsiders.

Similar effects can also be obtained by using governmental measures. By setting up minimum safety requirements for machinery and equipment, a market can be so defined that only one or several cartel enterprises can supply that market. Such requirements often result from a suggestion of the cartel's large enterprises.

[23] See Chapter 12.

The Conclusion of License and Supply
Contracts with Third Parties

Another effective method of binding third parties to the cartel's contractual system is to conclude license and supply contracts with them. While these contracts grant the third parties access to certain procedures or products of the cartel enterprises, they also restrict the third parties in their economic freedom of movement. The enforcement of these contracts, and therefore this element of the cartel's contractual system, can be secured with the assistance of the judicial system even if the cartel parties might prefer an appeal to the arbitration tribunal.

8 ～～～～～

Parties to the Contract

The interpreter of international cartels often encounters difficulties in defining the parties bound into a cartel, even though the agreement specifies those subject to it. If a basic regulatory agreement is to be concluded, all firms necessary to enforce the planning agreement must be included. The breadth of a planning agreement often makes it necessary to bring more or different partners into the contract itself to insure a really effective and efficient market regulation.

Formal Parties to the Contract

Because of the oligopolistic structure of international markets today, a rather small number of enterprises is necessary to effectuate a strong cartel, capable of regulating a specific market. Far-reaching international relationships between business entities, corporate or otherwise, permit greater economic influence by an enterprise in many commercial fields. This was not as true in previous decades, when corporate influence was narrow and localized. However, these few members of modern international cartels are not isolated enterprises, but regular entities controlling commercial combines; frequently these are parent companies with numerous integrated subsidiaries, but other "combine heads" have been used.

Because of the multipartite character of the individual cartel members, a question can arise as to the extent to which a parent or a subsidiary can bind other members of its corporate family to the cartel agreement. The draftsmen of cartel agreements apply a rather formalistic method to solve this problem. Whenever the parent company or a subsidiary subjects itself to the rules of an international cartel, only the entity that has formally entered into the cartel agreement is bound by it.

Of course, parties to the cartel agreement may also be obligated under the agreement if their agent was authorized to bind them. For the organizers of international cartels it is only a question of fact as to how far such an agency power exists. Few controversies ever arise between the agent and the principal as to the power of the agent.[1] For instance, a number of cases can be found where a subsidiary initially appears as the party to the cartel but also guarantees that the parent company and its other subsidiaries will act in accordance with the contract. Often the parent will later appear as a party to the contract and ratify all the acts of the subsidiary as fully within the scope of its authorization. This is particularly apparent in the oil industry. National subsidiaries would guarantee that the parent company and other subsidiaries would follow the contract provisions. Later, the American parent would act so much like a party to the contract that the acts of the subsidiary would be considered ratified and accepted as binding on the parent corporation itself.

Supplementary Parties

In addition to the actual parties to the international cartel, other persons often are bound to and benefited by the contract to the same extent as the real parties, without being formal parties to the cartel agreement itself. For example, express provisions in some cartel agreements provide that a particular subsidiary, in addition to the parent company, shall be bound to the agreement and shall also receive the benefits of it. When distribution of licenses is made under the planning agreement, for instance, it may be agreed that certain subsidiaries shall have the same benefits as the parent; however, they are obligated to pay royalties and will accept certain measures of control. This type of clause is often found in cases where a company acting as head of the entire enterprise enters into a cartel agreement.[2] It can also be found in contracts of subsidiaries that have the legal power to benefit or bind the parent or other subsidiary companies.[3]

[1] This may be different in the relationship between principal or agent and third parties; see DECA case, *Wirtschaft und Wettbewerb/Entscheidungssammlung* (WuW/E), p. 107, in which a group of Dutch construction firms acted as the agent for a subsidiary and its sister corporation in the Federal Republic of Germany, Belgium, and Italy without authorization.

[2] See, for instance, Act. 18 of the 1948 Lamp Agreement, which replaced the Phoebus cartel, in Monopolies and Restrictive Practices Commission, *Report on the Supply of Electric Lamps* (Oct. 4, 1951), App. 9; Art. 18 of the Phoebus cartel, *id.*, App. 8. In connection with a licensing agreement see citations in the U.S. Cong., Senate Comm. on the Judiciary, Subcomm. on Antitrust and Monopoly, *Hearings on Administered Prices in the Drug Industry*, 86th Cong., 2nd Sess., Pt. 15, pp. 8364 ff. (1960); Pt. 17, pp. 9664 ff. (1960); Pt. 26, pp. 15392 ff. (1961).

[3] See *Hearings on Administered Prices in the Drug Industry*, n. 2 above, Pts. 17, pp. 10090, 10107, and 26, pp. 15392, 15441.

Responsibility for Actions by Affiliated Enterprises

Normally cartel agreements contain express statements delineating the parent company's liability for the behavior of affiliated enterprises so as to ensure that their behavior is consistent with the cartel agreement.[4] Furthermore, express provisions usually prescribe the extent to which certain technological information acquired as a result of a cartel agreement may be transfered by one enterprise to its related enterprises. The reverse situation is also true. Contracts made by a subsidiary corporation may provide for its liability in the event of any violation of the cartel agreement by its "shareholders."[5] These contracts provide for a procedure that gives the interested parties the opportunity to substitute a new entity in the agreement because of changes within a particular enterprise structure.

Parties Affiliated with the Contract

From the foregoing, it is clear that the substance and importance of the international cartel cannot be fully explained by describing the formal structure and parties of the contract. Around the formal and exposed core of the international cartel exists a shell of those who must be included in the cartel because they are "in fact" under the control of one of the cartel parties. These parties are not outside the cartel arrangement, but rather, because of technology, distribution, or other relationships, are at least partially united with one of the partners of the cartel in a commercial unit and therefore are for all practical purposes subject to the cartel contract. This extension of the cartel relationship, and thereby indirectly of the cartel power, is an essential characteristic of modern international cartels which has not been sufficiently studied. The reason may be that in general the permanently increasing integration of the markets in the modern economy is not being given sufficient consideration. The different elements of this integration have already been referred to several times: the establishment of political or commercial communities; the integration of the several vertical levels of production; the integration of horizontal fields of development and

[4] For instance, §8 of the contract between Britain's M.O. Valve and Radio Corporation of America, Feb. 25, 1962, cited in Monopolies and Restrictive Practices Commission, *Report on the Supply of Electronic Valves and Cathode Ray Tubes* (Dec. 20, 1956), p. 98; for further examples, see *Hearings on Administered Prices in the Drug Industry*, n. 2 above, Pts. 15, pp. 8395, 8446, 8488, and 17, p. 9664.

[5] *Hearings on Administered Prices in the Drug Industry*, n. 2 above, Pts. 17, pp. 10090, 10107, and 26, p. 15756.

production or of adjoining markets; or the integration of the means of distribution. This integration makes it necessary for the organizers of international cartels to extend the cartel's sphere of influence in order to achieve an effective market regulation. This integration also leads to a coordination and combination into a larger commercial unit that can be used by the organizers of the cartel to regulate the total market.

Subjection to the Contract from Adherence to a "Commercial Unit"

A "commercial unit" can be described as the coordination of single or corporate persons or of their plants (regardless of formal ownership) for the exercise of market influence in a specific commercial sector. It makes no difference whether influence in a commercial sector is based on the relationship between individual companies in the same enterprise, a technological relation, or an integrated distribution system.[6] The decisive point is that on the basis of a centralized leadership a centralized unit is formed or at least parallel or complementary behavior is secured in a definite commercial field. Two conditions would appear to be necessary. The unity must relate to a "certain commercial field," and it must be a true "unity." However, it should be pointed out that both of these conditions should not be strictly defined, since what is at issue is the intent of the cartel organizers.

The parties also establish the "commercial field" or market covered by the cartel regulation. The parties must decide whether only one market or several horizontal or vertical markets are to be regulated. This regulation may be undertaken with the knowledge that related markets may be affected. Obviously, the commercial unit must be of significant relationship to the economic sector under cartel regulation in order to be useful. But that does not mean that there has to be complete identity of commercial activities between the unit and the cartel regulation. It is quite possible that one enterprise could belong to different commercial units in different market fields.

The necessary "unity" may arise out of the coordination of unilateral management, or in exceptional cases out of coordinated management, in such a way that parallel or complementary action occurs. This

[6] See H. Kronstein, *Die abhängige juristische Person* (Munich, 1931), pp. 72 ff., and for literature on the law of corporations with more than one enterprise see E. R. Latty, *Subsidiaries and Affiliated Corporations: A Study in Stockholders' Liability* (Chicago, 1936), *passim*; R. S. Stevens, *Handbook on the Law of Private Corporations* (2d ed.; St. Paul, 1949), pp. 85 ff.

parallel action must arise independently from the creation of the cartel; however, it is sufficient if the action exists only within the framework necessary for the purposes of market regulation.

Commercial unit arising from a factual subjection

If a cartel member has complete control over another enterprise, it becomes the duty of the cartel member to use this control in the interest of the cartel.

The most significant examples in this area are the companies dominated by a member of the cartel through corporate control.[7] The cartel partner (the parent company) exerts control over one or several companies (the subsidiaries) by means of shareholder ownership. Thus, the concept of the "combine unit" emerges, a concept which goes beyond that of the commercial unit. The combine unit covers all of the activities of the "concern," while the commercial unity only covers those areas regulated by the cartel. On the other hand, it is possible to establish a commercial unit of several persons or companies for the purpose of market regulation even if they do not form a unit. Thus, it can be seen that the combine unit and the commercial unit are two intersecting circles. The concept of the combine unit is important only if a commercial unit also exists in which the parent corporation and its subsidiaries complement each other from a commercial, industrial, or other point of view. A conglomerate control in which controlling and controlled companies, for the time being at least, are operating in other fields of business is exactly the opposite and may be helpful to examine our point. The American copper producers illustrate the concept of the combine unit. These companies, which own copper sources in the United States, Canada, and in other countries, have acquired complete control of enterprises that manufacture products mainly from copper, such as cables. The copper mine companies treat these other companies as part of their own enterprises by allotting definite quantities of copper to them. Further, the copper producers set the price at which merchandise manufactured from the copper is to be sold on the market and establish other conditions that buyers of the product must meet to obtain delivery.

This structure in the copper industry is a typical example of vertical enterprise control. The companies that produce products manufactured from raw materials are subject to the control of the raw material

[7] See L. Raiser, 33 *Schriften des Vereins für Sozialpolitik*, 51 ff. (n.s., 1946).

producers who through their stock holdings are in a position to influence the management of the subsidiary. As a consequence, the modern subsidiary corporation, while remaining an independent corporate entity from all outward appearances, has only such free will as its controlling interests permit. It must be accepted that the subsidiary is not a free agent. The parent in clearly capable of influencing the subsidiary to act in accordance with the cartel contract.[8]

In addition to direct corporate control, there are other cases of dominance which may or may not be combined units. But in any case, they are commercial units because of coordinated action under central management for the purpose of market regulation. In these cases control of the enterprise is removed from its formal owners and given to another entity so that the latter can subject it to the control of the commercial unit. To accomplish this it is not necessary to transfer legal title for the plants to the management of the commercial unit; it is sufficient that the management be given extensive control over these shares. Such control may be obtained by such legal devices as voting trust, trust agreements with a bank which then votes in the interests of the management of the commercial unit (especially in connection with appointment of officers or agents of the corporation), or an irrevocable power of attorney which may be limited to the appointment of the board and to the execution of certain policies that are in accordance with the wishes of the commercial unit.

Société Bull in France is a good example for this situation. Bull owned important research laboratories and plants that were engaged in research and development in the electrical industry. A plan was conceived to sell the majority of the shares of this company to General Electric, which was interested in obtaining a position competitive with the International Business Machine Corporation (IBM) in the computer field. Had this plan been carried out, General Electric would have been able to elect a new board at Bull, thus gaining access to the various products and research undertakings of Bull. The French government objected to this arrangement, whereupon it was agreed that certain phases of Bull's operations would be isolated from the general management of its operations and, although still finally under Bull

[8] For this reason the Reichsgericht (the former German Supreme Court on Civil and Criminal Law) in several cases ordered the sole shareholder of the corporation to take certain actions which were only possible of performance by the corporation itself (99 RGZ 232; 160 RGZ 257; compare however 142 RGZ 219).

ownership, these operations, primarily research and production in the computer field, would be subject to a special management which would insure that the research results would be used in the interests of French industry and the French government.

While this example is not typical because of the existence of political and military considerations, still it is an excellent case to illustrate the point that corporate entities may agree to put certain plants, research facilities, or work in connection with the manufacture of new products into a special division subject to the management of a new commercial unit that includes portions and parts of several legal personalities and corporations. This type of unity is especially prevalent in fields of new technological development that might later become the basis for a new technological cartel.

The integration into a commercial unit of a "negative" type can also take place by means of patents and trademarks. It is clearly possible to distribute patent licenses in such a way that the licensee, even if otherwise controlled by a third party, can be limited by the patent itself. A good illustration of how a company formally controlled through capital investment may be transformed into a subsidiary made dependent on patents is the General Aniline and Film Corporation.[9] Originally, this company was a subsidiary of I.G. Chemie in Basel, which in turn was a subsidiary of I.G. Farben. The General Aniline and Film Corporation acted on behalf of I.G. Farben in the United States in the field of dyestuffs and special pharmaceutical products. General Aniline and Film Corporation manufactured and distributed certain products on its own and also distributed products of the parent corporation. It also did certain research work assigned to it.

Later, General Aniline and Film Corporation was placed under the control of the alien property custodian, and the relationship with I.G. Farben was severed. As far as the ownership of shares in General Aniline were concerned, they had only been owned or associated with I.G. Chemie anyway, which was now called Interhandel. Interhandel had also abandoned its connection with I.G. Farben. However, what latitude did this really leave the General Aniline and Film Corporation? The corporation had access only to the processes and information given to it by I.G. Farben over the years. It had only those patent rights and licenses and only those trademarks that it had received from

[9] Kaufmann v. Société International Pour Participations Industrielles et Commerciales S.A., 343 U.S. 156 (1951).

I.G. Farben. Thus, the General Aniline and Film Corporation was restricted in its movements within the scope of the I.G. Farben interests, no matter who its official owner might be. As long as General Aniline depended on I.G. patents and procedures, it could not control its own future. Similarly with respect to trademarks, as long as General Aniline was obligated to sell its photocopy products with the trademark "Agfa," General Aniline was restricted as to the quality and manner of distribution, and especially in the territory to be supplied.

In short, through a combination of patent and trademark powers, the licensee can become so dependent on the licensor that the licensor can, at will, include the plants of the licensee in the system of market regulation regardless of formal ownership and control of these companies. As a result, the freedom of action of these companies and of their legal owners can become so circumscribed that there can be no opposition to the direction of the management of the commercial unit and its integration into the market-regulating system.

Aside from corporate control and control by means of patents and trademarks, there are other methods in the field of technology whereby enterprises can be included in a commercial unit. An enterprise may subject some of its plants to the unilateral technological management of the commercial unit in spite of continuously existing legal title in an "independent" company.[10] This subjection can also occur if utilization of developments, inventions, or patents is placed under the management of the commercial unit. This is true only if the plant has a clearly defined function easily adapted to the purposes of the economic unit, which is certainly the case whenever the direction of research, the distribution of research work, or the methods and conditions imposed on the use of research results are the responsibility of the management of the commercial unit.

The above result may be accomplished legally by granting to the owner of the plant a license for certain patents or processes with the stipulation that the owner will only be entitled to use this license with the approval of the management of the commercial unit. Or a formal partnership or joint venture agreement may be concluded in which the commercial unit is appointed as managing partner. While this type of contract gives quite a strong position to the one outside partner, it is tolerated because of the access granted to certain research results and

[10] As for instance in the Société Bull controversy described earlier.

because of the payments received for the agreement to permit management by the commercial unit.[11]

An example of the contractual constructions which in law or in fact make it impossible for the owner to oppose orders of the management of the commercial unit is the exclusive-dealing clause prevalent in gasoline supply contracts with gas stations. Such clauses stipulate that in return for supplying gasoline, the owner will not sell any other oil or tires than those designated by the management of the commercial unit. As a result, this management for all practical purposes controls the gasoline station.

Commercial unit based on contractual obligations

The parties to the cartel agreement can have contractual relationships with other parties which are so expensive that these other parties have no chance to use freely their own plants in opposition to the desires of the cartel partners in their market regulation. Here contractual obligations concerning production, distribution, services, and technological research may be of such a magnitude that the enterprise subject to these obligations no longer has any freedom of action. In effect, the cartel partner may use the plants of the other contracting party as if they were a part of its own operation. While the enterprise subject to the contractual obligation does not have the "right" to disobey the command of the dominating enterprise, it may still have the "power" to do so; however, in practice, no enterprise would assume the consequences of such defiance.

Four examples taken from the areas of production, distribution, services, and technological research aptly point out this type of contractual obligation. All of these examples show how a party to the contract arrangement may subject plants to the cartel regulation without ever having title to or actual legal control of the plants.

With respect to regulation of production, arrangements are made between the management of the commercial unit and each of the participating parties providing that the plants of these individual parties my only produce certain definite products, in a definite amount, and in a definite place.[12] A relationship between the management and the

---

[11] This kind of contract has now been acknowledged by the West German legislature (292 § I Nr. 3 AktG 1965; cf. G. Loss, "Betriebsführungsverträge und damit verbundene Generalvollmacht," 1963 Der Betriebs-Berater 615 ff.).

[12] In this connection the problem of regulation of supplying certain firms with essential material is in point.

enterprises obligated under the various patent licenses may be so far-reaching that the enterprise can no longer develop a field of activity on its own. These contractual restrictions upon production in combination with patent licenses can easily give a third person the power to coerce this producer into the market regulation scheme as a controlled unit.

With respect to distribution, trading companies often are bound by contract provisions that stipulate the area, manner, and conditions under which they can sell. Consequently, the cartel partner to whom such a company is obligated can include the dependent operation in its own organization.

With respect to services, shipping companies are often bound by contract to use their shipping space only in accordance with the orders of another enterprise, which is usually one of its largest clients.

In the area of research and development, it is often provided, by contract, that a firm will undertake specific research projects to the exclusion of other firms and with the restriction that any change in the program requires the consent of the management of the unit. Frequently, each of the individual companies is only given a small part of the total development program which can only be profitably used in coordination with the other parts, under the management of the unit. While these individual companies might obtain patent licenses from the total development program in order to carry out their limited research, these are of little help because the contractual agreements so limit the firm that it is basically confined to the utilization of the results of its project.

The existence of such obligations as these is not conclusive proof that a commercial unit exists between obligee and obligor. The basis of the unit described herein is that one party to the contract can influence the other party so strongly that if the first enters into a cartel agreement with third parties he can be assured that his obligor will be encompassed within the cartel structure. This is particularly true when one the contracting parties is a powerful firm and likely to be a member of an international cartel. Thus, the cartel can also regulate the market through those dependent enterprises that are tied to the cartel by contracts with the individual cartel members.

Commercial unit based on coordination of activities

In addition to vertically organized commercial units or those based on control and dependence, commercial units occasionally are organized along the lines of a federation of independent states as found in international law.[13] In this federation the members are relatively equal and, through a specified division of duties among the parties, each protects the interests of the entire federation within its own particular sphere. This is especially true in the area of market regulation. As a result, a commercial unit is born not out of dependence but simply because the parties do not desire to act any other way than as a unit.

A clear example of this "positive" type of unit is the relationship between the Aluminum Corporation of America (Alcoa) and Aluminium, Ltd., of Canada.[14] To understand the current form of this relationship, it is necessary to go back to the beginning of the cooperation between the two enterprises. Originally, during the development of aluminum, the Canadian company was part of the American company. Later the two companies became "independent" of each other; however, the same persons controlled the majority shares in both companies. Later, with the growing extension of American antitrust legislation to cover international agreements on restraint of trade, the Canadian company was entrusted with the task not only of protecting its own interest on the international market but also of protecting the interests of Alcoa in such a way that Alcoa would be a party to the international regulation just as if it had concluded the agreement itself.

Evidence introduced in the famous antitrust case *United States v. Aluminum Co. of America* [15] leaves no doubt that during the period between the two world wars the Canadian company organized the world market not only for itself but also for Alcoa. The Canadian company entered contracts with the German, English, and French aluminum producers, which agreed that the United States should not be supplied with aluminum without consent of the American firm. It was also agreed that bauxite should only be imported into the United States under the control of Alcoa.

In order to fully understand the present situation, it is necessary to realize that when parties are forced by national legislation to change their relationship, they only change as much as necessary to meet the requirements of the legislation. Thus, when Alcoa and Aluminium,

---

[13] Raiser, n. 7 above, p. 56.

[14] See Chapter 4; also testimony of H. Kronstein, *Hearings on Economic Concentration outside the United States before the Subcomm. on Antitrust and Monopoly of the Senate Comm. on the Judiciary*, 90th Cong., 2d Sess., Pt. 7 p. 3651 (1968).

[15] 148 F. 2d 416 (2d Cir. 1945).

Ltd., of Canada were forced to separate before World War I due to increasing unfavorable antitrust legislation in the United States, it should not be a surprise that this separation was merely formal and did not really change the essence of the relationship between the two companies. But an uninformed observer would have paused before the spectacle of the Canadian company entering agreements with companies from numerous other countries concerning commitments not to supply the United States.

Today the Canadian export price governs international business transactions with countries that do not have an aluminum production of their own. Further, this price governs in countries like England that do not have enough of their own production to determine the price within their own market. This world price is not established on the basis of any real market developments or upon competitive conditions. It is a price determined to a large extent by the Canadian enterprises and is considered as binding on "competitors." This price relationship is coordinated with other elements of market regulation, such as participation in joint bauxite ventures or in a division of markets in European and other countries.

Alcoa, which generally sells at a higher price in the United States than the Canadian price, respects the Canadian price whenever it or one of its subsidiaries appears on the world market. Alcoa would expose itself to the danger of dumping procedures in Canada if it were to supply Canada at the Canadian price. At the same time, the Canadian company does not do what independent enterprises in a competitive relationship would normally do, namely, sell at the American price in sales in the United States and thereby evolve a uniform North American price. In any case, true competitors would not utilize export prohibitions to prevent exports to the United States. The Canadian company has agreed to rules similar to those of a federation and is then entrusted with the task of regulating the international market, particularly with respect to prices. Alcoa accepted the same federation rules and its task is the regulation of the United States market.

Indeed, this is a special new form of a relationship between two companies. It is not an enterprise or a concern relationship, as there is no centralized management; neither is this a cartel, because these are not two independent firms concluding an agreement on market regulation. But it is a unit that has developed between these independent partners, a type of federal unit in which the Canadian company exercises one function and Alcoa another. They have coordinated their activities to such an extent that they appear as a unit in their relationship with third parties. While in the case of the first two commercial units mentioned, the parties are not able or were not allowed to deviate from the wishes of the unit, here is a commercial unit in which the parties do not desire to exceed the functions granted to them within the unit.

Lastly, this type of unit can not be regarded as an oligopoly, which structure suggests itself at first glance. The distinguishing characteristic of an oligopoly is the independence of decision of each of the enterprises in the so-called oligopoly. This independence exists even though it is assumed that each enterprise will be influenced in its market behavior by the expected behavior of the other enterprises and will direct its own actions accordingly. In the case at hand, however, there are two enterprises which appear on the international market as a commercial unit and which act under the expectation that each will exercise functions for itself and for the other.[16] One might refer to this phenomenon as a synthetic oligopoly, that is, a combination of enterprises which appear to be an oligopoly to the observer but which in reality form a system similar to a federation of independent states.

Borderline cases

Often it is difficult to determine whether the company is actually part of a commercial unit or not. In describing the restrictions on the world copper market, it was noted that American Metal owns about 49 per cent of the shares of Roan Selection Trust (RST). This company, together with the Anglo American Corporation, was responsible for the production restrictions and for the supporting purchases on the London Metal Exchange during the years 1956 to 1963. With respect to this relationship between RST and American Metal, four possibilities exist: they might have been two independent companies that concluded a cartel agreement with each other; RST may possibly have belonged to a commercial unit under the management and direction of American Metal; RST conceivably was acting not only for its own interest but at the same time as a representative of the interest of American Metal; finally, there may have been an oligopolistic coordination of independent enterprises even though participation by the American company was unusually strong.

[16] See Chapter 4 above, n. 62.

The determination of this question is not a legal but a factual one. The facts to be taken into account to resolve the question are, in addition to the participation of 49 per cent of the shares of the RST, the close cooperation of both companies in the financing and sale of the copper produced and certain personnel entanglements between the two companies.

In any event, it is almost certain that RST, as well as American Metal, benefited from the restraints of competition in the copper field. Restraints of production not only took place in Rhodesia but also in the American plants of American Metal. It is almost impossible to imagine that these two companies did not belong to the same commercial unit, considering their close cooperation and their parallel interests and activities. However, it seems to be impossible to establish exactly which type of commercial unit characterizes the case, whether it is just a dependence in fact or a coordination within which each partner has the power to exercise some of the joint functions. In any case, it would be wrong to designate a case of this type as a genuine oligopoly. The notion of the oligopoly presupposes that the management of each enterprise determines its market behavior independently of other competitors. Indeed, this complete and real independence of the enterprises is an absolute precondition for the existence of an oligopoly, even though it is true that any decision by one of the independent enterprises will influence the others. In the case of the Roan Selection Trust in its relationship to American Metal, this independence is not present. The only question is how far does this dependence go and whether there is some coordination under a management of outsiders. The parties were perhaps influenced by American antitrust legislation or by the development policies of a producing country, such as Zambia. The parties may have considered it useful not to show any clear relationship but at the same time wanted to establish an effective coordination of the actions of the two enterprises in the market.

In conclusion, it should be noted that the commercial unit is important in any case where an enterprise that is or may become a partner in an international market regulation is in a position to influence the behavior of several enterprises or plants in such a way that the unit's actions complement the market regulation of the cartel. This can be accomplished either through vertical control or other forms of dependence or by consent to coordinated actions. It is not really important whether these enterprises are otherwise independent or whether they belong to another commercial unit. The decisive point is that in the pertinent commercial field the dominating and powerful enterprise of the unit influences the other member enterprises. Therefore, in the negotiation of the regulatory international cartel agreement, the dominating enterprise of the unit may not only rely on its own power but also on the power elements resulting from the integration of enterprises into a commercial unit.

Internal Organization of the Commercial Unit

In order to discuss profitably the influence of the commercial unit upon the making and effectiveness of international cartels, a brief discussion of the internal organization of the commercial unit is necessary. The first factor to note is that a commercial unit is an entity forged by means of power. The participating parties are not—except in the typical cases of the federation of enterprises—parties of equal power. On the contrary, the parties are of unequal status and consequently internally organized into a hierarchy with the most powerful enterprises influencing all other parts. As a result, many lower-echelon plants and companies belonging to the commercial unit may be inclined to believe that the management decisions to which they are subject are not made or influenced by them but are made from the "outside." Nevertheless, the enterprises that belong to the commercial unit cannot be considered as third enterprises which are merely exposed to and affected by the actual forces present in the market. As part of the organization of the commercial unit, they are directly subject to the direction of the management of the unit.

Regardless of the formal-legal basis of the position of the managing agency of the commercial unit, power is always concentrated in one place where it can be exercised and enforced to obtain specific market behavior of the individual enterprises. In practice, the management can allocate the exercise of this power in any manner it chooses. This power may be largely delegated to others. For example, a simple accounting agency may be assigned an important function or a special agency may be entrusted with far-reaching power to enforce interests of the management.

Of special significance are cases in which the exercise of power of the commercial unit is decentralized among different agencies, including the various companies in different countries. This type of structure is almost a necessity in the federated type of commercial unit.[17] For example, in the field of aluminum, prior to World War II and the American antitrust action, the internal relation between Alcoa and Aluminium, Ltd., was organized in this way. As shown, Aluminium, Ltd., organized the world market outside of the United States in a manner compatible with the interests of Alcoa. Today, Aluminium, Ltd., again represents the interests of this continuously existing commercial unit. Often, Aluminium, Ltd., acts against its own interests when pricing its exports to the United States.

The Commercial Unit and Market Regulation

Capacity to act in relationship to third parties

An analysis of the internal organization of the commercial unit offers only slight assistance in resolving the question of who is authorized to act on behalf of the commercial unit in its external relations and, in particular, who has the power to bind the commercial unit to market regulation agreements. While the internal management may utilize all the plants and instrumentalities of the commercial unit in connection with the making of a cartel, still, it is not at all necessary for it to act as the contracting agent with third parties. Often subsidiaries make market-regulating contracts with third parties which include the understanding that their parents shall be bound. The subsidiary guarantees that the parent company will act in accordance with the contract; this function of the subsidiary may only be formal, since the subsidiary on its own would normally never assume such an obligation.

Today a frequent method used in making market-regulating contracts is one in which one of the parties or perhaps both of the parties are Swiss or Luxembourg holding companies. It is unimportant which interests are formally owned by the holding companies. The important point is that while as a matter of form the holding company alone is bound to the agreement, the agreement is actually made in the interests of the commercial unit, and the management thereof considers itself bound just as if it had concluded the agreement. Thus, as in the example above of the subsidiary, the holding company acts for the entire commercial unit on the basis of delegated power.

Inclusion of the commercial unit in the market regulation

Regularly in former times and sometimes even today there have been cartel contracts that explicitly provide for the extent to which each

17 See text at n. 13 above.

cartel partner must exercise its power over the commercial unit under its control for the overall market regulation of the cartel. Specifically, this takes place either by a direct formal obligation on the part of the dependent companies or by the acceptance of an obligation by the party to the cartel to ensure that these enterprises and plants will abide by the contract. In these agreements it is not at all unusual to enumerate all those plants or enterprises that are actually part of the commercial unit of the cartel partner. Moreover, in some cases the cartel partners even obligate themselves to ensure that enterprises becoming part of the commercial unit after the conclusion of the cartel agreement will abide by the requirements.[18]

But modern cartel agreements, which usually relate to only the most essential points, have no regulations governing the extent to which the cartel partners are required to bring the members of the commercial unit under their control to assist actively in achieving the aims of the agreement.[19] Generally, however, an agreement between the parties exists that no plant or enterprise subject to the control of a party to the cartel agreement may be used for a purpose inconsistent with its cartel obligations. It is not necessary that the obligations be imposed on the entire commercial unit. Often only a part of the commercial unit is considered bound by the agreement. It all depends on the purposes and aims of the international market regulation, as well as on the geographic and factual conditions of the market. If, for example, the German subsidiary of an American oil enterprise were to enter the European market regulation with French or Italian firms as the authorized agent for the American oil concern, the entire commercial unit would be bound to enforce the market regulation in the international field only enough to guarantee the execution and performance of the contract involved.

Each of the cartel partners is obligated to use its voting power plus its organizational and contractual influence over its subsidiaries to assure compliance with the cartel regulations. The cartel partners are also committed to defend the cartel agreement against violations taking place in a plant belonging to the commercial unit, even if the owner of this plant is not entirely a part of the commercial unit. In cases of the

[18] According to the German law, subsidiaries are obligated to abstain from acts which are prohibited to its parent corporation (H. Rasch, *Deutsches Konzernrecht* [3d ed.; Cologne, 1966], pp. 197 ff.).

[19] In general, see Kronstein, n. 6 above, pp. 72 ff. The specific problems of the modern industry have not yet been investigated.

coordinated (or federated) unit, it can be assumed that the members of the unit will freely abide by the cartel regulation. If they do not so conform to the regulation or only abide by it for a short time, or if a substantial interference in the cartel structure takes place, there is a certain danger that the cartel may break apart.

Examples of control over corporate management in the
interest of each of the basic cartel types

Partners in a technological cartel assume certain obligations on behalf of the commercial units dependent on them. They guarantee that all technological research undertaken in one of the plants or companies under the partner's command will be available to other members of the cartel. They have to prevent the enterprises of the commercial unit from undertaking research from which the cartel partner itself is excluded. They must insure that no plant or enterprise will use technological information it has received in a manner inconsistent with the cartel's provisions of purpose. On the other side, the cartel partners are given freedom to direct research projects or to distribute the results within the commercial unit. They may in some instances distribute among members of their commercial unit all information obtained from the technological cartel. However, there may be exceptions to this disclosure; for instance, certain research projects might only be carried on in the country of the parent company for reasons of national security.

The subsidiary has no rights of its own based on the technological agreement to demand from the cartel partners the transfer of research results and developed processes. Any right or claim against the parent company or management corporation depends on the structure of the total enterprise or contractual relations within the commercial unit, particularly when the subsidiary itself has contributed substantially to the research work.

The responsibilities of the cartel partners in a raw material cartel include the behavior of the enterprises that process the raw material or use it in manufacturing. In the American copper market it was considered only natural that the copper producers would fix the sales prices of the products made from copper by their subsidiaries. And there is an equivalent obligation among the cartel members to make their price rulings consistent with the purposes and aims of the cartel.

The members of an industrial products cartel assume the obligation to see that no measures are taken in the national distribution agencies that would be inconsistent with the aims and purposes of the cartel. It does not matter whether these violations of cartel rules are by one of the subsidiaries or by another dependent party.

In each of these three cases, the dependent entities must adhere to the regulations of the cartel, but have no legal right to benefit from the cartel agreement.

Legal consequences of behavior inconsistent with the cartel agreement

Underlying all of these cases is the question of how the international cartel as a whole or the cartel partners individually may react if an enterprise integrated into a commercial unit of one of the cartel partners acts inconsistently with the cartel regulations.

The first line of defense against such acts is for the cartel partner who is a member of the commercial unit of the nonconforming company to use all measures within its power to assure relief or to find a satisfactory solution within its own organization. If the partner is unable to reach a solution, then collective involvement by the cartel is possible.

A greater difficulty arises, however, when a subsidiary or holding company is called upon to assure obedience to cartel regulations by its parent company. As already mentioned, such a guarantee may be assumed by a subsidiary even though not explicitly written into the formal agreement. But only an uninformed outsider would ask how the cartel would react if the subsidiary said that it was not able to exercise enough influence over the parent company to guarantee behavior in accordance with the wishes of the cartel. It has already been pointed out that the making of an international cartel agreement is such an important and far-reaching decision for the enterprise that it can only be made with the approval of the parent enterprise. All the other parties to the cartel base their decisions on this fact. The other parties can not only be sure that the parent enterprise has given its approval at the time the contract was made, but they can also be sure that the parent company will not undertake commercial measures that will disturb the balance of power within the cartel. If such measures are taken almost no effective sanctions can be taken against the subsidiary. The members of the cartel will simply try to reach in the formal mediation proceeding a settlement that produces somehow a new balance of power. And thus again the subsidiary in issue will have to look after the interests of the entire enterprise.

The effects of market regulation on the commercial unit

A market-regulating agreement certainly will not make the commercial unit and the enterprises comprising that unit formal parties to the contract or even collateral parties to the agreement. But, by virtue of the fact that the management of the commercial unit enters into such a contract, the members of the commercial unit are either benefited or harmed by the contract and consequently affiliated with it.

These component enterprises are affected by the general rules and regulations of the cartel agreement, not because the cartel as such confronts them with its commercial and economic power, but because of their association with one of the parties to the cartel agreement. The subsidiary or dependent enterprise is restricted in its freedom of action merely by its dependence on one of the parties to the cartel. Consequently, its obligation goes only as far as directed by the cartel partner through its management of the commercial unit. Since these integrated enterprises are used by the management as instruments of restraint of competition, their freedom is very limited.

As far as a commercial unit is concerned, in which the elements shall not act against the rules of the cartel while they have the power to do so, it often experiences effects from the cartel regulation similar to those of third parties. This is because these enterprises are, in general, on the opposite side of the market regulation.

But it must be noted that often these dependent enterprises are not directly subject to the market regulations of the planning contract; if they are subject to these regulations, it is only to achieve the aim of market regulation toward third parties. This becomes obvious when the cartel partners enforce a price regulation upon their exclusive retailers. Here the real third party is the consumer. The retailers are, as affected enterprises, only participating in the execution of the price regulation under the direction of a cartel partner. In the case of commercial units organized horizontally, with equal rights, the cartel agreement concluded by one member of the unit is also binding on the others but not because of the exertion of force. The obligation results from a diversion of tasks based on the will of the equal partners of the unit.

Lastly, it must always be kept in mind that while the members of the commercial unit are restricted in their freedom of action, they do derive many benefits from affiliation with the cartel arrangement through membership in that unit.

9 〰〰〰〰

Cartels and Conflict of Laws

Enterprises today may avoid being drawn into judicial proceedings where the substantive law of the forum is disagreeable to them. They are completely free to decide among themselves upon the specific foreign substantial law, foreign court, or arbitration tribunal which will determine any disputes that may arise.

Manipulation of Conflicts of Rules

An American observer of this development has to understand fully the extent to which as a matter of fact and practice the organizers, including the American organizers, are fully authorized to use not only their own law but any law they wish. The following are basic points of the eventual utilization of legal institutions and legal rules for the purpose of the organization of international market regulation: (1) The rules of international conflicts of law authorize generally an American or foreigner to include in any contract or agreement the express provision that the performance of a contract or agreement be subject to any law the organizers may stipulate. (2) The freedom of the organizers to establish legal entities whether corporations or otherwise, protected by principles of international public law, including international treaties on commerce and friendship, gives organizers the chance to designate and determine the nationality of their "partners" to any agreement of cartel character. (3) The parties are free to distribute industrial property rights, patents, trademarks, copyrights, or rights in know-how or unpatented technological development—protected by the different laws on industrial property as well as the pertinent international treaties. (4) The organizing parties are fully free to enter into arbitration agreements subjecting contracts, agreements, or individual litigation as to license rights or the validity of industrial property rights, or the results of exchange of information and know-how, or any other type of disputes in organizations to the "whim of friendly courts." [1]

[1] G. Kegel, *Internationales Privatrecht: Ein Studienbuch* (Munich, 1964), pp. 212, 410, 413-414; E. Steindorff, *Sachnormen im internationalen Privatrecht*

This power of the parties to utilize rules on conflicts of law, corporations, or distribution of industrial property rights as well as the subordination of all these points in full or in part under arbitration tribunals convenient to their interest, are effective instrumentalities of the organizations designated as international cartels.[2] It is obvious that the organizers themselves know very well which laws are more beneficial to them with respect to corporations and their activities, or to the distribution of industrial property, or to arbitration. The rules for conflicts of law are just another legal instrument of international market regulation.

The present trend of the conflicts of law in the United States, in Germany, and in Switzerland, making conflicts of law a tool of business power, will be reviewed in this chapter.

If a transaction has implications in more than one state, conflict of law provides rules to decide which national law is to be applied to the set of facts giving rise to contact. A "point of contact" is used to determine whether the legal system of a given country can be applied to a transaction. The following analysis will deal with two types of contact points: objective (those the parties cannot change at their own will, e.g., change of citizenship) and optional (those the parties can influence or even determine at will, e.g., agreements on the application of foreign law).

Property, Family, and Inheritance Law

For multistate property under family and inheritance law, the parties must leave it to the judge to determine the law; the judge "chooses" the law. The parties themselves, in these areas of the law, cannot affect the principal elements of the facts to bring the case under a desired jurisdiction. In property, the *lex rei sitae* governs, and the laws

---

(Frankfort on the Main, 1958), pp. 11 ff.; E. Rabel, "Das Problem der Qualifikation," 5 *Zeitschrift für ausländisches und internationales Privatrecht* 241 ff. (1931); G. Kegel, "Der Gegenstand des internationalen Privatrechts," in *Festschrift für Leo Raape* (Hamburg, 1948), pp. 13 ff.; W. Goldschmidt, 4 *Österreichische Zeitschrift für öffentliches Recht* 121 ff. (1952); P. H. Neuhaus, *Die Grundbegriffe des internationalen Privatrechts* (Berlin, 1962), pp. 50 ff., 68 ff.

[2] W. Dörinkel, *Internationales Kartellrecht* (Berlin, 1932), pp. 54, 65–66 ff.; A. Nussbaum, *Deutsches internationales Privatrecht* (Tübingen, 1932), p. 281; H. Friedländer, *Konzernrecht* (Mannheim, 1927), pp. 310 ff.; M. Wolff, *Private International Law* (Oxford, 1950), p. 122; B. Aubin, "Internationale Kartelle im internationalen Privatrecht," 1940 *Kartell-Rundschau* 33 ff., 65 ff., 97 ff.

of citizenship, domicile, and inheritance are equally difficult to manipulate.

Corporation Law and the Law of Obligations

Mutual exchange contracts

In contract and corporation law, the parties do have the power to influence the determination of applicable law, either directly or indirectly, by so arranging the points of contact that the facts fit a given national choice of law rule. In this way it is possible to influence the applicability of substantive law. When the conflict rules of a country do not permit parties to a contract or organizers of a corportion to choose a foreign law, the manipulation of contact points (such as the place of performance or the seat of the corporation) may permit the desired effects. These points of contact are clearly manipulable, even by one of the parties alone, and they are generally the basis of the courts' determination of which law shall be applied.

The power to influence points of contact is not of course unlimited. Ordinary exchange or sales contracts in the regular course of business, or the organization of subsidiaries in the normal expansion of an enterprise, are limited by commercial and economic realities and by reasonable commercial judgment. There is probably good reason for a legal system to support the freedom of the parties to choose the applicable law in ordinary business transactions, because such determinations generally affect only the parties themselves and the public interest is not in question.

Contracts of market-regulating organizations

On the other hand, market-dominating enterprises, or groups of such enterprises, or their responsible agents may choose a legal system other than that of the countries affected and may effectively enforce this legal order. This is made possible by the general rules of international law on contracts and corporations. Thus a legal system of one state with a purely formal connection to a set of facts may replace that of other states more vitally interested in the business at hand.[3] Even for ordinary exchange contracts in the course of business, where the choice of law is limited by strict factual indicators, an organization of corporations regulating world markets may so manipulate the de-

[3] United States v. General Electric Co., 82 F. Supp. 753, 827 ff.

terminant facts (such as the place of performance of the apparent prevailing interests) as to make even these contracts subject to the law it chooses.[4] It is remarkable that parties to international cartels have a greater power to choose and enforce legal systems convenient to them than do parties to regular exchange agreements. There is an important distinction between the legal character of the power to choose applicable law in a case of a cartel agreement and that power in the case of a simple exchange contract. When the parties to an exchange agreement determine the law to be applied to their contract, they affect only the relationship between themselves. But when the organizers of a long-term market-regulating cartel choose the applicable law, they determine the law to be applied not only between themselves but to the entire market. Thus the power to choose the applicable law in the case of a cartel amounts in practice to the power to establish a quasi-public order.[5] Therefore the conflicts-of-law rules in all the agreements dealing with more or less "pure" international private law must be separated from conflicts-of-law rules governing the fields covered by private market regulations. In the latter case, these rules serve to give the market-dominating enterprise or group of enterprises the legally recognized power to determine the legal order under which they themselves will operate and to which they will subject others dealing with them.

The use of the principles of conflicts of law to enforce economic power depends completely upon the recognition by the court before which the case is pending that this exercise of power is "legal." The question of choice of law cannot be separated from the designation of the forum before which the cases are to be litigated. Conflict of laws is inseparably related to international procedural law. Two devices insure not only that the *lex fori* will not conflict with the interest of the parties to the cartel, but also that it will be helpful in the enforcement of cartel order. The first involves arbitration: a great number of countries grant to contracting parties a broad freedom to choose the court to enforce the arbitration award. The second device involves the designation of arbitrary places of performance or the creation of member corporations in favorable jurisdictions to utilize conflict rules that pre-

---

[4] H. Kronstein, "Kartelle, internationale," in K. Strupp and H.-J. Schlochauer, eds., *Wörterbuch des Völkerrechts* (Berlin, 1960), II, 206.

[5] A. L. Corbin, *A Comprehensive Treatise on the Working Rules of Contract Law* (St. Paul, 1962), V A, 91 ff.

fer the law of the place of performance or that of the seat of one of the corporations. While the inseparability of the substantive and procedural conflicts-of-law rules cannot be overlooked, for convenience of presentation they will be discussed separately.

Conflicts-of-law rules in the leading industrial countries, as interpreted by their courts, are useful for international private market regulation. As a result, the autonomy of the parties to international cartels is almost without limitation and is not seriously affected by the *ordre public* (public policy) restriction on private autonomy (considered essential by some writers). How could such a development possibly come about? This development is presented below along with the description of the current law of the major countries, without attempting to set forth a new theoretical orientation for the field of conflicts of law.

Development of American Law

In comparing European, especially German, law with American law in the matter of market-regulating contracts, it is important to understand the difference in approach of the two legal systems. While under German law each party to a contract may file a suit for a specific performance of the contract and is only referred to damages as a secondary remedy, the plaintiff acting under American law generally has only the right to recover damages. An American judge in equity may grant specific performance only in a limited number of special cases, such as the sale of real property. No way has been worked out to obtain specific performance of contracts restraining business activity or maintaining prices.

This legal situation is an important reason why it did not appear advisable to enter international cartel agreements under American law. In the mid-thirties, this reason was more important than the antitrust legislation, since antitrust laws were not actually applied to international agreements until 1945, when the National Lead case was decided. Before 1945 only the American Tobacco case, far more important for other reasons, had discussed the illegality of market divisions along national lines under the Sherman Act.[6]

Indeed, there was no need to enter complete market-regulating agreements in the United States. Since, according to the generally

[6] United States v. National Lead Co., 63 F. Supp. 513 (S.D.N.Y. 1945) American Tobacco Co. v. United States, 328 U.S. 781.

recognized principles of American conflicts of law, the law of the place of contracting governed the validity of the contract, the parties were invited to enter their contracts in countries having legal systems favorable to the validity of cartel agreements. In addition, patents and other industrial property rights were available to accomplish results not obtainable by simple contracts. Finally, contracts without formal participation of American parties could, by inclusion of foreign subsidiaries or affiliated companies, accomplish the desired market regulation. The Alcoa case makes this clear.[7]

American conflicts-of-law rules can be important in any system of contractual market regulation, because the regulatory structure can easily be established in the legal order most convenient to the parties involved. As in Europe, American courts and writers tend now to accept a more or less unlimited party autonomy in the choice of law. This development is particularly true in the field of arbitration, to the point that private international law has lost a good part of its former practical importance.

Place of Contracting: Opening Step of American International Conflicts of Law

Justice Story's doctrine and the older jurisprudence

The early American conflicts-of-law rule stated that the law of the place of contracting governs contracts involving several states. This doctrine was developed in 1834 by Justice Joseph Story, who was strongly influenced by Dutch scholars. Story, in discussing this problem, pointed out:

Generally speaking the validity of a contract is to be decided by the law of the place where it is made. If valid there, it is by the general law of nations (jure gentium) held valid everywhere by tacit or implied consent. The rule is founded not merely in the convenience but in the necessity of nations; for otherwise it would be impractical for them to carry on an extensive intercourse in commerce with each other.[8]

By logical extension Story suggested that the same rule also governs the law applicable to the illegality of contracts: contracts illegal or void at the place of contracting are illegal or void everywhere.[9] Story

---

[7] United States v. Aluminum Co. of America, 148 F. 2d 416 (1945).

[8] Joseph Story, *Commentaries on the Conflict of Laws, Foreign and Domestic, in Regard to Contracts, Rights and Remedies* (8th ed.; Boston, 1883), p. 201.

[9] *Id.*, p. 203.

based his doctrine on the principle of comity. Recognizing the place of contracting as controlling the law applicable to the contract, Story developed a parallel doctrine, later designated as the vested rights theory, but this was generally applied to contracts among the several states of the union rather than to international contracts. The vested rights theory had special appeal because it seemed logical that rights and obligations resulting from a contract legally entered into under the law of one state should be valid and enforceable in every state of the union. This logic was further reinforced by analogy to Article 4, Section 1, of the United States Constitution, which provides, "Full Faith and Credit shall be given in each State to the public Acts, Records, and Judicial Proceedings of every other State." One limitation of the vested rights theory was that the forum could refuse to enforce contracts if they violated the public policy of the forum.

But Story's doctrine was also based on the intention of the parties: "The ground of this doctrine, as commonly stated, is that every person contracting in a place is understood to submit himself to the law of a place and silently to assent to its action upon his contract." [10]

Story emphasized, however, that the application of the law is not an immediate effect of the intention of the parties, but is based on the sovereignty of the states, since each state is free to regulate transactions within its borders. It is up to the contracting parties to choose the state where they wish to enter into their contract; having done so, their contract is subject to the law of that state. Thus the intention of the parties is used to localize the contract. It is important to remember that the realities of transportation, communication, and business in Story's time made it almost impossible to choose the place of contracting arbitrarily.

Before Story's treatise the courts had already referred to the place of contracting, and later extended it.[11] But it was never an exclusive rule. In *Scudder v. Union Bank* the Supreme Court pointed out: "Matters bearing upon the execution, the interpretation and the validity of a contract are determined by the law of the place where the contract is made." [12]

In *Milliken v. Pratt*, Chief Justice Horace Gray, of the Supreme Judicial Court of Massachusetts, described the same principle most emphatically:

10 *Id.*
11 J. H. Beale, *A Treatise on the Conflict of Laws* (New York, 1935), 1105 ff.
12 91 U.S. 406 (1875).

The general rule is that the validity of a contract is to be determined by the law of the state in which it is made; if it is valid there, it is deemed valid everywhere, and will sustain an action in the courts of a state whose laws do not permit such a contract. Even a contract expressively prohibited by the statutes of the state in which the suit is brought, if not in itself immoral, is not necessarily nor usually deemed so invalid that the comity of the state, as administered by its courts, will refuse to entertain an action on such a contract made by one of its own citizens abroad in a state the laws of which permit it.[13]

At the beginning of this century, Justice Oliver Wendell Holmes was a champion of the doctrine of the place of contracting. In *Slater v. Mexican National Railroad Co.* (1904) he explained his theoretical grounds: "Although the act complained of was subject to no law having force in the forum, it gave rise to an obligation, an obligation, which, like other obligations, follows the person, and may be enforced whereever the person may be found." [14]

In *Mutual Life Insurance Co. v. Liebing* (1922), Holmes stressed that under the Constitution and basic law, the place of contracting, not the intention of the parties, determines the law applicable to the validity and effects of the contract.[15]

Beale and the First Restatement

At the beginning of the twentieth century, J. H. Beale, later the reporter of the First Restatement, extended Justice Story's doctrine and made the place of contracting the exclusive point of contact in establishing the law applicable to the validity of the contract. His opinion appears to be based on the principle of territoriality: Each state has exclusive legislative jurisdiction within its territory, and statutes promulgated under this jurisdiction are recognized everywhere. Closely connected with this doctrine of legislative jurisdiction, the vested rights theory maintained that the courts of every state must recognize all interests and rights created under the law of other states, provided these other states remaining within the scope of their territorial jurisdiction. The issue of the validity of a contract, which is the source of definite rights and obligations, depends on the question of the contract's validity at the place of contracting. Once that validity is established, the contract must be recognized as valid everywhere.[16] If

---

[13] 28 Am.R. 241 (1878).   [14] 194 U.S. 120, 126.   [15] 259 U.S. 209.
[16] See, however, Scudder v. Union Bank 91 U.S. 406 (1875).

this principle were not accepted, there would be no right to seek legal protection in any other state. As Beale says:

The question whether a contract is valid, that is, whether to the agreement of the parties the law has annexed an obligation to perform its terms, can on general principles be determined by no other law than that which applies to the acts, that is, by the law of the place of contracting.

If the law at that place annexes an obligation to the acts of the parties, the promisee has a legal right which no other law has power to take away except as a result of new acts which change it. On the other hand the law of the place where the agreement is made annexes no legal obligation to it, there is no other law which has power to do so.

So far is this the case that it is everywhere agreed that where a statute of the place where the agreement is made annexes no legal obligation to law, whether that of the place of performance or any other, can avoid the effect of the statute. This doctrine gives full scope to the territoriality of law, and enables each sovereign to regulate acts of agreements done in his own territory.[17]

One logical conclusion of this principle is that the forum is obliged to enforce prohibitory statutes existing at the place of contracting. This necessarily covers statutes usually designated as public law. But the forum will not assist an enforcement of statutes existing at the place of contracting, in so far as these statutes are actually political claims expressed in terms of contract, for instance, tax or tariff laws.[18]

The consequences resulting from Beale's doctrine are indicated in the case of *Holzer v. Deutsche Reichsbahngesellschaft* (1938).[19] Holzer, employed by the Deutsche Reichsbahn in a managerial capacity, was dismissed on account of his race. He brought suit in New York for performance of his contract, claiming that the United States could not recognize a public law promulgated by the Nazi government. The court, however, took the position that it is exclusively up to the state where the contract is entered into to determine whether the contract is valid and whether the contract is terminated. The New York court dismissed the complaint. The contract in question, however, did not have any genuine international elements.

This First Restatement faithfully reflected the opinion of its reporter, T. H. Beale. Section 311 is exclusively based on the concept of the place of contracting. However, it soon became obvious that the

17 Beale, n. 11 above, pp. 1090 f.
18 The Antelone, 10 Wheat. 66, 123 (U.S. 1825).   19 14 N.E. 2d 798.

doctrine of the place of contracting could not be maintained, entirely apart from the difficulties inherent in defining the "place of contracting." Even at the time the First Restatement was issued, a large number of jurisdictions had already accepted positions irreconcilable with the doctrine of the place of contracting.[20] Furthermore, there were almost no cases in which there was an express choice of law. Beale was certainly aware of this and may have been hoping to induce judicial acceptance of his position, but his hope was not fulfilled.

A legal analysis of this type is incomplete without consideration of the political, economic, and social background that influences the development of rules of law. Interstate litigation has influenced American conflicts-of-law rules more than international litigation. The legal conflicts with which Justice Story was concerned were between the several states of the Union, which all basically shared the common law tradition. It is important to consider carefully the reasons behind rules of illegality or prohibition prevailing at the place of contracting, which, according to Story, are to be accepted by the forum. Liberal economic principles prevailed in the America of Story's time, which contrasted sharply with the mercantilistic system established under the British colonial government. Trade between the states of the Union was subject to few governmental limitations. The United States, despite the War of 1812, traded primarily with Great Britain, a country which had outgrown the period of mercantilism. This situation prevailed until the beginning of World War I.

In such a situation it was easy to accept the principle that the place of contracting should determine the validity of a contract, much easier than it had been in the mercantilistic period or in the period following the economic crisis of 1932. It is not at all surprising that Cheatham and Griswold's casebook on conflicts of law presents only cases dealing with a minor or wife who, at the place of contracting, was not supposed to act without the consent of a parent or husband,[21] or cases dealing with the prohibition of gambling or usury.[22] Restraint of trade, although originally set out in English law, developed later as a peculiarly American illegality.

Economic reasons also played a part in the acceptance of the doctrine of the place of contracting. The United States was dependent

[20] Beale, n. 11 above, pp. 1172 f.   [21] Milliken v. Pratt, 28 Am.R. 241 (1878).
[22] E. A. Cheatham and A. N. Griswold, eds., *Cases and Other Materials on Conflict of Laws* (5th ed.; New York, 1963), pp. 483 ff., 510 ff.

upon Europe, and especially Great Britain, in financial matters. Under these circumstances, it was advisable for the debtor-country courts to protect contracts entered into validly in Great Britain according to British law, in order to ensure the continued flow of credit. Comity was not only a matter of altruism but also of self-interest. This is perhaps also why the American courts often did not regard their own law on usury as protected public policy with respect to loan agreements entered into in a foreign country or another state.[23] The law at the beginning of this century was interpreted by experts to permit the largest American match manufacturer to enter into a contract dividing world markets with the Russian government, provided the contract was made under English law and in England. Such a contract would be valid in England and, in the opinion of the experts, everywhere else in the world.

Place of Performance and Intention of Parties as Contact Points in Earlier Periods of American Law

Justice Story recognized that the law of the place of performance might be preferred to the law of the place of contracting in certain instances.[24] He said that the law of the place of performance should apply when "the transaction is entered into with an express view to the law of another country." In American law, the place of performance is where the parties undertake the actions necessary to fulfill their obligations. In Story's time, it was practically impossible for the parties to manipulate the determination of this place of performance.

American courts have referred to the law of the place of performance with regard to questions of actual performance, for example, with respect to impossibility and frustration.[25] In *Scudder v. Union Bank* the Supreme Court pointed out, "Matters connected with the performance are regulated by the law prevailing at the place of performance."[26] The distinction became lost, however, and some courts, once having accepted the law of the place of performance, applied this law with respect to all the other issues, including the validity of the contract. In 1935, according to J. H. Beale, the law of the place of performance was accepted by almost half as many states (nine) as the recognized law of the place of contracting (twenty-one).[27]

---

[23] Seeman v. Philadelphia Warehouse Co., 274 U.S. 403 (1927).
[24] Story, n. 8 above, pp. 233 ff.   [25] Beale, n. 11 above.
[26] U.S. 406 (1875).   [27] Beale, n. 11 above, pp. 1105 ff.

The consideration of the place of performance led increasingly to consideration of the will of the parties as to the law applicable to the contract in decisions rendered after 1850. This progression from place of performance to intention of the parties appeared logical: the parties determined the place of performance by agreement, so that it is in a sense by their agreement that the law of the place of performance affects the contract.[28] The parties could only choose the law of the place of performance in preference to the law of the place of contracting; and at first it was required that the law of the place of contracting permit this choice of foreign law. Later, it was said that a contract made within the United States could stipulate the law of another state regardless of the role in the state of contracting, as explained in *Adam v. Robinson:*

The Laws of the country where a contract is made are obligatory upon the parties, and upon principle no contract declared void by those laws ought to be enforced in any other country. . . . The laws of every country allow parties to enter into obligations with reference to the laws of the country where such obligations are to be performed; although such obligations may not be in accordance with the laws of the country where they are made as regards obligations to be performed in that country they may be strictly in accordance with such laws as to obligations to be performed in other countries. The right to enter into contracts with reference to the laws of another country is one allowed by nations for the convenience of those transacting business within their respective territorial limits, to enable them to obtain such rights as they could have secured in the country where the contract is to be performed by a just observance of its laws. No nation can be justly required to allow persons subject to its laws to enter into contracts without reference to and not in accordance either with its own laws or with the laws of the country where the contract is to be performed.[29]

Beale made the following statement in 1935: "The prevailing tendency of the American cases is to regard the intention of the parties as controlling; and this intention is often conclusively found to be in favor of the law of the place of performance." [30]

Nevertheless, the parties were not entirely free in their choice of the applicable law. Their intention was only one of the elements in the localization of the contract: their intentions were not given considera-

[28] *Id.*, p. 1100.   [29] 37 Ill. 45, 60 (1865).   [30] Beale, n. 11 above, p. 1100.

tion when the applicable law chosen had no connection with the contract itself.

Thus, though the First Restatement, under the influence of Beale, decided to accept the place of contracting as the best test for the applicable law, this rule cannot be said to have been national in scope. The rule of the place of contracting has had even less sway since, eroded by political and economic development and attacked by philosophies in law.

Disintegration of the Rule of the Place of Contracting

Weakness of the rule

Difficulties in the application of the rule as to the place of contracting became apparent during the 1930's. At that time neomercantilistic philosophies of autarchy brought about severe restrictions on international trade. Extensive currency regulations and governmental export restrictions invalidated international commercial agreements and jeopardized the choice-of-law rule, favoring application of the law of the place of contracting. Americans did not want to expose vital international commercial contracts to the restrictive trade policy of other countries, while Europeans wanted to prevent any circumvention of their trade regulations. Therefore the American courts refused to apply restrictive regulations of the (foreign) place of contracting, such as currency regulations. These courts held that such statutes were political laws, expression of the executive power of foreign states, comparable with penal or tax laws.[31] Furthermore, the comity of nations did not require application of foreign law that was directly in conflict with the interests of the United States. The refusal of American courts to apply foreign currency laws was so firmly established at the end of the war that courts have even hesitated to apply currency laws of the member states of the International Monetary Fund, though the Bretton Woods Agreements expressly provide for such recognition.[32]

---

[31] R. A. Leflar, "Extrastate Enforcement of Penal and Governmental Claims," 46 *Harv. L. Rev.* 193 ff. (1932); A. N. Sack, " 'Non'-Enforcement of Foreign Revenue Laws, in International Legal Practice," 81 *U. Pa. L. Rev.* 559 ff. (1933).

[32] T. D. Trickey, "The Extraterritorial Effect of Foreign Exchange Control Law," 62 *Mich. L. Rev.* 1232 ff. (1963/64).

Criticism of scholars

The first expression of the view that conflicts of law should not allow restrictive national regulations to interfere with free and open international trade came from European jurists forced to emigrate to the United States. International trade, they said, would benefit by being freed from mandatory, restrictive national policies, which influence the validity of contracts having significance far outside the national boundaries. The stronger the nationalistic philosophy of autarchy grew in Europe, the stronger grew the conviction among scholars that international contracts should not be subject to these national rules. Further, if a contract's validity were to be governed by the law of the place of contracting, it would be subject to all the uncertainty of political and social change; a frame of law favorable or neutral toward the purposes of the contract might at any moment be replaced by decrees inimical to it.

These dangers were insuperable so long as the place of contracting remained the index for determining the applicable law. To replace it, three immigrant scholars, Rabel, Rheinstein, and Nussbaum, put forward the rule they had advocated in Europe: party autonomy, or reference to the intention of the parties for determination of the applicable law. As Rabel said: "There is practically no doubt that the parties to a contract have a right to determine by agreement the law applicable to their contractual relationship. Only the limits may be controversial." [33] Rheinstein wrote:

If we regard it as one of the principal purposes of the conflict of laws to protect the justified expectations of the parties, then the intention of the parties rule is the one which fulfills that purpose better than any rival rule, and quite particularly better than the place of contracting rule. If the parties have agreed upon the application of some particular law, then they have thought and acted in accordance with it. The place of contracting, on the other hand, may be dependent upon completely accidental circumstances which have no connection whatsoever with the thoughts, disposition, and acts of the parties.[34]

[33] E. Rabel, *The Conflict of Laws: A Comparative Study* (Ann Arbor, 1945–1958), II, 367.

[34] Book review by M. Rheinstein of J. D. Falconbridge, *Essays on the Conflict of Laws*, 15 *U. Chi. L. Rev.* 478, 486 (1948).

Finally, in Nussbaum we find: "In Private International Law few ideas are as time honored and as universally adopted by courts as this one [the party autonomy]. . . . This theory, so universal and so well supported in American law and practice, is not even referred to in the Restatement or its Comment. The Reporter considers it 'theoretically indefensible' and 'absolutely impracticable.' " [35]

This new jurisprudence rejected the old international law foundation of conflicts theory with which Story and Beale had supported their preference for the law of the place of contracting. The scholars pointed out that conflicts rules are purely national law and up to each nation to determine. They argued, however, that it is in the interest of all nations participating in international trade to determine the validity of contracts according to the law chosen by the contracting parties. These criticisms of the vested rights theory fell on fertile soil; the suggested solution, however, was unworkable from the start.

The decisive blow to the law of the place of contracting came from the Realist, sociological school of law. Reacting against the ossification of the common law into invariable precedents, this school sought to adapt the case-law method of decision to new social realities. In the field of conflicts, the most radical Realist was Walter Wheeler Cook. He opposed the thesis that the principle of territoriality, upon which Beale based his choice of the law of the place of contracting, bound governments in the area of conflicts. Lacking a treaty, there was nothing to compel a state to recognize any law but its own. Each legislature might determine independently the extent to which its courts would apply foreign laws or respect foreign-based rights.[36] Cook also opposed fixed rules in conflicts of law; the judge should determine which law, from the point of view of his forum, should apply. To do this, he should consider and evaluate the interests involved. This became known as the local law theory of conflicts.[37] Despite his philosophical basis, Cook did not prefer application of the *lex fori*, and felt that the intention of the parties should be given due consideration.[38]

The decisions of Judge Learned Hand on the Second Circuit Court

[35] A. Nussbaum, "Conflict of Contracts: Cases versus Restatement," 51 *Yale L. J.* 893, 895, 897 (1941/42).

[36] W. W. Cook, *The Logical and Legal Bases of the Conflict of Laws* (Cambridge, 1949), pp. 59 ff.

[37] See also D. F. Cavers, "The Two 'Local Law' Theories," 63 *Harv. L. Rev.* 822 ff. (1950).

[38] Cook, n. 36 above, pp. 391 ff.

of Appeals develop a conflicts theory much like that of Cook, though less radical in principle. Hand's position was that a court in referring to foreign law does not apply that law *in toto,* but works foreign principles into the forum law in order to arrive at "correct" decisions consistent with the forum's judicial philosophy. His opinion in *Guiness v. Miller* best represents his conflicts-of-law theory.[39] There a servant had been whipped in Florida by her employer's wife. Under Florida law, the husband is liable for the torts of his wife; however, the husband could only be sued in New York, where he resided. The servant sued the husband in New York, basing her complaint on Florida law as the law of the place of contracting. Judge Hand ruled:

No court can enforce any law but that of its own sovereign and, when a suitor comes to a jurisdiction foreign to the place of tort, he can only invoke an obligation recognized by that sovereign. A foreign sovereign under civilized law imposes an obligation of its own as nearly homologus as possible to that arising in the place where the tort occurs.

Judge Hand's statement in *Gerli & Co. v. Cunard Steamship Co.* shows his criticism of party autonomy:

People cannot by agreement substitute the law of another place; they may of course incorporate any provisions they wish into their agreements— a statute like anything else—and when they do, courts will try to make sense out of the whole, so far as they can. But an agreement is not a contract, except as the law says it shall be, and to try to make it one is to pull on one's bootstraps. Some laws must impose the obligation, and the parties have nothing whatever to do with that; no more than with whether their acts are torts or crimes.[40]

It is interesting to note that the sociological school developed a method in conflicts of law somewhat like the European jurisprudence of interests (*Interessenjurisprudenz*). There is a distinction, however: the American sociological school does not ask for a determination of whether foreign law shall be applied *in toto,* but rather to what extent forum or to what extent foreign law shall apply in any one case. The effect sought is not doctrinal nicety but substantive justice.

[39] 291 Fed. 769, 770 (S.D.N.Y. 1923).   [40] 48 F. 2d 115, 117 (2d Cir. 1931).

The Results

Promises

It became increasingly clear from the cases applying the rule of the law of the place of contracting that, from the public interest point of view, the rule is only acceptable in a static, predominantly national economy. The place of contracting is too easily manipulable in an age where rapid transport and communications and the international organization of so many enterprises exist. Where private and public interests clash, the latter, as expressed in law, can be too easily avoided by making the place of contracting a place where the contract is most likely to be held valid. Under American law, the final act that creates a binding contract determines the place of contracting,[41] and it is clear how easy this is to manipulate. Subsidiaries abroad can be used to avoid the parent's domestic law regulations. Therefore, as the international economy grew, the rule of the place of contracting became increasingly a device of party autonomy in choice of law and represented a serious threat, particularly to the U.S. domestic economic and social order.[42] That this threat was not recognized is shown by the remarkable fact that the opposition to the place-of-contracting rule in the United States came mostly in reaction to the protectionism and autarchic philosophy of European governments. There was no discussion of protecting the public interest expressed in domestic U.S. law. The development might have been different had antitrust law been applied to international restraints before 1938.

In a 1949 article I expressed doubts that fixed conflicts rules for international contracts could be established.[43] It seemed to me that such rules would solve no public policy problems, as almost all contact points could be manipulated by parties bent on evasion. I took the position that the decisive test should be the effect of contract provisions on the social and economic order of the forum. The doctrines of the sociological school might have been utilized to put this suggestion into effect. As it has turned out, the recent development of American conflicts law has been quite different.

[41] S. Williston, *A Treatise on the Law of Contracts*, I (Mount Kisco, N.Y., 1957), 356 ff.

[42] H. Kronstein, "Staat und private Macht in der neueren amerikanischen Rechtsentwicklung" *in Festschrift zum 70. Geburtstag von Franz Böhm* (Karlsruhe, 1965), pp. 137 ff.

[43] "Crisis of Conflict of Laws," 37 *Geo. L.J.* 483 ff. (1949).

Actual development

The doctrines of Rabel, Rheinstein, and Nussbaum have had this effect: party autonomy in the choice of law applicable to contracts is increasingly the rule, though not without changes and limitations. Only two leading texts in conflicts law remain loyal to the old place-of-contracting doctrine, that of Judge Goodrich, and Cheatham's casebook.[44] Of Rabel, Cheatham says:

Though Dr. Rabel's general approach is needed, I do not find acceptable the specific method he recommends in contracts—the use of the rule that the intention of the parties as to the governing law shall prevail. . . . If actual intent is meant, this runs into the objection that freedom of contract has been increasingly restricted in local law, and there seem to be no reasons why it should continue to have unrestricted operation in conflict of laws, and the author's proposal to restrict it only by the conception of public policy is too vague to serve as more than a stopgap until more definite restrictions can be developed.[45]

But other writers increasingly recognize the power of the parties to choose the law of their contracts.[46] It is true that the American "philosophy" of international contract law is not as developed as that of Europe, and no one has "discovered" here that the intention of the parties is really a contact point. Reese alone seems to be an exception.[47] But he will not allow the parties to evade the public policy of the law that would apply but for their choice.

But although theory has lagged, in practice American law has come to similar results as the European. The principal vehicle for accepting

[44] H. F. Goodrich, *Handbook of the Conflict of Laws* (3d ed.; St. Paul, 1949); and n. 2 above.

[45] Book review of Rabel's *The Conflict of Laws: A Comparative Study*, 48 *Colum. L. Rev.* 1267 ff. (1948).

[46] A. A. Ehrenzweig, "Contracts in the Conflict of Laws," 59 *Colum. L. Rev.* 973, 989 ff. (1959); *id.*, "The Lex Fori Basic Rule in the Conflict of Laws," 58 *Mich. L. Rev.* 637, 644 f. (1960); Rheinstein, n. 34 above; H. E. Yntema, " 'Autonomy' in Choice of Law," 1 *Am. J. Comp. L.* 341 ff. (1952); Donald T. Trautmann and Arthur T. Von Mehren, eds., *The Law of Multistate Problems: Cases and Materials on Conflict of Laws* (Boston, 1965), pp. 246 ff.; D. F. Cavers, "Re-Restating the Conflict of Laws;" *Legal Essays in Honor of Hessel E. Yntema* (Leyden, 1961), pp. 349, 360; M. J. Levin, "Party Autonomy: Choice-of-Law Clauses in Commercial Contracts," 46 *Geo. L.J.* 260 ff. (1957/58).

[47] American Society of International Law, 54th Conference, Washington, D.C., Apr. 1960, *Power of Parties to Choose Law Governing Their Contract* (Washington, D.C. 1960), p. 51.

the decision of the parties as to the applicable law has been the theory of validation, the cornerstone of recent U.S. decisions accepting party autonomy.

Local law theorists, following Cook and Learned Hand, have come to agree with followers of Rabel in recognizing party autonomy, however much they disagree on other matters. When, with Cook, they reject all fixed conflicts rules, they leave party autonomy in a relatively strong position among the indicators upon which the court should base its choice of law. Here Ehrensweig is particularly important, since he obliges the court of the forum to base its decision upon the interest of the parties in the validity of the contract.[48] Ehrenzweig does attack the validity of party autonomy in adhesion contracts;[49] but he is silent as to other areas where forum social and economic policy is affected by the choice of law, despite his local law view of the forum's role. Of course a judge should seek to protect contracting parties from undue exercise of economic power as in contracts of adhesion, but the law's function is to protect not only private, but public, interests.

Currie's theory that the forum is bound to consider its own "governmental interests" in its decision could be a basis for a more active protection of domestic economic order.[50] Although he did not take up the problem of the law applicable to contracts, by implication he rejected reference to either the law of the place of contracting or place of performance as binding on the forum. He did not mention that these points of contact have been in effect superseded by party autonomy.

Modern American conflicts theories agree surprisingly on the question of party autonomy. Not even the local-law theory has given courts stronger guidelines for protecting their domestic economic order. Party autonomy is still not as absolute as in some European laws, because usually some reasonable relation between the contract and the chosen law is required, and there is the consideration of forum public policy. But the latter is weakening.

Siegelmann v. Cunard White Star, Ltd.

Today there is a tendency toward broader recognition of the will of the parties in the jurisprudence of the courts, but no one goes so far

[48] Ehrenzweig, n. 46 above.

[49] "Adhesion Contracts in the Conflict of Laws," 53 *Colum. L. Rev.* 1072 ff. (1953).

[50] "Methods and Objectives in the Conflict of Laws," 1959 *Duke L. Rev.* 171.

as to permit the parties by choice to transfer their entire contract to another legal order. Courts will follow the intention of the parties but will first examine the validity of the contract. Before we discuss this at length, there are two caveats: first, as a result of the increasing scope of arbitration tribunals, the number of actual decisions dealing with the international field (as distinguished from trade between the states) is rather small. Second, the decisions in this area come from relatively few jurisdictions and may not be representative of all of American law; but these decisions are very important as they come from the jurisdictions most often dealing with cases.

The leading case today is *Siegelmann v. Cunard White Star, Ltd.*,[51] although the recognition of the will of the parties is only dictum therein. The suit was for damages resulting from the death of plaintiff's wife as the result of an accident aboard a ship belonging to the Cunard White Star Line. The decedent had recognized and signed the contract of passage on her ticket, the conditions of which excluded any claim of damages after the lapse of one year and further submitted the contract to English law. The plaintiff justified the delayed filing of his complaint by alleging that the defendant waived the exclusionary clause by negotiation of a settlement beyond the limitation period. The court, however, pointed out:

Here, of course, the question is neither one of interpretation nor one of validity, but instead involves the circumstances under which parties may be said to have partially rescinded their agreements or to be barred from enforcing them. The question is, however, more closely akin to a question of validity. Nevertheless, we see no harm in letting the parties' intention control.

Instead of viewing the parties as usurping the legislative function, it seems more realistic to regard them as relieving the courts of the problem of resolving a question of conflict of laws. Their course might be expected to reduce litigation, and is to be commended as much as good draftsmanship which relieves courts of problems of resolving ambiguities. To say that there may be no reduction in litigation because courts may not honor the provision is to reason backwards. A tendency toward certainty in commercial transactions should be encouraged by the courts. . . .

Where the law of the parties' intention has been permitted to govern the validity of contracts, it has often been said (1) that the choice of law must be bona fide, and (2) that the law chosen must be that of a jurisdiction having some relation to the agreement, generally either the place of making or the place of performance. The second of these conditions is obviously

[51] 221 F. 2d 189 (2d Cir. 1955).

satisfied here. The fact that a conflicts question is presented in the absence of a stipulation is some indication that the first condition is also satisfied. Furthermore, there does not appear to be an attempt here to evade American policy. We have no statute indicating a policy contrary to England's on this subject.

And there is no suggestion that English law is oppressive to passengers. We regard the primary purpose of making English law govern here as being not to substitute English for American policies, but rather on the one hand, to achieve uniformity of result, which is often hailed as the chief objective of the conflict of laws, and on the other hand, to simplify administration of the contracts in question.[52]

The recognition of party autonomy in the choice of law expressed in this opinion, written by Judge (today Justice) Harlan, is even more remarkable because the contract involved is a contract of adhesion, dictated by one of the parties. A more recent opinion in the Southern District of New York expressly refused to consider the intention of the parties in adhesion contracts.[53] It is true that the latter case may be distinguished insofar as the plaintiff there, by his lack of knowledge of English, did not understand the contents of the contract and could not have been said to intend to subject himself to the "chosen" New York law.

The Cunard case has been followed in several recent cases, for instance, in the opinion of the U.S. Court of Appeals of the Third Circuit, in *Valdesa Compania Naviera v. Frota Nazional de Petroleiros* where, referring to the Cunard case, the will of the parties was expressly recognized as governing the applicable legal order.[54] Several other recent cases in this line recognize the express choice of the applicable law even as to the issue of the validity of the contract.[55] The legal theory remains the same, however: the law of the place of contracting determines the law applicable to the contract, and the will of the parties is considered only as a highly persuasive contact point in determining that law.

[52] *Id.*, pp. 195 f.

[53] Fricke v. Isbrandtsen Co., 151 F. Supp. 465 (S.D.N.Y. 1957).

[54] 348 F. 2d 33, 38 (3d Cir. 1965).

[55] Standard Register Co. v. Kerrigan, 119 S.E. 2d 533 (1961); Consolidated Jewelers, Inc. v. Standard Financial Corp., 325 F. 2d 31 (6th Cir. 1964); In re Lea Fabrics, Inc., 226 F. Supp. 232 (D.N.J. 1964); Cooper v. Cherokee Village Development Co., 364 S.W. 2d 158 (1963); Admiral Corp. v. Cerullo Electric Supply Co., 32 F.R.D. 379 (1961); National Chemsearch Corp. of New York, Inc. v. Bogatin, 233 F. Supp. 802 (E.D.Pa. 1964).

In this connection one should not overlook Ehrenzweig's "rule of validation" [56] under which the courts should always act so as to find a contract submitted to them valid.[57]

The Second Restatement

This interpretation is in full agreement with Section 187 of the Second Restatement of Conflict of Laws (Proposed Official Draft, 1968). This provision reads:

(1) The law of the state chosen by the parties to govern their contractual rights and duties will be applied if the particular issue is one which the parties could have resolved by an explicit provision in their agreement directed to that issue.

(2) The law of the state chosen by the parties to govern their contractual rights and duties will be applied, even if the particular issue is one which the parties could not have resolved by an explicit provision in their agreement directed to that issue, unless either (a) the chosen state has no substantial relationship to the parties or the transaction and there is no other reasonable basis for the parties' choice, or (b) application of the law of the chosen state would be contrary to a fundamental policy of a state which has a materially greater interest than the chosen state in the determination of the particular issue and which, under the rule of section 188, would be the state of the applicable law in the absence of an effective choice of law by the parties.

We should not forget, however, that the Second Restatement is not really the prevailing present law, but often the personal opinions of the reporter and of the members of the American Law Institute.[58] The interpretation of the reporter Willis L. M. Reese in regard to the recognition of the will of the parties cannot be accepted as stating the present American law, especially when he says that the American courts at present recognize the agreement of the parties as a basis for their conflicts-of-law decisions. However, in substance one must admit that the courts tend to uphold the validity of contracts and regard agreements, as to the applicable law, as an important element in localizing the contract.

[56] Ehrenzweig, "Contracts in the Conflict of Laws," n. 50 above; and *A Treatise on the Conflict of Laws* (St. Paul, 1962), pp. 353, 444 f., 458 f., 465 ff.

[57] See also Global Commerce Corp. v. Clark Babbit Industries, 239 F. 2d 716 (2d Cir. 1956).

[58] "Reporters bear a major share of responsibility for a restatement but the authoritativeness of a restatement as opinion about existing laws comes from decisions of the institute." ("Preface," *Restatement of the Law*, Second, 1965).

The Uniform Commercial Code

The Uniform Commercial Code (UCC) provides in Section 1-105:

(1) Except as provided hereafter in this section, when a transaction bears a reasonable relation to this state and also to another state or nation the parties may agree that the law either of this state or of such other state or nation shall govern their rights and duties. Failing such agreement this Act applies to transactions bearing an appropriate relation to this state.[59]

The adoption of this provision by the majority of the states is a very important development in American conflicts of law. It is the first far-reaching codification of an important principle of conflicts. At least in commercial matters, the parties can within limits agree on the law applicable with respect to validity, performance, and interpretation of their contracts. Discussions of the drafts of the UCC show that it was intended to recognize the freedom of the parties to choose the law in the broadest sense. Nicholas Katzenbach, in discussing this issue, stated in 1956:

In a society which believes in the widest freedom of contract on the one hand, and the enforceability of business promises on the other, the role of the courts is to discover and enforce the understandings of the commercial world, and rules of law are the handmaidens of this task. . . . We are within that area of law where . . . business men are free to "make their own law." They do so expressly through contract, implicitly through a course of dealing, collectively through custom and resultant business understanding. Presumably the law which courts enforce reflects, or consistent with its basic policy orientation ought to reflect, this merchant law. Hence the frequent references in substantive doctrine and decision to the "intent" of the parties. The conflicts doctrine is, of course, simply a reflection of the same policy and concept. . . . More often than not courts rule in conflicts cases to use it to protect a good-faith deal which violates, for example, a local or foreign usury law, a statute of frauds, or capacity provision.[60]

Legal writers

Recognition of the intention of the parties by legal commentators is becoming stronger. But most writers still consider the parties' intention as an element of localization of the contract. Reese suggests that

[59] Uniform Laws Annotated, Uniform Commercial Code, Arts. 1–3, 1965 Pocket Part, p. 5.
[60] 12 *Business Lawyer* 68, 71 f. (1956).

the agreement of the parties as to the applicable law establishes a contact point in itself.[61] Very few writers contend that forum is actually
bound by the parties' choice. The pragmatic tendency of American
lawyers not to indulge in general theoretical considerations has also
tended to slow down the development of American conflicts law.

Limitation of the Power to Choose Applicable Law

Cases and restatement

American courts, in contrast to continental European legal systems, often limit recognition of contractual determination of the applicable law to a *bona fides* choice or one that has an essential or
reasonable relation to the contract.[62] Generally the courts have recognized agreements as to the applicable law if the parties chose either
the law of the place of contracting, of the place of performance, or
of the residence of one of the parties. The draft of the Second Restatement requires a transaction to have a "substantial relationship" to the
chosen law. If such relationship does not exist, the courts recognize any
other "reasonable basis" for the choice of law.[63] Reese, the reporter of
the Restatement, stresses that a territorial relationship between the contract and the chosen law, e.g., the place of contracting, the place of
performance, or the residence of one of the parties, is not absolutely
necessary. The choosing of a certain legal order may also be reasonable
on the ground that none of those laws that have territorial relationships
to the contract could reasonably be expected to apply because the
parties could not agree upon one of them.[64] Should this opinion prevail, there would be little important difference between American and
European attitudes.

The Uniform Commercial Code

The law the parties can choose under the Uniform Commercial
Code is limited to that of jurisdictions with which the transaction in
issue has a "reasonable relation." The U.S. Supreme Court in *Seeman
v. Philadelphia Warehouse Co.* suggested that the recognition of a

---

[61] Cf. nn. 46 and 47 above.
[62] Siegelmann v. Cunard White Star, Ltd., 221 F. 2d 189 (2d Cir. 1955); Consolidated Jewelers, Inc. v. Standard Financial Corp., 325 F. 2d 31 (6th Cir. 1964);
Cooper v. Cherokee Village Development Co., 364 S.W. 2d 158 (1963); Hal
Roach Studios v. Film Classics, 156 F. 2d 596 (2d Cir. 1946); Rheinstein, n. 34
above, pp. 478, 485 ff.; Nussbaum, n. 35 above, p. 893.
[63] Sec. 332 a(1)(b).   [64] Reese, n. 47 above, p. 53.

chosen law having no actual relation to the transaction in issue may amount to an interference in the constitutionally protected rights and interests of those states that do have a direct interest.[65] But this is also generally recognized in international cases, where the constitutional objection is not applicable. When there is no contractual agreement as to the chosen law, the UCC appears to be applicable if there is an appropriate relation between the contract and the forum. It seems particularly significant that this UCC formula follows not only the U.S. Supreme Court rule, but also harmonizes with the Second Restatement's "substantial relationship." [66] The UCC does not define the concept of reasonable relation, but the official comment states that the concept of reasonable relation is similar to the test in the Seeman case, that generally the parties may choose the law of a state in which either a substantial part of the making or performance of the contract takes place.[67]

Doctrine of the Grouping of Contracts

Even today, short of an express designation, the law of the place of contracting or of the place of performance will generally govern the contract.[68] The opinion of the New York Court of Appeals in *Auten v. Auten*, however, opened a new development in regard to the law applicable to contracts as well as torts.[69] The Auten case itself deals only with a domestic-relations separation agreement, but the court used this opportunity to establish a number of general principles on the law applicable to performance, interpretation, and validity of contracts. The court stated that under a theory of "the center of gravity" or "grouping of contacts," the law of the place with the most significant contacts with the matter in dispute should be applied;

[65] 274 U.S. 403 (1927); see also Home Insurance Co. v. Dick, 281 U.S. 379 (1930).

[66] See also Mass. Gen. Law., Chap. 106 §1–105 and Massachusetts Code Comment; see Shinner v. Tober Foreign Motors, Inc., 187 N.E. 2d 609 (1963).

[67] Secs. 1–105, No. 1; see also R. A. Anderson, *Uniform Commercial Code* (Rochester, 1961), I, 17; H. F. Goodrich, "Conflicts Niceties and Commercial Necessities," 52 *Wis. L. Rev.* 199, 207 (1952).

[68] Fricke v. Isbrandtsen Co., 151 F. Supp. 465 (S.D.N.Y. 1957); Watts v. Swiss Bank Corp., 252 N.Y.S. 2d 196 (1964); Hazel Bishop, Inc. v. Perfemme, Inc., 314 F. 2d 399 (2d Cir. 1963); S. D. Hicks & Son Co. v. J. T. Beker Chemical Co., 307 F. 2d 750 (2d Cir. 1962); In re Fields Estate, 172 N.Y.S. 2d 740 (1958).

[69] 124 N.E. 2d 99 (1954); also Babcock v. Jackson, 12 N.Y. 2d 473 (1963); Griffith v. United Airlines, Inc., 203 A. 2d 796 (1964).

other cases have followed this reasoning.[70] The Second Restatement adopts this rule in Section 188:

(1) The rights and duties of the parties with respect to an issue in contract are determined by the local law of the state which, as to that issue, has the most significant relationship to the transaction and the parties under the principle stated in section 6.

(2) In the absence of an effective choice of law by the parties (see section 187), the contacts to be taken into account in applying the principles of section 6 to determine the law applicable to an issue include: (a) the place of contracting, (b) the place of negotiation of the contract, (c) the place of performance, (d) the location of the subject matter of the contract, and (e) the domicile, residence, nationality, place of incorporation and the place of business of the parties. These contacts are to be evaluated according to their relative importance with respect to the particular issue.

(3) If the place of negotiating the contract and the place of performance are in the same state, the local law of this state will usually be applied, except as otherwise provided in sections 189–199 and 203.

However, the Restatement does not follow the Auten opinion in an extremely important situation: the latter suggested that an objective test should prevail even over an express contractual choice of law on the question of the contract's validity. The courts have utilized the theory of center of gravity to set aside the contractual choice of law in only one case, involving a pledge—in reality a contract in which the parties are not free to decide the *lex rei sitae*.[71]

It must be recognized that the present means of transportation and present types of business enterprise make it very difficult to use old devices, such as the place of contracting, to determine the applicability in the absence of an agreement by the parties. As a matter of fact, the theory of the center of gravity is basically an admission of this fact.

---

[70] Richland Development Co. v. Staples, 295 F. 2d 122 (3d Cir. 1961); In re Campbell's Trust, 232 N.Y.S. 2d 522 (1962): Ketcham v. Hall Syndicate, Inc., 236 N.Y.S. 2d 206, affirmed 242 N.Y.S. 2d 182 (1963); S. D. Hicks & Son Co. v. J. T. Baker Chemical Co., 307 F. 2d 750 (2d Cir. 1962); Hazel Bishop, Inc. v. Perfemme, Inc., 314 F. 2d 399 (2d Cir. 1963); Perrin v. Pearlstein, 314 F. 2d 863 (2d Cir. 1963); Fleet Messenger Service v. Life Insurance Co. of North America, 315 F. 2d 593 (2d Cir. 1963).

[71] In re J. E. Schecter Corp., 334 F. Supp. 474 (E.D.N.Y. 1965).

Disintegration of the Concept of Public Policy

Justice Story and the early cases

Story explains what public policy once meant:

But there is an exception of the rule as to the universal validity of contracts which is that no nation is bound to recognize or enforce any contracts which are injurious to their own interests or to those of foreign subjects. This exception results from the consideration that the acts and contracts done in other states as well as the laws by which they are regulated are not proprio vigore of any efficacy beyond the territories of that state, and whatever is attributed to them elsewhere is from comity and not of strict right and every independent community will and ought to judge for itself how far that comity ought to extend. The reasonable limitation is, that it shall not suffer prejudice by its comity. Mr. Justice Best has with great force said, that in cases turning upon the comity of nations (comitas inter communitates), it is maxim, that the comity cannot prevail in cases, where it violates the law of our own country, the law of nature, or the law of God. Contracts, therefore, which are in evasion or fraud of the laws of a country, or the rights or duties of its subjects, contracts against good morals, or religion, or public rights, and contracts opposed to the national policy or institutions, are deemed nullities in every country, affected by such considerations; although they may be valid by the laws of the place, where they are made.[72]

While Story fully realized America's economic dependence on England, he was too close to the events of 1789 to overlook the necessity of protecting American institutions from English mercantile policies. Among these jealously guarded institutions were many public organisms not created by the Constitution.

The consequences of Loucks v. Standard Oil

Step by step, however, the courts began to limit the substance of the public-policy concept. Nussbaum, who has traced this narrowing road from "local" public policy through "strong" public policy, explained it by the liberal tradition built up in America from the Napoleonic Wars to World War I.[73] But it appears that the concept only began to lose substance gradually, after the beginning of the twentieth

[72] Story, n. 8 above, p. 203.
[73] A. Nussbaum, "Public Policy and the Political Crisis in the Conflict of Laws," 49 Yale L.J. 1027, 1048 (1940/1941).

century. The leading case is *Loucks v. Standard Oil Co. of New York* (1918).[74] The language is Justice Cardozo's:

The Courts are not free to refuse to enforce a foreign right at the pleasure of the judges, to suit the individual notion of expediency of fairness. They do not close their doors unless help would violate some fundamental principle of justice, some prevalent conception of good morals, some deep-rooted tradition of the common weal.

Cardozo expressed the growing conviction that rights acquired abroad should be refused recognition only in very extraordinary situations. The forum must have a "strong public policy," and its violation must be that "which in its nature offends our sense of justice or menaces the public welfare." [75]

Owing in part to the multiplicity in American courts, this rule is not universally the law. Many courts continued to protect forum interests by express reference to public policy, for the protection of domestic holders of foreign insurance policies and local labor laws.[76] But today the Loucks case is uncontested authority.[77] In a related development, the definition of public policy was changed; it was once defined as expressed in the Constitution, in statutes, or in judicial decisions.[78] Today it is more generally defined as a prevailing social and moral interest of the community.[79] But while the definition is broadened (the validation principle may be called a public policy), the concept is less used, as offensive violations of "strong public policy" are necessarily rare.

Public policy of the forum

The power of the parties under American law to choose the applicable law is limited by considerations of public policy.[80] This con-

[74] 120 N.E. 198, 202 (1918).   [75] See also Beale, n. 11 above, III, 1647, 1651.
[76] See "Conflict of Laws: 'Party Autonomy' in Contracts," 57 *Colum. L. Rev.* 553, 555 ff., 573 f. (1957).
[77] See Mertz v. Mertz, 3 N.E. 2d 597 (1936); Dym v. Gordon, 209 N.E. 2d 792 (1965).
[78] People v. Hawkins, 157 N.Y. 1, 12 (1898); Mertz v. Mertz, 3 N.E. 2d 597 (1936).
[79] Millsay v. Central Wisconsin Motor Transport Co., 189 N.E. 2d 793 (1963); Lilienthal v. Kaufmann, 395 P. 2d 543 (1964); International Hotels Corp. v. Golden, 203 N.E. 2d 210 (1964).
[80] The term "public policy" was defined in Loucks v. Standard Oil Co., 120 N.E. 198, 202 (1918); see also M. G. Paulsen, " 'Public Policy' in the Conflict of Laws," 56 *Colum. L. Rev.* 969 (1956); Griffin v. McCoach, 313 U.S. 498 (1941).

cept coincides generally with the European concept of *ordre public*. It dictates the implication of the mandatory public and private laws of the forum, but is resorted to whenever forum law is to be applied instead of the foreign law indicated by conflicts rules. The judge must determine that the issue is of such essential importance that foreign law must not apply.

Despite the theoretical breadth and suppleness of the notion of public policy, all American jurisdictions have developed precedents delimiting the situations in which public policy may actually be used. These cases generally circumscribe narrowly the scope of public policy; *Richland Development Co. v. Staples* is a good example of this tendency: A contract dealing with the utilization and disposition of real property in Alabama had been concluded while the parties were in an airplane flying over Missouri.[81] The parties to the contract were a real estate agent, licensed in Missouri but not in Alabama, and a customer. Under the law of Alabama, a local license is required for transactions in real property situated in Alabama. The Court of Appeals for the Fifth Circuit, in discussing the problem of public policy, stated:

It is undeniable that a state may refuse to enforce a contract valid in a state where made if the contract conflicts with the public policy of the state. The application of this doctrine, however, is limited to cases where strong reasons of public policy support it. Of course, a state has a certain latitude in declaring what foreign contracts violate its public policy but if the asserted policy is nothing more than the fact that the forum state has prescribed a different law to govern a particular transaction the foreign law will usually be enforced.

In applying a public policy test, the court considered the type of illegality involved, the degree of guilt of the parties involved, the weight of legislative interest, the amount of protection to be accorded to those in whose interest the rule was established, the losses resulting from the refusal to recognize the contract, and also the public interest.[82]

Other courts are less expressive in their arguments, but they, too, state that the chosen law can only be excluded on account of public policy if the policy interests involved are "fundamental" or "strong." [83]

[81] 295 F. 2d 122 (3d Cir. 1961).   [82] *Id.*, p. 127.

[83] In re Lea Fabrics, Inc., 226 F. Supp. 232, 237 (D.N.J. 1964); see also International Hotels Corp. v. Golden, 203 N.E. 2d 210 (1964).

Courts regularly refer to public policy of the forum in the following cases: (1) in contracts of insurance entered with foreign insurance companies whenever the chosen law deviates essentially from the law of the forum in regard to the protection of the insured person; (2) in cases of long-term contracts of employment whenever the chosen law places a lighter burden upon the employer than does the forum in regard to obligations toward the employee, especially as to liability for accidents; (3) in cases in which the forum considers a loan to be usurious,[84] or in fraud, gambling, or violations of Sunday Blue laws; (4) in cases of violations of ethical principles;[85] (5) in cases where the economic power of one party enables it to dictate the applicable law (adhesion contracts).[86]

It is surprising how seldom the problem has been raised as to whether a contract violates antitrust legislation or otherwise restrains trade. In *Lynch v. Bealy* it was decided that a contract valid by foreign law violates the public policy of New York whenever it restrains trade in New York.[87] This case deals with interstate commerce, however, and there are no cases of an international character deciding this point. There are in fact very few cases applying the antitrust laws to international cartels. Another explanation is that arbitration has excluded potential application of the regular judicial process.

It is remarkable that the UCC contains no express provision that the power of the parties to choose applicable law is limited by considerations of public policy. Of the official commentaries, only that of New Jersey addresses the question.[88] It says that a "strong public policy of the state" should be considered a limitation of the choice of law. The explanation in the commentary, that there would be a lack of reasonable relation between the transaction and the state of the chosen law whenever the public policy of New Jersey is involved, is not entirely convincing. It would at least require that the meaning of the word "transaction" be expanded to include litigation resulting from such transaction.

[84] See, however "Conflict of Laws," n. 76 above, p. 553.   [85] *Id.*

[86] A. A. Ehrenzweig, "Adhesion Contracts in the Conflict of Laws," 53 *Colum. L. Rev.* 1072 ff. (1953); Rheinstein, n. 34 above, pp. 478, 487.

[87] 90 N.Y.S. 2d 359 (1949), affirmed 90 N.E. 2d 484 (1949); J. R. Watkins v. McMullan, 6 S.W. 2d 823 (1928).

[88] N.Y.S.A. 12A: 10105 and New Jersey Study Comment.

Public policy of the displaced law

Very recently a tendency has developed to protect not only the public policy of the forum but also the public policy of other states having natural contacts with the transaction, or states having laws that would apply absent agreement. This tendency indicates that even today choice of law is only an element of localization of the contract and not a determination to submit the entire contract to the chosen law, which differentiates American from European theories of conflict law. *Richland Development Co. v. Staples* is a case in point, showing the consideration of public policy of another state.[89] The forum was Missouri, while all the public policy taken under consideration by the court dealt with Alabama law. The Second Restatement recognizes this principle in Section 187(2)(b). The choice of law is no permissible whenever

application of the law of the chosen state would be contrary to a fundamental policy of a state which has materially a greater interest than the chosen state in the determination of the particular issue and which under the rule of section 188, would be the state of the applicable law in the absence of an effective choice of law by the parties.

It is doubtful whether American courts would apply this principle to international contracts, thereby enforcing a foreign public-policy against an express choice of a foreign law; there are no cases which have resolved this issue.

German Law

Principle of Party Autonomy

German courts seeking the law applicable to cartel agreements apply the same general principles they apply to regular contracts, since they consider cartel contracts to be normal ones. This is true of conflict rules.[90]

According to the general German conflicts-of-law rule, the law applicable to agreements and contracts is determined on the basis of the express or implied will of the parties. The parties may not only

[89] 295 F. 2d 122 (3d Cir. 1961); see also In re Lea Fabrics, Inc., 226 F. Supp. 232, 237 ff. (D.N.J. 1964).

[90] Friedländer, n. 2 above, pp. 311 ff.; R. Wolff, *Die Rechtsgrundlagen der internationalen Kartelle* (Berlin, 1929), pp. 53 ff.; Dörinkel, n. 2 above, p. 65 f.

stipulate that a particular foreign substantive rule shall apply, but may choose to apply a complete foreign legal order *in toto*.[91] Agreement of the parties to apply a particular law has been considered as one of the substantive terms of the contract; it has also in practice been the weight of a point of contact in conflicts-of-law theory. It is the prevailing opinion that there is an unwritten German conflicts-of-law rule in contracts by which the choice of foreign law completely excludes whatever other legal order would be applicable, thereby superseding all other contacts determining the applicable law, whether they are subject to the parties' disposition or are of an objective character. The only limitation that remains is the *ordre public* clause which is rarely invoked.[92]

Party autonomy in the general law of contract

With only limited exceptions, German courts today apparently recognize the power of the parties to choose the applicable law. No decision of the German Federal Court deals directly with the scope and the basis of this choice of law; there can be no doubt that the decisions at least recognize the freedom of choice.[93]

The Federal Supreme Court points out in its opinion of April 14, 1953, that once jurisdiction is established, the applicable law is determined first according to the express or implied intention of the parties or, if necessary, according to the hypothetical intention of the parties, and only as a substitute for these is the law of the place of performance utilized.[94]

Contracts sufficient to support a choice of law have been found in citizenship or domicile of the parties by the place of contracting or of performance.[95] The courts have not yet expressly stated that the agreement on the choice of a legal system should be considered a special

[91] 7 BGHZ 231, 234; 17 BGHZ 89, 92; 19 BGHZ 110, 111; 22 BGHZ 162; W. Haudek, *Die Bedeutung des Parteiwillens im internationalen Privatrecht* (Berlin, 1931), p. 6; L. Raape, *Internationales Privatrecht* (5th ed.; Berlin, 1961), pp. 455 ff.; G. Römer, *Gesetzesumgehung im deutschen internationalen Privatrecht* (Berlin, 1955), pp. 160 ff.; Rabel, n. 33 above. pp. 362 f., 367 f.

[92] 31 BGHZ 367, 370 ff.; F. Gamillscheg, "Rechtswahl, Schwerpunkt und mutmasslicher Parteiwille im internationalen Vertragsrecht," 157 *Archiv für die civilistische Praxis* 303 ff., 307 ff. (1958/59); R. Heiz, *Das fremde öffentliche Recht im internationalen Kollisionsrecht: Der Einfluss der Public Policy auf ausländisches Straf-, Devisen-, Konfiskations-, und Enteignungsrecht* (Zurich, 1959), pp. 68 ff.; Steindorff, n. 1 above, pp. 136 ff., 206 ff.

[93] For citations see Gamillscheg, *id.*, pp. 303 ff.   [94] 9 BGHZ 221, 222.

[95] M. Wolff, *Das internationale Privatrecht Deutschlands* (Berlin, 1954), p. 139.

contract distinguished from the substantive contract, although the Court of Appeal of Cologne has pointed out that the contract to choose an applicable law is to be considered of a different character than the contract dealing with substantive provisions.[96] This principle should be applied by the court even if the substantive contract would become illegal or ineffective as a result of the application of the chosen law.

Some writers have even contended that the contract need have no connection at all with the jurisdiction, the law of which has been stipulated by the parties.[97] Some think this rule should apply to cartel agreements, especially because international cartels rarely have center of gravity in any one country.[98]

Party autonomy in a contract of partnership or personal services

Partnership agreements are also interpreted in deference to the principle of party autonomy. The intention of the parties will usually determine the law governing the partnership agreements, although in the case of a partnership having corporate attributes, most authors favor the use of the seat of the partnership as the point of contact.[99]

The Federal Supreme Court has recognized the seat of the partnership as the principal point of contact; however, a special agreement between the partners providing otherwise has been permitted, even in regard to relations of the partnership with third parties, including the question of the liability of the partner for obligations of the partnership.[100] The court apparently views as self-evident the power of the partners to choose the law applicable to the relation between themselves. From this we can assume that the Federal Supreme Court considers the intention of the parties to be the primary point of contact in all kinds of associations.

In the area of personal-services contracts, the intention of the parties in regard to the applicable law may not be decisive. In these cases, the obligatory contact point is the place where the services are to be

[96] "Rechtsprechung zum Wiedergutmachungsrecht," 1959 *Neue juristische Wochenschrift* 46, 47.

[97] Rabel, n. 33 above pp. 402 ff.; Gamillscheg, n. 92 above, pp. 303, 313.

[98] Aubin, n. 2 above, pp. 33, 68 ff.

[99] Rabel, n. 33 above, pp. 100 ff.; Kegel, n. 1 above, p. 212; H. T. Soergel, W. Siebert, and G. Kegel, eds., *Bürgerliches Gesetzbuch mit Einführungsgesetz und Nebengesetzen*, Art. 10, n. 42 (1959).

[100] The decision is published in 1959 *Aussenwirtschaftsdienst des Betriebsberaters* 106; see also 23 RGZ 31, 33.

rendered.[101] This rule closely follows the opinion that the parties have no power to choose the law whenever a set of facts so strongly involves problems of public law that the public interest must prevail even in the private law aspects.[102] It is interesting to observe that this consideration has not been applied to cartel agreements, in spite of the fact that there is a whole set of public rules regarding cartels. On the whole then, we have here only random disturbances of the power of the parties to choose the applicable law.

Hypothetical Intention of the Parties

The Federal Supreme Court, following the former Imperial Court, refers to the "hypothetical" intention of the parties whenever it cannot find an express or implied intention of the parties choosing the applicable law.[103] The Federal Supreme Court has pointed out that one should not try to find hypothetically some subjective opinions of the parties involved, but one should reasonably consider the interest of the parties involved on a purely objective basis.[104] This rule should not be considered a genuine deviation from the principle of private party autonomy. As a matter of legal method, all that is involved is a standard rule for the interpretation of substantive provisions of contracts.

Limitations on Party Autonomy

Rules not subject to disposition by the parties

The principle of party autonomy is even applied by the Federal Supreme Court in cases involving rules that are to be applied without party agreement and which are not subject to the intention of the parties under German law. This is shown in an opinion of the Federal Supreme Court of January 30, 1961.[105] The litigation concerned an exclusive agency contract between a Dutch enterprise and a West

---

[101] L. Schnorr von Carolsfeld, *Arbeitsrecht* (Göttingen, 1954), pp. 52 f.; the majority of the writers and courts have, however, taken a different position (see decisions of the highest appellate court for labor matters in West Germany, published in *Arbeitsrechtliche Praxis, Internationales Privatrecht*, Nos. 3, 4, 6, 9 and F. Gamillscheg, *Internationales Arbeitsrecht* [Berlin, 1959], pp. 101 ff., 140).

[102] K. Neumeyer, *Internationales Verwaltungsrecht* (Munich, 1910–1936), IV, 487, 488; F. Vischer, *Internationales Vertragsrecht: Die kollisionsrechtlichen Regeln der Anknüpfung bei internationalen Verträgen* (Bern, 1962), pp. 27 ff., 63 ff.

[103] 152 RGZ 53; 131 RGZ 41, 48.   [104] 7 BGHZ 231, 235; 9 BGHZ 221, 223.

[105] Published in 1961 *Neue juristische Wochenschrift* 1061, 1062.

German agency. The contract stipulated the application of Dutch law, and the issue was whether the court should apply the obligatory provision of Section 89(b) of the German Commercial Code, providing for a minimum compensation of commercial agents. The opinion states:

The agreement of the parties to apply the law of the Netherlands and to recognize the Dutch court as having jurisdiction cannot be set aside because the defendant, in entering this agreement, intended to evade the rules of section 89(b) of the German Commercial Code which is a rule not subject to the freedom of the parties (which alleges a violation of section 134 BGB). We must assume that, absent an agreement between the parties, the substantive German law would have been applied and the German courts would have had jurisdiction. Further, it is to be assumed that the defendant, by agreeing to make Dutch law applicable and to grant jurisdiction to the courts of the Netherlands, intended to exclude section 89(b) of the German Commercial Code and to see the corresponding rules of the Dutch law applied because these are more convenient for the defendant. However, in the pending case this does not render illegal the agreement providing for Dutch law and for Dutch courts under section 134 BGB. Plaintiffs, in attacking the opinion of the lower court, refer to the hypothetical case of two Germans, who, having domicile and property within Germany and no contact with foreign countries, may subject their contractual relationship to a foreign legal order and foreign jurisdiction merely for the purpose of evading German law. It must be admitted that there would be substantial objection to the legality of such an agreement under section 134 BGB. However, the case before us is quite different. In our case, the defendants gave their principal plants which were situated in the Netherlands and the principal part of their property to the corporation organized under the Dutch law, and which had its principal seat in the Netherlands. All these are essential reasons justifying the defendant's insistance on submitting his contract with the plaintiff to the law of the Netherlands and to the jurisdiction of Dutch courts. Therefore this contract is permissible and section 134 BGB is not applicable. The position of plaintiff would substantially extend the scope of *ordre public*, expressly recognized in only a very limited way in article 30 EGBGB, or section 134 BGB. Such extension would be inconsistent with the intent of the statute.

The court seems not to have considered that this case involved what might well be regarded as a contract of adhesion.

Ordre public

Article 30 EGBGB, discussed in the opinion of the Federal Supreme Court, represents a limitation on the power to choose foreign law. It provides that foreign law shall not be applied if such application would be incompatible with moral law or the objectives of a German statute. However, under the standard formulation of the Federal Supreme Court and of the former Reichsgericht (Imperial Court), it would only be applicable "whenever the difference of political and social opinions between the chosen foreign legal order and the German legal order is so substantial that by application of foreign law basic principles of German governmental or social life would be attacked." [106] It is not difficult to judge how rarely these conditions occur, and writers have attacked the opinion.[107] In effect, *ordre public* poses no obstacle to the choice of law today.

The Federal Supreme Court does recognize that a German law not subject to the parties disposition will prevail over party autonomy if there is a public-law aspect.[108] Sometimes such a decision is based on Article 30 EGBGB.[109] In most cases, the decision is based on the provisions and the intent of the statutes in issue.[110] So it was held that the parties cannot abrogate provisions concerning international currency transactions,[111] protecting the value of money,[112] and establishing minimum prices.[113] The prevailing opinion holds that German cartel law is equally obligatory.[114] But dicta in more recent opinions show that

[106] *Id.;* 22 BGHZ 1, 15; 28 BGHZ 375, 384; 60 RGZ 296, 300.

[107] Staudinger J. and Leo Raape, *Kommentar zum bürgerlichen Gesetzbuch mit Einführungsgesetz und Nebengesetzen,* Art. 30, nn. 811 ff. (11th ed.; Berlin, 1957); M. Wolff, n. 101 above, pp. 62 ff.; Soergel, Siebert, and Kegel, n. 99 above, Art. 30, n. 11.

[108] Cf. Neumeyer, n. 102 above, and Vischer, n. 102 above.

[109] For citations see Soergel, Siebert, and Kegel, n. 99 above, nn. 102, 109 before Art. 7.

[110] *Id.;* 31 BGHZ 367, 370 ff.; 104 RGZ 50, 53.

[111] 104 RGZ 50, 53.

[112] Decision of the Federal Supreme Court, reprinted in 1960 AWD 217, 218.

[113] 27 BGHZ 249, 256.

[114] Decision of the Federal Cartel Office (Bundeskartellamt), 1963; *Wirtschaft and Wettbewerb, Entscheidungssammlung zum Kartellrecht* 704 ff.; Annual Reports of the Federal Cartel Office 1959 (p. 44), 1960 (pp. 18, 40), 1961 (pp. 37, 52), 1962 (p. 41), 1963 (p. 25); see also E. Rehbinder, *Extraterritoriale Wirkungen des deutschen Kartellrechts* (Baden-Baden, 1965), pp. 213 ff., 274 ff.; Kegel, n. 99 above, pp. 410, 413, 414; J. Seidl-Hohenveldern, "Völkerrechtliche Erwägungen zum Deutschen Internationalen Kartellrecht," 1963 AWD 73, 74.

the Federal Supreme Court intends to limit even this restriction of party autonomy to those legal rules that have a clear-cut commercial and political purpose.[115] While the Court has expressed this opinion only with regard to the application of foreign law, logically it should also be applied to the *lex fori* where the legal rules are not to be subject to the intention of the parties.

Territorial limitations

A further limitation on private autonomy in the choice of law is the refusal of courts up to now to apply a completely arbitrarily chosen foreign law. The courts insist that the chosen legal order must have some contact with the business transaction involved. The character that this relation must take, however, remains very much an issue. There is a dictum by the former Berlin Court of Appeals that the contacts must be either territorial or based on citizenship.[116] But there is reason to believe that the opinion of the Court of Appeals in Hamburg will become the prevailing law: Any substantive material interest of the parties in the chosen law is sufficient.[117]

Swiss Law

Swiss conflicts of law do not contain express rules as to the law applicable to contracts. However, legal writers have long expressed their opinion that the parties may agree on the applicable law but only with regard to particular substantive rules. The parties cannot affect the decision as to the legality or illegality of the contract.[118] The Swiss Federal Supreme Court for many years took the position that a legal order chosen by the parties may affect only the terms of the contract and not its validity.[119] The latter was governed only by the law of the place of contracting. This contrast between the two aspects of the contract has been designated as the theory of the great division.

In 1952 the Swiss Federal Court abandoned its previous decision and

---

[115] 31 BGHZ 367 ff.

[116] Published in 1957 *Neue juristische Wochenschrift* 347.

[117] Published in 1954 *Monatsschrift für deutsches Recht* 422.

[118] G. Boerlin, "Die örtliche Rechtsanwendung bei Kaufverträgen nach der Rechtsprechung des Bundesgerichtes," 33 *Zeitschrift für schweizerisches Recht* 214, 215 (1914); A. F. Schnitzer, "Die Parteiautonomie im internationalen und im nationalen Privatrecht," 35 *Schweizerische Juristenzeitung* 305 ff. (1938–1939).

[119] 32 II BGE 418; 38 II BGE 519; 39 II BGE 167; 46 II BGE 493; 49 II BGE 73; 50 II BGE 281, 282; 56 II BGE 41.

began to determine the validity of the contract also on the basis of the law chosen by the parties. The court pointed out:

Once we have recognized the autonomy of the parties as regulating the applicable law in the field of contracts, it is not understandable why we should limit our application of the chosen law only to the effects of the contract. It is perfectly possible that the parties, by choosing another law, may intend to evade certain provisions which, under the law which would apply absent agreement, would not be subject to the free decision of the parties. But choosing a foreign law in regard to both contracting and the terms of the contract does not mean that the parties are able to avoid regulation by law. They merely subject themselves to the rules and provisions of a different legal order, chosen by themselves.[120]

The extent of party autonomy in regard to bringing entire contracts under foreign law was explained in a later opinion of the Swiss Federal Court:

The majority of writers contended for a long time that the agreement of the parties can have no power to bring contracts in a totality under other laws. It has been described as a logical impossibility to permit parties to a contract to determine the law applicable as to the validity of the contract they themselves have entered into.

Recently, however, the power of the parties to choose the applicable law with respect not only to the substantive provisions of the contract, but also its validity, has come to be more widely accepted by the writers. This change of position is based principally upon the recognition that there is not simply one contract at issue but two: one with substantive provisions and a supplementary contract containing only the submission of the contract to another legal system. It makes no difference whether, as a matter of form, this supplementary contract is separated from the main contract or combined in a single contract. In this way the allegation of logical error, made by the opponents of party autonomy in conflicts law, has been overcome. The law to be applied on the question of the validity and consideration of the main contract is not to be found by examining that contract, it is contained in a separate contract choosing the applicable law. This set of contracts will be based on the conflict of law rules of the forum.

Once this system of choosing foreign law by a special contract of submission is considered lawful, it is not clear why it is not also possible to submit the contracts to another law later on. For instance, during litigation. The principle of freedom of contract naturally governs the contract of

[120] 78 II BGE 74, 85.

submission; this follows from its nature as a contract. Since it is a contract, the parties have the power to change the contents of the contract at any point, by choosing a legal order other than the one they originally decided on. This can even be done retroactively, insofar as the main contract is not in effect fully performed.[121]

Later court decisions have supported this theory, which is in full accord with the opinions of the commentators and the writers.[122]

From this theory of the nature of choice of law it follows, in the interpretation of the courts, that the parties by agreement may avoid even rules of law not subject to the determination of the parties which are contained in a legal order applicable if there were no contracts of submission.[123] The courts do stress that the parties to the contract may not avoid all legislative systems; they must choose an existing legal order and they must abide by it. Furthermore, at least until recently, it was required that the contract have a "natural and not insignificant contact" to the legal order chosen.[124] The Swiss Federal Court in 1965 abandoned this requirement and now demands only that the parties have a "reasonable interest" in the chosen law.[125] It adds, however, that whenever the parties choose the *lex fori* this interest will generally exist.

The *ordre public* clause could serve to limit the freedom of the parties to choose the law, but the limitation is not great, since this clause is regarded the same way as it is in Germany.

French Law

French statutory conflicts law has no special reference to the law applicable to contracts, and thus the courts have developed the pertinent rules. At first, the place of contracting or the place of performance was considered the primary contact point.[126] Party autonomy was recognized as a secondary point of contact. In 1910 the French Supreme Court (Cour de Cassation) stated: "The law applicable to a contract, whether it pertains to its formation or its provisions and con-

---

[121] 79 II BGE 295, 298 ff.

[122] 80 II BGE 179; 81 II BGE 391; 82 II BGE 129; 82 II BGE 552; 91 II BGE 44; and H. W. Widmer, *Die Bestimmung des massgeblichen Rechts im internationalen Vertragsrecht* (Zurich, 1944), pp. 62 ff.; Vischer, n. 102 above, pp. 24 ff.

[123] 78 II BGE 74, 85.   [124] *Id.*   [125] 91 II BGE 44.

[126] Decision of the French Supreme Court, published in 7 *Revue critique de droit international privé* 395 (1911); see also H. Batiffol, *Traité élémentaire de droit international privé.* (3rd ed.; Paris, 1959), pp. 639 ff.

ditions, is that which the parties have chosen." [127] The court repeated this formulation in 1932 and the Chambre des Requètes adopted this ruling.[128]

Since World War II, the opinion of the courts has been less uniform and appears to be inclined to deviate from the earlier formulation. But the court decisions all deal with cases in which the parties have not expressly made a choice of law, and in these cases the courts use objective tests to find the applicable law. They stress, however, that any contractual choice of law will be given effect.[129]

The French Supreme Court in an opinion of April 24, 1952, following Batiffol, enunciated the principle that the parties have no power to choose the applicable law themselves, but can only localize the contract.[130] The judge may find this localization to be one element in establishing the applicable law, but he must give consideration to all other points of contact as well. Again, in the case in issue, the parties have made no express selection of the law.

This opinion abandons only the theory brought earlier in the formulation of the rule on party autonomy. The limitations imposed by the new opinion are not so broad; in fact under French law the power of the parties to choose the applicable law is really no less effective than in other big commercial nations.

Even the old rule of complete autonomy in the choice of law was not consistently applied whenever provisions in the chosen law not subject to the disposition of the parties would render the contract void.[131] In effect the chosen law was not considered a legal order under which the case was to be decided, but was treated only as a fact and applied only as long as it did not conflict with the interest of the parties. We have here a kind of "rule of validation." Furthermore, it is no longer held, as the writers once suggested,[132] that the contracting

---

[127] Id.
[128] The decision is published in 29 *Revue critique de droit international privé* 909 (1934); see also 1938 *Receuil Sirey* I, p. 30.
[129] Decision of the French Supreme Court, published in 48 *Revue critique de droit international privé* 708 (1959); decisions of the Appellate Court of Paris, 44 *id.* 330 (1955), 49 *id.* 72 (1960).
[130] 41 *id.* 502 (1952); H. Batiffol, *Les conflits de lois en matière de contrats* (Paris, 1938) pp. 46 ff.; and Batiffol, n. 126 above, pp. 621 ff.
[131] Decisions of the French Supreme Court, published in 49 *Revue critique de droit international privé* 202 (1960); 39 *id.* 609 (1950).
[132] P. Arminjon, *Précis de droit international privé commercial* (Paris, 1948) pp. 253 ff.; E. Bartin, *Études sur les effets internationaux des jugements* (Paris,

parties cannot by agreement avoid those rules not subject to the parties' disposition, contained in a legal order which would be applicable to the contract lacking their agreement.

Even the older court decisions allowed the parties to exclude rules and regulations that they would have been bound to, lacking agreement.[133] The examples are the inclusion of gold clauses or arbitration clauses that would otherwise be void. The result is not different under the more recently developed concept of choice of law as a mere localization of the contract. Laws that would have applied to the contract regardless of the will of the parties, for example the *lex fori,* can be rendered inapplicable by the localization of the contract in a different state. This principle was recognized by the French Supreme Court in its opinion of April 24, 1952. This opinion agrees fully with the proponents of this doctrine among the legal writers, particularly Batiffol.[134]

Under French jurisprudence, there are some limitations in the choice of the legal system to which parties wish to subject the contractual relationship: The parties to the contract have only the power to choose the applicable law on international contracts or, as stated by the French Supreme Court, whenever interests of international trade are involved.[135] Furthermore, the French Supreme Court in 1950 stated expressly that an international contract by the parties involved may not be put in a space empty of law, but must necessarily be related to a definite legal system.[136] Batiffol from this decision draws the far-reaching conclusion that French jurisprudence is not going to permit the choice of the so-called neutral legal order.[137] This conclusion is even more justified if one is acting on the basis that the right of the choice of law does not mean more than the right to localize the contract. Localization necessarily cannot be inconsistent with the realities of the

---

1907), pp. 201 ff.; A. Pillet, *Principes de droit international privé* (Paris, 1903), pp. 436 ff.; E. Audinet, *Principes élémentaires du droit international privé* 2d ed.; Paris, 1906), pp. 297 ff.; M. Calets, *Essia sur le principe de l'autonomie de la volonté en droit international privé* (Paris, 1927), pp. 79 ff., 427 ff.

[133] 1933 Cass. civ. 1re 41; 39 *Revue critique de droit international privé* 609 (1950).

[134] 41 *Revue critique de droit international privé* 502 (1952); also Batiffol, n. 130 above, p. 161, and n. 126 above, pp. 626 f.; J. Donnedieu de Vabres, "Remarques sur la théorie du conflit des lois," 1943 I *Juris Classeur Périodique* 375; M. Planiol and G. Ripert, *Traité pratique de droit civil français* (Paris, 1952) IV, 641.

[135] 1931 Cass. civ, 1re 41.

[136] 39 *Revue critique de droit international privé* 609 (1950).

[137] Batiffol n. 126 above, p. 626.

concrete contract of relation. It is an entirely different issue that these realities may be manipulated in cartel contracts.

Another limitation of private autonomy is *ordre public* beside the so-called *Sonderanknuepfung* of private rules not subject to the disposition of the party connected with principles of public law.[138] It is true that modern jurisprudence accepts the rule that *ordre public* only excludes law otherwise applicable whenever application of this law and the concrete case would be inconsistent with "the political and social basis of French civilization," whenever French interests of existence are really involved.[139] *Ordre public,* however, serves to protect a definite statutory aim. The courts seem to have gone one step beyond and equalize often the international *ordre public* with the national *ordre public.* However, the cases decided do not deal with the field of private autonomy. The objection that the judicial approach abuses *ordre public* is certainly not correct here.[140] We refer especially to the decision of the French Supreme Court of June 21, 1950.[141] Here the court chose to apply a devaluation rule and a prohibition of the gold clause of Canadian law applicable in reference to the *ordre public,* although there were similar rules in France itself. The court reasoned that international commerce calls for a different legal order from domestic commerce. In international trade the inclusion of gold clauses in contracts was considered absolutely necessary.

Article 57 of the French draft of an international conflict of law ratifies and renews essentially the attitude and approach of courts to the question of private autonomy.[142] Under this draft the parties may choose the law applicable to the validity of the contract even on legal principles outside the disposition of parties, provided they have legitimate interests in this choice of law.

English Law

The English courts, beginning with Lord Mansfield's opinion in *Robinson v. Bland,* which was followed by several opinions in 1865,

[138] Decisions of the French Supreme Court, published in 4 *Nouvelle Revue de droit international privé* 53, 55 (1937).
[139] Wengler, "Die Anknuepfung des zwingenden Schuldrechts im Internationalen Privatrecht," 54 *Zeitschrift fuer vergleichende Rechtswissenschaft* 168 ff. (1941); Batiffol, n. 126 above, pp. 413, 414.
[140] Batiffol, *id.,* p. 416.
[141] 39 *Revue critique de droit international privé* 609 (1950).
[142] Reprinted in 1 *Am. J. Comp. L.* 416 ff. (1952).

considered the contractual choice of law to be unobjectionable.[143]
However, the older cases in which this problem arose contained no express agreement on the applicable law. The courts, therefore, had to
look for "the proper law of the contract." In doing so, they stressed
the points "obviously borrowed from the workshop of the objectivists." [144] (Subjectivists look for the intention of the parties; objectivists look for objectively established elements.) The courts spoke of
the "probable," "presumed," or "expressed or implied" intention of the
parties; this was mere fiction. The judge himself found the applicable
law from the main point of the contractual relationship as based on
such objective criteria as the place of contracting, the place of performance, the nationality of a ship, or headquarters of the parties involved, and so forth. The judge presumed that the parties intended to
submit the contract to the legal order that could reasonably be deduced
from these objective criteria. The reference to the "hypothetical" will
of the parties amounted to nothing more than finding the "proper
law" by an objective consideration of the interests involved. It can
even be assumed that it was merely dictum when a judge found what
he called the express will of the parties in such a case.[145] The "rule of
validation," e.g. the doctrine that one should always seek to apply a
legal order that will maintain the validity of the contract, was of substantial importance in these cases.[146]

Recognition of an actual contractual choice of law begins to show
itself much later, especially in cases in which the parties had agreed
upon the jurisdiction of a British court or British arbitration tribunal.
The courts considered this submission of the contract to British courts
as an implied, "not hypothetical," agreement to apply British law.

---

[143] 2 *Burrows Rep.* 1077, 1078 (1760); and peninsular and Oriental Navigation
Company v. Shand, [1865] 3 Moo.P.C. 272; Lloyd v. Guilbert [1865] L.R. 1
Q.B. 115, 120 ff.; In re Missouri Steamship Co., [1889] 42 Ch.D. 321; The Industry
[1894] P. (C.A.) 58; The Adriatic [1931] P. 241, 245; The Njegos [1936] P. 90,
103; Mount Albert Borrough Council v. Australasian Temperance and General
Mutual Life Assurance Society [1938] A.C. 224.

[144] E. J. Cohn, "The Objectivist Practice on the Proper Law of Contract," 6
Int. and Comp. L.Q. 373, 374 (1957).

[145] See also W. Lorenz, *Vertragsabschluss und Parteiwille im internationalen
Obligationenrecht Englands* (Heidelberg, 1957), pp. 61 ff.; Cohn, n. 144 above,
pp. 373, 374.

[146] In re Missouri Steamship Co. [1899] 42 Ch. 331, 333, 337; The Adriatic [1931]
P. 241; The Assunzione [1954] All E.R. 278, 292 (C.A.); contra: British South
Africa Co. v. De Beers Consolidated Mines, Ltd. [1910] 2 Ch. 502, 513 (C.A.).

At first the courts considered this agreement of submission to a British court to be a factual contact point between English law and the contract that carried greater weight than other objective contact points.[147] "Even here, it may be noted, the arbitration constitutes a factual connection with the law applied."[148] Since the case of *Speenier v. La Cloche* (1902), however, it must be assumed that English courts have recognized the power of the parties to choose the law as a decisive element in conflicts of law.[149] In this case we read: "That the intention of the parties to a contract is a true criterion by which to determine by what law it is to be governed is too clear for controversy."[150]

Lord Phillimore spoke more directly in his opinion in *N.V. Kwik Hoo Tony Handel Maatschappij v. James Finlay & Co., Ltd.* (1927), where he said: "What shall be the law which shall govern a contract is (except in some instances, where positive mandatory or prohibitory provisions are dictated as matter of public policy by the State) a matter to be regulated by the intentions of the parties."[151] In *Rex v. International Trustee for the Protection of Bondholders AG* (1937), Lord Atkin even stated that the judge is bound by the will of the parties expressed in the contract.[152]

Since 1921, English courts in several opinions have affirmed their recognition of express choice of law.[153] However, these opinions deal with cases similar to the arbitration cases referred to above, in which English law was applied and in which the courts were influenced by the well-known "homeward trend" of English courts. The Privy Council in the case of *Vita Food Products, Inc., v. Unus Shipping Co.* (1939) sets forth the broad recognition of party autonomy in the choice of law.[154] In this opinion, which has no power of precedent in England, Lord Wright considered it "well settled by English Law" that the will of the parties determines the applicable law. But, he said, this choice of law will only be recognized "provided the intention expressed in bona fide and legal, and provided there is no reason for avoiding the choice on the ground of public policy."[155]

There are several objections to this opinion, however. First, the

---

[147] Hamlyn and Co. v. Talisker Distillery [1894] A.C. 202.
[148] R. H. Graveson, *The Conflict of Laws* (5th ed.; London, 1965), p. 360.
[149] [1902] A.C. 446.   [150] *Id.*, p. 450.
[151] [1927] A.C. 604, 609.   [152] [1937] A.C. 500.
[153] Jones v. Oceanic Steam Navigation Co. [1924] 2 K.B. 730; Ocean Steamship Company, Ltd. v. Queensland State Wheat Board [1941] 1 K.B. 402 (C.A.).
[154] A.C. 277.   [155] *Id.*, pp. 289, 290.

validity of the contract did not depend upon the application of English law, as the contract would have been valid had Nova Scotian or Newfoundland law been applied, as would have been the case had there been no agreement.[156] Furthermore, Lord Wright said that the choice of law must be "bona fide" and "legal," which opens the road to the interpretation that the parties, by choosing the applicable law, may not evade legal rules over which they would have no power of disposition in the legal order which would have been applicable, lacking agreement.[157] This caveat was reinforced by dictum in the case of *In re Claim by Helbert Wagg & Co., Ltd* (1956), where it is said that the will of the parties will not be decisive whenever the contract has no "real or substantial connection" to the chosen law.[158]

There are other indications that the opinion of English judges is not as uniform as the opinion of Lord Wright indicates. Take for example the dictum of Lord Denning in *Boissevain v. Weil* (1949):

The proper law of the contract is the law of England, and he cannot escape the effect of that law by stipulating in the contract that it is governed by the law of the United States. Notwithstanding what we said in Vita Food Products, Inc. v. Unus Shipping Co., I do not believe that the parties are free to stipulate by what law the validity of their contract is to be determined. Their intention is only one of the factors to be taken into account.[159]

It should be noted that this was the case involving the application of English currency law, and in such a case the rule of *ordre public* may not become the chosen law even under the theory of the objectivists.[160]

The subjective theory of party autonomy in contract is not supported by any clear majority of the writers either. Cohn, F. A. Mann, Schmitthoff, and M. Wolff are proponents of this doctrine; Cheshire, Morris, Graveson and the Canadian scholar Falconbridge and all critical.[161] The latter all hold that the validity of the contract can only be

156 J. H. C. Morris and G. C. Cheshire, "The Proper Law of a Contract in the Conflict of Laws," 56 *L.Q. Rev.* 320 (1940); Lorenz, n. 145 above, p. 96.

157 A. V. Dicey and J. H. C. Morris, *Conflict of Laws* (7th ed.; London, 1958), p. 864; Morris and Cheshire, n. 156 above; cf. M. Wolff, n. 2 above, p. 419; Lorenz, n. 145 above, pp. 98, 99.

158 1956 Ch. 323, 341.   159 1949 1 K.B. 482, 490 (C.A.)

160 Lorenz, n. 145 above, p. 373 ff.

161 18 *B.Y.I.L.* 97 ff. (1937); 3 *Int. L.Q.* 60, 597 (1950); C. M. Schmitthoff, *English Conflict of Laws*, 109 ff. (3rd ed.; London, 1954); Wolf, n. 2 above, pp. 414 ff; G. Cheshire, *Private International Law* (7th ed.; Oxford 1965), 192 ff.; Morris, n. 156 above; Graveson, n. 148 above, pp. 320 ff.; J. D. Falconbridge, *Essays on the Conflict of Laws* (2d ed.; Toronto, 1954), p. 380.

determined under the "proper law of the contract." Perhaps the best general statement is that the will of the parties governs *prima facie* [162] and is enforced by the judges, but that English law has not gone as far as the Continental legal systems in the recognition of the scope of party autonomy.[163] The parties are most constrained by the public policy limitation in England, which goes far beyond the corresponding rules in Germany; this is a great help to British trade regulation rules, over which the parties have no disposition, as they are outside the "proper law" as formulated.

Impact of Present Legal Interpretation on International Cartels

Our survey of the present legal interpretation has shown how in the field of conflicts of law a broad tendency to harmony has developed among the leading trading nations. Once we have analyzed the law in the field of procedure, private litigation, industrial property, and corporate entities, we shall see that they lead to the same result. It is doubtful whether this harmonization results simply from its reasonableness. Very powerful interests have exerted influence in its favor in all countries and before all courts.

To what extent do present legal conditions favor the organizers of the international cartels? The issue from the point of view of German law is that there were only a few, very ineffective special rules of cartel law at the time the trend toward recognition of private autonomy in conflict of law began. The acceptance of party autonomy finally ended in the full recognition of the choice of a legal system that is practically unrelated to the contract. There was no limitation other than *ordre public* in German law, and it was so limited by interpretation that it is of no real help. The difference of opinion on the character of *ordre public* in Section 8 of the Cartel Decree of 1923 demonstrates this.[164]

International cartels in practice are subject to no particular legal system; they live under their own autonomous law. Restrictive cartel statutes, developed in leading industrial nations, have not changed this

---

[162] O. Kahn-Freund, in Dicey and Morris, n. 157 above, p. 725.

[163] See also Re United Railways and Regla Wearhouses, Ltd. (1961) A.C. 1007.

[164] H. Kronstein, *Law and Economic Power: Selected Essays*, (Karlsruhe, 1962), pp. 247 ff.; cf. R. Isay, "Anwendung der Kartellverordnung auf international Kartelle," 1925 Kartell-Rundschau 117.

much. Even if a given statute was intended to reach international situations, it would be applied only by the forum of the state that enacted the statue. The parties from their point of view need a bridge to some other legal system or to better rules of conflicts of law, by virtue of which they obtain unrestrictive private autonomy in contracts.

It is not difficult to reach this bridge. We will see that the possibility of choosing a foreign court or arbitration tribunal appears to run parallel to the development of conflict of law. Since the foreign court applies only its own rules of conflict of law (except in rare cases of *renvoi*) and courts of arbitration very often decide only under "equitable principles," parties need only consider the legal opinion of courts, carefully selected by themselves, as to the legal rules which are beyond the disposition of the parties or pertain to *ordre public*. In all other cases, they live on the basis of and within their own legal aid.

IO

Establishment of Jurisdiction by Contract

The establishment of jurisdiction by contract is a most important device for circumventing mandatory legal provisions. By these contracts the contracting partners agree to submit their litigation to a certain court. At the same time, jurisdiction of other courts is excluded. Since the court must apply, to a certain extent, the mandatory provisions in force in the territory where the court is located, establishment of jurisdiction implies in some aspects selection of the applicable law. International arbitration is an additional device to exclude the application of unfavorable legal provisions and to determine the application of the most convenient legal system.

American Law

American law distinguishes significantly between interstate venue and municipal venue. Interstate venue, or venue as between different places in the same jurisdiction, is regarded as a procedural matter. In questions of municipal venue the parties have always been accorded wide discretion as to selection of the most convenient forum; whereas in questions of interstate venue some states have tried to exclude jurisdiction of other states in certain matters. In an early Supreme Court case, the Court was faced with the question whether the full faith and credit clause of the U.S. Constitution prohibited the courts of Georgia from enforcing a course of action provided by the Alabama code to the servants against the master for injuries occasioned by defective machinery when another section of the same code provided that suits to enforce such liability must be brought in a court of competent jurisdiction within the state of Alabama and not elsewhere.[1] The Supreme Court stated, "There are many cases where right and remedy are so united that the right cannot be enforced except in the manner and before the tribunal designated by the act." The Supreme Court found this law was not applicable to the case before it; it held:

[1] Tennessee Coal, Iron and Railway Co. v. George, 233 U.S. 354 (1914).

245

The courts of the sister state trying the case would be bound to give full faith and credit to all those substantial provisions of the statute which inhered in the cause of action or which name conditions on which the right to sue depends. But venue is no part of the right, and a state cannot create transitory cause of action and at the same time destroy the right to sue on that transitory cause of action in any court having jurisdiction. That jurisdiction is to be determined by the law of the court's creation and cannot be defeated by the extraterritorial application of a statute of another state even though it created the right of action.

The Former "Non Ouster" Rule

The American courts originally refused to recognize contractual establishment of jurisdiction in transitory actions. This was especially true with respect to agreements whereby the parties established jurisdiction of a foreign court. The courts argued that their jurisdiction was based in law and could therefore not be excluded by a private agreement.[2] The courts argued further that any stipulation between contracting parties distinguishing between the different courts of the country was contrary to public policy and could therefore not be enforced by the courts.[3] This line of reasoning is still accepted by some courts.[4] In any case, the courts rejected recognition of establishment of jurisdiction by contracts between parties of different bargaining power.[5]

Modern Development

A substantial change has appeared in recent court decisions. New York State courts and federal courts decided that there is no absolute

[2] Bartlett v. Union Mutual Fire Insurance Co., 46 Me. 500 (1858); Benson v. Eastern Building and Loan Association, 66 N.E. 627 (1903); State ex rel. Kahn v. Tazwell, 266 p. 238 (1928).

[3] Ranborg v. Indussa, 260 F. Supp. 660 (1966); Nashua River Paper Co. v. Hammermill Paper Co., 11 N.E. 678 (1916); Mutual Reserve Fund Life Association v. Cleveland Woolen Mills, 82 F. 508 (6th Cir. 1897); Nute v. Hamilton Mutual Insurance Co., 72 Mass. (6 Gray) 174 (1856); Nippon Ki-Ito Kaisha v. Ewing-Thomas Corp., 170 A. 286 (1934); see also A. L. Corbin, *A Comprehensive Treatise on the Working Rules of Contract Law*, Vol. VI A (St. Paul, 1962), §1445; J. H. Beale, *A Treatise on the Conflict of Laws* (New York, 1935), p. 1660 and Second Restatement, Tent. Draft No. 4, 1957, *contra* Restatement §617; 14 *Am. Jur.* 2d, "Courts," §§196, 389.

[4] Carbon Black Export v. The S.S. Monrosa, 254 F. 2d 297 (5th Cir. 1958), certiorari granted 358 U.S. 809, certiorari dismissed 359 U.S. 180; Kyler v. United States Trotting Association, 210 N.Y.S. 2d 15 (App. Div. 1961).

[5] Standard Pipe Line Co. v. Burnelt, 66 S.W. 2d 637 (1933), certiorari denied 292 U.S. 649 (1934); Parker v. Krauss Co., 284 N.Y.S. 478 (1935); State ex rel. Kahn v. Tazwell, n. 2 above.

prohibition against contracts provided for jurisdiction of a special court. The courts held that the enforceability of such agreements depends upon their reasonableness.[6] The courts recognize the reasonableness of an agreement if the court the parties choose seems capable of deciding the case justly and reasonably.[7] Such reasonableness may, for instance, be based on the favorable location of the court.[8] The decisions thus have some connection with the so-called doctrine of *forum non conveniens*.[9]

These decisions were often justified by an analogy to arbitration contracts. It was pointed out that the court decisions and even a federal statute [10] accorded the parties the right to submit their disputes to arbitration and to agree upon a particular arbitration tribunal. Therefore, the argument goes, the same should be true with respect to contractual settlement of jurisdiction.[11] This view neglected the fact that arbitration contracts were admitted because of their private nature.[12] In addition, contractual settlement of jurisdiction and arbitration clauses may be based on different motives and induce different results in the legal protection of the parties.[13] Finally it should be observed

[6] Wm. H. Mueller and Co. v. Swedish American Line, Ltd., 224 F. 2d 806 (2d Cir. 1955), certiorari denied 350 U.S. 903; but see Ranborg v. Indussa, 260 F. Supp. 660 (1966) which would seem to overrule Mueller; Euzzino v. London and Edinburgh Insurance Co., 228 F. Supp. 431 (N.D. Ill. 1964); Sociedade Brasileira, et al. v. The S.S. Punta Del Este, 135 F. Supp. 394 (S.D.N.Y. 1955); Krenger v. Pennsylvania Railroad Co., 174 F. 2d 556 (2d Cir. 1949), certiorari denied 338 U.S. 866 (1949) (concurring opinion J. Learned Hand); Schwartz v. Zim Israel Navigation Co., 181 N.Y.S. 2d 283 (1958); Nieto v. The S.S. Tinnum, 170 F. Supp. 295 (S.D.N.Y. 1958); Chemical Carriers v. L. Smit and Co.'s Internationale Sleepdienst, 154 F. Supp. 886 (S.D.N.Y. 1957); Skins Trading Corp. v. The S.S. Punta Del Este, 180 F. Supp. 609 (S.D.N.Y. 1960); Aetna Insurance Co. v. The S.S. Satrustegui, 171 F. Supp. 33, rehearing 174 F. Supp. 934 (D. Puerto Rico 1959); see also Central Contracting Co. v. Maryland Casualty Co., 242 F. Supp. 858 (W.D.Pa. 1965); Central Contracting Co. v. C. E. Youngdahl and Co., Inc., et al., 209 A. 2d 810 (1965).

[7] Nieto v. The S.S. Tinnum, 170 F. Supp. 295 (S.D.N.Y. 1958).

[8] Daley v. People's Building, Loan and Savings Association, 59 N.E. 452 (1901); Mittenthal v. Mascagni, 66 N.E. 425 (1903).

[9] P. Blair, "The Doctrine of Forum Non-Conviens in Anglo-American Law," 29 *Colum. L. Rev.* 1 (1929); A. A. Ehrenzweig, *A Treatise on the Conflict of Laws* (St. Paul, 1962), pp. 121 ff.

[10] U.S. Arbitration Act, 9 U.S.C.A. §1.

[11] Central Contracting Co. v. Maryland Casualty Co., 242 F. Supp. 858, 861 (W.D.Pa. 1965); Monte v. Southern Delaware County Authority, 335 F. 2d 855, 857 (3d Cir. 1964); Mittenthal v. Mascagni, 66 N.E. 425 (1903).

[12] Gilbert v. Burnstine, 255 N.Y. 348 (1931).

[13] Note "Testatrix's Devise of Husband's Property under the New York State Decendent Estate Law," 45 *Yale L.J.* 1147, 1151 (1936).

that arbitration clauses were even recognized where the law provides for compulsory jurisdiction of the courts—for example, in connection with separation agreements between husband and wife and custody over infants.[14]

British Law

In British law arbitration contracts and contractual settlement of jurisdiction have been equated to a large extent.[15] The courts originally denied recognition of contractual settlement of jurisdiction,[16] with the exception of a few cases in maritime law.[17] After the Common Law Procedure Act, permitting arbitration contracts, had entered into force in 1854, the course of decisions changed. Thereafter, the courts equated contractual settlement of jurisdiction with arbitration contracts and admitted agreements providing for jurisdiction of a foreign court under the same conditions as arbitration contracts were permitted according to the Common Law Procedure Act.[18] This development started with the case *Law v. Garrett*.[19] The same applies to court decisions in Canada and Australia.[20]

More recent decisions, however, show a tendency of the courts to refrain from equating contractual settlement of jurisdiction with arbitration contracts.[21] The courts argued instead that they were obligated to enforce contractual obligations and therefore not permitted to admit actions raised in violation of an agreement providing for jurisdic-

---

[14] Hill v. Hill, 104 N.Y.S. 2d 755 (1951).

[15] Z. Cowen and D. M. da Costa, "The Contractual Forum. A Comparative Study," 43 *Can. Bar Rev.* 453 (1965).

[16] Gienar v. Meyer (1796) 2 H.Bl. 603; Johnson v. Machielsne (1811) 3 Camp. 44.

[17] Horton v. Saver (1859) 4 H. and N. 643; Lee v. Page (1861) 30 L. J. Ch. 857; Edwards v. Aberayron Mutual Ship Insurance Society, Ltd. (1876) 1 Q.B. 563; Doleman and Sons v. Ossett Corp. (1912) 3 K.B. 257.

[18] 8 Ch. 26 (1878).

[19] (1878) 8 Ch.D. 26; see also Brand v. National Life Assurance Co. (1918) 44 D.L.R. 412; Compagnies Des Messageries Maritimes v. Wilson (1954) 94 Comm. L.R. 577.

[20] Austrian Lloyd Steamship Co. v. Gresham Life Assurance Society, Ltd. (1903) 1 K.B. 249; Logan v. Bank of Scotland (No. 2) (1906) 1 K.B. 141; The Cap Blanco (1913) P. 130; The Athenee (1922) 11 L.L.R. 6; The Vestris (1932) 43 L.L.R. 86; Brand v. National Life Assurance Company (1918) 44 D.L.R. 412.

[21] Racecourse Betting Control Board v. Secretary for Air, 1 Ch. 114 (1944); Hannessian v. Lloyd Triestino Societa Anonima Di Navigazione, 68 W.N. (N.S.W.) 98 (1951).

tion of another court.[22] This was the holding in the Fehmarn case [23] although the plaintiff was not a contracting partner of the defendant but an assignee of the original contracting partner. Judge Denning indicated that the court had to investigate which country was most closely connected with the substantive contract of the parties. The contractual establishment of jurisdiction of a foreign court had to be recognized if the British court came to the conclusion that the agreement was reasonable and did not improperly exclude jurisdiction of the British court. This view is very similar to the American position.[24]

German Law

According to the rules of German civil procedure, the parties may, in principal, agree on which courts shall have jurisdiction over the litigation.[25] Such agreements are excluded in very few cases, where the law establishes compulsory jurisdiction of certain courts.[26]

The development of German law is characterized by wide discretion in establishing and excluding jurisdiction of courts.[27] The parties may exclude jurisdiction of normally competent courts and establish jurisdiction of another court instead. This right is confined to litigation where an immediate pecuniary interest of the parties is involved.[28] In addition, there are some cases where law provides for compulsory jurisdiction.

German courts and writers have always distinguished between two types of contracts: the contract containing the substantive provisions of their agreement, and the contract by which the parties establish jurisdiction of a certain court. This method is even applied in cases where the substantive and procedural provisions are parts of one

---

[22] Racecourse Betting Control Board v. Secretary for Air, *id.*

[23] 1 W.L.R. 159 (1958).

[24] See cases cited in n. 6 above.

[25] E. Riezler, *Internationales Zivilprozessrecht und prozessuales Fremdenrecht* (Berlin, 1949), pp. 296 ff.; M. Pagenstecher, "Gerichtsbarkeit und internationale Zuständigkeit als selbständige Prozessvoraussetzungen," 11 *Zeitschrift für ausländisches und internationales Privatrecht* 337, 381 ff. (1937); W. Kralik, "Die internationale Zuständigkeit," 74 *Zeitschrift für Zivilprozess* 2, 36 ff. (1961); L. Rosenberg, *Lehrbuch des deutschen Zivilprozessrechtes* (9th ed.; Munich, 1961) 146, 167; A. Baumbach and W. Lauterbach, *Zivilprozessordnung mit Gerichtsverfassungsgesetz* (28th ed.; Munich, 1964) §38, n. 1.

[26] See German Code of Civil Procedure, §§24, 606; German Patent Act, §51; see also Pagenstecher, n. 25 above, pp. 410 f.

[27] German Code of Civil Procedure, §§38–40. [28] *Id.*, §40, n. 2.

formal agreement. Consequently, the legality and validity of the procedural contract have customarily been examined without consideration of the contract containing the substantive provisions. This course of decisions has changed slightly in recent years. In one case decided by the German Supreme Court, the parties had agreed on the application of Dutch law and established jurisdiction of a court in the Netherlands in order to circumvent an obligatory provision of the German Commercial Code.[29] The German Supreme Court set forth that the legality of such agreements was very doubtful if these agreements did not have any connection with the contractual forum.[30]

Jurisdiction of German Courts in International Private Litigation

The framers of the German Zivilprozessordnung (Civil Procedure Act) intended to regulate jurisdiction of German courts in their relationship with each other. Nevertheless, the German courts have also applied the provisions of this act to questions concerning the jurisdiction of foreign courts.[31] The parties thus may exclude jurisdiction of German courts and establish jurisdiction of a specific foreign court instead.[32] Such agreements are even permitted in some cases where the German law provides for compulsory jurisdiction.[33] On the other hand, contractual establishment of jurisdiction is restricted to cases where an immediate pecuniary interest of the parties is involved. This limitation, however, is of no significance for international cartels.

Comparison with International Arbitration

Contractual establishment of jurisdiction has to be distinguished from arbitration contracts. The conclusion of arbitration contracts was permitted early under German law. When the German Civil Procedure Act came into force, it was argued that arbitration contracts had to be permitted according to the principle of private autonomy. On this principle, the parties were entitled to settle disputes privately. It was argued that they were also entitled to subject themselves to the decision of an independent umpire.[34] Since such arbitration tribunals are

---

[29] 1961 *Neue juristische Wochenschrift* 1061 f.   [30] 44 BGHZ 46.

[31] 37 RGZ 371; 159 RGZ 254, 256.

[32] 126 RGZ 196, 199; 150 RGZ 265, 268; 14 BGHZ 286, 289; 22 BGHZ 1, 13.

[33] Riezler, n. 25 above, p. 239; Rosenberg, n. 25 above; Pagenstecher, n. 25 above, pp. 384, 399, 401 ff.

[34] C. Hahn, *Die gesamten Materialien zur CPO und zu dem Einführungsgesetz*, Pt. 1 (2d ed.; Berlin, 1881), p. 490.

entirely different from state courts, restrictions imposed on contractual establishment of jurisdiction were not applied to arbitration contracts. Therefore, jurisdiction of arbitration tribunals was even recognized in cases where the law provided for compulsory jurisdiction of a certain court in the relationship among courts.[35] This is indeed an awkward result. The parties were in the position to evade compulsory jurisdiction of a certain state court by providing for the settlement of the disputes by an arbitration tribunal. They were not in a position, however, to evade compulsory jurisdiction by establishing jurisdiction of a court of their own choice. To avoid these inconsistencies, the former German Supreme Court of Labor Law and a well-known German writer have argued that the parties should be entitled to establish jurisdiction of a foreign court, even where German law provided for exclusive jurisdiction of a certain German court, if there was some link with the foreign country concerned.[36] Since the German courts and the majority of writers have not accepted this argument, German law accords wide discretion in establishing jurisdiction of foreign courts and excluding jurisdiction of the German courts.[37]

The Public Interest

In order to limit the influence of international cartels, it would have been necessary to restrict private discretion in establishing jurisdiction of courts. Such restrictions have to be guided by the public interest.

Certain restrictions were made by the courts in cases where parties of different bargaining power were involved. In these cases the party in the weaker bargaining position had signed a form that contained a clause establishing jurisdiction of a court not linked in any way with the litigation. The courts held that these agreements were unconscionable according to Section 138 of the German Civil Code.[38] These cases aimed at protection of parties with weak bargaining power. There may, however, also be cases where the public interest requires that disputes

[35] A. Troller, *Das internationale Privat- und Zivilprozessrecht im gewerblichen Rechtsschutz und Urheberrecht* (Basel, 1952), pp. 276, 277; E. Reimer, *Patentgesetz und Gebrauchsmustergesetz* (2d ed.; Munich, 1958), §51, n. 2.

[36] 13 RAG 29; Pagenstecher, n. 25 above, pp. 384 ff. See also M. W. Berliner, *Vereinbarungen über den Gerichtsstand im internationalen Rechtsverkehr* (Heidelberg, 1936), pp. 63 f.

[37] Decision of the former German Supreme Court, published in 1894 *Juristische Wochenschrift* 369; Riezler, n. 25 above, p. 86.

[38] Decision of the Appellate Court of Frankfurt, published in 1960 *Betriebs-Berater* 1223; decision of the Civil Court of Dortmund, published in 1955 *Monatsschrift für deutsches Recht* 112.

between parties of equal bargaining power be decided on the market position of the parties or on the nature of the applicable substantive law.[39] The courts and the majority of the writers have neglected these viewpoints by investigating the legality of contractual establishment of jurisdiction without considering the nature of the litigation, the parties involved, or the applicable law. The German Civil Supreme Court has indicated that a contractual clause establishing jurisdiction of a foreign court might be illegal if the purpose of such a clause was to enforce an agreement unenforceable under German conflict-of-law rules.[40] This decision is significant since it re-establishes the relationship between determination of jurisdiction and the applicable substantive law.

Nevertheless, the principle that public interest prevails over private autonomy with respect to the establishment of jurisdiction has not been generally recognized. This is astonishing, since legislators have always shown a public interest in certain actions, such as divorce cases, or other actions concerning questions of family law or industrial property rights. Consequently, the powerful trade associations and enterprises are in a position to use the instrument of contractual determination of jurisdiction in order to deprive the state courts of their opportunity to maintain and protect competition in the market.

French Law

Article 14 of the French Civil Code provides that a French citizen may file a complaint against any foreigner in French courts on the basis of contractual rights even if the contract was concluded abroad and even if the foreigner is not a resident of France.[41] Aliens are also entitled to file complaints against French citizens in French courts (Article 15). This is to provide a forum for French citizens if the foreign forum has attempted to exclude French jurisdiction. Since the provisions of Articles 14 and 15 of the Civil Code are considered a privilege of the French plaintiff, he may agree to exclude jurisdiction of French courts and establish jurisdiction of a foreign court instead.[42]

---

[39] G. Schiedermair, *Vereinbarungen im Zivilprozess* (Bonn, 1935), p. 89.

[40] 1961 *Neue juristische Wochenschrift* 1061; 1965 *Neue juristische Wochenschrift* 1665.

[41] The provision applies also to corporations.

[42] H. Batiffol, *Traité élémentaire de droit international privé* (3d ed.; Paris, 1959), 768, 769; Riezler, n. 25 above, pp. 304, 312 f.

The majority of writers and the courts do not consider this principle incompatible with the *ordre public*.[43] As establishment of jurisdiction is not incompatible with the *ordre public* with respect to domestic French courts, the same is held to be true in regard to foreign courts.

Accordingly, contractual establishment of jurisdiction of foreign courts is even permitted if there is no substantial link between the contract and the respective foreign court. Objective reasons of whatever kind, for example a specific contract of the respective court, may justify contractual establishment of jurisdiction. According to one writer, this right is limited insofar as the agreement may not aim solely at circumventing obligatory substantive provisions of French law. In addition, the French courts reject the enforcement of such agreements if the establishment of jurisdiction was not based on the free will of the contracting parties.[44] Contractual establishment of jurisdiction is illegal where the law provides for compulsory jurisdiction of certain courts. Such compulsory jurisdiction exists with respect to actions based on title to real property located in France, decedents' estates where French law of inheritance applies, French patents, and certain insurance contracts.[45] All the French writers have drawn parallels to arbitration contracts. These ideas have, however, not gained the same importance as in common law countries.

The legal situation is the more difficult where aliens provided for the jurisdiction of French courts. Since the beginning of the nineteenth century, French courts have considered this problem an issue of the law pertaining to the treatment of aliens in France. As, according to Articles 14 and 15, aliens may sue only French citizens before French courts, it was argued that French courts do not have jurisdiction in litigations between aliens.[46] This opinion was finally abandoned by the courts in the Patino case.[47] The courts now recognize contractual establishment of jurisdiction by aliens under the same conditions that apply to contracts between French citizens.

Swiss and Italian Law

In Swiss law contractual establishment of jurisdiction is subject to the procedural regulations of the various cantons. The parties do not

[43] Batiffol, *id.*   [44] *Id.*, pp. 649, 772 f.
[45] Coure de Paris, 1904 II *Dalloz Period* 273; Riezler, n. 25 above, p. 313.
[46] P. Lerebours-Pigeonnière, *Droit international privé* (Paris, 1962), pp. 496–497.
[47] 1948 II *Juris Classeur Periodique* 4422.

have the right to choose a particular court if the law of the cantons or if federal law stipulates compulsory jurisdiction of certain courts. Such prescriptions can be found for all matters where the public interest is involved, such as real estate, affairs of minors, and divorce.[48]

Actions on a debt are transitory under Swiss law, but Article 59 of the Swiss Constitution provides that each solvent debtor (Swiss and foreigner) must be sued only in the canton where he resides unless he waives the right.[49] The purpose of this rule is twofold: it limits the jurisdiction of the cantons, and it provides constitutional protection for each person domiciled in Switzerland against judicial harassment within another canton. As the purpose of this provision is to protect the solvent debtor, the debtor may renounce this privilege and agree to the jurisdiction of a particular foreign court. Article 59, however, refers only to actions with respect to money obligations.

As in German law, the agreement establishing jurisdiction of a certain court is a procedural agreement and does not depend on the validity and legality of the other, substantive part of the contract.[50] The laws of some cantons provide that the procedural agreement has to be in written form.[51] With printed form contracts, the courts accept such agreements only if they are unequivocal and clearly visible.[52] In Swiss law, too, some writers hold that a contractual establishment of jurisdiction should be admitted in all cases where an arbitration contract would be lawful.

The designation of Swiss courts is held to be a privilege of people living in that country. Swiss courts may reject the jurisdiction of cases that do not have sufficient connections with Swiss people or Swiss territory.[53]

Italian law prohibits contractual establishment of jurisdiction in certain cases.[54] Article 2 of the Italian Code of Civil Procedure of April

[48] A. F. Schnitzer, *Handbuch des internationalen Privatrechts einschliesslich Prozessrecht* (4th ed.; Basel, 1957–1958), II, 826 ff.; 36 I BGE 588, 590, 600; 71 I BGE 26.

[49] F. Fleiner and Z. Giacometti, *Schweizerisches Bundesstaatsrecht* (Zurich, 1949), p. 857.

[50] Schnitzer, n. 48 above, p. 828; 62 I BGE 230; 59 I BGE 179, 224.

[51] Code of Civil Procedure of Bern, §27; see also 76 II BGE 249; Schnitzer, *id.*, pp. 827 f.

[52] 52 I BGE 268; 49 I BGE 48.

[53] Riezler, n. 25 above, p. 311; Schnitzer, n. 48 above, p. 829.

[54] Riezler, *id.*, pp. 305, 313; Schnitzer, *id.*, p. 827; H. Arnold, "Die Gerichtsstandsvereinbarung im internationalen Rechtsverkehr," 1958 *Aussenwirtschaftsdienst des Betriebs-Beraters* 238.

21, 1942, provides that contractual establishment of jurisdiction of a foreign court or of an arbitration tribunal requires a written agreement between aliens or between an alien and an Italian citizen who is not a resident of Italy.

International Agreements

The Hague Conference of Private International Law accepted at its tenth session, which ended on October 28, 1964, a draft convention on the choice of court. Article 4, paragraph 3, of this convention provides: "The agreement on the choice of court shall be void or voidable if it has been obtained by an abuse of economic power or other unfair means." According to Article 5, paragraph 2, of the draft convention, a chosen court may decline jurisdiction in cases where under the internal law of the state of the excluded court the parties were unable, because of the subject matter, to agree to exclude the jurisdiction of the courts of that state. Article 4, paragraph 3, reflects the legal situation in most of the states, but neglects the fact that public interest may require the exclusion of contractual choice of court even in cases where parties of equal bargaining power are involved. This may be true with respect to certain contracts, for example in the fields of property rights and antitrust law. Whether public interest will prevail in these cases depends on how the courts will interpret Article 5, paragraph 2, of the draft convention.

II ～～～～

The Corporation as an Instrument of International Market Regulation

The policy of the economic units of a cartel, which is determined by the interests of the entire organization and directed by a central management, takes advantage of a basic principle of international law: Corporations are subject to the law of the state under which they are incorporated or in which they have their headquarters, even if the shareholders are not citizens or residents of that state. Economic entities are therefore in a position to act through numerous seemingly independent corporations, each of which purports to be subject only to the law of its domicile. Just as in the other legal institutions discussed, the initiative of utilization of a legal instrument is with the organizers, while the legislators, courts, or administrative officials in the different national states are able to determine their interest only after the corporate entity has developed into an instrument of international market regulation. Chapter 8 indicated the varied roles corporate entities in different countries may play in the organization of international market regulation and how easily real or apparent changes may be implemented.

Before World War I, it was settled practice in international law that governments did not claim any other nationalities for a corporation than the nationality of the seat. During the world wars, however, governments claimed the right to protect the interest of the controlling group of a corporate entity having its seat in another country, especially against expropriation in revolution or war. A certain inconsistency developed in the approach of many states. Although they desired to increase the impact of their regulation on states where the subsidiary of their "own" corporations operated, they themselves endorsed the fiction that a local subsidiary organized and incorporated under their law should be subject only to local law.

The organizers of international market regulation are in an increasingly secure position. It is necessary to evaluate this point in line with the development of the relationship between the "corporate entity" and "its government" on the one side and the larger economic unit to which the corporation is economically and practically subordinated on the other.

Enemy Corporations and Expropriation of Their Assets

Modern war encompasses not only the states and people on the various sides, but also those business entities organized or resident in the belligerent states. During World War I, the British House of Lords held in *Daimler Co. v. Continental Tire and Rubber Co.*[1] that a corporation organized under British law was nevertheless an "enemy" under the Trading with the Enemy Act because all shares, and thereby effective control, were in German hands. American law originally recognized the independence of corporations more specifically. The United States Supreme Court decided in *Behn-Meyer & Co. v. Miller*[2] that a corporation organized under Costa Rican law, but fully controlled by a German corporation, was not to be treated as a German enterprise with respect to property situated in the United States. The Supreme Court held that the place of incorporation determined the nationality with respect to vesting of property in the Alien Property Custodian. This attitude, however, while fully consistent with classical corporate theory, proved incompatible with the necessities of war, and the United States eventually adopted the so-called control theory in the Mexican Oil case. In this controversy, the Mexican government had expropriated without compensation Mexican corporations owned by British and American shareholders.[3] The Mexican government justified this measure under the traditional rule that a corporation was to be treated as a national of the state under which it was incorporated. The government of the United States suggested that the citizenship of the shareholders should determine whether an expropriation without compensation violated international law. Although this case was settled between the respective governments, it nevertheless had a substantial impact on later developments.

Prior to American entry into World War II, the United States adopted regulations freezing the assets of certain nationals. The nationality of corporations was to be determined by the nationality of controlling shareholders. During World War II, Section 5a of the Trading with the Enemy Act and the implementing executive orders, as

[1] [1916] 2 A.C. 307; see also H. Kronstein, "The Nationality of International Enterprises," 52 *Colum. L. Rev.* 983 ff. (1952).
[2] 266 U.S. 457 (1925). [3] Kronstein, n. 1 above, pp. 983, 987.

well as the numerous court decisions considering this act, all accepted the concept of related corporations forming an economic unit.[4] English law during World War II followed the judicial decisions of World War I.[5]

In some instances, each side in World War II treated a unit of its own as a citizen of its state, although normally corporations were considered citizens of the state where the management of the entire unit had its headquarters. The case of the Dutch corporation Philips provides an interesting exception. Immediately after the occupation of the Netherlands by Germany, European nations continued to consider Philips a Dutch corporation, while the United States considered all assets of Philips situated in the Western Hemisphere as part of an American enterprise.[6] Immediately prior to American entrance into the war, the management of Philips had assigned all of its assets situated in the Western Hemisphere to a trust.

In the case of *Kaufmann v. Société Internationale pour Participation Industrielles Commerciales S.A.*[7] an attempt was made to examine even more closely the nationality of a corporation. Ninety-seven per cent of the shares of the General Aniline & Film Corporation, organized under Delaware law, were owned by the Swiss I.G. Chemie Corporation. The German firm I.G. Farbenindustrie owned a majority of the shares of I.G. Chemie until 1940. Plaintiffs were some of the small shareholders who together owned the other 3 per cent of the shares. After the entrance of the United States into World War II, the U.S. government confiscated all the assets of the General Aniline Corporation in spite of the fact that I.G. Farben had assigned its shares to Swiss I.G. Chemie. The United States government contended that the German I.G. Farben still exerted technological control over the American corporation. The minority shareholders argued that it was illegal to impair their interest in the corporation since they were American citizens. The Supreme Court accepted this argument and held that 97 per cent of the assets of General Aniline ought to be considered enemy property, while the rest of the assets were to be considered American property. It ruled that the government must protect the rights of the American minority shareholders in any disposition of General Aniline.

[4] 12 U.S.C. 95 (a) (1970); see Clark v. Übersee Finanzkorporation AG, 332 U.S. 480, 488 (1947).
[5] Trading with the Enemy Act, 1939, 2 & 3 Geo. 6, c. 89, Art. 2(1).
[6] United States v. General Electric Co., 82 F. Supp. 753 (D.N.J. 1949).
[7] 343 U.S. 156 (1961).

The provisions of the peace treaty between the Allied Powers and Italy, signed in 1947, shows again the application of the economic unit doctrine, even during peacetime. The treaty provided that Italy was to re-establish the interest of any citizen of any member state of the United Nations to its position as of July 10, 1940. The term "citizen" in the meaning of this treaty included all corporations established according to the law of any member state at the time of enactment of the treaty.[8] Thus, at this point, the theory of the independent nationality of a corporation was recognized. Article 78(4)(d) deals with the situation where corporations, not citizens of a member state, have suffered damage to property situated in Italy, and where citizens of a member state have an interest in such a corporation. In these situations, that part of the damages of the corporation which corresponds to the percentage of the shares held by member-state shareholders must be restored to the corporation. In effect, this is the same type of split nationality of a corporation as was found in the General Aniline case.

After World War II, Switzerland concluded a number of treaties with Eastern European nations to protect the property of Swiss nationals situated in these countries.[9] These treaties are based on the concept of control of property rather than on the form or place of incorporation. The treaties also included cases of indirect control and thus are applicable if the corporation organized under the law of one of the Eastern Bloc countries is controlled by Swiss citizens, and also in situations where the corporation owning the Eastern Bloc corporation is in turn owned by a corporation 50 per cent of the shares of which are controlled by Swiss citizens.

Confiscation on the Basis of Foreign Interest in a Corporation

The confiscation of corporate assets of German corporations arising out of World War II has caused a development of the so-called splitting theory within the Federal Republic of Germany. This theory is based on the concept that a determination of nationality requires analysis of economic and commercial influences on the corporation. The splitting theory is accepted today in Germany; however, it has led to substantial difficulties, especially in cases involving the expro-

[8] Treaty of Peace with Italy, Feb. 10, 1947, 49 U.N.T.S. 1, pp. 161–163.
[9] R. Bindschedler, *Verstaatlichungsmassnahmen und Entschädigungspflicht nach Völkerrecht* (Zurich, 1950), pp. 48 ff.

priation of the interests of minority shareholders. Courts and many writers overlooked these difficulties in order to protect domestic shareholders against the expropriation of enterprises by foreign states. The splitting theory has been accepted by other countries as well with respect to problems of expropriation or the vesting of enemy assets.[10]

United States Export Controls on Trade with Communist Countries

United States restrictions upon trade with Communist countries have caused some problems for American foreign subsidiaries. The Export Control Act prohibits the export to Communist nations of certain types of commodities and technical data unless a license is granted by the President.[11] The act applies to re-exports from third countries to Communist nations and includes all goods containing U.S. component parts or using U.S. technical data. The act by itself affects equally foreign subsidiaries and unrelated foreign companies. It applies whenever the component parts or technical data are involved, whether the transaction is undertaken by an American or by any foreigner. The re-export provision, however, has caused some minor problems with respect to U.S. subsidiaries in Canada, because the large American ownership of Canadian business has resulted in many products using U.S. components and technology. Hence, a high proportion of potential Canadian exports are subject to the U.S. law.

The administration of the Trading with the Enemy Act[12] has also caused serious strains on Canadian-American relationships. This act regulates all commercial and financial transactions made by Americans with certain types of foreigners. Two acts of regulation issued under this act have importance for U.S. foreign direct investment: the Foreign Asset Control Regulations (trade with Communist China, North Vietnam, and North Korea) and the Cuban Assets Control Regulations.[13] These regulations prohibit unlicensed trade with the nationals of these four countries and are applicable to foreign affiliates and subsidiaries whenever Americans have actual or potential effective control of the subsidiary. Thus, the United States exerts its jurisdiction over a foreign corporation even for exports containing no U.S. com-

[10] G. Beitzke, 1956 *Juristenzeitung* 673, 677.
[11] Export Control Act of 1949, as amended, 19 U.S.C. §§2021–32 (1970). This authority has been delegated by the President to the Secretary of Commerce.
[12] Trading with the Enemy Act, §5(b), 40 Stat. 411, as amended, 50 U.S.C.A. App. §5(b) (1970).
[13] 31 C.F.R. §§500.101–500.808.

ponent parts or technical data in any case where the U.S. shareholders are deemed to control the corporation.[14]

Canadian export trade, again, has been seriously affected by American ownership of Canadian industry and by the assertion of U.S. jurisdiction with respect to that ownership. The most controversial incident that has arisen under this act concerned an offer from Communist China to purchase a significant quantity of trucks from the Canadian subsidiary of the Ford Motor Company. Canadian foreign policy is more liberal than U.S. policy with respect to trade with Communist China, and the Canadians were anxious to conclude the agreement with the Chinese for the trucks. However, when the Ford Motor Company of the United States applied to the U.S. Department of Commerce for a license so that its subsidiary could enter into an arrangement with the Chinese, the license was denied. Since American interests owned almost all the Canadian trucking capacity, Canada found itself unable to engage in trade it desired.

The furor of Canadian public opinion over this incident led to an accord between the United States and Canada, known as the Eisenhower-Diefenbaker Statement. However, this arrangement has not proved entirely satisfactory to the Canadians. The United States did agree to grant a license for specific transactions if the Canadian government certifies that no Canadian enterprise is capable of carrying out the transaction and that the particular order is important to the Canadian economy. The United States, therefore, still has retained its right to regulate foreign subsidiaries while Canada has tacitly recognized this right. While the arrangement does provide a *modus vivendi* for resolving specific controversies, it does not settle any problems concerning the overlapping assertions of jurisdiction upon foreign subsidiaries.

United States Foreign Direct Investment Restrictions

Another area of the law which has caused some concern, in principle, with respect to the assertion of jurisdiction over foreign subsidiaries by the United States is the Foreign Direct Investment Regulations, announced January 1, 1968.[15] To alleviate the U.S. balance-of-payments deficit, the Department of Commerce promulgated a

[14] "Back Door Trade," *Wall Street J.*, May 10, 1966.
[15] Exec. Order 11387, Jan. 1, 1968. Pursuant to this the Secretary of Commerce issued the Foreign Direct Investment Restrictions (FDIR), 15 C.F.R. Pt. 1000.

complicated set of regulations which prohibit the transfer of capital abroad unless licensed by the Secretary of Commerce, and which require the repatriation of earnings from abroad and the reduction of bank deposits and other short-term financial assets abroad.[16] One significant factor applicable to the repatriation-of-earnings provision is that it applies in any situation where American ownership or control exceeds 10 per cent of the total ownership of the corporation. The assertion of jurisdiction over a foreign corporation, even though 89 per cent of its stock is owned by foreign nationals, would seem to be an intolerable interference by the United States in the control of corporations operating in the host country. Despite this interference, the FDIR's have provoked relatively little controversy to date: in part because United States ownership is generally well above the 10 per cent limit of the regulations; in part because the nations have a significant stake in maintaining the stability of the world monetary situation (a stability which could be further weakened if the United States failed to cure its balance-of-payments deficit); and in part because the host countries are delighted to see the restriction of American overseas investment. Nevertheless, this expansion of U.S. jurisdiction creates one more problem for the foreign government viewing American foreign direct investment.

United States Antitrust Laws

The administration of United States antitrust law has created a second area of conflict with the law and policies of other nations. Although only a few of these cases have involved assertion of jurisdiction over foreign subsidiaries of U.S. corporations (and this factor by itself is important only with respect to the question of service for due process considerations), the jurisdiction issue is raised frequently in connection with discussions of American foreign direct investment and as such should be discussed briefly.

Section 1 of the Sherman Act deals with contracts, combinations, or conspiracies in restraint of trade or commerce *among the several states, or with foreign nations.*[17] Section 2 of that act regulates monop-

16 FDIR, Subpt. B, §§ 1000.202–1000.203.

17 26 Stat. 209 (1890), as amended, 15 U.S.C. §1. Congressional authority to regulate foreign commerce is found in subsection 8(3) of Article 1 of the United States Constitution. Section 73 of the Wilson Tariff Act of 1894, 15 U.S.C. §8, specifically provides for control of imports when they are intended to oper-

olies or attempts to monopolize the trade or commerce *among the several states, or with foreign nations.* Section 7 of the Clayton Act prohibits a corporation engaged in commerce from acquiring the stock or assets of another corporation, also engaged in commerce, where in *any section of the country* the effect of such acquisition may be substantially to lessen competition or to tend to create a monopoly.[18] The Sherman Act applies to foreign commerce specifically, while the Clayton Act does not. A violation of Section 1 of the Sherman Act can occur whenever a restraint of trade affects either the foreign commerce or interstate commerce of the United States. Foreign commerce is generally defined to cover imports into, or exports from, the United States, although it may be expanded to include activities such as transportation.[19]

A number of jurisdictional requirments must be met before Section 7 is applicable: acquisition of stock or assets; acquisition of a company engaged in commerce by a company engaged in commerce; and acquisition of a company where the effect in any section of the country may be substantially to lessen competition. Any mergers involving foreign corporations must have some effect on competition within the United States. It has been suggested that the acquisition of a foreign firm not previously buying or selling in the United States would not be subject to Section 7 because the requirement that the acquired company be engaged in commerce has not been satisfied.[20]

One incidence of extraterritorial application of U.S. antitrust laws has particularly exasperated the Canadians. This is the so-called Canadian Patent Pool case in which a federal district court ordered the

---

ate in restraint of trade. This provision is only a form of control and is dependent upon a determination of restraint in accordance with the Sherman Act. See Reliable Volkswagen Sales and Service Corp. v. World Wide Auto Corp., 182 F. Supp. 412 (D.N.J. 1960).

[18] 38 Stat. 731 (1914), as amended, 15 U.S.C. §18.

[19] The Attorney General's committee to study the antitrust laws concluded that the phrase "trade or commerce with foreign nations" "should be construed broadly to include not only the import and export flow of finished products, their component parts and adjunct services, but also, as in domestic commerce, capital investment and financing. So interpreted, foreign commerce would also comprehend all types of industrial property rights in patents, trademarks, trade secrets and know-how and other technological information" (*Report of the Attorney General's National Committee to Study the Antitrust Laws* [1955], pp. 79–80).

[20] K. Brewster, Jr., *Antitrust and American Business Abroad* (New York, 1958), p. 192.

dissolution of a patent pool, established among a number of Canadian subsidiaries of primarily American corporations, even though the patent pool was legal under Canadian law.[21] The case was overruled by the Supreme Court on February 24, 1971, and sent back for further consideration, without clarifying the issue.

While the issue of extraterritoriality is clearly present in this case, the fact that most of the members of the pool are subsidiaries of American firms is not a crucial element in the case. Assuming that the United States could secure jurisdiction over them, the result in this case would be the same, even if no U.S. subsidiaries are involved. The famous Swiss Watchmakers case, in which most of the corporations involved were Swiss domiciliaries and were not owned by American shareholders, makes this point clear.[22] Nevertheless, this distinction is not generally made by foreign observers. In their eyes, direct investment means the possibility of extending U.S. antitrust laws to their domestic economic situation. While it is impossible to judge accurately, this belief may have some merit, since the propensity of American antitrust officials to bring suit may be greater when U.S. subsidiaries are involved. The broad reach of the Sherman Act in foreign commerce is clearly defined by three cases: *United States v. Imperial Chem. Industries, Ltd.* (ICI); *United States v. Aluminum Co. of America* (Alcoa); and *United States v. Minnesota Mining & Mfg. Co.*[23]

One of many issues in the Alcoa case involved two agreements among foreign aluminum producers. The court specifically found that the only U.S. producer, Alcoa, was not a party to these agreements. The court found that the foreign producers intended to affect imports into the United States through a system of production quotas and royalty payments to maintain the price of aluminum, that imports were affected, and thus that the agreements violated Section 1 of the Sherman Act. The court noted that this concept is but one manifestation of a clearly settled principle of law: "Any state may impose liabilities, even upon persons not within its allegiance, for conduct

21 Hazeltine Research, Inc. v. Zenith Radio Corp., 239 F. Supp. 51 (N.D. Ill. 1965), reversed on other grounds, 388 F. 2d 25 (7th Cir. 1967), reversed and remanded 401 U.S. 321 (1971).

22 Civil Action No. 90-170 (S.D.N.Y.), unreported. Final amendment of decree reprinted in 1965 CCH Trade Cas. ¶71, 352.

23 100 F. Supp. 504 (S.D.N.Y. 1951); 148 F. 2d 416 (2d Cir. 1945); 92 F. Supp. 947 (D. Mass. 1950).

outside its borders that has consequences within its borders which the state reprehends; and these liabilities other states will ordinarily recognize." [24] This case appears to be the only one in which the proscribed activity did not have some relationship to the United States, other than the effect on U.S. commerce.[25] In each of the other cases, one of the parties was an American citizen, as in the ICI case, or else the proscribed agreement of conspiracy was entered into in the United States.[26]

The principle to be derived from the Alcoa case is that the United States antitrust laws apply to conduct outside of the United States which affects imports into the United States. The G.E. Incandescent Lamp case added one refinement to this principle: If the foreign firms knew or should have known of the anticompetitive effect, the antitrust laws are applicable. Actual knowledge of the antitrust laws is not necessary.[27]

Judge Learned Hand suggested in the Alcoa case that Congress had not seen fit to regulate contracts made abroad which were not intended to affect the foreign commerce of the United States, but which did, in fact, affect that commerce. The proposition has never been tested. It should be noted, however, that the suggestion is made with reference to "conduct outside the United States of persons not in allegiance to it." [28]

The ICI and Minnesota Mining cases both involved acts that had an effect on exports from the United States. In the ICI case, DuPont and its British competitor (ICI) formed a corporation in Canada to develop the Canadian market for commercial and military explosives. The district court found that DuPont was already established in the Canadian market and that one of the purposes of the formation of the Canadian corporation was to affect the exports from the United States by limiting DuPont's right to export to Canada.[29] This was one of

[24] 148 F. 2d 416, 443.
[25] Some have argued that the close connection between Alcoa and Alcan gives this case a closer connection with the United States than the statement of the principle indicates. See R. C. Barnard, "Extra-Territoriality and Antitrust Law in the United States," 1963 Int'l and Com. L.Q. 95 (Supp. Pbl. No. 6), reprinted in S. D. Metzger, Law of International Trade (Washington, 1966) 1453, 1460. See also United States v. General Electric Co., 82 F. Supp. 753, 842-43 (D.N.J. 1949).
[26] For example, United States v. National Lead Co., 332 U.S. 319 (1947).
[27] United States v. General Electric Co., n. 25 above, p. 891.
[28] 148 F. 2d 416, 443.   [29] 100 F. Supp. 504, 557.

the basic factors in the finding of a violation of Section 1 of the Sherman Act. Jurisdiction was discussed in terms of the effects upon American commerce, without making any distinction between foreign and interstate commerce.

In the Minnesota Mining case, the creation of a joint manufacturing subsidiary owned by the dominant United States firms in the manufacturing of coated abrasives was found to be a violation of Section 1 of the Sherman Act because the agreement among these firms provided that they were not to export into the territory served by their joint subsidiary. The court found that the export trade of the United States was restrained by the "united forbearance from supplying to certain areas American-made goods when other companies owned jointly by the manufacturing defendants could supply to those same areas equivalent foreign-made goods." [30]

In both the ICI and Minnesota Mining Cases, the effects on exports were intended by the joint venturers, and U.S. nationals were involved in the arrangement. It is unlikely that the antitrust laws would ever be applied to restraints on U.S. exports undertaken solely by non-nationals if these parties were not doing business in the United States. Judge Hand's suggestion that an extension of anti-trust regulation to non-nationals would have international complications seems to be a relevant, and perhaps controlling, consideration. In addition, it is questionable under international law whether the United States has the power to prohibit restraints abroad by non-nationals which affect U.S. exports. Section 18 of the Restatement of the Foreign Relations Law of the United States provides in part:

A State has jurisdiction to prescribe rules of law attaching legal consequences to conduct that occurs outside its territory and causes an effect within its territory, if . . . the conduct and its effect are constituent elements of activity; the effect within the territory is substantial; it occurs as a direct and foreseeable result of the conduct outside the territory; and the rule is not inconsistent with the principles of justice generally recognized by states that have reasonably developed legal systems.[31]

It is doubtful whether an effect on U.S. exports constitutes a substantial effect within U.S. territory.

The issue of service of process under U.S. antitrust law also shows

[30] 92 F. Supp. 947, 961.
[31] Restatement of the Foreign Relations Law of the United States, Proposed Official Draft, May 3, 1962.

the American approach of looking at a multinational corporation as an economic unit. Thus, it has been held that service upon a subsidiary doing business in the United States is sufficient to bring the foreign parent within the jurisdiction of American courts if the parent exercises substantial control over the operations of the subsidiary.[32] Even if, in a rather roundabout way, the American position is extending the extraterritorial effects of U.S. legislation as far as its own corporations or their subsidiaries are concerned, this policy is substantially modified by the superiority and prevalence of the domestic policy of the state in which the subsidiary is either organized or active.

Consent judgments entered in several litigations add a further refinement to the extension of U.S. antitrust law over foreign corporations.[33] These consent judgments involved, in one situation, a number of companies in the petroleum industry and, in another, the United Fruit Company.

The provisions of the Texaco consent judgment, an example of all other consent judgments in the petroleum cases, apply specifically to subsidiaries of Texaco (Article VI of the consent judgment). The consent judgment of United Fruit contains a similar regulation providing for the publication of the provisions of the consent judgment by the Central and South American subsidiaries of the United Fruit Company. Thus, it is clear that the American antitrust authorities view these laws as applicable to foreign subsidiaries of American parent corporations, even though these subsidiaries are organized as legally independent entities. The American enterprise is treated as one economic unit, although it is very often split up into several corporations. This is true not only with respect to prohibitions laid down in the consent judgment but also in regard to provisions exempting the parent corporation as well as the subsidiaries from the application of certain legal provisions.

Most of these exemptions are employed to take account of foreign

[32] United States v. Scophony Corp., 333 U.S. 795 (1946); and United States v. Watchmakers of Switzerland Information Center, 133 F. Supp. 40 (S.D.N.Y. 1955).

[33] 1958 CCH Trade Cas. §68,941 (E.D.La. 1958) (United Fruit); 1960 CCH Trade Cas. §69,851 (S.D.N.Y. 1960) (Gulf Oil); 1963 CCH Trade Cas. §70,819 (S.D.N.Y. 1963) (Texaco); see H. Kronstein, "Staat und private Macht in der neueren amerikanischen Rechtsentwicklung," in *Festschrift zum 70. Geburtstag von Franz Böhm* (Karlsruhe, 1956), pp. 154 ff.; 1963 CCH Trade Cas. §70,609 (S.D.N.Y. 1963) (Watchmakers of Switzerland).

legal regulations that apply to subsidiaries doing business abroad. The consent judgments provide, for instance, that the parent corporations and their subsidiaries shall not be liable under the American antitrust laws for doing anything outside the United States that is required, or for not doing anything outside the United States that is unlawful under the laws of the country where the corporations or their subsidiaries are doing business. To this extent, the consent judgments in United Fruit and in the petroleum cases contain the same provisions. Section VIII(E) of the petroleum cases also exempted subsidiaries from the application of the American antitrust laws with respect to obligations under petroleum concessions pertaining to the fixing of prices and allotment of markets. Moreover, Section VIII(D)1 takes account of the governmental policy of certain petroleum producing or consuming countries. If these countries have officially proclaimed certain market regulations, the petroleum companies subject to the jurisdiction of these countries do not violate the antitrust laws by complying with these regulations.

The scope of the term "violation of foreign law" as used in the above-mentioned provisions is unclear. The consent judgments exempt corporations from the application of the antitrust laws if the corporations would violate foreign law by taking or not taking certain actions. The American antitrust authorities presumably intended to confine the scope of this term to a violation of governmental regulations. This presumption is supported by the provisions pertaining to the acknowledgment of the policies of foreign governments. In European civil law countries, the terms "violation of law" or "illegal" also include violations of civil code provisions and of private contracts. It would make sense to apply the exemptions also to these cases, since the corporations would become liable for damages if they violated their contractual obligations in order to comply with the American antitrust laws.

A further issue is raised by the interpretation of the words "official proclamation" of governmental policy as used by the consent judgments in the petroleum cases. The West German Federal government, for instance, is interested in keeping petroleum prices high in order to protect the German coal production. At first, the German government tried to initiate the organization of a German national petroleum cartel under Section 8 of the German Antitrust Act. Since the German government has abandoned this attempt, it has confined itself to issuing unofficial, nonbinding recommendations with respect to petroleum prices.[34] Only if these unofficial recommendations are considered proclamations of a governmental policy within the scope of the consent judgments can the American subsidiaries comply with these recommendations without running the risk of being prosecuted by the American antitrust authorities with respect to oil exported to the United States.

A more difficult problem is whether the subsidiaries of the petroleum companies are exempted from the application of the American antitrust acts according to the above-mentioned consent judgments when the European Economic Community (EEC) authorities have granted a waiver according to Article 85, Section 3, of the EEC Treaty. Article 85 of the EEC Treaty generally prohibits trade-restricting practices, such as the direct or indirect fixing of purchase or selling prices, the limitation or control of production, markets, or technical development or investment, the sharing of either markets or sources of supply, the application of unequal conditions to parties undertaking equivalent engagements in commercial transactions, and so forth. Article 85, Section 3, allows a waiver of these prohibitions if the respective agreement helps to improve the production or distribution of goods or to promote technical or economic progress, while allowing consumers a fair share of the resulting profit. It could be argued that the exemption of certain practices from the application of the EEC antitrust provisions never constitutes the expression of a general governmental policy within the scope of the above-mentioned consent judgments, since such an exemption is based on the assumption that the practices concerned are generally in violation of the antitrust provisions. On the other hand, an exemption can only be granted on the grounds that the cartel agreement furthers the public interest. The exemption therefore involves the statement that the cartel agreement is compatible with the public policy of the EEC authorities.

Despite these unanswered questions, American authorities have acknowledged by these consent judgments that a state under the law of which a corporation has been organized or is doing business exerts primary jurisdiction over this corporation even if the corporation is under the control of an American parent corporation.

[34] K. H. Biedenkopf, "Zur Selbstbeschränkung auf dem Heizölmarkt," 1966 *Betriebs-Berater* 1113.

Maritime Exception to the Economic Unit Approach

An exception to the economic unit approach exists in the field of maritime law. The right of a ship to travel under a specific flag is recognized in Article 5 of the Geneva Convention on the High Seas (1958):

Each state shall fix the conditions for the grant of its nationality to ships for the registration of ships in its territory and for the right to fly its flag. Ships have the nationality of the states whose flag they are entitled to fly. There must exist a genuine link between the state and the ship, in particular the state must effectively exercise its jurisdiction and control in administrative, technical and social matters over ships flying its flag.[35]

A ship owned by a corporation organized within the flag state is considered to have a sufficient link between the flag and ship within the meaning of Article 5, even if the shares of this corporation are entirely held by citizens foreign to the flag state. In *McCulloch v. Sociedad de Marineros de Honduras*,[36] the U.S. Supreme Court recognized the general principle of international law that the law of the flag state governed the internal affairs of the ship. The court was unwilling to extend the national labor relations law to cover such a situation absent the clear intent on the part of Congress.

An even clearer recognition of this principle occurred under the charter of the Intergovernmental Maritime Consultative Organization which came into force on March 17, 1958. Article 28 of this charter provides that the eight largest shipping nations are permanent members of the Maritime Safety Committee of the organization.[37] A meeting was held in London in 1959 to elect the members of the Maritime Safety Committee. The participants at this meeting were charged with deciding the eight largest shipping nations under the charter. The basic issue was whether the formal registration of the ships and of the corporations owning the ships would constitute the decisive criteria, or whether the nations active in shipping from a substantive point of view were to be represented on the Maritime Safety Committee. If

[35] L. F. Ebb, *Regulation and Protection of International Business* (St. Paul, 1964), p. 212.

[36] 372 U.S. 10 (1963).

[37] Official Report of the U.S. Delegation, First Session of the Intergovernmental Maritime Consultative Organization (IMCO), Jan. 1959, reprinted in Ebb, n. 35 above, pp. 208 f.

the first criterion were to be accepted, Liberia and Panama had to be considered as eligible members of the committee, whereas France and Germany would rank only as ninth and tenth shipping nations. The United States took the position that Liberia and Panama were necessary members of the committee, while the majority recognized the right of France and Germany to such membership. The question was referred to the International Court of Justice. The Court declared the resolution adopted by the London meeting in violation of the Convention and declared Panama and Liberia permanent members of the committee. It held that the "genuine-link" test of Article 5 of the Geneva Convention of 1958 had to be applied in connection with Article 28 of the Intergovernmental Maritime Consultative Organization.[38]

The doctrine of piercing the corporate veil is utilized in American maritime law under the Jones Act, however. For example, this doctrine was applied in *Bartholomew v. Universe Tank Ships Inc.*[39] decided by the Court of Appeals of the Second Circuit in 1959. The plaintiff, a citizen of the British West Indies, was a seaman on board a vessel owned and operated by a Liberian corporation and flying the flag of Liberia. In 1952, as the vessel was proceeding within the three-mile limit and hence in the territorial waters of the United States, the plaintiff was assaulted by a fellow member of the crew who had previously attacked other seamen.

The court had to consider the question of whether the Jones Act applied to the defendant corporation, since its stock was held by a Panamanian corporation, the stock of which was owned by American citizens. Justice Medina held that the practice in this type of case was to look through the facade of foreign registration and incorporation to the American ownership. Justice Medina explained: "This is essential unless the purposes of the Jones Act are to be frustrated by the American shipowners intent upon evading their obligations under the law by the simple expedient of incorporating in a foreign country and registering their vessels under a foreign flag." [40]

The device of setting up legally independent, interrelated corpora-

---

[38] Advisory opinion of June 1960 on the Constitution of the Maritime Saftey Committee of the IMCO, 1960 *I.C.J. Repts.* 150, 171. See generally "The United Nations Maritime Conference," in 1 *Transport. and Communicat. Rev.* No. 1, pp. 17-21 (1948) (historical background of IMCO Convention).
[39] 163 F. 2d 437 (2d Cir. 1959).   [40] *Id.*, p. 442.

tions was termed by Justice Medina "the mechanics of an evasion scheme." This was the crucial point of the decision, which aimed at preventing the defendant from evading the provisions of the Jones Act by choosing a specific legal device. The German courts would have probably come to a similar solution, since in German law the doctrine of piercing the corporate veil is applied to prevent the circumvention of compulsory legal provisions.

Corporations and Industrial Property Rights

Customary international law pertaining to the protection of industrial property rights is generally based on the territorial principle, but the German courts have admitted certain exceptions in the fields of trademarks and patents.[41] The courts have decided that an enterprise cannot prevent the importation of goods designated with its own trademarks if it has distributed the same goods in other states, and the same is true of subsidiaries.[42] A domestic subsidiary cannot prohibit the importation of goods that its parent corporation has distributed abroad. This principle does not apply when the domestic subsidiary is producing the goods concerned.[43] In these cases, the courts took account of the fact that the goods imported and the goods produced by the domestic subsidiary were manufactured by legally different entities which both had the right to legal protection of their trademarks under the territorial principle.

Economic Entity Concept under American and German Securities Law

American law imposes very limited obligations on the disclosure of business abroad. In 1964, Congress amended the Securities Exchange Act of 1934 by inserting Section 12(g)(1) to provide that a foreign issuer of securities engaged in interstate commerce or in a business

---

41 See esp., A. Troller, *Immaterialgüterrecht* I (Basel, 1959–62), 137 and "Die territoriale Unabhängigkeit der Markenrechte im Warenverkehr," 1960 *Gewerblicher Rechtsschutz und Urheberrect (Auslands- und internationaler Teil)* 244 ff.; "Arrondissements-Rechtsbank te Rotterdam," 1964 *id.* 265.

42 41 BGHZ 84; W. Miosga, "Territorialitätsprinzip und europäisches Markenrecht," 1963 *Der Markenartikel* 510 ff.; E. Gerstenberg, "Konzernmarke und Territorialitätsprinzip," 1961 *id.*, 507 ff.; "Revlon," Düsseldorf Oberlandesgericht, 1963 *Betriebs-Berater* 489.

43 "Persil," Hamburg Oberlandesgericht, 1964 *Gewerblicher Rechtsschutz und Urheberrecht (Auslands- und internationaler Teil)* 636.

affecting interstate commerce, or whose securities are traded by use of the mail or any means or instrumentality of interstate commerce, must register such securities with the Securities and Exchange Commission if the assets of the issuer exceed one million dollars and if the issuer has a class of securities held of record by 750 or more persons.[44] According to Section 12(b)(1) of the Securities Exchange Act, the registration statement must contain information as to the issuer and any person directly or indirectly controlling or controlled by the issuer and any guarantor by the security as to principal or interest or both.[45] Subsection (3) of Section 12(g) grants the Commission the authority to exempt any security of a foreign issuer if the Commission determines that the exemption is in the public interest and is consistent with the protection of investors.[46] A temporary exemption from compliance with Section 12(g) was granted by the SEC.[47] The present regulation with respect to foreign securities was adopted on May 31, 1967. It exempts any securities with fewer than three hundred holders resident in the United States and in specific circumstances permits the filing of information previously prepared by the foreign issuer instead of the registration statement, provided the information supplies sufficient facts upon which to base an investment decision.[48]

On the other hand, American parent corporations are subject to very limited obligations with respect to the disclosure of information concerning foreign subsidiaries. The corporations are admittedly committed to file a statement with the Securities and Exchange Commission concerning affiliated companies abroad and foreign subsidiaries. The Securities and Exchange Commission does not insist on detailed disclosure of business abroad by international affiliated groups of corporations.

Since World War II, it has generally become accepted in Germany that the public interest and protection of shareholders, prospective investors, and creditors require that corporations disclose significant details concerning their financial status.[49] This also applies to

[44] 15 U.S.C. §78 12(g) (1) (Supp. 1969).   [45] *Id.* §78 12(b) (1) (Supp. 1969).
[46] *Id.* §78 (g) (3) (1964).
[47] Reg. 240, 12g3-1, adopted Sept. 30, 1964, 29 F.R. 13461.
[48] Reg. 240, 12g3-2, adopted May 31, 1967, 32 F.R. 7848.
[49] E. von Caemmerer, "Publizitätsinteressen der Öffentlichkeit und Gesellschaftsrecht," in *Das Frankfurter Publizitätsgespräch* (Frankfort on the Main, 1962), pp. 141 ff.; G. Döllerer, "Zweck der aktienrechtlichen Publizität," 1958 *Betriebs-Berater* 1281 ff.; H. Kronstein and C. P. Claussen, *Publizität und Gewinnverteilung im neuen Aktienrecht* (Frankfort on the Main, 1960), pp. 11 ff.

an affiliated group of companies. According to Sections 329 and 338 of the West German Corporation Act, the central management of an affiliated group of companies is obligated to prepare annually a consolidated balance sheet and a consolidated profit and loss statement as well as a consolidated business report. All these obligations are confined to the territory of the Federal Republic, however. Foreign corporations are not subject to these provisions. The German members of an international affiliated group of enterprises are only committed to prepare partial reports and statements (Section 330 of the German Corporation Act). This is even true if the affiliated group of companies is under German control. The parent corporation, as the central management of the affiliated group, is not required to make disclosures of the business and financial status of foreign subsidiaries. The consolidated financial statements include only group members domiciled in Germany (Section 139 of the German Corporation Act). The same applies to consolidated business reports, according to Section 334 of the German Corporation Act.

Because of these deficiencies in the German Corporation Act, the financial and economic situation of the affiliated groups under German control will not be disclosed in the future. During the recent shareholder meeting of Farbwerke Hoechst, it was stated:

Preparing our business reports and financial statements, we shall consider our business interests abroad. In view of the different interests in the countries concerned and considering the interest of our respective partners, we shall not publish figures concerning the profits of specific corporations. Because of the same reasons, we shall not go beyond our legal obligations and hence shall not prepare financial statements and business reports with respect to our foreign subsidiaries.[50]

With such restricted disclosures, the situation of affiliated groups under German control will remain unknown to the public [51]—for no good reason.

The argument that sovereignty of state prohibits the imposition of obligations to disclose business through foreign subsidiaries is untenable. It neglects the fact that the states have become economically interrelated; regulations confined within national boundaries cannot cope with international economic problems.

50 "Reden und Berichte," 1966 *Das Wertpapier* 405.   51 *Id.*, p. 406.

The foregoing discussion has indicated that there are a few areas in which the regulation of a corporate structure, spanning several national jurisdictions, is possible. For the most part, however, state regulation of this type of corporate structure is not sufficient to achieve effective regulation. This result is based partly on political considerations, such as distaste for encroachment by extraterritorial application of particular laws within the sovereign domain of other nations, whether developed or developing. An even more important reason, however, is that it is merely a part of an overall development inherent in existing law. It is part of the increasing penetration of the state by business enterprises and of the increasing influence of economic and commercial interests upon governmental policy. Acceptance of the independence of corporations based on purely formal structure enables the central management of the economic unit to choose the government most favorable to its operations. This contradiction between effective control and formal independence is an important element and instrument in the maintenance of power by private commercial organizations.

12 ～～～～～

Role of Industrial Property Rights in the Implementation of Cartels and Market Regulation

The markets for products of the United States, Canada, England, Western Europe, and Australia in the fields of radio, television, and medical equipment are regulated by the establishment of patent pools in countries permitting such pools and in countries (such as the United States) which do not permit this type of pool by appropriate distribution of the licenses on patents or other industrial property rights. This parallel distribution divides the market by excluding any import or local product that requires the use of the particular patents, if the manufacturer is not subject to the system of regulation. Certain producers thus are able to regulate the utilization of technological development, including export to, and production in, underdeveloped nations. Because of this market regulation, comparable prices are charged for these products in each country.

Role of Patents

Industrial property rights, of whatever kind, can guarantee the execution of organized market regulation of any type. Indeed, in most cases the different industrial property rights, such as patents, trademarks, or—under modern definition—the right in protected know-how, even if unpatented, once recognized as proprietary interests, may be distributed among different persons and countries under various contingencies. As a matter of fact, these industrial property interests are seldom used singly. Usually the different types of right are combined to guarantee the effectiveness of a market regulation system. The patent, however, has been an especially effective device since the end of the last century.

William Meinhardt, the founder of the Phoebus Cartel more than thirty years ago, pointed out that agreements on the joint use of patents have often been the crystallization point of international cartels and are an essential instrument of the cartel.[1] Meinhardt suggested that the national light bulb cartel was an excellent example. Hermann Isay noted a few years earlier that the patent had developed into an important asset for exchange and compensation in reaching international cartel agreements. He cited the agreements between the General Electric Company and AEG as well as those between Westinghouse and Siemens.[2]

The institution of the patent, established by legislation in approximately one hundred countries,[3] grants to the inventor for a period of time (usually fifteen to eighteen years) the power to exclude others from the manufacture, use, or sale of patented products (product patent), or from the use of patented processes (process patent). This protection is offered to the inventor in return for publication of his invention, so that it may eventually be used by everyone. The patent serves, as stated in the United States Constitution, "to promote the progress of science and useful art." [4] The purpose of a patent grant is not, however, to create a system of market regulation.

The exclusive rights granted to the patentee can lead *eo ipso* to a regulation of the market if the patented product or process prevents competition in the country in which the patent has been granted. In this instance, the mere existence of the patent achieves control. This situation is relatively rare, since only a few patents are strong enough to exclude others from an entire market. Normally, an effective market regulation requires the use of several patents in accordance with an agreement on patent exchanges or pooling or on the licensing or sale of patents.

The patent is, however, an important device for market regulation, because a patent granted in one nation permits the patentee to obtain an exclusive right of similar character in many other countries. This opportunity is provided under the treaty establishing the so-called Paris Union, the Convention of Paris for the Protection of Industrial

[1] W. Meinhardt, "Patentfragen bei Internationalen Kartellen," 1931 *Gewerblicher Rechtsschutz und Urheberrecht* 1222.

[2] H. Isay, *Die Funktion der Patente im Wirtschaftskampf* (Berlin, 1927), p. 46. See also C. Edwards, *Economic and Political Aspects of International Cartels*, Monograph No. 1, 78th Cong., 2d Sess. (1944).

[3] See, for example, J. M. Lightmann and R. Y. Lee, "Patent Laws Worldwide," 71 *International Commerce*, No. 8, pp. 4, 5 (1965).

[4] In connection with the legal nature of patents see F. Machlup, *An Economic Review of the Patent System*, 85th Cong., 2d Sess., pp. 17–18 (1958).

Property of 1883, as amended on a number of occasions.[5] This treaty
provides for equal treatment for nationals of any contracting nation
(Article 2). Any patentee filing an application for a patent in any
signatory country is given the right for a period of one year to apply
for patent protection in any other contracting country (principle of
priority, Article 4). The Paris Union now numbers more than sixty
member countries, including the Soviet Union.[6]

Anyone seeking to establish a system of market regulation through
use of patents can do so by the same method in which limited patent
or license rights are distributed. Despite the consensus on the essential
points regulated by the Paris Treaty, especially in regard to the beginning and length of the period of patent protection, the so-called
independence of patents of each country permits a certain variety in
each country. This strengthens the use of patents as a device for international market regulation.[7] As long as patents remain in effect in
one or two of the important industrialized countries, they remain an
essential device for market regulation, which can be felt in other
countries because of the close interdependence of industrial markets.

A patent declared void in the United States or whose use is prohibited for a certain period under some antitrust provisions may
make the international market regulation more difficult. However, as
long as the patent exists in one other country which is of importance
in the field involved, the market regulation may nevertheless be in
full force and under the protection of the patent. The contents of
the patent power show this.

Contents of the Patent Power

Possible uses of the patent right

The patentee can make use of his patent right by the following
positive actions: (a) The patentee may undertake new development

[5] H. Kronstein, "Reevaluation of the International Patent Convention," 12 *Law
and Contemp. Prob.* 765 (1947); U.S. Cong., House Comm. on the Judiciary,
Subcomm. No. 3, Statement of Francis Browne in *Hearings on General Re-
visions of the Patent Laws*, 90th Cong., 1st and 2d Sess., Pt. 2, p. 236 (1967–68);
there are suggestions for a new convention on pp. 239–242.

[6] United Nations, Secretary-General, Department of Economic and Social
Affairs, *The Role of Patents in the Transfer of Technology to Developing Countries.* U.N. Pub. No. 65, II B 1, p. 14 (1964).

[7] In the United States a patent is protected for 17 years, and in the Federal
Republic of Germany for 18 years. This period is counted in the United States
from the grant of the patent and in Germany from the day following the day on
which the application is filed.

programs sufficiently protected by a far-reaching patent grant without fear of disturbance by patent claims of others. Furthermore, he will not be disturbed by competition from any other competitor before he has earned enough in profits to cover the substantial expenditures incurred in the original research work. (b) The patentee can expand the scope of the protection afforded by the patent to competition in fields only partially related to the patent grant.[8] (c) The patentee may regulate the next level in the claim of protection so that his customers or the team with which he is working obtain a more advantageous position vis-à-vis their competitors. This regulation is accomplished through control of the supply of patented products or of products produced by patented processes. (d) The patentee may control the terms of distribution of his products. This may include the grant of licenses only to those customers who agree to use the patented information for narrowly defined purposes or to sell the patented products at prices established by the patentee.[9]

The patent allows the following negative actions: (a) The patentee may exclude everyone from use of the patented article or of the patented process in connection with new research or with the production of new or improved products. (b) The patentee may, through the creation of patent licenses, impose certain conditions upon his competitors in regard to distribution of patented products, such as price or production limitations, or may impose some other conditions upon the use of patented processes. (c) The patentee may refuse to grant any license unless the licensee agrees to inform the patentee of any new development in the entire field of the patented product and may secure a commitment from the licensee that he will confine himself to a relatively narrow market in the event that he should obtain a patent for any new development. (d) The patentee may prohibit the grant of any sublicenses or may require that any sublicenses be made only on the condition that the sublicensees assume similar obligations with respect to quality of goods or prices as those of the licensee. (e) The patentee may require that he be granted a license on any subsequent improvements on the patent either for no consideration or for a fixed amount, or he may grant the license only in exchange for other licenses (cross-licensing).

[8] See testimony of Dr. Herbert Hollomon, *Patent Hearings*, n. 5 above, Pt. 1, pp. 28, 32.

[9] In some countries these agreements are prohibited by the antitrust laws.

Effects of a great number of patents being held by one patentee

Originally, enterprises generally applied for patents only with respect to a particular invention. They did not apply for other patents primarily for the purpose of protecting the field of the basic invention. This method of operation has changed today.[10]

Enterprises now very often apply for a great number of additional patents, solely to protect the basic patent. In the case of process patents, many different methods that can lead to the same result are made subject to patent applications, provided that these processes can be sufficiently distinguished to justify separate patent applications. In some cases, enterprises do not even disclose the basic invention but rather apply solely for the protection of a process that is of some importance, but not the decisive part of the invention. In the field of product patents, all products that may be used for the same purpose are included in the patent application. Furthermore, after filing the application for the basic invention, enterprises often apply for many supplemental patents, thus in effect extending the enforceable period of the original patent. Patent applications occasionally refer only to partial processes or products, although this approach is not permissible in all countries. It is very difficult to prove such a partial application in courts and patent offices.

Improvement patents are of great importance, because they protect the technological advancement of the patentee, since each improvement patent has its own period of protection. Because it is generally possible to manufacture the respective product or to apply the respective process on a profitable basis only if the improvement patents are available, the registration of improvement patents in effect leads to an extension of the protection period of the original patent.

Any patentee holding a great number of patents can exert a powerful influence on the market. Newcomers, as important as their invention may be, have only very limited opportunities, since there is generally some need for existing patents in order to develop a particularly new product. In addition, there are always questions as to whether a new product is patentable, and the threat of expensive litigation is often present. This discussion deals only with products and processes

10 This approach does occasionally occur; United States v. Huck Manufacturing Co. and Townsend Co., 214 F. Supp. 776 (E. D. Mich. 1963); 227 F. Supp. 791 (E.D. Mich. 1964), affirmed 382 U.S. 197 (1965).

developed in the plants of the applicants themselves. In these cases the applicants generally disclose only as many details as are necessary to obtain a specific patent. They do not disclose numerous technical procedures and methods that are essential to exploit the patent economically.

The patentee, having developed a number of patents within his own enterprise and thus having gained a strong influence in the market, may additionally strengthen his position by acquiring patents from other enterprises. The independence of patents in each country makes it possible to seek control of patents in a number of countries. The enterprise may purchase the patents outright or may even acquire the enterprises that control these patents. Furthermore, it may enter into patent exchanges with other enterprises, either on a case-by-case arrangement or under general agreement to exchange large numbers of patents.

The patent power of an enterprise may be based not only on the patents it has developed but also on the patent licenses it has acquired, since the licensee in effect exercises the same powers as does the patentee. The rights granted under an exclusive license may even extend to permit exclusion of the patentee himself from the manufacture, use, or sale of the patented product, or from applying the patented process.[11]

In any case, the holder of an exclusive license is entitled to exclude third persons from the exploitation of the patent. In other cases, the licensee may acquire only the right to use the patent without obtaining a right to exclude the patentee or third persons receiving similar grants from the patentee. In this case, a licensee is entitled to exclude any nonlicensed party, which also will eventually lead to substantial market power. Even a nonexclusive licensee may obtain substantial power. Because of the numerous methods by which power may be gained through the use of patents, it is not so much control over a particular individual patent but rather control over many patents that produces real power.

Patent power and concentration of enterprises

The giant corporations of today, with their large financial resources and pools of manpower, generally hold the greatest number of patents

[11] With respect to the German Law see W. Bernhard, *Lehrbuch des deutschen Patentrechts* (2d ed.; Munich, 1963), p. 181.

and hence exert a strong influence on the market. This is especially true in the chemical and electrical industries, where continuous research is very important. In Germany, the five largest enterprises controlled 49.4 per cent of all domestic patents in force on April 30, 1962, in the electrical patent class and 49.5 per cent of all patents in the chemical processes and industrial equipment construction class.[12] The situation is similar in other industrial countries; the General Electric Company, for example, obtained 10,757 patents in the United States between 1939 and 1955.[13]

The statistics show the increase in patent grants very clearly. Since most patent applications are being filed in all industrial countries, the U.S. and German figures indicate the total extent of patent applications. In 1963, 85,833 patent applications were filed in the United States, while 61,111 applications were filed in the Federal Republic of Germany.[14] It is estimated that 100,000 applications will be filed in the United States by 1972.[15] Patent concentration is especially beneficial to large enterprises. The patent position of the large enterprises in the United States was substantially strengthened during the last decades. As previously pointed out, the U.S. government has tended to rely more on private contracts for research and development work than on governmental laboratories. This is especially true with respect to atomic energy, research, and the space and defense programs, but the government has also been concerned with development of new methods for utilization of coal, purification of water, and the development of modern railroad techniques.

This procedure gives the large enterprises new opportunities to acquire additional patents without bearing any costs other than the

[12] Table III, 3, of the supplementary volume to the West German Report on Concentration, p. 786 (Bundesamt für Gewerbliche Wirtschaft, *Anlageband zum Bericht über das Ergebnis einer Untersuchung der Konzentration in der Wirtschaft*, Bundestagsdrucksache zu IV 2320 [Bonn 1964]).

[13] P. J. Federico, "Distribution of Patents Issued to Corporations (1939–1945)," in Study No. 3 of the Subcomm. on Patents, Trademarks, and Copyrights of the Comm. on the Judiciary, U.S. Senate, 84th Cong., 2d Sess., p. 19 (1957). Comparable figures are 8,539 patents obtained by American Telephone & Telegraph Co. and 7,894 patents by the Radio Corporation of America in the same period.

[14] H. B. Fay, Jr., 71 *International Commerce*, No. 8, p. 2 (1965), and the basic survey "Historical Patent Statistics, 1791–1961," 46 *J. of the Patent Office Soc'y* 89 (1964).

[15] Patent Hearings n. 5 above, Pt. 1, p. 35.

patent application fees.[16] This accumulation of patent power at the expense of the government is highly significant, since the participating enterprises had already obtained large numbers of patents and acquired a strong position in the market. This approach merely solidifies the power of these giant corporations, as described in Chapter 3.

Effects of patent practice

A final point must be considered in evaluating the significance of the power granted under a patent. The national patent statutes are based on the concept that the public interest will be served through the competition among patent applicants for protection of their particular invention. This competition for patents influences competition at other levels as well. Numerous procedures exist to prevent patent interference or to permit one patentee to attack the impact of other patents. These devices permit the patentee to protect himself against the grant of new patents that would permit one company to gain patent power unjustifiably. Under German law as well as some other legal systems, a patent appplication must be published in order to enable third persons to file objections on the ground of prior patents, lack of newness, or other deficiencies.[17] Under American law, the patent application is not published; however, the patent office is supposed to advise holders of patents in related areas of patent applications and also those applying for pertinent patents in the preceding year.[18] Any person or firm affected by the new patent application has the right to intervene to challenge the proposed patent grant. The basic purpose of this procedure is to prevent illegal grants of patents.[19]

[16] The supremacy of the American industry in the technological field is shown by a "technological balance of payments" of all West European countries and the United States. C. Freeman and A. Young, *The Research and Development Effort in Western Europe, North America and the Soviet Union* (Paris, 1965).

[17] Sections 27 ff. of the West German Patent Act, as amended on May 9, 1961, BGBl., 1961, I, p. 550.

[18] Interference proceedings, compare 35 U.S.C.A. §§135 ff.; see also E. Goldstein, *Cases and Materials on Patent, Trademark and Copyright Law* (Brooklyn, 1959), pp. 186–187. See testimony of the Commissioner of Patents, Patents Hearings, n. 5 above, Pt. 1, p. 131, for possible changes of the U.S. law.

[19] The United States Department of Justice stated in United States v. Singer Manufacturing Co., 205 F. Supp. 394 (S.D.N.Y. 1962); 374 U.S. 174 (1963), plaintiff's post-trial brief, p. 63: "The patent laws of the United States are an intricate system of checks and balances, which together in unison do function and protect from patent monopolies which exceed the contribution of the inventor.

It is true that in Germany the opportunities to protect against a new patent application are greater than in the United States. American law, however, gives more effective remedies to attack patents previously granted, since the issue of the propriety of the original grant may be investigated in either a suit for patent infringement or a declaratory judgment before the courts. Under German law, avoidance of a patent once granted can be obtained in only a very limited number of cases through a special procedure.

In reality, however, the legislators' concept of a balance of interests between patent applicant and the public has not proven to be the case. An outstanding authority spoke of "a tendency for a self-serving interpretation of past events by the parties to an interference." [20] The enterprise and inventors involved have sought to limit or eliminate the possibilities of attacks on patent applications or on patents previously granted. This objective is accomplished through the conclusion of patent-license, patent-exchange, or patent-sale agreements granting far-reaching protective rights to each of the parties and guaranteeing exploitation by each party of its rights. It is interesting to quote from a contract between the Vereinigte Österreichische Eisen- und Stahlwerke (VÖEST), the OAM (another Austrian enterprise), and the Brassert Oxygen Technik in Zurich (BOT), dated 1952.[21] In this agreement the contracting parties promise to do everything necessary "to secure the widest possible scope for each right to be protected." A similar clause is included in the agreement signed in 1956 between the Singer Manufacturing Company in New Jersey and the Swiss firm, Fritz Gegauf AG Bernina Nähmaschinenfabrik:

Singer and Gegauf each undertakes not to do anything, either directly or indirectly and in any country, the result of which might restrict the

---

These checks require that patent applicant swears that he believes himself to be the first inventor, and provides for an extensive system of examination by the patent office. It is recognized that these procedures are not infallible, especially since patents are obtained in an ex-parte manner so parties believing that they are being subjected to an undue broad patent have their remedy in the courts where they may seek to invalidate such a patent. Interference proceedings, however, are not ex-parte, but are adversary proceedings. An interference proceeding is the sign to compare the conflicting subject matter of applications disclosing and claiming substantially the same subject matter."

20 *Patent Hearings*, n. 5 above, p. 32.

21 Defendant's Proposed Findings of Fact in Henry Kaiser Co., Vöest and Bot v. McLouth Steel Corp., U.S. District Court, E.D. Mich., Civil Action No. 16-900, p. 38.

scope of the claims of the other party relating to the subject matter of the above mentioned patents and patent applications. . . . Singer and Gegauf each undertakes, in accordance with the laws and regulations of the Patent Office concerned, to facilitate the allowance in any country of claims as broad as possible, as regards the subject matter of the patents and patent applications referred to above.[22]

Nicholas Katzenbach, then Acting Deputy Attorney General, commented on this problem in a letter to the Chairman of the Judiciary Committee of the House of Representatives:

Recent experience has indicated that parties to interferences have, in some cases, used those proceedings to serve their own ends with little or no regard for the public interest. Interference settlement agreements have been entered into for the purpose of obtaining patents as broad as possible in order that they may be used by the parties to eliminate competition.[23]

As a result of such procedures the patent office does not receive information from any competitor of the patent applicant which could raise doubts as to the legality of the patent application. The participating parties may even make misleading statements in favor of the applicant.[24]

In the United States in recent years, parties involved in an interference procedure before the patent office have amended the papers submitted in the proceeding and agreed who should be designated officially as the inventor.[25] The party or parties not being granted the

[22] United States v. Singer Manufacturing Co., U.S. Supreme Court, Oct. Term, 1962, Motion of the Singer Manufacturing Co., p. 37a.

[23] U.S. Cong. Senate Comm. on the Judiciary, Subcomm. on Patents, Trademarks and Copyrights, *Hearings on Patent Interference Settlements*, 87th Cong., 2d Sess. p. 4 (1962).

[24] Memorandum of the Solicitor General (Dept. of Justice) in the case Walker Process Equipment v. Food-Machinery and Chemical Corp., in Dec. 1964, p. 2, n. 2: "A recent report of a Senate Subcommittee on Patents, Trademarks, and Copyrights, expressed concern about fraud and other unfairness in proceedings before the Patent Office. S. Rep. No. 97, 86th Cong., 1st Sess., pp. 6–9. Last year, the Federal Trade Commission dealt with widespread restraints upon competition in an important industry traceable to a patent obtained through misrepresentations and deliberate withholding of material information from a patent examiner (American Cyanamid Co., 3 CCH Trade Reg. Rep. 16,527). . . ."

[25] Letter of Chas. Pfizer and Co. to Eli Lilly and Co., of Feb. 27, 1948, U.S. Cong., Senate Comm. on the Judiciary., Subcomm. on Antitrust and Monopoly, *Hearings on Administered Prices*, Pt. 26, p. 16357 (1960), which later formed the basis of an agreement between the two enterprises:
"2. At an appropriate time, depending on the advice of our respective patent

patent generally obtain an exclusive license to the patent in issue. These agreements are very important, because the patent office is authorized to make a finding as to whether a patentable invention exists and who the inventor is only if the parties have not agreed upon this point. The Patent Interference Settlements Hearings and the Drugs Industry Antitrust Act Hearings contain numerous examples of this type of agreement.[26]

One of the purposes of these licenses, especially in cases of cross-licensing between important enterprises, is that—at least for the time of the license agreement—the licensee guarantees not to contest the validity of the licensed patent or of all patents directly or indirectly connected with the license agreement.

For example, the agreement of November 30, 1954, between Columbia Broadcasting System, Inc., of New York, and Radio Corporation of America, licensing the U.S. patent for a "color picture tube," provides for arbitration in case of disagreement as to the determination of the royalty. The arbitration agreement points out:

RCA having by §7 of such license agreement of Nov. 30, 1954, agreed that the validity of U.S. Letters Patent No. 2,690,518 shall not to the extent RCA and its subsidiaries are licensed thereunder be contested during the term of such license agreement by RCA or its subsidiaries. The arbitrator in determining the royalty payment under such license agreement shall assume that U.S. Letters Patent No. 2,690,518 is valid for the purpose of the arbitration.[27]

---

attorneys, we will review the matter of priority of invention with regard to the United States patent applications and determine between ourselves to whom the patents should issue. In the event we are unable to reach an agreement, we will permit the interference to proceed in the Patent Office solely on the issue of priority of invention based on facts stipulated by and acceptable to both parties, and the Patent Office decision shall be taken as final. A determination as to the ownership of the United States patents shall govern the ownership of corresponding foreign patents.

"3. The one of us to whom any patent is issued hereunder hereby grants to the other a non-exclusive license under such patent. In case Pfizer is the licensee, it may sub-license others under those claims of the licensed patent covering dosage forms of procaine penicillin."

[26] N. 23 above, pp. 23, 27, 35, 42; 87th Cong., 2d Sess. (1962), pp. 1197–1883, *passim.*

[27] Plaintiff's Exhibit 23 in Columbia Broadcasting System v. Sylvania Electric Products, Inc., U.S. Court of Appeals for the First Circuit, Joint Appendix Exhibit, Vol. 2, p. 501a.

Compare for another formulation of this point Section 4 of the license agreement of February 21, 1956, between Sylvania Electric Products, Inc., and Columbia Broadcasting System: "Any admission of validity which may be implied hereunder shall be limited to the scope of such licenses granted and in the term during which such licenses are in effect." [28]

An interesting example of international license agreements excluding attacks on the validity of patents is an agreement between an American firm, Columbia Broadcasting, and the subsidiary of a foreign firm, Amperex Electronic Corporation, a wholly owned subsidiary of the Philips Company of Holland. Counsel for CBS expressly stated that the purpose of the license agreement was the exclusion of any attack on the validity of the patent.[29] Whether this agreement affects the relationship between Columbia Broadcasting and the Philips Company in other countries is a question of interpretation.

It is not surprising, then, that a relatively small number of patent applications result in the institution of interference procedures in the United States. It has been estimated that only 1 or 2 per cent of American patent applications collide with any other official patent or patent application.[30] About 75 to 80 per cent of the interference problems are settled without any participation of the patent office, through private agreements among the parties.[31] Only in the remaining 20 to 25 per cent of the interference cases is the patent office in a position to decide for itself who is entitled to obtain a patent grant. Quite often enterprises even reach an understanding on the treatment of all future patents without any involvement of the patent-office procedures.[32] Even more agreements of this kind are concluded after an interference procedure has been instigated.[33]

[28] Plaintiff's Exhibit 24, *id.*, p. 533a.   [29] *Id.*, pp. 168a ff., esp. p. 173a.
[30] *Patent Interference Settlements Hearings*, n. 23 above, p. 21. Less than 2 per cent of all patent applications are involved in interference proceedings (*Patent Hearings*, n. 5 above, p. 34).
[31] Testimony of the former Commissioner of Patents, David Ladd, in U.S. Cong. House Comm. on the Judiciary, Antitrust Subcomm. 1 *Hearings on the Drug Industry Antitrust Act*, pp. 1197, 1207, 1552, 1559 (1962) and the statistics of the Comm. on Chemical Practice of the American Patent Law Association, U.S. Cong. House Comm. on the Judiciary, Antitrust Subcomm. *Hearings on the Drug Industry Act*, 87th Cong., 2d Sess. (1962).
[32] Citations in n. 26 above.
[33] N. 31 above, citations at pp. 9, 303, 304, 325, 361, 367, 389, 618.

Similar developments occur in other countries. In a study concerned with economic integration, the German Federal Office for Industrial Commerce noted that some experts believed that large enterprises engaged in significant research and development programs, or connected by licensing agreements or by the exchange of patents, often agreed as to who would be entitled to obtain a patent in order to avoid disputes before the patent office or before the courts.[34] About 50 per cent of all patent applications in Germany are settled by withdrawal or rejection. Applicants often withdraw their applications when a competitor files an objection. On the other hand, quite often the opponent withdraws his objection.

Such agreements are also common in the international field. The licensing agreements between Singer Manufacturing Company, the Italian firm Vigorelli, and the German enterprise Messerschmitt are of substantial importance in this connection.[35] In addition, there are numerous examples of agreements not to oppose present or future patent applications or not to challenge existing patents.[36] A 1934 contract between IG Farbenindustrie AG, Frankfort, and the American firm Roehm and Haas Company in Philadelphia provided in part:

Both parties will not oppose directly or indirectly the existence and validity of the domestic or foreign industrial property rights of the other contracting party as long as this contract is in force . . . they will support each other in these patent rights if so requested. Pending patent litigation will be terminated as soon as this contract comes into force.[37]

The purpose of this contract was to avoid possible patent litigation between parties and to regulate the manufacture and conditions of sale in the field of acryl acids and related chemicals in U.S. and Canadian markets.

The license agreement between the New Jersey Zinc Company and Metallgesellschaft AG of September 16, 1935, provided that:

---

[34] N. 12 above, pp. 776, 777.   [35] N. 22 above.

[36] These agreements are quite usual in the national field. Section 7 of the licensing agreement between Telefunken and the "Funkverband" of 1929 provided that the parties were prohibited from bringing any actions or claims, or supporting the actions of third parties, with respect to property rights subject to agreement between the parties (1934 *Kartel-Rundschau* 264).

[37] U.S. Cong., Senate Comm. on Patents, *Hearings on Patents*, S. 2303, 77 Cong., 2d Sess., pp. 752 ff. (1942).

The Licensee undertakes that neither it nor its sublicensees will oppose directly or indirectly in the Patent Office of Germany the issuance of Letters Patent on or in connection with the said patent applications, including any and all subsequently filed patent applications under which the Licensee is licensed as herein provided, and not to raise or cause to be raised on any account whatsoever any question concerning or in objection to the validity of any Letters Patent which may issue in connection with the said patent applications; and to require similar engagements on the part of its sublicensees.[38]

Similarly, a licensing agreement between Parke, Davis and Company and Les Laboratoires Français de Chimothérapie, dated January 25, 1950, provided: "The parties to the presents hereby relinquish all rights to contest during the life of this agreement the validity of patents granted to and applications for patents made by the said parties." [39] This is an especially broad provision and covers all patents of the participating parties whether the license actually refers to them or not.

A further example of this type of provision is found in the licensing agreement between Singer and Vigorelli or Messerschmitt:

Each of the two parties mutually agree not to institute any opposition, nullity or invalidation proceedings in any country against or otherwise to attack each other's above-noted patents or patent applications and immediately to withdraw any such proceedings if it has already been instituted . . . provided, however, that if such two parties' patents and patent applications are or have become involved in a patent office priority-determining proceedings such as a United States interference or a Canadian conflict proceeding, then both parties will work together in order to settle such a proceeding in accordance with the laws and regulations of the patent office concerned and in the spirit of this agreement.[40]

A survey of the patent suits pending before the federal district courts in the United States in the years 1945 to 1954 indicates the importance of private agreements in patent procedures.[41] According to the survey only 20 per cent of all cases were settled by judicial decision; the remainder were settled by the parties. A more recent report by the U.S.

[38] *Id.*, pp. 1631, 1635.
[39] *Administered Prices Hearings*, n. 25 above, pp. 16,053, 16,061.
[40] N. 22 above.
[41] U.S. Cong., Senate Subcomm. on Patents, Trademarks and Copyrights, *Hearings on American Patent System*, 84 Cong., 1st Sess., p. 179 (1955).

Commissioner of Patents indicates that this situation has not changed:

The majority of civil suits, including patent infringement actions, in the U.S. courts are terminated without trial. Many of these are settled by the parties. In this respect, the practices in the Federal Courts and the Patent Office are parallel.[42]

The situation in Germany is quite similar. A supplement to the study on concentration, referred to earlier, notes that only 33 per cent of the patent cases are concluded by a final judgment, while about 50 per cent are solved either by judicial or extrajudicial compromise or by discontinuance of the suit.[43]

These agreements affect others than the participating parties, because research and technology are so highly specialized today. Only a very few competitors of the patent applicant or patentee, who are working in the same field, are capable of evaluating whether the application is valid or not. When these enterprises conclude an agreement with respect to various patents it is almost impossible for an outsider without the necessary experience to challenge a particular patent application.[44]

Because of the lack of publication of the patent application, the patent examiners in the United States are left in an extremely difficult position in determining whether there actually was a "pertinent art already developed and published in advance." A mere 1,050 patent examiners confront the 8-to-10 per cent annual growth of world technical literature.[45] Germany, on the other hand, has a more effective *ex officio* examination procedure of patent publication, while the definite determination of whether the invention is patent worthy in Germany puts the patentee in a stronger position there, at least after the patent grant.

Patent Agreements for Market Regulation

Not every agreement between different enterprises with respect to patents or licenses restricts competition. Production, even among the leading firms, can generally not be undertaken economically solely on the basis of patents owned by the particular firm. Even the large enterprises rely on patent-licensing agreements with other firms. Since these other enterprises face similar problems, it is logical for

---

[42] N. 31 above, pp. 1197, 1207.   [43] N. 12 above, p. 781.
[44] 1952 *Blatt für Patent-, Muster- und Zeichenwesen* 269, 272.
[45] *Patent Hearings*, n. 5 above, p. 132.

the parties to exchange patents and to enter mutual licensing agreements. These agreements are very common in the international field, where a firm may secure numerous patents held by foreign firms in exchange for patent licenses it holds in foreign countries. This type of agreement quite often takes the form of a licensing agreement.

But it is only a small step from "the mere" patent agreement to an anticompetitive market regulation. The borderline between these forms of agreement is very vague and fluid. Nevertheless it would seem clear that a market-regulating cartel agreement exists if the partners make provision for a division of markets or of fields of production and if they agree on the production or distribution (whether production or distribution shall take place at all, how much, using which process, where, and for what purpose, and so forth).

These market regulations need not be part of a cartel agreement. In many cases they may merely result from vertical licensing contracts of an anticompetitive nature. While the pooling of patents and the exchange of exclusive licenses occur normally within the framework of a cartel, this is not necessarily so with respect to all licensing contracts. Each case has to be investigated in the light of the contracting partner's objectives. A specific licensing contract is not necessarily part of an overall system of licensing agreements which can be classified as a cartel. Because of the anticompetitive effects in both cases, vertical contracts and patent cartels will not be distinguished in the following discussion.

Division of markets and fixing of quotas

The allotment of markets plays an important part in international licensing contracts. The contract between the British company Imperial Chemical Industries, Ltd. (ICI), and the American enterprise E. I. du Pont de Nemours and Company (du Pont), concluded on June 30, 1939, may serve as an example. The agreement included explosives, cellulose, acids, salts and other chemicals, insecticides, and alcohol. It provided for the exchange of information and licenses with respect to certain countries. ICI was to grant exclusive licenses for North and Central America, with exception of Canada, Newfoundland, and some other British possessions, in exchange for licenses granted by du Pont in other countries of the British Commonwealth, with the exception of Canada and Newfoundland. Furthermore, each enterprise obtained the corresponding right to sell in Ireland and

Egypt, and each party was entitled to enter into exclusive licenses with respect to certain other countries. A number of special provisions provided for the territories in which specific products were to be sold; sublicenses were to be granted only to subsidiaries of affiliated corporations. In addition, the parties agreed to assist in the protection of each other's patents in the securing of new patents and licenses.[46]

The division of products is exemplified by a licensing agreement between IG-Farben and the American firm Roehm and Haas Company dated October 30, 1934:

SECTION 2

The contract relates to the manufacture, sale, and use of the contract products. The I. G. will not use or put on the market the contract products for use in the preparation of nonsplintering glass. The marketing and use of methacrylic acid products either pure or containing plasticizers as glass substitutes and also the use of acrylic acid esters, methacrylic acid esters and mixtures thereof, either alone or containing plasticizers, for adhesives is reserved to R. & H.

R. & H. will not sell nor use the contract products for the preparation or improvement of

Photographic articles

Celluloid-like masses or products made therefrom

Dyestuffs

Artificial rubber (which also means polymerization products of polyenes)

Pharmaceutical articles

Abrasives.

SECTION 3

Territorial Extent.—The contract extends to the United States and Canada.

SECTION 4

Exchange of Licenses and Information.—The I. G. grants R. & H. and R. & H. grants the I. G. a license under their existing patent rights; with respect to the subject matter mentioned in Section 2, paragraphs II and III, the license is granted only to the party entitled thereto. An agreement on future patent rights will be made in each individual case. (In case of possible future connections through other contracts, an explanation will be given or an agreement reached by letter with R. & H.)

[46] *Patent Hearings*, n. 37 above, pp. 794–798, 800–801.

To the same extent the I. G. and R. & H. will exchange their information on the preparation and use of the contract products.

The I. G. may grant to "friendly firms" sublicenses under the license granted it by R. & H. for the preparation of the contract products. Furthermore, the I. G. is permitted to grant to third parties a non-transferable sublicense for the manufacture of contract products for use in the preparation of artificial rubber. To this extent it (I. G.) may divulge to others the information received from R. & H. regarding the preparation of contract products.

In other respects I. G. and R. & H. will only grant sublicenses for the preparation of the contract products and divulge information to third parties after a mutual understanding has been reached.

SECTION 5

Preparation and Delivery of Contract Products.—Both parties to the contract are free to manufacture the contract products within the scope of the fields granted them in Section 2.

Until further notice, however, R. & H. alone will manufacture the contract-products in the United States. R. & H. will deliver contract products to the I. G. and its "friendly firms" at cost plus 10%. If R. & H. should not be in a position to deliver the contract-products at as low a price as could be obtained if one of the I. G.'s "friendly firms" were to manufacture them, or if the manufacturing capacity of R. & H. were not sufficient to cover the requirements of the I. G. or its "friendly firms" in the United States and Canada, the I. G. would be free to manufacture the products themselves or have them manufactured by one of its "friendly firms." In such a case the I. G. will give R. & H. nine months notice. In case the I. G. or one of its "friendly firms" should desire one of the contract products which R. & H. does not manufacture and for the manufacture of which a new plant would have to be erected, then the notice period may be shortened by mutual consent or entirely eliminated. The right of the I. G. to grant a nontransferable sublicense to third parties for the manufacture of artificial rubber is not affected by these conditions.

The I. G. is not permitted to import the contract products from other countries into the United States and/or Canada.

R. & H. may not sell the contract products outside of the United States and Canada and will prevent such sales by their customers insofar as it is possible. On the other hand R. & H. is permitted, with the assent of the I. G., to deliver contract products to Röhm & Haas, Darmstadt, in case and to the extent that the I. G. cannot deliver such products to Röhm & Haas, Darmstadt.

Finished articles, in the preparation of which contract products are used, may be sold by the I. G. and its customers to all countries, also to the United States and Canada.

(This paragraph changed by letter of April 4, 1935, to I. G., making it reciprocal.)

SECTION 6

Patent Rights.—Both parties, neither directly nor indirectly, will undertake anything against the status of domestic and foreign patents rights of the other party within the subject matter and territory of the contract, but shall, on request, assist each other. Pending patent controversies shall be dropped after this contract becomes effective.[47]

Exchange of know-how and patents

In a patent-licensing arrangement, the licensee is often obligated to inform the licensor of all know-how acquired with respect to further development of the product or process subject to the license, but there is no similar obligation on the part of the licensor. In this manner the licensor obtains all improvements upon his patent, in some cases, with no payment to the licensee. The licensee is also often bound to forego any attack upon patents for which the license was granted.

Patent communities

The so-called patent community is the most important form of cooperation among enterprises in the patent sector. This is basically a simple form of organization in which the title and exclusive rights in existing and future patents remain with the original owner, while other members of the patent community obtain nonexclusive licenses. No license of any type is granted to outsiders. Existing licensing agreements with outsiders are not extended. The international light bulb cartel, which existed in the period between the two world wars, is a good example of this type of agreement. Under this agreement each cartel member was entitled to demand a license from other members if it could obtain "the benefits and advantages given to it by the cartel

---

[47] *Id.*, pp. 752–754. Compare the licensing agreements concluded between the American enterprise, the New Jersey Zinc Co. and (1) Metallgesellschaft AG, Frankfurt/Main (including its subsidiary American Lurgi Co.) (*Patent Hearings* n. 5 above, pp. 1631 f., 1637 f.); (2) Unterharzer Berg- und Hüttenwerke GmbH, Oker-Hartz (pp. 1639 f.); (3) Société Générale de Minérail S.A., Brussels (pp. 1646 f., 1653 f., 1661 f., 1668 f., 1690 f.); (4) Società Italiana del Piombe et dello Zinco, Mailand (pp. 1683 f.) and (5) Financial and Investments Co. "FinInCo" S.A. Luxembourg (pp. 1692 f.).

agreement" only by the use of the patent. The royalty to be paid by the licensee was fixed by the cartel arbitration tribunal. The licensee was entitled to use the patent even before the amount of royalty had been established, if it deposited a sufficient security with the central agency of the cartel, the Phoebus Corporation.[48]

A more complicated arrangement is the so-called implementing patent community. Here all patents and all exclusive licenses of the participating parties are transferred to a joint managing agency of the cartel, a patent trust company, or a similar institution, which is empowered to grant licenses to each member. In some cases the cartel members are obligated even to transfer patents acquired from third persons. This form of patent community is appropriate only for cartels having a legally independent cartel managing agency or at the least a central patent office. On the other hand, it is more effective than a mere patent community.[49]

A number of difficult problems arise in the functioning of such an agreement. Since the cartel members are committed to transfer new patents to the central agency, their zeal to improve products and to obtain new patents may abate. The solution to this problem has been to authorize the inventing enterprise to demand royalties from other cartel members for the use of improvement patents.[50] Another delicate issue involves dealing with patent complications and existing patents of competing cartel members. Unlimited discretion to intervene in this situation would be inconsistent with the spirit of close cooperation among cartel members.[51] On the other hand, the absolute prohibition of any intervention against the patent or patent application is not advisable because it would require the payment of royalties in situations where no patent should have been granted.[52] The cartels generally take the middle road. The consent of the cartel is required before a cartel member may proceed against the industrial property rights or a patent application of another member. Before the individual member may contest another party's patent, the legality of the patent or patent application in issue is examined at a meeting of

[48] Meinhardt, n. 1 above, pp. 1222, 1224–1225.

[49] H. Isay, *Die Patentgemeinschaft in Dienste des Kartellgedankens* (Mannheim, 1923), pp. 12 ff.; F. Neumeyer, *Patentgemeinschaften und deren Aufbau bei amerikanischen Industrieverbänden* (Marburg, 1932), pp. 26 f.

[50] Isay, *id.,* pp. 16, 27.

[51] Patentfragen, 1931 *Gewerblicher Rechtsschutz und Urheberrecht* 1225.

[52] Meinhardt, n. 1 above, p. 1226.

the cartel members, by the managing board of the cartel, or by an arbitration tribunal. Suits concerned with patents in force at the time the cartel agreement is concluded are generally not permitted.[53] The central agency of the executed patent community generally protects the combined industrial property rights against outsiders. The patentee in this case is usually entitled to demand such action be brought by the cartel agency and is obliged to assist in this action. When a member withdraws from the cartel, it loses all licenses and rights granted by other members or by the central agency. The withdrawing member does secure all patents and exclusive licenses it had previously transferred to the central agency.

Two recent cases concerned with international patent cartels may help to illustrate the diversity of modern market regulation through patent and other industrial property rights.

In the first, the concentration of radio patents enabled the patentees to extend their influence to a new market (television) without any opportunity for outsiders to compete effectively.[54]

The cartel, which still exists today, has its origin in the 1920's. The following enterprises participated in the cartel, although some did so only temporarily:

U.S. firms: General Electric Company, Radio Corporation of America, Westinghouse, Western Electric, Hazeltine (Research) Corporation, ITT, and Zenith Radio Corporation;

British firms: Electric and Musical Industries, Ltd., The General Electric Company, Ltd., Marconi's Wireless Telegraph Company, Ltd., Murphy Radio, Ltd., Philips Electrical Industries, Ltd., Pye, Ltd., Rank Cintel, Ltd., and Standard Telephone and Cables, Ltd.;

Australian firms: Amalgamated Wireless (Asia), Ltd., Standard Telephones and Cables, Ltd., Philips Gloeilampen Fabrieken N.V., and Neutrodyne Propriety, Ltd.;

Canadian firms: Canadian General Electric Company, Ltd., Canadian Marconi Company, Ltd., Canadian Westinghouse Company, Ltd., Northern Electric Company, Ltd., and Standard Radio Manufacturing Corporation, Ltd.

---

[53] *Id.;* Isay, n. 49 above.

[54] The following explanations are based on the records in Hazeltine Research, Inc. v. Zenith Radio Corp., 239 F. Supp. 51 (N.D. Ill. 1965), reversed on other grounds, 388 F. 2d 25 (7th Cir. 1967), reversed and remanded, 395 U.S. 100 (1969); on remand, 418 F. 2d 21 (7th Cir. 1969); reversed and remanded, 401 U.S. 321 (1971); and United States v. Radio Corporation of America, U.S. District Court, S.D.N.Y., Criminal Action No. 155-107.

The principal member of this long-standing cartel is the Hazeltine Corporation and its completely owned subsidiary, Hazeltine Research. The Radio Corporation of America also played an influential role until it withdrew from the cartel. The Hazeltine Corporation and its subsidiary exert great influence in the American radio and television industry as a result of the five hundred important patents and patent applications it owns.

The cartel members regulated and divided markets in Great Britain, Australia, and Canada by establishing large patent pools, and in the United States, because of the strict antitrust legislation, by methods of parallel coordination of patents. The British enterprises listed above dominate the British radio and television market and are members of the British patent pool. The Hazeltine Corporation participates indirectly in this pool through an agreement with the English firm General Electric Company, Ltd. The agreement provides for the exchange of exclusive licenses and know-how. Each party grants exclusive licenses for the use of its patents in the other parties' territory. The British patent pool, organized in form of joint ventures, covers several thousand different property rights. Its members grant global licenses, so-called standard package-licenses, covering all patents combined in the pool under uniform conditions. The licensees are obligated not to export any radio or television equipment from the United States or other countries to Great Britain nor to export any of these products from Great Britain. The royalty payment is based on the total production of the licensee, not merely on the output related to the use of the particular license.[55]

The general purpose of this pool, as noted by the Federal District

[55] Section 4b of the licensing agreement A 8-T (Defendant's Exhibit No. 71) provides: "The Licensee agrees with the Grantors as follows: To pay to the Grantors: Royalties on the Licensee's net turnover as hereinafter defined at the rate of 0.5% (nought point five per centum). The expression 'net turnover' where herein used shall subject to Provisos (ii) and (iii) hereof mean the total of net invoice prices (whether or not paid and before deduction of settlement discounts) of all Television Receivers hereunder manufactured by or for the Licensee during the subsistence of this License and sold, let on hire or put into use by the Licensee whether or not such Television Receivers embody or utilise any invention the subject of any of the said letters Patent including in such prices the value of everything (for example cabinets valves and cathode ray tubes) normally incorporated in or forming part of complete Television Receivers and actually included as part thereof at the time of sale shall not include Purchase Tax or Customs Duties thereon"; in addition section 4g provides: "Not to contest or assist others to contest the validity of any Letters Patent under which the Licensee receives licenses hereunder."

Court in a suit brought by Hazeltine Corporation against Zenith Radio Corporation, is "to amass all of the patents for assertion against anyone not licensed, to prevent importers or foreign manufacturers from entering the market and to preclude the possibility of any attack by licensees on the validity of any one patent." [56]

The Canadian patent pool is organized in the form of a corporation under the name Canadian Radio Patents, Ltd. The shareholders are primarily subsidiaries of large American enterprises: The Canadian General Electric Company is a subsidiary of the American General Electric Corporation; Canadian Westinghouse is a subsidiary of the American firm of the same name; Northern Electric is affiliated with the AT & T subsidiary Western Electric; and the Standard Radio Manufacturing Company is a subsidiary of the Dutch firm Philips. In addition, the Hazeltine Corporation and several other foreign enterprises participated in the Canadian patent pool by exchanging exclusive licenses on all future patents with Canadian Radio Patents. Canadian Radio Patents grants licenses to its Canadian shareholders under uniform conditions generally similar to those of the British pool. The primary purpose of the Canadian pool was to protect its members and licenses against imports from foreign countries, especially the United States. This is pointed out in the findings of fact in the Hazeltine case:

XXVII. The Pool's campaign against importation of radio and television receivers from the United States is highly organized and effective. Patent agents, investigators and agents of the conspiring companies as well as the Canadian manufacturers and distributors trade associations at the behest of the Pool have systematically policed the market in order to locate and stop the sale of imported receivers and have immediately attacked by infringement suit or threat thereof any dealer found to be selling imported receivers. Warning notices addressed to importers, vendors and users of radio and television receivers advise the trade and the public that only the products of certain named local manufacturers are licensed by the Pool under "basic patents" and that even "users" of unlicensed products are subject to suit on account of patent infringement. Many advertisements run by the Pool went much further. They contained disparaging statements about imported receivers to the effect that they were cheaply made, unsatisfactory in operation, caused fires and were dangerous to use because of "shock hazard."

[56] 239 F. Supp. 51, 73 (N.D. Ill. 1965).

XXVIII. Mass attacks in the form of infringement suits were made on dealers found to be selling imported American made radio and television receivers. Suits or the threat of suits effectively prevented dealers from handling American made sets.[57]

The Australian patent pool, organized under the name Australian Technical Services and Patents Company, Pty. Ltd., also has the subsidiaries of a number of large foreign enterprises among its members. For example, Neutrodyne Proprietary is a 70 per cent subsidiary of Hazeltine. The foreign parent corporations contribute their patent rights to the Australian pool through their subsidiaries or affiliated corporations. The Australian pool in turn grants licenses upon uniform conditions similar to those in Great Britain and Canada. The licensees are obligated "not to export or sell or offer for sale in Australia any radio or television receiving apparatus not manufactured in Australia." [58]

The U.S. market was not regulated through a patent pool. The leading American enterprises, Hazeltine and RCA, granted licenses to other American firms on uniform conditions. These licenses referred not only to patents and licenses owned by the American firms but also to those patents and exclusive licenses received from foreign enterprises as a result of participation in the Canadian, British, and Australian pools. These license agreements also contain strict export and import prohibitions. The leading American enterprises, such as General Electric, Westinghouse, and AT & T, agreed in 1954 not to compete with RCA in the United States in the granting of radio patent licenses to third parties. They agreed either to grant sublicenses on their patents to RCA or to conclude licensing agreements with other American firms on conditions that recognized the superior position of RCA on the market. The other large American patent power, Hazeltine, followed a similar policy. These various pools and the participating enterprises controlled the essential patents in the respective geographical markets. Therefore, each competitor had to obtain licenses from the cartel members. These licenses were granted, however, only under the conditions referred to above. Since these provisions contained strict export and import prohibitions, the cartel members effectively regulate and divide the entire market. It is important to realize that enterprises in most other countries, such as

[57] 239 F. Supp. 51, 74–75.   [58] *Id.* 51, 76.

Germany, are related to the large patent cartels through contracts with respect to the exchange of patents and know-how. Thus, RCA and Telefunken in Germany entered into a cross-licensing arrangement in which the parties promised to help maintain each other's market position by inserting the necessary restrictive conditions into any licensing agreements concluded with third parties.[59]

The U.S. Supreme Court upheld the Zenith Radio Corporation's claim that the Canadian patent pool violated U.S. antitrust laws in a patent infringement suit brought by Hazeltine Research, Inc.[60] The court was primarily concerned with the measure of damages, but did describe the operation of the pool:

The Canadian patent pool, Canadian Radio Patents, Ltd. (CRPL), was formed in 1926 by the General Electric Company of the United States through its subsidiary, Canadian General Electric Co., and by Westinghouse through its Canadian subsidiary. The pool was made up largely of Canadian manufacturers, most of which were subsidiaries of American companies. The pool for many years had the exclusive right to sublicense the patents of its member companies and also those of Hazeltine and a number of other foreign concerns. About 5,000 patents were available to the pool for licensing, and only package licenses were granted, covering all patents in the pool and strictly limited to manufacture in Canada. No license to importers was available. The chief purpose of the pool was to protect the manufacturing members and licensees from competition by American and other foreign companies seeking to export their products into Canada.

[59] Sections 19, 20, 44, 45 (pp. 5, 6, 12, 13), file of the attorney of the government, Feb. 21, 1958.

[60] "The Court of Appeals did not disturb, nor do we, the findings of the District Court that HRI and Hazeltine conspired with the Canadian pool to deny patent licenses to companies seeking to export American-made goods to Canada. Accepting these findings, we have no doubt that the Sherman Act was violated. *See,* e.g., Timken Roller Bearing Co. v. United States, 341 U.S. 593, 599 (1951); Continental Ore Co. v. Union Carbide and Carbon Corp., 370 U.S. 690, 704 (1962). Once Zenith demonstrated that its exports from the United States had been restrained by pool activities, the treble damage liability of the domestic company participating in the conspiracy was beyond question. Continental Ore Co. v. Union Carbide and Carbon Corp., *supra. Compare* American Banana Co. v. United Fruit Co., 213 U.S. 347 (1909); United States v. Aluminum Co. of America, 148 F. 2d 416, 443 (C.A. 2d Cir. 1950). Although patent rights are here involved, the same conclusions follow. *See for example* United States v. Line Material Co., 333 U.S. 287, 305–315 (1948); United States v. Singer Mfg. Co., 374 U.S. 174, 196 f. (1963)" (Zenith Radio Corp. v. Hazeltine Research, Inc., 395 U.S. 100, 113, n. 8 [1969]).

CRPL's efforts to prevent importation of radio and television sets from the United States were highly organized and effective. Agents, investigators, and manufacturer and distributor trade associations systematically policed the market; warning notices and advertisements advised distributors, dealers, and even consumers against selling or using unlicensed equipment. Infringement suits or threats thereof were regularly and effectively employed to dissuade dealers from handling American-made sets.[61]

The patent litigation between Columbia Broadcasting System and Sylvania Electric Products, Inc.,[62] related to the color television tube, indicates that, under the leadership of RCA, the same group acquired control of technology and patents not only in black and white television but also those to color television. While this is not a patent pool, the industry speaks, however, of "a group" and "a group meeting" arranging a system of licenses and cross-licenses in this field (see Chapter 3).

The second example in this discussion of patent cartels can be drawn from the arrangements arising out of the use of the oxygen process in the manufacture of steel, the so-called L-D Steel Making Process. This has been referred to as the "only major technological breakthrough at the ingot level in the steel industry since before the turn of the century." [63] The oxygen process was developed by the Austrian enterprise VÖEST in the latter part of the 1940's. At the same time, the Austrian firm OAM and the German H. A. Brassert and Company were working on a similar research project. In order to avoid possible litigation among these firms and to protect and exploit the new invention, Brassert Oxygen Technik AG (BOT) was established in Zurich.[64] The parties indicated that their purpose was to accomplish "an aggressive world-wide patent policy to protect the developments of the group as fully as possible by patents and to secure the widest possible scope for each right to be protected." [65] This was accomplished by the conclusion of numerous agreements with leading steel firms.

[61] Id., 114–115.

[62] 294 F. Supp. 468 (D. Mass. 1968), 415 F. 2d 719 (1 Cir. 1969), certiorari denied 396 U.S. 1061 (1970).

[63] Kaiser v. McLouth, n. 21 above, Plaintiff's Findings of Fact, section 40, p. 17.

[64] Id., Plaintiff's Findings of Fact, p. 61. See also the Defendant's Findings of Fact, p. 33: "Plaintiffs admit that this 'large patent pool' (p. 9381), which put 'the utilization of the pertinent patents in one hand (BOT) outside the territory of Austria', was formed in order 'to eliminate the possibility of one single patent holder being played off against the other' (Dx 15, p. 65)."

[65] Id., Defendant's Findings of Fact, p. 33.

VÖEST and OAM transferred all necessary patent rights and know-how with respect to all foreign countries to BOT on May 9, 1932.[66] In June, 1952, BOT entered into an agreement with British Miles Company, which controlled a number of important inventions in the steel industry and possessed significant know-how. Under these agreements, the British firm granted exclusive rights in all its existing and future patents to BOT. On July 21, 1952, BOT acquired from the German firm H. A. Brassert and Company the exclusive rights in the German Schwarz patent and other similar inventions as they related to foreign countries, with authority to acquire supplementary or improvement patents and to grant licenses. Brassert agreed "not to contest the validity or protest the application of any patent owned or controlled by BOT relating to oxygen steel." In October, 1952, BOT acquired the present and future patent and know-how in the field of steel production from Mannesmann Hüttenwerken.

In May, 1954, BOT entered into an agreement with the American steel firm Henry J. Kaiser Company by virtue of which Kaiser became the American partner and representative of BOT. Kaiser obtained an exclusive license with respect to all patents, patent applications, and know-how of BOT in the United States and had authority to grant sublicenses. In exchange for this, Kaiser granted an exclusive license on its improvement patents in all countries outside of the United States to BOT. Furthermore, Kaiser promised to require exclusive licenses on all improvement patents secured by its sublicensees, with the additional right to grant sublicenses on these improvement patents to BOT. Similar arrangements were concluded with leading enterprises in Canada, Japan, India, Belgium, Luxembourg, Holland, France, Norway, Sweden, Spain, Italy, Brazil, Australia, and the British Commonwealth. The representatives of BOT in each country, for example Kaiser in the United States, entered into agreements with domestic enterprises in which these enterprises were committed to grant exclusive licenses on their patents in foreign countries to BOT.[67] By January 1, 1962, BOT had obtained more than 720 patents and 290 patent applications in thirty-eight countries.[68] Thus, BOT was in a

---

[66] Id.

[67] "All of these licenses, exclusive or non-exclusive, including all of the sublicenses, provided for a flow-back to BOT or some other member of the combination of all knowledge or inventions or patents of the licenses in the field of oxygen blowing" (id., p. 35).

[68] Id., p. 36.

position to establish a system of private market regulation in the international steel market.

Significance of Patents in Relationships among Cartel Partners

The impact of patents upon the relationships among parties to the cartel will vary according to the nature of the cartel. Therefore, the situation with respect to technological, raw material, and industrial product cartels must be investigated separately.

Technological cartels

The purpose of the technological cartel is to exchange and develop new and valuable technological information. The problem, therefore, is not one of the exchange of existing patents but rather the application of existing know-how to joint research programs. This does not mean that the parties may not grant cross-licenses to each other. The primary purpose of the cartel, however, is the determination of how the results of joint research are to be utilized. The cartel members may decide this question generally, without consideration of the extent to which the results of the development can be patented. The parties must eventually decide, however, whether the results of the joint research are to be patented and who is to be the holder of the patents. The primary purpose of these patents is generally to exclude third parties from the results of the research. These patents do not serve to regulate relations among the cartel members. There are other far more effective means of securing cooperation among the cartel members themselves.

Raw material cartels

Technological development is not very important in the field of raw material cartels. Its only purpose generally is to protect the raw material from competition from substitute products. Patents are therefore of minor importance in the relationship among members of raw material cartels.

The only exception to this may occur where base materials derived from a raw material are very similar to industrial products. In these cases the rivalry among the cartel members generally prevents any exchange of new patents. The lack of exchange of existing patents, however, does not affect cooperation within the cartel.

Industrial products cartels

Where there are a large number of cartel members, industrial products cartels occasionally utilize patents to secure execution of cartel regulations when there are no other appropriate means of control. In this case the cartel members distribute the patent rights in such a manner as to accomplish a division of markets or allocation of production. Whether detailed provisions with respect to production and distribution can be protected by patent agreements depends upon differing national laws. In numerous countries, cartel agreements on prices, quantity, and quality of licensed products are protected by the patent itself, so that a violation of one of these obligations constitutes an infringement of the patent. A suit for patent infringement presents many fewer possibilities for defense than a suit on the normal cartel contract, and thus, the position of the defendant is much less secure. By combining the licensing agreements and cartel obligations, these agreements are placed under jurisdiction of the same courts or arbitration tribunals that have jurisdiction in determining violations of the patent-licensing agreements.

The right of the patentee to enjoin further use of a patent because of a contract violation is of special importance. The danger of losing the opportunity to use a patent can be a significant regulating force for the members of the cartel. Of course the patent power of the cartel is greatest and most effective when the parties to the cartel put their patents into pools administered by an independent agency of the cartel, which is free from the will of the individual members.

The observer of the industrial products cartel cannot overlook the fact that in spite of all the stabilization accomplished by the cartel, technological development continues and that improvement and application patents are continuously registered by individual members of the cartel. Each participating enterprise in its entire commercial and economic activities depends upon access to all patents granted to any member of the cartel. This is true even if a member has undertaken its own research or has combined with other members in joint research.

The situation is somewhat different where only a few enterprises participate in the industrial products cartel. Here a mere exchange of information may suffice to secure sufficient cooperation among the cartel members.

Impact of Patents on Relationships with Third Parties

In all international cartel agreements, patents are an important means of protecting the agreements against third parties. A mere concentration of patents in the cartel or cartel agency may often be sufficient to accomplish this objective. The significance of patent concentration was pointed out in connection with the discussion of the patent power of single enterprises. The significance of patents is in effect raised to a higher power when a cartel succeeds in pooling all important patents of the cartel members. Thus, the cartel deters competition from outsiders in the protected field. If any enterprise should attempt such competition, it would run the risk of a suit for patent infringement.

Threat of patent infringement suits

The manner in which patents are distributed among the cartel members determines which member is obligated and authorized to bring suit for patent infringements. These obligations may be established specifically in the agreement or may follow generally from the manner in which the patent rights are distributed. In every country the patentee is entitled to sue for infringement. In some countries the licensee is authorized to bring suit. In cases where the licensee, and particularly the exclusive licensee, may not sue in its own right, it does have the right to require the patentee to bring suit.

Exclusion of potential competition by the licensing system

Even more important than the exclusion of potential competitors by patent infringement suits is the conclusion of licensing agreements with third parties. These licensing agreements enable the third party to work in a specifically defined area upon conditions imposed by the cartels and in such a manner as to prevent disturbances of the cartel market regulation. Enterprises that intend to become active in a special field generally prefer to conclude such licensing agreements with the cartels, instead of initiating a competitive fight on the basis of their own research developments.

The bargaining position of the cartel and its members is very strong in those cases where the party seeking a licensing agreement is a medium-sized or small firm. It is much more difficult to impose restrictive conditions in those situations in which the third party exerts con-

siderable patent power in its own right and is willing to defend patent
infringements suits. Agreements concluded between cartel members
with a strong patent position and potential competitors often follow
similar lines. The licensee receives a license for a definite product
or process and his use is limited to certain countries. He generally
agrees not to compete in other contiguous fields and is committed to
transfer future know-how and patents. In this way the cartel members
permanently strengthen their power, while the licensee does not
necessarily secure access to improvement patents of the cartel. When
the licensee is dependent upon access to these improvement patents,
the cartel members have an effective device to enforce their cartel
policy.

In certain cases, it may even be in the interest of the cartel members
to grant licenses covering the whole range of cartel products, provided the third parties' sphere of influence can be clearly defined and
limited geographically and factually, and that the prices and conditions of sale are not incompatible with the interests of the cartel.[69]
These agreements are often concluded with respect to developing
countries. In this situation imports are often hampered by import restrictions arising out of balance-of-payments difficulties. The organization of a subsidiary in the developing country may not be desirable.
The only reasonable possibility in this situation is to conclude a
licensing agreement along the lines described above. The developing
country is in effect exempted from the system of private market regulation, while the licensee agrees not to disturb the cartel policies in
other countries.

These territorial limitations in licensing agreements are more efficient
when the imposition of high royalties for sales affectuated by the licensee in third countries is made. If the high royalty approach is used,
the licensee often may sell the patent product below cost in an attempt to make profit through the sale of supplementary material
or replacement parts. On the other hand, the cartel members may con-

---

[69] The case Permanent Magnet Association Agreement, L.R. 3 R.P., pp. 119,
134 (1962) indicates the course of the negotiations between the Philips Co. and
the British Permanent Magnet Association on the granting of a license for a
patent on an alloying process developed by the Dutch enterprise. Philips demanded: (1) the right to fix sales prices of all alloys produced under the patent
and furthermore of all alloys produced by the Association; (2) 5 per cent of all
prices charged on alloys produced under the patent or not; (4) all licenses on
future improvement patents developed by the Association.

trol licensees, as well as potential competitors, by influencing the prices not only of the licensed product but also of total production and by the establishment of quantitative restrictions. This guarantees that the licensee remains under the control of the cartel in all aspects of its economic growth and thus cannot become a threat to the cartel.

Influence on succeeding levels in the chain of production

Through patent control, the patentee may influence not only his own buyers but also succeeding levels in the chain of production, provided these levels require the patented product for manufacture of their own products. In this way, the cartel members may regulate the price of the final product, may exclude competitors from all other business transactions with the licensee, and finally may bring contiguous markets under their control. In many nations, patentees use their patent power to enforce vertical price-fixing agreements, including sales to the ultimate purchaser. Such transactions are forbidden in the United States.[70] The American antitrust laws do not, however, prevent American enterprises from concluding price-fixing agreements through their distributing subsidiaries in foreign countries. The effect of price-fixing agreements based on patents is much greater than a general contractual price agreement not only because the impact is more far-reaching factually, but also because the arrangement has more justification in the eyes of national legislators and courts.

Licensing agreements as a first step to participation in a cartel

Licensing agreements with third parties often become a bridge to later full membership in a cartel for the licensee. When an enterprise having a strong market position generally enters a new field, it is usually interested in joining established firms in the common fight to exclude newcomers. This is especially true when the enterprise acquires, through new technology, entrance to a new field. This enterprise may initially require access only to certain individual patents or technical know-how. Once the new entrant has obtained a competitive standing technologically, the opportunity to join the cartel is open to it.

---

[70] S. Timberg, "International Patent and Trademark Licenses and Interchanges: The United States Approach," *Cartel and Monopoly in Modern Law*, II (Karlsruhe, 1961), 751, 764 ff.

Role of Unpatented Technical Secrets

More and more, the large quantity of unpatented know-how, subject to agreements discussed in the chapter on technological cartels, may be a perfect device for the protection of the agreement. The utilization of a patent often requires access to significant quantities of know-how and technological experience. Between the two world wars, many enterprises obtained patents without these prerequisites, since patent offices often applied a liberal policy with respect to patent applications and improvement patents. Because of this need to acquire know-how, the enterprises that granted patents very early began entering into licensing agreements with respect to know-how. By the close of World War II, exchange agreements with respect to know-how and technical experience were closely related to the exchange of patents. The light bulb and match cartel agreements each contained clauses to this effect.[71] These agreements clarify the important supplementary function of the exchange of information. For the reasons discussed in the analysis of technological cartels, the impact of the patent cartels has decreased. Today enterprises often confine themselves to the exchange of information or to licensing only of know-how, and even in those situations where an exchange of patents is still necessary, the patents have only a supplementary function. This trend is obvious in the technological cartels, as was indicated earlier in this chapter.

As in the case of patents, there are different types of licensing and exchange agreements dealing with technical experience, including know-how.

Vertical licensing agreements often contain the same anticompetitive clauses as those relating to patents. The licensor even has more discretion in imposing restrictive provisions than with patents, since the cartel authorities generally apply a more liberal policy with respect to the autonomy of its members in these instances.

Agreements providing for the exchange of information generally do

---

[71] Art. 4 (Exchange of Inventions and Experience) of the Phoebus Agreement, reprinted in The Monopolies and Restrictive Practices Commission, *Report on the Supply of Electric Lamps*, Oct. 4, 1951, p. 126; §10 of the Trading Agreement (British Isles) concluded between the British Motor Corporation and the Svenska Tändsticks Aktiebolaget in 1938, §8 of the Trading Agreement (overseas), reprinted in The Monopolies and Restrictive Practices Commission, *Report on the Supply and Export of Matches and Match-Making Machinery*, May 12, 1953, pp. 104, 109.

not establish additional obligations in those cases where the participating enterprises have equally strong research and development positions. When one enterprise is not as advanced as its partners, it is normally relegated to a supplementary position, which generally includes the payment of royalties to the other partners. The greater the exchange of information, the more the partners feel the necessity to guarantee certain price levels. When the parties are technologically equal, they will often fix the highest price that can be obtained on the market.

A division of markets, either on geographical or other lines, cannot be accomplished merely by the exchange of information, as is true in the field of patents. The reason is that know-how is not a territorially limited right granted by the government, and it is not possible to bring suit for violation of confidential know-how as with a patent infringement suit. Admittedly, some protection is offered to trade secrets, but it is not as extensive as is true with patents. Furthermore, once the secret know-how has been published, the owner is deprived of any control based on this knowledge. Second, the licensor of know-how will often be reluctant to bring suit for violation of a licensing agreement, since part of the proof of violation will entail disclosure of the valued know-how. Therefore, international agreements on the exchange of know-how are generally concluded only between related corporations or in cases where an allotment of markets can be made on other grounds, as through the use of the trademark device.

Cooperation among parties in a joint research program is to be distinguished from the regular exchange of information, although in some circumstances such a differentiation may be difficult. In those situations where enterprises cooperate in a joint research program either through a joint laboratory or through an integrated research program, the knowledge and patents arising from this research belong to all participating enterprises. Thus, the enterprises must agree on the distribution of research results. This generally means that competitors of the contracting parties are excluded.

Formal Implementation of the Exchange of Know-How

There are numerous difficulties inherent in attempts to license or exchange information. While contracts with respect to the assignment or licensing of patents refer to a clearly defined device, the situation is different in the field of know-how and technical experience. Know-how is not clearly definable and its value decreases immediately when a competitor acquires similar know-how. From the legal standpoint, the owner of know-how transfers this commodity to others either by a license or by an agreement of sale. The transfer may include drawings, formulas, or other informative material on products and processes. It may also include the oral exchange of some information. Prior to World War II, American firms had already begun sending technicians to consult with European firms with which they had some form of relatively permanent relationship in order to exchange particular information. The feedback this method entails leads to a very close cooperation between the parties and to a blurring of the origins of specific know-how.

In those cases where the know-how is merely licensed, it is often necessary to disseminate this information by actually sending technicians of the licensor to the licensee or by training employees of the licensee in the licensor's plants. It is essential in these licensing or exchange agreements that the participating parties are obligated not to disclose pertinent information to third parties. The protection offered under the patent laws may be of help in this connection because there will generally be some patents related to the know-how upon which the producer may rely in protecting his know-how. Some states have enacted strict provisions against the disclosure of industrial secrets so that the distinction between patented and unpatented information has diminished gradually.[72]

In discussing licensing agreements of know-how, it is important to define the third parties. Generally, subsidiary corporations are not regarded as outsiders, since they are either covered by the licensing agreement or at least entitled to sublicenses under it. In addition, these agreements often provide that the licensed know-how may be transferred to third corporations in which the licensee has only a partial interest. In these cases the licensee is committed to assure that the information will not be used to the disadvantage of the cartel.

Occasionally, a special agreement may be concluded in which the licensee is authorized to conclude an agreement divulging certain know-how to third parties, provided certain royalties are paid or an assurance is given that all know-how or inventions developed by this third party will be placed at the disposal of the cartel members.

The accumulation of know-how in the hands of a very few en-

[72] See also the provisions of §§17, 18 UWG (West German Antitrust Act) and Art. 273 of Swiss Penal Code.

terprises strengthens and enlarges the technological gap between these enterprises and newcomers. Accordingly, new entry into this market is for the most part excluded. Furthermore, the concentration of know-how and patents enables the cartel members to increase their competitive power, and thus they are better able to enforce their business policies against outsiders.

Significance of Trademarks and Similar Exclusion Rights

In the foregoing discussion of patents it was pointed out that cartel members regulate and divide markets through the concentration of patents and licensing arrangements. Similar market regulation can be accomplished through the use of trademarks and other similar exclusive rights which serve to designate and to distinguish the products of different enterprises. The significance of these exclusive rights as a device in dividing markets must be seen in light of the integration of markets which has been so typical for the period after World War II. The integration of markets affects production and manufacturing methods in three different ways:

(1) The cartel members are in a position to establish uniform market regulations including the advertisement and distribution of goods for whole territories. These regulations need not be restricted solely to vertical or economic communities. Their application is also possible where the countries concerned have reduced their tariff and other trade barriers.

(2) Technological development and marketing methods have led to a far-reaching standardization of goods and services which stretches beyond the borders of a particular state.

(3) The goods and services offered on the international market are increasingly under the control of groups of affiliated enterprises that have little difficulty enforcing uniform regulations in several geographic markets.

The influence of trademarks, commercial names, or other exclusive rights in the modern integrated market depends very much on advertising. Solely because of its advertising, a standardized product can obtain such a strong position in a particular market that other firms within a particular geographic territory find it very difficult to compete even if there are no patent or other technical barriers to competition. *Lever Brothers Co. v. Monsanto Chemical Co.*[73] indicates some of the effects advertising can have. The court found that Procter and

[73] U.S. District Court, S.D.N.Y., Civil Action No. 135–219 of Apr. 30, 1963.

Gamble by its enormous advertising campaign was able to make it extremely difficult if not impossible for any competitor to appear in a
particular market.

Exclusive Rights Used to Exclude Competitors

The following exclusive rights are used for market regulation purposes: the trademark; the trade name (firm name under which an enterprise offers its goods); the brand name under which a certain class
of goods is offered; the packaging of particular goods which serves to
enhance its marketability by symbols under which certain services
are offered; and the copyright.

The primary purpose of a trademark is to permit purchasers to distinguish the goods of the mark's owner from other goods. In addition,
the trademark guarantees a certain quality of the product offered because of its close relationship with a specific producer or distributor
who has established a good name in the market and who is desirous of
maintaining this reputation. The trademark can fulfill this function
only if it is sufficiently distinguishable from other marks or words used
in normal language to describe types of goods offered under the mark.

The trade name can be distinguished from the trademark by the fact
that it does not relate to specific merchandise but designates the enterprise that disseminates a large class of products.[74] Very often the
trade name is nothing more than an abbreviation of the name of the
corporation; however, in some cases symbols are used as trade names.

The brand name should be distinguished from both the trademark
and trade name by the fact that it designates a certain class of articles,
as for example Nylon. It does not refer to a specific producer or distributor. In connection with trademarks or trade names, it is often an
important element of the good will of an enterprise.

The packaging and form of a product as well as the symbol for service develop increasingly into exclusive rights as a result of new statutes
or new interpretations of the general law of unfair competition. In ad-

[74] "The terms 'trade-name and commercial name' include individual names and
surnames, firm names and trade names used by manufacturers, industrialists, merchants, agriculturists, and others to identify their businesses, vocations, or oc-
cupations; the names or titles lawfully adopted and used by persons, firms, associations, corporations, companies, unions, and many manufacturing, industrial,
commercial, agricultural, or other organizations engaged in trade or commerce
and capable of suing and being sued in a court of law" (*Trademark Rules of
Practices of the Patent Office with Forms and Statutes* [U.S. Department of Commerce Patent Office, 1963], p. 99).

dition, important steps toward regulation can be found in the law of unfair competition with respect to industrial designs.

Originally, copyrights applied solely to the field of arts. However, when the film industry expanded and when illustrated papers, pocket books, and other forms of entertainment gained an increasing part of economic life, copyrights became more important. Today copyrights are used in the United States to protect designs of industrial products against imitation by competitors. This development started with jewelry and soon extended to glassware, lamps, artificial flowers, and other items.[75]

Common features

The enumerated exclusive rights are generally admitted by most legal systems, although the applicable regulations may differ in some essential points. It is important, however, that all legal systems recognize these devices as giving the owner some exclusive rights. This permits the owner to exclude anyone else from the application of his trademark, trade name, or other device. Because of this exclusiveness, these rights can be used as a device to regulate markets by licensing arrangements, contracts, or assignments.[76] The prior discussion with respect to patents as to the form this may take is relevant here as well.

Effects of International Treaties

The Paris Convention for the Protection of Industrial Property Rights of March 20, 1883, deals with the protection of patents, utility models, industrial designs, trademarks, service marks, trade names, and indications of source or appellations of origin, and with the repression of unfair competition (Article I). The Convention establishes the principle of national treatment according to which nationals of countries of the Union enjoy "in all the other countries of the Union the advantages that their respective laws now grant or may hereafter grant to nationals" (Article 2).

In addition, the Convention provides for a right or priority for each person who "has duly filed an application for a patent, or for the registration of a utility model, or of an industrial design, or of a trade-

---

[75] "New Concept of Design Protection," 8 *IDEA, The Patent, Trademark and Copyrights Journal of Research and Education* 173 (1965); Manes Fabrics Co., Inc., v. Miss Celebrity, Inc., 246 F. Supp. 975 (S.D.N.Y. 1965).

[76] W. Fikentscher, "Die Warenzeichenlizenz im Recht der Wettbewerbsbeschränkungen," *Festschrift für Engan Ulmer* (Munich, 1963), pp. 405 ff.

mark in one of the countries of the Union" (Article 4). With respect
to trademarks, Articles 6 and 7 provide that a trademark, legally
registered in the country of origin, is to be admitted and protected in
all other member states.

The Madrid Agreement on International Registration of Marks of
April 14, 1891, sets forth provisions for enforcement and protection
of these rights.[77] It makes registration of marks with the International
Bureau for the Protection of Property Rights a prerequisite of recognition and protection outside of the country of origin.

The impact of these agreements is enhanced in countries such as
Germany which protect registered trademarks solely on the basis
of registration, whether the trademarks are used on the market or not,
and not on the basis of use.

Nearly all the major trading nations of the world are members of
the Paris Convention, and most of them participate in the Madrid
Agreement. In addition, many bilateral treaties between member states
and nonmember states contain similar provisions to those contained in
the Paris and Madrid agreements. National trademarks are therefore
protected in many relevant markets throughout the world. This is the
reason why exclusive rights, especially trademarks, are an excellent device to regulate markets.

Market Regulation through a Combination of Marks and Patents

Exclusive rights are used in many territories and fields as a device to
restrict competition. In many cases, especially in the pharmaceutical,
electrical, and chemical industries, they have played an important role
in international agreements since the prewar period.[78]

A market regulation based on strong patents continues after the
period for which the patents are effective. After the rights granted under the patent have terminated, competitors of the patentee have difficulties marketing the formerly patented product because they are then
confronted with the trademarks and trade names of the former
patentee. These marks are well known to the public and closely associated with the particular product. It is very difficult for competitors
to break this association.

[77] 96 *British and Foreign State Papers* 839 (1902–1903).
[78] United States v. General Electric Co., 82 F. Supp. 753, 849 ff. (D.N.J. 1949);
United States v. Imperial Chemical Industries, 100 F. Supp. 504, 583 ff. (S.D.N.Y.
1951).

Under these circumstances it is not surprising that trademarks often become so well established on the market that they are used in common language to signify a particular category of goods. This development may deprive the respective trademark of its legal protection, because one legal prerequisite is that the trademark not be identical with the word used in everyday language. Therefore, enterprises began after World War II to market new patented products under two words, the trademark and a more general term normally used in scientific literature.

The question of whether protection by trademark and other exclusive rights should be legally possible after the expiration of their respective patent is a controversial one today in the United States. The cases discussing the point have dealt with whole industrial segments where many patents expired at different times. In practice, it has proven very difficult to exclude the mutual protections which patents and other exclusive rights give to each other.

Methods of Horizontal Market Regulation

Division of markets

The cartel agreement may provide that the cartel members are obligated to utilize certain symbols or marks in the marketing of certain goods. These agreements have the practical effect that a cartel member cannot sell the product in issue in the territories where it does not possess the described trademark. This results in a division of markets in those situations where the cartel members have sufficient control of the market or where the trademarks concerned are very strong so that enterprises not participating in the cartel have no opportunity to compete.[79]

In other cases, the cartel members may agree to sell a certain product under a single uniform trademark by distributing the exclusive rights connected with the trademark only to certain territories. This agreement may also lead to a division of markets under the same conditions pointed out under the foregoing case.

An especially effective device is the agreement to distribute certain products under different trademarks in each country with the under-

---

[79] A typical horizontal market division by patents and trademarks, especially occurring in the field of pharmaceutical products, was pointed out above in the section on industrial product cartels in the agreements between the Fabwerke Hoechst AG and the Upjohn Company.

standing that each enterprise is entitled to sell only a certain fixed quantity of the product under this trademark. This quantity may correspond to the quota fixed for the respective country or market. There are also cases in which a special symbol is used in international trade in addition to the trademark with the understanding that only a definite quantity is to be distributed under the symbol. It is also possible for the parties to agree that the rights under these trademarks or designs are to be used only with certain packing or in certain forms.

Price-fixing and the establishment of other conditions of business

Marks and symbols may be used not only to accomplish a market division or the establishment of sales quotas. It is also possible to enforce horizontal agreements in such a way that products are marketed by each of the cartel members to their own distributing organizations at agreed prices, qualities, and quantities. For this purpose a combination of trademarks and other symbols are used with certain standard mark labels. The parties to the contract agree to use this label only for goods distributed under the agreed market rules with respect to price, and the parties agree that none of the participating enterprises will bring any product on to the market without using this label.

These agreements may be strengthened and enforced through the use of the corporate form. There are numerous agreements in the patent and trademark fields in which the participating parties assign their exclusive rights to a corporation under their domination or organized for this specific purpose. This corporation is authorized to license each of the participating parties in such a way that the agreed market regulation is accomplished. It may be agreed that the trademark can be used to market only a specific quantity of a particular product.

For purposes of enforcing horizontal divisions of the market, other combinations of the use of symbols with the use of a corporate entity can be found in various countries. The Radio Corporation of America (RCA) has a minority interest in a Mexican corporation that uses the RCA symbol on the Mexican market. Although RCA has no right under Mexican law to give instructions to the Mexican corporation, it can at least supervise this corporation because of its position as a shareholder in order to guarantee a certain quality in the product sold under the RCA symbol on the Mexican market.[80]

In the United States, the Lanham Act provides that the registered

[80] See also United States v. Timken Roller Bearing Co., 341 U.S. 593 (1951).

trademark may be licensed or assigned for use in particular fields or geographic territories only if the original owner of the trademark gains effective control over the licensed firm so that it can guarantee that the merchandise sold by the licensee is of comparable quality to the product manufactured by the owner of the mark. Under this sanction, a strong and far-reaching market regulation can be accomplished.[81]

Methods of Vertical Market Regulation

Exclusive property rights can also be used for vertical market regulation. The so-called franchise system can be found on both the national and international levels. Under this system, the owner of a trademark imposes upon all enterprises manufacturing or distributing its product the quantities, qualities, and conditions of sale, especially the price of sale. The franchise agreement also establishes the extent to which the distributor can sell competitive products. The automobile, petroleum, and tire industries show the extent to which market-regulation systems may be based on trademarks or other symbols. A typical example of this type of franchise agreement is contained in the standard contract utilized by Lusterock International, Inc.:

I. (A) Lusterock hereby licenses the Manufacturer to use the LUSTEROCK Mark and Lusterock Trade Name, together with or separate from the design, in connection with the manufacture and/or distribution of natural stone and of stone-simulating materials, in the following geographical area. . . .

(B) Lusterock hereby licenses the manufacturer to use Lusterock patents and Know-how in the manufacture of finished products made with Lusterock resin in the above described geographical areas.

(C) Manufacturer hereby acknowledges Lusterock's entire right and title in and to the LUSTEROCK Mark and LUSTEROCK Trade Name, hereby agreeing to convey to Lusterock any right or rights which manufacturer may acquire in the use of said mark and Trade Name during the term of this Agreement, and upon termination of this agreement, Manufacturer will not use said mark or Trade Name, including its use as part of Manufacturer's trade name, and will not use any other marks confusingly similar. . . .

(E) Manufacturer agrees to maintain in force and effect a program with its own officers, employees and agents by which confidentially of all the Know-how disclosed by Lusterock will be kept confidential to the fullest extent possible consistent with law and the practicalities of conduct of busi-

[81] This market regulation is often incompatible with antitrust laws.

ness; that as a part of such program, it will promptly require all of its
officers and employees to enter into a contract of the form attached hereto
and entitled 'Employment Contract'.

II. (A) Manfacturer hereby agrees to purchase and Lusterock agrees to
sell the manufacturing equipment, tools, sales equipment, advertising material, training and a basic inventory of resin and subsidiary materials. . . .

(C) Manufacturer agrees to purchase ------ Lusterock resin material. . . .

(D) Manufacturer further agrees:

(1) To diligently develop the market for Lusterock in the above described
territory; and (2) Not to use the Lusterock mark or Trade Name in any
way contrary to the provisions of this contract; and (3) To properly keep
and mail an activity report for each month to Lusterock by the 10th day of
the following month; and (4) To follow the quality control, storage procedures, manufacturing methods and the finished job specifications as currently published and distributed to Manufacturer by Lusterock; and (5) To
immediately perform a Standard Resin Test upon receipt of each drum of
resin and to immediately forward to Lusterock a copy of such test. (6) To
allow Lusterock to inspect from time to time Manufacturer's stock of resin
and related products, the methods of storage, manufacturing techniques,
finished jobs and test records, to determine if current minimum standards
are being complied with; and (7) Manufacturer further agrees to appoint
all dealers using Lusterock's standard Dealer agreement from then in use
and to submit all appointments of dealers to Lusterock for Lusterock's approval which shall not be unreasonably withheld. (8) To display LUS-
TEROCK labels on all finished products in a prominent place and to place
such lawful patent notices upon said products as Lusterock may instruct, and
(9) To pay his account in full on the 10th day of each calendar month of
all sums due from the previous calendar month, with the exception contained in Paragraph II (A). . . .

X. Manufacturer hereby agrees to disclose promptly to Lusterock all
developments and inventions made by Manufacturer during the term of
this agreement and relating to materials or apparatus for or methods of
manufacture, installation or sale of stone or stone-simulating materials and
hereby authorizes Lusterock to make, sell, use and disclose and communicate
such inventions and developments as part of the Know-how to other licensees. Manufacturer also hereby assigns unto Lusterock all developments
and inventions it makes during the term of this agreement in materials,
techniques or apparatus for and in methods of manufacturing, installing or
selling of stone or stone-simulating materials, and hereby agrees at Lusterock's expense and in all lawful and proper to aid Lusterock in the obtaining and maintaining of ways patent protection on such inventions.

XI. Manufacturer is an independent contractor, devoting his time and activity at his own discretion and without direction or domination by Lusterock; and as an independent contractor, Manufacturer is not authorized to incur any indebtedness for which Lusterock might or could become liable. In no events shall Lusterock ever be liable to Manufacturer for any claim of any nature whatsoever that might be connected with damage in any way related to the storage, manufacture, transportation or installation of Lusterock materials, and Manufacturer agrees to indemnify, save and hold harmless Lusterock from any such claim or action on the part of third parties.[82]

It is clear that the franchise system of a single enterprise in itself is neither a national nor an international cartel. It may easily be used as an element of such a cartel, however. The most appropriate manner to show how such a franchise system may be used for this purpose is to analyze each of its elements and to show how each of them is used in particular cases. The following are the types of vertical market regulations that can be obtained through the use of trademarks and symbols or other exclusive rights. As already pointed out, each of these elements can be used alone or in combination with others.

Territorial division of markets or products

The owner of a trademark or other symbol may restrict the licensee to use of the symbol to specific territorial markets.[83] It is also possible to divide markets so that the licensee is permitted to use the symbol only in connection with certain products.

Agreements on quality of goods

In many cases, the owner of a trademark prescribes the quality or the form of distribution of goods manufactured under the license. For example, the licensor may require that certain drugs be produced only in the form of pills. These provisions are often supplemented by the transfer of know-how in addition to the mark or symbol.

[82] Hearing on Distribution Problems Affecting Small Business before the Senate Antitrust Subcomm., 89th Cong., 1st Sess., Pt. 1, *Franchising Agreements*, pp. 432 ff. (1965). Much material pertaining to recent years can be found here, esp. pp. 44 ff., 279–280.

[83] Susser v. Carvel Corp., 332 F. 2d 505 (2d Cir. 1964); Denison Mattress Factory v. The Spring-Air Co., 308 F. 2d 403, (5th Cir. 1962).

Agreements on price and other conditions of sale

Symbols provide a most efficient device for use in vertical market regulation. The licensor may prescribe or recommend prices. It may establish regulations concerning the use of credit, such as the interest rate or the form of security. The licensor secures compliance with the contract because of his control over the mark or symbol. This control can be exercised to cancel the licensing contract in the event that the licensee violates its commitment to adhere to these conditions of sale.

Tying clauses

In many cases, the use of a mark or symbol is permitted only on the condition that the licensee purchase all necessary materials from the licensor or other persons designated by it. This regulation may cover all, or only a part, of the goods manufactured by the user of the symbol.

Tying clauses can also be found in contracts with repair shops. These clauses may provide that the repair shop use only spare parts bearing the symbol of the enterprises that produced the original item, for example a car. The repair shop may be permitted to work only on goods bearing a certain trademark or combine only items with the same trademark. When these provisions are supplemented by a requirement that the repair shop conduct business under a specific trade name, the particular market is regulated with great efficiency.

Common features

The owner of exclusive property rights permits use of these rights only as long as the licensee fulfills its commitments. When the licensee violates the agreement, further use of the symbol is deemed to be without permission and continued use may be enjoined. In some cases, an even more effective method exists than merely the filing of a law suit. Often a licensee operating an automobile distributorship or a television repair shop depends upon supplies provided by the licensor or an affiliated enterprise. All merchandise supplied to the licensee bears the symbol of the licensor. Thus threats to cut off this source of supply because of alleged violations of the licensing agreement place severe pressures on the licensee. This same pressure can be exerted by the licensor if it leases property to the licensee or retains a security interest or mortgage on property of the licensee. Experience has shown that it is very difficult, if not impossible, for the licensee to secure a licensing arrangement with the owner of other trademarks after termination of one licensing agreement.

Development of the Law on Industrial Property Rights

In the foregoing it was indicated that utilization of industrial property rights and unpatented information is possible only if these interests are protected in different countries under the various systems of industrial property law. For this reason, the analysis of international market regulation in 1971 requires consideration of different systems of industrial property law to understand and evaluate the pertinent agreements and distribution of industrial property rights.

This analysis must determine whether the development of the pertinent legal systems supports or hinders the utilization of industrial property rights in international market regulation. The American observer cannot deny his interest in developments in other countries, because even a change in the regulation of industrial property rights within the United States would not basically change the structure of international market regulation.

It must be emphasized that this utilization of industrial property rights is taking place in combination with utilization of such legal institutions as subsidiary corporations and autonomy under conflict of law rules in choosing the applicable law and arbitration. It is necessary to understand the utilization of all these legal institutions together in order to place the discussion of this chapter in its proper perspective.

International Development

The use of patent law to carry out the aims of international market regulation has been based substantially on the "internationality" of national patent laws. In the field of patent law, international agreements were consummated very early. After extensive preparation which went back as far as 1872, the International Convention for the Protection of Industrial Property, the so-called Paris Union Treaty, was concluded on March 20, 1883.[84] Pursuant to Article 1 of this treaty, the participating countries established "a Union for the protection of industrial property." The first members included Belgium, Brazil, Spain, France, Guatemala, Italy, the Netherlands, Portugal, Salvador, Serbia, and

---

[84] 25 Stat. 1372 (1887), T.S. No. 378 (effective May 30, 1887). See Kronstein, n. 5 above.

Switzerland. The convention was revised at Brussels in 1900, at Washington in 1911, at the Hague in 1925, at London in 1934, and at Lisbon in 1958.[85] The United States entered the Union in 1887, and Germany, the last industrial power to join, became a member in 1901. By September 1966, more than seventy-four countries, including all the important industrial nations both Communist and non-Communist, had become members of the Union.[86]

One of the most important provisions of the convention is the equal-treatment clause of Article 2, whereby each member has agreed to grant patent treatment to nationals or residents of other member countries equal to the treatment it grants its own nationals.

The priority provision of Article 4 has extensive implications. This clause grants a "priority right" for one year to the prospective patentee who has filed his application in any member country. He is entitled to the convention's protection and cannot be deprived of his priority right by another filing, by publication or exploitation of the invention, by sale of copies of the design, or by use of the mark. In other words, the inventor has the convention's protection for a one-year period, during which he can apply for patent protection in any other member country's jurisdiction. Originally granted for six months, the priority period was extended to one year by the Brussels revision of 1900; the Washington revision of 1911 extended the priority-right protection to the assignees of the patent applicant. This one-year priority provision therefore greatly increases the probability that an applicant will acquire a legal monopoly not only in his own nation but also in the other member countries.

The principle of independence

Article 4(b) was established by the Brussels revision of 1900 and provides that patents applied for in various member nations by nationals of the country are to be considered "independent of patents obtained for the same invention in other countries." This independence clause is to be interpreted without any limitation. Once a patent has been granted on the basis of the priority provisions of the convention,

85 The version currently in force is found at [1962] 1 U.S.T. 1, T.I.A.S. No. 4931 (effective Jan. 4, 1962).

86 For a valuable survey see U.N. Pub. No. 65, n. 6 above. Also note that India and Pakistan, which are not members of the Business Association concluded in Paris, have similar obligations based on inter-Commonwealth arrangements.

the subsequent invalidation of the patent by the original granting nation will not of itself affect the validity of patents granted elsewhere on the same invention. This means that even if it were later determined that the patent in the first country of application should never have been granted, the patents proliferated in other countries on the basis of the convention priority rights remain unaffected by their invalidation in the original country of issue. Article 5(a) of the convention provides that the patent shall not be forfeited by importation by the patentee into the country that has granted the patent of goods manufactured in any member country.

Article 5(b) binds the member countries not to issue compulsory licenses to the patentee for failure to use the patent during the first three years after its grant. Thus, the convention prevents its members from taking steps to compel "working" in the first three years after a patent is issued. After that the convention requires its members first to resort to compulsory licensing at reasonable royalties rather than to cancel the patent grant altogether. Cancellation is permitted only as a last resort after the compulsory licensing technique has been tried for at least two years and failed. By these provisions the foreign patentee has a better chance of producing where he chooses and retaining his patent monopoly.

Increasing number of patents

As patent rights became easier to obtain, patent protection broader, and the extension of patent rights less a danger, the number of patents increased. The number of foreign patents also increased. For example, in 1963, in the United States, foreign patents amounted to 22 per cent of the total number of patents granted; in the German Federal Republic it was 41 per cent and in some member countries it was as high as 52 per cent. It is clear that the patent power of the economically most powerful enterprises, which are actual and future cartel partners, has substantially increased and will continue to do so.

Development in the United States

The modern American patent seems to have developed as an antithesis to the old English patent. The original English patent was an exclusive right granted by the king to sell certain specific merchandise and goods. This exclusive right was often granted in consideration for the "importation" of a particular foreign item such as machines or processes or for the establishment in England of entirely new industrial fields.[87] By so "stealing" industrial secrets, the king intended to overcome the then existing advantage of the continental European countries, especially Holland, in the industrial field. In the final result, the British Crown was successful. Patents were also granted for exclusive economic and commercial development and utilization of certain colonies. An example is the patent granted to Lord Baltimore for the territory of Maryland. Therefore, the English patent was principally used not only to protect a particular invention of the patent owner, but essentially to regulate a definite market. In fact, an invention was neither the requirement nor the subject of the patent grant.

This concept of a patent, by which many markets were exclusively regulated by a few enterprises, was rejected at the time of the great revolution at the end of the eighteenth century. This concept was just as detrimental to the economic development of the colonies in the fields involved as it was detrimental to the development of any genuine competition. In one of the first legislative drafts submitted to the French parliament during the revolution, Mirabeau proposed to limit patent protection to the temporary grant of a private and exclusive right to the use of a new invention or discovery.

In the United States, Madison and his supporters in the Constitutional Convention argued in favor of total abolishment of patents. They were influenced by their knowledge that the separation from England had in part been caused by the dispute over the English tea monopoly. Alexander Hamilton represented the opposite view and argued that the United States in the interest of a reasonable industrial development could not refrain from granting exclusive rights for the establishment of industrial fields. A compromise was finally reached under which the institution of the patent was retained but was limited to a temporary protection of really new inventions and discoveries. This marked a definite, conscious deviation from the use of the patent in order to regulate markets toward the establishment of a genuine patent for actually new inventions. This concept of the patent has remained in force under the present American patent law.

[87] E. W. Hulme, "The History of the Patent System under the Prerogative and at Common Law," 12 *L.Q. Rev.* 141–142 (1896).

Requirements for the grant of a patent

The United States Constitution authorizes Congress "to promote the progress of . . . useful arts, by securing for limited times . . . to inventors the exclusive right to their . . . discoveries." [88]

The first patent act of April 10, 1790,[89] submitted to Congress by Jefferson, then Secretary of State, provided that patents could be granted for applications having as their subject "any useful art, manufacture, engine, machine, or device, or any improvement thereon, not before known or used." The patent was only granted if the agency having jurisdiction—a group including the Secretary of State, the Legal Counsel of the State Department, and the Attorney General—concluded "the invention or discovery was sufficiently useful and important." The patent was looked on as an award given by the federal government to a private inventor; but it was granted only in cases in which "inventions and discoveries promote human knowledge." "Jefferson did not believe in granting patents for small details, obvious improvements, or frivolous devices. His writings evidence his insistence upon a high level of patentability." [90]

The patent act of February 21, 1793,[91] maintained the principle that a patent could only be granted if the applicant "invented any new and useful art, machine, manufacture, or composition of matter, or any new and useful improvement thereon not known or used before the application." However, the patent grant itself was made "a clerical act on the part of the Secretary of State." There was no longer the requirement of an examination to show that the claimed invention was a novelty.[92] The patent act of July 4, 1836,[93] established an independent patent office which had the statutory requirement to examine each patent application to insure "that the patent may be only for any new and useful art, machine, manufacture, or composition of matter." [94] Thus, the examination to determine whether the item was actually

[88] U.S. Constitution, Art. I, §8.   [89] 1 Stat. 109.

[90] Graham v. John Deere Co., et al., 216 F. Supp. 272, 274 (D.C.Mo. 1966), reversed 333 F. 2d 529, affirmed 383 U.S. 1 (1966).

[91] 1 Stat. 117.

[92] Statement of Senator John Ruggles, Chairman of the Select Committee to Investigate the Patent Office, partially reprinted in *Expediting Patent Office Procedure*, Study No. 23, 86th Cong., 2d Sess., p. 2 (1960).

[93] 5 Stat. 117.

[94] *Expediting Patent Office Procedures*, n. 92 above, p. 3.

novel was reestablished and remains in force today under the Patent
Act of 1952.[95]

The landmark 1850 Supreme Court case of *Hotchkiss v. Greenwood*
required that the invention be both novel and of substantial importance.
A patent would be denied "unless more ingenuity and skill were required than were possessed by an ordinary mechanic acquainted with
the business." [96] This principle developed by the courts [97] was made
part of Section 103 of the Patent Act of 1952:

A patent may not be obtained though the invention is not identically disclosed or described in section 102 of this title, if the differences between the
subject matter sought to be patented and the prior art are such that the
subject matter as a whole would have been obvious at the time the invention was made to a person having ordinary skill in the art to which said
subject matter pertains. Patentability shall not be negatived by the manner
in which the invention was made.[98]

A dispute arose among American lawyers as to whether Section 103
was only a restatement of the rule followed by the courts for more
than a century or whether the statute had established a "more relaxed
standard." Compared to judicial opinions rendered after the Hotchkiss
decision, Judge Learned Hand considered Section 103 a "watering
down" of the requirements for a patent grant in comparison to the
"stricter standard" of preceding years.[99]

The controversy, however, is not of great importance. The authorities have ceased strictly examining the patent applications to determine their novelty. In practice, the American patent office is more
favorable to the grant of patents than the statute actually requires.
Congressional committees speak of "the gap between the views of the
Patent Office and the U.S. courts as to what is and what is not patentable." [100] The Supreme Court in *Graham v. John Deere Co.* spoke

---

[95] 35 U.S.C.A. §1; note the wording of §101 of this act: "Whoever invents
or discovers any new and useful process, machine, manufacture, or composition
of matter, or any new and useful improvement thereof, may obtain a patent
therefore, subject to the conditions and requirements of this title."

[96] 11 How. 248, 267.

[97] See the survey in *Efforts to Establish a Statutory Standard of Invention*,
Study No. 7, 85th Cong., 1st Sess., p. 3 (1958).

[98] 35 U.S.C.A. §1.

[99] Cf. 63 *Colum. L. Rev.* 306 (1963). Lyon v. Bausch & Lamb Optical Co.,
224 F. 2d 530, 535 (2d Cir. 1955), certiorari denied 350 U.S. 911 (1955).

[100] *Analysis of Patent Litigation Statistics*, 86th Cong., 2d Sess., p. 1 (1961).

in a similar vein.[101] The Court of Appeals for the Second Circuit was even more explicit: "Since 1950, eighteen patents on different variations of hardware for use in reclining chairs with movable leg-rest have been issued. Obviously there have not been eighteen "inventions" in the narrow area in the last twelve years." [102] This development has occurred despite the fact that the actual requirements for a patent grant have not been changed since 1790.

The process of weakening the patent requirements has been slow. In the first decades of the patent statutes, officials undertook to examine strictly the requirements for a patent grant. The first year that the number of granted patents exceeded one hundred (158) was 1808; a clear and marked increase in the number of patents can be observed after 1854 (1853: 844; 1854: 1,755; 1860: 4,357; 1865: 6,088; 1866: 12,277).[103] In 1883 more than 20,000 patents were granted for the first time.[104]

It is certainly true that developments in technology and the intensity of research are very important elements in the increase of patent grants. However, this is not the only explanation. Another major reason has been the weakening of the requirements by the patent office itself. For example, whenever Supreme Court decisions called for stricter application of requirements for granting patents, the number of patent grants decreased for a few years, only to increase even more later.[105]

Unfortunately, it is too early to evaluate the effect of *Graham v. John Deere Co.;* the tendency is to urge stricter interpretation of the word "invention" by the patent office. It has often been alleged that the practices of the patent office are actually due to the procedural steps used in granting patents.[106] This appears doubtful. It must be admitted that some courts, especially courts of appeal, participate in the

---

[101] Cf. n. 90 above.

[102] Lorenz v. F. W. Woolworth Co., 305 F. 2d 102, 105 (2d Cir. 1962).

[103] 46 *J. of the Patent Office Soc'y* 89 (1964).

[104] Graham v. John Deere Co., et al., n. 90 above.

[105] Note the reaction of the patent office to the Hotchkiss decision, n. 96 above. In 1850, the patent office granted 883 patents; in 1851, after the decision, 752 patents were granted, and in 1853, 844 were granted. By 1854, the number granted had jumped to 1,755 (n. 103 above). The decision in the case Cuno Engineering Corp. v. Automatic Devices Corp., 341 U.S. 48 (1950) had the same effect.

[106] "The whole thrust of the administrative process in the Patent Office pushes the examiner in the direction of allowing, rather than disallowing, applications" (J. C. Stedman, "The U.S. Patent System and Its Current Problems," 42 *Texas L. Rev.* 450, 476 [1964]).

"debasement of the standard of invention." [107] There has been an intentional and conscious weakening of the statutory requirements for granting patents by the agencies having jurisdiction over the grant of patents. A lack of statutory device to protect certain "samples" may have led to the weakening of the patent requirement.[108]

To a certain extent, the national patent offices are confronted with an extremely difficult task. The Supreme Court formulation of a test for obviousness in *Graham v. John Deere Co.* shows clearly how difficult the problem is. The first step (which is to examine the prior art, compare it with the subject matter of the claims of the patent application, and then determine whether the differences would or would not be obvious to one skilled in the art) requires many difficult judgments and evaluations that the tendency of administrative officials or patent offices to take the approach of least resistance by granting the patent application is certainly understandable. In the case *Columbia Broadcasting System v. Sylvania Electric Products, Inc.*, U.S. District Court for the District of Massachusetts, the defendant referred to an article in a scholarly review as well as to two rather remote patents.[109] It was true that from a purely scholarly and scientific point of view the article involved already opened the door to the invention in issue. However, the patent office decided that this article was too mathematical and too theoretical to be really "prior art." It is obvious how difficult these decisions are and that at the present development of technology this decision becomes more and more difficult.

Increase in the number of patents

Patent applications and grants in the United States have increased greatly:[110] while in 1955 more than 580,000 patents were in force,[111]

---

[107] Calmar, Inc. v. Cook Chemical Co., 220 F. Supp. 414 (1963); affirmed 336 F. 2d 110 (1964); certiorari granted 383 U.S.1 (1966). In many respects the decisions of the courts are more generous that the decisions of the Patent Office. For example, the Court of Customs and Patent Appeals has granted processing patents without evidence that the particular processing methods were useful. Instead the applicants had only to prove that the method in question was not detrimental to the public interest. Application of Nelson, 280 F. 2d 172 (C.C.P.A. 1960); application of Manson, 333 F. 2d 234, 238 (C.C.P.A. 1964). The Supreme Court reversed this holding in Brenner, Commissioner of Patents v. Manson, 383 U.S. 519 (1966), Justices Harlan and Douglas dissenting.

[108] A. Scher, *Handbuch des amerikanischen Patentgesetzes* (Basel, 1952–1953), p. 7.

[109] C.A. 66-35-c (1966).   [110] *Patent Hearings*, n. 5 above, Pt. 1, p. 35.

[111] Federico, n. 13 above, p. 3.

in 1970 the patent office estimated the number at 897,000. Each American patent has an average of approximately four and a half "claims," [112] and there are more than three million patent claims in force in the United States at this time. New applications increase each year not only in the United States but also in the other developed countries. Because of this great number of patent applications, it is not easy to examine exactly all the requirements for patent registration. The computer and data-processing systems, which have greatly improved in recent years, will be of immense help in these cases.

Conditions in other countries are very similar to those in the United States. An English patent attorney has expressed the opinion that "at least 90 per cent of the patents in the engineering field are normal improvements expected of any competent engineer and of no greater merit than other commercial, financial, organizational, and unpatentable technical innovations used in industry." [113] Even if this estimate is too high and should not be generalized, it does illustrate the point.

The research policy of the U.S. government in the fields of space, atomic energy, and national defense is another cause of the continuously increasing number of patent applications and patent grants. Private enterprises employed by the government to implement, at government expense, certain research and development programs questioned whether and to what extent they are entitled to a U.S. patent on the products of processes developed in connection with the programs. A second question is whether, even if patenting in the United States is refused, patents in foreign countries would be open to them, since their invention would be used for general civilian consumption.[114] Earlier statutes contained certain protective provisions favoring the American public.[115]

---

[112] Federico, "Size of Applicants and Patents," 35 *J. of the Patent Office Soc'y* 804–805 (1954); *The Examination System in the U.S. Patent Office*, Study No. 29, 86th Cong., 2d Sess., p. 48 (1961).

[113] M. C. Dobbs, Letter to the Editor, London *Times*, Sept. 3, 1965.

[114] There has been extensive discussion on this point; see Presidential Memorandum and Statement of Government Patent Policy, 28 Fed. Reg. 100 (1963).

[115] Section 4(b) of the Saline Water Conversion Act, H.R. 7916 (1961) provides: "All research within the United States contracted for, sponsored, co-sponsored, or authorized under authority of this Act, shall be provided for in such manner that all information, uses, products, processes, patents and other developments resulting from such research developed by Government expenditures will (with such exception and limitation, if any, as the Secretary may find to be necessary in the interest of national defense) be available to the general

A Patent Advisory Panel has been established under the National Council for Science and Technology to work out general principles for each of the different fields. Each individual agency, however, pursues its own policy.[116] The National Aeronautics and Space Administration (NASA) holds the opinion that pertinent patent applications shall not be submitted to foreign countries whenever NASA desires otherwise. However, the Department of Defense has left it up to the individual enterprises whether or not they file the application. This same development and attitude can be found in civilian agencies such as the Department of Agriculture and the Department of the Interior.

Description of the invention

Under American patent law, the applicant is required to set out an exact description of his invention and to attach drawings to his application.[117] This specification must contain a written description of the invention and the method of use and manufacturing "in such full, clear, concise, and exact terms" that each and every expert could apply the invention and implement the process. The applicant is also bound to report the best mode of the invention. This description, which will be published at the granting of the patent, is the *quid pro quo* for the grant of the exclusive right to the patentee. As the Supreme Court has repeatedly stated,[118] this description serves a twofold purpose: It enables every expert after the end of the patent period to make use of the invention, while at the same time protecting a competitor during the time of the patent from falling into negligent violation of the patent. However, this requirement of presenting such a specification has been gradually weakened.[119]

---

public. This subsection shall not be so construed as to deprive the owner of any background patent relating thereto or such rights as he may have thereunder." Similar provisions can be found in the Helium Gas Act, 50 U.S.C. §167 (1965) and the Arms Control and Disarmament Act, 22 U.S.C. §2551 (1965).

116 For details see Patent Advisory Panel, *Progress Report to the Federal Council for Science and Technology* (Washington, 1964), p. 11.

117 35 U.S.C.A. §§112–113.

118 For example, Fall Universal Oil Products Co. v. Globe Oil Refining Co., 322 U.S. 471, 484 (1944).

119 "If an improvement of a well known appendage to a machine is fully described in a specification, it is not necessary to show the ordinary master of attaching the appendage to the machine; the patent is to be read as if the machine and its appendage were present or in the mind of the reader, and he a person skilled in the art" (Webster Lorm Co. v. Elias Higgins, 105 U.S. 580) (1882).

An example of the weakening of Section 112 is the opinion of the Seventh Circuit Court of Appeals in the Flick-Reedy case.[120] Here, a patent had been granted for a machine. The applicant described the invention: "The outer surface of the reduced thickness section is formed with a 'special tool' "; he did not, however, disclose or describe the "special tool." Thus, the patentee was able to keep this special tool a secret, and a general utilization of the invention was not practically possible. However, under the formulation of Section 112 there is no doubt that such a possibility of general utilization is required. An expert opinion presented to the court during the course of the proceedings concluded "that a person skilled in the art would not know from reading the patent specifications what was meant by the term 'special tool.' " The patent was therefore finally declared invalid.

In the United States, the definite description of the invention and the patent is of greater importance than in any other country because, unlike the situation in most other industrial countries, a patent already granted can be attacked on the ground that someone else had previously made the invention. If an attack is made on this ground, it is especially important that the description of invention in the patent is definite enough to give a clear differentiation from the previous invention.

Exceptio pacti

In the United States, as in Germany, patent registration procedure and patent protection is based on the assumption that the competitors of the patent applicant will file objections if the requirements for registration of such patents are not fulfilled. In other words, it has been assumed that the market will take care of itself. The effectiveness of the patent registration procedure depends to a large degree on the initiative of the interested parties.

There is a difference in the method used for patent registration in Germany and in the United States. An American patent application is not published prior to a close examination of the application and a grant of the patent. Thus, eventual competitors of the applicant in this phase cannot present their objections to the application. However, the patent office under Section 135 must *ex officio* open a so-called interference procedure, to clarify the problem of priority. Whenever an

[120] Flick-Reedy Corp. v. Hydoline Manufacturing Co., 351 F. 2d 546, 550 (7th Cir. 1965).

application in the opinion of the commissioner may conflict with other patent applications or with patents granted within the previous year, the commissioner informs the other applicants or patentees, giving them an opportunity to object to the new application. After an extensive hearing and taking of evidence, a Board of Patent Interferences decides the question of priority of application. From this decision a complaint before the regular civil courts or an appeal to the U.S. Court of Customs and Patent Appeals can be taken. The competitor of a patentee in the United States may, with very few limitations, attack a patent even after it has been granted whenever he contests the legality of the grant.

Under German law it is easier to file an objection in the proceedings on the grant of the patent, but after the grant an attack on such a patent is very limited. In the United States, however, despite the final grant, anyone can attack the patent before the regular courts. An example would be a complaint for declaratory judgment on grounds that the patent granted is illegal and void. A competitor can also proceed in another way. He can use the patented invention, thereby exposing himself to an infringement complaint by the patentee and using as his defense the claim that the patent was granted without justification.

We have explained in detail how the interested parties—the patent applicant, the patentee, and their competitors—succeeded in improving the relatively weak position of the patentee and patent applicant. The parties settle their disputes concerning priority of inventions by arbitration or private proceedings without the participation of the patent office. In these cases, the winning party files the patent application while the losing party waives the filing of any objections to the patent and is paid off by the grant of a license. Such a private settlement of priority questions may also be reached in later phases of the "interference proceeding." In this case, the losing party discontinues its application or admits the priority rights of the other side, thereby ending the interference proceeding. This method leads to the grant of a large number of patents, despite the fact that there might be no real invention of sufficient merit to be patented, since only a competitor of the applicant who has undertaken extensive research in the same field is able to give a reasoned judgment on the degree and importance of the invention in question.

The interested parties are willing to do everything to retain a patent granted without justification. Usually this is accomplished by entering an agreement not to attack the industrial property right and specifically not to bring a suit declaring the patent void. This type of settlement is found in license and other similar agreements and today has become an almost permanent part of this type of agreement. The American legislation and practice not only allowed these agreements, but actually favored them for a long time. Admittedly, the necessity has been pointed out that exclusive rights such as patents should only be granted if all the legal requirements are fulfilled, since these exclusive rights have a far-reaching effect for the competitors, the market, and the whole public. The Supreme Court of the United States has stated that every participant in an interference proceeding, especially every patent applicant, is obliged in the public interest to inform the patent office of all facts "concerning possible fraud or inequitableness underlying the applications in issue." The Court further pointed out that a private settlement of such priority questions "lacks that equitable nature which entitles it to be enforced and protected in a court of equity" if the patent office has not been informed of the pertinent facts. However, the Court at the same time stated that private agreements or settlements of priority questions are not generally illegal.[121]

In practice, these kinds of agreements between interested parties occur every day. Approximately 80 per cent of all interference proceedings have been settled by understandings between the different patent applicants.[122] Disclosure of some important violations of antitrust legislation through this type of patent agreement in the pharmaceutical field led to congressional action. Section 135 of the Patent Act of 1952 was amended by Subsection c in 1962,[123] and the section now reads as follows:

Any agreement or understanding between parties to an interference, including any collateral agreements referred to therein, made in connection with or in contemplation of the termination of the interference, shall be in writing and a true copy thereof filed in the Patent Office before the termination of the interference as between the said parties to the agreement

[121] Precision Instrument Manufacturing Co. v. Automotive Maintenance Machinery Co., 324 U.S. 805, 818 (1944).

[122] *Patent Interference Settlements Hearings*, n. 23 above, p. 21. Approximately 1 to 2 per cent of all patent applications use the interference procedure. The reason for this relatively low rate may be that the participants agree before the official application of the invention which one will act as inventor.

[123] 76 Stat. 958.

or understanding. If any party filing the same so requests, the copy shall be kept separate from the file of the interference, and made available only to Government agencies on written request, or to any person on a showing of good cause. Failure to file the copy of such agreement or understanding shall render permanently unenforceable such agreement or understanding and any patent of such parties involved in the interference or any patent subsequently issued on any application of such parties involved.

This new provision applies solely to agreements whereby the parties settle their disputes before the patent application proceeding has been initiated: it does not apply to agreements settling disputes after the proceeding has begun. The effectiveness of this new provision is doubtful because the parties will certainly avoid any written detailed agreement and avoid informing the patent office of it.[124]

American courts have always upheld agreements not to attack present or future patents. Whenever one of the involved parties violates this agreement and claims that a certain patent is illegal or void, such a suit or a corresponding defense is excluded by estoppel.[125] This is also true with respect to licensing agreements between the parties where the agreement does not contain an express provision not to attack the patents involved. During the period of the license agreement, neither the licensor nor the licensee may successfully allege the illegality or invalidity of the patents. It is irrelevant whether the licensing agreement is simple or exclusive.[126] The principle of estoppel enjoins the licensee from alleging lack of novelty of the patent.[127] The same principle of estoppel is appiled in the relationship between the seller and buyer of a patent whenever the illegality or validity of the patent is alleged.[128] The prohibition against contesting the deficiency of the patent also includes all allegations of lack of novelty or usability of the invention.[129] However, the prohibition against attacking the validity of a patent is not only applied as far as the partner in a purchase or sale of a patent or in a license agreement is involved: the prohibition against attacking certain patents is extended to partnerships in which the buyer or licensee is decisively interested.[130]

---

[124] This is the position of the Chicago Bar Association expressed at *Patent Interference Setlements Hearings*, n. 23 above, pp. 32–33.

[125] 35 U.S.C.A. §261.   [126] *Id.*

[127] Scibba-Del Mac, Inc. v. Milius Shoe Co., 145 F. 2d 389 (8th Cir. 1944).

[128] 35 U.S.C.A. §261.

[129] Cook Electrical Co. v. Parsons, 60 F. Supp. 124 (D.Mo. 1945).

[130] 35 U.S.C.A. §261.

Overall, this principle amounts to a very far-reaching guarantee of the existence of every patent subject to an expressed or implied agreement not to attack. Generally, there is an exception in cases in which the illegality of the patent is based on an alleged violation of the antitrust laws. The Supreme Court has several times stated that the licensee-estoppel doctrine is not applicable in illegal price-fixing agreements in licensing contracts, or in other cases of violation of the antitrust laws.[131]

The patent license

The antitrust laws limit the effectiveness and validity of a patent and of a patent license. It is always difficult to draw a clear and useful distinction between permissible and unpermissible settlements on the use of patents, since every patent, by its very definition, amounts to a limitation of competition. Therefore, any permission to use such a patent affects the free competition of others.

The obligation of the licensee to follow the sales prices prescribed by the licensor has been declared lawful when the products involved are actually subject to the very same patent licensed in the contract.[132]

The Supreme Court's opinion in *United States v. General Electric* had often been used by lower courts as the rationale for permitting price-fixing agreements even for unpatented goods provided the patents involved "were reasonably related to commercially successful production and marketing of the article."[133] The Court's statement that such a price-fixing agreement is "reasonably within the patentee's reward" was probably an invitation to such a development. However, by the late 1940's the lower courts had changed their position.[134] Today, price fixing by the licensor of merchandise other than that actually patented is illegal; it is also considered illegal to include in license contracts an

[131] Sola Electric Co. v. Jefferson Electric Co., 317 U.S. 173 (1942); Edward Katzinger Co. v. Chicago Metallic Manufacturing Co., 329 U.S. 394 (1947); MacGregor v. Westinghouse Electric and Manufacturing Co., 329 U.S. 402 (1947). United States v. U.S. Gypsum Co., 333 U.S. 64 (1948); Automatic Radio Manufacturing Co. v. Hazeltine Research, Inc., 339 U.S. 827, 836 (1950).
[132] The two leading cases are Bement & Sons v. National Harrow Co., 186 U.S. 70 (1902); United States v. General Electric Co., 272 U.S. 476 (1926).
[133] United States v. General Electric Co., *id.*, p. 489; G. R. Gibbons, "Price Fixing in Patent Licenses and the Antitrust Laws," 51 *Va. L. Rev.* 273, 290 f., nn. 45–46 (1965).
[134] Gibbons, *id.*, p. 291, nn. 47–48.

agreement by which the licensee promises to impose certain resale prices on his customers.[135]

Price-fixing agreements in licensing contracts are illegal whenever the patents involved are mutually licensed or subject to pools.[136] However, the so-called grant-backs, which are agreements in licensing contracts by which the licensee promises to give the licensor sublicenses in all pertinent improvement patents the licensee may obtain, is not illegal. This rule, according to one of the federal district courts, shall also be in effect whenever price-fixing agreements and grant-back clauses are combined in one license agreement. Gibbons, however, makes clear that such a combination has the same basic effect as an illegal cross license. It is evident that the interested parties, despite apparently very strict decisions in antitrust matters, still have sufficient room to set up their own market regulations through patent and licensing agreements if they are skillful enough.[137]

The utilization of patent and patent licenses for international market regulation would be very much strengthened by enactment of the proposals of the President's Commission on the Patent System.[138] In this proposal it is permissible under the antitrust legislation to include any condition in a patent license "the performance of which is reasonable on the circumstances to secure to the patent owner the full benefit of his invention and patent grant. This recommendation is intended to make clear that 'the rule of reason' shall constitute the guidelines for determining patent misuse." The former Assistant Attorney General, Antitrust Division, Professor Donald F. Turner, objected strongly to this proposal.[139] As a matter of fact, nothing shows more the almost logical interdependence between the different patent systems, especially between the U.S. patent system and the German or Canadian patent systems. Once a limitation of the use of patents and production or quantity of import, export, and so forth is established under the license agreement in country A, the decisive element is achieved for inter-

---

[135] Ethyl Corp. v. Hercules Powder Corp., 232 F. Supp. 453, 459 (D.Del. 1963); Standard Sanitary Manufacturing Co. v. United States, 226 U.S. 20 (1912).

[136] United States v. Line Material Co., 333 U.S. 287 (1948); United States v. Neue Winkle, Inc., 342 U.S. 371 (1952).

[137] "Legality of Grant-Back Clauses," 55 *Mich. L. Rev.* 697 ff. (1957); United States v. Huck Manufacturing Co., 227 F. Supp. 791, 803 (E.D.Mich. 1964); Gibbons, n. 133 above, p. 297.

[138] Report of Nov. 17, 1966, reprinted in *Patent Hearings*, n. 5 above, Pt. 1, pp. 51 ff., 94.

[139] *Id.*, Pt. 2, pp. 619–621.

national market regulation. The German provision of the German cartel statute under Section 21 is discussed in Chapter 13. These types of agreements are permitted to a broader extent than at present in the United States. The American participants in the organization of a technological cartel are vitally interested in having one country at least to implement and guarantee the operation of the international market regulation. One other very strong element to be considered is the difficulty or even impossibility of applying the rule of reason in this line of patent licenses without having an idea of the organization of the patents in other countries. If through the parallel build-up of patents and patent licenses the market is closed down, especially for Americans, the rule of reason would require American courts to decide against the validity of license agreements in the United States. Professor Turner is quite right in his fear that cases under such a law would take a long time and would not give sufficient protection.

Know-how

The know-how agreements have vastly increased in importance in recent years. In the United States there are no fixed federal rules for dealing with know-how agreements. There are no statutes covering this point; nor are there any judicial decisions dealing with the legality or illegality of those agreements at the federal level in regard to restraint of trade. This may be because these agreements usually contain arbitration clauses. Professor Stedman has suggested applying a more relaxed common-law doctrine for know-how licenses than is applied to ancillary agreements not to compete and to patents.[140]

German Patent Law

Since the German Patent Act entered into force on May 25, 1877,[141] the number of patent registrations has increased tremendously. While under the former Prussian patent law, only 10 per cent of all patent applications had been successful, the percentage of patent registrations amounted to 25 per cent a short time after the federal patent law had been enacted in 1877, and increased to 61 per cent by 1900.[142] The situation has not changed since that time, and thus in 1951 an inflation

---

[140] 29 *ABAJ* 247 (1965).   [141] 1877 *Reichsgesetzblatt* 501 ff.

[142] Patentenquête, Protocol of Aug. 29, 1876, pp. 8–9; C. Duisberg, *Abhandlungen Vorträge und Reden aus den Jahren 1882–1921* (Cologne, 1923), I, 635, 639.

of patent registrations was noted in West Germany.[143] This development is further due to a tremendous increase of patent applications. In 1963, 61,031 patent applications were filed in West Germany. In 1964 the patent applications totalled 64,775.[144] Since 1955, patent applications steadily increased. At the end of 1970, 330,000 patent applications were pending before the German patent office.[145] This development results from a continuous relaxation of the legal requirements pertaining to patent applications and registration, which has favored the big and powerful firms in the market.

Requirements for the grant of a patent

According to Section 1 of the German Patent Act, any new invention that is useful for economic purposes can be patented. Inventions of chemical products or compounds cannot, however, be patented unless they concern a new process for the manufacture of such products. Although the purpose of this exception was to secure competition in the chemical industry and further the development of new products, this provision appears to foster monopolization in the chemical market. The chemical industry has developed chemical and technical processes in which it was possible to produce a vast variety of products. In the field of aniline dyes, for example, nine thousand different compounds are produced on the basis of a relatively small number of chemical processes.[146] This enabled the producers to monopolize whole sections of the production by acquiring patents for the essential chemical processes. This development was supported by an amendment to the Patent Act in 1891,[147] which established the presumption for the patentee that products of the same quality were manufactured on the basis of the same chemical process. A competitor of the patentee, marketing the same products as the patentee, has to prove that his products were manufactured by a chemical process different from the patented process.

The increase of patent applications and patent registrations has fur-

[143] Patentgesetz §1, n. 53.

[144] Compare the summary in 1964 *Blatt für Patent-, Muster- und Zeichenwesen* 135–136, with that in 1965 *id*. 99–100.

[145] Address by President Haertels before the National Ass'n of Manufacturers, New York, June 11, 1965.

[146] R. Sonnenmann, *Der Einfluss des Patentwesens auf die Herausbildung von Monopolen in der deutschen Teerfarbenindustrie (1877–1904)* (Berlin, 1923), pp. 119–121. See also p. 121 (Professor Hofmann's explanation and examples).

[147] 1891 *Reichsgesetzblatt*, I, 79.

ther been facilitated by relaxation of the requirement of novelty as established in Section 1 of the German Patent Act.

Formerly, an invention could not be patented if the invention was known or used by others in Germany or patented or described in a printed publication in Germany or in a foreign country before the filing of a patent application. This provision was changed in two aspects: the prior invention must be published within the hundred years before the filing of the application; and a publication within six months before the filing of the application is deemed irrelevant if it is based on the invention of the applicant or his predecessor.[148] In addition, administration of the requirements with respect to novelty and usefulness of inventions have been continually relaxed in the last decades.[149] Patents are therefore very often granted for processes and products of minor significance. Patent applications are filed in these cases because the novelty may be important for the marketing of the respective product and hence for the exclusion of competitors.

Proceedings before the German patent office

According to the German Patent Act, each patent application has to be published by the patent office provided the patent applicant fulfills the formal requirements of the Patent Act, and the patent office does not consider the patent application to be inadmissible on its face.[150] Motions against registration of patents must be filed within three months after publication of the patent application. If no motions are filed, the patent office must decide on the patent application. If, however, the patent application is opposed by other persons, the whole matter is referred to another section of the patent office which investigates thoroughly the reasons for denial or approval of the patent application.[151] If the patent office dismisses the motions filed against the patent applicant, the complainant may appeal to the patent court.[152] After the patent office has approved the patent application, no appeal from this decision is possible. However, every person whose rights

---

[148] Id., II, 117.

[149] Commentary on law of patents and registered designs, Patentgesetz, §1, n. 53.

[150] Patentgesetz, §30.

[151] Id., §32, as amended by regulation of Aug. 1, 1953 (Bundesgesetzblatt I, at 715). According to this regulation the investigation is done by the same office in order to accelerate the entire proceeding (R. Busse, Patentgesetz und Gebrauchsmustergesetz [Berlin, 1956], pp. 376, 385, 389).

[152] Patentgesetz, § 34 in connection with § 21.

are affected by the granting of the patent may institute an action to have the patent declared null and void.[153] Such complaint may be based on the following arguments: the invention was not patentable according to Sections 1 and 2 of the German Patent Act; the invention had been already patented by a prior applicant; or the application was based on descriptions, models, drafts, devices, institutions, or processes owned by another person.

Proceedings before the German patent office and courts are based on the idea that the public itself will prevent the registration of illegal and improper patents by filing the necessary complaints and motions. Earlier in this chapter, it has been pointed out that this assumption of the legislature has not been realized in practice. The big firms very often protect the applications and patents by conclusion of agreements with their competitors and these manipulations are not effectively prevented by the law in force. Motions and complaints can be freely withdrawn in patent proceedings even when the withdrawal occurs in complicance with a compromise concluded between competitors. Furthermore, the majority of the writers contend that the right to file defenses against patent applications may be waived in advance. This opinion has, however, been opposed by the patent office.[154]

A more controversial issue is the legality of covenants not to bring suit to have patents declared null and void. The former German Supreme Court dismissed several complaints on the grounds that such covenants had been concluded between the parties.[155] In 1949 and 1950,

[153] *Id.*, §35(1) as to final decision, §13 as to actions open to every impaired person (Busse, n. 151 above, pp. 173, 236, 405).

[154] Among the writers, see *Patentgesetz und Gebrauchmustergesetz* (2d ed.; Munich, 1958), § 32, n. 4; H. Krausse, F. Katluhn, and F. Lindemaier, *Das Patentgesetz vom 5.5.1936 und 18.7.1953* (4th ed.; Cologne, 1958); W. Müller in 1961 *Gewerblicher Rechtsschutz und Urheberrecht* 535. Müller suggests that the creation of a federal patent court should provide an opportunity for investigation into and possibly even revision of patent office practice. But see J. Kohler, *Handbuch des deutschen Patentrechts, in rechtsvergleichender Darstellung* (Mannheim, 1900), p. 770; Kohler suggests that the federal patent court renounce such an investigation. For the opinion of the Patent Office, see 1933 *Gewerblicher Rechtsschutz und Urheberrecht* 101, 102; 1927 *id.* 889; 1955. *id.* 90.

[155] H. Robolski, *Theorie und Praxis des deutschen Patentrechtes* (Berlin, 1890), pp. 160, 161. Twenty years ago, Robolski pointed out that the procedures before the patent office had developed in a way which did not correspond to the objectives of the legislation. Instead of giving the application official treatment, the right of the patent office to investigate the patent application was more and more restricted out of a fear of undermining the existence of the acquired patents.

the West German Supreme Court reversed this position, pointing out that covenants not to sue were contrary to the public interest. This interest required that the legality of patent applications be investigated thoroughly and that such investigations be not subject to the discretion of private persons.[156] In 1953 the Supreme Court returned, however, to the position of its predecessor. The Court pointed out that patent proceedings are very often cumbersome and extremely complicated and that therefore covenants not to sue ought to be considered justifiable from the economic viewpoint. This opinion has been supported by most writers.[157]

A covenant not to sue thus recognized by the highest German court has gained tremendous importance in many fields. The German Supreme Court and the majority of the writers have argued with respect to exclusive licenses that the licensee is not entitled to oppose and file complaints against the patentee.[158] The German Act Against Restraints of Trade has expressly acknowledged the legality of covenants not to sue between licensor and licensee.[159] With respect to simple licenses, the German Supreme Court has held that the licensee may be obligated to abstain from opposing the licensor's patent because of the specific nature, purpose, or contents of the licensing agreement.[160] Such obligations may further follow from the relationship between proprietors of the same patent, from agreements whereby the contracting party

---

The investigation increasingly depended on the litigating parties' own initiative, and the investigation of the patent application by the patent office itself became increasingly significant. The facts were regularly investigated only on the basis of the litigating parties' own files, and evidence uncovered by the patent office itself was not considered. See also 1914 *Blatt für Patent-, Muster- und Zeichenwesen* 348; 1923 *id.* 146; 1928 *id.* 253–254.

[156] 1952 *Blatt für Patent-, Muster- und Zeichenwesen* 269 ff.

[157] 10 BGHZ 22. An agreement not to oppose a patent may be void if the parties were aware of the patent's illegality (BGB, §138). See, e.g., remarks of G. Alexander-Katz in 1954 *Gewerblicher Rechtsschutz und Urheberrecht* 23; 1956 *id.* 292 ff.; H. Schippel, "Die Berechtigung zur Erhebung der Nichtigkeitsklage im Patentrecht und ihre Beschränkung durch Lizenzverträge," 1955 *id.* 322; Müller, n. 154 above, p. 535.

[158] Kohler, n. 154 above, pp. 379 f.   [159] GWB §20(2)4.

[160] Bundesgerichtshof, 1965 *Gewerblicher Rechtsschutz und Urheberrecht* 135 ("Vanol Patent"); Reichsgericht, 1913 *Blatt für Patent-, Muster- und Zeichenwesen* 458; 1921 *id.* 92; Bundesgerichtshof, 1957 *Gewerblicher Rechtsschutz und Urheberrecht* 485 ("Chenille-Maschine"); *id.* 812 ("Chenillefäden"); 1958 *id.* 177 ("Aluminiumflachfolien"). Parties may be prohibited from bringing an action against the patent even after the expiration of the licensing contract. See Bundesgerichtshof, 1964 *Der Betrieb* 1809.

undertakes to defend the property rights of the patentee, or from other contracts.[161]

Protection of patents

The protective rights of the patentee have been continuously extended since the first German patent act in 1877. According to the act in its original version, a recovery of damages was possible only for an international infringement of the patent. Lobbyists of the chemical industry then persuaded the legislators to extend the right of recovery to grossly negligent infringement. An amendment of May 1936 finally laid down the right to recover damages resulting from negligent or intentional infringement.

In 1898 the former German Supreme Court held that the damages of the patentee are measured by the royalties the licensee would have reasonably paid for the use of the patent.[162] This was, however, not the end of the development. In 1909 the former German Supreme Court held that the patentee could sue for the benefits the infringer gained by illegal use of the patent.[163] The Supreme Court held also that the patentee had a right to sue for such benefits even when the infringement was due to slight negligence, and the West German Supreme Court has reaffirmed these holdings.[164] In addition, many writers have argued that even the non-negligent infringement of patent rights creates a liability for the reasonable value of the patents rights used.[165] The former Supreme Court, however, rejected this view,[166] and it cannot be predicted which position the new German Supreme Court will take.

Patent licenses

The development has been the same with respect to patent licenses. At first the writers and courts argued that the licensee had no rights against third persons because the licensing agreement only created

[161] Kohler, n. 154 above, pp. 379–380.   [162] 43 RGZ 56, 59.

[163] 70 RGZ 249, 251 f. On the controversy over whether or not one may bargain for compensation damage, see Krausse, Katluhn, and Lindenmaier, n. 154 above, Vol. 5, §47, n. 22 (with detailed citations).

[164] 70 RGZ 249, 251 f.; 130 RGZ 108, 110; 156 RGZ 65, 67; 20 BGHZ 345, 353.

[165] E.g., H. Scheffler, Reichsgerichtsrätekommentar §812, n. 21; Soergel, Siebert and Mühl, id., n. 165; J. Esser, Schuldrecht (2d ed.; Karlsruhe, 1960), p. 774; E. J. Mestmäcker, "Eingriffserwerb und Rechtsverletzung in der ungerechtfertigten Bereicherung," 1958 Juristenzeitung 521, 524.

[166] 43 RGZ 56, 58; 121 RGZ 258, 261.

rights between the two contracting partners. The licensing agreement was, in other words, treated like a normal contractual relationship, as for example a lease.[167] In 1904 the former German Supreme Court overruled its former holdings with respect to exclusive licenses.[168] The Court argued that the licensing contract created a "quasi" property right in favor of the licensee, which enabled the licensee to sue third persons in his own right for infringement of the patent license. In later sessions, the Supreme Court explained that a licensing agreement creates a property right of special nature in favor of the licensee; this development was concluded by an amendment of the Patent Act in 1953 that provides for discretionary registration of exclusive licensing agreements.[169]

Legal limitations of patent rights

The Patent Act of 1877 provided for compulsory withdrawal of the patent three years after its registration when the patentee refused to grant a license for the purpose of the exploitation of the invention and when the granting of such license was in the public interest. According to Section 15(1) of the Patent Act, as amended in 1911, the patent office may grant a license without consent of the patentee.[170] A withdrawal of the patent is possible when the invention is exclusively or primarily used outside of German territory and when the public interest cannot be served by the issuance of compulsory licenses. The amendment has rendered the sanctions of patent withdrawal and obligatory licenses practically irrelevant, and it is therefore not astonishing that they have found the approval of business associations.[171]

Further limitations concerning patents and licenses can be found in Section 20 of the German Act Against Restraints of Trade. Section 20 renders agreements concerning the acquisition or the use of patents and registered designs invalid if these agreements "impose upon the acquirer or licensee any restrictions in his business conduct which go beyond the contents of the said privileges." This provision does not include "restrictions pertaining to the type, scope, quality, territory, or period of exercise of the privilege." Further it does not apply to the following, provided that these restraints do not remain in force beyond

[167] 17 RGZ 53 f.   [168] 57 RGZ 38, 40 f.
[169] 82 RGZ 431 f.; 134 RGZ 91, 96; Bundesgesetzblatt, I, 615 (1961).
[170] A. Magen, Lizenzverträge und Kartellrecht, (Heidelberg, 1963), p. 43.
[171] P. Zimmermann, Patentwesen in der Chemie (Ludwigshafen, 1965), p. 127.

the expiration of the privilege that is the subject of the acquisition of the license: (1) restrictions imposed upon the acquirer or licensee in so far and as long as they are justified by any interest of the seller or licensor in the technically unobjectionable exploitation of the matter protected by the privilege; (2) obligations of the acquirer or licensee with respect to the price to be charged for the protected article; (3) obligations of the acquirer or licensee to exchange know-how or to grant licenses for improvements or related inventions if these correspond to reciprocal obligations of the patent owner or licensor; (4) obligations of the acquirer or licensee not to challenge the protected privilege; (5) obligations of the acquirer or licensee relating to the regulation of competition in markets outside the area of the applicability of this law.

Finally, the cartel authority may approve an agreement rendered void under Section 20 "if the freedom of economic action of the acquirer, licensee, or any other enterprises is not unfairly restricted and if competition in the market is not substantially restrained through the restrictions involved." The exception renders the provision of Section 20 relatively insignificant. On the other hand, agreements falling within the scope of the exceptions have still to comply with Sections 1 to 14 of the German cartel law, which are not abrogated by Section 20.

It should be noted that Section 20 applies also to agreements concerning the transfer or exploitation of legally unprotected inventions, manufacturing processes, and technical designs if these constitute business secrets.[172]

Development of Legal Structure in Trademark Law and Other Exclusive Rights

International Development

The International Convention for the Protection of Industrial Property, the Paris Union Treaty of 1883, not only established rules for the protection of patents but also set out the rules for "trademarks or factory marks and trade marks." [173] The Washington Amendment of

---

[172] GWB, §21.

[173] Convention of Union of Paris of March 20, 1883, as revised for the protection of industrial property, Lisbon, Oct. 31, 1958 (effective Jan. 4, 1962), [1962] 13 U.S.T. 1, T.I.A.S. No. 4931, Art. 2.

1911 extended the scope of the Paris Treaty to "designation of origin" and "the oppression of unfair competition." [174] The Hague Conference of 1925 substituted the global concept of "industrial property right," which had already been used in Article 1, for the previous enumeration of particular cases. This meaning of industrial property right was expanded in Article 1, Section 2, by protecting all "statements as to origin or symbols of origin." Section 3 of the same provision expressly states that the concept of industrial property is to be interpreted in its broadest meaning. The Washington Amendment added protection for the "association mark," and the Lisbon Amendment finally included "service marks." [175]

The principle of priority

As we have seen, the priority protection of Article 4 of the Paris Convention has been expanded several times. Originally the protection period was three months for trade marks and factory marks. It was extended to four months by the Brussels Amendment and to six months by the Hague Conference.[176]

The principle of independence

The London Amendment established the principle of national trademark independence.[177] Whenever there is a trademark or factory mark in the country of origin as well as in other member countries registered pursuant to statutory provisions, each of the national marks is to be considered independent from the mark in the country of origin beginning from the day of their registration, provided that the mark meets the requirements of the domestic legislation of the country involved.[178]

Protection of the mark in detail

Under Article 6 of the Paris Convention each trademark or factory mark registered in the country of origin was "admitted to registration" or protected in all other member countries. The reasons for refusing such a registration, which were enumerated at the Paris Convention,

[174] Id., Art. 10 bis.   [175] Id., Art. 6.
[176] 38 Stat. 1645, T.S. 579; 47 Stat. 1789, T.S. 834, 74 L.N.T.S. 289.
[177] 53 Stat. 1748, T.S. 941, 192 L.N.T.S. 17.
[178] Convention of Union of Paris of March 20, 1883, as revised for the protection of industrial property, Lisbon, Oct. 31, 1958, [1962] 13 U.S.T. 1, T.I.A.S. No. 4931.

have been limited from convention to convention, while the degree of protection given the mark has increased. The Hague Amendment provided that the registration of a trade or factory mark is to be denied or, if already allowed, is to be declared illegal whenever such a mark "is the copy of or equally confused with another mark." This decision depends on the opinion of the agency of proper jurisdiction in the country of registration that the mark in question is already considered as "belonging to a national of another contracting country or is being used for the same or similar mechandise." The London Amendment extended the protection to those marks "which appear to be a copy, translation, or reproduction" of another mark. The Lisbon Amendment obligated the member countries to enjoin "the use" of pertinent marks.[179]

The Paris Convention provided for sanctions against the importation of merchandise symbolized or designated in an unlawful way. Article 9 provided that each product bearing any trademark or trade name in an illegal way shall be confiscated on importation into those member states in which this mark or this trade name has acquired a right to legal protection. The Brussels Amendment permitted each country to substitute for the right to confiscate a general prohibition against importing whenever its laws would not permit such seizure. The Washington Amendment required the member countries either to confiscate or to prohibit importation. It also provided that whenever the laws of a country permit neither seizure on importation, nor prohibition of importation, nor seizure within the country, then these measures are to be replaced by legal remedies available in these cases to nationals under the law of the country. In Article 9, Section 2, the amendment provided that the seizure has to occur in the country where the unlawful application of the mark took place or in the country into which the goods have been imported. Article 10 of the original treaty applied Article 9 to:

any producer, manufacturer or trader, whether a natural or juridical person, engaged in the production or manufacture of or trade in such goods and established either in the locality falsely indicated as the source or in the district where this locality is situated, or in the country falsely indicated, or in the country where the false indication of source is used, shall in any case be deemed an interested party.[180]

179 *Id.*, Art. 6 bis §1.   180 *Id.*, Art. 10, §2.

The Lisbon Amendment extended this protection to every case of direct or indirect use of a false statement of the origin of the product or the identity of the producer or trader.[181]

All the agreements discussed here have shown a clear attempt to extend the protection of trademarks. A description of any further agreement would exceed the purpose and intent of our analysis.[182]

Development in the United States

The American trademark is not acquired by registration but by "appropriation and use." The evolution of American trademark law clearly shows that the different stages developed gradually without the aid of specific legislation.

The basis from which the law evolved was not very favorable. The common law rule held that it was acceptable for anyone to copy the merchandise, package, or symbol of a competitor. The only exception was the prohibition against "passing" or "palming off": "It is unfair to pass off one's goods as those of another person or to imitate a rival's trade-name or label." [183] An essential element for the application of this rule of prohibition, however, was that the trademark or symbol had become so well known on the market that the public associated this trademark exclusively with the enterprise of the person claiming damages. Even in this situation there was no genuine protection of symbols as there is today. The concept of trademarks covered only the name of the producer of the goods and the place of production but not its symbol or descriptive name. There was

no right to an exclusive use of any words, letters, figures or symbols, which have no relation to the origin of ownership of the goods, but are only meant to indicate their name or quality. . . . no right to appropriate a sign or symbol which, from the nature of the fact which it is used to signify, others may employ with equal truth, and therefore have an equal right to employ, for the same purpose.[184]

That meant that any person violating a trademark was prohibited and enjoined from letting his goods appear as the goods of the plaintiff,

---

[181] *Id.*, Art. 10, §1.

[182] See generally R. Busse, *Warenzeichengesetz* (3rd ed.; Berlin, 1960), App. V, B, MMA, T, and App. V, D, MHA, CII.

[183] H. D. Nims, *The Law of Unfair Competition and Trade-Marks* (4th ed.; New York, 1947), p. 3.

[184] Amoskeag Mfg. Co. v. Spear, 2 Sandf. 599 (1849).

but he was not under any prohibition against using symbols developed by the person subject to the alleged infringement. The case of *Williams v. Adams* illustrates this point.[185] Here the infringer of the product "Yankee Soap" copied the symbol and make-up of the plaintiff-infringee and even used his name. The court, however, only enjoined the violator from designating his soap as the infringee's soap. He was not enjoined from further use of the symbol "Yankee Soap."

New York courts were the first to change their line of reasoning. The case of *Burnett v. Phalon* can be considered the "first modern case of production of a symbol." [186] Here the plaintiff, under the symbol "Cocoaine," which it prepared itself, introduced on the market a hair lotion and spent a considerable amount of money on advertising. The defendant under the symbol "Cocoine" then brought out on the market a lotion with almost the same composition as the plaintiff's lotion. Although the symbols used in the packaging of both products could not be confused, the court enjoined the defendant from making further use of the symbol "Cocoine" for his product. The plaintiff had acquired proprietary interest in this symbol by working out the word "Cocoaine." Despite criticism by scholars and caution by the courts, the recognition of the symbol as independent from any direct statement of the origin of the goods began to gain acceptance. The symbol increasingly acquired the function of guaranteeing quality and of being an important element of advertising.[187]

Symbols are still subject to substantial limitations however. Symbols that are not distinguishable, especially those of a descriptive character or family name, have generally been neither recognized nor protected. But even in this area protection of symbols has been extended under the doctrine of "secondary meaning." If a producer's trademark cannot be legally protected, he may under this doctrine bring an action for injunctive relief against another company using the same trademark, provided the plaintiff company was the first user of the trademark and the products sold under the trademark are associated by the public with the plaintiff's company, and provided the defendant's

185 8 Biss. 452 (Ill. 1879).

186 3 Keyes 594 (1867); W. Derenberg, *Warenzeichen und Wettbewerb in den Vereinigten Staaten von Amerika* (Berlin, 1931).

187 See Shredded Wheat Co. v. Humphrey Cornell Co., 244 F. 508 (Conn. 1917), affirmed 250 F. 960 (2d Cir. 1918); Standard Oil Co. v. California Peach & Fig Growers, 28 F. 2d 283 (Del. 1928).

products also became associated with the plaintiff's company.[188] The Waltham Watch case employed the "secondary meaning" theory to limit the general prohibition against the use of geographical words as trademarks.[189] The American Waltham Company had already gained a strong market position for its watches produced in Waltham under the trademark "Waltham," when the defendant U.S. Watch Company started producing its watches in Waltham also under the trademark "Waltham." The Supreme Court of Massachusetts, Justice Oliver Wendell Holmes presiding, enjoined the defendant from using the word "Waltham" on its watches unless he made perfectly clear on the watch itself that it was not a product of the plaintiff. The decision in the Elgin case was more extensive.[190] The court recognized that the complaining watch manufacturer was entitled to demand that the defendant, having only a formal office in Elgin, refrain from using the word Elgin on its products.

Legislative development

The increasing extension of production for symbols can be seen in statutory development. Article 1, Clause 8, of the U.S. Constitution authorized the government "to promote the Progress of . . . useful arts by securing for limited Times to Authors and Inventors the exclusive right to their respective Writings and Discoveries." It did not give the federal government jurisdiction to enact legislation in the field of trademarks. However, the government believed it could regulate the trademark field because of its similarity to patent law and enacted the first federal trademark statute in 1870.[191] Another statute was enacted in 1876, containing criminal sanctions.[192] Both were declared unconstitutional by the Supreme Court in 1879, the Court ruling that there is no affinity between trademark law on the one side and patent or copyright law on the other.[193] The Court pointed out:

The trade-mark may be and generally is the adoption of something already in existence as the distinctive symbol of the party using it. At common law the exclusive right to it grows out of its use and not its mere adoption. By the act of Congress this exclusive right attaches upon registration, but in

---

[188] Crescent Tool Co. v. Kilborn & Bishop Co., 247 F. 299, 300 (2d Cir. 1917) (definition of "secondary meaning" doctrine given by L. Hand, J.).

[189] The American Waltham Co. v. U.S. Watch Co., 53 N.E. 141 (1899).

[190] Elgin National Watch Co. v. Elgin Jewelry Co., 132 F. 41 (N.D. Iowa 1904).

[191] 16 Stat. 198.   [192] 19 Stat. 141.   [193] Derenberg, n. 186 above, p. 11.

neither case does it depend upon novelty, invention, discovery, or any work of the brain. It requires no fancy or imagination, no genius, no laborious thought. It is simply founded on priority of appropriation.[194]

In 1881, Congress enacted a new trademark law that covered only actual commerce with foreign countries and with Indian tribes; it did not cover commerce between the states.[195] The statute was based on the "interstate commerce" clause of the Constitution, which authorizes the government "to regulate commerce with foreign nations, and among the several states, and with the Indian tribes." [196] Only in 1905 was the trademark as used in interstate commerce made subject to federal law by an "act to authorize the registration of trademarks used in commerce with foreign nations or among the several states or with Indian tribes, and to protect the same." [197] Under Section 1 of this act, the owner of a trademark used in interstate commerce or in foreign trade or in trade with Indians may register his trademarks, provided he lives in one of the states or in another country that grants by statute or by international treaty the same protection to the citizen of the United States as it gives to its own citizen. Section 5 (1) provides that "a symbol in itself distinctive" should not be refused registration "because of content or form of the symbol" unless: "c) the symbol is identical to an already registered trademark for the same type of goods or is so similar to another mark that it might cause confusion in the public mind."

Under the provision of Section 5 (2), registration of a mark may take place even in cases of confusion, "provided the mark was used by the petitioner or his assignor effectively and exclusively for a 10 year period" before the act was passed. The registration of a symbol in itself fit for registration should "not be excluded from such registration merely because this mark is at the same time the name or portion of the name of the petitioner."

Extension of legal protection by the 1905 act

Despite the clear and restrictive statutory language of Section 5 (1), the legal protection of symbols continued to expand. Originally the patent office took the position that any geographical area was open to common use and could not be protected by a trademark even if the reference to a particular place was arbitrary and unrelated to it. Slowly this position changed. By the end of the 1920's, the patent office

194 United States v. Steffens, 100 U.S. 82 (1879).   195 21 Stat. 502.
196 U.S. Constitution, Art. I, §8.   197 33 Stat. 724.

permitted registration of those trademarks that arbitrarily used a geo-graphical word and were not related to "a reasonably well-known geographical" district.[198] The statute stated that "merely" names or geographical areas cannot be without property interest. This induced the higher courts at an early date to allow those symbols in which geographical references are used entirely separate from their original meaning. An example is the mark "Philadelphia Cream Cheese," which is produced in New York by the Phoenix Cheese Company and has no relation at all with Philadelphia. The courts protected this symbol as a trademark against a competitor who later started to produce the same cheese in Philadelphia.[199]

Symbols developed from the firm name of a corporation had a similar evolution to acceptability. Originally, the 1905 Act excluded from allowable trademarks or signs those symbols "merely composed out of the name . . . of a firm, or a corporation, or an association." [200] Thus, the courts enjoined the registration of the word "Champion" by the Champion Safety Lock Company.[201] Congress amended the act in 1911 [202] by expressly providing that the registration of a symbol otherwise fit for registration could not be denied on the mere ground that the symbol is at the same time the name of the applicant. The courts then permitted the registration of a symbol containing the name of the firm. However, they enjoined later applicants from using the same firm name of a corporation already registered even if the ap-plicants intended to use this symbol for entirely different products.[203] The Supreme Court finally changed judicial thinking in its "Simplex" decision.[204] The Court concluded that the registration of a symbol, which is at the same time in whole or in part the name of another cor-poration, is subject to the principle of descriptive properties. Under this principle, the same symbol may be applied and used for other essentially different classes of merchandise than those which were to be protected by the first owner of the mark. Only in cases of "famous and well-known" marks is the registration of the mark for other classes of products not permissible, since the public is bound to connect the

[198] Ex parte Semet-Solvay Co., 151 Md. 938 (1928).

[199] Phoenix Cheese Co. v. Kunedy, 7 T.M.R. 587; Phoenix Cheese Co. v. Samuel Dirpe and Morris Pearl, 164 N.Y.S. 71 (1917).

[200] 33 Stat. 724 §5 (1d).

[201] 153 *Official Gazette* (U.S. Patent Office), p. 1109.   [202] 61 Stat. 919.

[203] Asbestone Co. v. Cary Mfg. Co., 41 App. D.C. 507 (1914).

[204] American Foundries Co. v. Robertson, 269 U.S. 372 (1926).

owner of the famous mark with the products of other merchandise classes.

Under Section 5 (1d) of the 1905 Act, a symbol could not be registered that was identical with a trademark or symbol already registered for the "same descriptive properties." [205] The prevailing interpretation of this clause held that goods belonged to the same descriptive properties whenever the products involved belonged to the same class of merchandise as listed by the patent office.[206] The principle that everyone may register for certain goods a mark already known for other goods was abandoned step by step. In the Aunt Jemima decision [207] the Court no longer relied on the mere objective fact that certain merchandise belonged to the same class on the patent list, but instead relied on an evaluation of whether the public would connect or affiliate the goods with each other. An applicant, who applies for the registration of a mark already registered by someone else, is denied permission whenever the public may conclude that the goods come from the same source or origin.

In later decisions, applications have sometimes been denied on the ground that the first owner of the symbol could not be deprived of the power and interest to manufacture and distribute these additional goods if he decides to extend the scope of his business activities. There began a distinction between strong and weak symbols. Slowly the prevailing opinion changed to the view that any registration should be considered illegal if the public might be induced "to wrong conclusions as to the origin and identity of merchandise." It was considered unimportant "whether this public opinion was based on the singularity and fame of the mark . . . or whether it is based on the close affiliation of the goods involved." [208] The Lanham Act of 1946 provided that the registration of a mark already used should not be permissible whenever such a registration might "cause confusion and mistakes or deceive purchasers as to the source or origin of the goods." [209] If the identity of the

205 The interpretation of this principle has been hotly debated by scholars. Derenberg calls the situation "chaotic" (Derenberg, n. 186 above, p. 184).

206 Hump Hairpin Co. v. The de Long Hook and Eye Co., 39 App. D.C. 484 (1913). Other courts have decided differently; see, e.g., Wm. A. Rogers, Ltd., v. Majestic Products Corp., 23 F. 2d 219 (1927).

207 Aunt Jemima Mills Co. v. Rigney, 247 F. 407 (2d Cir. 1917).

208 Derenberg, n. 186 above, p. 200.

209 15 U.S.C. §1051 (1964). This language of §2 of the act was almost identical with a proposed draft for a new statute in 1930 which was rejected by Congress.

merchandise was involved, there was *prima facie* evidence of danger of confusion.[210]

Under Section 5 (2) of the 1905 Act, the registration of a symbol illegal under the general rule could be permitted whenever the "mark of the applicant or of his assignor was used for at least 10 years before the enactment of the Act exclusively in interstate commerce, or foreign trade, or trade with the Indians." Derenberg justifiably considered this ten-year clause as an expression of the "secondary meaning" doctrine.[211] This doctrine made it possible to register trademarks that could not have been registered under general principle of law. The ten-year clause became not only a procedural regulation of trademark law, as the legislators intended, but actually developed into a new basis of substantive law for trademark registration. The majority of the scholars contended that the usage of such a trademark by a third party before its registration had no legal effect as long as the usage constituted "an unsuccessful effort to steal the trademark." [212]

The ten-year clause of the 1905 Act only referred to such use before 1905. It did not cover the situation where the mark won general recognition on the market after 1905. The 1920 Amendment [213] extended registration authority by authorizing the owner of a symbol registered under the ten-year clause to demand that this symbol be registered for his other classes of merchandise whenever he expanded his business after termination of the ten-year period. For the extension of this registration privilege it was required that the symbol have been used for the new product for at least one year in interstate commerce or foreign trade or trade with Indians and that no one else have used the symbol for similarly new merchandise in the year prior to the filing of the application. The proposed 1930 federal law intended to permit the registration of any symbol unlawful under the 1905 Act "which . . . shall be shown . . . to have acquired a secondary meaning distinguishing the applicant's goods."

Section 2(f) of the Lanham Act of 1946 used similar language.[214] Symbols failing to meet the requirements for registration under Section 2(e) of the act could be registered if they are "merely descriptive,"

---

[210] In exceptional cases the same or similar trademarks may be registered by several applicants (§2d, p. 2).

[211] Derenberg, n. 186 above, p. 148.

[212] Davids Co. v. Davids, 190 F. 285 (S.D.N.Y. 1912).   [213] 41 Stat. 535.

[214] U.S.C. §1051 (1964).

or "primarily geographically descriptive," or "deceptively misdiscriptive," or "primarily merely a surname," yet are "used by the applicant and have become distinctive of the applicant's goods in commerce." "The commissioner may accept" as *prima facie* evidence of a general market recognition "proof of substantially exclusive and continuous use thereof as a mark by the applicant in commerce for the five years next preceding the date of the filing of the application for its registration." It should be noted that the Lanham Act, in contrast to the 1905 Act, not only refers to foreign trade or trade with the Indian tribes but also to the trade between the individual states.

Step by step, certain combinations of colors, words, pictures, and symbols acquired protection against use by competitors of the first owner. Originally, this protection was only granted in cases of "passing off." It was based on the principle that every color, form, or equipment could be used by anyone in commerce as long as there was no deception to the public. It later developed that pictures could acquire the character and protection of trademarks whenever they gained by means of a secondary meaning "a primary purpose to make the merchandise attractive." [215]

The collective mark

The collective mark, which is basically the same as the German "association mark," is one under the control of several persons having a certain definite legal relationship. Originally, this type of mark could only be obtained if and when the "association" itself functioned as manufacturer or trader of the involved product.[216] In practice, this mark developed into a kind of "group use" of trademarks. The 1938 law [217] amended Section 1 of the 1905 Act to the effect that each natural or corporate person "which exercises legitimate control over the use of a collective mark may apply and obtain registration of such mark." A similar provision is found in Section 4 of the Lanham Act, which says that the applicant himself does not necessarily own or control an "industrial or commercial establishment." This view that the use of a trademark registered for an association by another affiliated enterprise is generally not harmful to the mark had become the prevailing opinion before World War II [218] and was given a statutory basis by Section 5 of the Lanham Act.

215 Nims, n. 183 above, pp. 393, 608.   216 Derenberg, n. 186 above, p. 146.
217 75 Stat. 638.
218 Keebler Weyl Baking Co. v. J. S. Ivins Sons, 7 F. Supp. 211, 214 (E.D.Pa. 1934).

Legal protection of marks and symbols

Prior to 1905, the registration of a mark pursuant to several federal statutes had only declaratory effect. By Section 16 of the 1905 Act, however, registration became *prima facie* evidence of ownership for the person who registered the mark. The Lanham Act, Section 15, strengthened this evidenciary power by providing that the *prima facie* evidence becomes unattackable and incontestable if the registered mark has been used permanently for at least five years after registration without meeting objections, complaints, or other attacks by third parties.

The protection of the mark was also strengthened by the new statutory ability to use the federal courts without meeting the usual diversity requirements. Section 17 of the 1905 Act had provided that all district courts as well as the Supreme Court of the District of Columbia were to act as courts of first instance. The Circuit Court of Appeal and the Court of Appeal for the District of Columbia (the present day Court of Customs and Patent Appeal) were to act as appellate courts "in all litigations under common law and equity which concern trademarks or symbols registered under this statute." Section 18 gave the Supreme Court of the United States final jurisdiction. This federal jurisdiction, however, only covered actual trademark litigation within the scope of the existing trademark laws. The jurisdiction was not extended to cases decided under common law principles or to claims of unfair competition that were more important in practice. Thus, the court had to dismiss a complaint once it concluded that the trademark in issue was not legally admissible even though there was a good case for unfair competition.

The Lanham Act in Section 43(a) had a jurisdictional clause similar to the old act. However, this act allowed a complaint to be filed on account of "false designation of origin and false descriptions":

Any person who shall affix, apply, or annex, or use in connection with any goods or services, or any container or containers for goods, a false designation of origin, or any false description or representation, including words or other symbols tending falsely to describe or represent the same, and shall cause such goods or services to enter into commerce, and any person who shall with knowledge of the falsity of such designation of origin description or representation cause or procure the same to be transported or used in commerce or deliver the same to any carrier to be transported or used, shall be liable to a civil action by any person doing business in the locality falsely indicated as that of origin or in the region in which said locality is situated, or by any person who believes that he is or is likely to be damaged by the use of any such false description or representation.[219]

The question then presented was whether the jurisdiction of the federal court extended this far. In the lower courts, there are cases on either side [220] and the Supreme Court has denied *certiorari* on this point.[221]

The owner of trademarks has strengthened his position regarding the protection of registered marks. The problem of identity of goods and confusion of merchandise was discussed earlier. The doctrine of misrepresentation and unclean hands has slowly been weakened.[222] In its original interpretation this principle amounted to a substantial limitation on the power of the owner of a trademark if he made false statements in using this mark or sign. In regard to trademarks, express or implied agreements not to attack particular marks are illegal.

The law on unfair competition has been substantially extended. In this connection there are two problems: product simulation, and the importation of foreign products that would violate American patents if produced within the United States.

Under the common law, an unpatented product could be copied by anyone, since the old theory was based on the principle of free competition.[223] Slowly, an exception emerged in cases where the goods of the first producer gained such a strong position on a certain market that in the eyes of the public the product was already considered a product coming from a particular producer. In effect, a "secondary meaning" had developed. Whenever other producers brought out an exact or at least confusing copy of the merchandise involved, the possibility of confusion existed and the first producer was given the opportunity to sue.[224] This suit, however, presupposed that the copying was of a "functional feature" and not of an unessential or ornamental part of the

---

[219] 15 U.S.C. §1125(a) (1964).

[220] Compare S. C. Johnson and Son, Inc. v. Gold Seal Co., 230 F. 2d 832 (D.C. Cir. 1956), affirmed sub nomen, Gold Seal Co. v. Weeks, 129 F. Supp. 928 (D.D.C.1955) with L'Aiglon Apparel v. Lana Lobell, Inc., 214 F. 2d 649 (3d Cir. 1954), and Chamberlain v. Columbia Pictures Corp., 186 F. 2d 923 (9th Cir. 1951).

[221] S. C. Johnson and Son v. Gold Seal Co., 352 U.S. 829 (1956).

[222] Nims, n. 183 above, p. 1223.

[223] Candy Swan and Co. v. Deree and Co., 54 Ill. 439, 461 (1870); T. Arnold, "A Philosophy in the Protections Afforded by Patent, Trademark, Copyright and Unfair Competition Law," 54 *Pat. and T.M. Rev.* 413–414 (1964).

[224] See Note, "Uniform Deceptive Trade Practices Act: Effect of Sears and Compco," 50 *Iowa L. Rev.* 836–838 (1965).

product involved. The Uniform Deceptive Trade Practices Act [225] states that in the case of product simulation it is not expressly required that a secondary meaning in favor of the producer already be in existence, although the requirement is not expressly waived.[226]

Two recent Supreme Court decisions on product simulation are important for the law of unfair competition.[227] In the Sears case, the Stiffel firm had manufactured a "pole-lamp." This lamp was exactly copied by Sears and Roebuck and put on the market, using different packaging, which expressly referred to Sears as the manufacturer of the lamp. The first producer, Stiffel, had meanwhile obtained "a design patent" for the lamp. Stiffel brought a suit against Sears asking for an injunction under the principle of patent and unfair competition law. In the Compco case, Compco copied a "commercial fluorescent lighting fixture" produced by the complaining firm, Day-Brite Lighting, and incorporated it into its own "light fixture." Day-Brite possessed a "design patent." The District Courts and the Courts of Appeal declared the "design patents" void since they did not protect a new design important enough for such protection; however, they decided for the complainant on the basis of unfair competition.[228] The decisions amounted to "granting the equivalent of patent protection in state unfair competition principles." [229] The Supreme Court overturned the lower courts and dismissed the complaints:

An unpatentable article, like an article on which the patent has expired, is in the public domain and may be made and sold by whoever chooses to do so. What Sears did was to copy Stiffel's design and to sell lamps almost identical to those sold by Stiffel. This it had every right to do under the federal patent laws. That Stiffel originated the pole lamp and made it popular is immaterial.[230]

[225] This act was promulgated in 1964 by the National Conference of Commissioners on Uniform State Laws and is included in the Council of State Government's publication *Suggested State Legislation* for 1965, pp. 186–190. As of 1971, the act had been adopted by the legislatures of eight states.
[226] See, generally, R. F. Dole, Jr., "Uniform Deceptive Trade Practices Act: A Preparatory Note," 54 *Pat. and T. M. Rep.* 435–436 (1964) (general discussion of this act); see also 50 *Iowa L. Rev.* 845 (1965) (discussion of product simulation).
[227] Sears, Roebuck & Co. v. Stiffel, 376 U.S. 225, 231 (1964); Compco v. Day-Brite Lighting, 376 U.S. 234 (1964).
[228] 313 F. 2d 115 (7th Cir. 1963); 311 F. 2d 26 (7th Cir. 1962).
[229] 50 *Iowa L. Rev.* 836–838 (1965).
[230] Sears, Roebuck & Co. v. Stiffel, n. 227 above.

The Court did not deny that individual states may enjoin a product simulation through unfair competition rules. However, the Court, especially in the Compco decision, emphasized that such a step is permissible only under certain conditions.[231] These conditions curtailed the extension of unfair competition law into the field of product simulation.

It may be too early to assess the final impact of these decisions. For the time being, however, the courts are inclined to limit the development of "protected interests" against copying of unpatented articles.[232]

Section 337 of the Tariff Act of 1930 [233] contains certain prohibitions against importations that appear as an expression of unfair competition law:

(a) Unfair methods of competition and unfair acts in the importation of articles into the United States, or in their sale by the owner, importer, consignee, or agent of either, the effect or tendency of which is to destroy or substantially injure an industry, efficiently and economically operated, in the United States, or to prevent the establishment of such an industry, or to restrain or monopolize trade and commerce in the United States, are hereby declared unlawful, and when found by the President to exist shall be dealt with, in addition to any other provisions of law, as hereinafter provided.[234]

The Court of Customs and Patent Appeal (C.C.P.A.) originally held that this import prohibition not only referred to product patents but also to process patents where the imported good was manufactured in the United States by virtue of this process patent.[235] In the *In re Amtorg Trading Corp.* decision,[236] the C.C.P.A. reversed its stand and held that Section 337 cannot be applied whenever the patent involved protects only a process. However, when potash was imported from Russia to the American West Coast, and the prices were substantially

[231] 50 *Iowa L. Rev.* 850 (1965); R. Urey, "Product Simulation before and after the Stiffel Case," 9 *Idea* 131 (1965).

[232] Remco Industries, Inc. v. Toyominga, Inc., 158 *U.S. Pat. Q.* 455 (S.D.N.Y. 1968); Servo Corp. v. Fellino, 158 *U.S. Pat. Q.* 618 (N.Y. Sup. Ct. 1968).

[233] 19 U.S.C. §1000 (1964).

[234] U.S. Tariff Commission, Investigation No. 337-18, p. 5 (1962) (regarding importation or domestic sale of certain foreign-manufactured, self-closing containers).

[235] Re Frischer & Co., Inc., 17 C.C.P.A. 494 (1930), certiorari denied, 282 U.S. 852 (1930).

[236] 22 C.C.P.A. 558 (1934)

lower than the world market or cartel price, Congress amended the law to expressly state:

The importation hereafter for use, sale or exchange of a product made, produced, processed, or mined under or by means of a process covered by the claims of any unexpired valid United States letters patent, whether issued heretofore or hereafter, shall have the same status for the purposes of section 337 of the Tariff Act of 1930 as the importation of any product or article covered by the claims of any unexpired valid United States letters patent.[237]

The Senate Commerce Committee had reasoned:

This bill is designed to correct the present problem which was created when the Court of Customs and Patent Appeals in the case In re Amtorg Trading Corporation reversed its former decision and held that the importation of products made abroad in accordance with a United States process patent, without consent of patentee, was not regarded as an unfair method of competition. . . .

This will give to [owners of American process patents] the same rights which the owners of product patents have.[238]

At first the courts required as a condition for applying the prohibition against importation that the American patents, on which basis the prohibition takes place, not be subject to attack.[239] Later, the Tariff Commission accepted the view that Section 337 should be applied if the patent in issue has not been invalidated by final judgment, though a case might be pending. The Commission pointed out that it had the power and authority to stay the proceeding started under Section 337 but was not bound to stay such proceedings.[240]

The formulation and history of Section 337 seem to clearly indicate that the purpose of this provision was the protection of "industry inefficiently and economically operated in the United States." However, the Commission and the courts later went so far as to protect an American trader and merchant if he was the owner of the patent on the basis of which the merchandise in issue was being manufactured in the United States.[241]

[237] 19 U.S.C. §1337a (1964).
[238] U.S. Tariff Commission, Investigation No. 337-13, p. 7 (1954).
[239] "As . . . no attack [was] made . . ." , In re Orion Co., 22 C.C.P.A. 149, 159 (1934).
[240] U.S. Tariff Commission, n. 338 above, p. 18.
[241] U.S. Tariff Commission, n. 234 above, pp. 22, 44 (dissenting opinion of Chairman Dorfman).

The President's Patent Commission unsuccessfully proposed an amendment to U.S. law to provide "that the importation into United States of a product made abroad by a process patented in the United States shall constitute an act of infringement." [242] Under this bill, the owner of a U.S. patent covering the process for making an unpatented product could have blocked the importation into the United States of that product, if the product had been made in the foreign country by a process identical to the process patented in this country, provided the country in which the product was made did not offer patent protection for the general class of invention in which the process falls. This apparently refers to laws such as the Italian or Indian law excluding patent protection for pharmaceutical processes.

In the field of trademark law, there is a similar provision. Section 27 of the 1905 Act provided:

Merchandise imported from abroad containing or copying the name of a merchant or manufacturer active in the United States or bearing a trademark registered under this law, or bearing the name or mark inducing the public to the false assumption that the merchandise is being manufactured in the United States or in another country or place than the country or place designated . . . is to be refused at the port of import into the United States.[243]

Section 42 of the Lanham Act is similar:

That no article of imported merchandise which shall copy or simulate the name of any domestic manufacture, or manufacturer, or trader, or of any manufacturer or trader located in any foreign country which, by treaty, convention, or law affords similar privileges to citizens of the United States, or which shall copy or simulate a trade-mark registered in accordance with the provisions of this Act, or shall bear a name or mark calculated to induce the public to believe that the article is manufactured in the United States, or that it is manufactured in any foreign country or locality other than the country or locality in which it is in fact manufactured, shall be admitted to entry at any customhouse of the United States.

Section 526 of the 1940 Tariff Act is important in this respect:

(a) It shall be unlawful to import into the United States any merchandise of foreign manufacture if such merchandise, or the label, sign, print, pack-

<hr>

242 Testimony of Francis Browne, n. 5 above, p. 623.
243 Derenberg, n. 186 above, p. 377.

age, wrapper, or receptacle, bears a trade-mark owned by a citizen of, or by a corporation or association created or organized within, the United States, and registered in the Patent Office by a Person domiciled in the United States under the provisions of sections 81 to 109 of Title 15, and if a copy of the certificate of registration of such trade-mark is filed with the Secretary of the Treasury, in the manner provided in section 106 of said Title 15, unless written consent of the owner of such trade-mark is produced at the time of making entry.

The tariff agencies, which have a list of all American trademarks, are bound to act *ex officio;* but for patented goods there is no prohibition, absent the initiative of the American patentee.

Both of these provisions are of great importance. In practice they force the government to secure and guarantee a distribution of trade-marks as provided for in the cartel agreements. It is disputed whether the prohibition against imports covers goods lawfully manufactured and fixed with a trademark under the law of the country of origin but imported into the United States without license from the American owner of the trademark. Originally, an import of this type was not considered a violation of the law.[244] However, in the landmark case of *Bourjois & Co. v. Katzel,* Justice Holmes laid down the opposing view, which has prevailed up to today:

If the goods were patented in the U.S.A. a dealer who lawfully brought similar goods abroad from one who had a right to make and sell them there could not sell them in the U.S. The monopoly in that case is more extensive but we see no sufficient reason for holding that the monopoly of a trade-mark, so far as it goes, is less complete. It deals with a delicate matter that may be of great value but that easily is destroyed and therefore should be protected with correspondent care. It is said that the trade-mark here is that of the French house and truly indicates the origin of the goods. But that is not accurate. It is the trade-mark of the pl. only in the U.S. and indicates in law and, it is found, by public understanding, that the goods come from the pl. although not made by it. It was sold and could only be sold with the good will of the business that the pl. bought.[245]

The importation of original foreign goods is not covered, however, by the import prohibition as long as the American trademark and the foreign trademark are owned by the same person or corporation.[246]

---

[244] Fred Gretsch Mfg. Co. v. Schoening, 238 F. 780 (2d Cir. 1917).

[245] 260 U.S. 689 (1923).

[246] 19 C.F.R. 11.14(b) (involving the importation of French powder).

Section 526 has also been applied to cases in which an individual imported product, such as an automobile, was brought into the United States not for resale purposes but only for the personal use of the importer.[247]

Section 43 of the Lanham Act states that "any goods marked or labeled in contravention of the provisions of this section [false designation of origin, false description or representation, and so forth] shall not be imported into the United States or admitted for entry at any custom house of the United States." [248] The violation of a trademark that is not registered may be considered a case of unfair competition.

Licensing and transfer of trademarks

Section 10 of the 1905 Act, closely following the common law, provided that each mark registered or at least reported may only be transferred to other persons "jointly with a business enterprise and the good will." A license for a trademark in its real meaning was not considered possible. There were exceptions, however, in cases where the particular product was manufactured on the basis of a patent, copyright, or secret formula. In these cases, the court permitted an assignment without transfer of the business enterprise as long as the trademark was transferred jointly with the patent.[249] In one of the well-known Coca Cola cases, the Court decided that the owner of a mark may permit the use of this mark by another person as long as the owner of the mark retains enough of an effective quality control.[250] By the end of the 1920's, some scholars were arguing for the abandonment of the strict principle of inseparability of trademark and business enterprise.[251] In practice, the transfer of marks without the transfer of the original owner's entire business enterprise began to be permitted, provided at least part of the business enterprise was transferred and the mark or sign belonged to this part of the business enterprise. This option was incorporated in Section 10 of the Lanham Act:

A registered mark or a mark for which application to register has been filed shall be assignable with the goodwill of the business in which the mark is used, or with that part of the goodwill of the business connected

247 Sturges v. Clark D. Pease, Inc., 48 F. 2d 1035 (2d Cir. 1931).
248 15 U.S.C. §1125 (1964).
249 Hoffmann v. Kuppenheimer & Co., 183 F. 597 (N.D.Ill. 1910).
250 Coca Cola Bottling Co. v. Coca Cola Co., 269 F. 796 (Del. 1920).
251 Derenberg, n. 186 above, p. 253.

with the use of and symbolized by the mark, and in any such assignment it
shall not be necessary to include the goodwill to the business connected
with the use of and symbolized by any other mark used in the business or
by the name or style under which the business is conducted. Provided, that
any assigned registration may be canceled at any time if the registered mark
is being used by, or with the permission of, the assignee so as to misrepre-
sent the source of the goods or services in connection with which the mark
is used.

As pointed out earlier, the licensing of trademarks was generally
permissible long before enactment of the Lanham Act.[252] Trademark
licensing in the United States plays a very important role, especially in
regard to the very extensive advertising on radio and television. The
legal development has not yet completely settled. Generally, scholars
and courts are taking a rather liberal attitude. In some cases, the parties
to a trademark licensing agreement are even freer than the partners
to a patent license agreement.[253]

German Law of Trademarks
Registrable trademarks
The German law of trademarks is laid down in the German Trademark Act as amended in 1961.[254] According to Section 1, the owner
of a trademark used or intended for use in commerce may register his
trademark provided the trademark is capable of practical use and intended to distinguish the products of the owner from those of his
competitors. Section 4 of the act specifically prohibits registration of
words used generally in business to designate a certain kind of goods;
marks of a purely descriptive nature, such as numbers, letters, or words
describing the time or place when the goods were produced, or the
quality, quantity, purpose, price, and weight of such goods; the flag,
insignia, coat of arms of the Federal Republic of Germany, or of the
states of the Federal Republic, or of a municipality; marks that consist
of or compromise immoral, deceptive, or scandalous matter; marks
resembling trademarks currently registered or previously used in the
Federal Republic by another firm. Furthermore, marks whose primary
effect would be to distinguish the goods of one manufacturer from

[252] See B. B. and R. Knight, Inc. v. Milner, 283 F. 816 (N.D. Ohio 1922).
[253] This is seen in evaluation of certain obligations of the licensee to buy certain
goods from the licensor.
[254] *Bundesgesetzblatt* I, 574 (1961).

those of its competitors can be registered only if not already used by other unrelated corporations.

German courts have traditionally given broad interpretations to the provisions of the trademark laws. Since the first trademark law was enacted in 1874, the courts and writers have construed the Trademark Act as excluding any requirement that the trademark registered actually be used in business.[255] A corporation may thus register trademarks it intends to use some time in the future, or trademarks whose sole purpose is protection of other similar trademarks actually in use (defensive trademarks).[256] Taking advantage of the laws' permissiveness in this regard, the larger corporations in particular frequently register a great number of trademarks for the sole purpose of protecting their trademarks in use.[257]

Some efforts have been made, however, to limit registration of trademarks intended for future use. The former Supreme Court, for example, pointed out that such trademarks may not always be protected if reasonable business interests do not require their registration.[258] In determining the reasonableness of such interests, the size and the kind of business involved, among other things, are taken into account.[259] Some writers and some courts have claimed that trademark owners lose their rights if the trademark is not used within a reasonable time after registration.[260] This contention has not been adopted by the West German Supreme Court,[261] which has argued that such requirement of obligatory use could be established only by amendment of the law in force. The same court also pointed out, however, that where a trademark has not been used for a very long time—decades, for example— the trademark owner carries the burden of proving he still has an equitable interest in its protection.

---

[255] P. Kent, *Das Reichsgesetz zum Schutze der Warenbezeichungen vom 12. Mai 1894* (Berlin, 1897), §1, n. 43.

[256] 69 RGZ 376; 97 RGZ 90 ("Pecose/Pecho"), 302 ("Strahlenkranz"); Kent, n. 255 above.

[257] H. Tetzner, *Warenzeichengesetz* (Heidelberg, 1958), §1, n. 36.

[258] 97 RGZ, pp. 90, 95.

[259] Reichsgericht, 1926 *Gewerblicher Rechtsschutz und Urheberrecht* 77 (Fex/ Fix"); K. Hartung, *Defensivzeichen und Vorratszeichen in wettbewerbsrechtlicher Sicht* (Frankfurt/Main 1963), pp. 43–44.

[260] W. Pinzger and K. Schroeter, *Das deutsche Warenzeichenrecht* (Munich, 1937), §1, nn. 9, 10; 1949 *Gewerblicher Rechtsschutz und Urheberrecht* 375 ("Lunex"); 1951 *id.* 414 ("Caballero").

[261] 1957 *Gewerblicher Rechtsschutz und Urheberrecht* 224.

More incisive are the limitations that have been imposed on the owners of so-called defensive trademarks. The former German Supreme Court held that the owner of a defensive trademark may forbid the use of only such trademarks as are similar to the trademark the defensive trademarks were intended to protect.[262] In one case, for example, an owner had registered the defensive trademark "Grammofox" for the protection of the main trademark "Grammophon." The Supreme Court held that the owner could not interdict the use of the trademark "Vox" because his trademark was similar only to the defensive trademark "Grammofox," not to the main trademark, "Grammophon." [263]

These holdings have been confirmed by the West German Supreme Court, which has further held that defensive trademarks may be registered only to protect new trademarks. Once protected trademarks become known on the market, no rights can be derived from the defensive trademark, which could not be inferred from the main trademark itself.[264]

Protection of trademark rights

The owner of a registered trademark has several remedies against infringement of his trademark rights. First, he may file a notice of opposition against the registration of trademarks that resemble his own trademark, or he may apply for cancellation of the opposing trademark's registration (Section 5 of the Trademark Act). Second, he may file a complaint before a civil court for an injunction or for damages. Third, he may bring a suit in criminal court. An investigation of these remedies shows that protection of trademark rights has been extended considerably since the first trademark law was enacted in 1874.

Under the Trademark Act of 1874, the owner of a registered trademark had no right to oppose registration of another trademark. If an application for registration fulfilled certain formal requirements, the new trademark was registered without further investigation. The Trademark Act of 1894 then introduced the "notice of opposition," by which the owner of a registered trademark could protest registration of another similar trademark. Under this act the patent office, which ad-

[262] 112 RGZ 160.   [263] 114 RGZ 360.
[264] 1957 *Gewerblicher Rechtsschutz und Urheberrecht* 228; Hartung, n. 259 above, p. 43; 32 BGHZ 133.

ministered the trademark register, was obligated to formally advise the owner of the registered trademark of any application for a similar trademark. The holder of the existing trademark then had one month in which to file a notice of opposition. If no such notice was filed, the new trademark was registered by the patent office. If such a notice was filed, the patent office had to then decide whether or not the two trademarks were distinguishable. If the trademarks were found to be distinguishable, the new trademark was registered. If not, the application was denied. If he so chose, the applicant was then entitled to file a complaint against the holder of the registered trademark.

The above proceeding was changed by an amendment in 1949, which provided that the holder of the registered trademark need not be personally informed of the application. Instead, general notice of new applications is given by publication in the German *Journal of Trademarks*. Within three months after such publication, the holder of a trademark may file a notice of opposition. Later he may even apply for cancellation of the new trademark's registration.

Protection of trademark owners by the criminal laws has been enhanced to the largest extent. The Trademark Act of 1874 provided fines for persons intentionally infringing the trademark or name of another domestic producer or businessman by illegally designating his goods with this trademark and by trading these goods on the market. The Trademark Act of 1894 raised these fines and extended application of this provision to illegal use of trademarks on or in connection with wrappings, advertisements, price lists, business letters, recommendations, and invoices.[265]

In 1924 the fines that could be imposed for infringements of trademarks were again raised by amendment of the Trademark Act, and since 1925, individual complaints by holders of infringed trademarks are no longer necessary for initiation of criminal proceedings.[266]

Furthermore, under Section 24 of the Trademark Act, the owner of a trademark may bring a civil suit to enjoin all persons infringing his trademark. Under paragraph 2 of the same section, the trademark owner may also recover damages for intentional or negligent infringements. The requirements of this provision have been relaxed continuously since the first Trademark Act of 1874, which allowed re-

---

[265] Sections 25 and 26 of the same law regulate liability for damages to equipment caused through fraud in trade or commerce (see Chapter 12).

[266] 1925 *Reichsgesetzblatt* II, 115.

covery of damages only for intentional infringements. In 1894 recovery was extended to cases of gross negligence, and a 1936 amendment [267] provided for damages complaints based solely on negligent infringement of trademark rights.

The development was similar with respect to the second requirement of an illegal trademark infringement. The former German Supreme Court had originally held that use of a registered trademark is not illegal even if the registration had occurred in violation of prior trademark rights.[268] It was not long, however, before the Supreme Court reversed this holding and decided that the use of a registered trademark may constitute an infringement of prior trademark rights.[269]

Assuming the requirements of Section 24 of the Trademark Act have been fulfilled, the trademark owner may calculate his damages in several ways. According to Section 249 of the Civil Code, he may recover for actual economic loss including profits; or he may recover the reasonable value of the use of the trademarks in the amount of reasonable royalties; or he may ask for the profits accrued to the defendant by illegal use of the infringed trademarks.

Originally, the courts gave the trademark owner only the first of these remedies. In 1966, however, the West German Supreme Court held that the owner may calculate his damages on the basis of reasonable royalties and that this rule applies even in cases where the trademark owner would not have been entitled or willing to grant a license on his trademark.[270] But whether the owner may recover benefits accrued to the defendant by illegal use of his trademark remains a controversial question in legal writings.[271] Although the West German Supreme Court has not yet decided the question, other courts and writers have favored recovery by trademark owners for profits illegally earned on enfringement of their trademarks, and it is not unlikely that the West German Supreme Court will hold similarly.

Import prohibitions

The German Trademark Act of 1894 rendered unlawful the importation into Germany of any merchandise illegally bearing the trade-

---

[267] *Stenographische Berichte*, IX Legislaturperiode, II. Session, Vol. III, pp. 2162–2163 (1893–1894).

[268] 64 RGZ 275; 92 RGZ 386.   [269] 118 RGZ 76.   [270] 44 BGHZ 372.

[271] E.g., Kent, n. 255 above, §14, Nn. 566, 577; A. Seligsohn, *Warenzeichengesetz* (Berlin, 1925) §14, n. 8; C. Finger, *Warenzeichengesetz* (Berlin, 1926) §14, N. 24, §24, N. 29; *Wettbewerbs- und Warenzeichenrecht*, pp. 860–861.

mark or trade name of a German citizen. In accordance with the Paris Convention for the Protection of Industrial Property, a 1925 amendment further prohibited the importation of goods bearing trademarks or names that contained deceptive statements of origin, kind, or quality.[272]

Furthermore, the owner of a registered trademark may now sue to enjoin importation of goods that illegally bear his trademark. Whether he would be entitled to prevent importation of goods legally designated with his trademarks, however, has been long a controversial question. The former German Supreme Court originally took the position that trademark rights are not linked with any given territory but rather with the person of the trademark owner himself. Consequently, the Supreme Court concluded that the trademark owner could not prevent reimportation of goods designated with his trademark.

In the Hengstenberg case, however, the former German Supreme Court reversed this holding in favor of the principle of territoriality, under which the owner of a trademark who exports his goods abroad may now prevent reimportation of such goods by bringing suit against the importer.[273] The course of decisions changed again after World War II. In the Maja case,[274] the Appellate Court of Frankfurt decided that the trademark owner is only entitled to interdict reimportation of goods if the public would be otherwise deceived with respect to the origin of such goods. On the other hand, the court held that the trademark owner is not entitled to prevent reimportation for the sole purpose of enforcing private market regulations and securing a monopoly on the market. The West German Supreme Court affirmed this holding on the ground that the mere importation of goods legally designated with the trademark of the plaintiff does not constitute an infringement of that trademark. The Supreme Court pointed out, however, that there may be cases where illegal infringement of the trademark results from actions of the importer within the territory of West Germany or even within the territory of the country of exportation.[275]

In a later decision, the Civil Court of Bochum pointed out that the owner of a domestic trademark may prohibit importation of goods manufactured abroad if such goods were manufactured and marketed

[272] 1925 *Reichsgesetzblatt* II, 115.

[273] 118 RGZ 76; P. Säuberlich, *Die Warenzeichenrechtliche Problematik des Imports von Originalwaren* (Frankfurt, 1965), 19 ff.

[274] 1963 *Gewerblicher Rechtsschutz und Urheberrecht* 30 ff.   [275] BGHZ 84.

under special license from the trademark owner.[276] In the Revlon II case, the Appellate Court of Düsseldorf dismissed a complaint against importation of products marketed abroad under a legal trademark by an American parent corporation.[277] In another decision concerning the Revlon case, the Civil Court of Düsseldorf explained that the trademark owner is only entitled to prevent importation of goods legally designated with his trademark if the public might be deceived with respect to the origin of these goods.[278] Although the above decisions appear somewhat contradictory, it can nevertheless be stated that as a general rule, the courts will deny trademark protection when the sole interest of the trademark owner is to enforce a division of markets.

Transfer and licensing of trademarks

Although the Trademark Act of 1874 contained no provision for transfer of trademark rights, the Supreme Court has held that the transfer of a business and its goodwill includes transfer of trademark rights, since such rights can only exist in connection with a particular business.[279] Section 7 of the Trademark Act of 1894 then permitted expressly the contractual assignment of a trademark right, provided the business with which it was connected was transferred to the assignee. A 1936 amendment extenuated this requirement by providing that a trademark may be assigned with that part of the business to which it belongs.[280]

The contracting partners may circumvent these legal requirements, however, by having the "assignee" file a new application for registration of the trademark in his own name, while the "assignor" waives his right to file a notice of opposition and a complaint against registration of the new trademark. In such a case the patent office would not reject the application for registration *ex officio*. By such manipulation the contracting partners can achieve the effect of an assignment without transfer of the business connected.[281] One possible defect in

[276] 1964 *Aussenwirtschaftsdienst des Betriebsberaters* 369 ("Dixan"/"Pril").

[277] 1963 *Der Betriebsberater* 489.

[278] 1964 *Gewerblicher Rechtsschutz und Urheberrecht* (Ausland- und internationaler Teil) 146 ("Revlon III").

[279] E.g., 11 RGZ 141.   [280] E.g., Kent, note 255 above, §7, n. 210.

[281] Busse, note 182 above, §8, before n. 1. Regarding transfer of trademarks separate from the enterprises to which they are attached, see V. Tetzner, *Die Leerübertragung von Warenzeichen* (Munich, 1962).

such a transaction, however, would be resultant loss of the original trademark owner's priority rights.

In addition, the majority of writers and courts sanction the license of trademark rights even though the trademark acts do not provide for such a possibility.[282] Such licensing is not permitted, however, where the public would be deceived with respect to the origin of the product sold under the license.[283] The legal nature of such trademark licenses is a controversial issue. The courts and the writers originally contended that a licensing agreement created a legal relationship only between the contracting parties, so that only the trademark owner himself could bring suit to enjoin infringement of his trademark rights.[284] But it was later argued that the licensee may bring suit in his own name on the basis of express permission of the licensor.[285] Finally, many writers have even taken the position that such permission is unnecessary and that the licensee is exerting the same rights as the trademark owner against third persons infringing the trademark right.[286] The courts, however, have not decided this question.

Designs

Designs have been protected in Germany since the Trademark Act of 1894. Section 25(3) of the act declares a misdemeanor the imitation for deceptive purposes of a product's design, wrappings, announcements, price lists, business letters, and invoices.

The term "design" has always been given a broad interpretation. Trademarks and trade names, for example, that are unregistered but capable of registration are considered designs within the scope of this provision. Thus, a formerly registered trademark may be protected as a "design" even after its deletion from the trademark register. A design may further consist of letters or figures or other signs not reg-

---

[282] 44 RGZ 71; 100 RGZ 3; 1 BGHZ 41 ("Hadef"); Kent, note 255 above, §12, nn. 382 ff.; Seligsohn, note 271 above, §7, n. 7.

[283] See §21, para. 1, No. 2, Warenzeichengesetz, in 3 Gesetz gegen unlauteren Wettbewerb; U. Krieger, "Die gemeinschaftliche Benutzung von Warenzeichen durch mehrere Unternehmen nach deutschem Recht," Festschrift für Eugen Ulmer (Munich, 1963), pp. 3, 28–29.

[284] E.g., 99 RGZ 90, 92–93 ("Gilette"); 102 RGZ 17, 24 ("Torgament"); Kent, n. 255 above, §12, nn. 383–384; Busse, n. 182 above, §8, n. 3; 87 RGZ 184.

[285] E. Reimer, Warenzeichenrecht (3d ed.; Cologne, 1954), pp. 347–348; Krieger, n. 283 above, pp. 45–46.

[286] Krieger, id., pp. 3, 49.

istrable as trademarks. Even the form and the color of the wrapping may be considered a design under the act.[287]

Furthermore, protection of designs has been extended continuously since the Trademark Act of 1894. Today, designs and trademarks are treated by the courts as equivalent to property rights.[288] Thus, under Section 25(1) of the act, the owner of a design may sue to enjoin an infringement without having to show that the infringement occurred intentionally or negligently. The owner may also recover damages for negligent or intentional infringements under Section 25(2) of the act.

[287] Kent, n. 255 above, §15, n. 698, 712–713; Finger, n. 271 above, §15, nn. 2–3; Seligsohn, n. 271 above, §15, nn. 2, 4; Pinzger and Schroeter, n. 260 above, §25, nn. 2 ff.; Busse, n. 182 above, §25, nn. 2, 6–7.

[288] E.g., 73 RGZ 253; 162 RGZ 347; Busse, n. 182 above, §25, n. 1.

13 ～～～～

Arbitration and Mediation

The arbitration of cartel agreements can be illustrated by a hypothetical example. An agreement by which markets in the United States, Europe, and Australia are allocated to various members of the agreement provides for arbitration under the procedures of the International Chamber of Commerce. Assume that one of the European firms achieves a technological break-through and is desirous of entering the American market. The American partner to the agreement requests arbitration and an arbitration tribunal in Norway is designated to hear the case.

The European partner appoints a famous American judge as its arbitrator. The American judge certifies that the entire agreement, including the arbitration provision, is a violation of American antitrust law and therefore void. The other arbitrators decide otherwise, and the European partner is enjoined from entering the United States.

Here an agreement exists between an American and a European enterprise under which the European enterprise is bound to stay out of the American market. This agreement is based partly on patents, partly on know-how, partly on trademark regulations. The arbitration agreement grants to the international organization the power to designate the country in which the arbitration takes place. An award allegedly in violation of U.S. antitrust law takes place, and the European firm eventually sells its interest to the large American firm.

When an institutional tribunal is involved, even more dangerous results are possible.

Reasons for Arbitration and Mediation

The international cartel can achieve its purpose of market regulation only if the members abide by the basic regulatory economic contract and by the planning contract. While the cartel members can usually rely on the voluntary compliance of all the members, since the cartel arrangement is for their mutual benefit, nevertheless certain disagreements do arise. This tension and conflict may result from the stronger

competitive position of one of the members in other markets or areas
of service not covered by the cartel agreement, or they may follow
from changes in the economic or legal circumstances, after execution
of the agreement, which affect one member of the cartel more than
others. In these circumstances one or more members of the cartel may
be inclined to pursue an independent course of action. This nonad-
herence to the cartel agreement cannot always be prevented by the
devices previously discussed. The members of the cartel therefore seek
other effective procedures to thwart attempts by individual members
to break out of the cartel arrangement.[1]

It is naturally in the interest of the cartel that such procedures work
quickly and quietly. This is true for any type of disagreement relating
to the cartel agreement or its implementation, whether among cartel
members or between the cartel order and one of the members. In essence, it is the aim of each cartel, whether national or international, to
settle these differences in a practical and efficient manner while giving
optimum consideration to the interests of the cartel.

The power and authority to make final and binding decisions arising
out of disputes among two or more persons belongs generally to
the state. The state generally entrusts such power to courts established
by it, which are bound strictly by defined procedures. In the interest
of justice and fair play, nearly all procedural statutes applicable to
courts provide (1) that the trial be public and (2) that the decision of
the court of first instance be subject to review by one or more courts.
However, the cartel seeks to avoid these two policies in settling its
controversies: a major concern of the cartel is to prevent outsiders—
competitors, customers, suppliers, or the general public—from learn-

[1] In this regard the explanation of W. Meinhardt, Chairman of the Board of
Osram-Gesellschaft, concerning the arbitration tribunal of the international light
bulb agreement, is conclusive: The worldwide cartel agreement provided for the
exchange of all inventions, patents, and especially experiences with manufacturing,
and for the typification and standardization of all lamp production. It not only
required the cartel members to be satisfied with a certain share of the world
market, but provided also to which countries or groups of countries and in what
amounts the cartel members were allowed to sell. The agreement established the
right to control all the business of the cartel members and required such members
to report in detail on their products including distribution to the retailer and
the consumer. Under such circumstances the manager of the plant concerned must
strive for the greatest possible legal security in order to prevent some gentleman
or his successor, having become sufficiently informed, from canceling and saying
thank you, but hands off.

ing how the cartel works and what its problems are. In addition, the cartel is interested in resolving controversies as quickly as possible so as to avoid the long uncertainty that accompanies a legal controversy in the courts. As the German writer Tschierschky remarked almost forty years ago, "Bad examples that cannot be prosecuted fast enough may ruin good cartel morals." [2]

In international cartels, other factors have to be taken into consideration. The participants not only live in different states but also live under different legal systems. Thus, it is possible that the law of one country may require a judgment different from that required by another country, even though the facts of the controversies were the same. Should the law in the two countries be the same, different interpretations of it could possibly be given by courts in the various countries. This diversity can lead to serious results, since the entire agreement may be considered as violating antitrust laws. These differences of law and interpretation are not helpful to the maintenance of cartel unity.

In spite of these obstacles, the organizers of national and international cartels have found two methods which achieve relatively speedy, efficient final settlements of internal disputes and which eliminate the necessity of resorting to courts of the individual countries while permitting choice of the country of arbitration and of the tribunal most favorable to the interests of the cartel. These two methods are arbitration and mediation.

Arbitration

Almost all legal systems permit the parties to a contract to delegate the power to make a binding decision in certain instances to private arbitrators. The majority of legal systems do not require the arbitration procedure to be public or to be in the form of a trial. The private parties usually have the power to determine the arbitration procedure and to relieve the members of the arbitration tribunal from applying the substantive law of the state or even of stating the reasons for their award. As a result, private arbitration has proved to be an ideal method for settling differences arising within the cartel.

Organizers of international cartels have the power to transfer control over their basic agreements into areas where no national law ap-

[2] Julius Flechtheim, *Deutsches Kartellrecht*, Vol. I: *Die rechtliche Organisation der Kartelle* (Mannheim, 1923), p. 117.

plies, once they succeeded in subjecting themselves to a "friendly" forum. As the chapter on the role of conflict of law showed, the organizers can in effect limit contact with any existing legal order to a mere formality. While the election of a friendly forum could be made successful at times by agreeing to the exclusive jurisdiction of a particular court, the parties usually prefer to utilize the concept of arbitration that gives them an even larger freedom of action independent from the "law" of the forum, especially freedom from the danger of any substantial change or amendment of what was the law where the agreements and contracts were made.

At the beginning of the cartel development, arbitration was much less subject to prejudice than prorogation and was thus an added reason for its preference by the cartel over prorogation. For a long time it was perfectly legitimate to make an agreement subjecting all controversies arising out of certain agreements to arbitration. Such arbitration agreements came into wide use in international agreements between merchants. The parties expected an equitable solution in the interests of all parties involved. Thus, it is not surprising that international cartels sought to benefit from the favorable attitude toward arbitration as the world economy and a world market developed.

The so-called permanent institutional arbitration tribunals, particularly those developed in associations having established procedures and a permanent list of persons available for participation in the arbitration tribunals, proved to be much more helpful to the cartels than the isolated arbitration tribunals established by parties to decide a particular case. "The institutional arbitration tribunal was able to develop a system and was an excellent instrument to achieve definite commercial objectives including price fixing as well as establishing sales quotas, production quotas, or other conditions of sale. Institutional arbitration tribunals were powerful enough to act against public interest." [3]

Private arbitration is usually alleged to be better than public courts for a number of reasons. One of the most persistent arguments is that determination of a case by arbitration is faster and less expensive than through resort to the regular courts. The problem with the regular courts, according to Georg Erler, is that the slow judicial proceedings, which give the parties three chances, lead to "posthume legal victories,

---

[3] R. Littauer, "Schiedsgerichtsbarkeit und materielles Recht," 55 *Zeitschrift für Zivilprozess* 1 ff. (1930).

entirely uninteresting to the economy." [4] As a result, "arbitrations are now encouraged as an easy, expeditious and inexpensive method of settling disputes." [5]

The special expert knowledge of the members of the tribunal is usually mentioned as another reason for the superiority of arbitration. It is argued that the regular judge today, in contrast to an arbitrator, is not "able to understand the complicated social and economic conditions of today merely on the basis of his own experiences in life." [6] F. Eisemann, a recognized expert in the field of arbitration, stated that as a result of increasing codification of customs of trade "by fixing conditions of sale and delivery through and for the trade," a new legal situation has developed. [7] The effect of this is that today "in most litigations very special economic factual situations and technical details are to be considered." These considerations have less and less to do with legal rules with which the judge is well acquainted than with trade practices and other factors familiar to experts coming from the same field of business as the parties to the case. It is argued that "it was this new development rather than criticism of the judicial machinery which led to institutional arbitration in almost every field."

In a similar vein, another argument often presented in favor of arbitration is that the parties to the proceeding have the benefit of seeing a person they know and trust decide their litigation, rather than absolutely unknown judges in the regular courts. Further, the adherents of private arbitration point out that cases decided by arbitrators may be done so on an "equitable" basis instead of strictly on the basis of "law." [8] Many people feel that an arbitration procedure has the advantage that it is not bound by all the details of regular judicial proceedings, and thus a fairer solution may be obtained by all parties concerned.

[4] G. Erler, *Grundprobleme des internationalen Wirtschaftsrechts* (Göttingen, 1956), p. 187.
[5] Fudickar v. Guardian Mutual Life Insurance Co., 62 N.Y. 392, 399–400 (1875).
[6] Littauer, n. 3 above, p. 4.
[7] F. Eisemann, "Die internationale Schiedsgerichtsbarkeit in Handelssachen," in F. Eisemann, E. Mezger, and D. J. Schottelius, eds., *Internationale Schiedsgerichtsbarkeit in Handelssachen* (Frankfort on the Main, 1958), pp. 9–10.
[8] A. Baumbach and K. H. Schwab, *Schiedsgerichtsbarkeit; Kommentar zu den Vorschriften der Zivilprozessordnung, Des Arbeitsgerichtsgesetzes, Der Staatsverträge und Der Kostengesetze über das privatrechtliche Schiedsverfahren* (2d ed.; Munich, 1960), p. 50.

Eisemann finds private arbitration absolutely essential in international trade:

In international commercial litigations before regular courts at least one of the parties must find himself before a court which is certainly foreign to him. It is not necessary to state in detail all the disadvantages, especially psychological burdens, developing from this fact. But this is not all: Decisions of regular judges relating to international trade are without great practical value. They are not helpful anymore, whenever execution of decisions becomes necessary outside of the country in which they have been rendered. A look into comparative law proves that most countries permit an enforcement of judgments of regular foreign courts only on the basis of bilateral agreements relating to the recognition and execution of foreign judgment. . . . Even today, bilateral treaties in this field are an exception and not the rule. . . . As long as there is no specific agreement, German judgments will not be executed and enforced in France and vice versa. We do not see the end of this condition, even though these two countries are closely related, have a not too different legal system, and have very extensive trade relations. Even as far as bilateral agreements exist, their practical application is so often subject to many difficulties and is, therefore, not too helpful. It would be an error to argue that international bilateral treaties on the enforcement of regular judgments are really much more important than the enforcement of awards, since arbitration even in the international field would become unnecessary if the enforcement of a regular judgment was secure. For many reasons there is not the slightest chance that the enforcement of a regular judgment outside of the country of the forum will become possible, either by change of legislation or by international agreements. Just now, in spite of many statements to the opposite, governments are especially zealous in the protection of their sovereignty, and due to the philosophical conflicts between the Eastern and the Western nations, the chances to improve the recognition and execution of regular judgments is very small indeed. A judgment of a regular court is considered again and again, and with a certain justification, as basically the expression of a foreign sovereignty.

However, we find quite a different approach by governments with regard to commercial arbitration which by definition deals with a limited field.[9]

C. M. Schmitthoff argues:

Contracts in international trade may be interpreted in a different way, and sometimes the regular courts may unconsciously prefer their own legal

[9] Eisemann, n. 7 above, pp. 20-21.

order on the basis of the so-called "homeward trend." For this reason, arbitration in international commerce is preferred, as the arbitration tribunals are not so much exposed to this temptation.[10]

A short statistical survey published by Eugen Langen indicates the present preference for arbitration.[11] In 1960 about 990,000 litigations were pending before the German courts, while the number of all published opinions of German courts in the field of conflicts of law amounted to about 120 annually. Only about one-sixth of this total actually deal with international trade, including all cases dealing with shipping, industrial property rights, and competition, but not labor law. Langen goes on to say that the twenty published decisions concerning international trade are only an extremely small percentage of the annual litigation in the field of German international commerce. Langen concludes by saying that this statistical survey proves that the prevailing belief in international law is that arbitration is far superior to the regular courts.

This survey shows only too well how right Ernst Rabel was:

International trade has practically developed an independent legal system which has more or less separated itself from the legal system of the countries as well as from conflict of law. International trade shows less and less interest in the legal rules including an international legal system, since arbitration is becoming more and more powerful and decides cases on entirely different tests than the regular court of the countries involved.[12]

Although the main purpose of this book does not call for a lengthy discussion of the legality and limitations of private arbitration, it may be helpful, in order to show the operation and efficiency of market-regulating agreements, to present some of the counterarguments by critics of arbitration.

Indeed, it is true that one of the most essential advantages of the arbitration procedure is the relatively short time needed for the completion of a case; however, this advantage is rapidly being lost because of the tendency toward an institutionalized extension of the arbitration procedure in some fields. This is especially true in institutional arbitra-

[10] C. M. Schmitthoff, "Das neue Recht des Welthandels," 28 *Zeitschrift für ausländisches und internationales Privatrecht* 47 (1964).

[11] E. Langen, *Studien zum internationalen Wirtschaftsrecht* (Munich, 1963), pp. 9–10.

[12] E. Rabel, *Das Recht des Warenkaufs* (Berlin, 1936), Vol. I (reprinted in 1957), p. 36.

tions that provide the opportunity for one or two appeals. A good example of this is arbitration in the Bremen Cotton Exchange and in the German potato trade.[13] It is obvious that such opportunities for appeal necessarily lead to substantial prolongation of the arbitration procedure.

In the area of costs, substantial doubt has been expressed as to whether the expenses for arbitration are measurably below the costs for regular court proceedings. While such doubts were raised decades ago, today the argument that arbitration proceedings result in substantial savings as compared with proceedings in a regular court should be subject to even more scepticism.[14]

As to the experience of judges in commercial matters, it is certainly true that few have adequate experience in such matters; however, it is because of arbitration that most commercial litigation has been taken from the regular courts, and arbitration is itself the very cause for the inexperience of the judges in matters of trade.[15] The fact that very often in Germany, for example, certain high-court judges are appointed to act as arbitrators seems to prove that a substantial number of judges apparently do have the necessary acquaintance with economic matters.

The allegation that members of the tribunals are "persons of special confidence to the parties to the litigation" appears rather tenuous. Anyone familiar with modern institutions of arbitration knows that since the arbitrators are appointed by the parties they are not at all objective judges. They consider themselves to be representatives or agents of the party who chose them. They fight for the interests of "their" parties in preparing the award. Their bias is often quite obvious.[16] A Prussian judge rightly pointed out years ago that an ar-

[13] E. Reimer and R. Mussfeld, *Die kaufmännischen Schiedsgerichte Deutschlands* (Berlin, 1931), pp. 76–77 *passim;* O. Mathies, *Die ständigen Schiedsgerichte des Hamburger Grosshandels* (Braunschweig, 1921), pp. 38–39; D. J. Schottelius, "Arbitration Activities of the Bremen Cotton Exchange," in M. Domke, *International Trade Arbitration* (New York, 1958), p. 271; F. Steckhan II, "Die Schiedsgerichtsbarkeit der deutschen Kartoffelwirtschaft," 1956 *Konkurs-, Treuhand- und Schiedsgerichtswesen* 3–4.

[14] Cf. R. Wassermann, "Die Schaffung staatlicher 'Schiedsgerichte' und die Kartelle," 1924 *Kartell-Rundschau* 65–66; H. O. de Boor and G. Erkel, *Zivilprozessrecht* (2d ed.; Wiesbaden, 1961), p. 198.

[15] A. Heilberg, *Schiedsgerichtsvertrag, Schiedsgericht und schiedsrichterliches Verfahren* (Leipzig, 1929), p. 15.

[16] Mathies, n. 13 above, pp. 6–7; Reimer and Mussfield, n. 13 above, pp. 80–81; W. Grimm and V. Rochlitz, *Das Schiedsgericht in der Praxis* (Heidelberg, 1959),

bitrator appointed by one of the parties "necessarily has to deal with the entire affair on the basis of the views and aims of his party." [17]

Furthermore, today most of the arbitration cases are handled by permanent institutional arbitration tribunals. Normally the rules of procedure of these tribunals do not permit the parties freely and directly to appoint the arbitrators. The parties are either limited in their choice to a list of persons selected by someone else, or the arbitrators are appointed by a third person or an agency.[18] In this connection the rules and regulations of the three most important international arbitration tribunals are very interesting indeed: The London Court of Arbitration has prepared a list of candidates for the office of an arbitrator. This list was suggested partly by the board of the London Chamber of Commerce and partly by the London City Corporation. The court of arbitration then appoints arbitrators for a particular case from the list. The parties have the right to express their wishes to the court of arbitration; however, the court is free to make its own choice. They may request the parties to suggest other candidates as members of the tribunal or as umpire.[19]

The American Arbitration Association, the biggest arbitration organization in the world, also uses a list system.[20] The arbitrators are chosen from the list of candidates whenever the parties themselves cannot agree on, or have not provided another method for, the appointment of arbitrators.[21] Each party in the case receives the same list of candidates and may then choose from this list persons convenient to it. Any person on the list is presumed to be acceptable if the parties do not designate some persons from the list within a certain period of time. Under Rule 12, the secretary of the court of arbitration may

---

p. 42. H. Krause, "Die ständigen Schiedsgerichte im Entwurf der neuen Zivilprozessordnung," in *Rechtswissenschaftliche Beiträge zum 25-jährigen Bestehen der Handels-Hochschule Berlin* (Berlin, 1931), pp. 73, 81.

[17] 1925 *Juristische Wochenschrift* 717, 718.

[18] Mathies, n. 13 above, pp. 35 ff.; Reimer and Mussfeld, n. 13 above, pp. 50–51, 60 ff.; H. Kronstein, "Arbitration Is Power," 38 *N.Y.U.L. Rev.* 661, 664 (1963).

[19] Rule 25 is reprinted in R. Marx, "Entwicklung und Aufgaben der internationalen Schiedsgerichtsbarkeit seit dem Kriege," in A. Schönke, ed., *Die Schiedsgerichtsbarkeit in Zivil- und Handelssachen in Europa* (Cologne, 1956), III, 91.

[20] For further details, see D. J. Schottelius, "Die American Arbitration Association als Gründerin eines internationalen Schiedsgerichtssystems," 1956 *Konkurs-, Treuhand- und Schiedsgerichtswesen* 150 ff.; N. Braden, *Policy and Practice of the American Arbitration Association* (Washington, D.C., 1956), *passim*.

[21] Rules 12 ff. are reprinted in Schönke, n. 19 above, Vol. III, App. 3, pp. 168 ff.

appoint one or several of these persons to be members of the arbitration tribunal.

The arbitration tribunals of the International Chamber of Commerce follow slightly different rules. The members of the tribunal are appointed by a so-called court of arbitration, which is "an international arbitration agency composed of members appointed by the administrative board of the International Chamber of Commerce." [22] The parties may agree that the entire case is to be decided by one arbitrator. Under Article 7, they may suggest the name of this arbitrator jointly "to the court of arbitration for confirmation." Failing such an agreement, the member of the tribunal is appointed by the court of arbitration. In more complex cases, three members are requested for the tribunal. Each party is called on to designate one arbitrator to the court of arbitration "for confirmation." The court itself appoints the umpire, who acts as chairman of the tribunal. If one of the parties does not suggest the appointment of an arbitrator, the arbitration court is called on to appoint this member of the tribunal *ex officio*. But as a rule, cases are handled and decided by one umpire.

In reality, the general statement that the members of the arbitration tribunal are really "persons of special confidence" to the parties bears little truth in many cases. The relation between the arbitrators, especially relations involving a "third arbitrator" appointed by the two "party-appointed arbitrators," came up in a recent Supreme Court case, *Commonwealth Coating Corp. v. Continental Casualty Co.*[23] In this case the "third arbitrator," considered a person of special confidence and neutrality, did not disclose to the parties that he had prior dealings with one of the parties and that these dealings were connected with the general operation in issue in the case to be decided by the arbitration tribunal.

In the case, decided under the Federal Arbitration Act, the majority of the Supreme Court took the position that the award had to be set aside even if the lack of disclosure was not based on any international wrong, since arbitration rests on the premise that any tribunal permitted by law to try cases and controversies must not only be unbiased but must avoid even the appearance of bias. The dissenting justices would set aside the award if the lack of disclosure was "cal-

[22] Art. 6 of the arbitration rules is reprinted in Baumbach and Schwab, n. 8 above, pp. 355 ff.
[23] 21 L.Ed. 2d 301 (1968).

culated." The dissenters argued that the principal point in arbitration is that it is essentially consensual and practical and that the U.S. Arbitration Act was designed to protect the integrity of the process with a minimum of insistence upon set formulae and rules. The majority of the court applied to this process rules applicable to judges and not to a system characterized by dealing on faith and reputation for reliability. Such formalism was not, in the view of the dissenters, contemplated by the act nor was it warranted in a case where no claim of partiality, unfairness, or misconduct was made. In the arguments in this particular case it was suggested that an arbitrator is not a "judge-like person" but a "juror-like person" and that no more strict rules can apply than to the jury system.

One of the advantages proclaimed by the adherents of arbitration is that the tribunal can decide cases on the basis of equity rather than law and that such a course is not open to the courts. However, when this did become possible to the courts as well, the representatives of trade and commerce were the first to complain. German judicial proceedings are a good illustration. On the basis of many examples during the last decades in Germany, a very substantial change in the function within the judicial proceedings has been observed. The legislature authorized the judges to act more and more like arbitrators by permitting them to base their decisions on equitable considerations. Coexistent with this development was "the continuous strengthening of the judicial law," which made possible a more careful consideration of "elements of justice in each particular case." [24] In 1963, Rittner correctly spoke of the "arbitrational function of the judge in civil matters." Rittner came to the conclusion that the German development "goes more and more in the direction of a jurisprudence based predominantly on equity." [25] This type of development appears to be taking place in most other countries.[26] Yet, it is the representatives of trade and commerce who complain most about the continuous ten-

[24] F. Baur, "Sozialer Ausgleich durch Richterspruch," 12 *Juristenzeitung* 193-194, 197 (1957).

[25] F. Rittner, "Ermessensfreiheit und Billigkeitsspielraum im deutschen Recht," *Ermessensfreiheit und Billigkeitsspielraum des Zivilrichters* (Frankfort on the Main, 1964), pp. 21, 27, 50.

[26] P. Riedberg, *Der amiable Compositeur im internationalen Schiedsgerichtsverfahren* (Cologne, 1962), p. 6, and lectures on judicial discretion in civil procedures in France, the Netherlands, and Denmark in Rittner, n. 25 above, pp. 53 ff., 85 ff., 105 ff.

dency of regular judges to make unpredictable decisions on the basis of general clauses. As a result, these representatives are turning to the arbitration tribunal for the predictability they seek in litigation.[27]

Quite often, critics of private arbitration are met with the argument that the parties themselves have agreed to resolve their disputes by arbitration, and that this being "the free will of the parties involved," it should be respected. But this so-called freedom of the party is very often theoretical rather than real.[28] In many cases, the commercially weaker party to the contract has to accept the demands of the stronger party. The one party is given a "take it or leave it" agreement. Since its very commercial life often depends on maintaining its commercial relations with the stronger party, there is no choice but to sign the agreement.[29] According to Judge Bankes in *Czarnikow v. Roth, Schmidt & Co.*, "Powerful trade organizations are encouraging, if not compelling, their members and persons who enter into contracts with their members to agree, as far as they can lawfully do so, to abstain from submitting their disputes to the decision of the Court of Law." [30]

In conclusion, it can be said that behind an understanding that the arbitration tribunal can decide a case free from strict obedience to the law is often concealed "the intention of the parties to evade any kind of binding law under the guise of the so-called equitable decision." [31] It makes little difference whether the reason for this evasion is that both parties to the litigation dislike any provisions designed to protect the public, or if one of the parties is stronger and can thus deprive the weaker party of his lawful remedy. The result is that through arbitration commercially influential groups can build up their own legal order. These problems will be investigated in more detail in the section of this chapter dealing with the development of arbitration law in the

[27] *Report of the Commission Preparing the Reform of the German Civil Procedure Act*, edited by the German Federal Ministry of Justice (Bonn, 1961), p. 183.

[28] Even E. Mezger, a strict supporter of private arbitration, had to admit this. See his "Die jüngsten Bemühungen um ein internationales Statut der Handelsschiedsgerichtsbarkeit und der Anerkennung ausländischer Schiedssprüche," in Eisemann, Mezger, and Schottelius, n. 7 above, pp. 18, 20.

[29] H. Kronstein, "Business Arbitration—Instrument of Private Government," in his *Selected Essays* (Karlsruhe, 1962), pp. 37 ff.; Kronstein, n. 18 above, pp. 661 ff.; and "Staat und private Macht in der neueren amerikanischem Rechtsentwicklung," in *Festschrift zum 70. Geburtstag von Franz Böhm* (Karlsruhe, 1965), pp. 144 ff.

[30] 2 K.B. 478, 484 (1922). [31] 55 *Zeitschrift für Zivilprozess* 26 (1930).

United States, Germany, Switzerland, and Great Britain, as well as in treaties between the governments involved.

It may be stated once more that the various national laws are examined not for reason of comparative law, as interesting as it may be, but to show the various opportunities and possibilities which the parties have to bring the opening of the cases, the trial as well as the enforcement, under "friendly" rules.

Extent of Arbitration in Cartel Agreements

Agreements prior to World War I

The first work on modern cartels, published in 1883 by Friedrich Kleinwächter, shows arrangements for settling controversies of the cartel by arbitration.[32] Another later and valuable source illustrating the great importance of arbitration in cartel agreements is a report in 1906 by the German Department of the Interior. This report was the result of an investigation undertaken between 1903 and 1905. Volume 1 of the annex attached to this report contains cartel agreements from fifteen industries. Seventy-five of these agreements contain arbitration clauses. One out of every two published cartel agreements in the leather, rubber, timber, and china industries provided for arbitration. In the roofing and electrical industries the percentage was even higher.

Arbitration clauses were even more usual and necessary in countries where cartels were prohibited or where their agreements were unenforceable. In 1894 the well-known political economist Adolf Menzel reported at the general meeting of the Verein für Sozialpolitik in Vienna that the unfavorable legal atmosphere in Austria did not prevent the formation of cartels. He noted that the usual method for evasion of the Austrian statutory provisions on cartels was for the parties to submit all controversies resulting from the agreement to an arbitration proceeding and to waive all rights to court review of the arbitral award.[33] Lehnich, a German writer discussing the World War I period, reported that arbitration clauses were filed in the vast majority of cartels, including the large raw material syndicates and the numerous organizations within the manufacturing industry.[34] From this back-

---

[32] F. Kleinwächter, *Die Kartelle* (Innsbruck, 1883), esp. p. 127.

[33] A. Menzel, "Die wirtschaftlichen Kartelle und die Rechtsordnung," 61 *Schriften des Vereins für Socialpolitik* 23, 29, 39 (1895).

[34] F. Kestner and O. Lehnich, *Der Organisations-zwang* (2d ed.; Berlin, 1927), p. 124.

ground, it can be seen that arbitration has had a significant impact on the organization of the cartel system from its beginning.

Agreements concluded between the two world wars

There are numerous instances of cartel arbitration agreements between the two world wars. The agreement among the breweries of Rheinland-Westfalen in 1931 provided penalty and arbitration provisions for interference by members of the cartel with customers of a particular member.[35]

The important automobile industry cartel which came into force in 1924 established an arbitration court of its own composed of several panels. One of the most far-reaching systems of private courts ever developed was created under this agreement. Over 2,900 cases were submitted to it. Of these, an arbitration award was made in almost 2,000 cases, over 300 were settled and another 400 were concluded by the withdrawal of the action or admission of violation. The remainder of cases were not disposed of because of the outbreak of World War II.[36]

Recent cartel agreements

Since 1958 the system of cartel arbitration, particularly in Germany, has advanced. In that year the German statute dealing with restraints of trade replaced the complete prohibition of cartels established by Allied regulations. Under the new statute, cartel agreements must be registered with the federal cartel office.[37] A significant number of the agreements registered contain arbitration clauses. This is particularly significant since under Section 91 of the new statute, arbitration clauses are void if they prohibit the parties from submitting their controversies to the ordinary courts. Even without this additional inducement, however, the percentage of arbitration clauses in existing cartel agreements is notably high.

International agreements

Much of the previous discussion of German cartel agreements is also true with respect to international cartels. As early as 1828, one of the first modern international cartels, the Neckar-Salinen-Verein,

[35] W. Bernhard, "Brauerei-Verträge in Geschichte und Gegenwart," in *Festschrift für Max Metzner* (Cologne, 1963), pp. 223, 238.
[36] Cf. J. H. von Brunn, "Ein Konditionenkartell der Automobilwirtschaft 1931–1945," in *id.*, pp. 245, 253.
[37] Cf. articles in *Bundesanzeiger* and *Wirtschaft und Wettbewerb*.

provided in Section 13 of its contract for the jurisdiction of an arbitration court with respect to all controversies among the parties arising out of the contract.[38]

The most important international cartels in the field of ocean shipping all contain arbitration clauses. Similar provisions are also in wide
use in the cartel agreements in the technical and pharmaceutical industries,[39] the iron and steel industry, as well as other metal industries.[40]
The electrical industry has also utilized arbitration clauses, the most
important agreement being the international light bulb cartel and its
predecessor, the international light bulb cartel of 1924.[41]

The general attitude toward arbitration in international cartel agreements between the two world wars was expressed in a resolution of the
Conference on International Trade of 1927.[42] The resolution declared
it "desirable" for members of the cartel to voluntarily submit to arbitration, as the arbitrators, with their understanding and familiarity
with the economics of the situation, could best guarantee a settlement
furthering the general interest of commerce. A similar statement by
the International Law Association recommended that the members of
the international cartel call as often as possible on the international
courts of arbitration, as these tribunals were best able to lead to a
unification and harmonization of international cartel law.[43]

[38] Reprinted by R. Liefmann in 21 *Vierteljahresschrift für Sozial- und Wirt-
schaftsgeschichte*, 414, 424 (1928).

[39] E.g., A. Plummer, *International Combines in Modern Industry* (3d ed.; Lon-
don, 1951), App. III, pp. 272–273; H. Wagenführ, *Deutsche, ausländische und in-
ternationale Kartellverträge im Wortlaut* (Nuremberg, 1391), No. 20, p. 82; U.S.
Cong., House Comm. on the Judiciary, Subcomm. No. 3, *Hearings on Revision of
Patent Laws*, 77th Cong., 2d Sess. (1942); U.S. Cong., Senate Comm. on the
Judiciary, Subcomm. on Antitrust and Monopoly, *Hearings on Administered
Prices*, 86th Cong., 2d Sess. (1961).

[40] *International Cartels*, Bulletin No. 4 of the International Chamber of Commerce, pp. 51, 53 (1937); see also G. Kiersch, *Internationale Eisen- und Stahl-
kartelle* (Essen, 1954), pp. 140, 148, 156, 169, 180; The Monopolies and Restrictive
Practices Commission, *Report on the Supply and Export of Certain Semi-Manufactures of Copper and Copper-Based Alloys*, pp. 193, 195 (1955).

[41] See, by W. Meinhardt, *Entwicklung und Aufbau der Glühlampenindustrie*
(Berlin, 1932), pp. 87, 97, 127–28; "Die rechtliche Gestaltung internationaler Kartelle, insbesondere der Glühlampenvertrag," 1928 *Zeitschrift für ausländisches und
internationales Privatrecht* 460, 462; "Das Schiedsgericht der internationalen
Glühlampenvereinigung," 2 *Nussbaums Jahrbuch* 166 ff. (1928).

[42] A. Benni, C. Lammers, L. Marlio, and A. Meyer, *Internationale Industriekar-
telle: Völkerbundsdenkschrift* (Geneva, 1930), App. CI 1, p. 120.

[43] See also R. Callmann, "Die Lage der internationalen Kartelle auf der 38.
Tagung der International Law Association in Budapest 1934," 1934 *Kartell-Rundschau* 579, 591.

Because of the technological developments since World War II, problems related to research and development have arisen among the members of international cartels. This is especially true with respect to industrial property rights, particularly patents obtained through research and development. As a result, patent controversies have become a prime subject for arbitration. For example the German investigation into concentration has noted that the leading enterprises have appeared as a plaintiff or defendant in very few patent litigations in recent years.[44] In 1960, the one hundred largest enterprises controlled 29 per cent of all German patents owned by domestic persons. Yet these firms appeared in only 2 per cent of the patent cases. To avoid patent litigation, they frequently agreed to arbitration or mediation.

International licensing agreements often contained arbitration clauses. A good example is the arbitration clause contained in the contracts between Parke, Davis and Company and Les Laboratoires Français de Chimiothérapie concluded in 1950.[45]

Contents of the Arbitration Clause

Typical clauses

The arbitration clauses found in cartel agreements generally provide that all controversies directly or indirectly arising out of the cartel agreement will be resolved by arbitration. This is true whether the controversy is between either the cartel agencies and its members or between several members of the cartel. The jurisdiction of the cartel arbitration tribunal may even go beyond this point if the cartel members provide for the jurisdiction of the tribunal in their contracts with third parties.

The arbitration clauses are often very explicit in delineating the circumstances under which arbitration is to be used. This can be seen in a contract concluded by Grasselli Chemical Company, Farbenfabriken Bayer, Grasselli Dyestuff Corporation, and Farbwerken Hoechst AG concluded March 3, 1925:

If the parties hereto shall at any time be unable to agree upon the interpretation of any word, clause, provision, covenant, agreement or restriction in this contract, or the effect thereof, or the manner or the time of per-

[44] 1964 *Anlagenband zur Konzentrationsenquête* 780.
[45] Point 15 of the agreement, *Administered Prices Hearings*, n. 39 above, pp. 16053, 16065.

formance of any agreement herein, or upon anything relating to this contract, then the disagreement shall be referred to a board of arbitrators.[46]

A provision in the contract between the British Imperial Chemical Industries and E. I. du Pont de Nemours and Co. of July 1, 1929, reads:

Should any difference or dispute arise between the parties hereto touching this agreement, or any clause, matter, or thing relating hereto, or as to the rights, duties, or liabilities of either of the parties hereto, the same shall be referred to the President for the time being of E. I. du Pont de Nemours & Company and the President for the time being of Imperial Chemical Industries, Limited, who shall arbitrate, and their award shall be final.[47]

An even more complex clause occurs in the present trading agreement between the British Metal Corporation, Ltd., and Svenska Tändsticks A.B.:

If any dispute or difference shall at any time arise between the parties hereto touching these presents or the construction thereof or any clause, provision, or thing herein contained or any matter in any way connected with or arising out of these presents or the operation thereof or the rights, duties or liabilities of either party in connection with the premises then and in every such case the matter in dispute shall be referred to the arbitration of a single arbitration.[48]

Meinhardt reports that the jurisdiction of the arbitration tribunal in the light bulb cartel covered practically all possible litigation or differences of opinion resulting from the basic contract or so-called special contract. The jurisdiction was extremely comprehensive. The basic contract, especially in its connection with the special contract, was fashioned in such a way that not only litigation arising from the original contracts was under the jurisdiction of the arbitration tribunal, but also any differences that arose out of the basic contract after it had been amended.[49]

Originally, most courts refused to accept the proposition that the arbitration tribunal had authority to determine the validity of the arbitration clause upon which the tribunal itself was based. Meinhardt

[46] *Patent Hearings,* n. 39 above, Pt. 5, pp. 2169, 2174.

[47] *Id.,* Pt. 2, pp. 787 ff.; see also p. 800; Pt. 5, pp. 2192, 2209.

[48] The Monopolies and Restrictive Practices Commission, *Report on the Supply and Export of Matches and the Supply of Match-Making Machinery,* 100, 105 (1953).

[49] Meinhardt, "Das Schiedsgericht der internationalen Glühlampenvereinigung," n. 41 above, pp. 166–168.

declared that this was the only loophole in the jurisdiction of the arbitration tribunal of the international light bulb association.[50] Ehlers states that the electrical appliance cartel endeavored to circumscribe this loophole by establishing a special arbitration contract between the parties. This special contract explicitly stated that the parties intended the arbitration contract to be an independent agreement. This separate arbitration agreement did not depend on the validity or invalidity of some or all the provisions of the main contract. Such an arbitration agreement continued to exist in its own right after the termination of the main contract, until all questions or disputes with respect to liquidation were settled.[51]

Until recently, arbitration tribunals appeared to have the authority under most national laws to determine the validity of the arbitration agreement upon which its own authority was based. This determination was subject to court review, if at all only by way of defense to a motion for execution of an award. Outside of the United States, discussed later in this chapter, far-reaching international agreements prevent the courts from undertaking such a review to overrule the award on the ground that the merits of the case, including the legality of agreements, were decided improperly.

The arbitration clause may also include within its scope torts committed by the members in derogation of their obligations under the contract. It may also provide for arbitration of administrative details of the cartel, such as general principles of cartel organization and cartel policy.

The arbitration tribunals' scope of activity

As can be inferred from the previous section, the arbitration agreement may provide for a very broad scope of authority for the arbitration tribunal. An analysis of arbitration clauses contained in national and international cartels shows that arbitration tribunals have one or more of the following functions:

(1) They must interpret the basic cartel agreement. This interpretation must be flexible enough to adapt to changed conditions so that the purpose of the cartel is maintained.

---

[50] *Id.*, pp. 166–167.

[51] Heinrich Ehlers, "Praktische Gesichtspunkte für Schiedsabreden bei Internationalen Dauerverträgen," 3 *Internationales Jahrbuch für Schiedsgerichtswesen in Zivil- und Handelssachen (Nussbaum's Jahrbuch)* 215 ff. (1931).

(2) The arbitration tribunal may be authorized to establish general rules and regulations binding on the management of the cartel and its agencies. Thus, it establishes cartel policy.

(3) In most cartel agreements, the arbitration tribunal must determine and enforce the imposition of fines and penalties for conduct inconsistent with the cartel contract. The tribunal must also determine the legality of other disciplinary measures, which may go as far as exclusion from the cartel. The arbitration tribunals thus have ultimate control over the interrelationship of the members and thereby control competition among the members. When a problem has become this serious, however, the proceeding before the tribunal is usually preceded by a hearing before other agencies of the cartel organization, such as the management, the board, a special committee, or a meeting of all the members. Disciplinary measures are taken by this group against the member who has acted inconsistently with the contract. The arbitration tribunal then becomes a kind of court of review over the disciplinary measures taken. Quite often a further appeal is open to a higher arbitration tribunal. There are cases, however, in which the arbitration tribunal itself is the primary agency for imposing fines or penalties. An appeal is usually also available from these decisions.

(4) The cartel arbitration tribunal often must act as an administrative agency in making a decision on the distribution and licensing of industrial property rights within the cartel. In modern international cartels, particularly in the field of technology, this function has a special significance.

(5) The other major function of the arbitration tribunal is the determination of genuine controversies between the cartel and its members and between the members themselves. This function is generally considered the traditional task of the arbitration tribunal.

The statutes on arbitration in every country require that an arbitration agreement be concluded between the opposing parties, before a private arbitration tribunal will be permitted to decide the case. Such an agreement need not be specially concluded to cover only the controversy at hand. As can be seen from the previous examples of arbitration clauses, it is sufficient to include a statement in the cartel agreement providing for arbitration in all litigation resulting from the cartel agreement to which the parties are members and thus legally bound. In this way the tribunal obtains jurisdiction over all the members of the cartel.

Third persons may subject themselves to the jurisdiction of the cartel arbitration tribunal expressly or implicitly. The cartel organization will very often urge its members to include an arbitration clause whenever possible in their contracts with suppliers or customers in order to give the cartel arbitration tribunal jurisdiction over all controversies arising out of their contract. In fact, many times there is a specific provision in the cartel agreement obligating the members to secure such a clause in their contracts with outsiders. It is not always possible to extend the jurisdiction of the arbitration tribunal in this way. The success of such endeavors depends on the power of the cartel.

The arbitration tribunal often abandons a purely judicial role and becomes for all practical purposes an administrative agency of the cartel. It may even be characterized as a legislature dictating rules and regulations for the management. As a result, the traditional lines between administrative, legislative, and judicial bodies is unclear in discussing an arbitration tribunal. For example, the arbitration tribunal functions as an administrative agency through a clause in the 1929 agreement between the association of German composers and the German cartel of music entertainers.[52] This agreement provides that the arbitration tribunal is to decide whether the rates provided for in this contract should be changed as a result of substantial economic changes or other conditions. The decision of the tribunal is final. The parties also agreed that upon termination of the agreement by one of the parties, the arbitration tribunal will establish new rates if the remaining parties are unable to reach agreement.

A similar clause exists in Section 13 of the charter establishing a cartel called the Hydromechanik GmbH Vertriebsgesellschaft für Ölhydraulik. The arbitration tribunal is given the authority to decide, in case of basic change of business conditions, whether new contractual rules are necessary and which rules are best adapted to serve the spirit and purpose of this association's contract.[53]

Lastly, a clause in the agreement between Deutsches Zuckersyndikat and the Syndikat Deutscher Raffinerien clearly illustrates the use of the arbitration tribunal as an administrative body. In this instance, the tribunal is called on to resolve complaints with respect to measures taken by the joint committee, to advise on joint and common matters

[52] Reprinted in Wagenführ, n. 39 above, pp. 51, 53–54.
[53] 31 *Bundesanzeiger* 3 (1964).

of the syndicates, and to issue rules and regulations for the purpose of exercising cartel control.[54]

Arbitration tribunals in patent matters

The role of the cartel arbitration tribunal in the field of industrial rights is particularly important. Even in the thirties, Meinhardt had noted that agreement on the joint use of patents and other industrial rights is often the "cornerstone" in the formulation of the cartel contract.[55] This is even more applicable to modern international cartels. Meinhardt found that the international light bulb agreement, as existing then, was essentially conditioned and supported by previous agreements relating to the joint use of patents.

The cartel arbitration tribunal has additional tasks when questions of patents are involved. One of the most important of these is to determine which member is entitled to file a patent application. When joint research and development is undertaken, controversy occasionally arises as to the actual inventor of the product. The cartel is especially interested in preventing such controversies from becoming public. Thus, they do not seek to resolve the issues through a hearing before the patent office. Instead, the cartel agreement usually provides that the cartel arbitration tribunal will have jurisdiction to settle such a difference of opinion.[56] As a result, the firm designated the "inventor" by the tribunal can be relatively certain that no member of the cartel will challenge its patent grant.

Following the arbitration tribunal's decision, the losing party withdraws any objections it has filed with the patent office if the losing partner is the patent applicant; it will withdraw its application or assign its patent rights, if it has already been granted a patent. Further, any

[54] §§7, 11, reprinted in 1905 *Anlagenband zur Denkschrift über das Kartellwesen*, No. 52. Cf. "Schiedsgerichts- und Gutachtenvertrag des nordrhein-westfälischen Brauereigewerbes of Dec. 1, 1950," cited in Bernhard, n. 35 above, pp. 234, 239–240. Although the agreed-upon arbitration tribunals and opinions in question, of which there are several, are basically optional (the parties theoretically can invoke the jurisdiction of the regular courts), as a practical matter, they will almost invariably consider the agreement as binding. Since the existence of these agreements, almost all disputes between breweries were decided by arbitration tribunals (Heinz Devin, *Schiedsgerichts- und Schiedsgutachtenverträge in der Brauindustrie* [Fribourg, 1954], p. 42).

[55] W. Meinhardt, "Patentfragen in internationalen Kartellen," 1931 *Gewerblicher Rechtsschutz und Urheberrecht* 1222.

[56] Cf. Hartford Empire Co. v. United States, 46 F. Supp. 541 (D. Ohio 1943); Re American Cyanamid Co., 3 CCH Trade Reg. Rep. ¶15,537.

objections by cartel members against a patent already granted, or the filing of a suit to declare patents void, or allegations of patent infringement by other cartel members are usually subjected to determination by the arbitration tribunal.[57]

Patent licenses also play a very significant role before cartel arbitration tribunals. Litigation between cartel members is often settled by the grant of a patent license to the losing partner. The winning partner may even be obligated to grant a license to all the other cartel members and to abstain from granting a license to any person not a member of the cartel. Cartel agreements often stipulate that each member must grant licenses to the other members on existing and future patents.[58] In this case, the cartel arbitration tribunal has the power to fix the license fee to be paid.[59] According to the International Chamber of Commerce, about 20 per cent of all arbitration proceedings that came before it dealt with questions of licenses on patents, trademarks, or know-how.[60]

Influence of the arbitration tribunals

The fact that the arbitration clause grants to an arbitration tribunal the power to decide all patent matters does not necessarily mean that the tribunal will be called upon to exercise this power. The arbitration clause is meant to be used only as a last resort. Carl Duisberg, the father of I.G. Farbenindustrie, commented in 1908 that even then the number of cases brought before the courts was decreasing. He indicated that the licensing agreements of I.G. Farbenindustrie contained arbitration

[57] With all these cases compare Meinhardt, n. 55 above, p. 1226; Benni, Lammers, Marlio, and Meyer, n. 42 above, p. 110; as well as the more recent statement of the German so-called "Konzentrationsenquête" (Bundesamt für Gewerbliche Wirtschaft, *Bericht über das Ergebnis einer Untersuchung der Konzentration in der Wirtschaft*, Bundestagsdrucksache IV 2320, Bonn 1964) under points 3.5.3. p. 776, 3.5.5. pp. 776–777, 3.7.1. pp. 780–781, 3.7.4. p. 781; *Hearings on the Drug Industry Antitrust Act*, 87th Cong., 2d Sess., pp. 303 f., 325, 361, 367, 389, 618 (remarks of the leading American industries), 1792 ff. (examples) (1962); *Administered Prices Hearings*, n. 39 above, pp. 9637 ff., 15356 ff. (examples).

[58] Cf. the discussion in Chapter 12. See also Hartford Empire Co. v. United States, 46 F. Supp. 541 (D. Ohio 1943); Re American Cyanamid Co., 3 CCH Trade Reg. Rep. ¶15,537; Meinhardt, *id.*; Benni, Lammers, Marlio, Meyer, *id.*; 1931 *Gewerblicher Rechtsschutz und Urheberrecht* 1222, 1226; H. Isay, *Die Patentgemeinschaft in Dienste des Kartellgedankens* (Mannheim, 1923), pp. 23 f.

[59] Cf. W. Meinhardt, *id.*, pp. 1222 ff.; H. Isay, *id.*, p. 21.

[60] International Chamber of Commerce, *Guide to ICC Arbitration* (Paris, 1963), p. 11.

clauses, and not because arbitration clauses were so beneficial to the cartel. In fact, he noted, the members avoided arbitrational awards, if possible, because of the fear of a wrong decision by the arbitration tribunal. He indicated that the arbitration provision was to compel the parties to an understanding in advance. This type of settlement and understanding was an important factor in establishing a "community of interests" within the cartel, which eventually led to the abolition of all litigation.

This basic approach to arbitration is still true of present-day cartel members. Through the use of a royalty-free, or at least favorable, license option, amicable settlement of disputes is reached.

Organization of the Arbitration Tribunal

There are two types of arbitration tribunals: One is established to hear and decide a specific dispute; the other is a continuing institutional tribunal. These institutional tribunals can take one of two forms. The tribunal may be part of an existing association, or the cartel itself may establish a permanent arbitration tribunal of its own. The arbitration tribunals of national chambers of commerce—especially important is the one established by the International Chamber of Commerce—or of produce exchanges are examples of the first institutional form.[61] Examples of the second institutional form are those established by the international light bulb agreement and the low-voltage appliance industry, discussed earlier in this chapter.

The cartel, naturally, has a definite interest in influencing the composition as well as the procedures of the arbitration tribunal in order to ensure that any award will fully protect the interests of the cartel. Indeed, the greater the impact and power of the arbitration tribunal over the cartel, the greater the pressure exerted upon the tribunal.

Composition of the tribunal

The composition of arbitration tribunals can best be discerned through a review of some cartel agreements. First, a look at all the Austrian cartel agreements published by the Verein für Socialpolitik in 1895 shows that the cartel did not usually go so far as to appoint any

[61] See the cartel statutes reprinted in the appendix of 61 *Schriften des Vereins für Socialpolitik* (1895); cf. R. Wolff, *Die Rechtsgrundlagen der Internationalen Kartelle* (Berlin, 1929), p. 185.

of its own members to the arbitration tribunal.[62] This was true with regard to regular members as well as the chairman.

In a similar vein, the seventy-five cartel agreements attached to the report on cartels prepared by the German Department of the Interior in 1906 show almost no case in which the arbitration tribunal was entirely or partly composed of members of the cartel. Only three cases provide that the members of the tribunal must be members of the cartel; in two others, they are to be elected by the cartel; five agreements provide that the chairman of the tribunal is to be appointed by the cartel; and in two cases the members of the tribunal, including the chairman, are to be selected from a list prepared by the cartel.[63]

Cartel agreements in the chemical industry, such as the contract on the community of interest between Farbenfabriken, Badische Anilin- und Sodafabrik (BASF), and Aktiengesellschaft für Anilin-Fabrikation (Agfa), provide for the appointment of a counsel composed of all the members of the management of the three enterprises. This body acts as an arbitration tribunal in all litigations that develop between the participating enterprises, provided the controversy has not already been settled by an agency operating on a lower level.[64]

The arbitration tribunal of the German, French, and Swiss tar cartel of 1929 was composed of the chairmen of the boards of the participating companies. This tribunal had jurisdiction to decide litigation between the members about "know-how and technical inventions." [65] Several cartel agreements published during the American patent hearings provide for a similar composition. As already mentioned, the agreement between Imperial Chemical Industries and du Pont de Nemours in 1929 appointed the presidents of the two companies as members of the arbitration tribunal.[66] The clauses of the Lausanne Agreements,[67] the agreements of the International Electric Association,

[62] 61 Schriften des Vereins für Socialpolitik 410 ff. (1895).

[63] Id., App. D 5, L 53, 56; B 212, K 6; H 8, K 17, 19, 21, L 66; N 9, O 9, 10.

[64] Cf. C. Duisberg, Meine Lebenserinnerungen (Leipzig, 1933), p. 96; F. Binder-nagel, "Die Zusammenschlussbewegung in der deutschen chemischen Industrie künstlicher Farbstoffe," diss., University of Frankfort (Johann Wolfgang Goethe University), 1923, p. 65.

[65] Cf. W. Gaeb, Die internationalen Kartellbestrebungen in der Nachkriegszeit (Berlin, 1933), pp. 62–63; Benni, Lammers, Marlio, and Meyer, n. 42 above, pp. 61–62.

[66] Patent Hearings, n. 39 above, Pt. 2, pp. 787 f.

[67] Monopolies and Restrictive Practices Commission, n. 46 above, p. 195.

and the 1948 Lamp Agreement [68] appoint either the international committee, the secretaries of these associations, or the general meeting of the cartel members as members of the arbitration tribunal.

The number of members on the tribunal is normally between one and five, but the appointment of a single arbitrator is rare. In Anglo-American cartels, the arbitration tribunal sometimes consists of two arbitrators, who then appoint another party to be chairman. This chairman, or "umpire," has authority to decide the case alone if there is no agreement between the two arbitrators.[69]

Tribunals appointed for the decision of particular cases

If the cartel agreement does not provide for a permanent, institutional arbitrational tribunal, but only for the establishment of a tribunal for particular cases, the refusal of the defendant to appoint his member of the arbitration tribunal may hinder the execution of any arbitration proceedings. Many agreements provide for this possibility by inserting a provision in the agreement which gives authority to another person or another agency to appoint the necessary arbitrators if one of the cartel parties refuses to exercise its appointive authority. Or the agreement may even authorize the plaintiff himself to appoint the other member or members of the tribunal if the defendant has not exercised his authority.[70] Occasionally, a provision will provide that the arbitrator appointed by the plaintiff himself may act as the exclusive arbitrator if the defendant refuses to appoint the second arbitrator. But in the majority of cases, an official of a high court, a bar association, or a chamber of commerce will be designated to appoint arbitrators if the defendant refuses.[71]

Seat of the Arbitration Tribunal

Obviously, it is desirable to establish arbitration tribunals, particularly in litigations dealing with international cartels, in places hospitable to arbitration proceedings. While nearly every continental law system

---

[68] Monopolies and Restrictive Practices Commission, *Report on the Supply of Electric Lamps* (1951); *Report on the Supply and Export of Electrical and Allied Machinery and Plant* (1957).

[69] For example, the cartel agreement between Imperial Chemical Industries and du Pont de Nemours in *Patent Hearings*, n. 39 above, Pt. 2, pp. 787–788.

[70] Cf. agreement between Friedrich Krupp AG and General Electric Co. of 1928, in *id.*, Pt. 1, pp. 281, 286.

[71] E.g., the agreements in *id.*, Pts. 1, p. 239, 5, p. 2209, 7, p. 3449.

gives the parties full autonomy to designate the specific law the arbitration proceedings are to apply, such autonomy is not permissible under Anglo-American law. Consequently, the parties establish the law to be applied through the choice of the arbitration tribunal's seat.

As a result, the cartel's arbitration proceedings are subject to the most convenient procedural law, whether through full recognition of direct party autonomy or through the power to determine the seat of the arbitration tribunal in each particular litigation. The international light bulb cartel and the low-voltage appliance industry are excellent examples of the extent to which Swiss law, especially Geneva law, was preferred because of its "progressive attitude and liberality." [72]

With respect to the substantive law to be applied by the tribunal, the international cartel agreement will often provide that the tribunal should not be limited to the application of any specific national substantive law. Instead, it should decide according to the principles of equity. For instance, the international light bulb agreement provides that the decisions of the arbitration tribunal should be based "on law and equity in full accordance with the intention and the contractual will of the parties as far as determinable." [73] Recently, there has been a tendency to subject international contractual agreements, including cartel agreements, to a supranational law by referring to "multinational general legal principles" as the rule to be applied by arbitration tribunals in deciding litigation.[74]

Enforcement of the Award

The cartel is concerned with enforcing the award without resort to the courts of the particular nation-state. While these courts generally do not review the merits of an award, there is always the danger of an investigation into possible violations of public policy or of violation of the basic principles of fair procedure. Therefore, the organizers of cartels try to guarantee voluntary compliance by other means.

[72] See n. 41 above.

[73] Meinhardt, "Das Schiedsgericht der internationalen Glühlampenvereinigung," n. 41 above, pp. 166, 170; see also J. Henggeler, "Die Schiedsgerichtsordnung des Internationalen Verbandes der Baumwoll-Spinner und Weber-Vereinigungen," 2 *Nussbaums Jahrbuch*, 159–162 (1928).

[74] Cf. R. B. Schlesinger and H. J. Gündisch, "Allgemeine Rechtsgrundsätze als Sachnormen im Schiedsgerichtsverfahren," 28 *Zeitschrift für ausländisches und internationales Privatrecht* 4 ff. (1964).

Enforcement through moral suasion

In a substantial number of cases the award is automatically enforced. For instance, it is often stipulated that a cartel member who has exceeded the production quota provided in the cartel agreement shall produce less during the next accounting period. Furthermore, moral suasion of the cartel is generally strong enough to guarantee the performance of an award by the losing party. Even if obedience to an award is not made a "duty of honor," a violent reprimand by one's peers is usually sufficient to obtain obedience by the recalcitrant party.[75] This pressure is a significant factor in keeping cartels together and thus should not be underestimated.

Enforcement through the power of the cartel

In addition to automatic enforcement and moral suasion, the power of the cartel association itself usually can compel all parties to a dispute to abide by an arbitration award.[76] The power of the cartel is exercised in a number of ways. For instance, a cartel member may forfeit a deposit made with the cartel members if it refuses to submit to arbitration or to perform in accordance with the award rendered against it. If the disloyal member belongs to a technological cartel, he may be excluded from further participation in research projects and be precluded from access to the results of these projects. The cartel agreement may provide for a specific fine in cases of refusal to perform an award,[77] the exclusion from further supplies or credit, or other discriminatory treatment with respect to purchases and sales.[78] Another method of enforcement is the publication of a black list containing the names of all parties not abiding by the cartel agreement.[79]

[75] The holding of the decision—in public law—of the appellate division of the stock exchange court of honor in 1921 reads as follows: "The non-application of the judgment of an agreed upon arbitration tribunal runs against the honor and the right to trust in commercial transactions" (2 *Nussbaums Jahrbuch* 309 [1928]). See R. P. Wolff, n. 61 above, p. 167.

[76] Wolff, *id.*

[77] See §21 of the Agreement of the Associated German Venetian Blind Manufacturers in the appendix of the *Kartell-Denkschrift* G 8.

[78] Cf. G. Viertel, *Die Vertragsstrafe im Kartellrecht* (Jena, 1935), p. 16.

[79] E.g., extensive references in this connection in R. Kahn, "Sanktionsverfahren bei Nichterfüllung von Schiedssprüchen nach dem Rechte Englands, der Vereinigten Staaten und Deutschlands," 3 *Nussbaums Jahrbuch*, 186 f. (1931).

And finally, the most extreme measure is the exclusion of the party from the cartel.[80]

Attempts to attack the validity of awards in a court of law are specifically prevented through the use of these methods.[81] In this manner, the state and municipal courts are successfully excluded from exercising the functions allotted to them to insure new process by arbitration tribunals.

Development of the Legal Structure of Arbitration

International Development

Since 1920 important private institutions dealing with international arbitration have come into being and have expanded with the ever increasing growth of international trade. Numerous intergovernmental agreements also exist regulating this matter.

The Arbitration Society of America was organized in 1921 in the United States. In 1925 the Arbitration Foundation came into existence. Then in 1926 these organizations merged into the biggest arbitration organization in the world, the American Arbitration Association (A.A.A.). In 1919 the International Chamber of Commerce, headquartered in Paris, was organized and developed jointly with the London Court of Arbitration into the leading European international

[80] "Anyone who does not comply with the judgment agreed upon by the arbitration tribunal, or who fails to sign the declaration, is faced with temporary exclusion from the stock exchange" (§33 of *Schiedsgerichtsordnung für die Produkten- und Warenbörse in Köln*, quoted in Krause, n. 16 above, p. 86, n. 32). This declaration provides that the undersigned "must recognize the judgment of the arbitration tribunal as binding in itself, with no explanation necessary." Although we are dealing here only with a regulation of the stock exchange arbitration tribunal, this interpretation is consistent with customary commercial and economic views once held and in principle still held today.

[81] The declaration *id.* contains the following passage: "I agree that the coercive means of §33 of the regulation of the arbitration tribunal (temporary exclusion) might apply to me, if I should nonsuit according to the regulations of the ZPO." The appellate division of the stock exchange court of honor provides in a 1925 decision: "Investors in the stock market who disregard the generally recognized establishment of the stock exchange, and the norms set forth by their peers, in this case by denying the competence of the arbitration tribunal, although they were obligated to recognize its competence, and the investors who try to undermine the efficacy of the arbitration tribunal's decision through appeal to the ordinary courts, act inconsistent with the honor and the right to trust in commercial transactions" (2 *Nussbaums Jahrbuch*, 311 [1928]).

organizations on private arbitration. All of these organizations are connected with each other as well as with other international institutions by different agreements on arbitration clauses.[82]

International agreements

The first important international agreement in the field of arbitration was the Geneva protocol on arbitration clauses in international trade, signed in 1923.[83] This was followed four years later by the Geneva agreement on enforcement of foreign arbitration.[84] Germany, France, Great Britain and Northern Ireland, Switzerland, and some other countries are member states, but the United States did not join.[85]

The endeavor to develop a more complete international private system of arbitration has been made, primarily by the Institute for the Unification and Harmonization of Private Law in Rome and the International Law Association, as well as the International Chamber of Commerce. In 1935 the Rome Institute published a draft statute calling for arbitration in matters of international trade. The draft was published in amended form in 1940 and 1953.[86] The International Law Association in 1938 published a draft of a uniform arbitration clause that is recommended for use in individual contracts. In 1950 the International Law Association prepared another form of arbitration agreement containing rules of procedure on arbitration, the so-called

---

[82] D. J. Schottelius, "Die Organisation des internationalen Schiedsgerichtswesens," 1955 *Konkurs-, Treuhand- und Schiedsgerichtswesen* 97 ff., and "Die Notwendigkeit und Möglichkeit der Bildung eines internationalen privaten Schiedsgerichtssystems," in Eisemann, Mezger, and Schottelius, n. 7 above, pp. 68, 83–85; R. Bruns, "Zur Reform der Vollstreckung internationaler Schiedssprüche," 70 *Zeitschrift für Zivilprozess* 7–9 (1957).

[83] *Reichsgesetzblatt* II, p. 47 (1925), reprinted in A. Bülow and H. Arnold, *Der internationale Rechtsverkehr in Zivil- und Handelssachen* (Munich, 1954), No. 231, and in Baumbach and Schwab, n. 8 above, pp. 20 ff.

[84] *Reichsgesetzblatt* II, p. 1068 (1930), reprinted in Bülow and Arnold, *id.*, No. 236, and Baumbach and Schwab, *id.*, pp. 26 ff.

[85] See, for example, survey in H. W. Greminger, *Die Genfer Abkommen von 1923 und 1927 über die internationale private Schiedsgerichtsbarkeit* (Winterthur, 1957), pp. 112 f.; Baumbach and Schwab, *id.*, pp. 244 f.

[86] A. Schönke, "Der gegenwärtige Stand und der weitere Ausbau der internationalen Schiedsgerichtsbarkeit in Zivil- und Handelssachen," in Schönke, n. 19 above, I, 1, 7; W. J. Habscheid, "Nationale oder supranationale Schiedssprüche," 70 *Zeitschrift für Zivilprozess* 25 f. (1957); E. Mezger, "Die jüngsten Bemühungen um ein internationales Statut der Handelsschiedsgerichtsbarkeit und der Anerkennung ausländischer Schiedssprüche," in Eisemann, Mezger, and Schottelius, n. 7 above, pp. 23 f.

Copenhagen Rules.[87] The rules were intentionally simple and short.

The International Chamber of Commerce in 1953 finally published a draft international agreement for the enforcement of international awards.[88] The unique element in this draft was the attempt to achieve a truly international award. Under the draft, the parties to the arbitration agreement are authorized to waive, by agreement, all reasons provided in each of the national laws for possible avoidance of an arbitration award. This includes even the *ordre public*. Only a limited number of clearly enumerated reasons are recognized as exceptions to the enforcement of an award. This draft provided for the most far-reaching recognition of party autonomy in the field of arbitration,[89] but it has not been accepted by any country.[90]

The Economic and Social Council of the United States, at the suggestion of the International Chamber of Commerce, prepared another draft [91] that finally led to the U.N. agreement on the recognition and enforcement of foreign arbitration awards of June 10, 1958.[92] This agreement cancels the Geneva Protocol of 1923 and the Geneva agreement of 1927 "among the contracting states which participate in the new agreement as soon and as far as it becomes binding on these states." [93] The Federal Republic of Germany and France signed the U.N. agreement, although the United States has not.

The European agreement of April 21, 1961, is the latest important agreement on international commercial arbitration.[94] It supplements the U.N. agreement and is basically devoted to the problem of execution and enforcement of foreign awards.

---

[87] E. Mezger, "Die Regeln von Kopenhagen über das schiedsgerichtliche Verfahren," 64 *Zeitschrift für Zivilprozess* 56 (1951).

[88] Brochure No. 174 of the International Chamber of Commerce is reprinted in Mezger, n. 103 above, App. III, p. 59.

[89] *Id.*, p. 30.

[90] Habscheid, n. 86 above, pp. 32 ff.; A. Bülow, "Zur Revision des Genfer Abkommens über die Vollstreckung ausländischer Schiedssprüche," 1956 *Recht der internationalen Wirtschaft* 37, 40 f.

[91] Reprinted in Mezger, n. 86 above, App. IV, p. 61; and Bülow, *id.*, p. 41.

[92] *Bundesgesetzblatt* II, p. 121 (1961), reprinted in Baumbach and Schwab, n. 8 above, pp. 35 ff.; and Bülow and Arnold, n. 83 above, No. 240a.

[93] 92 L.N.T.S. 301 (Sept. 26, 1927).

[94] *Bundesgesetzblatt* II, p. 425 (1964); see A. Bülow, "Das europäische Übereinkommen über die internationale Handelsschiedsgerichtsbarkeit," 1961 AWD 144.

Other tendencies

In addition to the international agreements on arbitration, attempts
are being made in various countries to harmonize the individual national statutes on arbitration procedure. This is designed to maintain
the sovereign power of each state to pass statutes concerning arbitration, but at the same time to achieve mutual recognition of arbitration
agreements and awards entered into under the law of a foreign country.
The European Council has even gone so far as to attempt to reach
an agreement on a uniform statute on arbitration.[95]

Recently, the resolution of controversies by arbitration between
governments or governmental organizations on the one side and private parties on the other has developed increasing importance.[96] The
culmination of this development came in 1965 with the World Bank
Convention on the Settlement of Investment Disputes between States
and Nationals of Other States. This convention is now in force after
ratification by twenty states. It provides for the establishment of the
International Centre for Settlement of Investment Disputes, which appoints arbitration tribunals on a case by case method to either decide or
to mediate the conflict.[97]

The constant expansion of the system of private arbitration is clear.
The long-established institutions, such as the International Chamber of
Commerce and the American Arbitration Association, are steadily in-

[95] European Treaty Series No. 56; see H. Arnold in 1967 *Neue Juristische
Wochenschrift* 142 ff. This European Convention, the adoption of which as uniform law by national legislatures is doubtful, regards the arbitration clause and
the arbitration agreement as equal. Furthermore, it acknowledges the principle of
private autonomy with respect to applicable procedural rules (Arts. 15, 21). On
the other hand, it contains provisions for the protection of the constitutional
rights of the contracting parties (Arts. 3, 8 ff., 25) which are not laid down in
other international agreements nor in the provision of the German Civil Procedure
Act (Sec. 1025 ff. ZPO). The German industry, the German Association of Industrial Enterprises and Craftsmen (Handelstag), the committee on arbitration of
the German group of the International Chamber of Commerce, and the International Chamber of Commerce itself regard the Convention of 1966 with great
reserve. See H. Arnold, "Die Ergebnisse der Zehnten Tagung der Haager Kon-
ferenz für internationales Privatrecht auf dem Gebiete des internationalen Zivil-
prozessrechts," 1965 AWD 145, No. 41, 146, No. 43.
[96] M. Domke, "Arbitration between Governmental Bodies and Foreign Private
Firms," 17 *Arbitration J.* 129 (1962); K. H. Böckstiegel, "Schiedsgerichtsbarkeit
in Streitigkeiten zwischen Staaten und Privatunternehmen," 1965 AWD 101 f.
[97] J. P. Sirefman, "The World Bank Plan for Investment Dispute Arbitration,"
20 *Arbitration J.* 68 ff. (1965).

creasing their activities, while everywhere new international arbitration organizations, like the European Court of Arbitration in Strassburg and the Court of Arbitration under the new London Rules, have come into existence.[98]

Development of Certain Aspects of Arbitration Law

A short survey of the development of the law in international private arbitration during the last decades may be helpful. The main points of reference are the arbitration agreement, particularly the elements necessary for its legality and enforcement, the determination of the applicable law, and the review and possible reversal of awards by regular courts.

Arbitration agreement

In providing for the resolution of disputes by arbitration, one must distinguish between two possible avenues to this end: the arbitration agreement, a separate contract providing for the determination of already existing litigation by arbitration (*compromissum*); and the arbitration clause, a clause contained within the basic contract between the parties providing for determination of all future litigation by arbitration (*clausula compromissoria*).

Originally the arbitration agreement was the usual way to provide for arbitration. In fact, arbitration clauses were at one time unenforceable or even void in many countries, particularly under the Latin American and Anglo-American legal systems.[99] But a far-reaching change, giving recognition to these arbitration clauses under national laws, developed during the last century.[100] This tendency has been expressed and stated also in international agreements. The Geneva Protocol of September 24, 1923, was the first modern international treaty on arbitration. Article 1 obligates each of the signing governments to recognize arbitration clauses, in addition to arbitration agreement, provided certain requirements are fulfilled. One of the re-

[98] *Guide to ICC Arbitration*, n. 60 above, pp. 8 ff.; 31 *ICC News*, Monthly Bulletin of the International Chamber of Commerce, No. 2–3, pp. 34 f., No. 8, p. 1 (1965); H. Benke, "Europäischer Schiedsgerichtshof der Vereinigung für europäische Schiedsgerichtsbarkeit und europäisches Recht," 1960 AWD 65; K. Dobratz, "Schiedsklausel und Vollstreckung im Aussenhandel," 1962 *id.* 188, 190; J. Trappe, "Das Schiedsgerichtsverfahren nach den 'London Rules,'" 1965 *id.* 353.

[99] Mezger, n. 86 above, pp. 12 f.

[100] This issue will be discussed later in connection with arbitration in France, Great Britain, and the United States.

quirements is that the parties be "subject to the jurisdiction of the contracting governments." While there is some dispute as to the meaning of this concept of jurisdiction, there is a general consensus that citizenship of the parties is not necessary. The prevailing opinion requires the existence of jurisdiction for a longer period of time, while Mezger tends to define the clause "subject to the jurisdiction of the contracting governments" as referring to the so-called international jurisdiction.[101] The French and English text of the protocol is different from the German text. It requires that the parties to the agreement be subject to the jurisdiction of different contracting states. It is also disputed whether arbitration clauses are covered by the Geneva Protocol if they are only included in by-laws and charters of associations.

Article 1 of the Geneva Protocol also requires that arbitration agreements and arbitration clauses deal with litigation "in matters of trade and other matters in which settlement by contractually agreed arbitration procedures is permissible." It is obvious that not all fields of law can be subject to arbitration. Whenever really important public interests are involved there have to be limitations to the private system of tribunals exercising, for all practical purposes, genuine judicial activity. Criminal law and, with some exceptions, public law [102] are not open to arbitration. The natural field of activity for arbitration is wherever the parties have the power to dispose of the matter themselves. This would include the entire field of civil law. Some states, however, as already mentioned, have not permitted arbitration clauses or at least have only permitted them in international commercial matters. As mentioned, Article 1 also refers to "other matters" than trade. But each contracting state is free to limit recognition "to those agreements which by the legislation of the state is considered matters of trade." Some states, especially France, make use of this privilege.

A more recent international agreement reaffirming the recognition of arbitration clauses is the U.N. Agreement on the Recognition and Enforcement of Foreign Awards of June 10, 1958. Under Article II, Section 1, each contracting member state recognizes "a written agreement by virtue of which the parties promise to submit to an arbitration

---

[101] Baumbach and Schwab, n. 8 above, pp. 250 f.; E. Mezger, "Zur Auslegung und Bewertung der Genfer Schiedsabkommen von 1923 und 1927," 24 *Zeitschrift für ausländisches und internationales Privatrecht* 222, 225 f. (1959).

[102] With respect to the German decision of the Bundesverwaltungsgericht (Supreme Court for Administrative Litigation), see 1959 *Neue Juristische Wochenschrift* 1985 f.

procedure all or particular litigation which develops between them." [103] This litigation may concern either contractual or noncontractual matters. It covers existing and future litigation, but again, like the Geneva Protocol, this agreement permits the contracting states to limit the obligation to recognize arbitration to litigations in commerical matters.

The European Agreement of April 24, 1961, also refers to "arbitration agreements in litigation resulting from international commercial transactions, no matter whether they have already arisen or may arise in the future." [104] The agreement requires that arbitration agreements be in written form: letters, cables, or teletypes. "This written form, however, is not required in the relationship between the states which do not require a written form under their own applicable law on arbitration agreements." [105] These agreements are valid and enforceable if they have been consummated in accordance with the formalities required under the legal order to which they are subject.

According to the U.N. agreement, the question of whether an agreement is subject to arbitration or not is decided: on the basis of the law applicable to the arbitration contract; [106] on the basis of the law of the country of the award; [107] or on the basis of the law of the country where the award is to be enforced.[108] This procedure was called by Mezger, the leading proponent of arbitration, "not wrong but really destructive"; in his opinion only the arbitration contract can determine whether an agreement is subject to arbitration or not.[109]

The applicable law

The problem of the applicable law is basic in arbitration proceedings which involve contracts among foreign countries. In this area three separate issues must be distinguished. First, it is necessary to consider which law is applicable to the arbitration agreement. Second, it is necessary to determine the substantive law applicable to the particular case to be decided. Finally, it is necessary to discern the procedural law applicable to the arbitration proceeding. Certainly one law may be applicable to all three; however, it may happen that two or even three different laws are to be applied.

[103] Art. 2, §1(a), 330 U.N.T.S. 38 (1958).
[104] Art. 1, §2(a); see n. 94 above.   [105] Art. 5, §1(a).
[106] Art. 5, §1(a), 330 U.N.T.S. 38, 40 (1958). This will be discussed later.
[107] Art. 5, §1(d), 330 U.N.T.S. 38, 42 (1958).
[108] Art. 5, §2, 330 U.N.T.S. 38, 42 (1958).
[109] Mezger, n. 101 above, pp. 222, 237.

Which law is applicable to the arbitration agreement depends upon how the arbitration agreement is characterized. Two sharply contrasting opinions exist on this matter: The arbitration agreement is considered either a matter of substantive law or a procedural agreement. If the agreement is viewed as substantive in nature, the applicable law is determined under the general rules of conflict of law. If the agreement is procedural, rules of conflict of procedural law apply. The practical development in cases of international character clearly favors the recognition of the will of the parties in determining the law applicable to the arbitration agreement. The U.N. agreement was the first international agreement to refer to this problem and to express this general trend toward party autonomy.[110] Under Article V, Section 1(a), the parties determine the law applicable to the arbitration agreement in all respects except the law applicable to the personal capacity of the party to enter into a contract. If for any reason the parties do not designate the applicable law, the law of the country "in which the award has been rendered shall govern." The European agreement is very similar on this point. Thus, it can be seen that those persons anxious to give the will of the parties predominance over any state laws have clearly succeeded.

Finding the applicable law with respect to arbitration procedure is more complicated. Article 2, Section 1, of the Geneva Protocol reads: "The will of the parties and the statutes of the country in which the arbitration proceeding takes place govern the law of procedure in arbitration matters, including the composition of the arbitration tribunal." While this provision is the most famous one in the protocol, it is also the most criticized. The different interpretations given to it are irreconcilable. Some writers believe that this article deals "only with domestic law of the contracting parties."[111] However, they believe that the contracting states are perfectly free "to apply their rules on conflict of law instead of their substantive internal law." That means that they will require the arbitration procedure to follow the rules of other countries because it has been chosen by the parties.[112]

Another group of writers hold that the rules of procedure are those

[110] This question was not decided in the Geneva Convention because of the divergent viewpoints of the participating nations; see Greminger, n. 85 above, p. 22.

[111] F. E. Klein, "Zum Begriff des internationalen Schiedsverfahrens," *Festgabe zum schweizerischen Juristentag 1963* (Basel, 1963), pp. 145, 148.

[112] Mezger, n. 101 above, pp. 222, 242 f.

found in the statutes of the country in which the proceeding takes place and that the parties are permitted to determine the course of procedure only as far as there are no binding procedural rules in that country.[113] The majority opinion on Article 2 §1 is that it favors the most extensive power of the parties to choose the law under which the procedure takes place.[114] Under this view, the parties are absolutely free to set the rules of the arbitration procedure. The law of the country in which the arbitration proceeding takes place only comes into force when there is neither an agreement of the parties nor any possibility to imply the will of the parties from the facts of the case, or whenever the *ordre public* demands it.[115]

The recognition of party autonomy in choosing the applicable procedural law is acknowledged in numerous other drafts and agreements on arbitration. In the drafts of the Institute for the Unification and Harmonization of Private Law in Rome the agreement of the parties determines the governing procedure, and only in case of lack of such agreement is it left to the arbitrators to determine the applicable procedural law.[116] The Copenhagen Rules of 1950 follow the same concept.[117] Article IIIb of the draft of the International Chamber of Commerce "accepts the prevalence of the will of the parties generally." [118] Even the U.N. agreement recognizes the unrestricted will of the party to determine the applicable procedural law.[119] Only when there is a "failing of any such agreement by the parties" does the law "of the country of the arbitral procedure" determine the applicable law of procedure. Some writers even suggest that the parties may provide for rules of procedure entirely independent from any definite law of procedure.[120]

The European Agreement of 1961 even exceeds the U.N. agreement in the support of party autonomy. Under the U.N. agreement, if the

---

[113] It is not clear whether these authors meant the unlimited establishment of procedural rules by the respective parties or whether they only meant the selection of the applicable national procedural law (see *id.*, pp. 222, 240 f.); Greminger, n. 85 above, pp. 33 f.; Klein, n. 111 above, p. 149, No. 13.

[114] Cf. Heilberg, *Schiedsgerichtsvertrag, Schiedsgericht und schiedsrichterliches Verfahren,* n. 15 above, p. 15.

[115] Cf. Gremminger, n. 85 above, pp. 33–34n.; Klein, n. 111 above, p. 149, No. 13; M. Guldener, *Das internationale und interkantonale Zivilprozessrecht der Schweiz* (Zurich, 1951), p. 162.

[116] Schönke, n. 86 above, p. 8. [117] Mezger, n. 87 above, pp. 56, 66.

[118] Mezger, n. 86 above, p. 29. [119] Art. V, §1d.

[120] Klein, n. 111 above, pp. 152–154, No. 4.

parties fail to agree on the procedural rules, then the procedural laws of the country in which the arbitration proceedings take place apply. But under the European agreement, in the event that the parties do not agree on the applicable procedural rules, the arbitrators themselves determine them.[121]

Once this autonomy has been accepted, the next issue to be resolved is whether the parties must choose the procedural law of a particular country or whether they have the power to establish their own rules of procedure. Mezger takes the position that they have the power to establish their own rules of procedure. In his opinion, the novelty of the European agreement was the "creation of real international arbitration awards," meaning the awards become effective merely on the basis of the European agreement and the will of the parties, even if they are not supported by the law of any country.[122]

The principles of conflicts of law, especially the rules on the power of the party to choose the applicable law, generally determine the substantive law to be applied by the arbitration tribunal in deciding the controversy. The European agreement contains the following provision on this subject:

It is in the discretion of the parties to choose the law to be applied by the arbitration tribunal on the merits of the case. Whenever the parties have not made any agreement on the applicable law, the arbitration tribunal shall apply such law based on those rules of conflict of law to be considered as justified from case to case by the arbitration tribunal.[123]

The finding of the law applicable on the validity and the interpretation of the arbitration agreement is based on the same theory for anyone who accepts the so-called substantive law theory of arbitration agreements.

In international trade, a peculiar institution developed within the scope of the arbitration process with respect to the determination of applicable law. This is the institution of the *amiable composition*. This institution was first developed in French law on the basis of Roman

[121] According to Mezger, the law of the state where the arbitration proceeding takes place has to be applied when there is no private agreement ("Das europäische Übereinkommen über die Handelsschiedsgerichtsbarkeit," 29 *Zeitschrift für ausländisches und internationales Privatrecht* 231, 275 f. [1965]).

[122] *Id.*, pp. 231, 255 f., 295 f.   [123] *Id.*, pp. 239 ff.

canon law and permits the arbitrator to make his decision free of any substantive law and therefore based on equitable principles.[124]

It must be noted that "equity" as a legal concept has quite different meanings in different countries. An arbitration tribunal called on to decide a case on the basis of equity may always take notice of all trade customs that have developed in the international field. Thus, the arbitrators have almost complete freedom in reaching their decision, subject to the restrictions set by *ordre public*.[125] Also, arbitrators appointed to act as *amiable compositeurs* are usually authorized to decide their own method of procedure. The *amiable composition* clause means that the parties have abandoned, as much as possible, any right to appeal or seek any other legal remedy against the award.[126]

Amiable composition requires the existence of an express agreement of the parties involved.[127] The legal rules of most countries permit this type of agreement, as will be shown later in this chapter; but the Anglo-American countries are an exception, since common law generally requires that the members of the arbitration tribunal be bound to follow the substantive law of a particular country. For this reason, *amiable composition* clauses are not found in international agreements.[128] Still, this has not prevented arbitration tribunals from applying a most "liberal" attitude in the application of the "law." The ingenuity of those interested in arbitration has succeeded in finding a suitable method for adapting this device. The arbitration tribunals simply do not give the reasons for their decision in the award. Consequently, when called upon to review the award, the courts have no way of evaluating whether the award should be reversed on grounds of a legal error. "This simple method practically makes

[124] P. Riedberg, n. 26, pp. 16 f., 27 ff.; H. J. Landolt, *Rechtsanwendung oder Billigkeitsentscheid durch den Schiedsrichter in der privaten internationalen Handelsschiedsgerichtsbarkeit* (Bern, 1955), pp. 17 ff.

[125] Landolt, *id.*, pp. 18 f., 22, 26.

[126] R. Marx, "Entwicklung und Aufgaben der internationalen Schiedsgerichtsbarkeit seit dem Kriege," in Schönke, n. 19 above, pp. 1, 19; Landolt, *id.*, p. 31.

[127] A clause saying that the arbitrators are supposed to act as "amiable compositeurs" is sufficient. Art. VII §2 of the European Convention provides that the arbitration tribunal may decide in its discretion when this type of decision corresponds to the will of the parties and to the law which is applicable to the arbitration procedure. Even without such an agreement the arbitration tribunal has to consider the provision of the contract and the commercial practice according to this article.

[128] Riedberg, n. 26 above, pp. 10 f.

awards unattackable." [129] It has thus proved to be most successful in countries dominated by common law.

Another method that parties use to free their contracts from the influence of one particular system is to designate "multinational general principles of law as the substantive law to be applied by the arbitration tribunal." Thus the parties can free the tribunal from the local substantive law, while binding it to apply these "general legal principles." [130]

This short survey on the international development of arbitration has shown how definite the recognition of party autonomy has been. As a practical matter, the parties have been fully able to deprive the regular courts of any jurisdiction over their litigation and to subject their case to an arbitration tribunal bound to make a final decision based on a substantive and procedural law that is most favorable to the commercially strongest party. The result is the establishment of a genuine legal and economic order outside of government control.

Recognition and enforcement of awards by regular courts

The recognition and enforcement of awards by the regular courts is the only possible remaining hindrance to full party autonomy in the field of arbitration. But this hindrance is limited to those few cases where judicial enforcement is necessary. As pointed out in Chapter 10, the so-called voluntary performance of awards, especially in the field of international cartels, is often due to threatened social ostracism by the parties involved or because of economic pressure of the association.[131] In many commercial circles it is considered a breach of honor to refuse to accept an award as final, thus compelling the winning party to bring a formal complaint in the regular courts.[132]

The rules and regulations of many arbitration tribunals require the parties to waive any legal remedy that might be sought in the regular

---

[129] *Id.*, p. 48.

[130] R. B. Schlesinger and H. J. Gündisch, "Allgemeine Rechtsgrundsätze als Sachnormen im Schiedsgerichtsverfahren," 28 *Zeitschrift für ausländisches und internationales Privatrecht* 4, 38 f., 44 (1964).

[131] H. Kronstein, "Gesellschaft und Recht," in *Selected Essays*, n. 29 above, pp. 105, 111; Mathies, n. 13 above, pp. 105 f.; Reimer and Mussfeld, n. 13 above, pp. 162 f.; F. Trops, "Grenzen der Privatgerichtsbarkeit," 52 *Zeitschrift für Zivilprozess* 273, 283 (1927); M. Domke, *Commercial Arbitration* (Englewood Cliffs, N.J., 1965), pp. 94 f.

[132] Mathies, *id.*

courts against the award. For instance, Article 29 §2 of the Settlement and Arbitration Rules of the International Chamber of Commerce provides that each party subjecting himself to the jurisdiction of their arbitration organization thereby "accepts the obligation to execute immediately the award and to refrain from the use of all those legal remedies about which he can dispose." Under Rule 14 of the London Rules, the arbitration tribunal has to present, on request, the reason for the award, but "no use shall be made by either party of the reasons [even if they disclose an error of fact or law or both] in any proceedings which may be taken or in connection with the award." As previously mentioned, the parties may decrease the risk of a court refusal to recognize an award by authorizing the arbitration tribunal to omit the presentation of the reasons for the award.[133] This authorization is perfectly permissible under most laws and even expressly recognized by Article VIII of the European Agreement of 1961.

The first international agreement to establish the obligation of the contracting states to recognize and enforce foreign awards was the Geneva Protocol of 1927. Article 1, Section 1 of this agreement provides that an award based on an arbitration agreement consistent with the provision of the Geneva Protocol is principally "recognized as effective and admitted for execution and enforcement in conformity with the rules of procedure of the country in which the award is presented for execution." But the award must have been rendered within the territory of one of the contracting states and be considered a "foreign" award. Except under Anglo-American law, an award is "foreign" whenever it is based on a foreign law of procedure.[134] Under the Anglo-American system, the place where the arbitration tribunal undertook its proceeding determines whether it is a foreign award or not.[135] Further, the recognition and enforcement of foreign awards under the Geneva agreement has been made dependent on a number of pre-conditions. The award must be based on a valid arbitration agreement and must follow lawful procedures.[136] It must be considered a final decision in the country in which the award has been rendered. Also, the recognition or the enforcement of the

---

[133] 1965 AWD 353.   [134] Baumbach and Schwab, n. 8 above, pp. 231, 255.
[135] Habscheid, n. 86 above, pp. 36 f.
[136] Convention of the Execution of Foreign Arbitral Awards, Sept. 26, 1927, Art. I(a), (c), 92 L.N.T.S. 301, 305.

award must not be inconsistent with the *ordre public* and the principles of public law of the country in which the enforcement is being demanded.[137]

Other reasons sufficient under the Geneva agreement for refusal to recognize and enforce a foreign award are: the award has been declared finally void in the country in which the award was rendered; there has been a lack of due process in hearing the case; or there was an involuntary lack of representation of a party.

The reasons sufficient to deny recognition or to reverse the award in the Geneva convention are generally the same as those in other international treaties or agreements on the subject. A few notable differences are to be found in the U.N. agreement and the European agreement. The burden of proving that the award falls within one of the categories for denial of recognition in the U.N. agreement is just the reverse of the Geneva agreement. The burden is not on the winning (creditor) party but is upon the losing (debtor) party against whom execution is sought. Further, under the U.N. agreement, a court may not refuse to recognize and endorse an award merely because it may be subject to reversal in the country of the award. This may, however, be a sufficient reason for a stay of execution in the event that proceedings are already underway in the country of the award with the aim of overruling the award. Along similar lines, the European Agreement on International Commercial Arbitration of 1961 limited the traditional reasons for reversal of an award by providing that even an award subject to reversal in the country where it was rendered is to be reversed in the second country only if the reversal is based on expressly stated reasons, such as illegality of the arbitration agreement or a violation of due process. Not even the argument of violation of the *ordre public* is a reason for refusal to recognize or enforce an award.[138] Thus, provisions tending to support private arbitration even at the expense of essential governmental interests permeate these international agreements.

Neither the Geneva agreement nor any other international agreement concerning arbitration awards permits a review of the award for a substantive legal error or lack of equity. On this point, a statement by the German Federal Supreme Court is as true in the international as in the national field:

---

[137] See pp. 424, 431, 442, below.   [138] Bülow, n. 94 above, p. 145.

A review of an award in regard to eventual error in law or fact is not open to the regular courts. It is exclusively up to the arbitration tribunal to make a finding of the fact, to interpret the contents and scope of the contractual agreement, and to apply the law in regard to the rights or obligations of the parties resulting from the contract. . . . Error by the arbitration tribunal in applying the substantive law does not in itself mean a violation of public order or of good morals.[139]

Even an award fully inconsistent with "the binding conflict of law rules of the country of enforcement" is to be enforced as a matter of rule unless such enforcement would violate "in a shocking way the opinion of the good morals and law prevailing in this state." [140]

Development of Arbitration in the United States

In recent years, the organizers of international market regulation found it especially effective to provide for arbitration, including the enforcement of arbitral awards under the rules of the State of New York, in spite of the existence of U.S. antitrust legislation and in spite of the fact that the United States was the only big industrial nation not a party to the several multinational agreements on arbitration and had entered only a limited number of bilateral agreements on this problem.

Private arbitration in the United States has not been uniformly regulated due to the federal structure. Each state has its own rules on the subject, and they can vary widely from state to state. The single federal law dealing with arbitration covers arbitration agreements only in shipping matters (excluding contracts of employment) and in interstate and foreign trade.[141] These rules can only be applied insofar as the litigation in issue falls under the general principles of jurisdiction of a federal court.

The arbitration agreement

In spite of the great importance of arbitration in the United States, the majority of states still hold that an "arbitration clause" is revocable by any one of the parties until the award is rendered.[142] This has tremendous significance for arbitration, since 90 per cent of all arbitration proceedings derive their authority from an "arbitration clause" rather

---

[139] 21 BGHZ 365.   [140] Greminger, n. 85 above, p. 63.
[141] 9 U.S.C. (1964).
[142] Christenson v. Cudahy Packing Co., 247 Pa. 207 (1926).

than from an arbitration agreement.[143] Today it is almost a standard statement of the courts that a decision on the scope of arbitration clauses is to be made on the basis of "our policy in favor of arbitration." [144] The rationale of this rule is that it permits the parties to reconsider their consent to exclude the regular courts. There are, however, some states, including New York in 1920 and Illinois in 1961, that have broken from this common-law tradition and have enacted statutes recognizing the arbitration clause as valid and irrevocable.[145] The Federal Arbitration Act takes the same position as these states. The Uniform Arbitration Act, as it was drafted by the Commissioners on Uniform State Laws, provides for the validity and enforceability of arbitration clauses too and has been adopted by several states.[146] Since a general trend favoring arbitration exists in the United States now, it can be expected that the number of states fully recognizing arbitration clauses will increase in the near future.

Under the statutes of the leading arbitration states, all commercial matters may be submitted to arbitration.[147] "Commercial" is used in the broadest sense of the word to include litigation in the field of patents, trademarks, corporations, and partnership law.[148] All of these fields were originally under the jurisdiction of the regular courts and considered ill-suited to arbitration procedure.[149] But this view is being abandoned today. Problems, particularly in the area of industrial property rights, are increasingly being taken out of the control of the regular courts and submitted to private arbitration for decision. Businessmen, including the organizers of cartels, support this development, for, as discussed in Chapter 12, patents, trademarks, and licenses became an extremely effective instrument of national and international cartels,

---

[143] Domke, n. 131 above, p. 32.

[144] Miletic v. Holm & Wonsild, Myren v. Cunard Steamship Co., 294 F. Supp. 772, 776 (1968).

[145] New York, New Jersey, Massachusetts, Oregon, California, Louisiana, Pennsylvania, Arizona, Connecticut, New Hampshire, Rhode Island, Ohio, Wisconsin, Michigan, Washington, Florida, Minnesota, Wyoming, Illinois. See Domke, n. 131 above, pp. 17 f.; F. Kellor, *Arbitration and the Legal Profession* (New York, 1952), pp. 9 ff.

[146] Domke, *id.*, p. 18.

[147] In some cases the acts provide that the competency of the state courts can not be excluded by private arbitration agreement; see, for instance, the Louisiana Insurance Code (LSA-R. S-22:1406, D [5]), concerning claims of insured persons against the insurance company.

[148] Domke, n. 131 above, pp. 41 ff.

[149] *Zip Manufacturing Co. v. Pep Manufacturing Co.*, 44 F. 2d 184, 186 (1930).

in part through the use of the device of arbitration.[150] Even though there is a special public interest in the field of patents which should be protected by the regular courts and not subjected to an arbitration tribunal,[151] the general development in the United States continues to be very much in favor of arbitration in the patent field.[152]

Form

Arbitration agreements generally have to be in writing. Arbitration clauses included in standard contract forms or conditions of sale are considered valid provided the parties accepting the standardized contract of the other party are aware that such arbitration clauses are usual in the trade involved.[153] Arbitration clauses are also considered as effective if included in purchase and sale agreements, even if these contracts have not been signed by the parties, as long as the forms containing the arbitration clause have been delivered to each of the parties and the contract has been substantially performed by one of the parties.[154] It is not sufficient, however, to specifically subject the contract to the general commercial rules of a particular trade.[155] Even if all in that trade would understand that agreement to arbitrate all disputes arising out of the contract is customary, a provision requiring arbitration must be included specifically in the agreement. An arbitration agreement is recognized as enforceable whenever the reverse side of the letter accepting an offer to buy contains the condition of delivery, including the arbitration agreement, provided the main page of the letter of acceptance contains a reference to the reverse side.[156]

The arbitration agreement and the main contract

There has been a clear tendency in the United States to uphold the arbitration agreement even though the main contract is void or unen-

[150] Kronstein, n. 29 above, pp. 37, 56–57.

[151] Compare Aero Spark Plug Co. v. B.G. Co., 130 F. 2d 290, 292 (2d Cir. 1942) (Frank, J. dissent) with Zip Manufacturing Co. v. Pep Manufacturing Co., n. 149 above.

[152] Re American Cyanamid Co., 1961 Trade Cas. ¶15,537 (FTC); S. Farber, "The Antitrust Claimant and Compulsory Arbitration Clauses," 28 *Fed. Bar J.* 90 (1968).

[153] M. Domke, "United States," published in I *International Commercial Arbitration* 196 ff. (1956).

[154] Re Huxley, 294 N.Y. 146 (1945).

[155] Riverdale F. Co. v. Tillinghost Stiles Co., 306 N.Y. 288 (1945).

[156] Re Central States P & B Co., 132 N.Y.S. 2d 69, affirmed 134 N.Y.S. 2d 274 (1954).

forceable. Originally the U.S. position was the same as that of England: the unenforceability of the main contract also meant the unenforceability of the arbitration agreement.[157] Judge Cardozo in *Finsilver, Still & Moss, Inc., v. Goldberg, Maas & Co.* stated: "If in truth there is no contract at all or none calling for arbitration, the self-constituted tribunal is a nullity, without power to bind or loose by force of its decision." [158] Slowly, however, a change emerged. In *Shanferoke Coal & Supply Corp. v. Westchester Service Corp.* the court intentionally left unresolved the issue of whether a party who repudiates a contract *in toto* cannot then insist on arbitration.[159] In the well-known decision *Kulukundis Shipping Co., A/S., v. Amtorg Trading Corp.*, the court commented: "It is our obligation to shake off the old judicial hostility to arbitration." [160]

Today, the arbitration tribunal has the power and authority to decide cases even where one of the parties alleges that the other party induced him to enter the contract by fraudulent misrepresentation.[161] Judge Gulotta rightly stated: "It is true that arbitrators are sometimes somewhat illogically allowed to determine the validity of the very contract on which their own status depends." [162] The question of the validity of the arbitration agreement nevertheless has been increasingly separated from the fate of the main contract. This is clearly apparent in *Robert Lawrence Co. v. Devonshire Fabrics.* In this opinion, Judge Medina points out:

The District Court held that there could be no finding of an agreement to arbitrage until it was judicially resolved whether or not there was fraud in the inception of the contract as alleged by Lawrence. But surely this is oversimplification of the problem. For example, it would seem to be necessary to answer the following questions before we can decide or affirm or reverse the order appealed from: (1) is there anything in the Arbitration Act or elsewhere to prevent the parties from making a binding agreement to

[157] 171 N.E. 579 (1930).   [158] *Id.,* p. 582.
[159] 70 F. 2d 297, 299, affirmed 293 U.S. 449 (1934).
[160] 126 F. 2d 978, 985 (2d Cir. 1942).
[161] Nelly v. Mayor & City Council of Baltimore City, 166 A. 2d 234, 238, 240 (1960); Amerotron Co. and Maxwell Shapiro Woolen Co., 162 N.Y.S. 2d 214 (1957), affirmed 148 N.E. 2d 319 (1957).
[162] Standardbred Owners Ass'n and Yonkers Raceway, Inc., 220 N.Y.S. 2d 649–651 (1961). Exercycle Corp. v. Maratta, 174 N.E. 2d 463 (1961), remark by Froessel, J.: "The only rationale which can justify the position of the majority is that the arbitration clause is an agreement separate and apart from the main agreement."

arbitrate any disputes thereafter arising between them, including a dispute that there had been fraud in the inception of the contract. . . .

That the Arbitration Act envisages a distinction between the entire contract, between the parties on the one hand and the arbitration clause of the contract on the other is plain on the face of the statute. . . .

It would seem to be beyond dispute that the parties are entitled to agree, should they desire to do so, that one of the questions for the arbitrators to decide in case the controversy thereafter arises, is whether or not one of the parties was induced by fraud to make the principal contract for the delivery of the merchandise. Surely there is no public policy that would stand as a bar to an agreement of such obvious utility.[163]

Here, the arbitration agreement is described for the first time as "a separable part of the contract." [164] This opinion has been accepted in the leading arbitration states and, as Martin Domke has pointed out, is "of great importance." [165]

A similar development in cases in which one of the parties alleged that the main contract was not only voidable, because of fraudulent misrepresentation, but void because of illegality, came much later. For a relatively long period of time, it was the general rule that the arbitration agreement in such contracts was also void or at least unenforceable.[166] The prevailing rule was that the arbitration tribunal could render no decision until a regular court established the validity of the contract.[167] Any awards rendered contrary to this rule were "void and unenforceable." [168] While this is still the rule in some states today, it has been abandoned to a very large extent.

The power of the regular courts to determine the alleged illegality of a contract has been curtailed even more when the arbitration tribunal has already decided on the existence or nonexistence of the claim. An interesting case in point is the New York case Matter of Gale.[169] The court of first instance refused the petition for leave to enforce the

[163] 271 F. 2d 402 (2d Cir. 1959), certiorari granted 362 U.S. 909 (1960), appeal dismissed per stipulation 364 U.S. 801 (1960).
[164] *Id.*, p. 410.
[165] American President Lines, Ltd., v. S. Woolman, Inc., 239 F. Supp. 833 (S.D.N.Y. 1964); Exercycle Corp. v. Maratta, 174 N.E. 2d 463 (1961); Amicizia Societa Navigazione v. Chilean Nitrate and Jodine Sales Corp., 274 F. 2d 805 (2d Cir. 1960); Domke, n. 131 above, pp. 47 f.
[166] Kramer v. Uchitelle, 43 N.E. 2d 493, 496 (1942).
[167] Standardbred Owners Ass'n v. Yonkers Raceway, Inc., n. 162 above.
[168] See notes in 5 *Am. Jur.* 2d §60 (1962).
[169] 28 N.Y.S. 2d 271, leave to appeal denied 30 N.Y.S. 2d 845 (1941).

award on the grounds that usury was clear in this case. The appellate division, however, held that the question of usury was a question of fact and that the arbitration tribunal and not the regular court had the exclusive right to decide this point. Thus, the award was confirmed and made enforceable.

This rule is being modified in New York, at least as regards consideration of the arbitration agreement by the regular court before the rendering of any award. Section 9503 of the New York Civil Practice Law and Rules of 1962 provides that a party may call on the regular court "for an order compelling arbitration" when the other party refuses to cooperate in the arbitration proceeding in violation of his former agreement. It is provided that the court has to decide in favor of the motion, "where there is no substantial question whether a valid agreement was made or complied with." The previous statute did not expressly provide that the arbitration agreement must be "valid." Some judges and some writers conclude from this change that the new word was inserted in order to change or at least to restate the law more clearly. This was the conclusion in *Durst v. Abrash*, in which usury was alleged. The court decided that it was exclusively under the jurisdiction of the court and not the arbitration tribunal to make a binding decision on this issue:

> If usurious agreements could be made enforceable by the simple device of employing arbitration clauses the courts would be surrendering their control over public policy. . . . Moreover, anyone desiring to make a usurious agreement impenetrable need only require the necessitous borrower to consent to arbitration and also to arbitrators by name or occupation associated with the lending industry. . . . In this way the statutes, and, where they exist, licensing agencies, would all be facilely bypassed. . . . If the arbitration clause device could be thus used, all the complicated legislative distinction in the statute civil and criminal, as well as the authority of the administrative regulating agencies, would be avoided by the simplest draftmanship. The welter of legislation in this area makes clear that the concern is one of grave public interest and not merely a regulation with respect to which the immediate parties may contract freely.[170]

The New York Court of Appeals held the main contract and the arbitration clause to be void. They regarded the arbitration agreement not as a separate agreement but as a subsidiary agreement. Recently,

[170] Durst v. Abrash, 253 N.Y.S. 2d 351, 355–356 (1964), affirmed 17 N.Y. 2d 445 (1965).

the problem of the eventual limits of the validity of the arbitration agreement in cases in which the main agreement is considered a violation of the antitrust legislation became a most active issue. This problem became important with respect to the power of the arbitration tribunals to decide their own jurisdiction.

American antitrust legislation and the power of the arbitration tribunal to decide on its own jurisdiction

Two recent cases have clarified the issue of whether an arbitration tribunal was competent to determine if it had jurisdiction to pass on the invalidity of the arbitration agreement because it violated antitrust legislation, or whether this issue was a matter for the courts to decide. In *Aimcee Wholesale Corp. v. Tomar Products, Inc.*, the New York Court of Appeals held that it would not permit the jurisdiction of the courts to be ousted by an arbitration agreement in any alleged violation of the antitrust laws.[171] The holding was based on the need for the courts to protect the public interest:

Arbitrators are not bound by rules of law and their decisions are essentially final. Certainly the awards may not be set aside for misapplication of the law. Even if our courts were to review the merits of the arbitrators' decision in antitrust cases, errors may not even appear in the record which need not be kept in any case. More important, arbitrators are not obliged to give reasons for their rulings or awards. Thus our courts may be called upon to enforce arbitration awards which are directly at variance with statutory law and judicial decision interpreting that law. Furthermore, there is no way to assure consistency of interpretation or application. The same conduct could be condemned or condoned by different arbitrators. . . .

The realities of the commercial arbitration process bolster the conclusion that commercial arbitration is not a proper mechanism for a determination as to whether the price rebate here was discriminatory and violated the Donnelly Act. Arbitrators are often businessmen chosen usually for their familiarity with the practices of a particular industry or for their expertise with the real issues in dispute, which are almost always unrelated to antitrust claims. This problem is aggravated by the fact that the enforcement of the State's antitrust policy has often been a by-product of Federal enforcement. Thus, even if we were to assume that we have knowledgeable arbitrators, who would willingly and earnestly seek to follow judicial precedent, we cannot ignore the fact that many of the most important issues in antitrust law, including specifically those in this case, have never been

[171] 21 N.Y. 2d 621, 237 N.E. 2d 223 (1969).

resolved definitely under New York law. This is shown by the fact that it has never been determined whether price discrimination would violate the Donnelly Act.[172]

In a proceeding involving the U.S. arbitration act, the U.S. Court of Appeals for the Second Circuit reached a similar conclusion.[173] The parties involved had entered a patent license agreement in 1963. It was alleged that some sections of the license agreement violated the Sherman Act because they unlawfully extended the licensor's trademark monopoly and unreasonably restricted the licensee's business. When the licensee refused to make royalty payments, the licensor demanded arbitration under the license agreement. The licensee sought a temporary, and later a permanent, injunction enjoining the licensor from proceeding with the arbitration on the grounds that the arbitration agreement was void.

The district court ordered the licensee to submit its allegations of an antitrust violation to arbitration.[174] The Court of Appeals for the Second Circuit, however, overruled the district court, noting that the question was dependent on the legality or illegality of the arbitration agreement and on the question whether the arbitration tribunal could determine its own jurisdiction and the validity of the same agreement on which the arbitration tribunal was established.

The court expressly stressed that it was not its intention to deprive the arbitration tribunal of jurisdiction on the validity of contracts on account of fraud.[175] The court denied the power and right of the arbitration tribunal to make a determination of the validity of a contract attacked under antitrust law:

> A claim under the antitrust laws is not merely a private matter. The Sherman Act is designed to promote the national interest in a competitive economy; thus, the plaintiff asserting his rights under the Act has been likened to a private attorney-general who protects the public's interest. . . . Antitrust violations can affect hundreds of thousands—perhaps millions—of people and inflict staggering economic damage. Thus, in the recent "electrical equipment" cases, there were over 1,900 actions, including over 25,000 separate damage claims, commenced by purchasers of equipment allegedly illegally overpriced. . . .

---

[172] 21 N.Y. 2d 623–625, 237 N.E. 2d 225–227 (1969).
[173] 391 F. 2d 821 (2d Cir. 1968).   [174] 271 F. Supp. 961 (1967).
[175] Robert Lawrence Co. v. Devonshire Fabrics, Inc., 271 F. 2d 401 (2d Cir. 1959).

We express no general distrust of arbitrators or arbitration; our decisions reflect exactly the contrary point of view. . . . Moreover, we do not deal here with an agreement to arbitrate made after a controversy has already arisen. . . . We conclude only that the pervasive public interest in enforcement of the antitrust laws, and the nature of the claims that arise in such cases, combine to make the outcome here clear. In some situations Congress has allowed parties to obtain the advantages of arbitration if they "are willing to accept less certainty of legally correct adjustment," . . . but we do not think that this is one of them. In short, we conclude that the antitrust claims raised here are inappropriate for arbitration.

There has been no case before the American, especially the New York, courts in which an arbitration agreement was entered pursuant to which arbitration was to take place in a foreign country or in which the arbitration procedure was subjected to rules such as the rules of the International Chamber of Commerce, and in which one of the parties alleged the illegality of the agreement under American antitrust law or under the antitrust law of one of the states, such as New York.

In the opening part of this chapter a hypothetical case was suggested in which an American corporation has entered an agreement with a European enterprise which, under the allegation of the European enterprise supported by a legal opinion of highest authority, is in violation of American antitrust law. It is suggested that the logical conclusion from the two New York cases is that the same injunctive relief for a staying of further arbitration proceeding until the question of antitrust violation is definitely decided could not be decided otherwise than in favor of the protection of the American antitrust legislation. Since at least a very important part of the effects of the contract involved would be in the United States or in regard to the foreign trade of the United States, exactly the same public and higher principles have to govern as did in regard to the application of New York or United States arbitration.

A prohibition enjoining the American party to such an agreement from participation in the arbitration proceeding would have the same practical effect as a stay order. If, however, the foreign arbitration tribunal should decide against the American party on the fraud issue, the problem of enforcing such an award would be of great importance. Injunctive relief in issue could not only be brought against the American party but also against an American member of a foreign arbitration tribunal. It would be up to the American court to determine as fast as possible in a declaratory judgment proceeding whether there is actually a violation of the American antitrust legislation. The development started with two New York cases, state and federal, and is certainly of substantial legal importance. However, the practical danger that may develop here through the role of arbitration and mediation in the enforcement of international cartel agreements will remain much less in doubt than could be expected, on account of the business policy and the enforcement of the determination of these agencies or private organizations.

Rules on arbitration procedure

The parties generally have the power to regulate the arbitration procedure, but a few limitations are imposed by the courts. These include orderly service with respect to all stages of the proceeding, opportunity to be represented by an attorney, and a fair hearing with the opportunity to submit all pertinent evidence in the presence of all the members of the tribunal.[176] The proceeding may, however, take place without a hearing through the exchange of briefs if the arbitration agreement so provides.[177] If one of the parties refuses to cooperate in the proceeding, an *ex parte* proceeding may take place.

Legality of arbitration awards based on equitable consideration

American arbitration practices are quite different from the English practice with respect to the applicable substantive law on the case. The parties may, and regularly do, agree that their case should not be decided under strict substantive law, but rather "on equity principles and in justice, based on the specific merits of the case." [178] Indeed, even if there is no agreement on this point, the arbitration tribunals are not bound to follow substantive law. This is clearly seen in the case *Bryson v. Highdon,* which states that arbitrators are a "law unto themselves." [179]

The institution of "statement of case" is practically never used in the United States, even though it is permissible under some arbitration statutes.

[176] Domke, n. 153 above, pp. 197, 207.
[177] H. Kronstein, "Arbitration Is Power," 38 *N.Y.U.L. Rev.* 694 (1963).
[178] Domke, n. 153 above, p. 205. See also Ruppert v. Egelhofer, 170 N.Y.S. 2d 785 (1958).
[179] 21 S.E. 2d 836–837 (1942).

Review of the award by regular courts

Arbitration awards may be subject to judicial review in certain narrowly defined circumstances—for instance, bribery of the members of the tribunal, excess damages, incompleteness of the award, procurement of the award through misconduct of the tribunal, or the violation of public policy. For example, a violation of the antitrust legislation may be a violation of public policy. Thus in two recent U.S. cases, American Safety Equipment and AMCO Wholesale Corporation,[180] the courts have enjoined the continuance of arbitration proceedings until the antitrust question has been decided by the courts; an award rendered in a proceeding in which an antitrust violation is found to exist must be set aside and hence would be useless. In other situations, the regular courts are rather liberal on this point. A judicial review on the basis of such an alleged violation is limited to whether such a violation of public policy is "on the face of the award." In contrast to the highest German courts, the U.S. courts refuse to review an arbitration award on its merits.[181]

The right of a party to revoke his consent to an arbitration clause is recognized as a matter of public policy in those states in the United States which have not enacted the more modern arbitration statutes, although it is not very difficult to avoid the effects of such statutes.[182] The party winning the award can be fully protected simply by having the court in one of the so-called modern states, such as New York, recognize the award in a petition on the award. Under the full faith and credit clause of the Constitution, the award will then be a regular judgment in form and thus be entitled to recognition in every state.[183]

As suggested, the number of successful attacks on awards is proportionally small due to the ever-increasing limitations on judicial review. New York is typical. In the two years from 1960 to 1962, only nine awards were successfully attacked before New York courts. Three were brought on the basis of alleged bias of the arbitrators, one on misconduct, two on indefiniteness of the award, one on disregard of the statute of limitations, and two on the basis of lack of an arbitration agreement.[184] The two recent antitrust decisions may have some effect on the situation.

[180] 391 F. 2d 821 (2d Cir. 1969); 21 N.Y. 2d 621, 237 N.E. 2d 223 (1969).
[181] See p. 438.   [182] Banton v. Singleton, 40 S.E. 811 (1902).
[183] McClure v. Boyle, 141 N.E. 2d 229 (1957).
[184] Kronstein, n. 177 above, pp. 695 f.

Even if a court does review an award, it does not review the merits of the case. As a result, it can truly be said that the arbitration tribunals have developed their own "law" outside the regular legal order.[185]

Enforcement of the award

A majority of the state arbitration statutes provide for a procedure for the enforcement of awards in the form of a confirmation by the regular courts. The statutes require that a petition be submitted before the regular courts within a definite period of time. The proceeding is a summary proceeding without any review of the merits of the award. The court examines only whether certain basic rules of procedure have been maintained or not. The same reasons described above that may lead to an attack of the award are also sufficient for refusing to confirm an award. Logic demands that the courts refuse to confirm an award issued in contradiction to the principles of the two recent antitrust cases.

Once a confirmation is granted, the award has the same effect as a regular judicial judgment and can be enforced in the same manner. The decision made in the confirmation proceeding is subject to appeal, but the appellate court is also limited in its review to insure that the minimum procedural rules were observed.

Modern arbitration statutes, again under the leadership of New York, contain remarkably liberal rules on the rights of the parties to make their courts the court of proper jurisdiction in determining the confirmation of the award. Simply by mutual agreement, the parties can give a court jurisdiction to grant this confirmation. They can agree on a particular court convenient to them even though neither the parties nor the subject matter of the litigation has any relation to the state involved.[186] This provides a means to effectively limit any objections

[185] *Id.*, p. 669. Judge Paul Hays, U.S. Court of Appeals for the Second Circuit, states in connection with labor arbitration: "There are positive reasons for the courts not exercising their enforcement powers in favour of arbitration. We know that a large proportion of the awards of arbitrators are rendered by incompetents, that another proportion, we do not know how large but are permitted by the circumstances to suspect that it is quite substantial, are rendered not on the basis of any proper concerns, but rather on the basis of what award would be the best for the arbitrator's future. We know also that there is another group of cases, though it is true that the courts are not called upon for enforcement in such cases, in which the arbitrator has rendered a rigged award, a practice so vicious as to be unacceptable in any system of justice" (74 *Yale L.J.* 1019 [1965]).
[186] New York Civil Practice Act 7b CPLR §§7501-14 (1963).

against the award, because when it is a foreign award the defendant debtor is practically deprived of any chance to bring any objection, with the exception of a violation of the public policy of the forum.[187]

Arbitration agreement and foreign law

In arbitration proceedings involving foreign contracts, the question of the applicable law becomes very important. Although the United States is the largest trading nation in the world, up to now it has not become a party to any of the multilateral international arbitration agreements. It is neither a member of the Geneva conventions of 1913 and 1927 nor of the U.N. Agreement of 1958. However, through a series of bilateral Treaties of Friendship, Commerce, and Navigation, the United States has agreed to reciprocal recognition of arbitration agreements and enforcement of awards.[188] Nevertheless, if the claim of illegality is based on the violation of antitrust principles, the U.S. courts may refuse to recognize the validity of a foreign award, even though a treaty exists.

Under the prevailing opinion of the American courts, the arbitration agreement is considered procedural in character and therefore subject to the law of the forum.[189] Writers, on the other hand, take the position that the arbitration agreement is substantive in nature and therefore subject to the law to be applied at the place of the arbitration proceeding.[190] Recently some courts have adopted this view.[191]

Arbitration proceeding and foreign law

The law applicable on the arbitration proceeding is generally governed by the law of the forum. Consequently, the parties desire to have

---

[187] Kronstein, n. 177 above, pp. 661, 695.

[188] In connection with the German-American Treaty of Friendship, Commerce and Navigation of Oct. 29, 1954, see Baumbach and Schwab, n. 8 above, pp. 275 f.

[189] Pioneer Trust & Savings Bank v. Screw Machine Products Co., 73 F. Supp. 578 (E.D. Wisc. 1947); Vitaphone Corp. v. Electrical Research Products, 166 A. 255 (1933). See also "Commercial Arbitration and the Conflict of Laws," 56 *Colum. L. Rev.* 902, 905 (1956); W. Lorenz, "Die Rechtsnatur von Schiedsvertrag und Schiedsspruch," *Archiv für civilistische Praxis* 265, 300 f. (1958–1959); W. Krohn, "Anerkennung und Durchsetzung deutscher Urteile sowie von Schiedsvereinbarungen und Schiedssprüchen in den USA," 26 *Montasschrift der Vereinigung deutscher Auslandsbeamten* 101, 112, No. 69 (1963).

[190] Restatement Second §354; Comments a, b, Reporter's Note; Domke, n. 131 above, p. 104.

[191] Miller v. American Insurance Co. of Newark, 124 F. Supp. 160 (W.D. Ark. 1954); Arnold Bernstein Shipping Co. v. Tidewater Commercial Co., 84 F. Supp. 948 (D. Md. 1949).

426 THE LAW OF INTERNATIONAL CARTELS

disputes heard in a forum that has a procedural law favorable to them. Under American law, it does not appear to be necessary for enforcement of a foreign award that the parties or subject matter have any direct or indirect relation to the place of the proceeding and its law. For instance, in the famous case *Gilbert v. Burnstine*, the New York court declared the decision of a London arbitration tribunal, which applied the English law of procedure, to be valid even though both parties were American citizens and the main contract was entered in New York and to be performed in the United States. This is exactly the type of thing which international cartels do to insure their interests and achieve their goals.[192]

Foreign awards

Generally, foreign awards may be enforced in the United States if they have been rendered in a proper procedural manner and are final. This is determined on the basis of the law applicable to the arbitration proceeding. A technical obstacle in the enforcement of a foreign award does, however, exist. The award cannot be enforced if it violates the public policy of the state in which enforcement is to take place. But in practice "in no instance has an American court refused to enforce a foreign arbitration award because of its inconsistency with public policy." [193] Even in states where revocation of arbitration clauses is considered public policy, foreign awards based on arbitration clauses are fully possible. All that the creditor has to do is to submit the award to one of the states friendly to arbitration and have the award judicially confirmed. As pointed out earlier, this is possible even if the parties or cases have no legal relation to the state. Once the award is confirmed, the judgment may be enforced in any other state under the full faith and credit clause. For this reason, parties in interest within the United States have to use the remedies of injunction, declaratory judgment, or a petition to set aside the award before they are exposed to the constitutional requirement of full faith and credit.

Development of Arbitration in Great Britain

Two contradictory principles govern the English law on arbitration: the principle of party autonomy and the principle that the regular

---

[192] Gilbert v. Burnstine, 174 N.E. 706 (1931); Standard Magnesium Co. v. Otto Fuchs KG Metallwerke, 251 F. 2d 455 (10th Cir. 1957).
[193] Kronstein, n. 29 above, p. 50.

courts may not be entirely excluded from jurisdiction over the field of arbitration. Consequently, English courts can intervene more in arbitration matters than other legal systems can.[194]

Arbitration agreement

Under common law, agreements to subject future litigation to arbitration were unenforceable.[195] Finally, in 1854, through the Common Law Procedure Act and the Arbitration Act of 1889 [196] this legal precedent was changed. Under the Arbitration Act, an arbitration agreement or an arbitration clause "shall have the same force as if this agreement or clause would be included in a judicial order" and may "only be repealed with the permission of the court or of a judge." Under the present arbitration act,[197] "the authority of an arbitration tribunal shall be irrevocable except by leave of the High Court or a judge thereof."

Arbitration agreements may be concluded covering all matters the parties may themselves dispose of by agreement. Those misdemeanors that can be pursued by a civil suit may also come within the ambit of arbitration.[198]

With respect to the legality of arbitration agreements in the field of restraint of competition, the leading English textbook on arbitration by Russell states:

A contract which is unreasonably in restraint of trade will be invalid, and if it contains an arbitration clause, that clause will fall with the contract. But a contract may simply provide for the settlement of disputes relating to area of trading by arbitration, and then if any restraint is imposed it is by the award and not by the contract. If the award is then neither *ex farcie turpis* or illegal or obviously an unreasonable restraint of trade the parties are bound by such award.[199]

No specific form is required in order to have a valid arbitration agreement, but if it is a written agreement, the arbitration acts are applicable; if it is oral, the common law rules are applicable. A refer-

---

[194] E. Wolff, "Die Schiedsgerichtsbarkeit nach englischem Recht," in Schönke, n. 19 above, II, 23, 27.

[195] See Vynior's Case, 8 Co. 82a (1609).

[196] Reprinted in Wolff, n. 194 above, App., p. 73.

[197] Reprinted in F. Russell, *The Law of Arbitration* (17th ed.; London, 1963), p. 373.

[198] Wolff, n. 194 above, p. 29.   [199] Russell, n. 197 above, p. 10.

ence to arbitration in an exchange of letters between the parties or reference in the contract to general conditions of sale or trade is enough to make the arbitration act apply. Thus, it is not necessary that the arbitration agreement be signed by all the parties involved.[200]

The arbitration agreement and the main contract

Under English law, an arbitration agreement has been considered a contract of substantive law. This does not always mean, however, that the illegality or unenforceability of the main contract will also make the arbitration agreement illegal or unenforceable. One of the first principal decisions on this subject was the Jureidini case. The defendant, an insurance company, alleged that the insurance agreement was void because of a misrepresentation made by the applicant. The defendant also alleged that the matter should be decided by arbitration, as provided in the contract.[201] The House of Lords took the position that the validity of the arbitration clause depended upon the validity of the main contract. Lord Haldane pointed out: "When there is a repudiation which goes to the substance of the whole contract I do not see how the person setting up that repudiation can be entitled to insist on a subordinated term of the contract still being enforced." [202]

The arbitration clause has also been considered unenforceable when performance of the contract becomes impossible. This position was taken in *Hirji-Mulji and Others v. Cheong Yue Steamship Co.*[203] In this case the parties had entered a charter agreement, but the chartered ship was confiscated by the government before the charter agreement could be substantially performed. The court found a frustration of the contract "which forthwith brought to an end the whole contract." Lord Sumner of the Privy Council stated:

The arbitration clause is but part of the contract and unless it is couched in such terms as will except it out of the results, which follow from frustration generally, it will come to an end too. . . . An arbitration clause is not a phoenix that can be raised again by one of the parties from the dead ashes of its former self.[204]

On the other hand, there are two cases indicating a trend toward upholding the validity of an arbitration agreement in the case of

[200] *Id.,* pp. 23, 25 f.

[201] "The insurance company repudiated the claim in toto on the ground of fraud and arson, . . . a ground going to the root of the contract" (Jureidini v. National British & Irish Millers Insurance Co., A.C. 499 [1915]).

[202] *Id.,* p. 505.   [203] A.C. 497 (1926).   [204] *Id.,* pp. 505, 510 f.

repudiation of the main contract, which is not a challenge to the validity of that contract as such. In the first, *Woodall v. Pearl Assurance Co.*, Lord Justice Bankes observed:

Here are two separate classes of cases. One class is where the insurance company is repudiating a contract in the sense that they are disputing the existence of any binding contract at all. . . . The other is where the company is repudiating liability under the contract, but is accepting the existence of the contract as a binding contract.[205]

In the second case, *Heyman v. Darwins*, the court showed great favor toward upholding the arbitration clause:

Where there has been total breach of contract by one party so as to relieve the other of obligation under it, an arbitration clause, if its terms are wide enough, still remains even though the injured party has accepted repudiation. The contract was not put out of existence though all future performance of the obligations undertaken by each party in favour of the other might cease. The contract survived for the purpose of measuring the claims arising out of the breach and either party might rely on the arbitration clause.[206]

The English arbitration tribunals do not have the power to decide on their own jurisdiction.[207]

The arbitration proceeding

The structure of the arbitration proceeding is primarily left to the parties. If they have not made any agreement on the procedure, the arbitration tribunal will determine its own procedure. But neither the parties nor the members of the arbitration tribunal can set aside principles of general law or of public policy or of "fundamental rules of natural justice." [208] Generally, the parties have the right to a hearing. At the hearing, the questioning of a party or a witness must not take place in the absence of the other party, unless such other party did not appear after proper notification.[209] A formal hearing, including the taking of oral evidence, is not necessary. The arbitration tribunal may, on its own, question parties, witnesses, and experts.[210]

---

[205] 1 K.B. 593, 604 (1919).   [206] A.C. 356 (1942).
[207] Wolff, n. 194 above, p. 59.
[208] L. Macassey, "England," in I *International Commercial Arbitration* 60, 75 (1956).
[209] *Id.*; see also Russell, n. 197 above, pp. 166 f.
[210] See Arbitration Act of 1950, §12, and Russell, *id.*, pp. 185 f.

One peculiar arbitration procedure in English law is the institution of "statement of case." The statement of case is the submission of an important legal issue in the arbitration proceedings to the High Court. The statement of case may take place in the motion of one of the parties or on the suggestion and motion of the arbitration tribunal itself. The parties may not waive this right in advance. While the legal opinion of the High Court is not absolutely binding on the arbitration tribunal, the refusal to give full consideration to the opinion of the High Court may lead to the reversal of the award on account of "misconduct." If the tribunal itself makes the statement of case it does so in the form of the so-called award case, meaning the submission of a particular legal question to the High Court with the understanding that the determination of the High Court will in one way or another decide in favor of one of the parties. The statement of the case plus the answer given by the High Court in effect become the final award.[211]

The institution of statement of case is not considered by everyone to be advantageous. Some argue that it requires more time and money, and consequently is equal to pursuing the whole litigation before the regular court.[212] In response, Riedberg argues:

The institution of statement of case is not only based on practical considerations, but just as much on the endeavor to remain as close as possible to tradition. Often in England, common sense and understanding tradition develop into an inseparable unity: The so-called special case of today is an expression of the traditional idea that there shall not be any legal proceeding on British soil fully excluded from the regular courts.[213]

At the beginning of the legal use of arbitration tribunals, it was doubtful whether they could issue decrees for specific performance of the contract. Under common law, there was no form of action for the performance of a contract, only an action for damages. When the equity courts were later developed, they did have authority to issue decrees for specific performance.[214] Today, under English arbitration law, the arbitration tribunals may issue decrees of specific performance except in cases relating to real property or interests therein.[215]

211 In re Knight and the Tabernacle Permanent Building Society, 2 Q.B. 613, 619 (C.A.) (1892).
212 B. A. Wortley, *Commercial Arbitration* (1937), p. 4.
213 Riedberg, n. 26 above, pp. 43 f.
214 See generally, E. Wolff, in 1946 *Süddeutsche Juristenzeitung* 133.
215 Wolff, n. 194 above, p. 51. "Unless a contrary intention is expressed therein, every arbitration agreement shall . . . be deemed to contain a provision that

The legality of arbitration awards based on equitable consideration

English law takes a very peculiar and special position on the question of the legality of *amiable composition*. Generally, the English arbitration tribunal is bound to follow the substantive law of England. This is due to the principle of equalization of the permanent arbitration tribunal with the regular court and the institution of statement of case.[216] During the last few decades, however, a number of English decisions have raised doubts as to the continuance of this restriction upon the arbitration tribunals.[217] More and more legal writers have demanded that the arbitration tribunal be set free from the strict observance of substantive law.[218] These writers refer to Rule 21 of the London Court of Arbitration, in which the parties to the litigation waive their right to demand statement of the case and authorize the arbitration tribunal to determine definitely and finally the legal problem involved. This waiver under Rule 21 was found to be objectionable as a violation of public policy, but an English arbitration tribunal may still base its award on equitable considerations by simply declaring an award without a statement of reasons for it: "This awkward, but customary approach makes the award practically unattackable." [219]

Review of awards by courts

An award may be reviewed to a certain extent by the motion of one of the parties to the High Court or to one of its judges. Whenever the court finds that an arbitration tribunal has violated certain principles, they may either remit the case to the arbitration tribunal or set aside the award. It is the practice of the High Court of today, in contrast to earlier times, to prefer remittance of the case if the arbitrational tribunal has erred. Only in exceptional cases is the award set aside.[220]

An award may be remitted or set aside when there is error on its face or because of misconduct of the members of the tribunal. The error may be in the finding of facts or in the determination of the questions of law.[221] If the arbitration tribunal rendered its award with-

---

the arbitrator or umpire shall have the same power as the High Court to order specific performance of any contract other than a contract relating to land or any interest of land" (Arbitration Act of 1950, §15).

[216] Riedberg, n. 26 above, pp. 40 f.   [217] *Id.*, p. 46, No. 9.

[218] H. Landolt, n. 124, p. 79.

[219] Riedberg, n. 26 above, pp. 46 f. (p. 47, n. 6, for further citations); Macassey, n. 208 above, pp. 60, 65.

[220] Macassey, *id.*, pp. 60, 91.   [221] Russell, n. 197 above, p. 314.

out giving any reasons, then an apparent error of the arbitration tribunal can almost never be proven. Thus, this seemingly important power of review by the court is in practice easily circumscribed.

Acts constituting misconduct would encompass violations of public policy.[222] For instance, such a violation has been found whenever the parties waive in advance the right of a statement of case or if the rules and regulations of an arbitration tribunal exclude this right. As indicated previously, this is a violation of public policy because it excludes the jurisdiction of the courts to review the matter. Actually, the number of awards reversed on account of an alleged violation of public policy is extremely small. Another example of misconduct would be when the arbitration tribunal submits a statement of case to the High Court and then totally disregards the legal statement of the High Court.[223]

Enforcement of the award through the court

Under Section 26 of the Arbitration Act of 1950, the enforcement of an award requires "leave" of the High Court or one of its judges. It is within the discretion of the High Court to grant this leave or not. It may be applied for in an older summary proceeding, but the court refuses the petition for enforcement whenever the validity of the award appears to be doubtful as "this summary method of enforcing awards is only to be used in reasonably clear cases." [224] The same reasons that permit the court to set aside or remit an award are also appropriate for refusing leave for enforcement. For instance, in one case a motion for leave to enforce was denied because of doubts as to whether the arbitrator had acted within his jurisdiction; in another, it was denied on the grounds that the main contract between the parties was unenforceable because of lack of the required governmental license, and therefore the validity of the award was subject to doubt.[225]

If the court grants leave, the award can be enforced in the same way as a regular judgment of a court. If leave is denied, the creditor must bring a normal action on the contract.[226]

---

222 *Id.,* p. 332.   223 Riedberg, n. 26 above, p. 42.
224 Lord Justice Scrutton, In re Boks and Peters, 1 K.B. 491 (1919).
225 May v. Mills, 30 T.L.R. 287 (1914); In re Boks and Peters, n. 268 above.
226 Wolff, n. 194 above, p. 60.

Arbitration agreement and foreign law

Whether the parties have the power to determine the law applicable on the arbitration agreement as well as on the main contract is determined by applying the English conflict-of-law rules.[227] There is, however, a limitation on this principle to the effect "that binding provisions of the law, which would be applicable to the contract if the parties had not made provision for another applicable law, cannot be evaded by such an agreement if the foreign law so designated by the parties does not have a sufficient relationship to the contract." Thus, the parties only have the power to subject the agreement to a law other than the British law if they are domiciled or have branches in different countries, or if the contract is to be performed in another country.[228] Mention should be made that the statement of case is not permitted whenever the litigation is to be decided under foreign substantive law. In this situation, the only question that may be submitted to the court upon a statement of case is which law, under English conflict of law, is applicable.[229]

Arbitration procedure and foreign law

The applicable procedural law is usually the law of the seat of the arbitration tribunal. In most cases that will be the same as the substantive law applicable on the arbitration agreement. Where the award was made in a foreign country but enforceable in Great Britain, the award must not have been made in violation of certain essential principles of English procedure.[230]

Foreign awards

Under common law, the enforcement of foreign awards requires a suit to be brought on the award in the regular court. Difficulties arise in these suits, for the general requirements for submission to

---

[227] Lord Maugham in N. V. Handels-en-Transport Maatschappij "Vulcaan" v. A/S J. Ludwig Mowinekels Rederij, 2 All E.R. 152, 156 (1938); Lord Phillimore in N.V. Kwik Hoo Tong Handel Maatschappij v. James Finlay & Co., A.C. 604, 609 f. (1927); Russell, n. 197 above, p. 34; G. Cheshire, *Private International Law* (7th ed.; Oxford, 1965), pp. 192 f.; C. M. Schmitthoff, *English Conflict of Laws* (3d ed.; London, 1954), pp. 128, 486; A. V. Dicey, *Conflict of Laws* (7th ed.; London, 1958), pp. 1060 f.

[228] Wolff, n. 194 above, pp. 52, 34.   [229] *Id.*, p. 55.

[230] Schmitthoff, n. 227 above, p. 486; Dicey and Morris, n. 227 above, pp. 1061 f.

English jurisdiction must be met.[231] Thus, a possibility of ordinary service is required. Under English law, service in a foreign country is only permissible if the controversy involves a real property situated in England, or if the complaint is based on a contract entered into in England or breached in England. Today, the refusal to perform in accordance with an award is considered a breach of contract taking place in England, and thus service in a foreign country is available.

Once the problem of jurisdiction is overcome, a suit for performance of the award may fail if there was no valid arbitration agreement, if the arbitration tribunal exceeded the scope of the arbitration agreement, or if the award is not final.[232]

There has been a recent tendency to permit the enforcement of foreign awards to the same extent that domestic awards are enforced. This has been done in one of two ways. The first is through an extended application of Section 26 of the Arbitration Act of 1950, which makes a mere leave of enforcement sufficient. It also can be done through the Foreign Arbitration Awards Act of 1930, which attached as an annex the Geneva Convention on the enforcement of foreign awards if certain enumerated requirements discussed earlier exist.

The recognition or enforcement of the award must not be inconsistent with public order or the legal principles of the country in which the award has been rendered. There is a difference between the Geneva Protocol and the English Foreign Arbitration Awards Act, since the Geneva agreement provides in Article I, Section I(e), that the recognition of enforcement of an award is not to take place in violation of *ordre public* "or to the principles of the law of the country in which it is thought to be relied upon." English law provides that the award is not to be contrary to the laws of England in the Arbitration Act of 1930, Section 3. This act thus exceeds the Geneva Protocol. If a foreign award contains a decree for specific performance in regard to real property that is situated in England, such a decree would be a violation of English law, but not a violation of the basic principle of English law. Since the Geneva Convention has been attached as annex to the English law of 1930, it can be assumed that the concept "law of England" included in the text of the statute shall have the same meaning as the concept "principles of the law" contained in the annex. That means that only violations of basic main

231 Wolff, n. 194 above, p. 61.
232 Russell, n. 197 above, p. 297; Macassey, n. 208 above, p. 95.

principles of English law shall prevent recognition and enforcement of the award in England.

Development of Arbitration in Germany

In Germany, private arbitration is regulated by the Code of Civil Procedure of January 30, 1877, as amended on September 12, 1950.[233] The crucial provisions can be found in Sections 1025 to 1044, which are much more comprehensive than the legal regulations in most of the other countries. German arbitration law is, therefore, important to practitioners and students of international arbitration.[234]

The arbitration agreement

German arbitration is based on the principle of private autonomy. Limitations of this right refer solely to such subjects as support of children and divorce, because of the public interest, and are of no importance with respect to cartel agreements. Section 1027 provides that an arbitration agreement must be in writing and must be laid down in a separate document. This provision is, however, of minor importance since it does not apply to so-called traders of full status. If the contracting partners are traders of full status, an oral agreement will generally suffice. The term "traders of full status" is defined in Sections 1–3 and 7 of the German Commercial Code and need not be explained in detail. For our purpose it is sufficient to state that in practice cartel members will always be treated as traders of full status because the German Commercial Code extends this term to limited partnerships, corporations, and merchants who do a considerable business.

Consequently, the cartel members may provide for arbitration in three different forms, which will be all regarded as valid. They may agree on private arbitration orally, in a separate document, or in the form of an arbitration clause. However, arbitration agreements with respect to future litigation must refer to a specific legal relationship, for example to patent rights or to a clearly defined contract (Section 1026).

Arbitration clauses may be further inserted into articles of incorporation. Section 1048 provides for application of the normal legal

[233] I *Reichsgesetzblatt*, pp. 83, 533.
[234] E.g., D. J. Schottelius, "Notwendigkeit," in Eisemann, Mezger and Schottelius, n. 3 above, p. 78.

provisions pertaining to private arbitration. Such clauses refer to litigation concerning the relationship of the shareholders to the corporation and its legal organs. Third persons are not bound by these clauses. Therefore, the corporation would have to conclude a special contract with these persons.

Invalidity of arbitration agreements

An arbitration agreement may be invalid under Section 91 of the German Act against Restraints of Competition, which provides that arbitration agreements on future legal disputes arising from agreements or resolutions, which are restraints of competition under Section 1 of the German cartel law, are void. Whether arbitration clauses of articles of incorporation constitute an arbitration agreement according to Section 91 is a controversial issue in legal writings. One writer has contended that Section 91 does not embrace clauses of this kind.[235] Furthermore, it has been contended that Section 91 has been superseded by the European Convention on Private Arbitration of 1961, because it is allegedly discriminating against arbitration agreements on future disputes.[236]

When enterprises use their dominant position in the market to force arbitration agreements upon partners with a weak bargaining position, the question may arise whether the arbitration agreement is rendered void by Section 138 of the German Civil Code. Section 138 provides for the invalidity of agreements and contracts that violate the principles of moral law. However, the provision has been applied infrequently by the courts. The former German Supreme Court has held one arbitration agreement void under Section 138 on the ground that the contracting partners had a different bargaining position, that the more powerful partner had the exclusive right to appoint the umpire, and that the partner in the weak bargaining position was forced to conclude the arbitration agreement.

A second approach to this problem is supplied by Section 1025 of the Civil Procedure Act, which voids arbitration agreements that favor one contracting partner with respect to the appointment and rejection of arbitrators. This provision is limited to those situations where the

---

235 W. Tiffert, "Gemeinschaftskommentar," 91, nr. 8, in H. Mueller-Henneberg and G. Schwartz, eds., *Gemeinschaftskommentar zum Gesetz gegen Wettbewerbsbeschraenkungen* (Cologne, 1958), p. 868.

236 Mezger, n. 121 above, p. 246.

stronger party forced the conclusion of the arbitration agreement and the acceptance of the onerous contractual conditions by taking advantage of its stronger bargaining power. The requirements for this provision are fulfilled when the disadvantaged party has joined into the agreement fearing that it may otherwise suffer economic detriment.[237]

According to the prevailing opinion,[238] however, the stronger party has to be aware of its superiority and of the fact that only this superiority and the fear of economic loss has induced the other contracting partner to accept the disadvantageous conditions.[239]

Whether the provision applies also to arbitration clauses in articles of incorporation is unclear. Many writers and the Munich Court of Appeal have declined application of Section 1025, paragraph 2, with respect to such clauses.[240] This opinion is, however, not convincing. Many enterprises are forced to join cartels, business associations, or corporations because they would otherwise suffer severe economic damages. The rationale of Section 1025, paragraph 2, should therefore apply also to clauses in articles of incorporation.[241]

Finally, the question arises how far invalidity of a contract would affect the arbitration clause connected with this contract. Formerly, German courts had held that such invalidity comprised the whole contract, including the arbitration clause.[242] Then the course of decisions changed, and the courts decided that parties were entitled to refer the question of whether their contract was valid or not to an arbitration tribunal.[243] Today the prevailing opinion presumes that the parties intended to extend their arbitration clause to this question.[244]

[237] A. Baumbach and W. Lauterbach, *Zivilprozessordnung mit Gerichtsverfassungsgesetz* (28th ed.; Munich, 1964), §1025, No. 7b.

[238] R. Wolff, 1934 *Kartell-Rundschau* 19, 23; Baumbach and Lauterbach, *id.;* Nikisch, *Zivilprozessrecht* (2d ed.; Tübingen, 1952), p. 592.

[239] But see text accompanying n. 236 above.

[240] E.g., F. Stein, M. Jonas, A. Schönke and R. Pohle, *Kommentar zur Zivilprozessordnung* (17th ed.; Tübingen, 1953), §1048, No. II 2; Baumbach and Lauterbach, n. 237 above, §1048, No. 4; A. Schönke, "Die Schiedsgerichtsbarkeit nach deutschem Recht," in Schönke, n. 19 above, I, 76, 86; 1939 *Kartell-Rundschau* 288.

[241] Cf. for example, V. U. Meyer-Cording, *Die Vereinsstrafe* (Tübingen, 1957), p. 128; Baumbach and Schwab, n. 8 above, p. 227.

[242] See citations by B. Weiczorek, *Zivilprozessordnung und Nebengesetz*, §1025.

[243] 27 RGZ 378, 393.

[244] See the survey of literature in Baumbach and Schwab, n. 8 above, p. 65. Details of the dogmatic construction, especially the application of BGB §139, are found in W. Lorenz, "Rechtsnatur von Schiedsvertrag und Schiedsspruch," 157

Hence the arbitration agreement has become a legal institution entirely independent of the substantive provisions of the contract in issue. This is even true where the arbitration tribunal would have to decide whether the main contract and the arbitration agreement are rendered void by German cartel provisions.[245]

The arbitral procedure

According to Section 1034, paragraph 2, the arbitral procedure will be determined by the arbitrators if the agreement does not contain any special provisions. The arbitrators may act like an ordinary court, even though they are not bound by the German Code of Civil Procedure. They cannot, however, enforce the appearance of witnesses before them or administer oaths (Article 1035). Furthermore, the parties are entitled to be represented by legal counsel (Section 1034, paragraph 1).

German arbitrators are not committed to apply German substantive law, except where this law is of a compulsory nature. Nevertheless, they usually adjudicate in conformity with German law, since they hold decisions based on these rules to be equitable.

In general, arbitration awards cannot be reviewed by the state courts unless the contracting parties have so provided. Only in very special cases will recourse to a state court be permitted without consent of the parties. Under Section 1041 of the Civil Procedure Act, the courts have jurisdiction (1) if there was no valid arbitration agreement or if the proceedings suffered from any other procedural irregularity; (2) if the award is incompatible with moral law or public policy; (3) if a party has been denied the right of properly presenting its case; or (4) if the award does not state the reasons on which it is based unless the parties have expressly assented to this proceeding.

Enforcement of German and foreign arbitration awards

Arbitration awards can only be enforced with the assistance of the competent German state court, according to the general provisions of the German Civil Procedure Act. The court can decline the applica-

---

Archiv für die civilistische Praxis 289 f. (1958–1959); K. H. Schwab, "Die Entscheidung des Schiedsgerichts über seine eigene Zuständigkeit," 1961 *Konkurs-, Treuhand- und Schiedsgerichtswesen* 17, 19.

[245] "Wirtschaft und Wettbewerb, Entscheidungssammlung zum Kartellrecht," *Bundesgerichtshof*, pp. 523, 526 f., 597, 602.

tion for enforcement only in very exceptional cases, which are out-lined in Section 1041 of the Civil Procedure Act. This is true with respect to German and foreign arbitration awards alike, because Section 1044 provides that foreign arbitration awards are principally reviewed and enforced through the same provisions that pertain to awards handed down by a German arbitration tribunal. Recognition of foreign awards does not demand reciprocity, and they can only be set aside in certain cases. German courts may merely declare a foreign award unenforceable if the award is invalid, if its enforcement would be contrary to public policy, or if one party was not given proper opportunity to defend itself in the arbitration proceedings.

Development of Arbitration in Switzerland

A considerable number of international cartels have chosen Switzerland as their headquarters or, at least, as the seat of their arbitration courts. Arbitration is generally considered to be a procedural matter and thus is subject to the law of the various cantons. Thus, a discussion of Swiss law pertaining to arbitration must encompass twenty-five systems of regulations that sometimes differ considerably.

Agreement to establish jurisdiction

The procedural provisions of all cantons provide for two different kinds of arbitration agreements, the arbitration contract and the arbitration clause. The parties can agree to establish jurisdiction in one of these two ways, but only in completely private matters where no public interests are involved.[246] The most extended application of arbitration is to be found with respect to monetary obligations, including the liquidation of companies, litigation on patents, and unfair competition.[247]

A new, more sceptical attitude toward arbitration is established in the recent cartel law put into force in 1964.[248] Article 15 of this law declares that all agreements providing for arbitration in the settlement of cartel obligations are illegal if they do not reserve the right for each

---

[246] Cf. *Zivilprozessordnung* Zürich, §359, reprinted in the appendix to M. Vischer, "Die Schiedsgerichtsbarkeit in Zivil- und Handelssachen in der Schweiz," in Schönke, n. 19 above, p. 128.

[247] Cf. M. Guldener, "Switzerland," in I *International Commercial Arbitration* 438, 441 (1956).

[248] Cf. 1 *Schweizerisches Bundesblatt* 1 (1963); Bekanntmachungen des Schweizerischen Bundesrates, Feb. 7, 1964, in *Amtliche Sammlung*, p. 53 (1964).

member to invoke jurisdiction of the regular courts. There are some exceptions to this basic rule, however. One exemption pertains to international cartels if the cartel agreement has provided for the jurisdiction of an international arbitration tribunal.

As a rule, the parties must establish the competence of the arbitration tribunal by a writing. Some cantons do not allow any exceptions to this rule.[249] In several cantons, an arbitration contract must specify certain details such as the appointment of the arbitrators. They cannot be appointed later, when a dispute arises.[250]

The same rules also apply to arbitration clauses. A special question arises when such clauses are made part of the charter of a corporation. The problem is whether members who joined the corporation after its establishment are bound by a clause that, in most cases, they never signed.[251]

Generally, an arbitration agreement is held to be invalid if one party reserved such a strong position for itself in the arbitral procedure that the arbitration tribunal can no longer be considered unbiased, as, for example, when one party has a greater influence in the appointment of the arbitration court than the other.[252] Thus, the executive board of any union or association can never be the arbitration court in cases between the union itself and its members.[253] The Swiss Supreme Court has taken a very strict position on such questions for many years, and its position has evoked some criticism.[254]

The substantive contract and the arbitration agreement

Even if the arbitration agreement is made part of the whole contract, the Supreme Court nevertheless considers the arbitration agreement as an independent part, of purely procedural character, which is separated from the question of the validity of the remaining parts of the contract.[255] The Court stated that even the question of whether

---

[249] E.g., Art. 381, ¶1, *Zivilprozessordnung* Bern, reprinted in appendix to Vischer, n. 246 above, p. 130.

[250] Cf. *id.*, ¶2, *Zivilprozessordnung* Luzern, reprinted in appendix to Vischer, *id.*, p. 132.

[251] E.g., *Zivilprozessordnung* Zürich §361; Art. 385 *Zivilprozessordnung* Bern; M. Guldener, "Die Gerichtsbaarkeit der Wirtschaftsverbände," 71 *Zeitschrift für schweizerisches Recht* 254a, No. 62 (1952).

[252] Guldener, *id.*, p. 254 a.   [253] Cf. *id.*, p. 255a; 57 I BGE 205; 67 I BGE 214.
[254] 72 I BGE 88; 76 I BGE 93; Guldener, n. 251 above, pp. 240a ff.
[255] Cf. Vischer, n. 246 above, p. 104; 41 II BGE 534, 537, 538.

the whole substantive contract is valid or not does not affect the related arbitration contract.[256]

Originally, the arbitration courts did not have the discretion to decide whether they were competent to decide a particular case.[257] Some cantons, however, changed this restrictive attitude and permitted their arbitration courts to decide this question; however, the determination is subject to judicial review in all cases.[258]

Proceedings

The parties usually have the right to determine the procedures to be followed by the arbitration tribunal. If this is not specified, most cantons provide that the tribunal can establish its own procedures.[259] Some cantons require the arbitration tribunal in such cases to act under the procedural rules established for the regular courts.[260] However the procedures are determined, the Swiss Supreme Court has developed some basic principles that must be guaranteed in each proceeding: appropriate notice of the proceedings must be given; each party must be assured of the right to be heard by the tribunal, the right to equal treatment, and the right to legal counsel;[261] and a transcript of the entire proceedings must be made.[262]

An arbitration tribunal has the power to subpoena witnesses; however, it must obtain the order of a civil court to enforce the subpoena.

The possibility of equity decisions

The parties generally have the right to waive their rights under substantive laws in order to enable the courts to decide a case solely on equitable principles. In three cantons, the arbitration tribunals apply the substantive laws only upon express request of the parties involved.

---

[256] 59 I BGE 177, 179.
[257] Cf. M. Guldener, *Das schweizerische Zivilprozessrecht* (Zurich, 1948), II, 521; A. F. Schnitzer, *Handbuch des internationale Privatrechts* (Basel, 1958–1959). II, 879 f.
[258] Cf. Vischer, n. 246 above, p. 104; Schnitzer, *id.*
[259] E.g., *Zivilprozessordnung* Zürich §364, No. 2.
[260] E.g., *Zivilprozessordnung* Bern, Art. 387.
[261] Cf. Guldener, n. 257 above, p. 445, No. 22.
[262] Cf. Vischer, n. 246 above, p. 115; Guldener, n. 247 above, pp. 438, 445.

Judicial review of arbitration decisions

Judicial review of an arbitration decision in Swiss law can proceed along three different lines: [263] (1) Appeal is used to correct an error concerning the substantive law; if the appeal succeeds, the former decision is replaced by a new one. (2) Annulment is used to correct a formal error; if it succeeds, the former decision is suspended and the lower court may have to start a new trial. (3) Reinstatement (*restitutio in integram*) is to be used if new and significant facts (which existed at the time of the trial but were not known to the losing party) are discovered only after the decision; if the court grants reinstatement, it can either decide by itself or refer the case to the arbitration tribunal for a new hearing.

Annulment is the main legal remedy against decisions of arbitration courts. No party can ever renounce in advance its right to seek a subsequent annulment. Each canton has its own rules with respect to an annulment of an arbitral award, but the differences are minor. The principal grounds are the lack of a wild arbitration agreement, the biased composition of the arbitration court, or violation of procedural rights, such as the refusal to hear the arguments of one party. Violation of the *ordre public* principle is sufficient reason for granting an annulment trial. This rule is considered to be inherent in all laws, and only one canton (Basel-Land, paragraph 258) names it expressly.

The possibility of correcting a substantively wrong decision is recognized only by a few cantons if the arbitration decision is in clear and obvious contradiction to the statutory laws.

Enforcement of awards

As a rule, each canton permits the enforcement of an arbitration decision issued in another canton. However, most cantons request a preliminary formal approval by the competent court of the canton in which the decision is sought to be enforced. This proceeding normally is called *execuatur*.

Arbitration contract and foreign law

The problem of which law to apply arises in Switzerland in international as well as intercantonal cases. As already stated above, the

[263] Vischer, *id.*, pp. 118 f.; A. Heusler, *Der Zivilprozess in der Schweiz* (Mannheim, 1923), pp. 150 f.

arbitration contract is normally subject to the same law as the arbitration proceeding. The Swiss Supreme Court stated in 1931 that the formal aspect of an arbitration contract must be considered under the principle *locus regit actum*, i.e., an arbitration contract is valid not only if it complies with the formal requirements of the place of contracting, but also if it complies with the corresponding requirements of the (other) law where the contract is supposed to have its effects.[264]
One influential European scholar has suggested that the validity of an arbitration agreement is a question of substantive law and that the only exception to this rule concerns the provision under which the parties agree to bring possible disputes before an arbitration tribunal.[265]

Proceedings in arbitration trials and foreign law

The seat of the arbitration court determines the applicable procedural law. This rule first was recognized only for permanent arbitration tribunals, but it was later extended to all such tribunals.[266] Only a minority of writers claim that the parties should have the right to choose the applicable procedural law. [267]

The seat of a permanent arbitration tribunal is subject to the law of this permanent body. The parties designate a special seat and thus a special procedure. If they establish a nonpermanent arbitration tribunal, however, they can, in effect, designate any seat for this court and thus are able to choose the proceedings according to their own will.[268] One influential writer has suggested some limitations upon this far-reaching theory that the parties are completely free in choosing the seat of the tribunal; if the parties have not determined the seat of the arbitration tribunal, then it is free to choose its seat by itself.[269]

---

[264] 57 I BGE 295, 303 f.; cf., for example, 76 I BGE 338, 349.

[265] Schnitzer, n. 257 above, p. 878.

[266] 57 I BGE 295, 301; 76 I BGE 338, 349; M. Guldener, *Das internationale und interkantonale Zivilprozessrecht der Schweiz* (Zurich, 1951), p. 108; Guldener, n. 251 above, p. 230a; Guldener, n. 247 above, pp. 438, 441; Schnitzer, n. 257 above, p. 748.

[267] Vischer, n. 246 above, p. 111; Guldener, n. 247 above, p. 441.

[268] Guldener, *Das internationale und interkantonale Zivilprozessrecht der Schweiz*, n. 266 above, p. 109.

[269] *Id.*, p. 109, n. 82.

Foreign arbitration decisions

The enforcement of foreign arbitration awards differs in the various cantons.[270] Most cantons permit enforcement if (1) the arbitration agreement is valid; (2) the procedural laws of the canton provide for the execution of such awards; and (3) no special reason exists to prevent the enforcement because the decision originates from a foreign body. It should be noted that some cantons will enforce foreign awards only if the foreign jurisdiction accords similar treatment to Swiss awards. The law on this point is not settled at the present time.[271]

The enforcement of foreign arbitration awards may be refused on the basis of public order or as a violation of moral law. The Swiss Supreme Court has refused to order a particular canton to enforce an arbitration decision in a case of speculation. The court, however, decided that the violation of a foreign economical statutory regulation would generally not consist in an impairment of the *ordre public*.[272]

The *ordre public* principle has its basic importance in safeguarding an unbiased (foreign) arbitration tribunal and the equal treatment of the parties. Several cases have considered the question whether an arbitration tribunal whose members are appointed by the Chamber of Commerce of only one country (the other party having failed to designate an arbitrator) is unbiased. The Swiss Supreme Court considered this problem as an aspect of the *ordre public* principle and declared that such an arbitration tribunal still must be considered neutral and its decisions therefore valid.[273] The position of the court, however, has been criticized by a number of writers.[274]

Mediation

A second way to resolve disputes arising within the international cartel, without recourse to the regular courts, is by mediation. Quite

[270] According to, among others, Schnitzer, n. 257 above, p. 884, foreign arbitration awards are those which are issued abroad.

[271] Guldener, n. 268 above, pp. 111 f.; Guldener, n. 257 above, p. 532; Guldener, n. 4 above, p. 451; cf. Vischer, n. 4 above, pp. 125 f.

[272] 61 I BGE 275; 72 I BGE 276; 76 I BGE 128.

[273] Reprinted in 1958 AWD 184 f.; 84 I BGE 39.

[274] E.g., H. Nef, "Unabhängige Schiedsgerichte": *Fragen des Verfahrens- und Kollisionsrechtes, Festschrift zum 70. Geburtstag von Hans Fritzsche* (Zurich, 1952), pp. 105 ff.; K. Bloch, "Die Anwendung der Vorbehalts- (ordre public) Klausel bei Vollstreckung ausländischer Schiedsgerichtsurteile in der Schweiz," 56 Schweizerische Juristenzeitung 337 ff. (1960).

often mediation is the first phase in the attempt to reach a solution of disputes within the cartel. Formal arbitration takes place only if the parties are unable to reach a compromise through the informal means of mediation. There are, however, real divisions of tasks and powers between mediation panels and arbitration tribunals. Resolution of "political" questions is often reserved for mediation. This includes questions regarding a change in the planned purposes of the cartel, the adaptation to new cartel legislation, or the decision to appropriate action with respect to outsiders. Arbitration proceedings are more often used to resolve the daily problems of administration and management within the cartel.

Some cartel agreements provide mediation as the exclusive remedy for disagreements within the cartel. The parties thus are obligated to resolve all differences through this device. The agreement will usually establish a special institution and procedure for assisting in achieving this compromise. A number of large international organizations have established such institutions and have provided for such compromise procedures. Cartel organizations have quite often made use of their facilities. For instance, the International Chamber of Commerce provides a mediation procedure for the settlement of all controversies submitted to it.[275] This compromise procedure has proven to be very effective in business practice. The Guide to International Chamber of Commerce Arbitration, published in 1962, reports that an average of 18 per cent of all patent cases have been resolved in this manner. Even higher percentages were reported in earlier publications.[276] In addition to these figures, about 40 per cent of the cases in litigation were resolved by direct settlement between the parties, after notice had been served that one of the parties had called upon the International Chamber of Commerce for use of its facilities. Thus, it is evident that the compromises arranged are not always entirely voluntary.

The mediation procedure is gaining wider acceptance because of its general lack of formal requirements. For that reason, arbitration has lost some importance in modern international cartels. In controversies that are not legal in nature, the cartel members very often prefer a procedure without the appearance of a regular judicial proceeding

[275] Art. 1–5 of the regulation reprinted in the appendix to Baumbach and Schwab, n. 8 above, pp. 355 f.

[276] See citations in E. J. Cohn, "The Rules of Arbitration of the International Chamber of Commerce," 13 *Int. and Comp. L.Q.* 132, 138, No. 17 (1965).

and which does not lead to a final award. One other type of mediation procedure will occasionally develop in situations where no formal cartel arrangement exists. In some cases of an oligopolistic market structure the enterprises have not concluded a detailed cartel agreement. Their cooperation is based on a mutual understanding resulting from formerly existing formal cartel arrangements. These types of cartels require only explicit *ad hoc* agreements when it is necessary to establish certain specific market regulations.

Under these circumstances, the parties do not establish formal procedures for the settlement of differences. Instead, they settle these problems in each case by direct and informal negotiations. These differences are regarded not in a legal sense but as political issues that must be handled as a part of business policy. This is especially true when the dispute involves fundamental issues pertaining to the entire relationship of the cartel parties. Nevertheless, the underlying agreements are of the same legal nature as in all other cartels.

14 ~~~~~

The Modern Industrial Fabric, on the Road to One Transnational "Market" (Uncontrollable by National Legislation, but Regulated by the Aggregate of Public and Private National and International Regulation)

The reader of this study is bound to inquire how American and European Common Market antitrust and cartel legislation, or that of the individual European countries, can influence or substantially change the industrial organization here described. He might ask what rules can prohibit the abuse of existing national or international private regulation.

Can the Market Be Controlled by National Legislation?

The enforcement of American antitrust law, in particular its application to the regulation of the international market, is basically not within the scope of this study. The shaping and effectiveness of American antitrust law, however, is of decisive importance for the structure of private regulation. There is no question that American antitrust legislation influences the behavior of the international market, and from this point of view it is interesting to see whether the function of these laws is being fulfilled. Keeping in mind the development of international regulation in recent years, we must express substantial skepticism as to the success of the present legislation. A brief look at the history of regulation may substantiate our findings. Antitrust laws are of a special character. They have been enacted to keep American domestic and foreign markets free from monopoly control and to facilitate the operation of an open, if not "pure," market economy. In their early years the Sherman Act of 1890,[1] the Clayton Act of 1914,[2] and the Federal Trade Commission Act of 1914,[3] were slowly but surely ap-

---

[1] 26 Stat. 209 (1890), as amended, 15 U.S.C. §§1–7 (1964).

[2] 38 Stat. 730 (1914), as amended, 15 U.S.C. §§13, 21 (1964).

[3] 38 Stat. 719 (1914), as amended, 52 Stat. 114 (1938), 15 U.S.C. §§41–58 (1958), as amended, 15 U.S.C. §45(f) (1964).

plied against giant enterprises, such as Standard Oil, American Tobacco, and American Sugar, all of which tried to dominate particular
markets. Besides this antimonopoly function of the antitrust laws, the
Antitrust Division of the Justice Department and the Federal Trade
Commission fulfilled several other economic and governmental functions: (1) as a substitute for price controls, particularly as an alternative to the New Deal price control mechanisms; (2) as an agency
of control over international cartels, particularly in raw materials;
(3) as an authority to assure American industry and defense contractors access to industrial property through control of the abuse of
American patent laws and international patent conventions; and (4) as
a collector of vital economic information about specific national and
international markets. The Federal Trade Commission's reports in such
fields as oil, copper, potash, and steel demonstrate the effectiveness of
this device. All of these and other discretionary powers of the antitrust
agencies were from time to time coordinated with the Bureau of the
Budget to facilitate concentration on one or another of the areas
enumerated above.

Under these conditions a decree (Judicial Decree, Section 4, Sherman
Act; or Section 15, Clayton Act; or Administrative Rules, Section 5,
Federal Trade Commission Act) usually had a reasonable chance to
re-establish conditions of free competition.

After periods in the twenties and thirties in which industry learned
to live with the antitrust legislation and very often used new, more
sophisticated and restrictive, business practices, the effects of the great
depression and of mounting governmental control during World War
II gave some hope for a new start and a total reopening of the economy.

During and immediately after World War II the so-called Cartel
Committee, comprised of members of the Antitrust Division, the State
Department, and other governmental agencies, prepared plans for a re-
structuring of the American and international economy. These plans
envisioned that antitrust would play a vigorous role. I speak with
special knowledge in this area, since I was closely associated with
Thurman Arnold, then head of the Antitrust Division, and with others
in formulating these plans.

In any event, plans were designed to prevent the reimposition of
the following strictures upon the economy in the postwar era: (1) the
division of the United States market among several large firms as part

of a scheme to divide international markets in nitrogen, steel, and aluminum,[4] as had occurred prior to the war; (2) the exclusion of American and foreign industry from technogical progress through misuse of the patent system as has occurred, for example, with the air-gasoline invention arrangements between Standard Oil and I. G. Farben;[5] (3) the restriction of access to vital raw materials such as copper or bauxite; and (4) the blocking of capital flows to and from the United States, essential to the establishment of industrial activities where they were economically most justifiable.

An analysis of the most recent decisions and pending cases in anti-trust and in the closely related field of industrial property laws seems to show, furthermore, that current administrative and judicial anti-trust decisions address themselves, in their substantive aspects, to the economy as it existed prior to World War II. This disjunction be-tween administrative and judicial determination on the one hand and the economic structure on the other has the result that, while the decisions strike down particular legal arrangements, the closed eco-nomic structure remains essentially intact.[6] Often its participants merely find new arrangements to accomplish the same ends supposedly prohibited by the decisions.

Today, unfortunately, we find that many of these strictures have tenaciously re-established themselves. As it appears in this study, the reality is often the opposite of what was planned at the end of World War II. We have seen the redivision of markets in the United States, Britain, Japan, and the Common Market, with the same forces also organizing access to raw materials in Latin America and South Africa. The case of aluminum and bauxite exemplifies the process of the verti-cal integration of multinational enterprise from raw material to finished product and the subsequent division of markets among themselves through what we call "synthetic oligopoly." Similar line-ups have happened in copper and oil, to mention just two other fields. The concomitant of this process has again been restriction of access to technology via patent and know-how licensing agreements.

Today, even high officials of the American government admit that only "dramatic new legislation" can give a "chance of meeting such corporate giantism." Several possible new methods of regulation are now under discussion: "a federal corporate licensing system that could deny permits to firms with undue economic power and monopolistic

[4] See Chapter 4.   [5] See Chapter 3.   [6] See Chapters 9 and 10.

position," "a new enforcement commission with broad powers to break up existing concentration," "adding more stringent guidelines to the old antitrust laws." [7] This movement points out the strong feeling that something is wrong and that something has to be done.

Recent Judicial Interpretation of United States Antitrust Law: A Chance of More Effective Application

The structural reasons for the present inefficiency of antitrust legislation become clear if we observe that a substantial number of procedural and legal points that ease the position of plaintiffs in antitrust cases have, for the moment, grown less and less effective in changing the structure of the market. For the purposes of this study, it is not necessary to analyze the question in full; some remarks should be sufficient.

Personal Jurisdiction and Service

Principles and rules prevailing today on jurisdiction or service on foreign business entities may subject a substantial part of the market organization described in this study to United States jurisdiction. The National Lead case [8] and *United States v. Imperial Chemical Industries, Ltd.,*[9] show the first symptoms of the adoption of a rule using the existence of a subsidiary corporation of a foreign business as sufficient basis for taking jurisdiction over the parent corporation.

For a long time, however, in regular government and private antitrust cases the transaction of business by a subsidiary corporation of a foreign corporation within the United States did not give American courts jurisdiction over the foreign corporation. But the subsidiary itself could be made a party to a case as a coconspirator of the parent corporation, provided that the subsidiary had sufficient business contacts within the United States.

However, the prevailing tendency of the courts in antitrust cases—

---

[7] Statement by Senator Philip A. Hart, Chairman of the Subcommittee on Antitrust and Monopoly, in Joint Economic Hearings, September 21, 1971: "Everyone agrees that if only one company produced all the manufactured goods in this nation, we would be a vastly different people and society. Currently we are at the point where two-thirds of our total manufacturing assets are in the hands of only 200 firms" (p. 594).

[8] United States v. National Lead Co., 63 F. Supp. 513 (S.D.N.Y. 1945), affirmed, 332 U.S. 319 (1947).

[9] 105 F. Supp. 215 (S.D.N.Y. 1952).

and in the so-called Robinson Patman price discrimination cases [10]—has been to consider the foreign parent corporation itself as transacting business here whenever the subsidiary is, practically speaking, an agent of the foreign combine and acting under the control of a parent corporation. An observer of modern combines, especially of multinational corporations, is bound to find that parent corporations regularly determine the policy of their subsidiaries in the United States, and that the parent corporation appoints the directors, officers, and employees of the subsidiary and, furthermore, pays their salaries.

The enlargement of American jurisdiction over foreign parent corporations in antitrust cases has developed parallel to a similar enlargement of American jurisdiction over cases dealing with product liability. In the *Hoffmann Motors Corp. v. Alfa Romeo S.p.a.* case (a price discrimination case in which the court based its jurisdiction over the Italian parent corporation on the existence of a New York subsidiary of Alfa Romeo),[11] the court refers expressly to an especially typical product liability case, *TACA International Airlines S.A. v. Rolls Royce of England, Ltd.*[12] The rapid enlargement of American jurisdiction over foreign corporations is best shown by a comparison of the TACA case of 1965 with a 1964 case, *Boryk v. Aerolineas Argentinas.*[13] This wrongful-death case arose out of an airplane crash in Brazil and was brought against a subsidiary of the British corporation, De Havilland Aircraft Company, Ltd. Jurisdiction over De Havilland, Ltd., was denied by the Federal District Court: "It is clear, under New York law, that mere ownership by a foreign corporation of a stock of the subsidiary doing business in the state does not subject the foreign corporation to jurisdiction. Nor may the parent be subjected to the jurisdiction of the New York court merely on the basis of the subsidiary. As long as the separation between the parent and the subsidiary, though formal, is real, the subsidiary's activities will not subject the parent to jurisdiction." [14]

Today this reasoning appears archaic, since "influence" also existed in the case *United States v. Watchmakers of Switzerland Information Center, Inc.*[15] The treatment of "combines" (parent corporation and

[10] See Hoffmann Motors Corp. v. Alfa Romeo S.p.a., 244 F. Supp. 70 (S.D.N.Y. 1965).

[11] *Id.* at 75.   [12] 15 N.Y. 2d 97, 204 N.E. 2d 329 (1965).
[13] 228 F. Supp. 528 (S.D.N.Y. 1964).   [14] *Id.* at 534.
[15] CCH Trade Cas. ¶69,988 (S.D.N.Y. 1962).

its group of subsidiaries as a unit for jurisdiction) in antitrust cases has long been an established fact.

Irrespective of the existence of subsidiaries or affiliated corporations in the United States, a foreign corporation may be subjected to American jurisdiction in claims for damages or for injunctive relief for violation of antitrust laws. *Hoffmann Motors Corp. v. Alfa Romeo S.p.a.* permits the application of the "long-arm statute" under Rule 4(e) and (f) of the Federal Rule of Civil Procedure.[16] A defendant may be served in a foreign country provided the law of the state in which the court is located permits such service. Special reference is made to Section 302(a) of the New York Civil Practice Law and Rules.[17] Similar rules exist in almost all states today. The Supreme Court of the United States has the opportunity to determine whether the long-arm statute in cases of this type where the service on a foreign corporation is made abroad, is consistent with the minimum standards of the federal courts on due process.[18] A certain limitation of the present practice in this matter is not entirely out of the question. It may influence the ever enlarging jurisdiction over foreign corporations through service of subsidiaries.

Another enlargement of American jurisdiction in antitrust cases is based on a new interpretation of certain provisions of the patent statute. In the pending case *United States v. Bristol Myers Co., Beecham Group, Ltd., Great Britain, and Beecham, Inc., New Jersey*,[19] the United States District Court for the District of Columbia and the Department of Justice alleged under the heading "Jurisdiction and Venue" that the Federal District Court has personal jurisdiction over Beecham Group, Ltd., solely on the grounds that Beecham holds an American patent. This patent allegedly had been employed as part of a scheme of agreements in violation of Sections 1 and 2 of the Sherman Act. The patent statute [20] gave the court personal jurisdiction by providing it with an opportunity to render an effective declaratory judgment for the purposes of contesting the validity of the patent held by a foreign patentee as well as for determining a patent infringement by a foreign patentee when it is alleged that the use of this patent is connected with the infringement of another one.

---

[16] See above n. 10.   [17] See 244 F. Supp. 70 (1965).

[18] International Shoe Co. v. State of Washington, 326 U.S. 310 (1945).

[19] Civil No. 822-70 (D.D.C., filed Mar. 19, 1970). This case has been consolidated with the case against Pfizer as the Multi-District Judicial Panel 45-70.

[20] 35 U.S.C. §293.

In the Beecham case, however, the Department of Justice asserts that the Beecham Group, Ltd., while having no place of business in the United States, is subject to service in England under 35 U.S.C. Section 293.[21] The complaint is based on the assumption that the use of a patent for purposes of restraint of trade permits a suit based on a patent or on rights resulting from this patent under the patent statute. Thereby Beecham Group, Ltd., becomes subject to the jurisdiction of the court. The Department of Justice has two precedents in favor of this argument: the cases *United States v. Bayer* [22] and *United States v. Glaxo*.[23] These cases, in contrast to a number of preceding decisions, take the position that the use of a patent for restraint of trade is to be considered under the patent statute, insofar as jurisdiction arises from a case "on the patents and rights resulting from the patent." [24] The patent chapter in this study shows in how many cases of national and international importance the jurisdiction of American courts could be based on this new interpretation of the law.

The Beecham case has another interesting point: The same Department of Justice that brings its antitrust suit on the grounds that a particular patent was used for antitrust purposes alleged that the same patent was invalid because of the fraudulent character of the patent application.

Some Improvements in the Law of Evidence in Favor of Plaintiff's Antitrust Case

The chances of the plaintiff in antitrust cases are improved by the rules relating to the submission of foreign documents or of information on foreign activities, once the court has acquired jurisdiction over the foreign corporation. I refer to the Glaxo case and the statement of the court there.[25]

The broad area in which an interested party in an antitrust case, especially a case pending before the Federal Trade Commission, may request information on foreign occurrences is well shown in the re-

[21] "Every patentee not residing in the United States may file in the Patent Office a written designation stating the name and address of a person residing within the United States on whom may be served process or notice of proceedings affecting the patent or rights thereunder. . . . The court shall have the same jurisdiction to take any action respecting the patent or rights thereunder that it would have if the patentee were personally within the jurisdiction of the court."
[22] 135 F. Supp. 65 (S.D.N.Y. 1955).   [23] 328 F. Supp. 709 (D.D.C. 1971).
[24] *Id*. at 712.   [25] *Id*.

quest of Litton Industries, Inc., addressed to the General Counsel of the International Business Machines Corporation (IBM): [26]

The Federal Trade Commission has challenged the acquisition of Triumph Werke Nuernberg A.G. and Adlerwerke, vormals Heinrich Kleyer A.G. of West Germany by Litton Industries, Inc.; we hereby request your co-operation in furnishing the documents and information specified in the enclosed questionnaire and an opportunity to interview IBM personnel, knowledgeable on the subject matters referred to therein.

The request goes so far as to require

documents or in lieu thereof a verified tabulation showing . . . for each year 1960 to 1969:
   a. The total number of units of each model IBM typewriter, including variation within models (all carriage widths, braille, OCR typewriters, etc., (1) manufactured and (2) reconditioned at each IBM plant worldwide;
   b. The total number of units of each model IBM typewriter sold or leased in (1) United States, (2) Canada, (3) Mexico, (4) each country in free Europe, (5) all of Europe, (6) Japan, and (7) rest of the world.

The formulation of the request leaves no doubt that information owned by a subsidiary or an affiliated corporation (e.g., information requested concerning IBM's non-United States subsidiaries and affiliates), may be included in this request, wherever the subsidiary or affiliated corporation may be.

   This case shows what it means to be subjected to personal jurisdiction in either the United States or in the Federal Trade Commission.

Examples of "Easing of Substantive Rules of Antitrust Law" from Point of View of Plaintiff

   The application of American antitrust laws, either to a foreign corporation or to an American corporation doing business abroad, can be shown in many cases. At present one case, *United States v. Westinghouse* [27] *and the Japanese Electric Combines,* is pending in the United States courts. In this case, the Antitrust Division attacked agreements through which Westinghouse, in agreement with Japanese firms, undertook to divide international markets of direct interest to the United States as a part of its foreign trade.

   There are a number of other new cases dealing with the application

[26] Federal Trade Commission v. Litton Industries, Inc., F.T.C. Doc. No. 8778 (Apr. 11, 1969).
[27] Civil No. 70–852 (N.D.Cal., filed Apr. 22, 1970).

of Section 7 of the Clayton Act, in which either two foreign corporations (e.g., Ciba and Geigy in Switzerland) [28] merge, or in which two
subsidiary corporations within the United States merge. Another example is the acquisition of the Standard Oil Company of Ohio by British Petroleum (BP).[29] BP had already been considered a domestic U.S.
corporation on account of its activities in Alaska. *Federal Trade Commission v. Litton Industries, Inc.,*[30] shows very clearly the new development in connection with the application of Section 7 of the Clayton
Act. The Federal Trade Commission demands that Litton Industries
divest itself of the two German companies on the grounds that this
acquisition not only limits eventual imports into the United States,
especially by the two German companies as independent units, but
also limits the chances for newcomers within the American market
itself. While the outcome of this case may be doubtful for other reasons, the principal position, that the United States law is applicable to
the acquisition of a foreign corporation abroad, is beyond doubt, provided there is a decrease of imports or other similar adverse effects on
the American market.

In Chapter 5 of this study, we referred to the importance of the
consent decree in *United States v. United Fruit Co.,*[31] as well as of the
consent decrees against Texaco, Gulf, and other individual American
oil companies.[32] We would like to repeat the following observation:
All these consent decrees presuppose that a restrictive practice undertaken in foreign countries may be subject to rules of prohibition under
United States law, provided there is an effect on American imports, or
that the American market is otherwise adversely affected. *Interamericana Corp. v. Texaco, Maracaibo, Inc.,*[33] is consistent on the decisive
point: it assumes that American law, enjoining restrictive practices, is
applicable to foreign corporations doing business abroad, provided
there is an effect on the American market.

Consent decrees bind only the United States government as plaintiff

[28] 1970 Trade Cas. ¶73, 269 (S.D.N.Y. 1970).
[29] United States v. Standard Oil Co., CCH Trade Cas. ¶72,988 (N.D. Ohio
1969) (consent decree).
[30] F.T.C. Dorket No. 8778 (April 11, 1969), Hearing Examiner ordered dis-
missal of complaint on Feb. 22, 1972; see CCH Trad. Reg. Rep. §19,918 appeal
pending before Commission.
[31] 410 F. 2d 553 (C.A. La. 1969), certiorari denied, 396 U.S. 820 (1970).
[32] CCH Trade Cas. ¶89,889 (S.D.N.Y. 1971).
[33] 307 F. Supp. 1291 (D.Del. 1970).

and as a particular defendant. Therefore, these cases, especially those involving oil, bind neither the courts nor the Department of Justice in the consideration of other cases. In a recent letter from Assistant Attorney General McLaren to Senator Proxmire, the Department of Justice leaves no doubt that it is entirely up to the discretion of the Department whether or not they wish to bring an antitrust suit. Therefore, the implied recognition of an enlarged principle of substantive application of United States law to "foreign cases" which directly interfere with United States trade does not change the fact that the Department remains in complete control of the decision whether or not to use its improved position.

Elements Hindering Application of American Antitrust Law

Most private restraints on international trade remain effective in the present structure of industry. These private restraints, inasmuch as they are based either on agreement or mutual acceptance, fall within our definition of "cartel." These "cartels" are strengthened by the structural set-up of modern industry on the national and partly international levels which are to a large extent out of the reach of American or other antitrust legislation.

The United States administration, not without support from the courts and the Federal Trade Commission, has increasingly approved, or at least practically exempted from the application of antitrust legislation, acts of restraint directly or indirectly resulting from acts of foreign governments or even from the desires of a government or group of governments. In Chapter 12, we cited the consent decree in *United States v. United Fruit Co.*,[34] as well as the oil consent decrees against Texaco,[35] Gulf, and other individual American oil companies. These decrees contain the express provision [36] that American-controlled companies doing busines in oil or fruit will not be subject to United States antitrust attacks when complying with the demands of a foreign government which has jurisdiction over them. That provision refers at least to those rules on prohibition provided in the antitrust legislation, which are repeated in the language of the consent decrees, such as rules on price fixing, the allocation of markets, and the limitation and allocation of production, sales, imports, and the like. Whenever parties to the consent decrees can show that restrictive practices, agreed to and used by them, are required by foreign law and under-

[34] See above, n. 31.   [35] CCH Trade Cas. ¶89,889 (S.D.N.Y. 1971).   [36] *Id.*

taken as the result of compulsion by foreign governments, or even the expressed desire of a government or group of governments, they are not subject to American antitrust law.

It cannot be overlooked that only American oil companies are parties to the consent decrees. The question arises whether we have, practically speaking, a special antitrust oil law for American international firms, and whether French, German, or British companies, if sued, could refer to the same defenses. It may be especially important, if, under the "license" of the consent decree, United States firms can enter into agreements with a group, such as the Organization of Oil-Exporting Countries, and if these agreements can be attacked under the antitrust legislation on the grounds that they exclude other American or foreign firms from access to certain oil wells. Here the problem presents itself whether or not United States law allows attacks on the participation of the British Petroleum Company, Ltd., the Compagnie Française des Pétroles, or Shell Petroleum Company, Ltd., in the so-called pool proposal of oil companies in negotiations with the Organization of Oil-Exporting Countries on January 16, 1971.[37]

In any case, these consent judgments give protection to important parts of American-controlled industry in the world. Certainly, one has to observe carefully whether, irrespective of this consent judgment, defendants in antitrust cases have a good chance to use foreign governments' demands or desires or foreign law as defense. We refer to the case *Interamericana Corp. v. Texaco, Maracaibo, Inc.*[38] Subsidiaries of American oil firms in Venezuela, such as American International Oil Company (AMOCO), defended themselves against a suit for treble damage brought by an American corporation, Interamericana, controlled by a Venezuelan shareholder. The subsidiaries argued that a foreign government, the government of Venezuela, required in essence the boycott of the plaintiff after the defendant had entered a contract for long-term supply of oil to the plaintiff, and that the defendant had broken this contract. The oil firms answered that they had acted on the demand of the Venezuelan government, which claimed an interest on the grounds that the oil to be supplied was Venezuelan and that the government of Venezuela had reason to fear that the oil could be supplied to a customer in Europe at prices below the so-called posted

[37] 10 *International Legal Materials* 243, 245 (Mar. 1971); see also the Teheran and Tripoli agreements.
[38] See above, n. 33.

458

prices.[39] The District Court of Delaware, as a court of first instance, decided against the plaintiff, on the grounds that the demands of the Venezuelan companies upon foreign oil companies doing business in Venezuela were of decisive importance in the case. The oil companies acquired their licenses to do business and to exploit oil mines from the Venezuelan government under the condition that rules and decrees of the Venezuelan government, especially in the Department of Mines, be expressly and clearly kept. The defendant oil companies alleged that, under Venezuelan practice, a mining concession would be revoked whenever the Venezuelan rules and regulations for the export of oil from Venezuela were violated. These rules, however, were allegedly set up by the Venezuelan Department of Mines. The logical conclusion of this case is that participation of an American firm on the suggestion of a foreign government in a worldwide oil cartel or in American foreign markets would be exempt from attack in the United States.

The District Court justified its decision on the basis of *United States v. Watchmakers of Switzerland Information Center, Inc.*[40] In this case the court had stated that United States courts would not do anything that might interfere with acts of the defendant which are actually required by Swiss law.[41]

Thus, today the application of American antitrust laws is limited by the recognition of mandatory provisions of foreign law or foreign institutions.

The problem of the impact of international law on the American concept of antitrust law was indicated in the decision of the International Court of Justice, February 5, 1970, in the so-called Barcelona Traction case [42]—which dealt with whether the Canadian government has the exclusive right and power to give diplomatic protection to the Barcelona Traction Light and Power Company, Ltd., a holding company incorporated under the law of Canada. The problem of diplomatic protection here also includes the bringing of claims against the Spanish government on account of interference in property of this corporation. The alternative is whether the Belgian government may deal with this diplomatic and legal protection, because the majority of the shareholders of the pertinent corporation are allegedly Belgian citizens.

The court, at least pro forma, decided unanimously that there is no

[39] *Id.*   [40] See above n. 15.   [41] *Id.*
[42] Belgium v. Spain, 9 *International Legal Materials* 227 (Mar. 1970).

general rule as to nationality of the corporation, but that one has to consider, from case to case, which national principal interest has to be protected.

A separate opinion of Judge Sir Gerald Fitzmaurice [43] is of special interest, particularly since Sir Fitzmaurice is a British judge and the United Kingdom has taken an extreme view against the application of antitrust law to international problems.[44] Judge Fitzmaurice points out: [45]

It is true that under present conditions international law does not impose hard and fast rules on states delimiting spheres of national jurisdiction in such matters (and there are of course others, for instance, in the field of shipping "antitrust" legislation, etc.), but leaves to states a wide discretion in the mattter. It does, however, (a) postulate the existence of limits, though in any given case it may be for the tribunal to indicate that these are with regard to the facts of that case; and (b) involve for every state an obligation to exercise moderation and restraint as to the extent of the jurisdiction assumed by its courts in cases having a foreign element and to avoid undue encroachments on a jurisdiction more properly pertaining to, or more appropriately exercized by, another state.

But, as a matter of fact, we do not believe that there are American cases objectionable under international law, with the possible exception of the first Swiss Watchmakers decision.[46]

We will now consider the problem of the act of state doctrine especially in the light of *Banco Nacional de Cuba v. The First National City Bank of New York*.[47]

The importance of the act of state doctrine as a legal problem is growing in connection with the new series of cases involving nationalization and expropriation, and in connection with the subjection of certain enterprises to certain definite rules in regard to their activities and form of business undertakings.

In *Banco Nacional de Cuba v. Sabbatino*,[48] the Supreme Court of the United States indicated that inquiry into the legality *vel non* of expropriations, as there involved, would be foreclosed by the act of state doctrine, which forbids the courts of one country from sitting

[43] *Id*. at 278, 286.
[44] Special reference is made to the British memorandum, submitted to the European Court, in the case Commission of European Communities v. I.C.I. et al., L 195 *Amtsblatt der Europaeischen Gemeinschaften* 11 (Aug. 7, 1969).
[45] 10 *International Legal Materials* 286 (Mar. 1970).   [46] See above n. 14.
[47] 431 F. 2d 394 (2 Cir. 1970).   [48] 376 U.S. 398 (1964).

in judgment on the acts of the government of another within its territorial bracket. In the opinion of the Supreme Court the act of state doctrine precludes the examination of the validity of the act of a foreign sovereign within its own territory, even when this act is allegedly a violation of international law.

In connection with *Banco Nacional de Cuba v. The First National City Bank of New York*, the Department of State submitted a very interesting brief to the Supreme Court: [49]

While the Department of State in the past has generally supported the applicability of the act of state doctrine, it has never argued or implied that there should be no exception to the doctrine. In its Sabbatino brief, for example, it did not argue for or against the Bernstein principle; rather it assumed that judicial consideration of an act of state would be permissible when the executive so indicated, and argued simply that the exchange of letters relied on by the lower courts in Sabbatino constituted "no such expression in state." [50]

This kind of act of state doctrine appears to be an obvious obstacle to effective antitrust enforcement.

Limited Effectiveness of Antitrust Application in the New Business Structure

This study has tried to show the forces that are bringing about the monopolization of industrial and commercial processes, from basic raw materials and technology and services, such as transportation, distribution, or banking, to the supply of the ultimate customer with products and services of any kind. "Markets" formerly independent are becoming subdivisions of a total market, while certain supplementary enterprises, such as real estate agencies or soft drink markets, continue to represent an "independent relevant market." In practice, even these independent markets function independently only so long as they are licensed by the "total fabric."

The structural hindrances to integration are obvious. (1) The territorial distance between continents or countries or cities, or between the sources of agricultural or mining products and the places supplied by them, is being reduced. A few decades ago an entire economic theory was based on the existence of these distances. During and after World

[49] Reprinted in 10 *International Legal Materials* 89 (Jan. 1971).
[50] *Id*. at 92.

War II, air transport of light but valuable goods and modern transport by ships (e.g., special tankers) helped unify markets, not only on account of the speed or large capacity of the means of transport but also on account of their fast loading and unloading. The relatively small impact of the closing of the Suez Canal in 1967, requiring circuit of the Cape of Good Hope, is the most illuminating experience in this field. (2) Technology itself integrates diverse industrial or commercial activities. Each observer has to realize to what extent a single scientific or technical process may be used in very different fields, for instance, in electronics, in the pharmaceutical industry, or in fertilizer companies. (3) The present trend in vertical business integration is to a large extent following the pattern of the integration of commercial activities (raw materials, refining, transportation). The system of modern distribution symbolized by the national and international franchise system, so-called, is embodied in a comprehensive system of integration.

Parallel to and partly as a result of the integration of areas and territories, an interdependent set of rules of a different character has developed, which determines important elements of behavior.

It is fully understandable that the thinking of generations of economists and legal observers has been directed by "faith" in an open-market system of special American character. They hope again and again that the regulation of the economy is only temporary in character.

The "franchise system" in parallel vertical forms of integration is becoming less and less vulnerable under the antitrust laws, whether operating on merely a domestic, or on both a domestic and international, basis.

The franchise system is best described by a citation from a New York State case, the *Triple T Service, Inc., v. Mobil Oil Co.*[51] The case deals with the gasoline station contract as a typical franchise case. The Mobil contract was divided into two agreements, the "retail dealer contract" and the "service station lease." The court employed the definition used in *The Impact of Franchising on Small Business.*[52] "The franchise system of distribution is an agreed arrangement whereby a franchiser (Mobil) extends to the franchisee the right to conduct such a business provided it follows the established pattern." "About 25 per

[51] 304 N.Y.S. 2d 191 (1969).
[52] Published by the U.S. Senate Small Business Committee, Vols. I and II (Jan., Mar. 1970).

cent of all retail sales [and] 10 per cent of the nation's gross national product are operated under this system." Today a substantial number of manufacturers have organized their industries from top to bottom, creating a closely integrated unit encompassing raw-material exploitation, technology, transport, and the like. The retail dealer, even if it is a corporation as in this case, is in a very weak bargaining position vis-à-vis such organizations.

The domestic retail bargaining system is an area where one would expect the American antitrust laws to be applied for the maintenance of competitive conditions. It is not an area impinged upon by foreign governmental sensitivity. The Supreme Court of the United States and all the other courts, following the rule of *United States v. Arnold Schwinn Co.*,[53] had clear legal grounds on which to outlaw the franchise system. The Supreme Court declared illegal per se, as a violation of Section 1 of the Sherman Act, a bicycle manufacturer's agreement limiting his wholesalers and retailers to particular customers and territories. This decision, rather than striking at the core of exclusionary devices in retail distribution, invalidates an isolated atypical structure while, as we have seen, the much more widespread and effective franchise device has not yet been outlawed. One might have expected the Schwinn decision to be a case leading in a direction that would eventually outlaw the franchise device itself; however, today the franchise practice has obtained so strong a hold over retail distribution that it is very improbable that later cases will outlaw the practice. In *Autowest, Inc., v. Peugeot*,[54] involving issues of geographical and price limitation imposed upon a retail automobile dealer, the Federal Court of Appeals, Second Circuit, had the opportunity to present its stand on the application of general antitrust principles and, instead, it fell back upon special federal legislation protecting automobile franchises. By implication the decision thereby "legalized" the same franchise limitation when imposed in other areas.

A foreign newcomer attempting to enter the American market will find his way closed by the franchise system of American firms, which in some cases have the special approval of the United States government. Swedish, Swiss, and German firms have attempted to establish a cash register distribution system in "competition" with National Cash Register, but the latter's stronghold on the repair field has led to the failure of this attempt. Certain National Cash Register distributors

[53] 388 U.S. 365 (1967).   [54] 434 F. 2d 556 (2d Cir. 1971).

brought an action for treble damage against National Cash Register alleging that via its franchise system the firm had developed a monopoly position. The Justice Department allegedly participated in reaching a settlement in the following peculiar manner: The independent retailers were permitted to sell foreign cash registers under the license and supervision of National Cash Register in consideration for which National Cash Register would agree to repair foreign cash registers up to the limits agreed upon in the consent judgment.[55]

The exclusive character of the combination of vertical integration with the oligopolistic set-up of industry proves to be so strong that even the nationalization of raw materials, such as copper, does not change anything for the country that consumes the expropriated raw material. An inquiry into the most recent arrangement in the copper industry in Zambia and the Congo shows the following: The Zambian government, desiring to destroy the power of multinational corporations by nationalization, took over 51 per cent of the Anglo-American subsidiary in Zambia. The Anglo-American combine, in addition to the agreement on compensation, entered into an agreement with the Zambian government for a practically exclusive agency position to dispose of the Zambian copper. In the Congo case, the Congolesian government after nationalization gave the former owners an agreement which, as a compensation, made them in effect the exclusive agent for the distribution of the Congolesian copper.

Foreign patents, whether granted to American corporations or to foreigners, according to rulings in recent cases, cannot be effected by courts of the United States, even if the patents are used for the regulation of an American domestic or foreign market. This issue has to be distinguished clearly from the question of the validity of foreign patents under foreign law. The grant of a patent is as much a governmental institution of a foreign country as, for instance, the activities of a foreign governmental sales agency. A comparison of the ICI–Dupont case [56] with the case *Carter Wallace, Inc., v. United States* [57] appears to be helpful. Carter Wallace, Inc., owns an American as well as a foreign patent for Meprobamate, a combination of drug

---

[55] Testimony of Bernhard Hellring, n. 52 above, at 45.

[56] United States v. Imperial Chemical Ind., Ltd., et al., 100 F. Supp. 504 (S.D.N.Y. 1951); see also United States v. Imperial Chemical Ind., Ltd., et al., 105 F. Supp. 215 (S.D.N.Y. 1952).

[57] 449 F. 2d 1374 (Ct. Cl. 1971).

products containing meprobamate, a leading tranquilizer for the treatment of neurosis, anxiety, and tension. In this case, Carter Wallace demands reasonable and entire compensation for unauthorized use of the compound in the United States. The United States government claimed the invalidity of the Patent 2724 720. Furthermore, the government alleged "that the patent is unenforceable because the plaintiff combined and conspired to restrain and monopolize a trade in meprobamate in violation of Sections 1 and 2 of the Sherman Act and that the plaintiff has misused its patent to secure a monopoly beyond the scope of the patent." By contract dated July 28, 1964, and amended February 10, 1965, the plaintiff granted to American Cyanamid and its foreign subsidiary "a non-exclusive royalty-free right and license under Carter's foreign meprobamate patent . . . to use and to sell but not to make meprobamate to the extent required to make the combination product . . . in any of the foreign countries listed. . . ." The contract listed foreign countries in which the plaintiff has been granted patent rights to meprobamate pending patent application. The 1965 amendment to the 1964 contract added the provision that "Canada is included with the countries listed. . . ." The contract provided that all the meprobamate made and sold under it will be manufactured outside the United States, and it also provided that the plaintiff would cause "our foreign subsidiaries to sell and that you and your sublicenses purchase from other . . . subsidiaries all quantities of meprobamate powder which you and they may require to make and sell the combination products so made throughout the world except in . . . Austria, Japan, South Vietnam, Taiwan and Thailand where we have existing commitments." The defendant contended that the requirement of the American firm and its foreign subsidiaries and sublicensees preventing the sale of the licensed combination drug product in Austria, Japan, South Vietnam, Taiwan, and Thailand violates Section 1 of the Sherman Act and constitutes misuse of the patent entrusted. The court decided in favor of the plaintiff on the grounds that the agreement alleged to be illegal under the Sherman Act was based on foreign patents, was related to operations and transactions outside the United States, and had nothing to do with the United States meprobamate patent, and was therefore not a misuse of that patent. "The contracts deal only with meprobamate made outside the United States by foreign corporations under foreign patents for sale and use outside the United States." It is obvious that the foreign corporations, at least to a very large extent, were subsidiaries and affiliates of American corporations, especially American Cyanamid itself, and that the patents, while foreign, were always under the control of the American parent corporation. It is furthermore obvious that the American export trade and the American international trade were affected by this license agreement.

Even if *Lear, Inc., v. Atkins* [58] was to be interpreted as a substantial limitation of protection of know-how and know-how agreements, the international relations between an American and a foreign firm as to know-how would not be affected at all.[59]

Examples of Modern Business Structure Indicating Practical Ineffectiveness of Antitrust Law

As has already been stressed, the economy of the present day is closely integrated and subject to interdependent rules of a kind very different from those which operated in the time of an open, liberal economy. The reader may wonder whether the basic position taken here with regard to the distinctive role of antitrust or other rules on trade and commerce has any application to the modern economy. Let us consider three hypothetical situations, extrapolated from the latest developments in the area of cartel law. Our sole purpose here is to suggest ways in which the reader might examine any potential application of antitrust or similar legislation in the light of the description and explanation of the total economic structure that is found in the present study. It should be obvious, moreover, that we would hinder rather than increase understanding of the problems at hand if we were to carry out a detailed investigation of the legal as well as economic conditions involved.

First, let us consider what the result might be if American oil companies subject to consent decrees (e.g., Texaco, Gulf, and the Standard Oil Company of New Jersey) were divested, in the interest of the reestablishment of an open and free oil market, of any vertical control of distributors, whether franchised or dealing in any other way with any kind of fuel, gasoline, or heating oil within the boundaries of the

[58] 395 U.S. 653 (1969).
[59] Special reference is made to the article of Henry P. DeVries, in *Columbia J. of World Business* (Mar., Apr. 1970), pp. 92, 93.

United States. Then, theoretically, retailers in oil would be permitted to buy whatever they desired, and in the general field of fuel and the like to distribute any goods they might choose.

As a second possibility, let us consider what might occur if IBM were divested of all patents and licenses used in connection with the production of magnetic tape selectric typewriters (MT/ST), and the patents were enumerated in a special judicial decree. For example, on the motion of any producer of electric typewriters, a compulsory license by judicial decree would be granted to an applicant in return for a certain royalty fee paid in return for the production of each typewriter subject to the patents, provided that the applicant can show his right to use the patent on the basis of his ability to manufacture, sell, and service electric typewriters of an economically competitive and technically successful kind.

As our third possibility, we might ask what the result would be if the producers of aluminum operating within the United States (e.g., the Aluminum Company of America, Alcoa, Reynolds, Kayser, Intalco Aluminum, Howmet, and Anaconda) were enjoined from entering into any cooperative agreements with one another in regard to the import or export into or from the United States from or to any other country, or to any limitation on the extent, method, or quality of production. The same American aluminum corporations would have to refrain from any cooperation with a foreign company, especially Aluminium, Ltd., of Canada, and any foreign governments, with regard to import, export, production, or transportation of bauxite, alumina, or aluminum.

A general observation can be made about all three of these hypothetical situations: under present legal and political conditions such measures may seem too radical, but if they were insufficient to open a market within the United States or in the foreign trade of the United States, any less all-embracing measures would have still less effect on the domestic and foreign markets of the United States.

Integration and interdependence will very probably keep in force all other elements of restraint. The substitution of one element of restraint for any other elements of restraint is necessarily a mutual and reciprocal process. Here we must limit ourselves to making a number of general observations about the mutuality in all three situations and, furthermore, to giving more detailed factual and legal background on the effects of integration and interdependence in each of them.

The structure of the industries involved is of decisive importance: in the oil and aluminum industries there is vertical integration from raw material to finished product. In the typewriter case, the patent and technology has practically the same importance as raw material as a basis for the same type of vertical system. In addition, in the typewriter case we have, to a very large extent, an almost exclusive seller, making profitable sales to the government, to some large business enterprises, and to schools.

In all three instances, patents and other exclusive rights based on technology and know-how are effective, while in the case of oil and typewriters, the brand name, the trademark, and the corporate name have very strong power to exclude any possible competitor.

In the oil and aluminum industries, control of transportation is of vital importance, such as control over tankers in the oil fields, control over pipelines or other means of transportation, and control over the specialized shipping requirements in the aluminum industry.

In all three industries, the system of capitalization of the corporation and combines is very important. Financial power is not only of decisive importance for the development of production and research, but also for the considerable cost of advertising, especially with oil and IBM products. Financial power is one of the decisive points of control in export and international business.

Finally, in all three situations, the supply of qualified labor and energy is important.

As we consider the interdependence of all rules and regulations, private and public, on oil, electric typewriters, and aluminum, we discern clearly the great number of factors which may exercise a restraining influence.

Oil

Vertical integration of fuel, heating oil, and related businesses is closely connected (1) with the public rules on the availability of oil within the borders of the United States, (2) with the dependence of "free" agents in oil distribution as well as industrial users of oil for production of finished products made from oil, and (3) with the opportunity to do business abroad, whether as buyer or as seller. The individual gasoline station is dependent on the supply of accessories for automobiles, such as tires, batteries, or the right to use certain brand names, or trademarks. For two additional reasons, the integrated economy, as well as the interdependence of rules and regulations, the system does not lead to far-reaching opening of the market.

It may be true that, within rather narrow limits, the so-called independent oil companies in the United States could establish "competitive" gasoline systems, but they would be always subject to the limitation of the available oil accessories.

In our chapters on raw material and government measures,[60] we have shown the operation of market regulation of oil within the United States by a special system of coordination as a result of public measures fixing the rate of production in oil wells or fixing the quantity of licensed imported oil, with measures regulating "synthetic'" oligopolistic corporations.

During the oil dispute of February 1971, which developed out of the demands of the Organization of Petroleum-Exporting Countries,[61] there was a consensus on one point: how the American domestic market in fuel oil and heating oil is actually regulated. The difference of opinion had been limited to the question of what measures should be taken in regard to the existing method of mixed private and public control, in order to deal with the present oil and energy conditions in the new world.

The availability of domestically produced oil is strongly affected by acts of state agencies, "in pursuance to the so-called Connally Act (enacted by Congress some thirty-six years ago to stop the movement of hot oil in industry and commerce, in much the same way that the Mann Act was directed at white slavery and the act against stolen automobiles)." [62] The most important state oil production control agency is the Texas Railroad Commission, which is elected "by the people of Texas every two years when one of the commissioners must run for reelection." [63] The procedure used by the Texas Railroad Commission in fixing the monthly rate of production was clarified once more in the discussion between Hendrik Houdhekker, a member of President Nixon's Council of Economic Advisors, and Congressman Silvio Conte on the one side, and Byron Tunnell, Chairman of the Texas Railroad Commission, on the other.[64] Houdhekker insisted that the Texas Railroad Commission should be very careful in setting the

[60] See Chapters 4 and 2.   [61] Compare Chapter 2.

[62] Statement of Byron Tunnell, Chairman of the Texas Railroad Commission, submitted to the Senate by Senator Hansen, in 92 *Congress. Rec.* S 5028 (daily ed. Apr. 19, 1971).

[63] See above n. 62.   [64] 92 *Congress. Rec.* H 400 (daily ed. Feb. 3, 1971).

March rate of production and avoid any "significant" reduction of the low rate of production for the next month. He went on to say: "The state has the authority to fix the rate of production and I don't think the companies would violate the state law, but," he added, "the companies would have to be extremely careful in submitting nomination for crude production after the Connally Law was suspended. Any symptoms of joint or concerted action by the companies in arriving at rates of production would be a violation of federal antitrust laws." [65] The supplementary statement of Congressman Conte, who submitted to Congress a pertinent bill on February 29, 1971, was designed to "end state production controls by repealing the so-called Connally Hot Oil Act." "Without the Connally Act," the Congressman said, "this prorating would be unlawful as an unconstitutional interference with industry and commerce, a field left to the exclusive control of Congress." Houdhekker had indicated that the oil companies would be in violation of the antitrust legislation if after the repeal of the Connally Act they should participate in submitting information or suggestions to the Texas Railroad Commission on the quantity of oil to be produced.

For our particular concerns, it is especially interesting that Tunnell, speaking of Houdhekker, points out: "This same economist then puts on his antitrust fright wig and intimates rather strongly to the companies who buy oil that in the absence of the Connally Act they might be running afoul of the law if they tell us how much oil they want to buy, but he doesn't seem to know if this is only one source of information, on which we base our judgment as to what the demand might be." [66] He leaves little doubt that if, after the repeal of the Connally Act, general coordination between the oil companies and the Texas Railroad Commission continued, an antitrust case would have practically no effect on the nature of the market system.

Parallel to the regulation of the quantity of oil mined in the territory of the United States, there is an oil import quota set by federal agencies on the suggestion of the participating oil companies, as we have learned in the case of the Texas Railroad Commission. In the President's Task Force on Oil Import Report, we find a detailed description of this procedure.[67] Indeed, this Task Force on Oil Import

[65] *Oil Daily*, Feb. 12, 1971, p. 1.
[66] 92 *Congress. Rec.* S 5029 (daily ed. Apr. 19, 1971).
[67] Compare Chapters 2 and 4.

Control has found the quotas unnecessary for national security. President Nixon agreed with this finding. On the basis of this, it can be said that the outlawing of the maintenance of vertical control over gasoline stations by oil companies would not change the quantity of oil available in different parts of the country. There might be somewhat greater opportunity for "independent oil companies" to act as "free agents" in the distribution of fuel, gasoline, or oil. Very strong pressures, however, would work against the effectiveness of any possible decree: (1) the gasoline station, free as far as supply of oil, fuel, and so on is concerned, remains bound in regard to tires or other accessories absolutely necessary for running a profitable operation; (2) under the Uniform Commercial Code, the sales contract entered into between the oil companies and the gasoline station, after setting aside all types of active vertical control, puts the big oil companies in an excellent position. We refer to the dictum in the case of the *Triple T Service, Inc., v. Mobil Oil Co.*[68] This case leaves no doubt that, whenever no franchise agreements are in effect, the rules on sales contracts ought to be applied; specifically, the rule of section 2–302 of the Uniform Commercial Code [69] is applicable. Under this section the courts can set aside contracts only if the "agreement was unconscionable." This Section 2–302 contains in paragraph 2 an exculpatory provision which reads: "When it is claimed or appears to the court that the contract or any clause thereof may be unconscionable, the party shall be afforded a reasonable opportunity to present evidence as to its commercial setting, purpose and effect to aid the court in making the determination." Anyone concerned with the issues of trade regulation must be especially skeptical of this section. In the discussion during preparation of the Uniform Commercial Code draft, Professor Robert Braucher of Harvard University expressed fear that the courts would use the power given to them in paragraph 1 of Section 2–302 to write their own contract, irrespective of the will of the business community.

Within an oligopolistic business society, protection against interference from the courts as the result of the "freedom of contracts" makes those contractual rules which the court considers "unconscionable,"

---

[68] 304 N.Y.S. 2d 191 (1969).

[69] "(1) If the court as a matter of law finds the contract or any clauses of the contract to have been unconscionable at the time it was made the court may refuse to enforce the contract, or it may enforce the remainder of the contract without the unconscionable clause, or it may so limit the application of any unconscionable clause as to avoid any unconscionable result."

indeed fully justified. This means that the large oil companies are powerful enough to make the grant of substantial credit for long periods of time dependent on the acceptance of many forms of restraint. Even without any vertical control the power over credit, as well as the power to guarantee a certain supply, will continue.

With regard to the gasoline station, patents or other technological information may be involved, especially where self-service or up-to-date equipment is used for the purpose of supplying customers. It may be helpful to add here a further hypothetical assumption: How might a decree become effective if and when one of the public regulatory measures concerning import and quantity of production were to be abolished? Here we recognize the mutual and reciprocal function of public and private restraints of many kinds. In such a situation the question would come up whether the oil importer (American, independent, or foreign) would actually be free to import oil into the United States at all, and especially under conditions competitive with the domestic prices. Tunnell referred to such a situation in his statement: "Right now the governments of the other major oil-producing countries of the world have formed a cartel to check up the prices which will soon be passed on to the American customer, and we find the President of the United States being advised to follow policies that will hasten the day when we have no barriers between us and the avarice of the Organization of Oil-Exporting Countries." [70]

Originally most members of the Organization of Oil-Exporting Countries, whether in Venezuela, Libya, or the other Middle East countries, were very much influenced by the governments of the United Kingdom, the United States, and France. It may be permissible to compare this original organization with the Yellow Union. Today they are in a position of a "fighting union." Once an agreement is reached, a situation may develop similar to one referred to in a recent Supreme Court decision, in which a labor union in cooperation with business had the power to exclude newcomers from entering into business. [71]

The new Teheran agreement, and also the Tripoli agreements, give

[70] See above n. 66.

[71] An especially interesting example has been and is the role of the Bundesrepublik Deutschland (Federal Republic of Germany); only one of their companies, jointly with Mobil Oil, contracts for actual production in Libya, and a few corporations have exploration rights there. Compare "Who Is Where in the Middle East," *Petroleum Press Service*, Dec. 1970, p. 447.

guarantees in regard to a certain increase of prices. We refer to sections
3(b) and 3(c) of this agreement. On the one hand it guarantees that increases in the price of crude oil will not exceed a certain amount, while
on the other hand it gives the governments a certain guaranteed minimum increased price. Furthermore, Section 5 of the agreement states
that "each of the Gulf states accepts that the companies undertaking
hereunder constitute a fair, appropriate and final settlement between
each of them and those of the companies operating within their respective jurisdiction of all matters relating to the applicable basis of taxation and the levels of posted price up to the effective date (February
15, 1971)."

We know of no cartel agreements or other price-fixing agreements
between governments and companies in which prices are fixed for the
future without an implied or corresponding guarantee for the "companies operating within their respective jurisdiction." The language
and practice of the Teheran and Tripoli agreements indicate that the
companies now involved will have an exclusive status. All in all, a
decree setting aside vertical control of oil through gasoline stations,
including fuel and heating oil and the like, would not basically change
the structure of the American oil market (even if the present coordinated control of the available oil in the United States should be
overruled).

It is too early to evaluate the effects of the agreements between leading oil companies (British Petroleum Co., Ltd., Compagnie Française
des Pétroles, Gulf Oil Co., Shell Petroleum Co., Ltd., Standard Oil Co.
of California, Standard Oil Co. of New Jersey, Texaco, Inc., Marathon
Oil Co., Continental Oil, Inc., Nelson Bunker Hunt, Occidental Petroleum Co., Amerada Hess Corp., Atlantic Richfield Co., and Grace
Petroleum Corp.) on January 16, 1971, with regard to the efforts made
to coordinate their negotiations with the Organization of Oil-Exporting
Countries as well as with the so-called Teheran Price Agreement of
February 14, 1971, between six Gulf exporting countries, Abu Dhabi,
Iran, Iraq, Kuwait, Quatar, and Saudi Arabia, which were essentially
identical with the participants in the pooling agreement as stated
above.[72] While the Teheran agreement deals with the Gulf states, the
Tripoli agreement of March 1970 deals especially with oil from Libya
and Algeria.

[72] The proposal of oil companies with regard to the negotiations of January 16,
1971, is reprinted in 10 *International Legal Materials* 243 (Mar. 1971); The
Teheran agreement is to be found in the same publication on pp. 247 ff.

The oil partners of the Tripoli agreement are the international market's seven leading oil companies, plus a few outsiders and individual participants. The Gelsenkirchener Bergwerks AG Erdoel has an interest administered through a joint venture with Mobil Oil.[73] It will be necessary to observe the ensuing developments to find out to what extent an "outsider" or a participant in the Teheran or Tripoli agreements has a chance to obtain sufficient control of oil production in excess of existing and proved mining rights or exploration rights to bring it into the United States and thus influence the general oil market.

It has been stated that the oil companies are now operating as a team [74] (the settlements in the first place established the precedent for the oil companies to negotiate as a team). They demonstrate the possibility of strong joint efforts and ended the practice whereby companies were being whipsawed individually by the unified action of producing countries. In the final analysis, they allowed the oil companies to use their control over transportation and marketing as effective levels against nationalistic control over production. It is a question of definition and interpretation as to what the statement of Chairman Tunnell of the Texas Railroad Commission actually means when referring to the protection of the United States market against the threat of the oil exporting countries. It is suggested that we have here three agreements, one among the countries, one between the countries and the companies, and one among the companies themselves. The last takes on the characteristics of a cartel.

IBM

In examining the possible effect on the office machine market of the hypothetical situation we described above, we may quote directly from the briefs of *Federal Trade Commission v. Litton Industries, Inc.*[75] The Federal Trade Commission has challenged the acquisition of the German corporations, Triumph Werke Nuernberg AG and Adlerwerke (formerly Heinrich Kleyer AG), in pursuance to Section 7 of the Clayton Act. The counsel for the respondent Litton Industries, Inc., argued that the typewriter market, especially in the field of the electrical and special electrical typewriters, is controlled by IBM to such an extent that neither the acquisition of the two West German companies by Litton nor a divestment of the acquisition would actually change market conditions. The statement in the respondent's trial brief

[73] F.A.Z., Mar. 17, 1971, No. 64.   [74] *Oil Journal*, Mar. 1, 1971, p. 16.
[75] F.T.C. Doc. No. 8778 (Apr. 11, 1969).

presents in an especially impressive manner the integration of the IBM system into the entire typewriter and office machine market, as well as the interdependence which exists between patents and distribution and the resultant closing of access to especially important customers, such as government agencies or schools.

We shall quote parts of pages 3 to 10 in this brief:

IBM is the leading manufacturer of typewriters in the world. By standard indicia, it already possesses monopoly power in the all-important office market in the United States. With the high quality of its production; its sophisticated research and development program; the effectiveness of its sales and service organization; and its economies of scale in research and development, production, marketing, and repair service, it has the power to sweep aside its few remaining competitors and to achieve a complete monopoly of the typewriter market.

IBM got its start in the typewriter market through its acquisition of the Electromatic typewriter patent and business in 1930. With the advent of World War II and the conversion of the traditional United States typewriter companies to the production of war materials, IBM became virtually the sole producer of electric typewriters in the United States. Starting with this 100 per cent entrenchment of the electric typewriter business, IBM continued to dominate the office typewriter market after the war. Based on the war-time reputation gained for its key-lever, basket-type typewriter, IBM set the standard of performance for electric typewriters at the conclusion of World War II.

In 1963, while its competitors, such as Royal, were still struggling to perfect their key-lever, basket-type typewriters based on an electrified manual design, IBM introduced the revolutionary single-element Selectric typewriter. Within seven years, the IBM Selectric typewriter captured approximately 60 per cent of the United States office electric typewriter market. No other typewriter company in the world has been able to develop and market a single-element typewriter, and IBM's unwillingness to license the know-how of this machine has inhibited competitive development. Litton, for example, was offered a patent license by IBM at a cost of about 6 million dollars, plus other substantial considerations. IBM, however, refused to license or otherwise make available its know-how.

IBM single-handedly has led the trend to new generations of typewriters. In 1967, it introduced the Magnetic Tape/Selectric typewriter (MT/ST); in 1969, it introduced the Magnetic Card/Selectric typewriter (MC/ST). . . . More recently, IBM introduced the Magnetic Tape Selectric Composer (MT/SC), which has the ability to automatically store, edit, and justify lines of type. These machines constitute the most advanced application of the single-element typewriter in word processing systems.

At present the IBM MT/ST and MC/ST, backed by their advanced design and IBM's unequalled marketing organization, account for well over four-fifths of the automatic typewriters installed in the office market each year; it is estimated that the current value of automatic typewriters installed annually is over 100 million dollars.

Concurrent with the growth of IBM's dominance of the full-featured, heavy-duty office electric market and the automatic typewriter market has been the development of the impactless printer, which operates noiselessly and at a speed four to ten times faster than conventional office typewriters. Early this year, IBM unveiled its next generation of high-speed, noiseless, impactless printers.

Technological advances in electric memories, displays and data transmission portend that in even small offices and typing pools, advanced typing systems of the future made up of conventional keyboards, electronic displays and memories, and high-speed, impactless printers will afford such savings in secretarial time and word-processing that they will be competitive in cost with the typewriters of today. The inevitable result will be an erosion of the market for conventional typewriters of today. Although presently used with stored-data accounting/billing machines, IBM's impactless printer of the future places it even further ahead of all other typewriter companies in the technological changes taking place in the office typewriter market. In the absence of effective competition in this area, IBM will continue its dominance of the market through new technology. . . .

Approximately 85 per cent of all sales in the office typewriter market are made on a direct distribution basis, as distinguished from sales through office equipment dealers; and a large portion of the sales in this market is made on a centralized, "national account" purchasing basis. Consequently, to be a strong competitive factor in the office typewriter market, it is important to have a direct national sales force. IBM has by far the largest typewriter sales and service organization in the United States; its sales and servicemen are assigned on a "block" or "building" basis in certain major cities. In the face of this substantial organization, typewriter companies such as Triumph-Adler, which are committed to distributing their products in the United States through an independent dealer organization, exist at the mercy of IBM and cannot provide substantial competition with IBM. Triumph-Adler's insignificant share of this market in the United States is proof of this fact.

The measure of IBM's virtual monopoly of the office typewriter market is its ability to set a price umbrella over all of its competitors. IBM maintains a rigid price structure with sales at list prices. Other typewriter companies, such as Royal, must offer substantial discounts and generous trade-in allowances, particularly on IBM typewriters, in order to achieve any degree of sales success. Sales by IBM are made predominantly on the basis of product performance, its reputation and image, maintenance and servic-ing considerations, ability to offer a broad range of office equipment and machines, and other factors not related to price. In short, it is in the envi-able position of being able to set its own price levels without significantly affecting its sales and market share.

IBM's predominance in the office typewriter market has also permitted it to gain inroads among school and other institutional purchasers of type-writers. While manual typewriters at one time made up a large portion of this market, their use in recent years has been declining. An increasingly important source of supply for school purchasers is used and reconditioned electric office typewriters traded in by office users on the purchase of new models. Since IBM has the largest sales of electric office typewriters, it follows that it also has the largest supply of used and reconditioned office electrics. It is aggressively marketing these typewriters to school and other purchasers through a nationwide network of franchised typewriter dis-tributors. Thus, IBM's dominant position in the office typewriter market is allowing it to extend that dominance into the school market. On the other hand, because of the natural desire of students to use IBM typewriters after school if they learned on an IBM during school, as IBM increases its posi-tion in the school market, it will strengthen its already dominant position in the office market in the future. In consequence, the extension of IBM's dominant position in the office market and the school market is adversely affecting sales by Royal and other manufacturers to school purchasers of new as well as used and reconditioned typewriters.

Royal's potential for survival as a competitor in the typewriter business must be measured against this background of IBM's dominance of the office typewriter market and its increasing penetration of the school market.

Aluminum

While our first hypothetical situation dealt basically with vertical concentration and the second with a special problem of utilization of patent and know-how for the purpose of regulation of markets, our third hypothetical situation deals with horizontal agreements.

In discussing this problem, I ask for understanding if I use my own testimony before the Subcommittee on Antitrust and Monopoly.[76] In

76 Testimony of Heinrich Kronstein, in Hearings before the Subcommittee on Antitrust and Monopoly of the Committee on the Judiciary, United States Senate, 90 Cong., 2d Sess., Pt. 7: *Concentration Outside the United States,* pp. 3651 ff.

this testimony [77] I refer to the power of vertical integration from raw material to final product to exclude any possible intruder in the market, even if there is no cooperation on the horizontal level between producer, wholesaler, retailer, and so on.

Vertical integration is only an element of concentration, subjecting the consumers and users of aluminum to the management of one aluminum producer. . . . Vertical integration of consumers of raw materials into an organization of the raw material producers is a well-known method leading to concentration everywhere. . . .

The interdependency of vertical integration and concentration of aluminum producers in the international market comes clearly into focus by virtue of the following example: Ardal, the Norwegian government-controlled producer (it was 100 per cent Norwegian government), tried to avoid vertical integration which resulted in the loss of its markets in Europe. This fact was one of the decisive reasons for the Norwegian government's decision to sell 50 per cent of Ardal to Alcan of Canada.

In the United States, Alcoa, Reynolds, and Kaiser, controlling 81 per cent of the American production, are fully integrated today. Until recently the nonintegrated users of aluminum were supplied by Alcan. The disappearance of independent producers of materials made from aluminum, as a result of this development, made it necessary for Alcan to accept integration also. Today Alcan is an integrated organization within the United States.

This vertical integration . . . is inseparable from the concentration between producers of aluminum.[78]

As a matter of fact, the full completion of vertical integration in the United States and in Europe would have been enough to reestablish a stable market, but much more was done to assure the permanent prevalence of the private international system of market regulation in which these elements in the process of concentration are but part of the total structure. Other important instruments and elements of the market regulation system in the international field exist:

Contracts of exclusive supply. An aluminum producer who is a party to an exclusive supply contract for bauxite, is no less a part of the total concentration process of the supplier than is an enterprise in which the supplier has a substantial shareholding. An example of this is the Alcan contract with the German government-owned Vereinigte Aluminum-Werke, which supplied about 40 per cent of the West German market.

This and other long-term supply contracts usually run over a considerable period of time and cover substantial quantities of material. A contract

[77] *Id.* at 3654. [78] *Id.*

extending over a period of 10 to 20 years is by its very nature restrictive, as it limits the operating freedom of the parties over the operational time of the agreement. To a certain degree these contracts give the supplier a definite influence on the business policy of the purchasing company, especially if the raw material price is rated as a percentage of the supplier's primary aluminum price, or if the purchasing company has to pay for its raw material with primary ingots.

Access to technology especially in the modern forms of production and of electricity. Prior to World War II, exclusive access to technology, patents and know-how in the transformation of bauxite into alumina and alumina into aluminum, and control over bauxite were the decisive elements of market regulation. Today, vertical integration plays a more effective part, but even today there cannot be any aluminum production which does not use the technological experience and development, especially of Alcoa and Pechiney, at some stage of production. An additional element of Alcoa's apparent superiority is its access to the most modern processes of the production of electricity. Since even the smallest cost advantage in electricity is of decisive impact on the price and costs of the final product, this is an important element of market regulation. The method of licensing this know-how has been described as one of the elements of controlling any newcomer.

The Canadian export price—a "silent regulator." The price aspect of the trade system has been reestablished. The first principle is that in each country the price of a producer, if there is any, should never be undersold. However, short of such a price, the Canadian export price is considered as a kind of posted price comparable to a similar regulating element in international oil trade. Since November 1964, Alcan's published world export price has been 24.5 cents per pound. From November 1957 to November 1964, the price moved in the narrow range of 24.63 cents per pound to 24 cents per pound.

Once more, it should be noted that the elements of parallel concentration in different segments of the world are part of a total private trade regulation system in aluminum. The more we recognize how powerful and closed this system is, the more important the observation of each of the elements, such as the process of concentration, becomes.

Despite these steps which re-created a stable market, two possible sources of disturbance remained: The U.S. stockpile, and the economic planners in the Soviet Union. In 1965, the U.S. Department of Defense threatened to release quantities of aluminum from the U.S. stockpile to counteract a price increase planned by the industry. In 1965, an agreement was reached between the stockpile administrator and the American producers of aluminum, except Intalco, Conaco, and Anaconda, on one hand, and the Canadian producer, Alcan, on the other. Under this agreement, each of the participating aluminum producers in the United States, with the exception of Alcan, agreed to take a quantity of the eventual stockpile releases, proportionate to its production capacity in relation to the capacity of each of the other firms. Alcan's proportionate share was based on its 1965 imports to the United States.

These agreements not only informed each of the producers of their competitor's relative capacity, but it in effect recognized and sanctioned the existence of a clearly organized and carefully regulated market.

A parallel in Europe to the American stockpile agreement is a gentlemen's agreement with the Soviet Union. The Soviet Union offered aluminum at 15 cents per pound at a time when the Canadian world price was 24 cents. Under this gentlemen's agreement the European group agreed to take the Soviet Russian aluminum supply in return for the promise of Soviet Russia not to supply Japan and to refrain from any disturbance of the group's trade with Japan. As a matter of fact, the Soviet Russian aluminum was supplied to Japan by the European group. It is interesting to note that soon after this agreement Japan ceased to be a purchaser in the European market and appeared instead in the U.S. market.

The law school case method has been used to show, through a review of international developments in the aluminum market, that each individual step of concentration, from whatever point of view, can only be evaluated if understood in light of its interdependence with other national or international steps of concentration or with market regulation agreements of a private system of trade.

My testimony refers to the system of joint ventures in bauxite;[79] in this statement it is shown that practically all available sources of bauxite are divided among all participants in the aluminum production. The fact that the other firms among themselves could continue as joint ventures, the effect of complete regulation of access of the reserved bauxite would in principle remain strong. I believe this material is sufficient to show our point: Even a decree as far-reaching as in the example, aluminum would not lead to any substantial change of the aluminum market within the United States or in the foreign trade of the United States.

Re-evaluation of National and International Business Structure: Precondition of New Public Policies on Trade

The practical observer of commercial and industrial organizations, including the legal draftsmen of the corporate structure, finds it disturbing that economists and sociologists, preoccupied with model

[79] Id. at 3656.

building and mathematical formulas, do not give him adequate research of the facts. Modern economists often believe that only adherents to an obsolete school of economics can undertake this type of factual research. The combination of an inquiry of economic facts with the study of the utilization of legal rules and institutions raises the principal questions that must be answered by the combined effort of practice and theory of law and economics: (1) Are legal rules, designated to direct the commercial behavior of powerful groups, effective enough within our society to maintain principles of constitutional standing on the relationship between state or federal government, on the one hand, and different groups in society, on the other, with the aim of remodeling the social fabric of the whole, or at least in part, whenever disturbed? (2) Do actual economic units, integrated by different devices and extending over political borders, exercise power of a governmental character by enacting rules and regulations of their own, and enforcing them?

This chapter suggests that the study in its entirety raises very substantial doubts whether antitrust or other governmental rules on unfair "competition" continue to be practical, or if they ever have been.[80]

In our inquiry, the power of multinational corporations, working in conjunction with many national domestic economic entities, to set effective regulatory rules and even to regulate governmental activities and economics, nationally and internationally, is not only the result of the political and economic power as well as the will of the managements of these enterprises, but it is also deeply embodied in the integration of the economic phases in an objective meaning. Nothing shows this point better than the relationship between consumer countries and nationalizing countries, in which governments come in control of raw material, whether they have a liberal or Communist economy. How the United States government or other governments shall deal with this new situation remains to be seen.

It is obvious that this study ends on a very difficult problem, the answer to which derives from the facts of economics and law marshaled in this study. As a matter of fact, President Theodore Roosevelt, in his dispute with the Wilsonites, especially Brandeis, but also with LaFollette, foresaw at an early stage the development of an economic

[80] Compare the Nader Study Group Report on Antitrust Enforcement, *The Closed Enterprise System*, Center for Study of Responsive Law, Washington, D.C., Vols. I and II (1971).

situation in which the executive and legislative branches would find themselves entrenched in a closed industrial society, international as well as national. He suggested new rules of trade behavior which today look very modern, and which could give us some idea of how to deal with the problem by the use of effective rules and regulations originating from American economic forces and by use of the rules of other countries or private powers within other countries. The period of time between Theodore Roosevelt's era and today shows that after two world wars, several economic crises, and the confrontation with the stresses of urban society, including its effect on the foreign trade of the United States as well as on international trade in general, has raised, again and again, the problem whether or not the United States and others should develop a new system of legal economic structure. The American desire to return to "normalcy," which in a practical sense existed only during relatively few years, and the faith in a unique American economic system and fate, are in fact temptations to leave everything as it was, and attempt to develop a new structure of trade and industry without creating a new and proper relationship between private and public national and international interest.

President Theodore Roosevelt, again, provides us with an important example: He established a "corporations office," which had done excellent work in a number of studies on the structure of the oil and other industries.[81] In an article in the *Detroit Law Journal* more than 10 years ago,[82] I suggested that the Federal Trade Commission apply Section 6 of the Federal Trade Commission Act to exactly the new structure of industry presented in this study and undertake full and comprehensive studies, even if that should mean that some cases of unfair competition may be left to other judicial and administrative proceedings to be undertaken by public or private groups. The Federal Trade Commission recently published a staff report on automobile warranties, including a structural study of the automobile industry.[83] This report describes an example of the industrial practices that develop once the industrial firms are set free from competitive pressure. An even more startling experience is the Federal Trade Commission's investigation of the methods of the Procter and Gamble Company,

[81] Public Act No. 87, ¶6, 32 P.L. 827 (1903).

[82] Heinrich Kronstein, Reporting on Corporate Activities, 38 *U. Det. L.J.* 589 (June 1961).

[83] F.T.C., *Staff Report on Automobile Warranties* (Nov. 1968); see generally, F.T.C., *Report on Auto Warranties* (Feb. 20, 1970).

Sears Roebuck and Company, and other similar large corporations. The Commission announced that they are preparing a structural study on chain stores. The reader may wonder, without any desire to minimize the importance of chain stores, automobile warranties, or other abuses of the economy, why the Commission, under Section 6 of the Federal Trade Commission Act, does not undertake a full study of such material as is presented here and elsewhere. The Commission has access to much broader material from governmental agencies as well as from many semigovernmental, totally governmental, or even private sources. It cannot be overlooked, however, that, whenever they need material for a full structural study, the Federal Trade Commission and other agencies are under an "undue application" of due process.

These structural studies should also clarify the question whether the 1971 national and international economic structure diminishes or even overcomes the difference between agricultural and industrial markets. The present dispute between the United States and the European Common Market, apparently and allegedly an agricultural market, could be much more easily solved if all participating parties would definitely understand and accept the inseparability of both the agricultural and industrial markets. It might be possible to give benefits in the industrial field in order to bring about an improvement of the agricultural situation, whenever the political condition permits it.

It is suggested that "private" groups, outside the Organization for Economic Cooperation and Development (OECD) and other governmental agencies, take the initiative to set up, parallel to the ten representatives of the leading monetary nations, a committee of experts to deal with the kind of problems presented in this study. Cooperation among the leading groups in the United States, Japan, and Western Europe, including the Common Market, could help to assure the reliability of tests. Such a report on the present structure is possible. One should not be too much impressed by the argument concerning the danger of "disclosing so-called secrets." I doubt that in the type of closed economic structure in which we live these so-called secrets exist in any way other than they existed in an open and liberal society.

No time should be lost; the only way is to proceed into a new understanding of legal rules and legal sociology in the real sense of word. Only after we agree on what is actually the present economic structure can we hope for economic control that will limit the public and private power in our economy.

Index

Achnacarry Agreement, 21, 92
Act-of-State doctrine, 459, 460
Adhesion contract, 216, 218, 227; *see also* Contract
Administered price, *see* Price
Advertising, 69, 311-313; *see also* Market regulation, international
Agreement, international, 9-10, 12-14, 22, 49, 82, 85, 89, 129, 172, 255; restrictive, 5; *see also* Arbitration *and* Commodity agreements
Agreements: arbitration, 198, 372, 385, 402, 403, 406-408, 411, 413-415, 416-418, 420, 423, 425, 427, 433, 434, 435-437, 440; bilateral barter, 3, 10, 16; cartel implementation, 156, 159, 163, 167, 168; contractual, *see* Contract; direct price, 86, 92, 133, 135, 136, 137, 161, 169, 307; government, 77; horizontal, 164, 316; licensing, 146; loan, 208; market regulating, 81, 145, 202, 378; planning, 156, 158, 159, 160, 161, 162, 163, 164-168, 170, 171-173, 177-178; planning, types of, 163; producer's planning, 164; production quantity, 82; research and development, 138; restrictive, 5; technological, 54, 66; trust, 5; types of, 41; vertical, 156, 317; *see also* Patent
—post-World War II: coal, 8, 13; cocoa, 16; coffee, 10-11; cotton, 14, 21; olive oil, 10-11; sugar, 10-11, 22-23, 83; tin, 10-11, 77, 83, 109, 117; wheat, 10-11, 14
—pre-World War II: beef, 11; cocoa, 11; coffee, 11; cotton, 11; rubber, 11; sugar, 11; tea, 11; timber, 11; tin, 11, 77; wheat, 11
Aid, foreign, 23-26; *see also* Market regulation, international
Alliance of enterprise, private, 3; *see also* Cartel
Aluminum, 17, 29, 35, 54, 79-80, 85, 93-95, 116-117, 171, 187-188; and bauxite, 54, 80, 90, 93, 171, 187; *see also* Raw materials

American law, international jurisdiction of, 245-248; *see also* Contract
Analysis, methods of, 53-55, 60, 67
Anticartel legislation, 9
Antidumping, 18, 30
Antitrust, 6, 113, 187, 192, 278, 336, 420, 423, 425; impact of international law on, 458; laws, 1, 8-9, 30, 45, 65, 104, 202, 227, 255, 262-269, 300, 307, 317, 335, 372, 374, 420, 421, 447-448, 450, 454, 465; legislation, 38, 45, 92, 187-188, 190, 201-202, 227, 262-263, 297, 336, 413, 419, 422-423; limited by mandatory position, 458; practicality of, 480; U.S. jurisdiction in, 450, 452, 455-456
Applied research, 43; *see also* Research and development
Arbitration, 4-6, 39, 121, 194, 201, 203, 238, 241, 372-446; amiable composition of, 409, 431; awards, 422-424, 432, 438, 442, 444; contracts, 247-248, 250, 405, 441-442; international commercial, 401; London Court of, 399, 431; main contract, validity of in, 415-418, 428-429; and mediation, 444-446; proceeding, 425-426, 429, 441, 443; procedure, 422, 425-426, 430, 433, 438-439; tribunal or court of, 160, 162, 171-172, 198-199, 217, 240, 244, 247, 250-251, 255, 372-446
Arbitration Association, American, 380, 399
Arbitrators, private, 374-375, 378, 402, 414, 436
Artificial order, 40
Automation, 44, 54, 72
Automobile industry, 125, 132
Automony, 39, 80, 138, 161, 174, 202, 211-218, 228-237, 239, 241-244, 250, 252, 308, 402, 406-408, 410

Balance-of-payment, 2, 119, 143, 261-262, 306
Bargaining, collective, 155

Barriers, trade, 6, 11, 27, 28, 70, 89, 97, 104, 106, 206, 311
Barter, *see* Commodity agreements, international
Base point system, 92
Basic regulatory agreement, 155-167, 170-173, 177
Basic research, 43, 45
Bauxite, 54, 80, 93, 171, 187
Blacklist, 173
Boycotts, 173
Brand name, 312
Bretton Woods Agreement, 17, 27, 210
Buffer stock, 12-13, 34, 115
Buy American Act, 31

Cartel, 1, 3, 8, 9, 12, 35, 42-58, 64, 74, 77-153, 162, 170, 183, 194-196, 201-202, 228, 231, 243, 256, 269, 303-304, 308, 337, 395; advantages and disadvantages of, 68; agreement, 41, 44, 99, 104, 143, 151-152, 168, 172, 177-179, 189, 191, 193, 195, 196, 201-202, 228, 231, 269, 395; barriers in, 71; and communication, 44, 66, 68-69; and conglomerate mergers, 54; and correlation of data, 44; defensive, *see* Cartel, defensive; definition of, 39, 41, 155, 179; and development, *see* Research and development; enterprises participating in, 78, 120-121, 144; independent existence of, 41; industrial product, 1, 8, 119-141, 170, 194, 304; and industries, old and new, 47; influence, 78, 193, 451; and inner group, 56; integration of, 1, 39, 78-80, 84, 86, 93, 97, 107, 108, 162-163, 174, 179, 460-461, 465-466, 473-479; internal regulation of, 41; and main customer, 84; obligations in, 56-57; and preferential treatment, 84, 99; private, 12, 77, 106, 159; raw material, 1, 8, 35, 38-42, 77-118, 162, 170, 303; regulation of, 158, 180, 195-196; and second industrial revolution, 46; and secondary enterprises, manufacturers, and retailers, 69; and surpluses, 77; and syndicates, 83-84; technological, 1, 8, 41, 43-76, 81, 119, 141, 170, 183, 194, 303, 308, 337; and technological expertise, 47; types of, 41
Cartel, defensive, 8, 14-15, 142-153; and concealed objectives, 152; decentralization of, 144; and exclusion of competitors, 145; exclusive licensing agreements in, 146; and export cartels, 145,

151-152; and Interest Equalization Tax, 149; and minimum-price countries, 145, 147; and parallel market regulation, 143; position of members of, 149; purpose of, 145, 152; relation to politics of, 143; traditional markets of, 145; and transfer of capital, 150
Ceiling price, 111, 113, 118
Centralization, 57, 188
Choice of law, 198, 200-201, 203-210, 212, 214-215, 217-218, 221-234, 236, 240, 257
Coal, 8, 13, 33, 79, 83
"Commercial unit," 40, 179-197
Commodity agreements, international: Achnacarry, 21, 92, 156; Bretton Woods, 17, 27, 210; Buy American Act, 31; Paris Union Treaty, 277, 321; *see also* Agreements *and* Arbitration
Communications, 44, 204
Contract, 6, 38-40, 62, 70, 73, 78, 84, 89, 99, 123, 137, 151, 157, 162, 167-170, 173-198, 200-232, 234-255, 262, 265, 410, 415-417, 421, 426-430, 433-434; adhesion, 216, 218, 227; adjustment clauses in, 137; antidumping, 18, 30; arbitration, 247-248, 250-251, 254, 405, 441-442; arbitration clauses in, 238, 384, 386-389, 394, 400, 414-415, 423, 427-429, 437; and combine unit, 181; and commercial field, 180; and "commercial unit" as means of subjection to, 180, 182; and contact points, 199-200, 205, 214, 216, 218, 221, 230, 236, 241; dumping 188; exclusive-dealing clause in, 185; formal parties to, 177-178; influence over subsidiaries of, 193; licensing, 169; long-term, 84; main, 415-418, 428-429; mutual exchange, 200; parties subject to, 179; and place of contracting, 203-212, 214-215, 218, 221, 223, 234, 236, 240; and place of incorporation, 257; and place of performance, 208, 209, 217, 221-223, 229, 236; planning, 159, 161, 196, 372; and preferential treatment, 84; sales, 169, 200; saving clauses in, 24; and Story Doctrine, 203-204; substantive, 440-441; supplementary parties to, 178-179; tying clauses in, 24-26, 320; validity of, 205-207, 212, 216-219, 223-226, 234-235, 240, 242, 250, 254; vertical, 168-169, 291; *see also* Arbitration *and* Law, international public

The Laws of International Cartels

Designed by R. E. Rosenbaum.
Composed by Vail-Ballou Press, Inc.,
in 10 point linotype Janson, 3 points leaded,
with display lines in monotype Janson.
Printed letterpress from type by Vail-Ballou Press
on Warren's 1854 text, 60 pound basis,
with the Cornell University Press watermark.
Bound by Vail-Ballou Press
In Holliston book cloth
and stamped in All Purpose foil.

Library of Congress Cataloging in Publication Data
(For library cataloging purposes only)

Kronstein, Heinrich David.
  The law of international cartels.

  An expansion of the author's Das Recht der internationalen Kartelle, published
in 1967.
  Includes bibliographical references.
    1. Trusts, Industrial—Law. I. Title.
Law   341.7'53   73-164642
ISBN 0-8014-0627-7